BTEC NATIONAL

Health Studies

Edited by Beryl Stretch

BTEC NATIONAL
Health Studies

Edited by Beryl Stretch

Beryl Stretch
Andrew Boak
Dr. Orla Dunn
Hilda Haws
David Herne
Lynda Mason
Neil Moonie
David Webb

Endorsed by Edexcel

Heinemann Educational Publishers,
Halley Court, Jordan Hill, Oxford OX2 8EJ
A division of Reed Educational & Professional Publishing Ltd

Heinemann is a registered trademark of Reed Educational & Professional Publishing Limited

OXFORD MELBOURNE AUCKLAND JOHANNESBURG BLANTYRE GABORONE
IBADAN PORTSMOUTH NH (USA) CHICAGO

© Andy Boak, Dr Orla Dunn, Hilda Haws, David Herne, Lynda Mason, Neil Moonie,
David Webb 2002

First published 2002
2006 2005 2004 2003 2002
10 9 8 7 6 5 4 3 2 1

A catalogue record for this book is available from the British Library on request

ISBN 0 435 45519 2

Typeset by 🗡 Tek-Art, Croydon, Surrey

Printed and bound in Great Britain by Scotprint, East Lothian

Tel: 01865 888058 www.heinemann.co.uk

Contents

* These units are externally assessed

Introduction

About this book

This book is designed to support students wishing to gain the Level Three BTEC National qualification in Health Studies for Edexcel. The book will also form a useful resource for other basic care courses.

Course Structure

The BTEC National Diploma in Health Studies is a specialist vocational qualification available for full-time study and is equivalent to three A Levels. A Certificate programme is available for part-time students who may be in employment.

The Diploma programme consists of eight core units (with a unit value of nine) and nine specialist option units. The Certificate course comprises seven core units (with a unit value of eight) and four specialist option units. Both the Diploma and Certificate programmes are designed to assist entry into the majority of health-care professions.

The BTEC programmes are particularly beneficial because they allow vocational theory to be put into practice. You will need to spend a minimum of four hundred hours in vocational work practice. You must demonstrate how you have improved your basic practitioner skills and how, through your study, you have linked theoretical knowledge and understanding to practice. Reflecting the importance of this, the Vocational practice unit runs throughout the length of the programme and has a value of two units.

This book covers the eight core units and five specialist option units.

The core units are:

- Equality, diversity and rights*
- Communication and supportive skills*
- Research and project
- Human anatomy and physiology

- Applied science
- Vocational practice
- Lifespan development
- Health promotion

The option units are:

- Health and society
- Environmental health
- Diet and nutrition

- Advanced physiology
- Health psychology

*These units will be externally assessed.

Assessment

For the externally assessed units your work will be sent to examiners appointed by Edexcel for marking. The assessment may take the form of short or extended questions, case studies or externally set assignments. The remainder of the units will be assessed internally by your teachers. You will need to produce a portfolio of evidence to meet the evidence criteria outlined in the specification. This book provides excellent guidance for you to match both the specifications and assessment criteria for each unit covered.

Features of the book

Throughout the text there are a number of features that are designed to encourage reflection and discussion and to help relate theory to practice in a care context. These features are:

What you need to learn	a list of the knowledge points that you will have learnt by the end of the unit
Think it over	thought-provoking questions and dilemmas that can be used for individual reflection or group discussion
Theory into practice	practical activities that require you to apply your theoretical knowledge to the workplace
Key issues	contemporary issues in childcare that you should be aware of
Case studies	examples of 'real' situations to help you link theory to practice
Assessment activities	activities that address the assessment requirements of the course

At the end of each unit there is a test to consolidate the knowledge you have acquired in the unit. Finally, there is a comprehensive glossary of key terms that you may want to refer to on the Heinemann website at www.heinemann.co.uk/BTECNatHealth/glossary.

A wide range of experienced professionals have contributed their expertise to this book; their purpose in doing so is to support you in your chosen studies and to provide you with a firm knowledge foundation from which you can extend and develop your particular interests.

We do hope that you enjoy your BTEC National in Care course and wish you good luck and every success in achieving your qualification and in your future work.

Beryl Stretch
Series Editor

Acknowledgements

Orla Dunn would like to thank Andrea, Chris, David and Sheila for their support and suggestions. Andy Boak would like to thank Gemma Brocklesby. The authors and publisher would like to thank the following individuals and organisations for permission to reproduce photographs:

Associated Press/Jacqueline Arzt – page 437; Gareth Boden – page 95; Format Photographers/Jacky Chapman – page 24; Format Photographers/Roshini Kempadoo – page 309; Format/Brenda Prince – page 500; Sally & Richard Greenhill – page 9; Sally & Richard Greenhill/Sally Greenhill – page 78; Help the Aged – page 226 (top); The Image Bank – page 267; The Image Bank/Terje Rakke – page 511; Impact Photos/Andy Johnstone – page 383; Impact Photos/Colin Jones – page 434; Impact Photos/Caroline Penn – page 47, 410; Impact Photos/Stewart Weir – page 335; PA Photos – page 10 (left), 346; Photodisc – page 84, 279; Rentokil Initial – page 411; Rex – page 515 (right); Rex Features – page 7, 515 (left); Rex Features/Tony Larkin – page 10 (right), 132, 214; Science Photo Library/Simon Fraser/Dept. of Neuroradiology, Newcastle General Hospital – page 215; Science Photo Library/Ruth Jenkinson/MIDIRS 348; Science Photo Library/Dr. Philippa Uwins, Whistler Research Pty – page 128; Stone/Tessa Codrington – page 225; Stone/Chris Sanders – page 352; Wellcome Trust – page 192 and WRVS – page 226 (bottom).

Crown Copyright material on pages 11, 105, 108, 109, 277, 335, 338 and 357 is reproduced under Class Licence Number C01W0041 with the permission of the Controller of HMSO and the Queen's Printer for Scotland.

Every effort has been made to contact copyright holders of material published in this book. We would be glad to hear from any unacknowledged sources at the first opportunity.

Websites
Please note that the examples of websites suggested in this book were up to date at the time of writing. It is essential for tutors to preview each site before using it to ensure that the URL is still accurate and the content is appropriate. We suggest that tutors bookmark useful sites and consider enabling students to access them through the school or college intranet.

Equality, diversity and rights

This unit introduces the rights of individuals, and how some groups in society are denied those rights as a result of individual and structural discrimination in society. It encourages you to think about the negative effects that discrimination has on all members of society, and the corresponding benefits of diversity.

It shows how equality, diversity and rights are central to the delivery of care services, and describes the systems, structures and policies which attempt to prevent discrimination and promote the rights of clients. It explains the statutory background to some clients' rights, and the circumstances in which the law allows those rights to be overridden.

This unit explains the role of the individual worker in promoting equality, diversity and rights, and how it is necessary for them to understand the origins of discriminatory behaviour and examine their own prejudices in order to do so.

What you need to learn

- The importance of equality, diversity and rights to care services
- How care services recognise and promote equality, diversity and rights
- How the individual care worker can promote equality, diversity and rights in their own practice

The importance of equality, diversity and rights to care services

Principle of equity

The principle of equity is that all people should have equal opportunities. This does not mean that everyone should have equal wealth, status and power. This is impossible to achieve in a free society. It does mean that everyone should have the same rights under the law, and the right to services provided by the state on the basis of their need. Individuals should be free from discrimination. Discrimination means treating someone differently because of something about them – their race, age or sex, for instance – which is not relevant to the situation. It results in people being unfairly denied opportunities.

Concept of tolerance

Tolerance is essential if everyone is to have equal opportunities. It means that people recognise and respect the rights of others who are different. Prejudice prevents some people from doing this. A prejudice is a judgement made without evidence, and sometimes in the face of evidence to the contrary. Prejudice results in discrimination. The law supports the rights of some groups which suffer from prejudice and discrimination. The Race Relations Acts, the Sex Discrimination and Equal Pay Acts and the Disability Discrimination Act make some forms of discrimination illegal.

Cycle of disadvantage

The cycle of disadvantage describes how inequalities combine and relate to each other in a way that makes it very difficult for people to escape from them.

Some sections of society suffer discrimination in many different aspects of their lives. The groups most likely to be over-represented in this excluded section of society are older people, people with disabilities, people from some ethnic minority groups, and single parents (the great majority of whom are women). A common feature of nearly all of these people is dependence on benefits.

Low income results in unequal access to education and health services, and an inability to afford good quality food and housing. Low educational achievement results in fewer job opportunities and a greater likelihood of unemployment, which limits income. Poor diet and housing result in ill health, which further damages employment prospects.

The effect is cumulative, and results in marginalisation (see page 6). Some commentators speak about the formation of an **underclass**. Others dislike this term, and say it blames the individual when the real cause is structural discrimination in society. They prefer the term **socially excluded**. The Black Report (1980) identified a strong link between membership of the lower social classes and poor health.

Think it over

Look at the factors which contribute to social exclusion (see Figure 1.1). Write a brief life story of an individual from birth to death. Your account should show how these factors work together to create a cycle of disadvantage over the individual's lifetime.

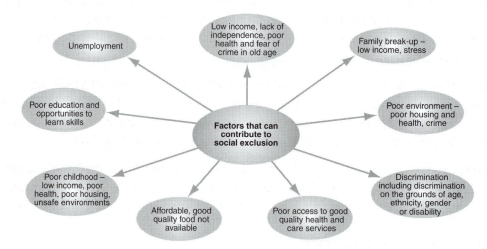

Figure 1.1 Social exclusion can have many causes

Care values

The basic care values are that services should be available to everyone on the basis of need and that they should be delivered in a way that promotes users' rights. Many people requiring services are members of vulnerable groups and suffer disadvantage. Care services must not exclude or discriminate against any group in society. The way care services are delivered should empower clients and promote their dignity.

This is achieved by applying the Care Value Base in every aspect of care work. The Care Value Base is embodied in health and social care qualifications and in the service standards of care agencies. There are three areas in which care workers have particular responsibility to respect clients' rights (see Figure 1.2).

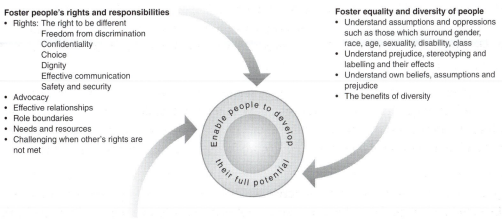

Foster people's rights and responsibilities
- Rights: The right to be different
  Freedom from discrimination
  Confidentiality
  Choice
  Dignity
  Effective communication
  Safety and security
- Advocacy
- Effective relationships
- Role boundaries
- Needs and resources
- Challenging when other's rights are not met

Foster equality and diversity of people
- Understand assumptions and oppressions such as those which surround gender, race, age, sexuality, disability, class
- Understand prejudice, stereotyping and labelling and their effects
- Understand own beliefs, assumptions and prejudice
- The benefits of diversity

Enable people to develop their full potential

Maintain the confidentiality of information
The legal framework: Data Protection Act, 1998
- The security of recording systems
- The need and right 'to know'
- Confidentiality can value and protect a client
- Policies, procedures and guidelines
- Boundaries and tensions in maintaining confidentiality

Figure 1.2 The Care Value Base – to promote equality, diversity and rights

Care work should empower clients in order to promote people's rights and responsibilities. This means that workers must recognise the right of people to make decisions about their own lives. Clients should have choices wherever possible. Nothing should be done without their agreement unless the law permits it (see page 19). Wherever necessary, clients should be provided with the necessary information to complain about infringement of their rights.

Workers should respect a client's individual and social characteristics and their views and beliefs to encourage diversity in people and further equality. They should challenge discrimination and oppression whenever it occurs. The worker should know how to get support for any clients who are being oppressed and discriminated against.

Workers need to understand service users' moral and legal rights to confidentiality, but also the limits to confidentiality. They should respect confidentiality, but be open with people about the limits resulting from agency policy and the law (see pages 22 and 24).

Moral rights of individuals

The principle of equity is based on the idea that individuals have the moral right to equal opportunities. There are a number of other moral rights which support this. There have been many attempts to define these rights. These include the United Nations Universal Declaration of Human Rights, the United Nations Convention on the Rights of the Child and the European Convention on Human Rights.

Some attempts have been criticised because some of the rights are thought too ambitious, and very difficult to achieve. The rights of one person imposes obligations on others. They are meaningless unless others accept these obligations, and the means exist to enforce them.

One attempt to define human rights which does appear to be realistic and is enforceable is the European Convention on Human Rights. The Convention was incorporated into UK legislation in October 2000 as the Human Rights Act. For the first time there is a statement of what constitutes human rights in UK legislation (see page 17). This means that people can go to court, if necessary, to enforce their rights.

Key issue

In small groups, spend ten minutes making a list of the moral rights which every individual should have. When you have finished, compare your list with the Articles of the European Convention on Human Rights (see pages 17–18).

How does your list differ?

Have you things on your list which do not fit into the Convention?

Are they true rights?

If there are rights in the Convention which are not on your list, say why they are important.

How people who use care services may be subject to inequality generally within society

Many service users will be subject to inequality in a number of ways. In the course of their everyday lives they may experience:

- individual discrimination because of the prejudices of others – this includes unfair treatment, exclusion, insults, harassment and violence
- institutional discrimination as a result of organisations failing to provide appropriate services because of prejudiced or ethnocentric attitudes of service providers
- structural discrimination or a general disadvantage because prejudiced attitudes are common throughout society and its institutions. An example of this is the way some ethnic minority groups experience discrimination in education, health, social care, housing employment and the law.

Effects of inequality on people

Despite anti-discriminatory legislation, people's life chances are still affected by prejudice and discrimination. National statistics on health, wealth, employment and education show it on a structural level. Regular press reports of Employment Tribunal findings and court judgments show it on a personal level. Individuals' prospects are directly affected because they are denied opportunities by overt or covert discrimination. Overt discrimination is open, though not always deliberate. Covert discrimination is more subtle (or hidden), such as failing to invite someone rather than deliberately excluding them.

There are further effects resulting from discrimination operating against the whole range of human needs as identified by Maslow (see Figure 1.3).

Exposure to discrimination may affect the individual's self-image. If people have a poor self-image, they will have low self-esteem which will further limit their opportunities.

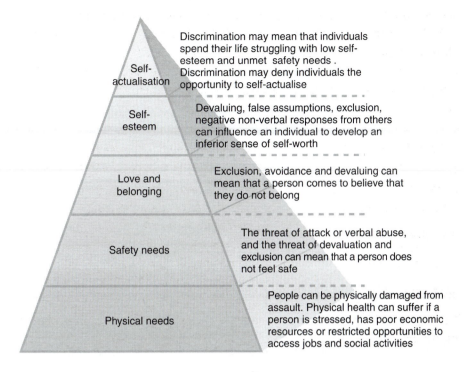

Figure 1.3 Discrimination can block human needs (as described by Maslow) and change people

They may believe that opportunities are not open to them, so there is no point in trying for them. If their self-esteem is poor, they may not present themselves to the best advantage. They may feel that others have low expectations of them, perhaps in education or work, and end up fulfilling those expectations (see Figure 1.4).

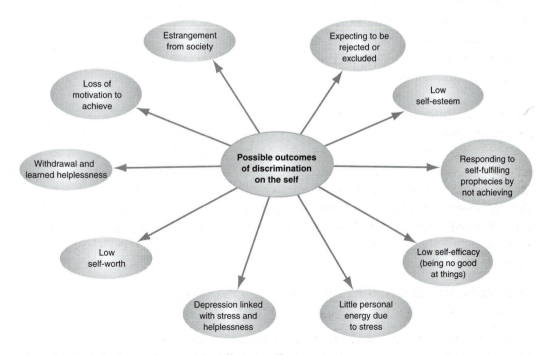

Figure 1.4 Discrimination can have negative effects on self-esteem

The following case study shows how low self-esteem may affect opportunities.

Case study

Sean and Daniel are both interviewed for a job, but neither gets it. Sean has high self-esteem. He is disappointed, but thinks that he was unlucky, or that he didn't have the skills the employer was looking for. He asks the employer for some feedback on his performance in the interview and looks at ways in which he can acquire the skills he needs, and present the skills he has in future applications. He is more confident the next time he applies for a job, and is successful in his application.

Daniel has low self-esteem. He gets very depressed by being rejected and thinks it must be his fault. He goes along to his next interview feeling very low and expecting to be rejected again. He doesn't present himself very well, and doesn't get the job. He is even less confident when the next opportunity arises.

- Suggest some ways to help Daniel raise his own self-esteem.

An individual with a good self-image and high self-esteem will see rejection as a short-term setback. But if a person's self-image has been eroded by constant exposure to prejudice, discrimination and abuse, then they may find it much more difficult to handle setbacks.

Stereotyping and labelling

Stereotyping is based on prejudice, and means holding beliefs that all members of a group are the same. Stereotypes are often based on inaccurate, negative and damaging beliefs about a group. They are damaging even when they appear positive because they make people unreceptive to the differences between individuals. The subject of the stereotype may be forced into a mould unsuitable to their interests and talents. Even qualities that are generally true of groups will not be true of all individuals in that group.

Labelling means applying a stereotype to a particular person. When one individual labels another, they are less likely to accept evidence which contradicts the label. This means that labels are often self-fulfilling prophecies. Prejudice, stereotypes and labelling result in individual discrimination, which is one individual treating another differently, usually worse, because of a physical characteristic or membership of a group.

Think it over
Consider one example when you have stereotyped an individual and, therefore, labelled that person. What prompted you to do this? If the individual had known of your action, how do you think that person would have felt?

Have you ever been knowingly labelled by someone else?

How did you feel about it?

The effects of marginalisation and disempowerment

The victims of prejudice and discrimination are often marginalised, which means forced to the edge of society. As a result they are cut off from economic, cultural, political and social activities, and do not enjoy the full rights or benefits of citizenship. They do not have the economic power to purchase services for themselves. Services provided by the state are not distributed fairly. The Acheson Report (1998) identified that it was often the communities with the greatest need which received the poorest services, and the better off communities which had the better services. Marginalisation is one of the mechanisms of the cycle of disadvantage, working to prevent people from improving their disadvantaged position.

Disempowerment results when people are denied choice. It usually happens when service users are expected to fit in with services, rather than services being designed to meet users' needs. Sometimes users are not given the information needed to make decisions about their lives. Many users do not have the money to purchase what they need for themselves. If the professionals they rely on to arrange their care do not consult them or offer them choice, individuals lose control over important parts of their lives. These may include things such as where and how they live, how they spend their day, who they associate with, what they eat and drink and what time they get up and go to bed. If people are disempowered they are likely to have a poor self-image and low self-esteem.

Think it over

Consider your own self-image and self-esteem for a few moments.

What questions would you ask yourself in order to assess these?

Identification of vulnerable groups

Discrimination takes place on the basis of sex, race, age, disability, sexuality, religion, health status and class. This does not mean that everybody in these groups experiences disadvantage as the following examples show:

- Although women are under-represented in higher paid jobs, many women do have successful careers.
- There is widespread racial discrimination in society, but not all groups suffer the same levels of disadvantage. Pakistanis and Bangladeshis experience the worst levels of economic disadvantage. People of Caribbean and Indian origin are not as seriously disadvantaged. African, Asian and Chinese people appear to suffer little economic disadvantage.

Many women do have successful careers

- Whilst many older people are poor, increasing numbers have occupational pensions and enjoy high standards of living.

If we think about these characteristics as playing cards, the more supposed positive cards a person holds (for instance a young, white heterosexual man in good health and without a disability), the greater their chances of success.

Groups open to structural inequality are those dependent on state benefits – the long-term unemployed, single parent families and older people relying on the state pension. The more supposed negative cards a person holds, the more likely they are to be a member of these vulnerable groups.

- Young Caribbean men may be over-represented amongst the long-term unemployed if they underachieve in education because of institutional racism in the education system. They may start in a less competitive position even in the absence of racial discrimination by employers.

- Older men who lose their jobs may join the long-term unemployed because of ageist attitudes of employers. Someone with a disability or from an ethnic minority group in this position would find themselves doubly disadvantaged.
- Women are very over-represented amongst single parent families as it is usually the mother who has the child care responsibility. Women from the lower social classes will find it harder to obtain work that pays well enough to pay for child care.
- People from the lower social classes, those with disabilities and members of economically disadvantaged ethnic minority groups are less likely to have a good employment record in a well paid job. They are less likely to have an occupational pension, and are more likely to be dependent upon state benefits in old age.

Equal access to services

Some groups are denied access to services because of institutional discrimination by organisations in society. Institutional racism was defined by Sir William McPherson in the Stephen Lawrence Enquiry Report (1999) as 'The collective failure of an organisation to provide an appropriate and professional service to people because of their colour, culture or ethnic origin. It can be seen or detected in processes, attitudes and behaviour which amount to discrimination through unwitting prejudice, ignorance, thoughtlessness and racist stereotyping which disadvantage minority ethnic people'. This does not mean that all the workers in an organisation are prejudiced against a particular group. They may have ethnocentric attitudes. This means they do not question ways of working which are based on incorrect assumptions that disadvantage some groups.

Many of the report's findings apply to education, health and social care services. The report raised awareness of the extent to which institutional discrimination exists in health and social care services.

There is evidence of institutional racism within the National Health Service. A number of studies have suggested that non-white patients are treated differently from white patients within mental health services. This has been confirmed by a recent Mental Health Act Commission report which found that non-white patients, and particularly people of Afro-Caribbean ethnicity, were far more likely to be compulsorily detained ('sectioned') under the Mental Health Act 1983.

Social services departments have also been accused of institutional racism. It is suggested that in some cases they have made incorrect assumptions about ethnic minority populations. One assumption is that ethnic minority populations are made up of stable, multigenerational families who care for their own older people through community organisations or the extended family. This has led to failures to make appropriate provision for elders from ethnic minorities. Children of Afro-Caribbean and mixed parentage are over-represented in the care system, and there is frequent failure to recruit sufficient foster parents and prospective adopters from appropriate ethnic backgrounds.

Other groups are widely discriminated against by public services. In March 2001, the Health Secretary launched a national framework for older people, to prevent older people being denied the services they need. Whilst there are good reasons why an older person should receive different health treatment from a younger one, there was evidence that this was often happening because of the prejudices of doctors and nurses. In October 2000 health workers were told they should stop deciding not to resuscitate older patients if they fell into a coma, without prior consultation with the patients or their families. People with learning disabilities have also experienced discrimination in the health service, and in particular children with Down's syndrome have been refused heart surgery.

Ensuring equal access to services requires structural changes in the way those services are provided. Many organisations which discriminate against groups in society have equal opportunities policies, but they are not working.

Assessment activity 1.1

What is the importance of equality, diversity and rights in health, care and early years success?

Write a report that looks at the issues faced by health, care and early years workers to ensure that all people are treated equally and receive the same rights to health care. Discuss the problems faced by different groups in receiving their right to be treated equally, and suggest solutions.

Advantages of diversity in British society

There are two reasons to respect the diversity of others. The first reason is that it is unfair, and often illegal, to treat members of minority groups in a discriminatory way. The second, equally important, reason is that there are positive benefits to diversity for all members of society.

The dimensions and advantages of diversity in British society

Ethnocentricity is the unthinking assumption that the individual's viewpoint from their own cultural perspective is normal or superior, without considering that there could be other points of view. It is a narrow and limiting attitude, the opposite of valuing

diversity – which enriches a person's life. Valuing diversity opens people to new experiences, and to new ways of looking at things. Being open to other cultures enriches everyone and means that our everyday lives are more interesting, even at such basic levels as the types of food we eat. Fashion often borrows from other cultures, and popular music has benefited from diverse cultural influences.

What are the benefits of diversity to our society today?

Many people find that experience of other philosophies, and the use of different therapies or techniques such as yoga, alters their view of the world and makes them more creative. Others benefit from forms of complementary medicine, such as acupuncture, massage and aromatherapy, which have their roots in other cultures.

Not only do we benefit culturally from being open to diversity, but we also benefit from the contribution of people as individuals who would otherwise be excluded. If people are excluded, they cannot make a full contribution to society, and everyone loses. For example:

- if people from some ethnic minority groups underachieve in the education system, society suffers as it is deprived of their potential contribution to the workforce
- if women are discriminated against in employment and are excluded from certain jobs, or do not achieve the highest positions, their contribution at this level is lost
- if people with disabilities do not have equal opportunities, they will have unrecognised talents which remain unused
- if older people are devalued, their skills and experience are lost to society.

David Blunkett and Stephen Hawking are known primarily for their important contributions to society rather than their disabilities

Assessment activity 1.2

Imagine you are a reporter for your local newspaper. Choose an aspect of culture that interests you – food, music, film, literature, fashion, medicine. Write an article on how it has been influenced as a result of being open to other cultures. How has it benefited? What are people's attitudes to it? Which cultures have influenced it?

How care services recognise and promote equality, diversity and rights

Formal policies on equality and rights

Formal polices on equality and rights include legislation, such as the following:

- Mental Health Act
- Children Act
- Race Relations Act
- Sex Discrimination Act
- Disability Discrimination Act
- Human Rights Act
- Data Protection Act.

The government issues Codes of Practice and Guidance alongside the legislation to advise care organisations and individual professionals about how laws should be implemented. All care organisations should have formal policies on equality of access and client rights incorporated into all their procedures.

All care workers are bound by the law and the Care Value Base, but workers in particular services will also be bound by Codes of Practice and Charters. Health service workers must comply with the Patient's Charter which promotes equal rights by stating patients' rights and the standards that they can expect from services (see Figure 1.5). The Community Care Charter fulfils a similar role for social services workers.

Some workers will be bound by codes of conduct issued by their professional organisations. The UK Central Council for Nursing, Midwifery and Health Visiting Code of Professional Conduct contains a number of provisions protecting patients' rights to equal treatment (see Figure 1.6).

Patient's Charter

Everyone has the right under the charter to:

- receive health care on the basis of clinical need
- be registered with a GP and change your GP easily and quickly if you want to
- get emergency medical treatment at any time
- be offered a health check when you join a GP's list
- ask your GP for a health check if you are aged 16 – 74 years and have not seen your GP for the past three years
- be offered a health check once a year in your GP surgery, or at your own home if you prefer, if you are 75 years or over
- receive information about the services your GP provides
- decide which pharmacy to use for your prescription and have the appropriate drugs and medicines prescribed
- get your medicines free if you are a pensioner, a child under 16, or under 19 in full-time education, pregnant or a nursing mother, suffering from one of a number of specified conditions, or on income support or family credit
- be referred to a consultant, acceptable to you, when your GP thinks it is necessary, and to be referred for a second opinion if you and your GP agree this is desirable
- have any proposed treatment, including any risks and any alternatives, clearly explained to you before you decide whether you agree to it
- receive dental advice in an emergency (if you are registered with a dentist) and treatment if your dentist thinks it is necessary
- receive a signed written prescription immediately after your eye test
- see your own health records, subject to any limitations in law, and know that everyone working in the NHS is under a legal duty to keep your records confidential
- choose whether or not you wish to take part in medical research or medical student training
- information about the standards of services you can expect, waiting times and local GP services
- have a complaint about NHS services investigated thoroughly and receive a full and prompt reply from the Chief Executive or General Manager
- be told before you go into hospital, except in an emergency, whether it is planned to care for you in a ward for men and women.

Figure 1.5 The Patient's Charter ©Crown Copyright

Summary

- As a registered nurse or midwife, you must respect the patient or client as an individual
- As a registered nurse or midwife, you must obtain consent before you give any treatment or care
- As a registered nurse or midwife, you must co-operate with others in the team
- As a registered nurse or midwife, you must protect confidential information
- As a registered nurse or midwife, you must maintain your professional knowledge and competence
- As a registered nurse or midwife, you must be trustworthy
- As a registered nurse or midwife, you must act to identify and minimise the risk to patients and clients

Figure 1.6 Summary of the UKCC Code of Professional Conduct *Source:* Nursing and Midwifery Council

Soon, all care workers will be covered by similar standards when the Care Standards Act 2000 sets up the General Social Care Council.

Documents such as the Wagner Report (1988), *Home Life* (1984) and *A Better Home Life* (1996) set standards for care in residential homes and nursing homes. *Community Life* (1990) sets standards for people being cared for in their own homes.

> ### *Think it over*
> Divide into four groups, each group finding the key points relevant to equality, diversity and rights, in the four documents mentioned above. At a plenary discussion find similar themes and discuss their importance to service users.

Positive promotion of individual rights

The positive promotion of individuals' rights is only possible if they know what their rights are. Care organisations should have policies on equal opportunities, confidentiality and access to records, and complaints. They must also have guidance for people whose rights are being infringed, for instance under the Mental Health and Children Acts. Organisations' policies must be widely available to service users. This means they must be accessible, readable and comprehensible. This may involve providing leaflets and translating them into ethnic minority languages and Braille to ensure equal access. Where clients are unable to represent themselves, it may be necessary for the organisation to arrange advocacy services for them.

Advocacy

In order to have choice, individuals must be able to understand what is available and express an opinion. Some individuals cannot do either of these things. Advocacy is the process by which they can be helped to do so. Sometimes an advocate may make decisions in their interests and on their behalf. The dictionary defines an advocate as someone who pleads, intercedes or speaks for another.

Clients may be unable to exercise choice for many reasons. For example:

- children may lack the maturity to understand the reasons for, or the implications of, things that are happening to them
- people with learning disabilities may be unable to fully understand their circumstances
- some older people may be confused or have a memory problem which calls into question the validity of choices they make
- some people with disabilities, for instance people who have had strokes, may be unable to communicate their wishes
- people from a different cultural background may not understand the systems and processes for securing their rights
- for a number of reasons clients may lack knowledge or confidence to deal with officials.

Many of these people will have friends or family to advocate on their behalf. However, if they do not, then they risk becoming disempowered and marginalised unless they have an independent person to support them.

Personal advocacy may take two forms:

- professional advocacy, such as a lawyer or other professional representing a person in court, or any other formal hearing, such as a tribunal or complaints procedure
- citizen advocacy, when an independent volunteer acts on behalf of a client with a service provider.

> ### *Think it over*
> Have you ever spoken on behalf of someone else? Why did you do that? Was the result satisfactory or did the individual wish they had spoken out for themselves?

Public advocacy is different, and is where a voluntary organisation represents a whole group. The purpose is to get a message across better than the members of the group could do as individuals. An example of this is the work of the Terence Higgins Trust in relation to people with HIV/AIDS.

Care workers may act as advocates for service users, but may have problems when there are conflicts between the role of advocate and the role of employee of a service provider. This is especially true when the client is complaining about that provider.

Think it over

Think about examples from your own care experience when a service user would have benefited from advocacy. Were there any arrangements in place for them to be represented? What were the arrangements? If there were no arrangements, what were the effects on the service user?

Work practices

The role of work practices in promoting clients' rights is particularly important. Services should be provided in a way that respects the privacy and dignity of service users.

- Service users should be able to protect their private space, to lock the door to their room, and expect staff to ask permission before entering.
- They should have choice over what to eat and wear, what activities they participate in, and how they are addressed by staff.
- Service users' needs should be more important than the routine of the organisation, and they should be able to choose when to get up, have meals and bathe.
- Dignity and privacy must be a particular consideration when helping service users with intimate care tasks.
- Care should be offered in a way that maximises independence and service users should be encouraged to do things for themselves, rather than the worker taking over to save time.
- Service users must be kept safe but not overprotected. They have the same right to take risks as others. They should only be discouraged from activities after a clear decision that a risk outweighs the client's right to independence.

Organisational policies

Employing organisations may include standards for staff behaviour in their contracts of employment. They will issue general guidelines which regulate workers' day-to-day relations with their clients. These will cover areas such as confidentiality, and when it is permissible to accept a gift from a client. There will be procedures for staff dealing with people who are particularly vulnerable, such as child abuse and elder abuse procedures. Organisations will also have mission statements and service standards which inform workers and service users about expected standards. All of these polices should include the organisation's policy on equal opportunities.

Staff development and training

Organisations set standards for their workers to promote the rights of clients. The organisation must have ways of ensuring that these standards are met. An important way they do this is through staff development and training. Staff development will normally take place through supervision, which enables workers and their managers to deal with issues which have arisen in the workplace. Part of a manager's role is to use their experience and knowledge of the organisation's requirements to advise and guide junior staff. Supervision is a way of supporting staff, but sometimes there is an element of discipline in the process, where a worker falls short of the standards which the organisation expects. Supervision should also identify the training needs of workers. These may arise for a number of reasons: as the worker develops and takes on more responsibility or when there has been a change in organisational policy, legislation or government guidance which requires a change in working practices.

Quality issues

Quality issues are about how well an organisation is meeting standards, here meaning how well it is respecting the rights and meeting the needs of its clients. They are about how the organisation complies with legislation, government guidance and policies, Charters, Codes of Practice and the rights of clients expressed in the Care Value Base. The performance of an organisation can only be judged if it has systems and structures in place that show the quality of the services it offers. These will include policies and procedures, staff development and training, and recording systems.

Systems and structures

Organisations need to check that they are meeting standards. This is called monitoring or internal audit. In larger organisations the systems for doing this may be formal and structured, and they may have specialised managers who are responsible for this. They must have systems in place to monitor the quality of work with clients. As well as staff supervision, these systems will also cover the quality of recording of the work that is done. The ability to check records to see what happened is known as an audit trail. It is a vital part of maintaining standards, and for the operation of a credible complaints procedure.

Organisations must have adequate record systems to meet the requirements of inspection, or external audit. This is where the performance of an organisation is checked by an outside body. There are a number of ways in which the performance of organisations is checked. Organisations have no choice about some forms of external audit, which are compulsory. These include:

- the Social Services Inspectorate inspecting the services provided by a social services department
- the National Care Standards Commission inspecting residential and nursing homes.

There are other forms of audit which are optional for organisations, and they volunteer for them by applying for awards such as the Charter Mark or Investors in People.

Theory into practice

Think about a care setting where you have worked. How did the managers explain to the staff what standards were expected of them? How did the management check that these standards were being met? If the answers to these questions aren't clear, what do you think the implications are for the way that service users' rights are protected?

Complaints procedures

If service users do not have the right to complain, they have no way of standing up for their rights. An accessible and easily understood complaints system is a basic part of any organisation's policy on equal opportunities. In the case of a social services department, for instance, a common form of complaints procedure would be as follows.

- In the first instance, to speak with the member of staff concerned or their manager to see if the issue can be resolved informally.
- If that does not resolve the issue, to make a complaint to a senior manager of the department.
- If the matter is still not resolved, to request the matter to be referred to a review panel, which will have lay members as well as a representative of the social services department.
- If the complainant is not satisfied, they have the right to refer the matter to the Local Government Ombudsman.

A similar system operates for the Health Service. The first stage is local resolution, if the complaint can be dealt with informally by the provider of the service. If not, the complaint moves to an independent review, when the complaint may be reviewed by a panel. Patients who are not satisfied with the outcome of their complaint may approach the Health Service Commissioner (Ombudsman). It is one of the roles of Community Health Councils to advise and assist patients who want to make a complaint about health services.

Theory into practice

Investigate how to make a complaint against a large service provider such as a social services department or an NHS Trust. How can you establish what your rights are? How can you get a copy of the complaints procedure? How easy is it for individuals to complain? How can individuals contact sources of support?

Affirmative action

Affirmative action is positive discrimination. It means identifying individuals or groups which are disadvantaged or marginalised and taking compensating action to promote the equality of their opportunities. This is often completely uncontentious, for instance in the case of services for older people and people with physical disabilities. Sometimes it may be more controversial. There have been cases where the provision of services to disadvantaged groups has been resented, usually by other marginalised groups who feel that they also deserve special treatment.

Sometimes affirmative action is very controversial. For instance, some political parties have attempted to redress the under-representation of women in Parliament by proposing all-women shortlists. Some men have complained about this on the grounds that it may exclude better qualified men. Some women have also felt uneasy because of concerns that people will think that they have not succeeded on their own merits.

The argument against this is that discrimination and disadvantage are so deep rooted in society that, without affirmative action, these inequalities will never be removed. The Race Relations Act allows affirmative action in the provision of services to ensure the

**AFRICAN CARIBBEAN SOCIAL WORKER –
ADOPTIONS PROJECT DEVELOPMENT**

Qualified social worker to recruit, train, assess and
support black adopters and support the adoption
needs of black children.

**We are an equal opportunities employer. This
post is advertised under Section 5(2) of the Race
Relations Act 1976**

**ASIAN SENIOR CHILD PROTECTION
TELEPHONE COUNSELLOR**

We are planning an Asian languages service. To
help us create this we are looking for two
qualified and experienced Asian social workers.

These posts are advertised under S5(2) of the
Race Relations Act 1976 and are only open to
applicants who are Asian and who are fluent
in at least one of the following languages:
Bengali, Gujarati, Hindi, Punjabi or Urdu.

Male Senior Practitioner

Young Abusers Counselling Project

Your role will involve risk assessment
and counselling of young sexual abusers,
provision of therapeutic help to young
people and their carers, and giving advice
and consultation to other professionals.

This post is advertised under Section 7(2) of
the Sex Discrimination Act 1975

Female Social Worker

Abuse Survivors Counselling Service

Counsellor required to provide individual
counselling to young women aged 12 to 21 and to
mothers who are survivors of sexual abuse.

**Section 7(2) of the Sex Discrimination Act
1975 applies**

Some job advertisements allow discrimination for special reasons

welfare of particular groups, or to promote the participation of under-represented
groups. Both the Sex Discrimination Act and Race Relations Act allow discrimination in
employment where there is a genuine occupational qualification.

Think it over

Look in the social work press for job advertisements claiming exemption under s5(2)d
Race Relations Act and s7(2) Sex Discrimination Act. Why are the advertised posts
exempt from the anti-discriminatory legislation? What are the arguments for and
against this type of affirmative action?

Think it over

Have you ever met affirmative action in your own life or heard a friend or relative
complain about someone else receiving affirmative action? How would you support
affirmative action if it disadvantaged someone you care for? It can be very difficult
under such circumstances.

Freedom from harassment

Harassment is an expression of prejudice in an intrusive form which is harmful to the
victim. It involves verbal or physical abuse, unwanted attention, bullying, jokes and
exclusion. Harassment on the bases of race and sex are illegal under the anti-
discrimination legislation, but all groups liable to discrimination may suffer from it. It is
often disguised in the form of humour, and people committing harassment will often
defend themselves by saying that they did not mean it, or it was only a joke, and that

people complaining about it have no sense of humour. Harassment is never acceptable and people have an absolute right to be protected from it. Employers should have a policy for dealing with harrassment which is known and understood by all their staff.

Assessment activity 1.3

Imagine that you are a single parent who has been offered a job working 3 days a week in the sales team of a local company. However, there are no nurseries that are able to look after your 4-year-old daughter and you cannot afford a child minder.

Write a letter to your local MP explaining how you feel you have been discriminated against and what effect this could have on you and your child.

What could your local health, care and early years services do to promote your rights and enable your return to work? How would they monitor this?

Human rights legislation

The Human Rights Act 1998

Until October 2000, UK law covered only three areas of discrimination: race, sex and disability. This changed in October 2000, when the European Convention on Human Rights (see page 3) was incorporated into UK law as the Human Rights Act 1998.

It is early yet to predict how the implementation of the Human Rights Act 1998 will affect the way that care organisations and individual care workers work with service users. It will enable people to enforce their rights under the Convention in British courts, and all other legislation must be compatible with the Act.

Main sections and implications for health, care or early years

These are some of the effects which the Human Rights Act may have on care practice.

Article 2: Protection of life

The right to life provision of the Convention will be very important in health settings. It will have to be considered in matters such as abortion and in end-of-life decisions, such as whether to switch off life support systems. It will question the legality of 'postcode rationing' of services on resource grounds, particularly of life-saving operations and medications. Children on the child protection register not allocated a social worker may be covered, as well as the closure of nursing homes or care homes which often results in residents being moved, perhaps reducing their life expectancy.

Article 3: Prohibition of torture and inhuman and degrading treatment

Neglectful treatment of clients in residential homes, the failure to provide proper health care or social care and failure to protect children from abuse may be covered by this article. It has been suggested that refusal of contact between parents and children in care may be contested on this ground. Life prolonging treatment which causes pain and suffering may also be covered.

Article 5: Right to liberty and the security of the person

The arrangements for compulsory admission to hospital under the Mental Health Act will have to meet the requirements of this article. Delays in making practical arrangements for the discharge of people no longer suffering from mental disorder may infringe it. It may have repercussions for locking the door of an elderly resident's room, even if they are at risk of wandering.

Article 6: Right to a fair and public hearing

Lack of openness or failure to involve service users in any proceedings, such as child protection conferences, adoption panels and mental health review tribunals may infringe this article. Disciplinary committees of professional bodies such as the BMA and UKCC will have to consider this article when the outcome would affect a person's right to work.

Article 8: Right to respect for private and family life, home and correspondence

This article will be important in any procedure removing children from their parents, and any refusal of contact. Closure of care and nursing homes will be covered. It may provide a positive duty on social services to help older people to stay in their own homes. It might be a breach of their rights if they have to go into hospital or residential care because care was not provided in the community. Older people kept in hospital when their needs could be better met by a care package at home may also argue that their rights under this article have been breached.

Article 9: Freedom of thought, conscience and religion

This article will promote the ability of clients to practise their religion. Matching children with foster homes and adoptive homes of the same faith may become a more important consideration. The right of residents in care homes to follow religious practices will also be protected.

Article 12: Right to marry and found a family

Organisations turning down people as prospective adoptive and foster parents may have to justify their decisions under this article. It may also cover people with physical or learning disabilities who are discouraged from becoming parents, or who have children removed from them.

Article 14: Prohibition of discrimination on the grounds of: sex, race, colour, language, religion, political or other opinion, national or social origin, association with a national minority, property, birth or other status.

This article cannot be applied on its own, but applies to all the other rights in the Convention. The term 'other status' may have a wide interpretation, and make discrimination illegal in a range of situations not otherwise mentioned in the Act.

Key issue

Watch the press for stories linked with the Human Rights Act, or use the Internet to search a newspaper archive. Write a report on how the Act is changing the way care services are delivered.

The rights of an individual may need to be overridden

Although the Human Rights Act guarantees the rights of individuals, not all of these rights are guaranteed in all circumstances. The right to life and the freedom from degrading and inhuman treatment are absolute. However, many other rights are called *qualified rights*. This means that they can be set aside in some circumstances. The right to liberty may be lost if detention is based in law, such as the Mental Health Act (see page 20), or if a crime is committed. The right to privacy may be limited by the need to prevent crime, to safeguard the individual or to protect others.

This recognises that not everybody's rights can be enforced as there may be tensions and contradictions between two rights of one individual, or between competing rights of different individuals. There is more about this on page 22.

The use of power and force

Carers have power over service users because they have control over some aspects of their lives. This power is not legitimate. It should be limited by giving service users choice whenever possible. Power that is not legitimate is oppression.

Force means using physical means to make someone do something, or to prevent them from doing something. It should only be used as an absolutely last resort, and when there is legal authority to do so (see below). It should be extremely rare for a care worker to use force of any kind with an adult. If things are serious enough to justify the use of force, the police will usually be called. There may be occasional situations in working with children when restraint is justified.

Everybody takes risks in their everyday lives; for example, driving and crossing the road are not risk-free activities. It is sometimes difficult for care staff to accept that clients should be allowed to take risks, because they feel responsible for them. In some ways this is true, and it is important that care organisations have a policy on what is acceptable risk, so that workers understand what the limits are.

A form of discrimination often applied to older people is to suggest that things should be done to them against their will, if it is for their own good. This is discriminatory, patronising and illegal. Client choice should always be respected, unless there are very good reasons for doing otherwise.

Think it over

An older person is living alone and at risk because she cannot look after herself and sometimes falls. She refuses to consider residential care. Should she be made to go into care? What is the difference between this older person and a younger person who wants to go rock climbing, which also involves risks?

Statutory powers

The law assumes that all adults are able to make decisions about their lives unless it is shown otherwise. This concept is known as **competence**. It does not automatically apply to children. The law demands that children show competence, or understanding, before they are allowed to make important decisions for themselves, such as consenting to medical treatment. Children of any age can consent to medical treatment, providing that they fully understand what is proposed. This principle was established by the Gillick case (*Gillick v West Norfolk and Wisbech Health Authority*). A child can refuse consent to treatment on the same basis, but the refusal can be overridden by anybody with parental responsibility giving consent.

Children Act

The Children Act 1989 introduced the concept of parental responsibility to replace parental rights. Although parental responsibility is not clearly defined, this is an important change because a responsibility is something which safeguards the rights of another. Here it is the rights of the child which are the more important. This reinforces the central principle of the Children Act 1989 which is the paramountcy of the welfare of the child. The Act has two main aims:

- to safeguard and promote the welfare of children
- to promote the upbringing of children by their families.

Parents and children have rights under the Human Rights Act (see page 17). The Children Act recognises that it is not always possible to reconcile everybody's rights, for example when a child is abused. Then the parents' rights take second place to the welfare of the child. If attempts to help a child within the family fail, then there are powers to remove them. To do this, the social services has to satisfy the court that:

- the child is suffering, or at risk of suffering, significant harm *and*
- this is the result of the care being given to the child, or because the child is beyond parental control.

The magistrates can only make a care order if they are satisfied that these conditions are met, and that it is in the best interests of the child to do so.

The police can also take a child into protection for up to 72 hours if they have reason to believe that the child would otherwise suffer significant harm.

The Mental Health Act
Because all adults are assumed to have competence, the law requires certain conditions to be satisfied before their right to choice is removed.

The Mental Health Act 1983 allows someone to be taken to hospital and kept there against their will for assessment or treatment if:

- they are suffering from a mental disorder *and*
- being kept in hospital against their will is the only way to protect their health, to prevent them from harming themselves or otherwise coming to harm, or to protect others from harm.

Two doctors and a social worker (or the patient's nearest relative) must agree compulsory detention is necessary. In an emergency, one doctor and a social worker may do so. The police also have powers to detain someone in a public place if they have reason to suspect that they are suffering from a mental disorder.

Case study

Mrs Greene has become very agitated. She has not slept for three nights and is not eating or drinking. She is talking continuously and constantly active with pointless tasks such as moving the furniture around. Her husband calls the GP. Mrs Greene is in danger of becoming exhausted and dehydrated, but refuses to take medication or go to hospital, as she does not believe she is ill. The GP calls the social worker and the psychiatrist.

- What should the doctors and social worker be considering before deciding whether it is justified to make Mrs Greene go to hospital? (It may help you to think about this if you read first through the section which follows.)

Common law

Some situations where clients' rights may be overridden are not covered by legislation (statute law), but by the common law. Common law is law that has built up over the years from custom and the decisions of judges. This does not mean that it is less important than statute law. There is no statute law against murder for instance, which is a common law offence.

The common law allows things to be done to people without their consent if they lack competence. They must be done in that person's best interests and only if they are unable to make the decision for themselves. This may be because they are prevented by a mental disability, or if they are unable to communicate a decision because they are unconscious or for any other reason. The safeguards are that, in deciding someone's best interests, consideration should be given to:

- their past and present wishes
- the need to maximise their participation in the decision
- the views of others (e.g. relatives) about the person's wishes and feelings
- the need to do what is least restrictive to their freedom.

It is an important role of advocacy (see pages 12–13) to make sure that these conditions are met.

Assessment activity 1.4

Write a report on how legislation can be used to protect an individual's rights, using four examples. Discuss particular situations where legislation can equally override the rights of the individual. Why is this? When can it be used?

Staff actively promote equality and individual rights

Treating people equally

Treating people equally does not mean treating everybody the same. It means to treat people in such a way as to give them equal access to services. It also means providing services in such a way that all service users get equal benefit from them.

These are some examples of how it might be necessary to treat people differently in order to treat them equally:

- a person who has English as an additional language may require a translator in order to understand the services available and to express a choice about them
- for cultural reasons, a Muslim client may require the services of a carer of the same sex to perform intimate tasks
- a child with a disability may be allocated a classroom assistant to enable them to take full advantage of mainstream education.

Theory into practice

Plan the development of a nursery to meet the needs of a diverse client group. Consider the staffing, building, equipment and activities required to provide an equal opportunities environment. Make notes of your reasons for each suggestion.

Confidentiality

There can be no such thing as complete confidentiality. Information about clients has to be shared between workers in health and care organisations in order to ensure continuity and good quality care. It has to be shared with managers to ensure worker accountability. Sometimes information will have to be passed to another agency to ensure that service users get the care they need. Clients should understand what information is held about them, with whom it will be shared, and under what circumstances. Their permission should be sought before sensitive information is passed to others. Whenever possible they should be able to control disclosure about themselves. Care staff should only seek information about clients on a 'need to know' basis.

There are circumstances where even very sensitive information may have to be passed on, even if the service user objects. This happens when there is a likelihood of harm if the information is not disclosed. This consideration will override the confidentiality of professional relationships. Examples are as follows:

- A GP has a patient suffering from a serious mental disorder, in need of hospital treatment but refusing it. The GP would have to provide information about the patient's condition to a social worker to enable the social worker to decide whether to make an application for compulsory admission to hospital.
- A social worker suspects that a client is physically abusing their children and a child protection case conference is convened. The professionals concerned must share information in order to protect the child.

Tensions and contradictions

For every right, there is a corresponding duty and responsibility on another person. The examples above show that there is no guarantee that rights and duties will never conflict. Because of this, care workers in all situations encounter tensions and contradictions in their roles. These differ from straightforward choices between right and wrong, because there is an element of right on both sides. These tensions arise for a number of reasons:

- The rights of one person may clash with the rights of others.

Case study

An older person is confused and wanders at night, repeatedly waking the neighbours with claims that he has been burgled. The neighbours demand something is done but when a social worker offers the older person residential care, he refuses it.

- The right of the person to choose conflicts with the right of the neighbours to lead an undisturbed life. Whose rights should take precedence?

- Two different rights a person has may conflict.

Case study

An elderly person in a residential home is confused and thinks that her parents are still alive. She insists on leaving the home at night to look for them. The weather is bad, and the home is on a busy road. The resident would not be safe outside.

*   The resident's right to choose is conflicting with the right to be protected from harm. Which right is more important?

*   Two obligations of a care worker may conflict.

Case study

A home care assistant has a good relationship with a service user who is severely disabled with a degenerative disease. The assistant calls one day to discover that the service user has taken a large overdose of medication, and left a note expressing a wish to be left to die. The care assistant knows that the service user has thought this through but the assistant has responsibilities as an employee of a social services department.

*   What is the first responsibility of the worker?

*   Cultural values may conflict.

Case study

A young child requires an operation. The parents are Jehovah's Witnesses and refuse permission for the child to have a blood transfusion. The doctors can either operate without a transfusion, which increases the risk to the child, or overrule the parents.

*   Is the parents' right to bring up the child as they wish more important than the duty of the doctors to carry out the operation in the safest way possible?

*   Resource allocation often has a moral dimension.

Case study

An NHS Trust has a limited budget, and cannot meet all the health needs of its population. A patient in a Persistent Vegetative State has a limited chance of recovery, and is taking up a scarce bed in an Intensive Care Unit. The patient has the right to life, but the bed could be used for other critically ill patients with a better chance of recovery.

*   How should this choice be made?

Think it over
In a group, choose one of the preceding case studies and discuss the arguments on both sides.

Staff development and training

One of the responsibilities of a manager is the professional development of their staff. This may be done formally through supervision sessions, or more informally in the course of day-to-day working. The manager should supervise the work of staff, offer advice and guidance in difficult situations and help the workers identify training opportunities to improve their practice.

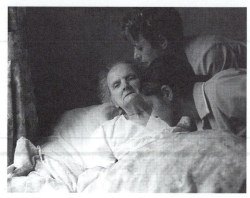

A manager is responsible for the professional development of staff

Education and training will help a worker recognise tensions in their work roles, how to begin to deal with them, and when to seek management advice. These tensions may go unrecognised without a sound knowledge of client rights and the Care Value Base. Workers who go on to further professional training will be equipped by their training to make more complex decisions that respect clients' rights in difficult situations. Professions have codes of conduct to guide their members in how to carry out their work, and there may be a controlling body with disciplinary procedures to deal with workers who do not meet acceptable standards (see page 10).

Practice implications of confidentiality

Every organisation should have a confidentiality policy to protect their clients and meet the requirements of the Care Value Base, and also the requirements of the Data Protection Act 1998.

The Data Protection Act 1998 has eight key principles which apply to both paper and computer records. These principles govern the way health and care services deal with information they hold about users.

1 **Personal data must be obtained and processed fairly and lawfully**
   Service users must be told that records are kept about them, and how and why these records are kept. They must be told who the information may be shared with, and why, and should be asked to give their consent. Service users must also be told of their rights of access to information held about them.

2 **Personal data shall be held only for one or more specified and lawful purposes**
   Organisations must have a lawful reason to hold data on individuals, for instance to enable them to provide, monitor and review services, and to provide statistical information to central government.

3 **Personal data must be relevant, adequate and not excessive**
   Organisations should only keep information they need to provide a service, nothing more and nothing less.

4 **Personal data shall be accurate and kept up to date**
   Facts should be checked before being recorded and the records of service users should be reviewed regularly to make sure that information held about them is correct. If service users' details change, the record must be amended as soon as possible.

5 **Personal data must not be kept for longer than is necessary**
Organisations should have a disposal date for records, and these should be destroyed when the date arrives. Some records, such as those concerning people who have received services, may be destroyed within a few years of the service ending. Others, such as adoption records and the records of people who have committed offences which may make them a danger to children, may be kept for as long as 100 years.

6 **Personal data must be processed in accordance with the rights of data subjects**
Individuals have rights of access to their records and rights about when information is passed to others. There are exemptions, which cover situations where people would be at risk, but generally users should be able to see information held about them, and have control over who that information is given to.

7 **Personal data must be kept secure from unauthorised access, alteration, disclosure, loss or destruction**
Paper records should be stored safely. There should be a system for removing and returning files. Electronic records should be protected by passwords and backed up regularly.

8 **Personal data shall not be transferred to a country outside the European Economic Area unless that country ensures an adequate level of protection**
Principle 8 is unlikely to affect health and care organisations, and is intended to ensure that data is only transferred to countries where there are appropriate safeguards about how it will be dealt with.

Every organisation should have a nominated member of staff to act as data controller. An individual who believes that their rights under the Data Protection Act have been infringed should complain to the data controller within the organisation. Anyone who is not satisfied with how the complaint is dealt with can complain to the Data Protection Commissioner.

Think it over
Think about an organisation with which you have come into contact. How well did the policies and procedures of the organisation protect individuals' confidentiality?

How the individual care worker can promote equality, diversity and rights in their own practice

The bases of discrimination and how these may be reflected in the behaviour of care workers

Every care worker should have an understanding of the bases of discrimination within society. Bases of discrimination are cultural features, so they will all have widely held stereotypes associated with them. Everyone will have been exposed to these at some level, and some of them will have been absorbed. If they are not questioned, then they will be reflected in our behaviour. It is important to identify your own beliefs and prejudices because much discrimination is unintentional – the result of learned attitudes and lack of knowledge.

Identifying one's own beliefs and prejudices

There is a natural tendency for human beings to classify things into groups. In the past, this had evolutionary advantages. When all humans were hunter-gatherers, it would have been extremely important to make quick decisions about what was a predator and what was prey, on the basis of very limited information. People unable to do this would either not eat or be eaten themselves. This is a skill which is still important today, for instance when crossing the road there is not time to consciously process a lot of information about size, shape and colour before deciding that the object approaching is a car.

In Figure 1.7, the pictures, although very different, are all chairs. In recognising them, we are demonstrating that we have a stereotype of a chair, and by calling them all chairs, we are labelling them.

This ability to classify objects and make judgements on limited information is very useful. However, it is damaging if applied to people. It may lead to discrimination through prejudice, stereotyping and labelling. We must accept that we all have this tendency.

Figure 1.7 These items can all be labelled as chairs

Changing one's own beliefs and prejudices

There are two steps to changing one's beliefs and prejudices. The first is for individuals to think about their own attitudes, and accept that some may be based on prejudice. The second step is to seek out accurate information about the issue, since prejudice can only flourish with ignorance. It will probably be necessary to do this in cooperation with others, perhaps in the context of support groups or awareness training. You may have the opportunity to check out your beliefs and attitudes about a group with a member of that group. This would have to be done with great tact.

Key issue

In a group, spend a few minutes thinking about what your life might be like when you are 80 years old. Write down some notes about your thoughts. Share these notes with the other group members. What do they tell you about your attitudes towards older people? Are the thoughts of the entire group similar? What does this tell you? Do any of the group have very different ideas? How might these have arisen?

Challenging oppressive and discriminatory behaviour

Good care practice is anti-discriminatory, not only non-discriminatory. It is important to challenge oppressive and discriminatory behaviour whenever it happens. Ignoring it or doing nothing about it is not a neutral option. If oppression is ignored and not opposed, this is the same as accepting it, and it will be reinforced in the minds of both the oppressor and the oppressed.

In order to challenge oppression, workers must be aware of their beliefs and prejudices, and have examined them. They have to be confident in their knowledge of the rights of clients, and of the values, laws, codes of practice and procedures which support them. To support clients, it may be necessary to know the means of redress open to them, such as complaints procedures, and the roles of support groups and statutory bodies such as:

- the Equal Opportunities Commission
- the Commission for Racial Equality
- the Disability Rights Commission
- the Data Protection Commissioner.

It is also necessary to have an assertive approach, as challenging people over discriminatory behaviour may lead to defensiveness and possibly even aggression. It is important for the worker challenging discriminatory behaviour to know how to get support from colleagues and from within the management structure of their organisations.

Think it over

In a group, consider the following situation. You are an assistant in a nursery class. One of the children makes racist remarks about another child. Discuss how you would deal with them.

Bases of discrimination in society and the links between discrimination and behaviour

All bases of discrimination have linked prejudicial attitudes which directly affect the behaviour of those who hold them. Below are some examples.

Older people may be thought of as a burden, or a drain on resources resulting in their being begrudged appropriate services, and preference given to younger people when resources are limited. Older people are often treated like children; they are patronised and not consulted when decisions are made about them, resulting in disempowerment. Sometimes illnesses are seen as an inevitable result of old age, and not investigated or treated appropriately.

People with disabilities may experience similar attitudes to older people. They are often patronised by others pitying them, regarding them as objects of charity or remarking on their bravery. This is a stereotype which, although apparently positive, is damaging. They may be treated as though their disability were general rather than specific, and ignored by others – the 'does he take sugar?' syndrome – and excluded from social contacts and decisions about themselves. People with learning difficulties are particularly vulnerable to being treated as children.

What is wrong here? Who should the waitress be speaking to? What effects will such discrimination have on the person in the wheelchair?

People with mental disorders may similarly be regarded as dangerous to others. Some may be, but so are many people without a mental disorder. Of those people with mental disorders who could harm someone, there are far more who harm themselves than harm other people. Fear may result in people being treated in a more restrictive way than is necessary for their own or others' safety.

People with HIV/AIDS will be open to discrimination if people do not understand how the virus is transmitted. If they wrongly believe it can be caught from touch, or sharing crockery and cutlery, they may exclude them from normal social contact. If care workers are not well informed, it will result in clients receiving a poorer service.

Appropriate use of language

No competent care worker will use overtly discriminatory language, but it is also necessary to be aware of more subtle ways in which language can devalue clients. Some words have fallen into disuse because they have acquired negative connotations. No one would use words such as cripple, imbecile or lunatic, though at one time all were in common use. Workers should be aware that this is a continuing process. A handicap now is regarded as a socially constructed disadvantage that results from a disability, because of the attitudes of others or the lack of appropriate resources and facilities. The two terms should not be confused. Similarly, learning difficulty is a more appropriate term to use than mental handicap.

Workers should also be aware of the danger of stereotyping and labelling service users by grouping them together in relation to a single characteristic – an illness, for instance. To call individuals schizophrenics, rather than people with schizophrenia, makes their

illness the most important thing about them, and devalues them by ignoring their other qualities. Individuals should not be described as suffering from an illness, because this makes them into passive victims. Referring to people as having an illness is more empowering and conducive to an open minded approach to them as individuals. Terms such as 'confined to a wheelchair' are similarly unacceptable and patronising. People with disabilities regard themselves as wheelchair users, and the wheelchair as something which enables – not confines – them.

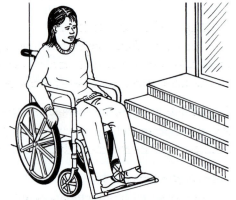
Disability or handicap?

Role modelling

Care workers are important role models because discriminatory attitudes are learned. We know that failing to challenge discriminatory behaviour will reinforce it, and the reverse is true. If discriminatory behaviour is challenged, then the person discriminating may rethink their attitudes – especially if their behaviour was unconscious or unthinking. The person discriminated against will at least know that not everybody shares the same discriminatory attitudes.

It is important that the worker does not just pay lip service to anti-discriminatory practice, but that they show it in their everyday working lives. This is particularly true when working with children, for whom role models will be more influential in forming their attitudes. If services are delivered in such a way that they conform to sexual stereotypes, or fail to respect different cultures, then whatever statements are made about equal opportunities, the message that will be learned is that it is all right to discriminate.

Practice implications of confidentiality

Every worker has a statutory and professional duty to protect information about service users.

Interviewing

When sensitive information is being discussed, interviews with clients should always be somewhere they cannot be overheard. Workers should always be aware that clients have the right to keep back information, and should not pressurise clients or be oppressive in their questioning if this happens.

Recording

Workers should take care to distinguish between facts and opinions when recording information about clients. They should only record information necessary for the organisation to carry out its responsibilities.

Storage of information

Electronic data should be protected with passwords. Workers must never use somebody else's password, and should not let anyone else use theirs. When using a computer, workers should make sure that screens are positioned so that unauthorised people cannot see them.

Files and other paper records should be kept securely where unauthorised people cannot get access to them, and never left lying around. Workers should only remove files from their secure location when there is a good reason for doing so.

Sharing of information

Workers should ask the client's permission before passing on sensitive information to others. They should check that any enquirer has the right to the information and the need to know. If in doubt, they should consult a manager. They should check the identity of people requesting information, to ensure that they are who they claim to be. Sometimes information may have to be given over the telephone, in which case it is good practice to ring back to confirm the person's identity.

Workers should take care when passing information to authorised people, so that sensitive information is not overheard by people who do not have the right or need to know. They should never gossip about the private affairs of clients, either between themselves or outside work with friends and family.

End of unit test

1 Why doesn't equality of opportunity lead to equality of outcome?

2 What are the problems in defining the moral rights of individuals?

3 Identify two reports which provide evidence for a cycle of disadvantage. State the main findings of each.

4 What is the contribution of the McPherson Report to our understanding of unequal access to services?

5 What is the difference between a prejudice and a stereotype?

6 What is the difference between statute and common law?

7 Identify three pieces of anti-discriminatory legislation.

8 How might the Human Rights Act cause a tension between the rights of children and their parents in cases of suspected child abuse?

9 How do the main aims of the Children Act meet the requirements of the Human Rights Act?

10 A very confused resident of a care home wants to go out in the early hours of the morning. The resident is very frail, the weather is bad, and the resident has nowhere to go. Do the staff have any right to stop the resident?

11 Why might it be necessary to treat people differently in order to treat them equally?

12 What are the arguments for and against affirmative action?

13 What are the limits to confidentiality in the client/carer relationship?

14 Which organisation assists patients who wish to complain about health services?

15 Describe a situation in statute law which allows someone to be compulsorily detained, other than if they are suspected of a criminal offence.

References and further reading

Bagilhole, B. (1998) *Equal Opportunities and Social Policy*, Harlow: Longman

Brading, J. and Curtis, J. (1996) *Disability Discrimination, A Practical Guide to the New Law*, London: Kogan Page

British Medical Association and the Law Society (1995) *Assessment of Mental Capacity – Guidance for Doctors and Lawyers*, London: BMA

Centre for Policy on Ageing (1984) *Home Life – a code of practice for residential care*, London: CPA

Centre for Policy on Ageing (1986) *A Better Home Life – a code of practice for residential and nursing home care*, London: CPA

Clarke, L. (1995) (2nd edn) *Discrimination*, Wimbledon: Institute of Personnel Development

Clements, P. and Spinks, S. (1997) *The Equal Opportunities Guide*, London: Kogan Page

Donnellan, C. (ed.) (1999) *Issues for the Nineties: Vol. 6 Racial discrimination; Vol. 13 What are Children's Rights; Vol. 17 Disabilities and Equality; Vol. 18 Gender and Prejudice*, Cambridge: Independence Educational Publishers

Family Welfare Association Guide to the Social Services 2001/2002

Fenwick, H. (1998) (2nd edn) *Civil Liberties*, Harlow: Longman

Linden, J. (1998) *Equal Opportunities in Practice*, London: Hodder

Mason, D. (1997) *Race and Ethnicity in Modern Britain*, Oxford: Oxford University Press

Moonie, N. (ed.) (2000) A*VCE Health and Social Care*, Oxford: Heinemann

Thompson, N. (2000) *Anti-discriminatory Practice*, Basingstoke: Macmillan

Wadham, J. and Crossman, G. (2000) *Your Rights*: *The Liberty Guide to Human Rights*, London: Pluto Press

Webb, R. and Tossel, D. (1993) *Social Issues for Carers*, London: Edward Arnold

Worsley, J. (1989) *Taking Good Care*: A *Handbook for Care Assistants*, London: Age Concern

2 Communication and supportive skills

This unit explores the skills of effective interpersonal interaction and communication. It examines the factors that enhance and inhibit communication and provides you with some guidance on how to communicate effectively with clients in many situations, including the support of distressed individuals.

In order to achieve this unit you must produce reports of interactions that you have undertaken which meet the grading criteria requirements. It may be easier to report a small range of different interactions that demonstrate different aspects of the criteria for passing this unit, than to attempt to meet all the criteria with just one report.

The criteria for this unit require you to demonstrate a number of practical skills. You must show that you have reviewed your own personal communication methods, demonstrated the use of supportive skills, used communication skills effectively and appropriately, demonstrated ways of overcoming or minimising barriers to communication and used examples from placement to explain how communication skills can support a distressed individual. In order to gather evidence of these criteria, it may be useful to maintain a logbook that records details of conversations and other interactions which have occurred in placement settings. These records can then be used to create detailed transcripts of interactions which can be evaluated in order to meet the grading criteria.

What you need to learn

- Interpersonal interaction and communication
- Supportive skills
- Communication skills
- Supportive skills with distressed individuals

Interpersonal interaction and communication

Many animals and insects communicate information in some way, but no other species can communicate in the complex range of ways used by human beings.

Types of interpersonal interaction

There are many different ways in which people communicate with each other. These can include: language, body language, signs and symbols, written communication, art and music. Recorded information also enables communication to take place.

Language

Spoken, signed or written language can communicate complex and subtle messages between individuals or groups of people. Language not only enables people to communicate information, but it also provides a basis for people to develop concepts. Concepts influence the way individuals think. Concepts enable us to group experiences together to help us understand events that we have experienced. Concepts also enable us to predict the future. Human civilisation has developed because of our ability to classify experience using language.

Language does not have to be based on sounds which are heard. Signing systems such as British Sign Language provide a full language system for people who do not use spoken language.

Body language

Facial expressions, body posture and muscle tone all provide messages as to how we feel and perhaps what we are thinking. Mime and drama use body language to communicate complex ideas and emotions.

Signs and symbols

Gestures made with hands or arms, written symbols or diagrams such as traffic signs all communicate messages to people.

Written communication

Books, email, text messages and so on, allow people to communicate around the world and even across centuries of time. Written communication does not have to be visual. Braille (a system of raised marks that can be felt with your fingers) provides a system of written communication for people who do not use visual systems of communication.

Artwork and other objects which are designed or built

Paintings, photographs, sculptures, architecture, ornaments and other household objects can communicate messages and emotions to people. People often take photographs or buy souvenirs to remind them of happy experiences. Many individuals earn their living by designing and developing artwork.

Music

Music can provide an effective communication system for expressing emotion. Music is sometimes called the language of emotion.

Recorded information

Books, magazines, newspapers, films, videos, tapes, CDs and other electronic media enable us to re-experience events or messages from the past.

Communicating simple messages

Some forms of communication involve simply sending a message within a fixed unambiguous system of meaning. An example might be an airline pilot trying to park an aircraft. The pilot might be guided by a member of the ground staff using arm signals.

The arm signal clearly indicates the direction that the aircraft must turn towards. Each arm signal will have a simple meaning, which is exactly the same for pilots, and for the ground crew – the message cannot be misinterpreted.

Communicating complex messages

Most communication between people is not simple and unambiguous. Artwork, for example, rarely communicates straightforward information. It is normal for people to experience completely different messages from the same piece of artwork. Paintings,

Some messages are simple and unambiguous

sculptures and poems are not designed to give people information but to stimulate thoughts and emotions in people. Beauty is said to be in the eye of the beholder – this phrase means that what we experience depends on the way we think, as well as what it is that we hear or are looking at.

Within health care settings a great deal of communication with members of the public will be complex. It is vitally important to understand that people will have their own ways of interpreting things that are said to, or done to them. Communication with members of the public should not be a simple matter of trying to pass on information. Effective communication will depend on engaging in a 'communication cycle', which takes into account the way information is being received by the other person. Different people will interpret messages in different ways. Effective communication requires much more than giving clear information.

The communication cycle

When we communicate with other people we become involved in a process of expressing our own thoughts and interpreting the other person's understanding of what we are communicating. This process should usually involve the steps set out in Figure 2.1.

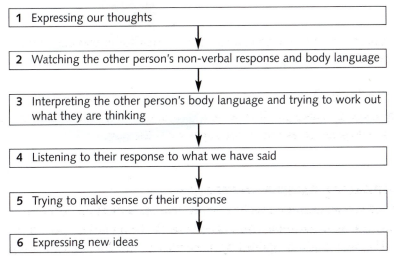

Figure 2.1 The process of expression and interpretation

Communication needs to be a two-way process where each person is trying to understand the viewpoint of the other person. The communication cycle requires professionals (at least) to have advanced listening skills and the ability to check their understanding of others' responses (see Figure 2.2).

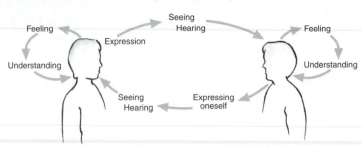

Figure 2.2 The communication cycle

Listening is not the same as hearing the sounds people make when they talk. Listening involves hearing another person's words – then thinking about what they mean – then thinking what to say back to the other person. Some people call this process 'active listening'. As well as thinking carefully and remembering what someone says, good listeners will also make sure their non-verbal communication demonstrates interest in the other person.

Skilled listening involves:

1 looking interested and ready to listen
2 hearing what is said
3 remembering what is said
4 checking understanding with the other person.

It is usually easier to understand people who are similar to ourselves. We can learn about different people by checking our understanding of what we have heard.

Checking our understanding involves hearing what the other person says and asking the other person questions. Another way to check our understanding is to put what a person has just said into our own words and to say this back to them, to see if we did understand what they said.

When we listen to complicated details of other people's lives, we often begin to form mental pictures based on what they are telling us. Listening skills involve checking these mental pictures to make sure that we understand correctly. It can be very difficult to remember accurately what people tell us if we don't check how our ideas are developing.

Good listening involves thinking about what we hear while we are listening and checking our understanding as the conversation goes along. Sometimes this idea of checking our understanding is called 'reflection' because we reflect on the other person's ideas (see Figure 2.3).

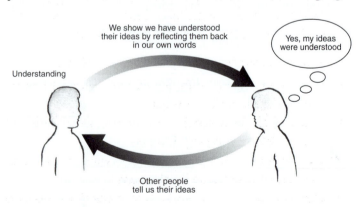

Figure 2.3 Reflection

Good listening is hard work. Instead of just being around when people speak, we must build up our understanding of the people around us. Although listening is difficult, people who are attracted to work in health care may often enjoy learning about other people and their lives.

Assessment activity 2.1

Identify two contrasting examples of interpersonal interaction that you have had. One could be spoken, for example a conversation with someone you know well. The other could be written, for example a letter you have received.

For each one, describe the interaction and evaluate how effective it was. Were there any barriers or difficulties to overcome? If it was successful and the meanings were clear, what factors contributed to its success?

Barriers to effective interpersonal interaction

Communication can become blocked if individual difficulties and differences are not understood. There are three main ways that communication becomes blocked:

1   A person cannot see, hear or receive the message.
2   A person cannot make sense of the message.
3   A person misunderstands the message.

Examples of the first kind of block, where people don't receive the communication, include visual disabilities, hearing disabilities and environmental problems, such as poor lighting, noisy environments, and speaking from too far away (see Figure 2.4).

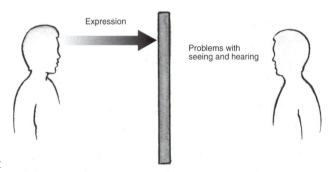

Figure 2.4 Environmental problems like noise and poor light can create communication barriers

Examples of where people may not be able to make sense of the message include:

- the use of different languages, including signed languages
- the use of different terms in language, such as jargon (technical language), slang (different people using different terms), or dialect (different people making different sounds)
- physical and intellectual disabilities, such as dysphasia (difficulties with language expression or understanding), aphasia (an absence of language ability), being ill, or suffering memory loss, or learning difficulty.

Reasons for misunderstanding a message include:

- cultural influences – different cultures interpret non-verbal and verbal messages, and humour in different ways
- assumptions about people – about race, gender, disability and other groupings
- labelling or stereotyping of others
- social context – statements and behaviour that are understood by friends and family may not be understood by strangers
- emotional barriers – a worker's own emotional needs may stop them from wanting to know about others
- time pressures which cause staff to withdraw from wanting to know about others
- emotional differences – these can sometimes be interpreted as personality clashes, or personality differences. Very angry, or very happy, or very shy people may misinterpret communication from others.

Effective communication requires that healthcare workers evaluate the possible barriers to communication and find ways of overcoming these barriers.

Assessment activity 2.2

Mr A, aged 75, came from Bangladesh to the UK to live with his daughter and son-in-law, ten years ago. Recently, he has become forgetful and has also had some difficulty in hearing speech when there is any background noise. His daughter has decided to take him to the doctor for an assessment. They are shown into the consulting room of the locum doctor, who is a young woman.

What barriers to communication might there be in this interpersonal interaction? Describe each one, giving reasons why they could prevent effective communication. Keep a record in your portfolio.

Communication and culture

Non-verbal communication is a type of language. There are many languages in the world and they do not all have the same concepts and sounds. Non-verbal communication is not the same everywhere. For example, in Britain the hand gesture with palm up and facing forward, means 'Stop, don't do that'. In Greece it can mean, 'You are dirt' and is a very rude gesture.

Why do the same physical movements have different meanings? The answer lies in culture. One explanation for the hand signs is that the British version of the palm-and-fingers gesture means, 'I arrest you, you must not do it'; whereas the Greek interpretation goes back to medieval times when criminals had dirt rubbed in their faces to show how much people despised them.

Without looking at the history and culture of a society, it is confusing to consider why gestures mean what they do. No one can know all the history and all the cultural possibilities of body language and non-verbal communication. But it is vitally important that carers should always remember that people have different cultural backgrounds. The carer's system of non-verbal communication may not carry the same meanings to everyone. We can easily misinterpret another person's non-verbal messages.

Personal space and culture

Sometimes cultural differences are very marked. British people are often seen as 'unusual' or odd by other cultures when they go outside Europe, because they keep a large personal space around them. Other people are not allowed to come too near when they speak, or to touch them. In many other cultures, standing close is normal and good manners – touching an arm or shoulder is just what people do. Some British people can feel threatened by such behaviour because it is not what they have grown up with. For some British people, strangers who come too close or who touch are trying to dominate or have power over them. They become afraid or defensive. However, things work out when this need for space and distance is understood and allowed for by people from other cultures.

From a caring viewpoint, the right attitude is to have respect for other people's culture. People learn different ways of behaving, and good carers will try to understand the different ways in which people use non-verbal messages. For instance, past research in the USA suggests that white and black Americans may have used different non-verbal signals when they listened. It suggests that some black Americans may tend not to look much at the speaker. This can be interpreted as a mark of respect – by looking away it demonstrates that you are really thinking hard about the message. Unfortunately, not all white people understood this cultural difference in non-verbal communication. Some individuals misunderstood and assumed that this non-verbal behaviour meant exactly what it would mean if they had done it – that is, it would mean they were not listening.

Learning the cultural differences

There is an almost infinite variety of meanings that can be given to any type of eye contact, facial expression, posture or gesture. Every culture develops its own special system of meanings. Health care workers have to understand and show respect and value for all these different systems of sending messages. But how can you ever learn them all?

In fact, no one can learn every possible system of non-verbal message – but it is possible to learn about the ones people you are with are using! It is possible to do this by first noticing and remembering what others do – what non-verbal messages they are sending. The next step is to make an intelligent guess as to what messages the person is trying to give you. Finally, check your understanding (your guesses) with the person: ask polite questions as well as watching the kind of reactions you get. So, at the heart of skilled interpersonal interaction is the ability to watch other people, remember what they do, and guess what actions might mean and then check out your guesses with the person.

- Never rely on your own guesses, because often these turn into assumptions.
- If you don't check out assumptions with people, you may end up misunderstanding them.
- Misunderstandings can lead to discrimination.

Think it over

Imagine you are working with an older person. Whenever you start to speak to her she always looks at the floor and never makes eye contact. Why is this?

Your first thought is that she might be sad or that you make her sad. Having made such an assumption, you might not want to work with this person – she is too depressing and you do not seem to get on. You might even decide that you do not like her. But you could ask: 'How do you feel today? Would you like me to get you anything?' By checking out what she feels, you could test your own understanding. She might say she feels well and is quite happy, and then suggests something you could do for her. This means that she cannot be depressed.

Why else would someone look at the floor rather than at you?

1 It could be a cultural value. She may feel it is not proper to look at you.
2 She may not be able to see you clearly, so she prefers not to try to look at you.
3 She may just choose not to conform to your expectations. Looking at the floor may be important to some other emotional feeling that she has.

So it would be unfair to assume that she was difficult or depressed just because she did not look at you when you talked to her.

Good caring is the art of getting to understand people – not acting on unchecked assumptions. So non-verbal messages should never be relied on; they should always be checked. Non-verbal messages can mean different things depending on the circumstances of the people who send them. But all messages are like this. Words can be looked up in a dictionary, and yet words do not always carry exactly the same meaning.

As well as looking at the whole picture of people's words, their non-verbal messages and where they are, it is also necessary to understand their culture, their individuality and how they see their social situation. This is why caring is such a skilled area of work. People can improve their skills constantly through experience, and through linking new ideas to their experience. The main thing is always to check out assumptions. It is important to remember that it is easy to misunderstand others. By checking out ideas it is possible to reduce the risks of being uncaring or discriminatory.

Culture, age and gender

A person's understanding of him or herself (a self concept) will be strongly influenced by past personal history and current social context. Socialisation into the rules of a culture has a major part to play in the way individuals form their self concept.

Perceptions of age-appropriate behaviour and gender-appropriate behaviour are strongly influenced by culture. Culture is the term used to describe the norms and values which belong to an identifiable social group. People are socialised into the norms and values of a culture; they learn the socially accepted rules of their group. Group norms and values – the 'rules' for behaviour – vary between different religious, ethnic, class, gender and age groups.

Norms and values which influence interpersonal interaction vary a great deal between different class groups and different regions of Britain. Not only do norms of interaction vary, but they also constantly evolve and change. It might be possible to invent a dictionary of rules for understanding the meanings of verbal and non-verbal behaviours; but such a dictionary would need constant revision for it to be accurate.

People of different age groups have usually been socialised into different norms with respect to interpersonal behaviour.

Case study

Florence Tucknell was born in 1912. When she was young there was a cultural norm that only close friends and family would call her by her first name. She was Miss Tucknell to everyone else. For a stranger to call her 'Florence' would be a sign of disrespect, a sign that they thought they were socially superior or more powerful than she was. When Florence went into a respite care home for a week she was upset that everyone used first names. She knows that this is what goes on nowadays, but this was not how she was brought up to behave.

However, Miss Tucknell was very pleased to be greeted by her carer who introduced herself by saying, 'I'm Anthea Shakespeare, may I ask your name?' Miss Tucknell replied, 'I'm Miss Tucknell, please.' 'Shall I call you Miss Tucknell then?' 'Yes please.'

The next day one of the other staff said 'Hello Flo, I've come to take you into lunch'. Miss Tucknell avoids this care worker whenever she can.

1 How do you think Miss Tucknell felt when she was addressed as 'Flo'?
2 What effect is this likely to have on her relations with this member of staff?
3 What actions could the member of staff have taken to avoid this problem?
4 Why is it important to use appropriate language with clients?

Martin Howarth was born in the north of England in 1949. He recently moved to the south east of England and took a job as a care worker. Martin was shocked to find that many of his younger female colleagues were complaining about his behaviour. Martin has been socialised into the norm of calling women 'Flower' or even 'Petal'. When Martin used these terms he was expecting to communicate approval, comradeship and warmth. Martin believed that these were universal terms of endearment, i.e. 'You are likeable, we're all working together, we get on – don't we?'

His new colleagues in the south had never been referred to as 'Flower' before and saw it as sexist and degrading: 'You are saying that I am weak, short-lived and that all that matters about my existence is my degree of sexual attractiveness!' Martin soon learned that age, gender and region affect how words are understood. Words change their value with time.

Supportive skills

Health care workers often work with people who are in pain, afraid, or who do not understand what might happen next. They are often vulnerable people – people who feel threatened by what they are experiencing. Health care staff must have advanced inter-personal skills if they are to be effective in meeting the needs of the people they work with.

Human needs are complex. Historically, health care staff often assumed that physical needs should always take priority over other social and cultural needs. Nowadays physical needs are often seen as the foundation for working with people, but not always the most important issue to address. One way of understanding human needs is through the work of Abraham Maslow (1908–1970). Maslow's theory was that the purpose of human life was personal growth. He believed that the quality of a human life can be understood in terms of an individual's development of their own ability and potential. Before a person can fully develop their potential, there are levels of need – called deficiency needs – which first have to be met. Maslow's levels of need are often set out as a pyramid as shown in Figure 2.5 on the left-hand side of the diagram. The role of communication in meeting these human needs is described on the right-hand side of the diagram.

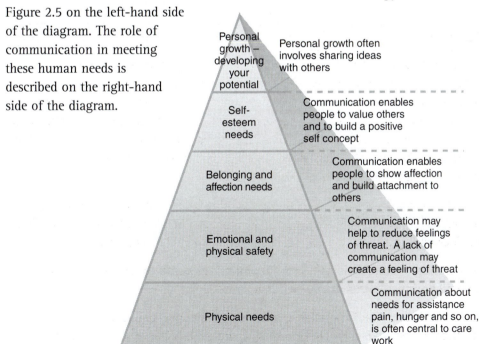

Figure 2.5 Communication within Maslow's levels of need

Effective communication needs to operate at every level of the triangle above. It is important to give and receive clear information about physical needs in order to respond to those needs. A lack of clear communication may result in a person's physical needs being unmet.

Listening skills are vital in order to create the basis for psychological safety and to reduce the threat that members of the public may feel. If a person does not feel that they have been listened to they may feel that they have not been shown respect as a person. A lack of respect may create a feeling of low self-esteem and emotional vulnerability. As well as this, the individual may feel that they are physically at risk because their needs have not been understood. Effective body language is vital to establish professional relationships and to create a sense of safety and belonging with people whom we work with.

Supportive skills are essential if workers are to meet the self-esteem needs of others. If workers can build an understanding of others' needs, then patients may feel that they have been respected and valued. Listening and supportive skills convey a sense of value to others.

An overview of supportive skills

Effective supportive behaviour will depend on a range of verbal and non-verbal skills, together with the ability to reflect on our own personal behaviour and to work in a context which enables effective communication.

Supportive body language

Muscle tone, facial expression, eye contact and posture can send messages of being friendly. When meeting a person it is usually appropriate to smile, to express interest through eye contact and to maintain a relaxed posture – free of muscle tension – indicating a readiness to talk and listen. It is difficult to define a simple set of rules for supportive body language because each individual will have their own expectations about what is appropriate and normal. Settings where conversation takes place can influence how people should behave. The most important thing about supportive body language is to learn to monitor the effects that our behaviour is having on the other person. Being supportive involves being aware of your own non-verbal behaviour and monitoring how your non-verbal behaviour is affecting others. The section on communication skills on page 47 explores the detail of components of non-verbal communication in more depth.

Think it over

Imagine that you feel sad about something and that you explain your problems to a friend. How would you feel if your friend did not look at you and instead seemed interested in what was happening outside the window? How would you feel if your friend just 'parroted' things you said back to you? How would you react if they just said things like 'I know, yes' all the time – without sounding at all sincere or interested?

Being a good friend involves supportive behaviour – how good are you at showing others that you understand their feelings?

Personal space

There are different social and cultural expectations about how close another person should be when they talk to you. For many British people, face-to-face contact where the two people are less than about 0.5 m apart suggests either intimacy (love and affection) or aggression. These interpretations are naturally suspended when a worker is performing a socially understood role, such as nursing or dentistry. Even so, some members of the public may feel threatened because their personal space has been entered. It may be important to establish a sense of trust through smiling and talking to the individual before coming closer than an arm's length.

Listening skills

Listening is an essential skill for supportive communication. As explained in the previous section, listening is an active process which involves thinking carefully about the content of the other person's speech and checking this understanding as the conversation progresses. It can also be important to plan even brief conversations so that there is an emotional structure to conversation (see Figure 2.6).

Usually we start with a greeting or ask how someone is. Conversations have a beginning, a middle and an end. This means that we have to create the right kind of atmosphere for a conversation at the beginning. We might need to help someone relax – we might need to show that we are friendly and relaxed. We then have the conversation.

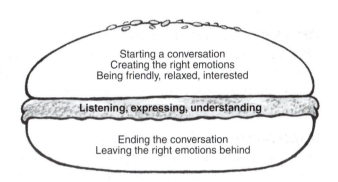

Starting a conversation
Creating the right emotions
Being friendly, relaxed, interested

Listening, expressing, understanding

Ending the conversation
Leaving the right emotions behind

Figure 2.6 The conversation sandwich

When we end the conversation we usually say something like 'See you soon'. When we end a conversation we have to leave the other person with the right feelings about what we have said.

Specialist skills for supportive communication

The skills for creating a sense of emotional safety were first identified by Carl Rogers (1902–1987). Originally these skills were seen as a basis for counselling relationships, but they have since become adopted as a basis for any befriending or supportive relationship. There are three conditions for a supportive conversation. These are that the carer must show (or convey) a sense of warmth, understanding and sincerity to the other person. These conditions sometimes have other names:

- warmth (sometimes called acceptance)
- understanding (originally called empathy)
- sincerity (originally called genuineness).

Conveying warmth

Conveying warmth means being seen as a warm, accepting person. In order to influence another person to view you this way you will need to demonstrate that you do not stereotype and label others. You will need to demonstrate that you do not judge other people as good or bad, right or wrong. This is sometimes referred to as a non-judgemental attitude. Warmth means not comparing people to see who is best!

Conveying warmth means being willing to listen to others. It means being able to prove that you are listening to a person because you can remember what they have said to you. Warmth involves using reflective listening. That is, you give your attention to the person when they talk, and remember what they say. You can then reflect the words back again.

Patient	'I hate it here, you don't know what it's like, there's no one to talk to, they're all too busy, no one cares about me.'
Worker	'I suppose they are busy and you feel that no one cares.'
Patient	'That's right, they don't – you aren't so bad, but you won't be here tomorrow.'
Worker	'Well that's right, I can't come in tomorrow but we could talk for a while now if you would like that.'

The worker is able to show the client that they are listening by repeating some of the things that the patient has said. The repetition is not 'parrot fashion'; the worker has used their own way of speaking. The worker has also avoided being judgemental. When the patient said that no one cared, the worker did not argue. The worker might have felt like saying, 'How can you say that – don't you know how hard we work for you? You want to think yourself lucky, there's plenty of people who would be pleased to be here, other people don't complain'. Such advice to think yourself lucky and make comparison with other people is judgemental; it does not value the other person, and it is not warm. If the worker had said these things it would have blocked the conversation. Warmth makes it safe for the patient to express their own feelings. Warmth means that the worker could disagree with what a patient has said, but the patient needs to feel safe in the conversation.

In developing the skill of showing warmth, it is important not to judge. Workers should accept that people have the right to be the way they are, and to make their own choices. While you may disapprove of a person's behaviour, you must show that you do not dislike them as an individual. This is particularly important when working with people with difficult behaviour. It is essential that individuals know it is the behaviour which is disliked, not them as a person.

Conveying understanding

Understanding means learning about the individual's identity and beliefs that a person has. Carl Rogers saw the idea of understanding or empathy as 'the ability to experience another person's world as if it was your own world'; the key part being the 'as if'. We always keep an idea of our own world and we know that other people have different experiences from our own. It is important to try to really understand the thoughts and feelings of others.

Reflective listening provides a useful tool to help staff to learn about people gradually. By keeping a conversation going, a person may feel understood; the worker is warm and non-judgemental, so it becomes safe for a person to tell the worker something personal. If the worker checks that they understand the person, the individual may feel valued. The person who feels valued may talk more. The more the person talks, the more the worker has a chance to learn about their views.

Patient	'So anyway, I said to the doctor, look these pills are only making me worse, I don't want them.'
Worker	'So you told him to stop them.'
Patient	'That's right, I don't believe in pills – you end up rattling round with all that lot inside you – if you're meant to get better you will, that's what I say.'
Worker	'Have you always believed that pills don't help?'
Patient	'Yes, well ever since I was young, I put my faith in God.'

By listening and conveying warmth the worker is being given the privilege of learning about the patient's religious views and perhaps even needs. Understanding can grow from a conversation which conveys value for the other person.

If you can get to understand people a sense of trust may develop. A person who is understood and not judged may consider it safe to share thoughts and worries with staff.

Conveying sincerity

Being sincere means being open about what you say and the way that you speak. It means not acting, not using set phrases or professional styles which are not really you. In some ways being sincere means being yourself – being honest and real! This has to involve being non-judgemental, trying to understand people rather than trying to give people advice. If being honest means giving other people your advice – don't do it! However, when you listen and learn about other people, do use your own normal language. Think about ways you might describe yourself and occasionally share details of your own life with people you are helping. Sometimes it is necessary to share your thoughts to keep a conversation going. Sharing information from your own life might help to convey sincerity or genuineness in some situations.

Patient	'But what's the point in talking to you? I mean you don't really care, it's just your job.'
Worker	'It is my job, but I do care about you, and I would be pleased to talk with you. I chose this work because I care and because I can make the time to listen if you want to talk about it.'

Understanding, warmth and sincerity have to be combined in order to provide a safe, supportive setting.

Learning to create a supportive relationship with people will involve practice and a great deal of self-monitoring and reflection. It will be necessary to get feedback from colleagues, supervisors and, most importantly, members of the public, when you practise conveying warmth, understanding and sincerity.

You may be able to tell if your communication is effective because the other person may reflect your behaviour. That is, if you are warm and understanding the other person may come to trust you; then you may find that this person is warm and friendly towards you. If you are honest and sincere, people may be honest and sincere with you. The quality of a supportive relationship can become a two-way process. You may find working with others more enjoyable because you become skilled at warmth, understanding and sincerity.

Theory into practice

The following are ideas for developing supportive skills.

1 Work with a friend. Take turns in imagining that you are upset or sad whilst the other person uses reflective listening skills. Tape record the conversation. Play the tape back and evaluate your performance in terms of warmth, understanding and sincerity.

2 Watch videos of conversational skills or counselling situations where warmth, understanding and sincerity are demonstrated – discuss how this is effective and how you might develop your own conversational skills.

3 Think about your own conversations with clients – keep a logbook to reflect on your own skills development.

4 Practise being warm, understanding and sincere with your supervisor or tutor – ask for feedback.

5 Work on supportive behaviour as part of a group project. Practise being supportive whilst undertaking some problem-solving work.

Assertive skills

Some people may seem shy and worried; they say little and avoid contact with people they don't know. Others may want people to be afraid of them, they may try to dominate and control others. Fear and aggression are two of the basic emotions that we experience. It is easy to give in to our basic emotions and either become submissive or aggressive when we feel stressed. Assertion is an advanced skill which involves controlling the basic emotions involved in running away or fighting. Assertion involves a mental attitude of trying to negotiate, trying to solve problems rather than giving in to emotional impulses.

Winning and losing

A simple way of understanding assertion is to look at people's behaviour when they have an argument. An aggressive person will demand that they are right and other people are wrong. They will want to win whilst others lose. The opposite of aggression is to be weak or submissive. A submissive person accepts that they will lose, get told off or put down. Assertive behaviour is different from both these responses. In an argument an assertive person will try to reach an answer where no one has to lose or be 'put down'. Assertion is a skill where 'win-win' situations can happen – no one has to be the loser. For example, suppose a member of the public is angry because they have been left alone for a while.

Person:	'Why have you left me all this time – I'm not putting up with it – I'm going to make a formal complaint about your behaviour!'
Aggressive response:	'Don't you talk to me like that! You're lucky I'm here at all – don't you know how hard we work? There are other people to look after as well as you, you know!'
Submissive response:	'I'm terribly sorry, I promise I won't be late again.'
Assertive response:	'I'm sorry that you're angry, but I really couldn't help it. Please let me explain why I couldn't get back to you any sooner.'

The assertive response aims to meet the emotional needs of both people without anyone being the loser. The aggressive response tries to meet the needs of the worker and not the member of the public – it aims to give the worker power and keep the other person vulnerable. The submissive response may allow the member of the public to control and dominate the worker. Assertive skills can help enable carers to cope with difficult and challenging situations.

To be assertive, a person usually has to:

- understand the situation fully – including facts, details and other people's perceptions
- be able to control personal emotions and stay calm
- be able to act assertively using the right non-verbal behaviour
- be able to act assertively using the right words and statements.

Learning to stay calm and use the right verbal and non-verbal behaviour is a skill which can be developed by watching other experienced professionals and copying their performance. Role play and reflection on practice can also help to develop assertive skills. Some verbal and non-verbal behaviours involved in assertion are summarised in the table below.

Aggressive behaviour	Assertive behaviour	Submissive behaviour
Main emotion: anger	*Main emotion:* staying in control of actions	*Main emotion:* fear
Wanting your own way	Negotiating with others	Letting others win
Making demands	Trying to solve problems	Agreeing with others
Not listening to others	Aiming that no one has to lose	Not putting your views across
'Putting other people down'	Showing respect for others	Looking afraid
Trying to win	Keeping a clear, calm voice	Speaking quietly or not speaking at all
Shouting or talking very loudly		
Threatening non-verbal behaviour including: fixed eye contact, tense muscles, waving or folding hands and arms, looking angry	**Normal non-verbal behaviour** including: varied eye contact, relaxed face muscles, looking 'in control', keeping hands and arms at your side	**Submissive non-verbal behaviour** including: looking down, not looking at others, looking frightened, tense muscles

Assessment activity 2.3

Use an example of a conversation you have had whilst on placement in order to provide examples of how you have used supportive skills effectively and appropriately in practice. You should explain what supportive skills were involved and describe how you have used listening skills to build an understanding of the other person's point of view.

You may wish to make a reference to the communication cycle and to the three conditions identified by Carl Rogers. You need to evaluate your own communication skills in order to achieve a distinction grade.

Advocacy

Sometimes, when people have a very serious learning disability or an illness (such as dementia), it is not possible to communicate with them. In such situations care services will often employ an advocate. An advocate is someone who speaks for someone else. A lawyer speaking for a client in a courtroom is working as an advocate for that person and will argue the client's case. In care work, a volunteer might try to get to know someone who has dementia or a learning disability. The volunteer tries to communicate the client's needs and wants – as the volunteer understands them. Advocates should be independent of the staff team and so can argue for the client's rights without being constrained by what the staff think is easiest or cheapest to do.

Advocacy often provides a way to make sure that people's needs are not overlooked. Advocacy is not straightforward however; volunteers may not always understand the feelings and needs of the people that they are advocating for. Some people believe it would be better if clients could be trained and supported to argue their own case. Helping people to argue their own case is called self-advocacy. Self-advocacy may work very well for some people, but others may need very considerable help before they can argue or explain their needs.

Another kind of advocacy is called group advocacy. This is where people with similar needs come together and receive support to argue for their needs as a group. Group advocacy may provide an answer for some people who need extensive support to be able to self-advocate. Different people may need different kinds of advocacy support.

Interpreters and translators

Interpreters are people who communicate meaning from one language to another. This includes interpreting between spoken and signed languages such as English and British Sign Language. Translators are people who change recorded material from one language to another.

Translating and interpreting involve the communication of meaning between different languages. Translating and interpreting is more than just a technical act of changing the words from one system to another. Many languages do not have simple equivalence between words or signs. Interpreters and translators have to grasp the meaning of a message and find a way of expressing this meaning in a different language system. This is rarely a simple task even for professional translators.

Think it over

There are many funny stories of misunderstandings that arise when translators fail to translate the meaning of a message and simply change words from one language to another. One story is of a drinks company which used the slogan 'turn it loose' in English. When this slogan was translated literally into Spanish it conveyed the meaning of 'this drink will give you diarrhoea'.

Interpreters can be professional people who are employed by social services or health authorities in order to communicate with people who use different spoken or signed languages. Interpreters may also be friends or family members who have sufficient language ability to be able to explain messages in different circumstances. A mother might learn sign language in order to communicate information to a deaf child. A child might have learned to speak a language such as English more effectively than their parents. It is possible for family members to interpret for each other.

Interpretation and translation are vital in any setting where communication is blocked because individuals rely on different languages or communication systems. Many people live in communities where English is an additional language. When these people need to access health care or social services, or when members of these communities need legal support, the services of translators and interpreters are likely to be needed. People who are deaf from birth often use a signed language such as British Sign Language (BSL). British Sign Language is not a version of the English language; it is an independent language system, which

A mother might use sign language to communicate with her deaf child

is as different from English as Spanish is. Many people from the deaf community rely on their own language system (BSL) and they may be unable to access written or spoken communication in English.

Interpreting, and communicating using interpreters raises a number of important issues (see page 55 for further details).

Assessment activity 2.4

Describe in your own words the role of advocacy, interpreters and translators in the care sector. Find out from your workplace how and when these services might be used. For each of the three roles, give an example of their use with a client. You can base these on actual examples from your workplace.

Communication skills

Verbal and non-verbal behaviour

Non-verbal communication

When we meet and talk with people, we will usually be using two language systems. We will use a verbal or spoken language and non-verbal or body language. Effective communication in care work requires care workers to be able to analyse their own and other people's non-verbal behaviour. Our non-verbal behaviour sends messages to other people – often without us deliberately meaning to send these messages. The eyes, the face, body posture, movement and gestures can give clues to how a person is feeling (see Figure 2.7).

The eyes

We can guess the feelings and thoughts that another person has by looking at their eyes. One poet called the eye 'the window of the soul'. We can sometimes understand the thoughts and feelings of another person by eye-to-eye contact. Our eyes get wider when we are excited, attracted to, or interested in someone else. A fixed stare may send the message that someone is angry. Looking away is often interpreted as showing boredom or lack of interest in European culture.

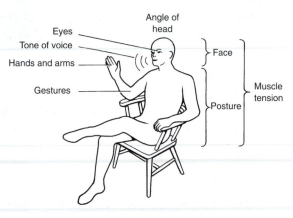

Figure 2.7 Non-verbal behaviour sends messages

The face

The face can send very complex messages which can be read easily.

Our faces often indicate our emotional state. When a person is sad they may signal this emotion with eyes that look down – there may be tension in their face and the mouth will be closed. The muscles in the person's shoulders are likely to be relaxed but the face and neck may show tension. A happy person will have 'wide eyes' that make contact with you – their face will smile. When people are excited they will move their arms and hands to signal their excitement.

Voice tone

It's not just what we say, but the way that we say it. If we talk quickly in a loud voice with a fixed voice tone, people may see us as angry. A calm, slow voice with varying tone may send a message of being friendly.

Body movement

The way we walk, move our head, sit, cross our legs and so on, sends messages about whether we are tired, happy, sad or bored.

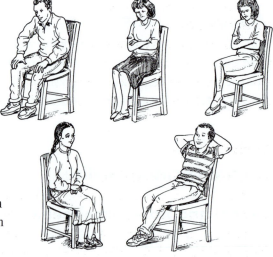

Posture

The way we sit or stand can send messages. Sitting with crossed arms can mean 'I'm not taking any notice'. Leaning backward can send the message that you a re relaxed – or bored! Leaning forward can show interest. The body postures in Figure 2.8 send messages.

Figure 2.8 Body postures that send messages

Muscle tension

The tension in our feet, hands and fingers can tell others how relaxed or how tense we are. If someone is very tense their shoulders might stiffen, their face muscles might tighten and they might sit or stand rigidly. A tense face might have a firmly closed mouth with lips and jaws clenched tight. A tense person might breathe quickly and become hot.

Gestures

Gestures are hand and arm movements that can help us to understand what a person is saying. Some gestures carry a meaning of their own.

Touch

Touching another person can send messages of care, affection, power over them, or sexual interest. The social setting and other body language usually help people to understand what touch might mean. Carers should not make assumptions about touch. Even holding someone's hand might be seen as trying to dominate them!

Proximity

The space between people can sometimes show how friendly or 'intimate' the conversation is. Different cultures have different behaviours with respect to the space between people who are talking.

In Britain there are expectations or 'norms' as to how close you should be when you talk to others. When talking to strangers we may keep an arm's length apart. The ritual of shaking hands indicates that you have been introduced – you may come closer. When you are friendly with someone you may accept them being closer to you. Relatives and partners may not be restricted in how close they can come.

Proximity is a very important issue in care work. Many clients have a sense of personal space. A healthcare worker who assumes it is all right to enter a client's personal space without asking or explaining, may be seen as being dominating or aggressive.

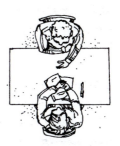

Face-to-face positions (orientation)

Standing or sitting eye to eye can send a message of being formal or being angry. A slight angle can create a more relaxed and friendly feeling (see Figure 2.9).

Figure 2.9 Face-to-face interaction

Verbal skills

Keeping a conversation going

It can be hard to get to know people unless you can keep a conversation going. Starting a conversation is often easy. We ask someone how they are today, we introduce ourselves or we ask a question. If we remember, we can mention things that have been talked about before such as, 'How did you get on at the dentist yesterday?'

Once a conversation has started, the trick is to keep it going long enough. Skills which help with this include turn taking, using non-verbal communication to show interest, being good at asking questions using prompts and using silence at the right times. Conversations involve taking turns to listen and talk. If you are trying to get to know a client you will probably do less talking and more listening. People need to take turns for a conversation to work. People normally show when they want you to talk by slowing down the rate at which they speak their last few words; changing the tone of the voice slightly and looking away from you. The person will then stop speaking and look directly at you. If you are sensitive to these messages you will be ready to ask a question or say something which keeps the conversation going.

It is also important to look interested in what a client is saying. Looking interested is one way we can show respect – carers should be interested in what people say because learning about others is part of the professional skill of a carer. So carers should show interest even if the member of the public is talking about things which would be boring in private life.

Showing interest involves giving the other person your full attention. Non-verbal messages which usually do this include:

- eye contact – looking at the other person's eyes
- smiling – looking friendly rather than 'cold' or frozen in expression
- hand movements and gestures that show interest
- slight head nods whilst talking – these indicate non-verbally, 'I see' or 'I understand' or 'I agree'.

Showing interest can be a good way of keeping another person talking.

Asking questions

Some questions don't really encourage people to talk. These are called closed questions. Closed questions are not very useful when trying to get to know people. Questions like 'How old are you?' are 'closed'. They are closed because there is only one, right, simple answer the person can give: 'I'm 84', and so on. Closed questions don't lead on to discussion. 'Do you like butter?' is a closed question – the person can only say yes or no. 'Are you feeling well today?' is a closed question – the person may only say yes or no.

Open questions ask for a broader response. Instead of giving a yes/no answer, the person is encouraged to think and discuss. A question like 'How do you feel about the food here?' means that the other person has to think about the food and then discuss it. Open questions keep the conversation going. Sometimes closed questions can block a conversation and cause it to stop.

The more we know about someone, the more we can be sensitive about the type of questions that we ask. Some people don't mind questions about their feelings or opinions, but do dislike questions which ask for personal information. Getting to know people often takes time and usually involves a number of short conversations – rather than one long conversation.

In some formal conversations it can be important to ask direct closed questions. The best way to ask closed questions is to ask open questions beforehand. There is a saying that if you really want to find out what someone else thinks then 'Every closed question should start life as an open one'.

There is a technique called **funnelling**, which uses this principle in formal interviewing. First, the interviewer asks general open questions, then narrower questions, then a closed question. The answer to the closed question can be followed up using probes and prompts (see Figure 2.10).

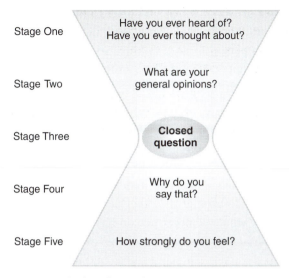

Figure 2.10 The funnelling technique

For example, a care worker might be trying to find out about the life history of an older client. Perhaps the worker wants to ask 'Were you interested in music?'. It can be 'cold' and even aggressive to just fire questions like this at people. Instead, the question could be funnelled.

Worker	'What was it like in the evenings before television came along?' [*open question*]
Other person	'Well, we used to get together and make our own entertainment.'
Worker	'So what sort of activities did you do?' [*open question*]
Other person	'Oh, gossip, talking to neighbours, sing-songs.'
Worker	'Were you interested in music?' [*closed question*]
Other person	'Well a bit. I used to have piano lessons – but we couldn't afford a piano at home.'

Funnelling is a skill which enables carers to lead into questions 'gently'; it is a good alternative to asking too many closed questions.

Silence

One definition of friends is 'people who can sit together and feel comfortable in silence'. Sometimes a pause in conversation can make people feel embarrassed – it looks as if you weren't listening or interested. Sometimes a silent pause can mean 'let's think' or 'I need time to think'. Silent pauses can be all right as long as there are non-verbal messages which show respect and interest. Silence doesn't always stop the conversation. Some carers use pauses in a conversation to show that they are listening and thinking about what the client has said.

Probes and prompts

A probe is a very short question such as, 'Can you tell me more?' This kind of short question usually follows on from an answer that the other person has given. Probes are used to 'dig deeper' into the person's answer; they probe or investigate what the other person just said.

Prompts are short questions or words which you offer to the other person in order to prompt them to answer. Questions such as, 'So was it enjoyable or not?' or 'Would you do it again?' might prompt a person to keep talking. Sometimes a prompt might just be a suggested answer – 'More than 50?' might be a prompt if you had just asked how many clients a carer worked with in a year and they seemed uncertain.

Probes and prompts are both useful techniques to improve questioning skill, when you are trying to keep a conversation going.

To sum up, if you need to keep a conversation going you can:

- use non-verbal behaviour, like smiling and nodding your head, to express interest
- use short periods of silence to prompt the other person to talk
- paraphrase or reflect back what the other person has said to confirm that you have understood them
- ask direct questions
- use probes and prompts to follow up your questions.

Listening skills

Listening means hearing another person's words, thinking about what they mean and planning what to say back to the other person. Hearing simply means picking up the sounds that another person is making. Listening and hearing are quite different activities. Listening involves hearing and then remembering what has been said; if we are going to remember what someone else has said we have to understand it first. Some psychologists believe that people usually only remember about one out of every 2000 pieces of information that are heard in a day. Most of the sounds that come to our ears are not important enough to bother about remembering.

Think it over

Last night you may have watched TV or talked to family and friends – just how much can you recall of what you heard last night? If you cannot remember much, perhaps it does not matter, a lot of conversation may just be for creating a social atmosphere.

Listening is a central skill in health care work. Listening enables workers to develop an understanding of the people that they work with. Listening provides a way of showing respect and value for others. Listening enables the worker to learn about the lifestyle, beliefs and personal needs of others.

Sometimes, getting ready to listen involves switching into a store of knowledge and understanding. For some people this is a conscious 'switching on' process. We switch on by remembering another person's name or face; perhaps we can recall when we last talked to them and what they said. Listening skills depend on being able to remember important details about other people. Listening can be hard mental work. Instead of just living in our own private worlds we have to think about other people. So, if someone is saying that they are sad about something we first have to hear their words and then imagine how the other person feels. We have to make sense of what is said, perhaps imagining how we would feel if it happened to us. Having thought through what we have been told, we have to think again before we speak. Listening takes time and effort; too often people do not bother to listen.

Communication differences and overcoming barriers to effective communication

Ways of overcoming difficulties in communication

It is always important to learn as much as possible about other people. People may have 'preferred forms of interaction'. This may include a reliance on non-verbal messages, sign language, lip-reading, use of description, slang phrases, choice of room or location for a conversation and so on. Everyone has communication needs of some kind.

Below are some ideas for overcoming barriers to communication.

Visual disability
- Use language to describe things.
- Assist people to touch things (e.g. touch your face to recognise you).
- Explain details that sighted people might take for granted.
- Check what people can see (many registered blind people can see shapes, or tell light from dark).
- Check glasses, other aids and equipment.

Hearing disability
- Don't shout, keep to normal, clear speech and make sure your face is visible for people who can lip-read.
- Show pictures, or write messages.
- Learn to sign (for people who use signed languages).
- Ask for help from, or employ, a communicator or interpreter for signed languages.
- Check hearing aids and equipment.

Environmental constraints
- Check and improve lighting.
- Reduce noise.
- Move to a quieter or better-lit room.
- Move to smaller groups to see and hear more easily.
- Check seating arrangements.

Language differences
- Communicate using pictures, diagrams and non-verbal signs.
- Use translators or interpreters.
- Be careful not to make assumptions or stereotype.
- Increase your knowledge of jargon, slang and dialects.
- Re-word your messages – find different ways of saying things.
- Speak in short, clear sentences.

Preventing misunderstandings
- Try to increase your knowledge of different cultures.
- Watch out for different cultural interpretations.
- Avoid making assumptions about or discriminating against people who are different.
- Use reflective listening techniques to check that your understanding is correct.
- Stay calm and try to calm people who are angry or excited.
- Be sensitive to different social settings and the form of communication that would be most appropriate in different contexts.
- Check your work with advocates who will represent the best interests of the people that you are working with.

Physical and intellectual disabilities
- Increase your knowledge of disabilities.
- Use pictures and signs as well as clear, simple speech.
- Be calm and patient.
- Set up group meetings where people can share interests, experiences or reminiscences.
- Check that people do not become isolated.
- Use advocates – independent people who can spend time building an understanding of the needs of specific individuals to assist with communication work.

Figure 2.11 outlines factors which enhance communication.

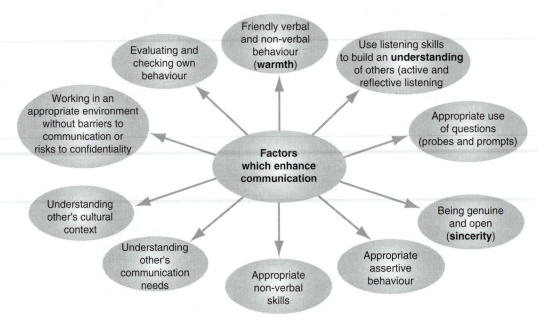

Figure 2.11 Factors which enhance communication

Emotional barriers which can inhibit communication

Sometimes it is very difficult to listen to and communicate with others. Clients often have very considerable emotional needs; they are afraid or depressed because of the stresses they are experiencing. Listening involves learning about frightening and depressing situations. Carers sometimes avoid listening to avoid unpleasant emotional feelings.

Communication can be inhibited because health and care workers:

- are tired – listening takes mental energy
- do not have sufficient time to communicate properly
- are emotionally stressed by the needs of clients
- do not understand the culture or context of others
- make assumptions about others or label or stereotype others.

Labelling and stereotyping

People who have difficulty hearing or seeing are sometimes assumed to be awkward or mentally limited. Older people are sometimes seen as demented or confused if they do not answer questions appropriately.

People can also be labelled or stereotyped when they use different language systems. Some people will shout at those who don't speak the same language, as if increasing the volume would help. People who sign to communicate are sometimes thought to be odd or to have learning difficulties, because they don't respond to written or spoken English.

Assessment activity 2.5

Choose an example of an interaction you have witnessed or been involved in whilst on placement. Use the grid below in order to identify factors which can create barriers to effective communication.

The Barriers to Communication Grid

Rating scale:
1 Good – there is no barrier.
2 Quite good – few barriers.
3 Not possible to decide or not applicable.
4 Poor – barriers identified.
5 Very poor – major barriers to communication.

In the environment	Barriers				
Lighting	1	2	3	4	5
Noise levels	1	2	3	4	5
Opportunity to communicate	1	2	3	4	5
Language differences					
Carer's skills with different languages	1	2	3	4	5
Carer's skills with non-verbal communication	1	2	3	4	5
Availability of translators or interpreters	1	2	3	4	5
Assumptions and/or stereotypes	1	2	3	4	5
Emotional barriers					
Stress levels and tiredness	1	2	3	4	5
Carers stressed by the emotional needs of clients	1	2	3	4	5
Cultural barriers					
Inappropriate assumptions made about others	1	2	3	4	5
Labelling or stereotyping present	1	2	3	4	5
Interpersonal skills					
Degree of supportive non-verbal behaviour	1	2	3	4	5
Degree of supportive verbal behaviour	1	2	3	4	5
Appropriate use of listening skills	1	2	3	4	5
Appropriate use of assertive skills	1	2	3	4	5
Appropriate maintenance of confidentiality	1	2	3	4	5

Once you have identified the factors which can create barriers to communication you need to write about ways in which you could have overcome or minimised these barriers. You should discuss how your own conversation created or reduced communication barriers. Your work for this task might provide evidence that you can analyse the potential effects of your communication style on communication barriers. Your work might also enable you to use a placement example in order to minimise barriers for a specific interaction.

Some issues associated with using interpreters

Translation and interpretation involves conveying what a person meant from one language to another. This is not as simple as just changing words or signs from one system to another. When interpreters work with people they will become part of the communication cycle. It will often be important that the interpreter can confirm that they have understood things correctly before attempting to pass that understanding on to another person. Much interpretation in health and social work settings is *consecutive interpretation*. Consecutive interpretation is when the first person pauses to allow the interpreter to make sense of what they have communicated. When the interpreter is clear about the message they communicate it to the second person. The interpreter will then listen to the response from the second person. The second person will need to pause so that once again the interpreter can make sense of what they wish to communicate.

Another kind of interpretation is called *simultaneous interpretation*, which is when an interpreter explains what one person is saying whilst they talk. Because of the need to clarify subject matter and emotions this kind of interpretation is likely to be more difficult in many health care settings.

Interpretation makes the communication cycle more complicated. There is a range of other issues which are critically important when considering working with an interpreter.

Knowledge of the subject matter

An interpreter who understands the issues involved is likely to be more effective. A professional interpreter may be able to explain details of legislation or procedures for claiming benefit because they understand the issues. If a relative or friend is acting as an interpreter they will have to make sense of the technical details before they can communicate clearly. Knowledge of languages alone is not always sufficient to enable clear and effective communication.

Trust

It is important that people have confidence in somebody who is acting as an interpreter. People from specific communities may find it hard to trust someone from a different community. Many women may not feel safe and confident discussing medical issues using a male interpreter. The issue may not be about the interpreter's language competence, but about the interpreter's ability to understand and correctly convey what a person wants to say.

Social and cultural values

Many people may wish to use a professional interpreter, or a specified member of their community or gender group because of social norms. Many people may feel that it is inappropriate to discuss health details using an interpreter of the opposite sex. Some deaf people do not feel confident using interpreters who have not experienced deafness themselves. Choice of an interpreter must support the self-esteem needs of people who need to access interpretation services.

Confidentiality

Confidentiality is a right enshrined in the 1998 Data Protection Act as well as an ethical duty on professional staff. Professional interpreters are likely to offer guarantees of confidentiality. Using a relative or volunteer may not necessarily provide people with the same guarantee of confidentiality. Confidentiality may be an issue which needs to be checked before interpretation begins.

Non-judgemental support

A professional interpreter who has trained in social work is likely to offer advanced interpersonal skills which include the ability to remain non-judgemental when undertaking interpretation work. Volunteers, relatives and friends may have language competence, but they may not necessarily be able to interpret meaning without biasing their interpretation.

Self-esteem and the development of self concept

As children grow they will come to be socialised into the beliefs, values and norms of their initial family or care-giving group. Later, children will be influenced by the beliefs, values and norms of the friends with whom they mix and play. Children adopt others' values and norms in order to be accepted into social groups. They will need to understand the rules of games or sports that they wish to join in. To be liked and to be popular, they have to show that they fit in with others. Mead (1934) believed that children come to learn general social rules and values at this stage. They might be able to imagine 'generalised others' or general social demands which they need to live up to.

Mead believed children might learn to display emotion as expected within the social roles and cultural context that they live in. They do not simply do what others teach them to do, however. They internalise values that are built into a sense of self. This sense of self determines what they actually do. These roles may become part of the child's self concept and social identity.

This sense of self will guide the individual to exaggerate, suppress or even substitute emotional expression. In some social classes and geographical areas, boys may learn to exaggerate feelings of anger and aggression in order to achieve social status. In another social class group, boys may learn to express anger in terms of clever verbal behaviour with little hint of emotion. Some girls may learn to suppress feelings of distress in order to look 'in control'.

It is tempting just to say that society does this to people – that people develop the emotions for which society trains them. Mead's theory provides an explanation of how social influences work on an individual. It is the idea of a self, a 'me' that explains how social values influence individual behaviour (see Figure 2.12).

During adolescence this sense of self becomes of central importance. Erik Erikson (1963) believed that biological pressures to become independent would force adolescents into a crisis which could only be successfully resolved if the individual developed a conscious sense of self or purpose. He wrote, 'In the social jungle of human existence, there is no feeling of being alive without a sense of ego identity.' Other theorists have regarded the development of self concept or identity as more gradual, and less centred on

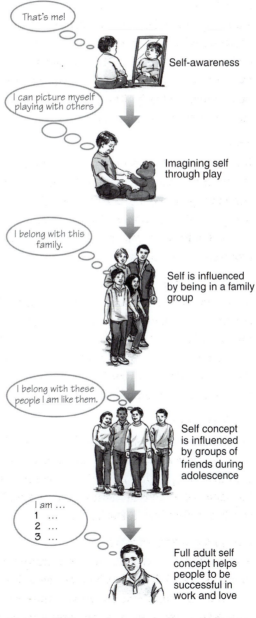

Figure 2.12 The development of self concept begins with self-awareness

biological maturation. A clear sense of self may lead a person to feel worthwhile and to have a sense of purpose. A sense of self might provide a person with the confidence to cope with changes in life.

The development of a secure sense of self may be needed in order to:

- make effective social and sexual relationships with others
- cope with work roles where we have to make independent decisions
- cope with complex interpersonal situations where 'emotional intelligence' (Goleman, 1996) is needed in order to use appropriate skills, such as assertion
- cope with our own internal or intrapersonal feelings in order to enable us to motivate ourselves
- develop self-confidence and self-efficiency in social or work settings.

General factors which will influence the development of self concept include those shown in Figure 2.13.

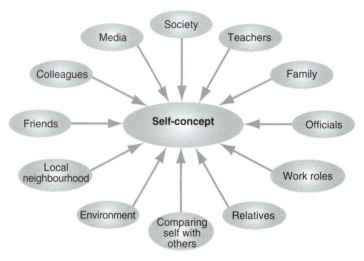

Figure 2.13 Influences on self concept

Think it over

Examine the list of influences in Figure 2.13. How have each of these issues influenced your own sense of who you are? What are the most important influences on your life?

An overview of the developmental stages of self concept might be summarised as in the table below.

Age	Stage of development
$1\frac{1}{2}$–2 years	Self-awareness develops – children may start to recognise themselves in a mirror
$2\frac{1}{2}$ years	Children can say whether they are a boy or a girl
3–5 years	When asked to say what they are like, children can describe themselves in terms of categories, such as big or small, tall or short, light or heavy
5–8 years	If you ask children who they are, they can often describe themselves in detail. Children will tell you their hair colour, eye colour, about their families and to which schools they belong

8–10 years	Children start to show a general sense of 'self worth', such as describing how happy they are in general, how good life is for them, what is good about their family life, school and friends
10–12 years	Children start to analyse how they compare with others. When asked about their life, children may explain without prompting how they compare with others. For example: 'I'm not as good as Zoe at running, but I'm better than Ali.'
12–16 years	Adolescents may develop a sense of self in terms of beliefs and belong to groups – being a vegetarian, believing in God, believing certain things are right or wrong
16–25 years	People may develop an adult self concept that helps them to feel confident in a work role and in social and sexual relationships
25 onwards	People's sense of self will be influenced by the things that happen in their lives. Some people may change their self concept a great deal as they grow older
65 onwards	In later life it is important to be able to keep a clear sense of self. People may become withdrawn and depressed, without a clear self concept

There are differences in the expression of self concept between the various age groups. These could be summarised as in the table below.

Age group	Expression of self concept
Young children	Self concept limited to a few descriptions, e.g. boy or girl, size, some skills
Older children	Self concept can be described in a range of 'factual categories', such as hair colour, name, details or address, etc.
Adolescents	Self concept starts to be explained in terms of chosen beliefs, likes, dislikes, relationships with others
Adults	Many adults may be able to explain the quality of their lives and their personality in greater depth and detail than when they were adolescents
Older adults	Some older adults may have more self-knowledge than during early adult life. Some people may show 'wisdom' in the way they explain their self concept

According to Maslow, the goal of living is **self-actualisation**. This means to fulfil one's potential and to become everything that a person is capable of becoming. Deficit needs such as physical illness, not feeling safe, not having a sense of belonging, or having low self-esteem prevent people from developing fulfilled and happy lives.

The way other people communicate with us will be one factor which can influence our feelings of safety, secure self concept and the ability to value what we think we are.

Think it over

Imagine you went into a shop and tried to pay for some goods. Imagine that the shop assistants were unfriendly and ignored you. Imagine that they told you to shut up and wait your turn when you tried to attract their attention. How would you react to this and what impact would this have on your self-esteem?

Most people would be very angry in this situation but their self-esteem would not suffer greatly because they would think to themselves, 'I'm not using this shop again, I'll take my business elsewhere'.

Now imagine that you are in pain and waiting on a hospital trolley. The health care staff are unfriendly and ignore you. When you complain, the staff tell you to shut up and wait your turn. How will this affect you and how will this affect your self-esteem?

Most people would be angry but they would also be afraid. If staff treat you as if you don't matter it is hard for you to value yourself. You will also feel very unsafe.

The key difference between being mistreated in a shop and mistreated in a health care setting is one of power. Where you believe that you hold the power, your self-esteem will not be vulnerable. If you think that other people have all the power, your self-esteem is likely to be at risk (see Figure 2.14).

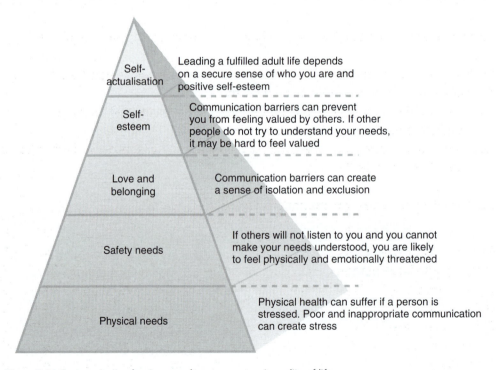

Figure 2.14 Communication barriers can damage a person's quality of life

A loss of general self-esteem is associated with depression and withdrawal (see the next section on learned helplessness).

Assessment activity 2.6

Prepare a role play or simulated discussion where one person interviews or leads a conversation with another person. Audio or videotape this conversation and use the rating scale below in order to analyse ways in which verbal and non-verbal communication affect the communications cycle and as a basis for evaluating your own skills with respect to different types of interaction.

The rating scale: how good were different aspects of non-verbal communication?

Eye contact	1	2	3	4	5
Facial expression	1	2	3	4	5
Angle of head	1	2	3	4	5
Tone of voice	1	2	3	4	5
Position of hands and arms	1	2	3	4	5
Gestures	1	2	3	4	5
Posture	1	2	3	4	5
Muscle tension	1	2	3	4	5
Touch	1	2	3	4	5
Proximity	1	2	3	4	5

How to rate behaviour:

Circle around the number 1 when you have seen very effective and appropriate use of a skill.
Circle around the number 2 when you have seen some appropriate use of the skill.
Circle around the number 3 when you have not seen the skill demonstrated or if it does not seem appropriate to comment on the area.
Circle around the number 4 when you have seen some slightly ineffective or inappropriate behaviour in relation to the area.
Circle around the number 5 when you have seen very inappropriate or ineffective behaviour in relation to the area.

How good were verbal communication and listening skills?

Encouraging others to talk	1	2	3	4	5
Reflecting back what others have said	1	2	3	4	5
Using appropriate questions	1	2	3	4	5
Use of prompts	1	2	3	4	5
Using silence as a listening skill	1	2	3	4	5
Clarity of conversation	1	2	3	4	5
Pace of conversation	1	2	3	4	5
Turn taking	1	2	3	4	5

(Use the same rating instructions as for non-verbal communication above.)

When you have completed your ratings you should discuss ways in which you might improve specific aspects of your communication skills in relation to the role play or conversation that you undertook. If you can make detailed plans for developing your skills this may help to meet the grading criteria for a distinction grade.

Supportive skills with distressed individuals

Health care needs are often associated with strong emotions. People who undergo tests or investigations may be anxious about what might happen to them. People who are ill or in pain may feel threatened or depressed. People who have experienced long-term ill-health may have become depressed to the point where they withdraw from human interaction.

Reasons for distressed behaviour

Some reasons for distressed, angry or withdrawn behaviour include the following:

- **Pain** People in pain often find it difficult to control emotion. Pain can cause people to become aggressive or to give up and withdraw.
- **Fear** Many people do not know what to expect. Fear of the unknown can cause people to feel out of control and become angry or upset. Most people fear pain; not all treatments and investigations are pain-free.
- **Grief** A major loss of a person or of a lifestyle may result in a feeling of being out of control. Emotions of anger, guilt, depression and withdrawal may result from a loss.
- **Frustration** Some people will become frustrated because they cannot do things as easily as they could before experiencing an illness or accident. Other people will experience frustration in having their needs attended to or being given services with limited resources. Frustration often leads to anger.
- **Communication differences** Where people use a different first language, or use a signed language, or where there are sensory disabilities there is always a risk of inappropriate assumptions stereotyping, or labelling. People may feel that their rights have been infringed.
- **Feeling vulnerable and threats to self-esteem** Some people may be afraid of losing their dignity, others may feel that they had been discriminated against, or simply that their needs have not been addressed. Pain, fear and grief can all create a feeling of vulnerability. Unwanted change can threaten self-esteem.
- **Past learning** Some adults and children may have learned that being aggressive is one way to get things that they need. Some people may be used to starting arguments or fighting as part of their way of life.

Anger and withdrawal

Case study

Mr Mansel is 84 and moved into a nursing home after having a stroke. Mr Mansel grew up in Jamaica but moved to Britain 50 years ago. Unfortunately, he has been placed in a nursing home some distance from his friends and receives few visits. None of the staff understand Mr Mansel's history or cultural background. The home has a number of staff vacancies and is currently short staffed. Staff have little time to talk to Mr Mansel. The stroke has affected Mr Mansel's speech and staff find communication difficult and time consuming. Other residents in the home have communication differences including hearing disabilities and disorientation and memory loss.

Some residents avoid Mr Mansel and appear to label him as different from themselves. Mr Mansel feels isolated and distressed.

Ineffective communication, such as Mr Mansel is experiencing, can result in:

- a loss of self-esteem – you can't be worth much if people don't communicate
- a loss of purpose in life – you may feel excluded, or alienated from others if you cannot communicate
- a loss of support – you may find life difficult to cope with if your social and emotional needs are not met
- a feeling of being threatened – if people do not communicate you may not be able to be able to predict what is likely to happen.

These problems may result in a belief that we can no longer control our life circumstances.

Martin Seligman (1975) published a theory of learned helplessness which explains how a loss of control over our life circumstances can result in a process of learning to become withdrawn, depressed and helpless (see Figure 2.15).

Helplessness starts when people find that no matter what they do they can't control what is going to happen. People can develop a general helpless attitude to daily living when major needs like communication are 'out of control'.

According to Seligman, the first stages in the process of becoming helpless are to react with frustration and anger. In the case study above, Mr Mansel may become aggressive, perhaps shouting at others or damaging property. In the past, such problems were often regarded as being due to 'confusion', 'age' or dementia. Seligman explains that aggression can be a last attempt to maintain control – when nothing else works you can lose your temper. In a 'stressed' care environment Mr Mansel's anger is unlikely to get him the attention he needs. Instead he may be labelled as disturbed or difficult and isolated further.

The next step in the process is learning to 'give up'. Giving up saves energy. Withdrawal from trying to communicate may be the best coping strategy. Being 'withdrawn' can protect a person. Mr Mansel cannot get his social and self-esteem needs met but there may be a sense of safety in not attempting to communicate. Ineffective communication may not matter so much if you come to expect no communication at all.

The process of learning to become helpless does not stop with withdrawal. A person who cannot predict what is likely to happen is likely to become anxious. The stress of anxiety can cause a deeper level of withdrawal, a withdrawal into depression. Seligman

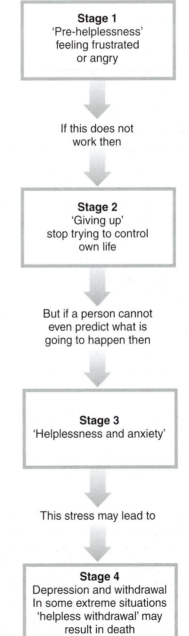

Figure 2.15 The process of learned helplessness

argued that helplessness and anxiety could result in clinical depression due to changes in brain chemistry.

A lack of communication could be enough to cause anxiety. Mr Mansel may not know what is happening around him or what to expect from staff. If he feels unable to respond to discrimination and exclusion he may experience anxiety and withdrawal. Serious mental ill-health may result.

Finally, Seligman believed that severe depression resulting from learned helplessness could be fatal. This may be particularly true when an individual is in poor health.

Effective communication is not just a right which clients may expect – not just a quality issue. Effective communication is necessary to protect the mental well-being of vulnerable people. Poor communication can be understood as a form of abuse. If Seligman's theory is correct, then it is possible to argue that this abuse may be enough to cause death.

Think it over

Many distressed individuals feel that they cannot control their situation. Consider the emotions of the people below.

- A mother attends A & E with her sick child. She fears that her child might have contracted meningitis and that the child could die. The mother feels that staff are not responding quickly enough to her demands for help. She may feel that she is failing to influence health care staff sufficiently. Emotionally the mother may feel panic and a desperate desire to be able to control the staff working in the A & E section of the hospital.

- An older person sits quietly looking at the floor in a waiting room. He does not respond to staff when asked questions except to move his head or to appear to agree with any statement that they might make. The man has had many hospital admissions for a long-term illness over the past years and his condition has failed to improve. The man feels that there is little he or anyone else can do to help him. He has given up and become withdrawn.

- A young woman is waiting to be collected from hospital by a friend, following a road accident. The woman was injured by a 'hit and run' driver and cannot see how she can obtain compensation. She will not be able to work for the next month and is worried and angry about how she will cope in the near future. Her emotions involve feeling that her life is – temporarily at least – out of control.

Can you recall a situation when you or someone you know well felt out of control? Evaluate the situation. What was the cause of the situation? How could it have been managed?

Can you see how a process of learning to give up could start in each of the above situations? Learned helplessness often starts with frustration and aggression. It is easy to see how the mother and perhaps the young woman may become angry and aggressive because of the need to control their situation. When aggression fails it is possible that these people's distress will turn into depression and withdrawal. The older man has already given up trying to influence his situation. He is further advanced in the stages of learned helplessness as set out above.

Much angry and aggressive behaviour experienced by staff in health care settings may be a result of members of the public feeling that they have lost control of the situation they are in. The theory of learned helplessness provides a useful way of understanding some causes of anger and withdrawal.

What happens when people become aggressive?

Anger is a powerful emotion and it often looks as if people suddenly lose their temper. A person in A & E will suddenly start shouting; a patient will suddenly start making abusive comments. In many situations a person will already feel stressed long before an outburst of anger. Frustration and tension can grow as an individual fails to control their own emotions and circumstances.

As tension mounts, it may only take a single remark or some little thing that has gone wrong to push the person into an angry outburst. People who feel stressed only need a trigger incident to set off an explosion of anger that has built up inside them.

After an explosion of anger, stressed people can still feel tense. Very often they may feel that is someone else's fault that they have been made to feel so angry. Anger can flare up again if the person is not given respect and encouraged to become calm. As time passes, tension may reduce as stress and levels of high emotional arousal decrease (see Figure 2.16).

Not all angry outbursts follow this pattern. Some people learn to use aggression to get their way and some people can switch aggressive emotions on and off as they wish. Being angry can sometimes be a reaction that a person has chosen. But it is wrong to assume that all aggression and anger are deliberate. A great deal of aggression experienced by health care workers will be an emotional response to not being able to control circumstances.

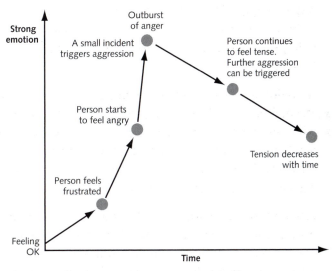

Figure 2.16 Stages in the development of aggression

When people are aggressive or abusive they may make health care workers feel threatened. The simple in-built emotional response to threat is to want to run or fight. An unskilled response to aggression is to be aggressive back. This will escalate into a conflict situation which is unlikely to have a positive outcome. For example, suppose an immobile patient has asked for a commode but has been left waiting. They may react aggressively with accusations such as, 'You don't care about me, you're too lazy to do your job properly' and so on. An unskilled response to this abuse might be to shout back at the patient, returning the abuse with statements such as, 'You're not the only person here you know, I've only got one pair of hands' and so on. The problem with responding to aggression by being aggressive is that one or both people have to lose. The purpose of health care is to improve the quality of life as well as the quantity of life that people may have. If a health care worker is successful in putting down a patient they are likely to increase that person's sense of being out of control and create increased helplessness in the individual. Depressed or withdrawn patients may seem easier to manage than aggressive ones, but turning aggression into depression can hardly rate as a satisfactory health outcome.

Even in mildly aggressive encounters one or both people are likely to feel resentment towards each other. It cannot be a good outcome for members of the public to feel that health care staff are rude and abusive. Equally, most workers are unlikely to have job satisfaction if they develop resentment towards a significant number of the people that they work with.

There is, of course, no guarantee that the health worker will be the winner in every conflict situation. Some members of the public become physically violent and cause physical as well as emotional injury to staff. Other members of the public may make successful formal complaints if they have received abuse. A professional skilled response is to stay calm, to be assertive rather than aggressive, calm the other person, and resolve the situation without creating resentment. This is easier to say than it is to do.

Skills for working with individuals

Emotional intelligence and staying in control

Daniel Goleman (1996) published a theory of emotional intelligence. Whilst people vary in their degree of intellectual ability, Goleman's theory is that people also vary in their ability to manage and use their own emotions. Education and training can improve intellectual performance and it can also improve emotional performance. One aspect of emotional intelligence is the ability to influence or even control the emotions that we experience. According to Goleman, emotionally intelligent people are likely to be able to control feelings of threat so that they can remain calm in situations involving people who are distressed or aggressive.

Humans have two systems to guide behaviour. We can think and reason using the outer part of the brain called the cortex and we can react to experiences with emotion – a system which is built into our mid-brain. Emotion is designed to enable us to respond rapidly if we are threatened. For example, if you switched on the lights as you entered a room in your house and you saw a large bear coming towards you, your emotional systems would make you respond with fear – you would attempt to run away. If you suddenly realised that this was a friend wearing a fancy dress costume, your fear response would switch off. You would probably laugh because your emotions had made you react inappropriately. Thought takes time and is much slower than emotional response. But thought can influence our perception of threat. Emotional intelligence involves the ability to use thought to moderate and control our emotional responses.

If someone is aggressive towards us the immediate emotional response is to feel threatened and to fight back or run. We do not have to be fixed by this first emotional reaction. It is possible to rethink what we are experiencing and re-interpret the threat. A professional person may see a distressed person who is in danger of becoming helpless – a person who they can help. An unskilled person may simply experience the emotions of threat and danger. The professional person can switch off the emotions associated with being attacked and can think, 'This person is distressed but I'm sure I can work with them, they will not harm me'. Learning to re-interpret threats means that professional people can choose the emotions that they need to be able to work effectively with others. Untrained and unskilled people may be controlled by their emotions. People who have developed good levels of emotional intelligence can often make their emotions work for them – they may literally be able to choose their emotional state.

Health care workers are unlikely to be able to switch off feelings of being threatened simply by wishing them away. Usually workers will switch off the threat by using positive thoughts about their own past experiences, their skills in being able to calm people, or just by using their own professional role to protect themselves from feeling 'got at'. If a health care worker can think that the person

It is not reality that creates emotions in us – the way we perceive and think controls what we experience

is distressed because of their situation, rather than 'this person is out to get me' they may be able to switch off the emotions that create a sense of being threatened.

Staying calm

Being calm depends on the thoughts that we have, but it is also a practical skill which can be acted out and rehearsed. If a worker can appear to be calm their own behaviour may have a calming effect on others. Non-verbal signs of being calm are summarised in Figure 2.17.

It is important to remember to breathe gently and slowly; slow, careful breathing can help to create relaxation and calmness as well as looking calm to others. Sometimes it is appropriate that body posture should be at a slight angle towards an angry person. A face-to-face posture is sometimes interpreted as an attempt to dominate or be threatening. The volume of speech should not be raised; it is important to talk in a normal tone and volume and to display that you do not feel threatened or angry.

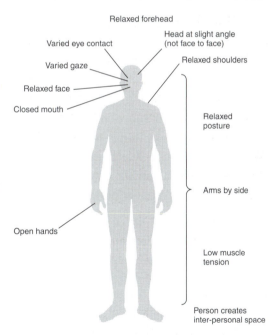

Figure 2.17 Non-verbal signs of being calm

Communicating respect and value

It is important to acknowledge the feelings and complaints that distressed people may be experiencing. If the other person feels that they are being taken seriously and are being listened to, this may have a calming effect. Reflective listening skills and the ability to keep the conversation going will be very important. A professional conversation should be warm and sincere whilst also seeking to build an understanding of the situation. Thanking a person for clarifying issues may be one way in which a worker can reduce the frustration that another person may feel. If a worker can communicate that they understand the other person's point of view, this may go a long way toward calming a situation and preventing further outbreaks of anger.

Assertion

Staying calm and in control of your own emotions, displaying respect and value for others, reflective listening and building an understanding of another person's viewpoint are central assertive skills. Assertion is the skill of being able to understand another person's viewpoint whilst being able to help them to understand your own viewpoint. Assertive skills create a situation where negotiation is possible. Assertive skills will therefore be very important when working with distressed individuals. More details comparing assertion with aggression and submissive behaviour can be found on page 44. More detail on listening skills can be found on page 52.

Creating trust and negotiating with distressed individuals

If you can successfully calm an angry or distressed person, the next step will be to try to establish a sense of common ground or liking between each other. It is at this stage that a skilled worker will attempt to build an understanding of the other person's viewpoint. Creating trust involves meeting the other person's self-esteem needs. In some situations it may be necessary to make the other person feel important. Sometimes it may be appropriate to say just a little about your own feelings, your background and so on if this helps to build bridges and create a sense of safety with the other person. It is usually appropriate to come across as open-minded and supportive but it is important that you do not agree with everything that the other person demands. It will be important to keep the conversation going and to keep the other person talking – perhaps using questioning and reflective listening skills.

Once you have built a level of understanding with a distressed person, it may then be possible to try to sort things out and to negotiate what kind of help or support you can offer. At this stage in the interaction it may be possible to take a problem-solving approach. Problem solving may start off by clarifying the issues that are involved and exploring alternative solutions.

Sometimes it may be necessary to structure expectations. This means gently introducing ideas of what is possible and not possible. It is important not to argue with a distressed person as this may only force them back to being aggressive or withdrawn. If you have to say 'no' to a demand, it may often be better to slowly lead up to the expectation that you will say no, rather than directly confronting a person with a 'stone wall' rejection of their views. For instance, 'I understand what you're saying and I'll see what I can do, but it would be wrong to promise anything' or 'We can try but I am not hopeful'.

Negotiation often depends on factual information and it may be important to bring factual information into the conversation at this stage. It will be important not to appear patronising when offering information. It will also be important to explain clearly any technical information that the other person may not understand.

Sometimes it will not be possible to reach agreement with a distressed person and in these circumstances it will be important to conclude the conversation leaving a positive emotional outcome, even if agreement has not been reached. It may be possible to agree to resume a conversation tomorrow, or to thank the person for their time and offer to talk again. It will always be important to leave the person with an increased sense of self-esteem even if they did not agree with your viewpoint.

Stages in managing a conversation with an angry person

1 Stay calm.
2 Try to calm the other person using appropriate non-verbal behaviour.
3 Listen to the other person.
4 Build trust and meet the other person's self-esteem needs.
5 Negotiate and try and solve problems.

Real conversations do not always follow simple stages but it is important not to attempt to negotiate and solve problems before listening and building trust.

Managing a difficult conversation

The brief example below is designed to illustrate some of the principles explained in this section. Real conversations may often be longer and more complex than this example. One way of developing skills in conversation management might be to analyse real conversations using the principles set out above.

Relative	'What have you done to my mother! She's so much worse than before. You aren't looking after her properly. She can't eat because of the rubbish food you give out.'
Worker	'Your mother does look worse today, perhaps you would like to sit down and we can talk.'
Relative	'Well, you tell me what is going on then and why the food is such rubbish!'
Worker	'I'll explain what we're doing if you like and I'm sorry that your mother doesn't like the food. Could you tell me what sort of things she really does like to eat?'
Relative	'Not the rubbish here.'
Worker	'Sometimes it's possible to increase a person's appetite by just offering a very small tasty piece of something they really like, perhaps fruit or a tiny piece of bread and jam?'
Relative	'What, and you are going to sort that out, are you?'
Worker	'I've found that it works for a lot of people – but can you give me some ideas of what your mother would like?'
Relative	'Well, she likes pears and cherry jam, but good stuff – not like here.'
Worker	'OK. Could you possibly bring some of her favourite things in and we could try and see if that would help?'
Relative	'Why should I?'
Worker	'Well, it might help, everyone is different and you are the person who would really know what your mother is likely to enjoy.'
Relative	'Can't you do something about the food here?'
Worker	'I'm afraid that the choice of food is limited, but we might be able to work together to improve your mother's appetite as a first step to making things better.'
Relative	'I suppose it's not up to you to change the food. I'll bring the jam in but I still think it's not right.'
Worker	'I'm sorry that you're not happy about the food but perhaps we can talk again tomorrow.'
Relative	'Well, thank you for your time – at least I could talk to you.'

This conversation starts with the relative making aggressive accusations. The worker responds by remaining assertive and not arguing, or going straight into discussing the complaints that the relative has raised. Instead the worker attempts to calm the situation and invites the relative to sit down. By inviting the relative to sit down the worker is taking control of the conversation and creating a situation where she can use her listening skills.

At several points the angry relative is still challenging the worker with complaints and aggressive statements. The worker is careful not to respond to these challenges and risk triggering more aggression. The worker is able to stay calm and to build a sense of trust by keeping the conversation going. The worker is able to ask the relative questions about his mother's needs. The worker is also able to meet the relative's self-esteem needs by pointing out that he is the person who would really know what his mother likes.

In this conversation the worker negotiates that the relative will bring some food in. The worker structures the relative's expectations by mentioning the limited choice of food. Because the relative has been listened to he is willing to stop complaining – he compliments the worker with the statement that at least she listened. The conversation ends on a positive emotional note, even though all the problems of catering in health care settings have not been resolved. The point of this conversation was to meet the emotional needs of the distressed relative and not to find technical solutions to catering problems!

Sources of support for carers

Working with distressed people is stressful. Even highly skilled and experienced professional staff sometimes fail to manage conversations appropriately, or to manage their own emotions. It is important that staff receive practical advice and emotional support if they are to develop or even maintain their skills.

It is difficult to provide emotional support for others if you do not receive emotional support yourself. An organisation that blames and criticises staff rather than supporting them is unlikely to employ staff that can provide effective support to its clients or customers.

Sources of practical and emotional support for staff include the following:

- **Formal supervision**   This is where a worker discusses their work with a senior member of staff. The supervisor may provide feedback on the quality of the worker's practice. Formal supervision may also be used to discuss training needs, or to review specific incidents which have occurred in practice. Formal supervision might be an appropriate setting to discuss the development of communication skills.
- **Peer support**   This involves the help and guidance that can be gained from colleagues. Sometimes this support can be formal, for instance where workers have a mentor or adviser, who may be a more experienced colleague. Very often peer support is informal – workers may talk through incidents that have happened during a coffee break. Workers may ask one another for ideas and advice or simply share experiences.
- **Counselling**   There is an old saying that a problem shared is a problem halved. Counselling services provide a service where individuals can discuss their thoughts and feelings in a totally confidential setting. Counselling can help people to make

sense of practical and emotional problems that they are experiencing. Many people experience emotional stress when working with people who are distressed. Counselling provides a vital support service to help cope with stress.

- **Training**   Most roles within health care work now require that workers undergo continuous professional development. Training enables people to reflect on their practice, to explore new ideas and to develop their own personal and professional skills. The development of new ideas and skills can help to increase confidence in working with people.

- **Support within own social network**   Many people rely on the emotional support that partners, family and friends supply. When things go wrong, friends and family can provide an emotional 'buffer' which takes the stress out of some aspects of life. Many people develop a positive sense of belonging and self-esteem through their relationships with friends and family. Friends and family can provide a useful source of emotional support which can promote self-confidence when working with other people.

Assessment activity 2.7

Using observations on other notes you have recorded in your logbook, you should explain how communication skills can support a distressed individual or contribute to the managing of challenging behaviour. For this piece of work you might write a theoretical account of how you might have worked. You might choose to base your account on a real situation which you have observed. You are not required to have demonstrated advanced emotional and conversation management skills for this exercise, but you are required to discuss the theory involved in communicating with distressed individuals.

End of unit test

Read the short conversation below between a nurse and patient in a hospital setting and then answer the questions which follow.

Nurse:	'Hello, how are you this morning?'
Patient:	'I'm not feeling well, I've got pain in my back.'
Nurse:	'Did your relatives visit yesterday?'
Patient:	'Er, no I haven't seen them.'
Nurse:	'I've just got to check your chart now.'
Patient:	'Can you do something for my pain please?'
Nurse:	'I'll ask the doctor later.'
Patient:	'But I asked for something yesterday and never saw the doctor.'
Nurse:	'Well, they are all very busy you know.'
Patient:	'But that is no use to me is it, can't you do something now?'
Nurse:	'Don't get worked up now, I'll see what I can do but we are all very busy you know!'

1   Identify some of the inhibiting factors which may prevent this conversation from meeting the client's needs.

2   List three types or levels of need that the patient may have had in a hospital setting.

3 Why are closed questions often inappropriate in caring conversations?

4 Identify one barrier to effective communication in the conversation above.

5 Name two consequences that may follow for the patient if they are constantly treated the same way as in this conversation and they are in hospital for a length of time.

6 Explain the difference between listening and just hearing.

7 List three important qualities that a supportive conversation should include.

8 What risks might a patient face if they felt that they were being ignored and could not control what was happening to them? Explain the process of learned helplessness.

9 What is an advocate and why might a person need the services of an advocate within a healthcare context?

10 List three types of support that staff might receive whilst working with people with challenging behaviours.

References and further reading

Goleman, D. (1996) *Emotional Intelligence*, London: Bloomsbury

Hargie, O., Saunders, C. and Dickson, D. (1987) *Social Skills in Interpersonal Communication*, London: Routledge

Maslow, A. H. (1970) (2nd edn) *Motivation and Personality*, New York: Harper & Row

Pease, A. (1997) *Body Language*, London: Sheldon Press

Rogers, C. R. (1951) *Client Centred Therapy*, Boston: Houghton Mifflin

Sanders, P. (1994) *First Steps in Counselling*, Manchester: PCCS Books

Seligman, M. (1975) *Helplessness*, San Francisco: W. H. Freeman and Co.

Thompson, N. (1996) *People Skills*, Basingstoke: Macmillan Press

3 Research and Project

The two units on *Research* and *Project* provide an understanding of research, the research process and its application as applied to health studies. Through increasing your understanding of research, and developing your research skills, you will be better placed to complete many of the activities required of you for other units, in particular the core units of Communication and supportive skills and Health and society as well as the optional project, Health promotion, Microbiology, Diet and nutrition, Complementary therapies, Health psychology and Current issues in health units.

What you need to learn

- Research methods
- The primary research process
- Statistical research information
- Ethical issues
- Your research as a presentation
- Producing a bibliography

Research methods

What is research?

Have you ever been shopping in your local high street and been pounced upon by someone with a clipboard who just wants a few minutes of your time and ends up asking a seemingly endless stream of questions? If so, then you will probably have been involved in market research to determine, for example, different people's shopping preferences.

You will almost certainly have completed a registration card after purchasing a new stereo or TV which will have involved ticking a number of boxes in answer to a variety of questions. This is another type of market research.

You may have taken part in the national census or even been interviewed about your views on some topic in the news. These are examples of social research.

Scientific research is used by many people, not just scientists. In science classes at school you will have carried out experimental investigations that are the basis of scientific research. Another example might be where you have been asked by your doctor to be involved in the trial of a new type of drug.

Think it over

Given the above examples can you think of any similar situations or other examples of research in which you have been involved? Working in groups, discuss your experiences.

Purpose and role of research

Research is used in all sorts of different ways and can be regarded broadly as a tool to develop a better understanding of the world we live in. In health care services it can help to identify need and highlight gaps in provision. Organisations and professionals concerned with health are continually undertaking research for many different reasons. These can include the following:

- Extending scientific understanding – in many cases scientific research may appear to have little to do with health or health-related matters and it is only later, often after many years of continued research and development, that their application to health becomes recognised. The ability to manipulate the genetic make-up of and the potential to clone humans stems from the elucidation of the structure of DNA by Watson and Crick in 1953.

- Developing new technologies – the increased range of new technologies available to health care specialists has grown from the application of computers to existing technology as well as the development of novel systems that have arisen from the application of pure science. The use of X-ray crystallography by Rosalind Franklin, that led to the determination of the structure of DNA by Watson and Crick, took several years, whereas the introduction of computer technology in the 1960s enabled complex structures to be determined in days.

- Carrying out clinical trials – according to the Association of the British Pharmaceutical Industry it takes 10 to 12 years to develop a new drug, at the cost of around £350 million, before it becomes available to the public.

- Health screening – health screening has been identified as helping to reduce the risk of disease and the subsequent burden on the NHS. Screening presently covers both general health checks as well as screening for specific conditions within life stage groups – antenatal, children, men, women and the elderly. However, many screening programmes are currently under review and it is envisaged that screening programmes should be more effective in identifying where health service provision should be targeted as well as gaps in provision.

- Evaluating services – up until the 1990s most health research was based upon scientific investigations and clinical trials. There is an increasing focus on assessing the effectiveness and efficiency of these and other aspects of health intervention including the provision of services, health care procedures and care settings.

Health research is vast and crosses political as well as international boundaries, although at any one time and in any one country it can often reflect issues of current political importance simply because a large amount of research is government funded. In the United Kingdom we have a publicly funded health service, the emphasis and culture of which changes with changing political ideologies.

An idea of the breadth of research carried out in different countries and by different organisations is exemplified by the following examples of recent studies that have been reported in the media.

Examples of recent research in health

Second thoughts on folic acid

Swedish researchers have found that women who take folic acid before and during pregnancy are more likely to have twins. Of 2569 women who used folic acid supplements 2.8 per cent gave birth to twins. This compares to a twin birth rate in the general Swedish population of 1.5 per cent. Bengt Kallen of the Tornblad Institute in Lund has calculated that if 30 per cent of 100,000 women in Sweden took folic acid there would be 225 extra pairs of twins. These twins would have a lower birth weight and an increased risk of cerebral palsy. This should be weighed against the benefit of avoiding 4 or 5 neural tube defect (spina bifida) cases. Not all researchers are convinced that the link between twins and folic acid is real though and further research is urged.

New Scientist, 28 July 2001, p. 19

ADVICE TO TAKE WITH A SMALL PINCH OF SALT?

Low salt and a healthy diet would benefit everyone in the western world, according to a US study that assessed the effects of a low sodium diet and a diet rich in fruit, vegetables, and low-fat dairy items and low in fat, red meat, and sugary foods.

Low sodium and the DASH (Dietary Approaches to Stop Hypertension) diet have been shown (*N Engl J Med* 2001; **344:** 3–10) to lower blood pressure in some groups of people such as women and African Americans, but detractors have argued that the results do not apply to everyone.

Reprinted with permission from Elsevier Science (*The Lancet*, 2001, vol 358, p2134)

Asthma linked to diet

Australian researchers have discovered that children whose diet includes a high level of polyunsaturated margarines and cooking oils are more than twice as likely to have asthma than children who consume less of these polyunsaturated fats. The researchers believe that omega–6 fatty acids, which metabolise into inflammation-causing prostaglandins, are the culprits. They estimate that as many as 17 per cent of all childhood asthma cases may be related to a high intake of omega-6 fatty acids.

New Scientist, 28 July 2001, p.19

Vitamin C prevents cataracts

Researchers at Tufts University, Boston, Massachusetts and the Harvard Medical School have confirmed that a high intake of antioxidants (from diet or supplements) helps prevent the development of cataracts (age-related nuclear lens opacities). Their recent study included 478 female nurses who had completed food frequency questionnaires every second year since 1980. The questionnaires included details of vitamin and mineral supplement use. During the period 1993 to 1994 the study participants all underwent a detailed eye examination and had blood samples taken for analysis of plasma concentrations of vitamins C and E and the carotenoids.

The researchers conclude that vitamins C and E, riboflavin (vitamin B), folic acid, beta-carotene, and lutein/zeaxanthin all protect against cataract development. However, after adjustment for other nutrients only the association with vitamin C remained statistically significant.

Jacques, Paul F., *et al.*, 'Long-term nutrient intake and early age-related nuclear lens opacities', *Archives of Ophthalmology*, Vol. 119, July 2001, pp. 1009–19

Smoking outside still causes second-hand smoke exposure to children

Research has shown that exposure to second-hand or environmental tobacco smoke (ETS) can be detrimental to a young child's health. But even if a parent smokes outside the home, children could still face a high level of ETS exposure, US researchers reported at the 2002 Pediatric Academic Societies' annual meeting (Baltimore, MD, USA; May 4–7).

Judith Groner (Columbus Children's Hospital, OH, USA) and colleagues assessed the extent of ETS exposure by analysing hair cotinine concentrations in 327 children aged 2 weeks to 3 years. Cotinine, a nicotine metabolite, has been used in previous research to quantify ETS exposure. Of the 41% of primary caregivers who self-reported being smokers, 20% said that they never smoked indoors.

Hair cotinine concentrations were strikingly similar whether the parent smoked indoors or outside.

Reprinted with permission from Elsevier Science (*The Lancet*, 2002, Vol 359, p1675)

Types of research

There are many different ways of undertaking research and all involve the use of what is termed **primary** and **secondary** research.

Primary research is the gathering of information by the person or persons carrying out the research. Primary research provides up-to-date and hopefully relevant information about the topic being studied.

Secondary research is the use of information that others have collected. You will undertake secondary research to gather information for the completion of much of your course work. The information you obtain may come from a variety of sources and will be based upon the published work of the original researcher or an interpretation of their work by someone else.

Secondary research is an essential part of primary research as the researcher needs to be fully aware of what other people have studied in relation to their own work. It may be that one piece of research is based upon the work of someone else or that the same research is being carried out in a different context, i.e. in a different place or with different people.

The type of information obtained by primary or secondary research can be identified as either **quantitative** or **qualitative**. Quantitative information describes information or data that is in the form of numbers, for example the number of births and deaths, whereas qualitative information is descriptive and in the form of the written or spoken word, for example experiences of cancer.

Further distinctions can occur as a consequence of research involving the study of people. These include **cross-sectional** and **longitudinal** studies. A cross-sectional study is based upon the investigation of people at a particular moment in time. Such research may form part of investigations into the differences or relationships that can occur between individuals or groups, for example finding out about the difference in reaction times between the young and old (see Experimental methods, page 93). Alternatively, longitudinal research studies individuals or groups over a period of time, in some cases many years, for example studying the development of a baby for the first six months of their life.

The problem with longitudinal studies is the time required to complete them. Whilst the development example of a baby for six months might be feasible for you to carry out, others may not, for example a lifetime study of the social and emotional development of twins. After all, your course has been designed to be completed within two years!

Secondary sources of data collection

As already stated, secondary research involves finding out facts and figures that have been produced by others, so some thought needs to be given to potential sources of such information.

Books, newspapers, magazines, specialist publications

Books obtained from your college will probably be your main source of information initially, particularly if you have not had experience of using other sources of information. Whilst your tutors may direct you to some books and give you lists, you will have to search out others for yourself. This can be quite a task if a library is well stocked. However, most libraries now possess computerised search facilities and the librarians can be a great source of help in finding resources that cover the area of work you are studying. As well as the college library your local library may have useful material and depending upon where you live it may be possible for you to access more specialist libraries, such as university libraries or your local NHS Trust (access to such facilities may be restricted or involve paying a subscription).

Libraries often subscribe to, and keep back copies of, one or more daily newspapers, magazines and specialist publications produced for people working in specific

Libraries are a good source of secondary data

industries/organisations. The types of publications you might find helpful include the following:

- *Nursing Times* – a weekly publication produced for nurses and other professionals in the health and caring services. Often contains specialist articles relating to children.
- *Times Educational Supplement* – published weekly, covering newsworthy topics and developments in education.
- *Social Trends* – published annually, this is an invaluable source of official statistics covering information on families, housing, health, education and work.
- *Regional Trends* – similar to *Social Trends* but contains information on a regional basis. Useful if you want data relevant to the area you live in.

People

By talking to people who work in health, your tutors, family and friends you can get different views and ideas on subjects. Such views may reflect changing attitudes towards health, parenting and education and as such support or refute information obtained from books, etc.

Organisations

There are voluntary and statutory organisations that you will have found out about by reading other parts of this book and through input from your tutors. They can be an invaluable source of help and information on specific topics.

Whilst the statutory services are available throughout the country, voluntary organisations may be concentrated in larger towns/cities. However, a good starting point to look for such organisations is your local newspaper or the library. The following are just some of the organisations listed in one local newspaper: Voluntary Action, National Asthma Campaign, Attention Deficit Hyperactivity Disorder, Autism Support Group, British Diabetes Association, Cancer Support Group, Charcot Marie Tooth Disease (Peroneal Muscular Atrophy), International Support Group, Childline, Coeliac Society, Cry-sis (support for parents with babies who cry constantly), Down's Syndrome Association. Whilst many of these organisations offer support to victims, sufferers and carers they are usually more than happy to talk to, or provide students with, information that helps to market their cause.

Computers

You can love them or hate them, but in terms of potential computers are probably the most readily available source of up-to-date information. Computers can be used to obtain information from CD-ROMs, DVDs, the Internet or intranets.

CD-ROMs (Compact-Disc Read Only Memory) are digitally recorded stores of information. They can be similar to encyclopaedias, containing textual and visual information on a wide range of topics. Others are digital copies of the publications mentioned above that are updated annually. CD-ROMs are now the usual source of computer programs, many of which have an educational content.

The Internet is a worldwide information base which anyone can contribute to or access. You name it and there is probably something on the Internet devoted to it. Accessing the Internet requires a computer to be fitted with a modem that links it to worldwide communication systems. Computer programs then allow the computer to gain access to the Internet via an Internet Service Provider (ISP). These enable you to use 'search engines' to find the information you require. However, you can waste an awful lot of time searching the 'web' and getting nowhere. You need to be quite specific in your search, but not so specific that the search engine comes up with nothing. Most search engines have help facilities to assist you in your quest. To use a search engine and find what you are looking for, follow the instructions in Searching the net below and look at a search engine home page in Figure 3.1.

Intranet sites are local versions of the Internet used by organisations for exchange of information within that establishment. The organisation may choose to allow access to others via an Internet website, but may limit use to specific parts of the site.

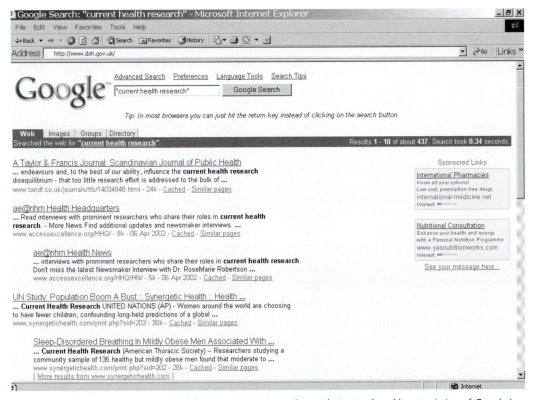

Screenshot reproduced by permission of Google Inc.

Figure 3.1 A search engine home page

Searching the net

This information assumes you are able to access the Internet and need some help with searching for information. It also assumes that you are already at the 'home page' of one of the search engines. If you are unsure how to access the Internet ask your tutor or a member of the IT staff at your college.

Enter the details of what you are looking for in the search box by typing in keywords, phrases, or questions. The search service responds by giving you a list of all the web pages, news, discussions and products relating to those topics. The most relevant content will appear at the top of your results. Always use lower-case text in your searches. When you use lower-case text, the search service finds both upper-case and lower-case results. When you use upper-case text, the search service only finds upper-case results.

Focusing your research

If you get too many results or the results aren't as specific as you would like, here are some strategies for focusing your search results.

- Put quotation marks around phrases or words that you want to appear next to each other in your results.

  Example: Putting quotes around the words "heart disease" ensures you get pages about heart disease and not about each separate word.

- Alternatively, create phrases using punctuation or special characters such as dashes, underscore lines, commas, slashes, or dots.

  Example: Try searching for social-emotional-development instead of social emotional development. The dashes link the words together as a phrase.

- Some search engines allow you to ask a question.

  Example: 'Where can I find a list of intelligence tests?'

- Include or exclude words. To make sure that a word is always included in your search, place a plus sign (+) immediately before the keyword (no spaces) in the search box. To make sure that a word is always excluded from your search, place a minus sign (–) immediately before the keyword (no spaces) in the search box.

  Example: To find recipes for chocolate cookies without nuts try: recipe chocolate +chips –nuts.

- Use wildcards. By typing an asterisk (*) at the end of a keyword, you can search for multiple forms of the word.

  Example: Try child*, to find children, childish and childlike.

Broadening your search

If you get too few results or do not find what you are looking for, here are some strategies for broadening your search results.

- Check your spelling. A single misspelled or mistyped word can turn an otherwise well-defined search into a dud.

- Use synonyms instead of the original words.

  Example: If a search on 'mental development scales' produced too few results try 'intelligence tests'.

Other media

TV, national and local radio are sources of up-to-date information which are often used to reflect current attitudes and opinions about different issues. However, like newspapers, they may reflect the biased views of the publishers and in order to attract a maximum audience will latch onto subjects that are topical, e.g. the global threat of bioterrorism.

Museums

Museums may often be disregarded but are potentially useful in terms of local history and the subsequent social changes in local communities. Such changes may reflect on a wide range of issues relating to parenting and the development, education and experience of children in a community. Many museums operate interactive displays or operate as living museums to reflect social history, e.g. Beamish Museum.

Where you look will depend on the topic you are studying. Generally you should be able to work on the premise that anything relating to education will be of use.

Using secondary research

Remember that information obtained from secondary sources is second hand. As such, it may be biased towards the views of the person or organisation that has produced it. In addition, the information may be out of date as the book or article may have been written some time after the original research was undertaken and you may be reading the material some years after publication. Therefore you should always treat such information with caution and have evidence from different sources to support your work and provide a balanced picture.

Avoiding plagiarism and summarising information

Plagiarism is the direct copying of someone else's work and is against copyright law. However, copyright does allow for other work to be used for research purposes as long as the original author is acknowledged. The use of secondary information means that you must produce a summary of the original. You can make a direct quote where the information contains specific facts or data relating to your study, but the information should be enclosed within inverted commas '...'. Whether you have summarised or used a direct quote you must also include a reference or acknowledgement to the author or producer of the information and its source (see page 117 on producing a bibliography).

With the advent of computers and the Internet plagiarism has become a widespread problem, with students cutting and pasting large chunks of material for inclusion in their work. It has been known for students to copy information from such publications as *Encarta,* not even taking the trouble to remove the copyright symbol! Teachers and lecturers are becoming more adept at spotting such transgressions and it is important that students do not 'cheat' in this way.

Key issue: Meningitis

Meningitis is an inflammation of the meninges, a lining tissue surrounding the brain. Many different organisms can cause meningitis, although bacteria and viruses are the main culprits.

Bacterial meningitis is fairly uncommon, but it can be extremely serious. It is fatal in 1 in 10 cases and 1 in 7 survivors is left with a serious disability, such as deafness or brain injury.

The bacteria that cause meningitis are very common and live naturally in the back of the nose and throat, or the upper respiratory tract. Only rarely do the bacteria overcome the body's defences and cause the illness. Five main groups of the more serious form of the disease have been identified. These are meningococcal meningitis A, B, C, W135 and Y, of which Group B is the most common, followed by group C.

The bacteria are passed from person to person by prolonged close contact and by coughing, sneezing and intimate kissing (saliva exchange). A vaccine that will give long-term protection against group C has been introduced to protect those at greatest risk, young children and teenagers. The numbers of cases of group C infection have rapidly decined as a consequence.

Assessment activity 3.1

To develop your research skills you should know how to conduct an information search. By undertaking this activity you will also gain a deeper understanding of meningitis.

An information search involves using a variety of sources to identify suitable secondary information. Go to your local or college library and look for texts on the subject or chapters or articles within books or publications. Note down the title of such publications, the author, date and place of publication (see the section on producing a bibliography on page 117).

Now carry out an Internet search. Use the Searching the net information above and try different search engines such as Google (www.google.com), Dogpile (www.dogpile.com) and Hotbot (www.hotbot.com) to identify online information on meningitis. Check out some of the website addresses that you see on screen and if they appear to contain relevant information note down or copy the titles of the research, together with their author and website address.

If you have not used the Internet ask your tutor, school, college or local library for help.

The primary research process

Secondary research can provide the background and basis for many of your studies but you will also need to be familiar with the process of primary research and the different primary research methods used. These include:

- surveys/questionnaires
- interviews
- experimental methods
- observations
- case studies.

You might find by reading specialist books on research that these methods are presented in different ways and that there are others. Each method has its own advantages and disadvantages and will consequently be used by researchers in different circumstances.

Before considering each method in turn, you need to be aware of the processes you must go through to plan your research effectively.

Research is regarded as a cyclical process that generally involves the stages shown in Figure 3.2.

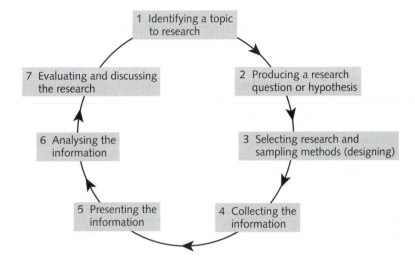

Figure 3.2 The research process as a cycle

Discussion and evaluation of the research can lead to further or continuing investigations to complete the cycle.

The first three stages are all about planning and the more effort put into planning and organising your activities, particularly where the research is a project for which you have been allocated a term or longer to complete, the better the end result. Once you have planned the research you are then ready to collect the data, after which you need to sort it out ready for presentation and analysis.

A checklist is provided on pages 118–19 to help you with the organisation and planning of any research or project you undertake.

Identifying a topic to research

This can be based upon:

- having read about something which you think would be interesting and enjoyable to find out more about
- your own ideas
- the ideas of others.

Your tutor may be able to get you started on suggesting topics that previous students have investigated but you and your fellow students could try a 'brainstorming' session as described below and in the case study example that follows.

Brainstorming

This is a popular technique used by businesses and organisations to generate ideas. You need flip chart paper and marker pens.

Your tutor may have given you a broad area to think about or left things very open. As a class group or in smaller groups of about four to seven agree who will write the ideas down (the person needs to write large enough for the whole class to see).

The group should then start to think about what they could research and any idea that is suggested should be written down by a 'scribe' for all to see, no matter how silly some of them may seem. (Who would have thought of a wind-up radio or a group of strange looking figures with odd-shaped aerials on their heads and television screens on their tummies?) Sometimes it can be difficult to get going but once the ideas begin to flow you shouldn't have a problem. Continue until the list is long enough or ideas begin to dry up. Don't worry if the list isn't very long since more ideas may be generated when you start to discuss the different topics.

If you divided into groups, now is the time to put each flip chart onto the wall for everyone to see. Some of the ideas will be repeated but there are likely to be others your group hadn't thought of which may give you further ideas.

From the list choose two or three topics that sound interesting. Either as a whole class, or in your original or like-minded groups, begin to discuss the ideas to see if they are realistic, i.e. would it be possible to investigate the idea in the time allocated, are there sufficient resources to carry out the investigation, are there any ethical or confidentiality issues that could prevent you completing the work, what research methods could be used? Your tutor will probably help you with this process.

You should hopefully end up with an idea that you can now begin to consider in more detail.

Case study

A group of students was asked to undertake some research into childhood infectious diseases. In order for each student to select a disease to investigate the tutor asked the group to brainstorm different childhood illnesses they knew or had heard about. The list they came up with was as follows:

Meningitis	Threadworm	Tonsillitis	Chicken pox
Whooping cough	Polio	Measles	Flu
Diarrhoea	Headaches	Scabies	Thrush
Gastroenteritis	Nits	Cystic fibrosis	Impetigo
Asthma	Coughs	Eczema	AIDS
Diphtheria	Mumps	Scarlet fever	Colds

The tutor then went through the list with the group to identify actual infectious diseases rather than non-infectious diseases or symptoms. Students individually selected a disease to study.

Another starting point for ideas is the course syllabus, which should be available through your tutor. The syllabus identifies the outcomes and assessment evidence requirements for the units you will be studying. By reading through these it should be possible to identify a topic that could be based upon a research project. Indeed, your tutor may give some direction or set specific assignments to ensure you meet such outcomes and assessment criteria. A number of units, both core and optional, refer to research projects as possible means of assessment.

Talking to other people can be invaluable for helping to generate ideas and may include any of the following:

- Family – your parents or guardians will have a wealth of life experience and discussing any project ideas with them may help you to focus in on your study. Other family members may also be of assistance, not only to talk things through, but possibly someone who works in the health sector.
- Friends – talking to each other about your work will help spark off different ideas and make you think more deeply about your work, which can help you become more focused.
- Tutors – your tutor will probably want you to study something that is related to the course, but their experience and understanding of the subject, and of past students' work make them an invaluable resource to be exploited at every opportunity (even though they may be busy!).
- Employers and workplace supervisors – if you work in a 'caring' organisation in a voluntary capacity, through an organised placement or as an employee you could ask for advice and may find that they would like you to carry out some research for them.

The research question or hypothesis

Having selected the topic or list of topics that you would like to study, or are thinking about studying, you must now begin to refine your ideas – focusing in on what you would specifically like to find out. This will lead to producing a research question or hypothesis.

A **research question** simply states the question or questions you want your research to answer.

A **hypothesis** is a special type of research question that tends to be used in surveys or experiments. It proposes the existence of a relationship between variables or factors and tends to suggest how the relationship will be tested.

Students often find that identifying a research question is one of the more difficult parts of the whole process and consequently try to opt out of making a decision about this until later. This is an error that results in students being unclear about the focus of their study. Time needs to be given to what you intend to find out. This part of the research process will involve you in doing some secondary research, reading around the topic, looking at recent research and talking to others. In this way you will begin to find out more about the area you are going to study that can then lead to the selection of a specific topic.

For example, suppose you have chosen disability as a subject area. There are as many different issues within disability to study as the number of ideas you came up with in the first place. So, deciding what to find out about a subject can involve further brainstorming or secondary research to identify a specific subject that would be worthwhile investigating, i.e. one you would enjoy. Look at the case study below, Focusing on disability.

In writing your research question or hypothesis you should simply start by noting what questions you would like your study to answer. If you have several questions, try to narrow them down to one or two. This will make your project more manageable.

Case study

Figure 3.3 represents the start of a spider diagram designed to focus in on a research topic related to disability. As you can see, there are many different strands to looking at this subject and this isn't comprehensive! In addition, it is possible to make connections between different subtopics that begin to show how complex a subject can become if it is not specific. However, by identifying the possible strands to a piece of work it allows you to focus on one or a small number of aspects that makes a research programme feasible. So, for example, this researcher chose to investigate the causes and support for children with cerebral palsy as a result of talking to people she knew through voluntary work at a day care centre.

• Are there any more links to be made between physical conditions and any of the other subtopics?

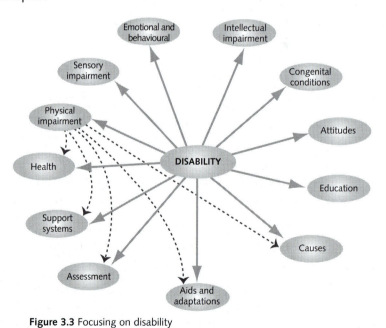

Figure 3.3 Focusing on disability

Think it over

Draw your own version of the spider diagram in Figure 3.3 and in a small group add any other subtopics you can think of. Then choose one subtopic and start to make connections to other subtopics. Whilst this may broaden the subtopic it allows you to see which connection or connections you could pursue in your research.

Assessment activity 3.2

Once you understand how to use a spider diagram, create one for your own research topic. Then complete a report for your research project which defines which primary and secondary sources of data collection you will use. Show that you have evaluated the strengths and weaknesses of each method and how you have decided on your methods and sources.

Primary sources of data collection

This section concentrates on information about the different methods of research and how to use them.

Surveys/questionnaires

Survey research is based upon asking questions of people. This can be in the form of a questionnaire or an intensive one-to-one, in-depth interview.

Questionnaires are usually a paper-and-pencil exercise that people complete. The completion of a questionnaire can be carried out through a mail drop or group activity or as a one-to-one structured interview.

The advantages of using a questionnaire are that:

* they are relatively inexpensive to administer, apart from the cost of photocopying and postage stamps
* you can send a questionnaire to a wide number of people
* they allow respondents to fill it out at their own convenience.

However, there are some disadvantages, such as:

* response rates from mail surveys are often very low
* postal surveys are not the best way of asking for detailed information.

The disadvantage of poor response rate can be overcome by carrying out the survey face to face, for example in your local high street. This also allows for questioning the respondent to clarify any questions or to gain a more insightful response. If you decide to use this method it is important for personal safety that you conduct the activity in a small group and that you have some form of identification (see Data collection, page 102).

Alternatively, a group-administered questionnaire is an effective way of getting people to respond to a questionnaire. It guarantees a high response rate and can draw on people who are readily available, such as in college, a school or workplace, though it may limit the total number of people surveyed and can create a biased sample. Respondents are handed the questionnaire and can be asked to complete it immediately or you can offer to collect it the following week or whenever convenient.

How you administer the questionnaire is relatively easy compared to producing it. You might think it's simple to run off a few questions about, for example, the views of parents on raising children and keeping pets. You will find that it takes time, thought and practice to ensure that the questions give you the answers you are seeking. You will also find that you need to undertake a trial to find out if the questionnaire works.

The types of question you can ask will vary and include the following:

1 **Closed and open questions.** Closed questions expect a yes/no answer, whereas open questions expect the respondent to say something more. For example, closed question, 'Are you married?'; open question 'What are your views on marriage?' Closed questions give information that can be easily quantified whilst open-ended questions allow the respondent to express their own views. The difficulty with open-ended questions is that respondents may have slightly different views, making the presentation of such information more difficult.

2 **Information gathering questions**, which usually ask for some numerical data. For example:
   i) How many children do you have?
   ii) What is your age?
   iii) In what year were you born?
   (*Note iii*) is regarded as a more sensitive way of asking someone their age than *ii*).)

3 **Category questions** offer a number of possibilities, only one of which the respondent can fit into. For example:
   i) Is the respondent:
         Male
         Female
   ii) Are you:
         Married
         Single
   iii) Tick which age group you fit into
         15–25
         26–35
         36–45
         46–55
         56+
   The use of categories such as age groups is another way of obtaining information that may be regarded as sensitive. It can also be useful to allocate people to age ranges if you want to see if there is any difference in response to your questionnaire between age groups, e.g. attitudes to euthanasia.

4 **Ranking questions** are used to place answers in order and are useful for obtaining information on views or attitudes. For example:
   i) Consider the following personal needs and number them in order of importance to you. How important to you is it to have:
         • a home
         • financial security
         • employment
         • friends
         • a car
   ii) In order of importance number your preferred method of pain relief in childbirth:
         • Gas
         • Pethidine

- Epidural
- Breathing and relaxation techniques

5 **Scale questions** can also be used to obtain information about attitudes and beliefs, but must be used with care. For example:

Tick the box that best describes how you feel about the following statements:

Euthanasia is appropriate when the person concerned:	Strongly agree	Agree	Disagree	Strongly disagree
Has a terminal illness				
Is a burden on the health service				
Has been in a coma for many months				
Is so depressed that they want to end their life				

The scale question above is quite controversial and may not be easy to do for a college-based project. However, it helps to illustrate how controversial topics may be investigated without having to ask someone directly about the subject, i.e. do you believe in euthanasia?

An alternative type of scale question is given below.

Tick the box that best describe your views on:

	Strongly agree	Agree	Neither agree nor disagree	Disagree	Strongly disagree
Breast feeding					
Fluoridation of water					
Homework for infant schoolchildren					

In this example an extra column has been added to include the neutral response of 'neither agree nor disagree'. Whilst this allows people to express a neutral view it can result in people avoiding the subject.

In addition to the style of questions used you also need to consider the construction and presentation of your questionnaire. The following pointers should be taken into account.

- Keep your questions as simple as possible. Two or three simple questions may be easier to answer than one difficult one.

- Do not ask too many questions. If there are too many, people will get fed up.
- Make sure your questions are unambiguous. For example, 'Should a child be disciplined for being naughty?' This question begs the response – what form of discipline are you referring to and how do you define naughty?
- Do not ask leading questions that imply a particular response, such as 'Should more money be spent on the health service?'
- Avoid grouping together questions that have a negative or sensitive context or if you are seeking a more personal view place them towards the end of the questionnaire, e.g. asking people's views on abortion, child abuse or drugs.
- Do not ask too many open-ended questions as they can take time to answer and are difficult to analyse. Again, these are best placed towards the end of the questionnaire and can be a useful way of getting a response to more contentious issues.
- Type or print your questionnaire in a format that is clear and legible.
- Order the questionnaire so that simple closed questions requiring yes/no or one-word answers come first, followed by ranking and scale-type questions and finishing with open-ended questions to allow subjects to express their opinions more fully.
- Ensure that you include an explanation of who you are, where you are from and the purpose of the questionnaire. Also provide clear instructions and a statement to assure respondents that the questionnaire is confidential (see Ethical issues, page 114).

You may be quite happy with your first draft of the questionnaire but problems can arise over the meaning of words or people misinterpreting the questions. Consequently, it is advisable to practise using your questionnaire on a small number of people to see whether questions need modifying to make them clearer. This is called a pilot or trial study, the results of which may still be used if you have not had to make any changes.

Be prepared to answer questions about your survey and remember to thank the respondent at the end.

Interviews

Interviews, particularly at their simplest level, can be seen as no more than extended survey questionnaires. However, interviews are a far more personal form of research and can provide more detailed information – particularly on sensitive subjects. They are usually carried out on a one-to-one basis.

Whilst interviews are generally easier for the respondent, especially if what is sought is opinions or impressions, they are not necessarily easier for the interviewer. Interviews can be very time consuming and they require good communication skills to complete effectively.

Interviews can be structured, semi-structured or open-ended. Structured interviews are based upon a set of questions requiring specific answers and are not very different from a questionnaire. Open-ended interviews may have little if any format and may take the form of a discussion, whilst semi-structured interviews are a bit of both. If you use this form of research, semi-structured interviews are probably the most appropriate procedure to follow.

You are most likely to use interviews to find out about people's feelings, attitudes and experiences of, for example, childbirth, postnatal depression, caring for a sick child or elderly relative, coping with bereavement or terminal illness. As a result, you will tend to choose one or more people to interview from those you know, have had contact with or have been put in touch with by your tutor or workplace supervisor.

As a consequence of knowing or having been introduced to the person to be interviewed you should give a brief explanation of the purpose of your interview and make arrangements as to the date, time and place of the interview. This will help prepare both the interviewee and yourself for the event. In addition you should make preparations for recording the interview. You can choose to use a tape recorder or take notes, both of which have their advantages and disadvantages – as shown in the table below.

Tape recording	Note-taking
Able to concentrate on interviewee and what they have to say and the questions to be asked	Need to give attention to both interviewee and note-taking
Can make respondents anxious and not able to talk about sensitive issues	Can be distracting
Provides a complete account of what has been said but can take a long time to transcribe and analyse	Allows a summary of what has been said to be noted and the main features identified so analysis is easier. Important facts or remarks may be missed

Whichever method is used, ensure you have the agreement of the interviewee and, if note-taking, have a spare pen or pencil and devise a system for abbreviating certain responses such as Q: for your question, A: for the respondent's answer, DK for don't know, etc.

In conducting the interview you need to take into account the beginning, middle and end.

The beginning includes making appropriate opening remarks that put the interviewee at ease and doesn't ask too much of them. This can be achieved by explaining who you are, where you are from and emphasising again what the research is for. The main thing here is not to be long winded. Also provide reassurance that the interview will remain confidential. This part can include asking simple questions that only require one-word or short answers such as 'How many children do you have?, 'What age and gender are they?' These simple questions can be memorised, enabling you to give attention to the interviewee and so helping to establish a trusting, honest, and non-threatening relationship that can lead into a more open-ended discussion about the main issues.

If you are interviewing more than one person for your research you must ensure that the questions asked are exactly the same, as altering them in any way can change their whole meaning and as a result alter the response you get.

Ask all the questions in the order arranged prior to the interview so that nothing is missed out either by you or the interviewee. Do not finish people's sentences for them because it might not have been what they were going to say.

If the beginning has gone well, it should lead naturally into the middle part of the interview where you hope to elicit a more open or detailed response. To help you do this the following techniques may be of use:

- Silence – one of the most effective ways to encourage someone to say more is to do nothing at all, just pause and wait. It works because people are generally uncomfortable with pauses or silence and it suggests that you are waiting, listening for what they will say next.
- Encouraging remarks – something as simple as 'Uh-huh' or 'OK' after the respondent completes a thought can encourage the respondent directly.
- Elaboration – by asking a question such as 'Is there anything else you would like to add?' can result in the respondent providing more information.
- Ask for clarification – by asking the interviewee to talk in more detail about something said earlier can allow the discussion to explore new areas. This type of question also shows that you have been listening and can elicit further information.
- Reflecting – by repeating back part of what the respondent has said. You say something without really saying anything new. For instance, if the respondent had just described a traumatic experience they had in childhood, you might say, 'What I'm hearing you say is that you found that experience very traumatic'. Then you should pause. The respondent is likely to say something like, 'Well, yes, and it affected the rest of my family as well. In fact, my younger sister...'.

When the interview ends, conclude by thanking the respondent and offering them the opportunity to read your completed work or at least a summary of it. Do give the respondent time to ask any further questions about you, your course or your research before you leave.

You may have observations about the interview that you weren't able to write down whilst you were with the respondent. As such, you should immediately go over your notes and make any other comments and observations, ensuring you distinguish these from the notes made during the interview.

Think it over

Interviews require good communication skills and take practice. If you are unsure about conducting an interview try this activity to practise the skills and gain confidence.

In groups of three, take turns at being an obsever, interviewer and interviewee. Choose a topic which each of you feels able to talk about. (What you did at the weekend tends to be a good one, but you could consider something related to the course.) Together jot down some questions that will require closed or open answers. Start by the interviewer asking a simple question, with the observer noting down how the interviewee responded. Move on to more open questions and again note the response, using the above techniques to see if the interviewee says more.

If you found this easy, try repeating the exercise, but this time choose a controversial or more sensitive subject such as abortion, embryo research or cancer.

Experimental methods

The experimental method is a standard scientific procedure whereby the researcher, possibly after some preliminary work, devises a research question in the form of a hypothesis by which they hope to explain the initial findings.

The hypothesis forms the basis of an experiment or series of experiments that enable the researcher to find the answers to the problem being investigated, i.e. the experiment tests the hypothesis. The hypothesis tends to be a very precise question, statement or prediction which the experiment can answer as probably yes or probably no. The word *probably* is used since you can never be 100 per cent certain that your study can be repeated over and over again to give the same answer.

A hypothesis suggests that there is a relationship or difference between two or more factors or variables, where a **variable** is something that changes or can be changed. A **relationship**, often referred to as a **correlation** or **association** between variables, results from changes in one variable being *related* to changes in another, for example the number of children suffering from asthma may be correlated to the increase in house dust mite infestations through increased use of central heating. A **difference** between variables can be regarded as changes in one variable causing an *effect* in another variable, for example ageing affects reaction times, often referred to as a cause and effect relationship.

The hypothesis can also be written in one of two formats, the **experimental** and the **null** hypothesis:

- The experimental hypothesis predicts the outcome of an experiment, for example the number of children suffering from asthma increases with increased numbers of house dust mites or people under 20 have quicker reaction times than people over 40.
- The null hypothesis does not predict an outcome, but states that there is no effect or relationship between variables, for example there is no relationship or correlation between the number of children suffering from asthma and the increased numbers of house dust mites or, there is no significant difference between the reaction times of people under 20 and those over 40.

The next step is to design a suitable experiment that will prove or disprove the hypothesis. The idea is to look at how one variable alters in response to changes in the other. With the cause-effect type of experiment the researcher deliberately alters the variable known as the **Independent Variable** (IV) that is thought to be causing the effect and measures changes in the other **Dependent Variable** (DV). The problem with this approach, particularly when applied to research on people, is that there may be many other factors that could influence the results. These are called confounding or extraneous variables. Consequently, the effect of such variables has to be eradicated or minimalised. This can be achieved by attempting to control as many of the factors as possible by ensuring the subjects are of the same or similar age, the same gender, etc. Alternatively the experiment can be designed using one of two approaches:

- Repeated measures design – this type of study is carried out by working with one group of subjects so that each subject experiences both experimental conditions, for example in an experiment (clinical trial) looking at the effect of a new drug, each person experiences both conditions, i.e. no drug and drug at different times.

- Independent subjects design – in this case each experimental condition is experienced by two different groups of subjects, for example in a drug trial, two groups of people would be chosen, one of which receives the drug and the other receives a placebo (sugar pill).

Think it over

Discuss the problems that might be associated with the repeated measures and independent subjects design approach.

Look at the case study below and consider which approach would work best.

Case study

The following experiment provides an example of how you could use the experimental method to investigate an aspect of your course. It shows how the experimental and null hypotheses are presented and the need to design a suitable test.

Suppose you want to find out whether young people actually do have faster reaction times than older people. As you are probably aware, the ageing process affects a wide range of bodily functions and one effect is the reduced speed of transmission of nerve impulses. However, you will also be aware that the ageing process is gradual and you might not be able to see a difference in reaction times if the people taking part are not from widely differing age groups. So, your experimental hypothesis might state that people under 20 years of age have quicker reaction times compared to people over the age of 40. The null hypothesis would state that there will be no difference in the reaction times of people under the age of 20 compared to people over 40 years of age.

You now need to design an experiment to test your hypothesis. This involves selecting the subjects (people) to take part in your study and designing a way of testing the hypothesis. Selecting the subjects involves taking a sample (see Sampling methodology, page 99) of young people under 20 years old and another group of over-40-year-olds. In selecting the subjects you also hope to manage or control some of the extraneous variables that could affect the outcome. The test is quite easy whether you use an electronic reaction timer or a ruler. If you are using rulers then you will hold the ruler vertically at some fixed point along its length whilst the participant will be asked to grasp the ruler when you let it go. The distance the ruler has travelled gives an indication of an individual's reaction time. The exercise should be repeated at least 10 times for each person taking part and you should have at least 10 people from each age group taking part.

Now you should produce an experimental and null hypothesis for a similar experiment on reaction times to investigate the effect of gender on reaction time. Design the method with a suitable sampling regime. With the availability of electronic reaction timers this type of experiment could be extended to investigate the effects of reaction times to different types of stimuli; also a number of Internet sites allow you to investigate reaction times when other thought processes are being stimulated.

Think it over

In the experiment in the case study what extraneous variables could there be that might affect the results? How could these be managed or controlled?

Observations

Observation can be defined as the recording of facts or data through close examination of situations or events.

There are two principal types of observation – **participant** and **non-participant**. In the former, you – as the observer – become involved in the activities you intend to observe. In non-participant or passive observation you observe as an outsider and do not become involved. Through different placements you may find yourself involved with one or both types of observation, depending upon the setting. In a school, nursery or playgroup observations of children undertaking activities in which you are also participating could occur, whereas on a hospital ward or in a residential/nursing home you may be observing the work of a nurse or a patient recovering from an operation.

Observations can also be regarded as either structured or unstructured. Structured observations are based upon pre-determined criteria that will measure the duration, frequency, type or consequences of events. Patient recording charts provide a typical example for recording observations of recovery or otherwise of someone in hospital whereas in a school, playgroup or nursery you may need to devise a form or other means of recording the observation of child behaviour (see References and further reading at the end of the unit).

Participant observation

The opposite of a structured observation is the open-ended, unstructured approach. At the extreme this method involves the researcher having some vague notion of what they wish to study, and through the observation process gathers information which provides a focus for developing a research question or hypothesis (the opposite of what has been suggested so far). The advantage of this approach is there are no pre-conceived notions or expectations about what the outcome of the research will be, as such a large amount of information is gathered which over time can begin to show patterns that can lead to broad generalisations. This is the problem with this type of research – you need time to both carry out the research and to analyse the information.

Observation as a method in general has low validity as the researcher(s) may view and interpret what is taking place in light of their own experiences, values and attitudes. For similar reasons, observation is not particularly reliable as reproducing the work would involve another researcher with a different perspective in terms of attitudes and experiences repeating the activity.

The advantages of observation are that it is adaptable to many situations, can reveal unexpected relationships, draw on data not available using other methods, and can be used in conjunction with the experimental method, for example the observation of behaviour before and after the introduction of a behaviour modification programme to evaluate its success or otherwise.

Case studies

The case study is not a method in itself, but an approach to research that is based upon the observation of an individual, organisation or culture. Case studies take into account historical evidence and are used to study the consequences of past and present events on the subject being studied. They can provide a unique insight into an individual or organisation but as such can be intrusive and care must be exercised in carrying them out to ensure you have informed consent and to maintain confidentiality (see Ethical issues, page 114).

The gathering of information for a case study should initially be focused upon the gathering of historical information to prepare what is called a case history. This will usually be based upon interviews of the parents, nurses, teachers or other people associated with the individual being studied followed by observations of the person in different settings depending upon their age, i.e. home, day centre, school, outdoors, in social groups.

Case studies are very useful for finding out about the effects of a disabling condition, such as Down's syndrome, cystic fibrosis or autism, on a person's physical, emotional and social development. More in-depth studies can also consider the effects on the family or carers and the implications for health, education and social services.

Case studies are particularly useful for students as they allow the opportunity to study something in depth over a relatively short space of time. They are also valuable for studying individuals as they enable a 'picture to be painted' from which conclusions about patterns of physical, emotional and social well-being can be drawn that can then be used to determine the appropriate level of care required.

A student's case study on a child with autism
The student chose to use an open-ended questionnaire to produce a case history, the record of which follows. This approach was chosen as the mother could answer the questions at her leisure, as she did not have the time free for an interview.

The child is 6 years old and was diagnosed officially with autism when she was $3\frac{1}{2}$ years old. She has a twin sister.

Before the child was diagnosed

The child was developing like a 'normal' child until she reached the age of $2\frac{1}{2}$. Soon after she reached this age she began to isolate herself from others, stopped talking and feeding herself, and started to hit her head and bite her hand. She would also avoid eye contact and have 'crying' episodes for long periods of time, then she would stop and laugh for no reason. She began to spend a lot of time sitting looking out of the window at clouds and trees as they moved.

Getting the child diagnosed

The child's mother had some knowledge of autism so took her daughter to the doctor. She told the doctor 'My child's autistic'. The doctor referred her to the child development centre. Here the child was observed by a psychologist, who confirmed that the child was 'severely autistic' and she underwent a 6-week assessment.

After the child was diagnosed

The child attended play/therapy at the child development centre. Here the staff attempted to write an educational statement for the child. But, due to the severity of her problems, the child became very distressed, so the sessions had to be stopped and the statement was not completed. The child started to attend a local special needs school in the mornings, where the statement was completed. This also found she had autism with profound learning difficulties.

How her mother felt during and after the diagnosis

Her mother felt and still feels very sad about the situation. She has had a variety of different feelings – anger, guilt and loneliness. She felt that all her dreams and hopes of her child were lost, but she realised that she had to try and not stop her daughter's twin from reaching her full potential. She sometimes feels isolated and she feels it is easier to stay at home as it's away from people who stare and pass comments. She will always be frightened for her child as she is very vulnerable.

Child's behaviour in situations

The child can get very upset when she is in crowds or when she is near a loud group of people. She does not like motorbikes, or cars that play loud music when they drive past. These things upset the child and make her cry. The behaviours are difficult to control, as these are everyday happenings. Her behaviour changes when she goes to her grandparents' house. When she visits she has a routine that she follows and things that she wants.

Routine of the child at morning and night

When the child wakes up she likes a drink and something to eat. She usually goes and asks for a video to be put on while she is getting ready. When she has got her bag and coat she goes to the window and looks for the bus. If the bus is late she becomes very cross and upset. At night the child has no set bedtime, but she does have a routine. When she is tired the child will fetch a certain pillow to her mum. She will place it on her mum, then lie across it. She places her mum's hand on her back to tell her to pat it. The child will sleep for four hours on average, never more than that.

Problems that have solutions

If the child gets upset, she likes music being played as it often calms her down. If that doesn't work then she likes to watch bubble lamps or lights; these calm her down. But as the child's problems are ongoing and are unpredictable it is hard to find solutions.

Communication used at home

The child uses PECS (Picture Exchange Communication System) at home but she has also found her own way of communicating. She does this by bringing what she wants or taking a person to it. The child can sometimes get cross if she has already brought her mum a cup and the juice, and is asked for the symbols. She will often just grab a symbol and give it to her mum, even if it is wrong.

The student then proceeded to carry out observations of the child in three different situations:

- watching a video in class
- in a school disco
- using the PECS.

The student used the case history and observations to confirm secondary research findings on autism.

Action research

Finally, a note on a specialised research technique that you may come across during your studies or be involved with at a later date. Called action research, and popular within education, this technique involves observing the effects of making a change or changes within an organisation with a view to improving the way things are done. It usually involves a number of people either as implementers, observers or participants. The implementer will introduce the change and the observer will record the effects on the participants. A simple example of action research is a teacher introducing a new teaching method to a group of pupils. The teacher acts as researcher, implementer and observer, whilst the pupils are the participants. The teacher hopes that the new method enables the pupils to learn more effectively, a result that may be measured by improved SATS test results or improved behaviour.

Action research is a very powerful tool aimed at improving work practice and focusing on specific problems whilst involving all concerned – allowing the processes of the research cycle to be linked together.

To complete this section on different methods try the assessment activity that follows to help you in selecting the most appropriate method or methods for your study.

Assessment activity 3.3

1 Look through the different research methods and identify the advantages and disadvantages of each.

2 Read the following research problems and decide which method would be most appropriate. Justify your reasons for choosing such a method.

Attitudes and experiences to female circumcision of young, single Somalis living in the UK

Female circumcision is a highly controversial and sensitive problem, affecting an estimated 126 million women worldwide. It refers to traditional practices of cutting and removing the clitoris or vaginal labia of girls, and in some countries the closure of the vagina using stitching or thorns. This more severe form is practised in Somalia, and with the immigration of substantial numbers of Somalis into the UK has become a problem here.

A collaborative study showed that 70 per cent of females had been circumcised, half with the most severe type. Those who arrived in Britain before the usual age of circumcision (less than 9 years old) were half as likely to be circumcised as others. The study highlighted the pain of the operation and the anguish of subsequent health and sexual problems. The study also describes how important family expectations are in the continuation of female circumcision and how the practice is intricately bound up with ideas about sexuality and marriage.

A normative study of children's injuries

The frequency and nature of minor injuries has been investigated in a community sample of children aged between birth and 8 years. Information on the nature of the injuries and details of the context in which they occurred was collected from families. This was followed by talking with the parent, during which standardised measures of child behaviour, parent effect and stress were completed. More detailed investigations took place in a sub-sample of families to investigate the role of parental actions and expectations of child behaviour on injury causation or prevention, as well as parental views of appropriate supervision, safety measures and expectations of child behaviour.

Drugs, crime and the fear of crime

In a new policy, Tackling Drugs Together, the Government highlighted drugs, crime and fear of crime as one of the three areas of concern for which data is limited. The aim of this project is to determine the feasibility of different forms of data collection. Major agencies, such as the police, probation service and drug agencies, were researched to determine currently available data and information requirements. The second part of the project was to investigate new data collection at a community level. Initially, this looked at households' current experiences of crime and the fear of crime. Also a number of drug users resident in the community were investigated in depth. The report of the project will be presented to the Drug Action Team and a paper prepared for publication after comments have been received on the findings from the research.

Sampling methodology

As well as choosing the primary research method, some thought has to be given to the subjects who will be involved with the research. It is necessary to consider some form of subject selection process since it won't be possible to include everyone. This selection process is known as **sampling**.

A sample is regarded as being representative of the group or population of people from which it is taken. Researchers hope to be able to draw conclusions about the population as a result of their work on the sample.

By way of example, suppose you want to find out about the development of a Down's syndrome child compared with a child who does not have Down's syndrome. It might be possible that the research forms the basis for making generalisations about the development of Down's syndrome children compared to children without Down's. However, as you are probably aware there are several types of Down's syndrome and all children are individuals. Therefore to make generalisations would mean comparing the development of every Down's syndrome child with every other child. As this would be impossible, the way forward is to study a small number of children that can be regarded as representative of both Down's syndrome and children without Down's. This group of children will become your **sample** and the group from which they are selected is the **population**. For your work to be truly representative of the whole population, the sample selected must be random. This means that everyone in the population has an equal chance of being chosen to take part in your study.

Not all forms of sampling are random and the method chosen to select your sample will for the most part be dependent on the nature of the study, how easy it is to gain access to the people you hope to research and how much time you have.

Random sampling

Subjects are selected at random from a list created by yourself or someone else, e.g. telephone directory or electoral register. It involves everyone in the list being allocated a number and then using a random number generator to select a sample of appropriate size. A random number generator is like 'Arthur/Guinevere/Lancelot', the machine that spews out the lottery numbers every week. Most calculators have a random number generator button that will perform this task for you or you can use a random number table like the one on page 101.

Systematic sampling

From a list, every *nth* case is selected, i.e. every fifth or tenth person. So if you wanted to choose 10 children from a group of 20 you would allocate everyone a number from 1 to 50 then select the fifth, tenth, fifteenth, twentieth, twenty-fifth, etc., person.

Stratified sampling

Stratified sampling involves taking a random or systematic sample from groups within a population. The reaction time experiment would involve taking a random sample from within the under-20 and over-40 age groups (see page 94).

Quota sampling

Quota sampling is more or less the same as stratified sampling, but relies on the groups coming from a conveniently available population. In the reaction time example, the college where you are studying would provide a convenient population from which to take your age group sample.

Opportunity sampling

This is the most common form of sampling employed by students as it simply relies upon the sample being drawn from the population with which the student is associated.

Random Number Table

20	17	42	28	23	17	59	66	38	61	02	10	86	10	51	55	92	52	44	25
74	49	04	19	03	04	10	33	53	70	11	54	48	63	94	60	94	49	57	38
94	70	49	31	38	67	23	42	29	65	40	88	78	71	37	18	48	64	06	57
22	15	78	15	69	84	32	52	32	54	15	12	54	02	01	37	38	37	12	93
93	29	12	18	27	30	30	55	91	87	50	57	58	51	49	36	12	53	96	40
45	04	77	97	36	14	99	45	52	95	69	85	03	83	51	87	85	56	22	37
44	91	99	49	89	39	94	60	48	49	06	77	64	72	59	26	08	51	25	57
16	23	91	02	19	96	47	59	89	65	27	84	30	92	63	37	26	24	23	66
04	50	65	04	65	65	82	42	70	51	55	04	61	47	88	83	99	34	82	37
32	70	17	72	03	61	66	26	24	71	22	77	88	33	17	78	08	92	73	49
03	64	59	07	42	95	81	39	06	41	20	81	92	34	51	90	39	08	21	42
62	49	00	90	67	86	93	48	31	83	19	07	67	68	49	03	27	47	52	03
61	00	95	86	98	36	14	03	48	88	51	07	33	40	06	86	33	76	68	57
89	03	90	49	28	74	21	04	09	96	60	45	22	03	52	80	01	79	33	81
01	72	33	85	52	40	60	07	06	71	89	27	14	29	55	24	85	79	31	96
27	56	49	79	34	34	32	22	60	53	91	17	33	26	44	70	93	14	99	70
49	05	74	48	10	55	35	25	24	28	20	22	35	66	66	34	26	35	91	23
49	74	37	25	97	26	33	94	42	23	01	28	59	58	92	69	03	66	73	82
20	26	22	43	88	08	19	85	08	12	47	65	65	63	56	07	97	85	56	79
48	87	77	96	43	39	76	93	08	79	22	18	54	55	93	75	97	26	90	77
08	72	87	46	75	73	00	11	27	07	05	20	30	85	22	21	04	67	19	13
95	97	98	62	17	27	31	42	64	71	46	22	32	75	19	32	20	99	94	85
37	99	57	31	70	40	46	55	46	12	24	32	36	74	69	20	72	10	95	93
05	79	58	37	85	33	75	18	88	71	23	44	54	28	00	48	96	23	66	45
55	85	63	42	00	79	91	22	29	01	41	39	51	40	36	65	26	11	78	32

To use the table, let us suppose you need a random sample of 10 under-20-year-olds from a group of 50 for the reaction time experiment (see page 94). Allocate each person in the group a number, then starting at the top left-hand corner of the table and moving down the column select the first 10 numbers that are 50 or less. You should get the numbers 20, 22, 45, 44, 16, 4, 32, 3, 1 and 27. These are the people that will take part in your experiment. Next time you use the table start at the last number you chose.

Voluntary and snowball sampling

This involves people volunteering to be part of the research sample and may lead to others becoming involved through word of mouth.

Purposive sampling

The selection of typical or interesting cases. This is particularly suited to case study research or the investigation of a specific problem, such as a congenital disease.

Whilst quota and opportunity sampling are the most likely methods you will use, whichever method you employ there may be people chosen who either don't start/join in or don't finish/give up. Never pressurise people into taking part.

Think it over

Look back at the examples of recent research in health on page 75 and selecting examples that do not identify the sampling method, suggest an appropriate sampling programme for each, noting the advantages/disadvantages of the methods chosen.

Data collection

Having determined what method or methods you will use and the sampling strategy you will employ, you need to start collecting your data/information.

It is important here to plan your activities. It would not be helpful if you decided to carry out a survey questionnaire in your local high street when the weather forecast is for gales and heavy showers, or to find you had forgotten your recording materials when carrying out an observation or interview.

Whichever method you use it will be necessary to carry out the following to ensure the research is undertaken in an effective and efficient manner.

- Check that your tutor is happy with what you are going to research and how you are going to do it. Make sure your tutor has vetted your questions for a questionnaire, interview or case study or the way you intend to conduct an experiment or observation.
- Obtain written permission from anyone who may have some responsibility for your research. Verbal permission is adequate for a simple survey.
- Organise when and where the research will be undertaken:
  - Is it at college, a local hospital, residential home, school, nursery or playgroup, your local high street or shopping centre, at your own house or that of a relation or friend?
  - Timing can be important. For instance, Mondays tend to be quieter in town centres, young children and the elderly may be more tired in an afternoon if you are conducting an observation or experiment, and adults may be in too much of a rush to get involved.
- Organise and prepare any materials or resources required:
  - Photocopy adequate numbers of questionnaires, having a few for spares if any get spoilt.
  - Have you got/do you need paper, pens or flip charts for you or the participants to write on?

- If you are conducting the research in a group make sure:
  - everyone knows what they are doing
  - everyone follows the same procedures
  - that in carrying out an interview or verbal questionnaire everyone uses the same style of questioning. The way a question is asked can alter its whole meaning.

Statistical research information

Data presentation

When you have collected all the information or data it will need preparing for presentation. Qualitative data is descriptive information and can therefore be regarded as information collected in the format of words, whilst quantitative data is based upon numerical information. You may find that your study produces both types of information.

Dealing with qualitative information

Qualitative information may be in the form of directly written words, such as may be transcribed from an interview or written notes that summarise what occurred. Both forms may reflect some selectivity on the part of the person who provided the information or by the researcher in summarising the information. In effect this shows that some analysis has already taken place and further analysis involves additional selection and refinement of the data.

Initially you should take time to organise or manage the data so that the analysis and refining process becomes easier. You can do this in many different ways but here are some suggestions to assist you with the process:

- Use different coloured highlighter pens to highlight words or passages that say the same thing, that support or refute your research question and support or refute theoretical arguments.
- Add notes or comments alongside highlighted words or phrases that can help you relate the information to the research question or theory. This can include adding references to articles or books on the subject.
- Use a coding system to process information that repeats itself or could be grouped, e.g. males and females, different ages.
- Use tables to categorise words or phrases in particular groups. Open questions from an interview or questionnaire may elicit a wide range of responses. However, it may be possible to identify words or phrases that mean the same thing, allowing them to be grouped together. You need to be clear about how you have done this in presenting the data to show that you have avoided being biased.
- Cross out information that is irrelevant.

Once you have processed the information in the above fashion you can begin to select and summarise those bits of data that support or refute your research. Whilst this might seem like doing the whole thing again it allows you to present a coherent argument in favour of, or against, your research question. It also enables you to tie your research into the information you will have gained by means of secondary research.

Where the information can be categorised into groups, as with words or phrases that occur frequently, then the information may be summarised as numerical values; for example, five respondents to an open-ended question on experiences of childbirth referred to the desire for giving birth naturally rather than with medical intervention, whilst four preferred intervention. In such cases the information can then be regarded as quantitative.

Dealing with quantitative data

Quantitative data will be based upon direct measurements: categories that have been assigned a value (e.g. the number of males, females, the number in specified age groups), percentages or averages. Percentages and averages may form part of the next step to summarise and refine the data in order to make it clearer. You may also have obtained data from secondary research that you need to prepare for presentation.

Such numerical information can be termed discrete or continuous. Discrete data is usually based on whole numbers that fit into categories, e.g. the number of males and females in a group. Continuous data is any numerical value within a range and can be a fraction of a whole number, e.g. heights and weights.

Methods of presentation

The purpose of data presentation – whether discrete or continuous – is to make it easier to digest. This can be achieved by following the list as detailed below:

1　Tables act as the first step in organising data. They allow information to be set out in a structured way and can show simple trends and differences between numbers where there is not too much information.
2　Graphs are used to summarise more complex information that is difficult to digest from a table.
3　Statistics are used to analyse data in order to establish the proof or otherwise of the research question or hypothesis.

Computer packages

Modern computer programs enable you to complete all the above by entering the data into a spreadsheet program. Such programs include Microsoft Excel, Lotus 1-2-3 and more specialised statistical packages such as MINITAB, SPSS (Statistical Package for Social Science) and STATVIEW.

Figure 3.4 shows some data entered into a spreadsheet that is easily formatted into a table. Graphs can then be produced and formatted to show off your results to best effect. The difficult bit is deciding which graph is

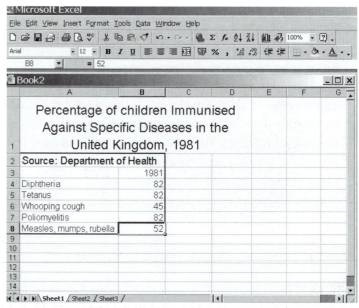

Screenshot reproduced with permission of Microsoft Corporation

Figure 3.4 Entering data into a spreadsheet (created in Microsoft Excel)

the most appropriate. The whole purpose of a graph is to make large amounts of data, or more complex data, more easily interpreted than might be possible from a table. This does not mean all data should be displayed graphically. However, pie charts, graphs, bar charts and histograms can all be used in addition to tables to present your information.

Pie charts

Pie charts are used when you have a single value for each category or set of data collected. They show each set as a percentage of the whole. The table below shows the use of different types of drugs amongst young people aged 16–19. It can be seen that each item of data is a proportion of the total. To produce a pie chart, each value in the table has to be converted into a percentage of the total. Each percentage has then to be converted to the number of degrees as part of the 360° that make up a circle prior to constructing the chart. Figure 3.5 shows the pie chart for this data, produced using a spreadsheet program that does away with the need for changing to percentages and degrees required for producing the chart by hand.

Numbers (thousands) of 16–19-year-olds using selected drugs in 1998

Type of drug	Numbers (thousands)
Cannabis	28
Amphetamine	9
Ecstasy	4
Poppers	4
Magic mushrooms	4
Cocaine	1
LSD	2
Total	52

Source: British Crime Survey

You should avoid a pie chart where there are more than six or seven sets of data as the information begins to look confused.

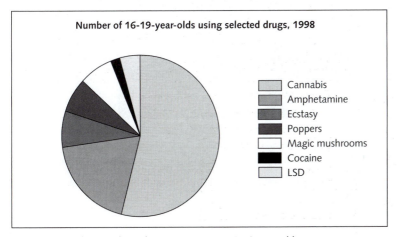

Figure 3.5 Pie chart to show drug use amongst 16–19-year-olds

Bar charts

These can be used as an alternative to pie charts for displaying data as either percentages or whole numbers, and can be used where there are too many categories to display in a pie chart. The table below shows the number of children who received support from the Children and Family Services Teams in England, during one week in February 2000. The types of care are distinct from one another so the resulting bar chart displays each group as a separate bar or line (see Figure 3.6). It doesn't matter how wide the bars or gaps between the bars are.

The number of children receiving support from Social Services in one week in February 2000, by category of need

Category of need	Numbers receiving support
Abuse or neglect	79,740
Disability	30,310
Parental illness/disability	13,800
Family in acute distress	26,685
Family dysfunction	31,155
Socially unacceptable behaviour	14,045
Low income	14,195
Absent parenting	7,340
Cases other than CIN*	12,065
Total	229,335

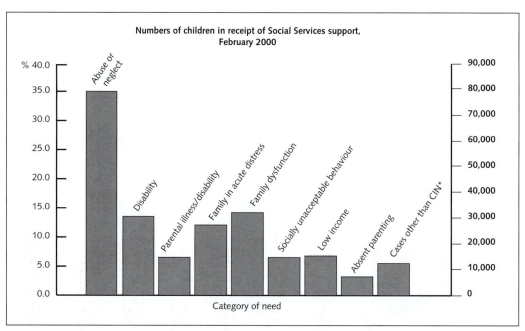

*Children in Need   *Source:* Department of Health

Figure 3.6 Bar chart showing the number of children receiving support from Social Services each week in February 2000

A more advanced form of bar chart is shown in Figure 3.7, illustrating the data on trends in HIV infection. This enables the trends in such provision to be easily recognised and visible to anyone looking at the graph, but not so easily seen from the table of data. With this type of bar chart you should not try to place too many categories together as the graph becomes untidy.

Numbers (thousands) of adults diagnosed with HIV in the UK by probable routes of transmission between 1990 and 1999

Year	Sex between men	Sex between men and women	Injecting drug use	Other/ not known
1990	1.667	0.531	0.197	0.101
1991	1.679	0.634	0.242	0.097
1992	1.602	0.771	0.182	0.116
1993	1.477	0.749	0.201	0.122
1994	1.451	0.780	0.166	0.116
1995	1.441	0.835	0.177	0.127
1996	1.518	0.815	0.169	0.121
1997	1.362	0.997	0.163	0.146
1998	1.331	1.129	0.126	0.157
1999	1.259	1.341	0.098	0.199

Source: Public Health Laboratory Service

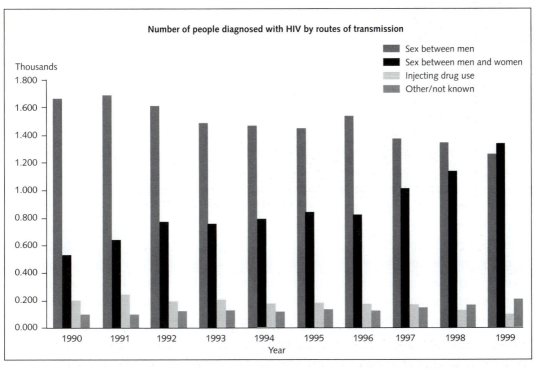

Source: Public Health Laboratory Service

Figure 3.7 Bar chart showing numbers (thousands) of adults diagnosed with HIV in the UK by probable routes of transmission between 1990 and 1999

107

Line graphs

When there is a considerable amount of data to display, especially when it is based on measurements taken over a period of time, the line graph is the best choice. Figure 3.8 shows the decrease in the number of live births since 1961. This type of chart allows several lines displaying changes to several groups of data over a period of time to be displayed. This should only be done if it is necessary to compare different groups of data. As with the pie charts it is best to avoid having too much data, i.e. too many lines.

Sometimes students aren't sure whether to join the data points with a line or a curve. A simple rule of thumb is that if the points for the graph when joined together look like a curve, then draw a curve. If the points form a line, connect the points to form a line. If points are scattered you can draw a best fit line (see Scattergrams, page 109).

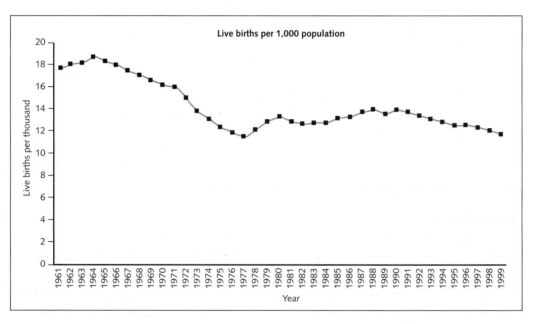

Source: Office for National Statistics

Figure 3.8 Line graph showing live births per 1000 population from 1961 to 1999

Frequency distributions (frequency histograms and frequency polygons)

Frequency distributions are rather more sophisticated graphs that are often confused with bar charts. They are used exclusively with continuous data. The data is grouped into what are termed class intervals, where the number or frequency of values falling into each class is found. In order to produce a frequency distribution the raw data requires some manipulation prior to entering into a spreadsheet. This involves producing a tally chart (see Figure 3.9) and then entering the class intervals and frequency into a spreadsheet. Creating the chart (Figure 3.10) is easier on some programs than others but an IT tutor should be able to help you through any difficulties.

If you wish to compare frequency distributions of two or more sets of data it is preferable to present the frequency distribution as a frequency polygon rather than a frequency histogram. A frequency polygon is simply a line joining the tops of each bar at their mid-points.

weights (g)	Tally	Frequency
1000–1499		0
1500–1999		0
2000–2499	II	2
2500–2999	JHT JHT IIII	14
3000–3499	JHT JHT JHT JHT JHT JHT JHT JHT JHT II	47
3500–3999	JHT JHT JHT JHT JHT JHT JHT JHT JHT	45
4000+	JHT JHT JHT JHT	20

Figure 3.9 Tally chart of live birth weights of babies born to a random sample of 128 women

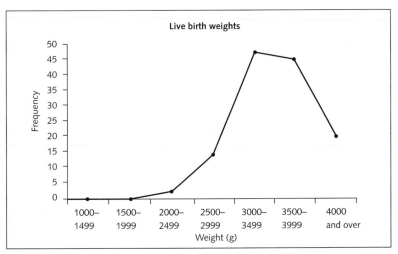

Source: Office for National Statistics

Figure 3.10 A frequency distribution to show live birth weights of babies

Scattergrams

Scattergrams are used specifically for displaying the results of correlational studies, i.e. data collected to compare one variable with another (see Experimental (research) methods, page 93). It simply involves plotting the results of one variable against the other as a series of markers. The pattern created by the marks once the scattergram has been completed can indicate whether or not there is a relationship between the two variables. If it appears possible to draw a straight line through the markers then a relationship exists. In a spreadsheet the computer can draw in the line. This trend line describes either a positive or negative correlation. If positive, it shows that as one variable increases so does the other, for example increase in asthma correlates with an increase in the use of central heating. If negative, as one variable increases the other decreases, for example the amount of media attention given to problems associated with vaccination correlates with a decrease in the number of children being vaccinated.

However, beware! Just because a correlation exists does not mean that a change in one variable results in a change in the other; for example, did you know that the amount of bananas imported into the UK after World War II correlates with the increase in the number of pregnant women! It is possible that the change in both variables is due to some other unrelated factor. Another example is the rise in asthma amongst children during the 1980s and 1990s. It has been found that this increase correlates well with the increasing use of diesel engine motor vehicles. Researchers proposed that this was due to the size of soot particles in vehicle exhausts which were polluting the air and irritating the lungs. However, there is also a correlation between the increase in rates of asthma and the use of double glazing in homes, central heating and fitted carpets, which encourage the increase in numbers of house dust mites that also irritate the lungs.

Consequently, don't be tempted to draw a conclusion about a correlation unless it is backed up by the research of others, i.e. your secondary sources.

Think it over

A line of best fit has been added to Figure 3.11 to show that there is a positive correlation between height and weight. How would the scattergram appear if:

1   the correlation was negative

2   there was no correlation?

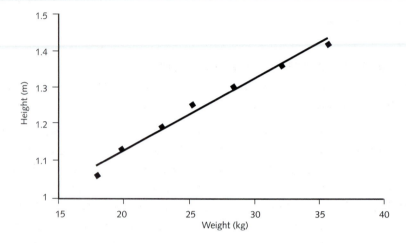

Figure 3.11 Scattergram to show relationship between height–weight for girls aged 5–11

Statistics

Mean, median and mode

Apart from graphs, numerical data can also be simplified and made more meaningful by determining the **mode**, **median** or **mean**. These terms describe different forms of averages known as measures of **central tendency**. The mode is the most frequently occurring number in a set. The median is simply the middle value in a set of results that have been arranged in ascending or descending order. The mean is calculated from adding up all the values and dividing by the number of values to give the 'average' value.

The mode is useful if the data contains very similar numbers, such as shoe size. The median is used where the data is discrete and is often used in conjunction with the **range** (the difference between the lowest and highest values in a set of data) to summarise the data. The range gives a measure of the spread of the data. Whilst this is satisfactory for many circumstances the range will include extreme values and as a consequence may not be representative of most of the data. As a result it may be more appropriate to use the **interquartile range** covering the middle 50 per cent of the data.

Standard deviation

The median and range or interquartile range are useful when working with discrete data but where the data is continuous, the mean and the **standard deviation** tend to be of more value. This is because the standard deviation, whilst giving an idea of how much the data is spread either side of the mean can be manipulated to exclude extreme values and as a result can be more representative of the majority of subjects in the sample.

Although it is difficult to generalise, the larger the standard deviation, the greater the spread of the data about the mean.

The standard deviation is rather more difficult to calculate than the mean. However, scientific calculators that have statistical functions can determine the standard deviation at the same time as the mean. Alternatively, the standard deviation can be obtained from data entered into a spreadsheet.

The standard deviation and mean can be used to determine whether two sets of data, e.g. skin surface temperature in stressed and unstressed conditions, are *significantly different* from one another. However, the Health Studies syllabus does not expect you to take your data analysis this far!

Discussing and evaluating your results

This is perhaps the most skilled part of the research process that is used by tutors to confirm decisions regarding the award of higher grades.

It is best to start the discussion with a restatement of the problem you chose to investigate, together with the research question or hypothesis. This sets the scene and also helps to focus your mind on what all the data collection and presentation were about. You should then look at your results and summarise what they show. The idea is to highlight those features of your results that are important to your research question or hypothesis i.e., whether the information supports or refutes the research question or hypothesis. Preparing your report for a presentation is a good way of summarising and picking out the most important features.

In the same way, you need to compare your findings with the information obtained through secondary research. Does this support your study or contradict it? Differences between your work and those of others may reflect real differences due to the local nature of your research or it may highlight weaknesses in your study. Alternatively, the results may reflect something you hadn't thought of which could lead to the need for further research. You should then attempt to suggest what that research could be.

If your results fail to support your research question or hypothesis, do not be tempted to manipulate them; instead draw on the information provided in the next two sections to evaluate the presentation of your data and the research and sampling methods used.

A further way of preparing your discussion is to talk to people who have had some involvement with your research, including your tutor, and see if they agree with your conclusions. You could also sit down with someone else on the course and tell them what you have found out. If it makes sense to them, then it should make sense on paper. You can do the same for them.

If your research was part of a group project, even better. Although you will probably expect to submit individual reports you can discuss your findings and help each other to draw relevant conclusions, evaluate and justify your approach to the topic.

If your research was based on interviews with just a few people, or a case study, then it can be appropriate to discuss your findings with them. Not only can they make suggestions or identify things you have missed, but it also keeps them fully informed in line with the ethical requirements for informed consent.

Assessment activity 3.4

Complete a table that shows:

- the methods of presenting statistics
- when you would use the methods
- the advantages and disadvantages of using particular methods.

Which computer packages could you use to present your statistics?

Use and misuse of statistics

'There are three kinds of lies: lies, damned lies, and statistics,' said Disraeli, who attributed it to Mark Twain.

The above quote implies that people are suspicious of statistics and statistical information. This may result from difficulties we had with mathematics at school and may be exacerbated by the amount of what appears to be statistical misinformation we read or hear about in the media.

However, statistics provide a valuable tool for presenting and interpreting information so that the results of research are more readily understood. Their use and misuse can arise as a result of problems with different aspects of the research process and not just the presentation and interpretation of the results. Such difficulties include the following:

- Lack of clarity in the research question or hypothesis, i.e. being unsure about what you want to find out. If you are unclear about the focus of your study it can lead to selecting the wrong methods and, consequently, the production of data or information that is difficult to explain. It may also lead to a misreading of the results in trying to make them fit the hypothesis or research question. For example, you may have chosen to undertake a survey on drugs, but not clarified what aspect of drugs it is you are interested in. The likely result of not being clear about the focus of your study will be to produce too much information to organise and simplify with ease.
- Use of inappropriate methods. The important point here is that the method allows you to gather information that will support your research question or hypothesis. This means choosing a method that enables you to find out what you want it to and which can be reproduced. These features of the method are known as **validity** and **reliability** and will be discussed in more detail below.
- Unrepresentative sampling. Remember that the purpose of sampling is to use people in your research who are representative of the whole population and this means obtaining a random sample of subjects. This is no easy task and there is often bias within a sample, whatever the sampling method chosen. In particular, the most common sampling method used by students is the opportunity sample. As the people chosen are probably following some further education course like yourself, then the sample is biased towards students and misses out other people.
- Inaccurate recording of information (sloppy techniques). Failure to construct a questionnaire with care or to undertake a trial can result in questions being misunderstood and answers being ambiguous. If you are administering a questionnaire as a group, failure of everyone to follow the same procedure can give misleading results. The results of an interview that you haven't prepared for in terms of questioning or recording may bear little resemblance to the actual

interview itself and is more open to being biased towards your own views. A poorly prepared observation sheet, or failure to conduct an experiment with care and precision, will give inaccurate results.

- Inappropriate presentation or misinterpretation of data. The following examples serve to show how results can be presented in such a way as to change their meaning or to give misleading information. Figure 3.12 compares the attainment of children at Key Stage 1 in two schools, A and B.

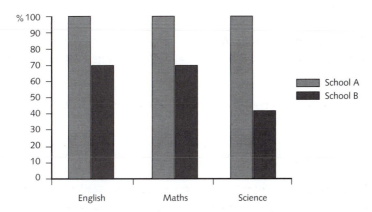

Figure 3.12 Percentage of children at National Curriculum level 2 (Key Stage 1) in two schools

You can see that school A appears to be far more effective at enabling the children to reach level 2 of Key Stage 1 than school B. However, what you don't know is that school A is an independent school while school B has three times as many pupils as school A and the children entering the school come from different social backgrounds.

Another example is based upon a media report stating that the effect of divorce on children was not as bad as might have been thought, since 80 per cent of children whose parents divorce become perfectly normal adults. What the report omits to mention is the other fairly significant 20 per cent!

Both cases do not falsify the results but deliberately seek to mislead. You may have noticed that both examples use percentages to summarise the data. This can be a rather neat way of presenting small amounts of data to prove a research question or hypothesis. However, it gives a false impression of the results and should be either avoided or at least explained to prevent the reader being deceived.

So to avoid misusing information, remember the following points:

- Be clear about what you are trying to find out, i.e. ensure your research is focused.
- Be sure to use the most appropriate method or methods for your study.
- Try to ensure your sample is representative of the population in which you're interested.
- Don't try to use statistical methods in presenting your data to make it fit your research question when it doesn't, i.e. be honest. In using graphs, make sure they are accurate.
- Don't misinterpret the data, i.e. don't say something is true when it blatantly isn't or say the results don't show anything when they do. This means that you should look carefully at – and use all – the results.
- Don't try to draw conclusions that don't exist. These can become discussion points for further research.

Assessment activity 3.5

Evaluate all of the different methods of presenting statistics, showing the benefits and disadvantages of each method. Discuss the use and misuse of statistics and show examples of where research has been misused.

Validity and reliability

These terms have already been mentioned with respect to one or two of the different primary research methods and they need to be taken into account when selecting the most appropriate research method for any research you undertake.

Validity is about whether the results you obtain using a particular method tell you what you want to find out. Reliability is to do with the method being reproducible, i.e. if someone else repeated your work would they get the same answers?

A method may be reliable but not necessarily valid. Whilst some methods are more reliable and others more valid, in the end it is probably true to say that the level of reliability and validity is dependent upon how carefully the research has been undertaken. This surprisingly comes down to the conscientiousness of the researcher! One way of improving reliability and validity is to use more than one method in your study.

Assessment activity 3.6

Read the brief evaluation of the reliability and validity of questionnaires above before evaluating the effectiveness of other research methods in terms of reliability and validity. This activity can be extended to consider how different methods could be combined to improve the reliability and validity. Explain why the issues of validity and reliability are so important when completing research.

Questionnaires can have high validity and reliability depending on how well they are produced. If the questions have been worded appropriately and the answers aren't ambiguous, then the results should tell you what you wanted to know and are therefore valid. By the same token it should also be feasible for someone else to repeat your work and get similar answers, making the research reliable. However, if you tend to get mixed responses to questions that you thought were straightforward, then the validity and reliability will be poor. The best way to ensure good validity and reliability with a questionnaire is to do a trial first in order to iron out any problems.

Ethical issues

Practice

Before undertaking any primary research that involves questioning, experimenting or observing people you must consider the ethics of conducting your research and any issues of confidentiality that may be raised.

Ethics has been an issue in research ever since World War II when the Nazis were found to have submitted individuals to horrific experiments that resulted in death, disfigurement or psychological trauma. The Nuremberg trials that followed the war made researchers aware of the dangers of carrying out experiments on non-consenting subjects and it led to the development of a code of ethics for working with human subjects. Even so, there have been many cases of research carried out since the war that have subjected people to physical and/or psychological pain.

One famous experiment on obedience, carried out during the 1960s by Stanley Millgram, involved allowing participants to administer electric shocks to other people they could see. Unknown to the participants, the subjects being electrocuted were actors faking increasing discomfort as shocks were applied. Participants were told that they had to continue applying shocks of increasing voltage even though the person being 'electrocuted' appeared to be in obvious pain. The experiment proved that people would follow 'orders' irrespective of the suffering they may cause, but the justification for such deceit of participants was regarded as immoral. Not only had Millgram deceived the participants, but he had attempted to alter their behaviour and used secret recordings to observe them.

Ethical codes

Deception may be considered unethical, but many drug trials rely on this to determine the effects of new drugs. Such trials, known as blind trials, involve two groups of volunteers, one of which receives the drug and the other a placebo (sugar pill). This experimental type of research works on the basis that any effect of the drug will only be seen in the group taking the drug as neither group knows whether they are taking the placebo or the drug under test. It has been found that some drugs have had as much effect on the placebo group as the test group!

Another feature of drug trials is that whilst participants are volunteers they do not know the potential consequences of taking the drug, even though it may have undergone extensive testing in a laboratory. Volunteers for drugs trials often participate in the hope that a new drug will work where others have failed and as such feel cheated if they end up in the placebo group, even though they don't know they are.

This dilemma is a major topic of debate that has yet to be resolved. One solution has been the use of 'double blind' trials where not even the experimenter knows who is receiving the treatment and who is receiving the placebo, the drug company having made that decision. This was originally introduced to prevent the experimenter influencing the results because they want to see a positive outcome for the patient. The effect of such bias is potentially present in any research situation and ultimately it comes down to the professionalism of the researcher to ensure they carry out and present the results of the research in an honest and open way. Anyone found deliberately changing the nature of their research or the results obtained could be severely reprimanded or even face criminal charges.

Anyone participating in research is now covered by the United Nations Declaration of Human Rights, which is supported by European legislation enshrined in the EU Directive on Data Protection (1995) and nationally by the Data Protection Act (1998). Organisations conducting research implement a code of ethics to ensure these rights are protected. Such codes include the need for participants to give their informed consent. This means that they are fully informed as to the nature and purpose of the research, what will happen and how and where it will take place. It also gives participants the right to refuse or to withdraw at any time and ensures that the anonymity of participants is preserved. Many researchers also include the requirement to debrief the participants about the nature of the research and why any deception may have been necessary.

As far as your research is concerned you would be unwise to set about collecting data if it were to cause distress to the people involved as a result of the methods chosen, the sampling process or the reporting of your work. It is important to:

1 gain permission from appropriate authorities (employers, teachers, tutors) to conduct the research. (This is important, as you may need the support of such people if any problems occur. It is generally recognised that research undertaken at this level will be underwritten by your tutors and/or workplace supervisors due to your inexperience.)

2 ask the subjects, or where children are concerned their parents or guardians, if they wish to take part

3 be in a position to explain your research as a consequence of 1 and 2

4 be able to reassure participants (or their guardians) about the measures taken to maintain confidentiality (see below).

Confidentiality

With regard to confidentiality you must ensure the anonymity of all participants.

- Change the names of subjects, particularly when using observation, experimental and case study methods where the sample size might be small. False names, letters or numbers can be used instead, e.g., Fred, Miss X, subject 9.

- Avoid descriptive language that could reveal a person's identity as can occur in case studies, e.g., 'Mrs Y, the leader of the local Labour party', does give the game away a bit! You need to think whether such information is important to your study and if so, how else it can be worded, e.g. 'Subject 8, a local politician'.

Another issue is what you may find out as part of your research. When gaining permission to conduct the research you need to be clear about what you must do in the event of being told or finding out something of a confidential nature. So, if you find out or suspect for example, that abuse has taken place you need to know what your responsibilities are and to whom you should refer. These responsibilities should also form part of the information given to potential participants, before the research is carried out.

Key issues: Human cloning and stem cell research

In 1997, scientists in Scotland cloned the first-ever animal, 'Dolly' the sheep. Since that time, developments in technology and understanding have created the potential for cloning human beings. Alongside this research has been the work on human stem cells. These are cells within the body that have the capacity to develop into any other type of body cell. Such cells are responsible for the growth and development of children and the replacement and regeneration of damaged tissues in adults. Stem cells are found in the embryo, foetus, child and adult, but it is the stem cells within the embryo that appear to hold the most promise for further research. Not only could these cells be used for cloning, but also to replace tissues that have been damaged in children or adults. However, the current state of research means that the embryo is destroyed in the process of obtaining the stem cells – an embryo that could have developed into a perfectly healthy person.

Assessment activity 3.7

Undertake a literature search to find out more about embryonic stem cell research and use this information to present arguments for and against such research. Evaluate the evidence on the basis of your own stated position on such research, for example belief in the rights of the unborn child or the rights of someone with bone marrow disease to treatment.

If the establishment you are studying at also has an Early Years course you or your tutor could consider arranging to debate this issue.

Now do this again on a piece of contemporary controversial research of your choice. What is the purpose of the research? Why are ethics so important in the research process for health, care or early years? What are the ethical issues of these pieces of research?

Your research as a presentation

You may have been asked to present the findings of your research to your peer group or others as part of the assessment process. You will not be alone if you dread this part of the project and are unsure about what you should put into the presentation and what to leave out. A good way of tackling this is to produce an **abstract** or summary of your work. This is a paragraph or two of 100–200 words that:

- states the purpose of your research, the research question or hypothesis
- describes the methods chosen
- states the most significant results that either support or refute your research
- gives the conclusions drawn, together with any suggestions for further work.

The abstract can then be the basis for your presentation, which can be expanded on with references to:

- aspects of secondary research
- interesting parts of the data collection process (the interview that went wrong!)
- tables, diagrams and charts that display quantitative findings to good effect
- an acknowledgement of the people who took part.

Producing a bibliography

In producing your work you will hopefully have used a range of books, articles, people and other sources. Since you will have summarised or extracted sections from such material for inclusion in your work it is essential that you acknowledge the producers or providers of this information. Consequently, you need to produce a reference section, bibliography and/or acknowledgements section. Although these words can be used to mean the same thing they are used here as follows:

- A reference section is generally used for acknowledging information taken from the original author(s)' work.
- A bibliography is used for information extracted from more general textbooks where the author(s) has/have drawn a wide range of material together from different sources.

- An acknowledgements section is to identify and thank those people who have given help or support (a shoulder to cry on) or have contributed directly to your work by being a subject (do remember not to identify anyone for whom confidentiality was promised).

You do not have to use this system and your tutors may prefer everything to be acknowledged within a bibliography only. However, whatever form you use you also need to adopt a style or format for identifying information and material used.

One of the most commonly accepted formats for referencing is known as the Harvard system. Within the body of your report any book/periodical/newspaper report, etc. used must identify the author, the year of publication and the page number(s) referred to, e.g.

> *'Observation is particularly suited to the study of phenomena such as non-verbal communication and tactile skills' (Lynes, 1999, p.315).*

If the author's surname is part of the sentence, then the date and page number(s) are sufficient, e.g.

> *Lynes (1999, p.315) suggested that observation is useful for studying non-verbal communication and tactile skills.*

If reference to a table or diagram is made, then the following is appropriate:

> *'Analysis of the results (White, 1995, p.13, table 2)' or 'White (1995, p.13, table 2) in his results showed that many single mothers . . .*

If you have copied or used part of a table or diagram from another source this must also be acknowledged. This is normally done by identifying the author of the work and year of publication after the title of the table or diagram.

At the end of the assignment the information sources referred to are listed alphabetically by surname. The format depends on the type of resource referred to and is best shown by example:

- For textbooks:
  Tortora G.J. and Grabowski, S. (2000) *Principles of Anatomy and Physiology.* John Wiley (Ninth edition).

- For articles from newspapers/periodicals/magazines:
  Lynes, D. (1999) 'Using observation for data collection' *Professional Nurse,* Vol. 14, No. 5, pp. 315–17.

You should seek advice from tutors with regard to other types of resource you may have referenced.

Some of this may appear rather confusing, but once you have got used to the idea you will find that it helps in organising and presenting your work in a logical manner.

A checklist for carrying out a research project

1   Find out how much time you have got. You may have been given a deadline that only allows you a few weeks or even days to complete the work, alternatively, you may be looking at a whole year. However, you will still need to plan your time

effectively to ensure the work is completed on time and is of the standard that you feel justifies the grade you are aiming for. Don't leave things to the last minute – particularly with a longer-term project.

2   Select a topic. If you only have a short period of time you need to select a topic that does not involve more complex secondary or primary research. For instance, it would be no good choosing a topic that involves obtaining information from obscure sources or relies on postal questionnaires. You may not get the information back in time, if at all.

3   Start reading around your chosen topic to help with focusing on your study in order to produce a research question or hypothesis.

4   Select the primary research and sampling methods appropriate to your study. With a short-term project you should choose just one or two research methods that will provide information quickly, whereas a longer-term study should involve a variety of methods and allow a more in-depth investigation to be carried out.

5   Identify what resources you will require to complete your study. Do you need specialist equipment? Where will you get such equipment? Will there be a charge and how long can you have it for?

6   Produce an action plan that identifies your research topic, research question or hypothesis, resources required for the primary research and secondary resources, an approximate time allocation for each section. Submit this to your tutor for approval.

7   Continue reading around the subject, making notes that provide background information and that supports or refutes your research question.

8   Draft an introduction and have it checked by your tutor.

9   Carry out the primary research.

10 Collate and present the results.

11 Analyse, discuss and evaluate your research.

End of unit test

1   Identify the difference between primary and secondary research.

2   Explain what is meant by these terms: qualitative, quantitative, cross-sectional, longitudinal.

3   Identify three forms of secondary information.

4   Identify the main primary research methods.

5   In surveys, how would you differentiate between a questionnaire and an interview?

6   What are the differences between a structured, semi-structured and unstructured interview?

7   Explain the difference between open-ended and closed questions.

8   Produce an experimental and null hypothesis for the observation that heart rate is affected by stressors such as exercise.

9   Re-read the case study about an autistic child (page 96). Using secondary data find out about the symptoms that are associated with autism. How do the child's symptoms match up with your findings?

10 Select the most appropriate graph/chart to present the following categories of data:

    a. The number of children being immunised against measles, mumps and rubella (MMR) between 1985 and 2000.

    b. The number of deaths from different diseases in different countries in 2000.

    c. Blood pressure changes related to stress levels.

    d. Reaction times of people under 25 compared with people over 40.

11 What is the most appropriate measure of central tendency for the amount of money spent on non-prescription drugs?

12 The diastolic blood pressure of 24 female students aged 16–25 was measured as part of a health awareness day. The results were:

1	2	3	4	5	6	7	8	9	10	11	12	13	14	15	16	17	18	19	20	21	22	23	24
70	70	88	88	96	94	75	85	90	85	64	85	75	86	85	85	80	90	70	75	70	80	74	78

Would the mean, median or mode best summarise the data?

13 Using the table and chart (on page 107) showing numbers of people diagnosed with HIV by different routes of transmission, 1990–1999, describe the changing trends over this period of time. Suggest why the changes have taken place.

References and further reading

Bell, J. (1993) (2nd edn) *Doing Your Research Project*, Buckingham: Open University Press

Blaxter, L., Hughes, C. and Tight, M. (1996) *How to Research*, Buckingham: Open University Press

Lynes, D. (1999) 'Using observation for data collection', *Professional Nurse*, Vol. 14, No. 5, pp. 315–17

Marshall, P. (1997) *Research Methods: How to Design and Conduct a Successful Project*, Plymouth: How to Books

Owen, D. and Davis, M. (1991) *Help with your Project: A Guide for Students of Health Care*, London: Edward Arnold

Peterson, R. A. (2000) *Constructing Effective Questionnaires*, London: Sage

Sharman, C., Cross, W. and Vennis, D. (1995) *Observing Children – A Practical Guide*, London: Cassell

4 Human anatomy and physiology

This unit introduces you to the basic structures and functions of the human body. You will learn about the fundamental unit known as the cell and the enormous variety of cell types and sizes that make up the tissues, organs and organ systems of the body.

Each cell is bathed in tissue fluid derived from blood, and materials are constantly exchanged between cells and fluid by important physiological processes. The chemical and physical properties of tissue fluid (also referred to as interstitial fluid) have to be carefully maintained within narrow limits in order for cells to function efficiently. The maintenance of this internal environment surrounding cells is known as homeostasis. The unit concludes with an exploration of the structure and function of all the major body systems. Further studies of some of these systems can be found in Unit 12.

What you need to learn
- Main components of the human body cell and tissues
- Tissues and their functions
- Processes involved in the exchange of materials
- Processes of homeostasis
- Human body systems

Main components of the human body cell and tissues

The structure and ultra-structure of cells in relation to their roles

Every individual is composed of billions of microscopic cells that carry out the vast complex chemical reactions and processes that make up the essence of life itself. The largest cell in the body is the ovum or egg cell of a female and this is only the size of a full stop on this page. Most other cells are many times smaller than this and thus need a microscope in order to be seen. Ordinary laboratory microscopes are excellent for viewing tissues, but not very useful for viewing the interior of human cells. An electron microscope is required to explore the detailed interior of a cell; this uses a beam of electrons rather than light and thus provides a far greater magnification that can be seen without blurring. These microscopes are highly specialised and very expensive as well as requiring a trained operator, so you are very unlikely to have one in your college. Photographs of the images seen through electron micrographs are, however, easily obtainable and you will be able to view the structures of the cell from these. It is usual to refer to the parts of a cell seen through an electron microscope collectively as the ultra-structure, signifying the very high magnification required, and the bodies which make up the ultra-structure are known as organelles.

A typical cell seen by a light microscope

There is a vast number of different types of cell in the body and strictly speaking there is no such thing as a typical cell. The term is used to mean a cell showing no specialisation at all.

The living material that makes up a cell is called protoplasm and it is enclosed within a thin cell membrane. Protoplasm can be subdivided into cytoplasm and nucleus; the latter is usually centrally placed and surrounded by its own nuclear membrane.

Under the light microscope both cytoplasm and nucleus appear grainy and granular, with no distinct features except for a darker patch called the nucleolus inside the nucleus (see Figure 4.1). Early biologists likened this cytoplasmic material to a kind of 'soup' with no specific structure.

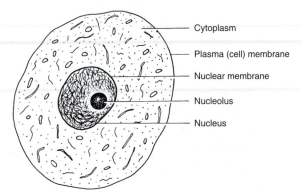

Figure 4.1 A cell viewed under a light microscope (magnified × 300)

They were very inaccurate in their thinking and when technological advances led to the electron microscope in the 1940s, a very complex structure was revealed (see Figure 4.2). The cytoplasm is the site of most complex chemical reactions, directed in the main by the nucleus which also contains the genetic material responsible for inherited characteristics and the instructions for the cell's metabolic processes. The cell membrane allows substances to move into and out of the cell and can be quite selective in its purpose.

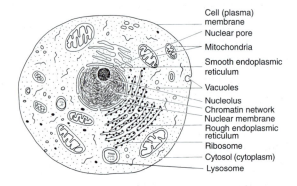

Figure 4.2 A cell magnified under an electron microscope (magnified × 1000)

Cell structure through the electron microscope

Cell ultra-structure is so complex and highly organised that a separate branch of science known as cytology (the study of cells) has arisen. Each type of organelle will be studied in detail.

The plasma or cell membrane

This was once thought of as a simple membrane, but can be seen to be a lipid-protein sandwich composed of 50 per cent of each material by weight (see Figure 4.3). However, the proteins are much larger molecules than the fats or lipids, which are far more

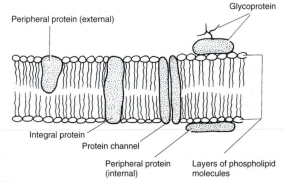

Figure 4.3 The cell membrane structure is known as the fluid mosaic model

numerous. Most of the lipids are phospholipids with a water soluble phosphate head and two water insoluble lipid (fatty) chains (see Figure 4.4). Two layers of these molecules line up with their lipid chains opposite each other and the phosphate heads lying externally and internally – this is often said to be a bi-layer.

Phospholipids are able to slide sideways in their positions and so repair any breaches in the membrane. Large protein molecules may be inserted into the top or bottom layer of phospholipids or all the way through. Many have sugar chains attached and are known as glycoproteins; they frequently line channels in the membrane that can act as passages for substances to move to and from the cell. Others carry different molecules through the membrane. Those inserted into the outer layer of phospholipids often act as identity markers or receptor sites for molecules, such as hormones, that are important to that particular cell.

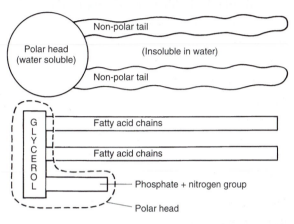

Figure 4.4 The structure of phospholipids

Plasma membranes exert selectivity over substances entering and leaving the cell, called *selective permeability*. Substances that dissolve easily in fatty substances also dissolve easily in the phospholipid layer and enter the cell interior with ease; these are said to be freely permeable. Charged particles or ions can experience difficulty in gaining access to the cell interior and have to locate suitable protein channels. In general, positively charged ions (called cations) are more favoured than negatively charged ions (anions).

Think it over
Make a list of common chemical ions that you know and say whether they are cations or anions. If you do not know many ions, research the following list of ions that are common in human physiology: hydrogen, chloride, phosphate, oxygen, sodium, potassium, carbonate, hydrogen-carbonate, hydroxyl, sulphate, nitrate.

Cytoplasm
Cytoplasm is a semi-fluid material capable of flowing slowly and in which many other substances are suspended. Many chemical reactions are carried out here. The sum total of chemical reactions is called metabolism, a term frequently used in biology and physiology text references. Melanin, a pigment responsible for hair or skin colour, and complex sugars, such as glycogen, are also found in the cytoplasm.

Cell organelles
Cell components with distinct structures and functions can be likened to miniature organs and so have been termed *organelles*.

Organelles include:

- endoplasmic reticulum
- ribosomes
- lysosomes
- mitochondria
- nucleus.

You will need to refer to Figure 4.2 as you study the organelles.

Endoplasmic reticulum (ER)

'Endo' means within and reticulum is a network. Hence the endoplasmic reticulum is a network of branching channels, which fills the cell interior. The membranes enclosing the channels have a similar structure to the plasma membrane and are continuous with the membrane surrounding the nucleus. The channels clearly represent a means of transporting materials from one part of a cell to another.

Electron microscope cell diagrams often show just a portion of ER for clarity, although the entire cell is filled with these channels.

There are two distinct types known as the rough and the smooth ER. Rough ER is studded along the membranes with tiny black bodies called ribosomes, whereas smooth does not. Rough ER together with its ribosomes makes the cell proteins and acts as a temporary storage area. It can also add on sugar chains to the proteins to manufacture glycoproteins such as those seen in the cell membrane.

Smooth ER has a different task and makes fatty materials such as phospholipids, steroids and fatty acids.

Ribosomes

These small dark bodies are attached to the rough ER (as mentioned above), but there are also large numbers floating freely in the cytoplasm. Those on the rough ER manufacture cell proteins, either used in the cell membrane or for export from the cell to be used elsewhere. Free ribosomes also manufacture proteins but this time for the cell's own use. Ribosomes contain ribonucleic acid, more commonly referred to as RNA, a close 'cousin' of the genetic material DNA.

Lysosomes

These are like tiny bags enclosed in just one layer of membrane and made in a specialised part of the ER (the Golgi apparatus). They contain enzymes capable of digesting all the major chemical components of living things.

Lysosomes can travel about the cell interior quite freely and are normally found in the cytoplasm. Some lysosomes secrete their enzymes outside the cell to digest externally; some digest substances internally and eliminate the digested material outside the cell. Some types of white blood cells (the phagocytes) are loaded with this type of lysosome to digest bacteria, viruses or carbon particles. Other lysosomes are capable of destroying old or damaged cell organelles, such as mitochondria, or even the whole cell itself. They both help to renew parts of the cell by removing debris and assist in cell protection.

Many disease-causing agents, poisons and carcinogens (substances that promote cancer) are believed to act by damaging the lysosome membrane, thus bringing about cell destruction from within.

Mitochondria

These bodies are very numerous in active cells, such as muscle and liver cells, because they are concerned with energy release.

Every body cell has at least one thousand of these rod-shaped or spherical bodies lined by a double membrane similar in structure to the plasma membrane. The inner layer is folded to produce shelf-like ridges (cristae) that hold the enzymes responsible for the last stage of respiration or glucose oxidation (see Figure 4.5). The first stages of respiration take place in the cytoplasm and the mitochondrial enzymes finish the process.

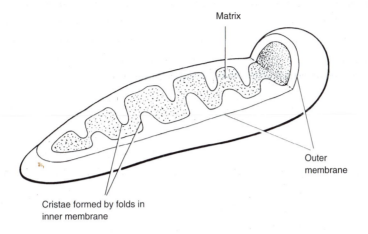

Figure 4.5 The structure of a mitochondrion

Nucleus

Usually the largest structure inside the cell, the nucleus takes up stains very easily and appears very dark. Mature red blood cells have no nucleus (but cannot divide and have a limited life span) and muscle cells may contain many nuclei. Some white blood cells have lobed nuclei but most are spherical or oval and central. Cells that become separated from their nuclei usually die, although you will learn that the mature red blood cell is an exception to this rule.

The double-layered membrane surrounding the nucleus also has a structure similar to the plasma membrane, but contains minute gaps or pores through which materials such as RNA and proteins can pass. One or more smaller bodies, which stain even darker, can often be seen in micrographs and these are the nucleoli that make RNA for the ribosomes (see above). The remainder of the nucleus of a cell between cell divisions looks like a tangled mass of material, called the chromatin network, and this only separates into distinct chromosomes during division. The chromatin network and the chromosomes contain genetic material composed of deoxyribonucleic acid (DNA) and protein; DNA and RNA, both present in the nucleus, are collectively known as the nucleic acids.

The nucleus of a cell controls all the activities of the cell; it can be likened to the blueprint of a building which in this case is the cell structure.

Assessment activity 4.1

Look back at Figure 4.2, the cell seen with the electron microscope, and produce your own large-scale diagram with labels, preferably on unlined A3 paper, leaving enough space around for notes to describe the functions of the plasma or cell membrane, the cytoplasm and the cell organelles. On a smaller sheet of unlined paper (A4) produce a diagram of a cell under a light microscope with similar added notes. Write one or two pages of notes describing the differences between the two diagrams. Keep this work for assessment.

Some cells have microscopic projections from their surface known as cilia (see Figure 4.6). They are capable of a whip-like action, known as beating, and are capable of moving materials along surfaces. Cilia are nearly always associated with sticky white or transparent mucus secretions and move towards an orifice or opening. The

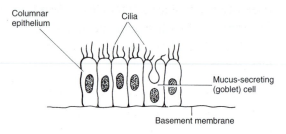

Figure 4.6 Ciliated cells

female ovum is transported in this way down the oviduct, and so are foreign particles that become trapped in the nose and respiratory tract. Inflammation, for instance when we have a severe cold, causes excessive mucus secretion and we notice this as we have to wipe it away.

Tissues and their functions

Cells carry out functions, but in practice they do not work in isolation. They usually form groups and work together carrying out their particular function. A group of similar cells carrying out a particular set of functions is called a *tissue*. The cells of a tissue can be fastened together in several ways, called *cell junctions*, but there is always fluid between these fastenings. The fluid is known as *interstitial* or *tissue fluid*. It transports materials to cells and carries out chemical reactions. This fluid is where bacteria are found in bacterial infections. Viruses, on the other hand, can reproduce only when inside living cells. This is why chemicals such as antibiotics are effective against bacteria, but not against viruses as the cell would be damaged as well.

The study of tissues is called *histology* and, for simplicity, tissues can be classified into four major groups:

- epithelial tissues
- connective tissues
- muscle tissues
- nervous tissue.

Epithelia

These tissues cover internal and external body surfaces, including the lining of ducts, body cavities, hollow organs and gland formation. Epithelia consist of closely packed cells either in single layers (*simple epithelia*) or in several layers (*compound epithelia*).

The lowest layer of epithelia always sits on a basement membrane. This is a thin membranous layer secreted by the epithelial cells themselves, which provides support and attachment. Epithelia have nerve supplies, but are nourished by diffusion from blood vessels in neighbouring connective tissue.

As epithelia line surfaces and organs, it follows that they are subject to considerable wear and tear, so their capacity for repair is greater than most other cells.

Simple epithelia

The simplest type is *squamous epithelium* which consists of cells so flat that the nucleus forms a lump in the centre, giving an appearance something similar to the yolk of a fried egg when viewed from above. They fit together rather like crazy paving with very little tissue fluid between them (see Figure 4.7).

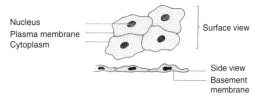

Figure 4.7 Simple squamous epithelium

Squamous epithelium cells are found in the wall of blood capillaries (in this location called *endothelium*), Bowman's capsule in kidney nephrons and lung alveoli. They are located in areas where diffusion and osmosis take place, or where filtration and secretion occur.

Other types of simple epithelia are *cuboidal* and *columnar epithelia* which have shapes like cubes and columns respectively (see Figure 4.8). Columnar cells are often associated with the presence of cilia and mucus-secreting cells (see Figure 4.6).

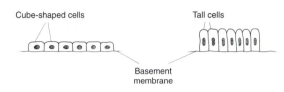

Figure 4.8 Cuboidal and columnar epithelium

Compound epithelia

These consist of several cell layers which can be cuboidal, columnar or mixed with squamous cells forming the upper layer. This last type is called *stratified squamous epithelium* (see Figure 4.9) and it lines the vagina, oesophagus, mouth and tongue. The skin is similar, but with the added protection of a layer of dead cells forming a barrier to the outside world (*cornified stratified squamous epithelium*).

The lower layers of stratified squamous epithelium are formed of cuboidal or even columnar shapes which gradually become flattened (squamous) as they near the surface. This is due to the multiplication of cells in the lowest layer as they divide. The newly formed cells are gradually pushed upwards. The lowest layer sits on a basement membrane.

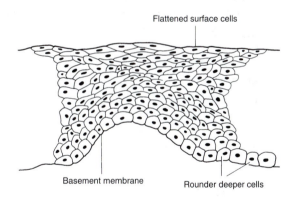

Clearly, by forming several layers, the main function of this type of epithelium is the protection of deeper structures.

Figure 4.9 Stratified squamous epithelium

Connective tissue

This is the tissue found most widely in the human body. Some connective tissues are liquid like blood, flexible like cartilage or rigid like bone. Connective tissues lie deeper than epithelial tissues. They support, connect and strengthen other tissues while some protect and insulate body structures.

Connective tissues consist of cells located in a matrix (background substance). The matrix surrounds cells, which are therefore not attached to each other, and is often called *intercullular matrix*, because it is between the cells. The matrix is usually secreted by the cells themselves and gives the tissue most of its characteristics. Matrix can be fluid as in blood, semi-fluid as in the general white, sticky connective tissue around muscle fibres, nerves, etc. (*areolar connective tissue*), flexible and firm as in cartilage, or calcified and rigid as in bone. Many types of matrix also contain fibres such as collagen, which give added strength, or elastic fibres, which give elasticity. Some contain both.

Blood

This connective tissue consists of a fluid matrix called *plasma* in which cells or fragments of cells are suspended. Plasma is a straw-coloured liquid consisting of water in which nutrients (like glucose and amino acids), ions (sodium, chloride, etc.), enzymes, hormones and gases are dissolved. Plasma proteins found in plasma have important functions in the body.

Blood cells have diverse functions and comprise the following:

- red blood cells, or *erythrocytes*, which carry oxygen to body cells and have a role in transporting carbon dioxide away from them (see Figure 4.10)
- white blood cells, or *leucocytes*, which come in different forms:
  - *phagocytes* which engulf foreign materials and microbes
  - *lymphocytes* which play an important role in immunity
  - *monocytes* which behave in a similar way to phagocytes
  - *basophils* which produce an anti-clotting agent
  - *eosinophils* which are involved in allergic reactions.

Cell fragments are the platelets (or *thrombocytes*) concerned with blood clotting mechanisms.

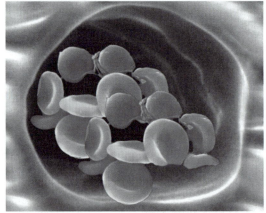

Figure 4.10 Scanning electron micrograph of normal red blood cells in a vessel lumen

Compact bone

This is the dense bone found on the outside of all bones and in the shafts of long bones of the skeleton.

The other type of bone is *spongy bone* (see Figure 4.11) which forms the bulk of the heads of long bones and irregular bones. Spongy bone contains spaces filled with bone marrow and is less rigidly organised than compact bone.

Compact bone is constructed to withstand the weight of the body carried by the long bones and to protect and support other tissues. Under the microscope, this tissue is seen to be made of series of concentric circles called *Haversian systems* (or *osteones*) each with a central canal containing blood vessels and nerves (see Figure 4.11). These connect with larger blood vessels and nerves which penetrate the bone from its outer covering, the *periosteum*.

Each Haversian system has rings of hard calcified material visible and these are called *lamellae*. At intervals close to the lamellae are small spaces, or *lacunae*, which house mature bone cells, or *osteocytes*. In the immature state, these cells are *osteoblasts* which secrete the matrix and become imprisoned in it. Running outwards in all directions from the lacunae are tiny channels (*canaliculi*) which are filled with fluid and contain long, finger-like processes from the osteocytes. These channels connect with other osteocyte canaliculi and eventually the Haversian canal, and in this way the cells are nourished and able to get rid of their waste products.

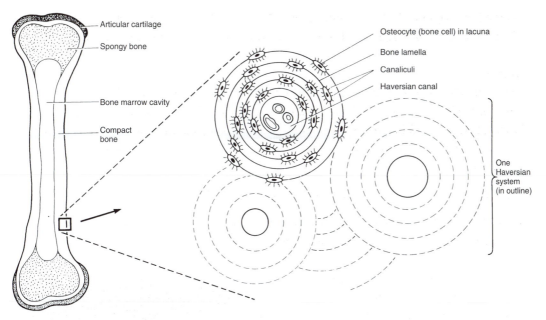

Figure 4.11 A long bone and the microscopic structure of compact bone

The matrix of bone has two major components:

- *mineral salts*, mainly salts of calcium, like calcium carbonate and a form of calcium phosphate, which form around collagen fibres and give the bone its hardness
- *collagen fibres*, which give bone its ability to bend under strain and prevent it from being too brittle like an eggshell.

Muscle tissues

There are three types of muscle tissue in the human body:

- skeletal muscle (also called voluntary, striated or striped muscle)
- smooth muscle (also called involuntary, unstriated or unstriped muscle)
- cardiac muscle.

Each type consists of special cells known as *muscle fibres* which are capable of contraction, or shortening. In this way they cause movement or help to maintain posture. All muscles generate heat as a side effect and this contributes to maintaining body temperature. All muscles have blood and nerve supplies.

Skeletal muscle

As its name suggests, this is always attached to bones of the skeleton – it is the familiar meat we see in butchers' shops. It can be made to contract or relax by an individual's conscious control via nerve impulses, hence the alternative name of *voluntary muscle*. The individual muscle fibres show alternate bands of light and dark, thus appearing striped or striated (see Figure 4.12). Fibres in a muscle lie parallel to each other and are cylindrical in shape. There are hundreds or thousands of fibres in each individual muscle, depending on its size. The thickness and length of individual muscle fibres is variable – the largest fibres can be up to one third of a metre long and one hundredth of a millimetre thick.

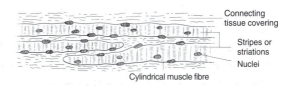

Figure 4.12 The microscopic structure of skeletal muscle

Each fibre is composed of many *myofibrils* and these are made up of tiny protein filaments. The cell membrane of a muscle fibre is called the *sarcolemma*. It encases the myofibrils and many nuclei are located close to the sarcolemma. The fibre is said to be *multi-nucleate*. Large numbers of mitochondria lie close to the myofibrils in parallel rows, able to supply energy (ATP, adenosine triphosphate; see page 136) to the fibre for the contraction process.

Smooth muscle

This type is found in the walls of arteries and veins and in sheets running in different directions around hollow organs such as the stomach, intestines, bladder and uterus. It is not attached to bones. If you think about it, you cannot control the contraction of these muscles, hence the alternative name – *involuntary*. There are also no bands visible so it is unstriped or unstriated.

Each fibre is spindle-shaped, with a central nucleus, surrounded by a sarcolemma (see Figure 4.13). They lie dove-tailed with one another in sheets. Although these fibres still contain protein filaments they do not lie in an orderly fashion so this is why there is no light and dark banding. Recent evidence suggests that shortening or contraction occurs because the fibre twists and coils up.

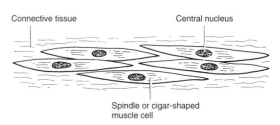

Figure 4.13 The microscopic structure of smooth muscle

Cardiac muscle

As its name suggests, this is found only in the walls of the heart. The fibres interconnect and branch with each other forming a network. Each cell is roughly rectangular with a central nucleus and packed with mitochondria. Like skeletal muscle, it shows banding but, like smooth muscle, it cannot be controlled at will. When isolated from a nerve supply, it is still able to contract and relax – a property known as *myogenicity*. The sarcolemma between adjacent cells is thickened to produce a disc-like appearance known as *intercalated discs*. This enables nerve impulses to pass very swiftly from one cell to another. When one fibre is stimulated, the impulse rapidly spreads through the network of cells (see Figure 4.14).

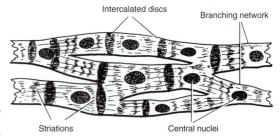

Figure 4.14 The microscopic structure of cardiac muscle

Nervous tissue

Surprisingly, this consists of only two types of cell – nerve cells (*neurones*) and supporting cells called neuroglia. The latter are not important at this level of study.

Neurones are highly specialised cells which are either sensitive to stimuli, converting them to nerve impulses, or capable of transmitting nerve impulses to effectors or other neurones. Effectors are structures which do (or effect) things in response. In practice, these are muscles which respond by contracting or glands which respond by secretion. So basically, there are three types of functional neurones – sensory, relay and motor neurones.

All types of neurone have similar structural components:

- cell bodies, which contain nuclei and other organelles
- axons, which are single, long processes which conduct nerve impulses away from the cell body
- dendrons, usually multiple processes which carry nerve impulses towards the cell body (see Figure 4.15).

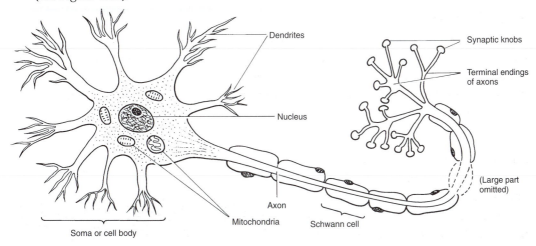

Figure 4.15 The general features of a nerve cell (neurone)

Sensory neurones are mainly located intimately with sensory receptors or have their terminal portions adapted to receive stimuli themselves (see Figure 4.16a).

They usually have quite long dendrons which carry the impulses close to the brain and spinal cord where their cell bodies are located. Axons, on the other hand, have only a small distance to cover inside the central nervous system, and are therefore short.

Motor neurones are intimately associated with effectors. Their axons are long, with specially adapted endings called *neuromuscular junctions* (see Figure 4.16b). The dendrons travel only a short distance within the central nervous system and are short.

Relay neurones, also called *connector* and *internuncial neurones*, have relatively short axons and dendrons as they lie completely within the central nervous system (see Figure 4.16c).

Nerve cells, like muscle fibres, are excitable cells capable of responding to stimuli by producing nerve impulses or contraction responses respectively.

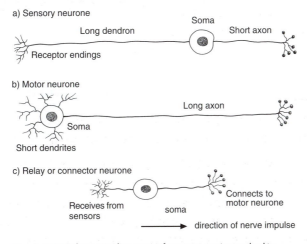

Figure 4.16 Schematic diagrams of sensory, motor and relay

Assessment activity 4.2

Study micrographs 1–4 below carefully. (A micrograph is a photograph of a microscope image.) Identify the type of tissue shown in each micrograph and describe, using your own words, the main features of the four main types of tissue. Relate these features to their functions.

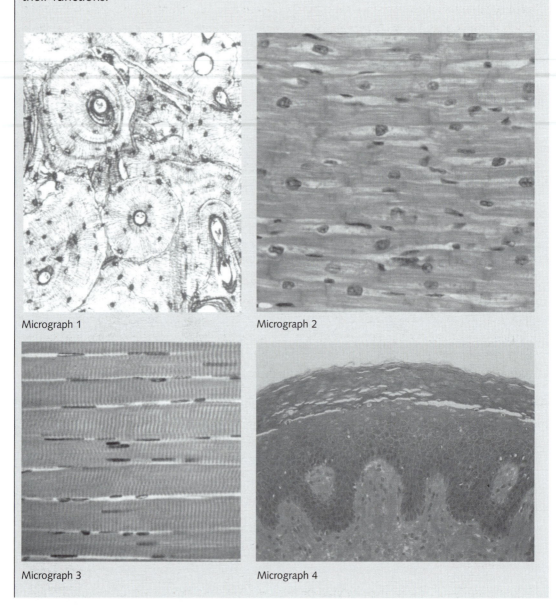

Micrograph 1

Micrograph 2

Micrograph 3

Micrograph 4

Processes involved in the exchange of materials

Cells are actively engaging in passing substances out of the cell and accepting other materials into the cell. They must, however, be quite selective in this exchange or they will not function efficiently or even die. There are three basic processes that are physiologically important to this exchange and you will explore each one in detail:

- diffusion
- osmosis
- active transport.

Diffusion

This can occur in gases and liquids, wherever there is a concentration gradient, time and a thin barrier (or no barrier at all) that separates the different levels of concentrations. Molecules of a substance are in a state of movement. In gases they move freely, bouncing off each other and the walls of any container. Liquid molecules also move a great deal, but not as much as gases. Molecules in a solid also move, but this is more of a vibration so there is no 'flow' as there is with gases and liquids. From this, it is easy to see how diffusion occurs: when you have a large number of molecules in one place (a high concentration) and a small number in another (low concentration), with the passage of time and little or no barrier between the molecules, the numbers will tend to even up. That is exactly how diffusion occurs. The scientific definition is: *Diffusion is the movement of molecules from a region of high concentration to a region of low concentration.*

Diffusion will only take place whilst there is a difference in concentration; as the numbers of molecules in the two regions become nearer to each other the *rate* of diffusion slows down. When the molecules have become evenly distributed between the two regions the overall rate of diffusion stops. At this stage equilibrium is said to have been achieved. This does not mean that the molecules become still, because molecules are in constant random motion. Equilibrium means that the net movement of molecules has stopped and they are moving equally between the two regions. Some parts of the body, such as the lungs and oxygen transport into the blood, depend on diffusion so it is important not to reach the state of equilibrium. The diffusing molecules must be carried away (usually by the bloodstream) to maintain the low concentration, and the high concentration must be refreshed constantly by inhaling fresh air containing 20 per cent of oxygen.

The diffusing molecules can traverse thin membranes but any process that thickens the barrier will slow down diffusion. When clients suffer from pneumonia where the lungs contain increased fluid, or if they are heavy smokers with increased mucus secretion, the rate of oxygen diffusion in the lungs will be decreased. This will mean that cells and tissues in other parts of the body will be less efficient. In pneumonia, the client may have to be given extra oxygen through a mask.

Molecular movement increases with temperature, so it is clear that at body temperature diffusion will take place at a faster rate than at room temperature in the laboratory.

When a diffusing membrane is present between the two regions of differing concentration, the surface area of the barrier is a factor affecting the rate of diffusion. The greater the surface area, the faster will be the rate of diffusion; you will find that where diffusion is important for the exchange of materials the membranes are usually folded, scalloped or carrying projections, such as the villi in the small intestine.

To summarise, the factors that affect the rate of diffusion are:

- increased temperature
- increased surface area
- thinness of barriers
- maintenance of the concentration gradient.

Assessment activity 4.3
Diffusion of gases

1 Moisten some strips of pink litmus paper and stick them at intervals along an open glass tube about 0.75 metres long. Place a bung in one end and a plug of cotton wool moistened with a solution of ammonia at the other end and leave for a few minutes. As the gas diffuses along the tube, it will turn the litmus paper blue. Take care not to get ammonia into the nose or eyes as this will be very uncomfortable. You can cork the 'cotton wool' end or work in a fume cupboard as well to minimise this.

How could you modify this experiment to measure the rate of diffusion along the tube? What other equipment will you need?

How could you adapt this experiment to investigate one of the factors, which influence the rate of diffusion? Design your own experiment and check it out with your tutor. Do not forget to include health and safety aspects.

2 It is difficult to demonstrate diffusion between liquids of different concentrations, because the act of pouring two liquids into one container causes them to mix and confuse the results. If two liquids are 'held' in gelatine by dissolving in warm gelatine solutions and then allowed to cool, one being dyed with a stain and one clear, diffusion occurs very slowly. You need to allow one gelatine solution to set before pouring the other solution on the top. It may be several days before a result is seen. You could also adapt this experiment to investigate one of the influencing factors.

Osmosis

Osmosis is a special type of diffusion that involves only moving water molecules in the presence of a selectively permeable membrane. It can be defined as:

Osmosis is the movement of water molecules from a region of high concentration of water molecules to a region of low concentration of water molecules through a selectively permeable membrane.

A selectively permeable membrane is a thin sheet that allows certain small molecules to pass through but not larger molecules. In the living body, there are many types of selectively permeable membranes such as the pleura, which covers the lung surface, and the peritoneum, which covers abdominal organs and lines the abdominal cavity. However, the most common selectively permeable membrane you will hear about is the cell membrane around every living cell. In the laboratory, we can mimic a cell membrane by using a commercial product known as Visking tubing that was developed for use in kidney machines for renal dialysis.

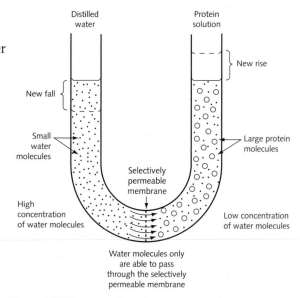

Figure 4.17 How osmosis works

Imagine a glass U-tube with a selectively permeable membrane partition in the centre (see Figure 4.17). On one side of the tube is distilled water and on the other side is the same volume of a protein solution, such as albumen solution. Albumen molecules are large and cannot pass through the selectively permeable membrane; water molecules are small and pass through easily. If the tube is left for a short time, water molecules will pass through from the region of high concentration of water molecules in distilled water to the smaller concentration in the albumen solution. Water molecules actually travel through the membrane in both directions, but because of the concentration gradient of water the *net* or overall movement is from high to low concentration.

The contents of a cell include proteins and other large molecules, whereas the fluid bathing cells (called tissue or interstitial fluid) contain much less. Therefore, one of the main ways in which water passes through the cell membrane is by osmosis. The 'extra' water that passes through the membrane exerts a pressure called *osmotic pressure,* and *osmotic potential* is the power of a solution to gain or lose water molecules through a membrane. Weaker or dilute solutions have higher osmotic potential than concentrated solutions; it must follow that water has the highest osmotic potential.

When tissue fluid returns to the capillary/venular blood, it does so by osmosis because the plasma proteins in blood exert a lower osmotic potential than the watery tissue fluid; in this case the single-celled lining of the capillary acts as the selectively permeable membrane.

Assessment activity 4.4

Cut a piece of Visking tubing about 12 cm long and soak in distilled water until soft. Tightly knot one end of the tubing to make a bag and open the other end. Pour in a mixture of starch and glucose solutions and either knot the open end or secure with a rubber band so that there are no leaks. Wash the exterior of the bag with distilled water to ensure that no contamination has taken place. Carefully place the bag inside a boiling tube half full of distilled water and test small samples of the water immediately for starch and glucose. You can do this using iodine solution that turns blue-black in the presence of starch and warming a second sample with Benedict's solution for glucose. If glucose is present there will be a colour change to yellow/orange or red. This test is the basis for testing urine for glucose (a condition called glycosuria) with chemically impregnated strips.

Continue testing samples of the water at 3-minute intervals for 15 minutes and record your results on a chart. Explain your results and draw clear conclusions.

Repeat the experiment but add an extra layer of Visking tubing and compare the two results charts you have collected. What influencing factor will you have investigated? You could also repeat the first experiment using starch solution that has been diluted with 50 per cent distilled water and compare the two sets of results again. What factor have you investigated this time?

Health and safety note: Starch and glucose are relatively non-toxic, but the chemical test reagents will have different properties and you must be aware of the health and safety aspects when handling these materials. Read the instructions on the reagent bottles or ask your tutor to supply you with the details. Ensure that you know the correct procedures for warming solutions over flames and never forget to wear protective clothing and goggles in a laboratory.

Physiologically, any large molecular substance present on one side of a selectively permeable membrane with a watery solution on the other can effect osmosis.

Active transport

There are many examples of materials passing through living cell membranes against a concentration gradient, i.e. passing from a low concentration to a high concentration, and this cannot utilise either the diffusion or osmosis process. Transporting materials against a concentration gradient is called *active transport* and it requires an energy source for the work done. For this reason, active transport can only take place in living cells that contain an energy store known as ATP (adenosine triphosphate). ATP is found inside cells, acting rather like a re-chargeable battery, releasing energy when it is required and 're-charging' from the energy released by the mitochondria of the cell.

In some physiological circumstances, molecules may need to be moved very rapidly and active transport can be used here. For example, glucose may need to be transported quickly across the lining of the digestive system and sodium ions need to be pumped out of neurones or nerve cells during the passage of electrical impulses.

Factors affecting the rate of active transport involve the difference in the concentration gradients (how much work is required), the surface area to be covered and the quantity of energy available to carry out the task. During respiratory difficulties – when oxygen is not so freely available – the rate of active transport slows.

Processes of homeostasis

This is the process by which the human body maintains a constant internal environment despite external changes. Body organs can only maintain their functions efficiently within a narrow range of conditions such as temperature, acidity, blood pressure and so on. When a condition varies from its set point for working optimally, automatic regulatory mechanisms are activated to counteract the disturbance and re-establish the set point. This is homeostasis.

Homeostasis is the process that maintains the constancy or stability of the body's internal environment (see Figure 4.18). Regardless of which body system is involved, there is the need for *receptors* to detect changes in the external environment, a *control centre* (usually in the brain) to receive and act on the information from the receptors and *effectors* to act to bring the system back to normal. This is known as the **negative feedback** effect as the change is always dampened down or lessened to return the system to normal. Negative feedback effects are the most common types of homeostatic control.

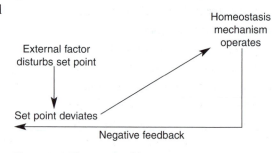

Figure 4.18 The process of homeostasis

Positive feedback effects are very rare in human physiology, because they stimulate greater deviations from normal and eventually result in a 'bust' situation. Childbirth, which involves the continued stimulation of uterine muscle, is an example of positive feedback, resulting in 'bust' – the birth or expulsion of the foetus. We will be concerned wholly with negative feedback situations in this unit.

Some important homeostatic mechanisms within the body are:

- maintaining blood glucose level
- body temperature regulation
- maintaining heart rate
- maintaining respiratory rate
- regulating water balance (osmoregulation).

When homeostatic control mechanisms fail, the physiology of the human body is in serious trouble.

Osmoregulation and body fluid composition

We have learned that osmosis relates to water and so the term osmoregulation refers to the regulation of the water content of the body. First, you will investigate where most of the water is held in the body. Figure 4.19 shows the water compartments in the body of an average adult male, but you must remember that there are wide variations in different people.

The total body water is either contained inside the living cells (intracellular water) or external to cells (extracellular water). Twice as much water is inside cells than outside; at first sight this may seem surprising as you will be more familiar with fluid outside cells, but thousands of millions of cells comprise the body structures and these are over 90 per cent water. Extracellular fluid can be further subdivided into the watery part of blood – the plasma – and the larger volume of tissue or interstitial fluid that bathes all cells.

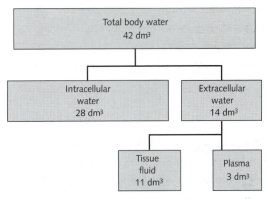

Note: 1 dm³ is equivalent to 1 litre

Figure 4.19 Distribution of body water in an average adult

How do these water volumes remain so steady from day to day? Food and drink on a daily basis add 2.2 dm³ and waste products from metabolic processes, chiefly respiration, add another 0.35–0.5 dm³, making a total input of 2.5–2.7 dm³ each day. Output consists of 1.5 dm³ urine, 0.1 dm³ faeces, 0.05 dm³ of sweat and 0.9 dm³ from expired air and the skin (often called insensible water loss as it goes unnoticed), again totalling 2.55 dm³ each day. So, the volume of water going into the body matches that leaving the body – *theoretically* (see Figure 4.20). You will be able to recall days when you haven't had time to drink much or – just the opposite – when you have spent more time than usual drinking fluid, be it alcoholic drinks, tea, coffee or just plain water.

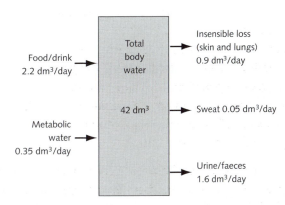

Figure 4.20 Average daily water gain and loss

At other times, you sweat more due to hot weather or hard exercise. Abnormal conditions can also upset this delicate balance, such as food poisoning causing vomiting or diarrhoea, bleeding from a wounds or even menstruation.

It is clear then that although theoretically water balance looks easy, massive individual variations can occur with different external and internal circumstances and the body must have a homeostatic control system for regulating body water.

So, how does the body handle changes in water loss or gain? Receptors are necessary to detect the change in water balance. These are known as osmoreceptors and lie in the hypothalamus of the brain close to blood vessels. How they work is largely unknown but they are modified neurones (nerve cells) that make anti-diuretic hormone (ADH) that is actually secreted by the posterior pituitary gland (see Figure 4.21).

ADH causes parts of the renal nephrons to become more permeable to water that can then be reabsorbed into the tributaries of the renal vein and thus returned to the extracellular body water. A lack of ADH causes these parts to become 'waterproofed', water is not reabsorbed and passes through the kidneys to the bladder and beyond.

When an individual drinks a litre of water, beer, juice or any liquid, it is absorbed into the bloodstream from the digestive tract. This increases extracellular blood volume and the osmolarity of the body fluids fall (they get more dilute) and ADH is inhibited due to reduced activity of the osmoreceptors. As less ADH is produced, more water passes into the urine. The excess water is eliminated in this way and osmolarity of body fluids returned to normal limits. Conversely, when the body is lacking in sufficient water, body fluid osmolarity rises and the stimulated osmoreceptors secrete more ADH which in turn acts upon the renal nephrons to cause more water re-absorption and a return to normal limits. Under these circumstances, urine becomes more concentrated and has less volume (see Figures 4.22 and 4.23).

ADH secretion is also influenced by other factors such as fear, excitement, pain and drugs. It is also acted upon by pressure receptors called baroreceptors, located within the kidneys and around major arteries and veins. Baroreceptors are also stimulated by lowered plasma volume.

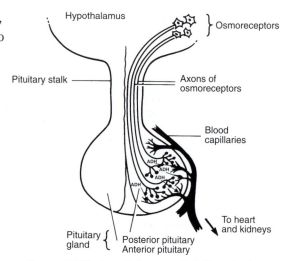

Figure 4.21 The hypothalamus and pituitary gland

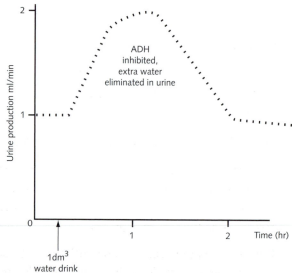

Figure 4.22 ADH secretion

The composition of tissue fluid is allied to the composition of plasma from which it is derived apart from the absence of plasma proteins. This bathing fluid is important in allowing the correct functioning of the cells. If its osmolarity falls (too dilute), then cells will increase in size by taking in more water through the cell membrane by osmosis. Conversely, if osmolarity rises above normal, the cell will lose water to the tissue fluid through osmosis and shrink or dehydrate. Cells that are surrounded by tissue fluid of the correct strength are said to be isotonic with their surroundings. Cells

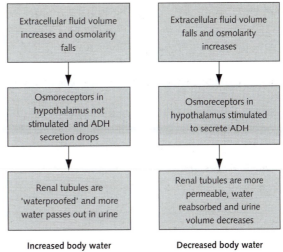

Figure 4.23 How water gains and losses are restored within normal limits

that are bathed by more dilute fluid are in a hypotonic environment and those in a more concentrated medium are in a hypertonic environment. Hypertonic and hypotonic environments will disturb the metabolism of cells and can even cause their deaths. Water, glucose and salts affect the tonicity of fluids (see Figure 4.24).

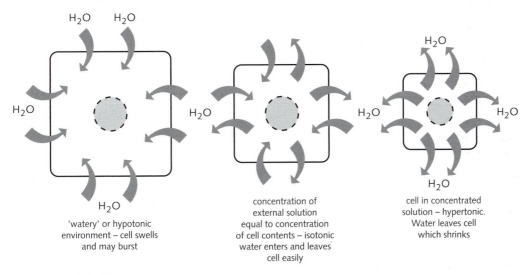

Figure 4.24 Cells in different environments

Composition of body fluids

Major body fluids comprise intracellular fluid, extracellular fluid (tissue fluid, plasma) and urine.

The major components of intracellular fluid and extracellular fluid are:

Sodium ions (Na^+)   Potassium ions ($K+$)   Calcium ions ($Ca2^+$)
Magnesium ions ($Mg2^+$)   Chloride ions(Cl^-)   Amino acids
Glucose   Protein   ATP
Hydrogen carbonate ions ($HCO3^-$)   Phosphate ions

However, there are considerable differences in some concentrations of these materials between the two fluids. Sodium and chloride are major ions of extracellular fluid (145 mM (millimoles) and 110 mM respectively) whereas in intracellular fluid they are only 15 and

10 mM. Hydrogen carbonate and glucose are also present in larger quantities in extracellular fluid. The remainder are higher in intracellular fluid than extracellular fluid, with potassium being the major ion (150 mM intracellular and 4 mM extracellular).

One might think that diffusion would cause these ions in solution to even up in time and, in fact, these ions do continuously leak into the other fluid compartment. Present in the cell membrane is a sodium/potassium pump that transports or ejects these 'leaked' ions back to their own fluid compartment. The pump uses energy from ATP in the cell to move these ions against the concentration gradient – a perfect example of active transport (see page 136).

This electro-chemical gradient is important in all cells, but particularly in nerve cells where it forms the basis for excitable nervous impulses. Calcium ions are important in nervous excitability as well and also in bone metabolism and blood clotting.

Blood plasma consists of water (93 per cent), electrolytes (ions) in similar quantities to extracellular fluid, plasma proteins (albumins, globulins and fibrinogen), dissolved gases (oxygen, carbon dioxide, nitrogen), nutrients (glucose, amino acids, lipids), vitamins, hormones and other trace elements. In addition, there are waste products of metabolism such as urea, uric acid, creatinine and bilirubin.

Urine derived from plasma contains similar substances, with the exception of the plasma proteins, the molecules of which are too large to be filtered through into the renal nephron, and nutrients that are reabsorbed from the nephron to be returned to the bloodstream. Once again, actual quantities of these substances in urine vary from plasma, as you will remember that one of the main functions of the renal system is to remove many waste products of metabolism. The table below illustrates some of the differences between plasma and urine.

Component	Plasma (per cent)	Urine (per cent)
Water	93	95
Urea	0.02	2
Uric acid	0.003	0.05
Sodium	0.3	0.6
Potassium	0.02	0.15
Chloride	0.35	0.5
Phosphate	0.003	0.12

Assessment activity 4.5

Look again at the table above and answer the following questions:

a Which components become more concentrated as they pass from the plasma into urine?
b What is the ratio of the percentage for urea concentration in plasma and urine?
c Account for the differences in water percentages between the two body fluids.
d Suggest reasons why the percentages of sodium and chloride ions are higher in urine than potassium.
e Construct a bar chart for the components of plasma and urine, excluding water.

The influence of blood glucose on metabolism

The production of more than 2.5 dm³ of urine per day is considered to be excessive and may have an underlying medical cause. Undiagnosed diabetics drink excessive volumes of liquid and produce excessive urine. As the level of blood sugar rises it might cross the 'threshold' level for the kidneys and spill over into the urine. A higher level of glucose in the urine (glycosuria) draws fluid with it, so consequently a person suffering from untreated diabetes mellitus produces larger quantities of urine loaded with sugar and constantly feels thirsty. If water/liquid cannot be supplied, dehydration can result with severe metabolic damage and risk to life. Similarly, body cells become surrounded by tissue fluid with a high concentration of glucose and water is drawn from them causing dehydration of cells and severe metabolic disturbance. Diabetes mellitus is a life-threatening condition if left untreated.

Think it over
Refer back to page 139 – how the tonicity of the environment affects cellular metabolism – and analyse this information in relation to the cells of an untreated diabetic.

Gaseous exchange

The composition of inspired and expired air

Although the atmospheric air that you breathe contains mainly gaseous nitrogen (unusable in this state by living organisms) there is enough oxygen to sustain life. Carbon dioxide is present in only small amounts, which at first sight may seem surprising – considering that carbon dioxide is a waste product of respiration and a well-publicised major cause of pollution. Water vapour content depends on the weather and climate.

Expired air reverses 4 per cent of the oxygen into carbon dioxide, saturates the gases with moisture and is warmer (and cleaner). The table gives a comparison of inspired and expired air.

Component	Inspired air (per cent)	Expired air (per cent)
Nitrogen	80	80
Oxygen	20	16
Carbon dioxide	0.04	4
Water vapour	Variable	Saturated
Temperature	Variable	Close to body temperature
Cleanliness	Variable	Fairly clean

Note: Percentages are rounded up so do not necessarily add up to 100 per cent.

The medulla of the brain contains clusters of neurones that represent the respiratory centre; one cluster is responsible for inspiration and the other for expiration. In normal quiet breathing, the inspiratory centre is active for approximately two seconds followed by the expiratory centre activity for three seconds.

Think it over
Calculate the normal breathing rate for an individual in normal quiet breathing and compare with the above timings.

141

You are aware that you can suddenly hold your breath, take deeper breaths than normal or speed up the rate of breathing. Above the medulla, in a part of the brain called the pons, there are two further centres associated with respiration; these are:

- the pneumotaxic centre – this inhibits the inspiratory centre as the lungs fill with air so allowing expiration to occur
- the apneustic centre that sends impulses to the inspiratory centre to prolong inspiration (see Figure 4.25).

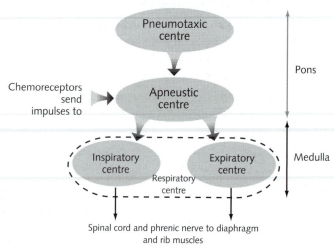

Figure 4.25 The location of the main centres for respiratory control

Expiration is often described as an elastic recoil of the lungs and a relaxation of the intercostal muscles and the diaphragm. This is so in quiet breathing, but in forced expirations, such as blowing into a peak flow meter, expiratory centre neurones actually send impulses to the muscles, causing expiration.

Cells require a constant supply of oxygen to carry out the oxidation of glucose or respiration. There is no storage facility for oxygen in the body, so breathing in supplies of oxygen every few seconds is vital to maintain the internal environment supply of dissolved oxygen. Waste products of metabolism, in this case carbon dioxide and water, must be regularly eliminated by exhalation to prevent an accumulation and disturbed metabolism. For more information on the respiratory system, refer to page 154.

Homeostatic regulation

In order for body cells to function properly, and indeed survive, conditions around their cell membranes must remain stable or within physiological limits. This is often called the *internal environment* and consists of the extracellular fluid which bathes cells. *Homeostasis* is defined as the maintenance of the constant internal environment. It means that concentrations of ions and nutrients, water, temperature, pH, and more must be kept within a range compatible with correct functioning of cells.

Homeostatic responses are controlled by the nervous and endocrine systems. The nervous system has receptors which detect when deviations from the normal start to occur, impulses are sent to a control centre, often within the brain, and impulses are then sent to effectors to counteract the change. Endocrine organs work in just the same way, but they use chemicals in the form of hormones instead. Such a system needs constant monitoring to ensure that the mechanism for counteracting the change does not act too far. Therefore a system incorporates a feedback loop of which there two types: negative feedback and positive feedback.

- *Negative feedback loops* check the original deviation to ensure that the original state has returned, such loops are very common in the body as we shall see. Example of negative feedback loops are body temperature regulation and water balance.

- *Positive feedback loops* enhance the original stimulus pushing the change onwards. This does not return the status quo, tends to produce a 'bust' situation and is therefore not in common use in the human body. An example is the uterine contractions leading to the birth of a baby.

Homeostasis of body temperature

Humans are the only animals that can survive in both tropical and arctic conditions and this is largely due to negative feedback homeostatic mechanisms for thermo-regulation, which means that under these conditions body temperature varies very little. The mechanism is shown in Figures 4.26 and 4.27.

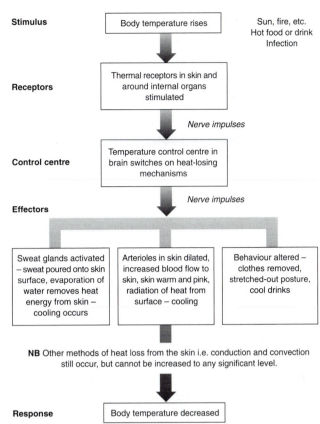

Figure 4.26 The homeostatic mechanism for regulating rising body temperature

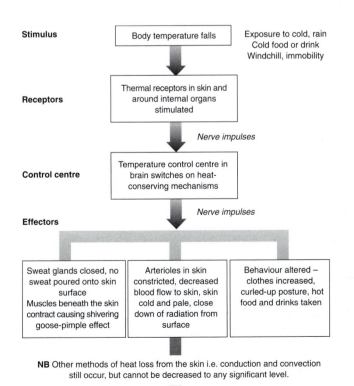

At all times, the main aim of the thermo-regulatory system is to maintain the vital organs of the human body (often referred to as the *core*) at a constant temperature, at the expense of the peripheral areas, chiefly the skin.

Figure 4.27 The homeostatic mechanism for regulating falling body temperature

Think it over

When you are feeling hot, you will often have a very cold drink or an ice cream; this cools the interior of the body and eventually the bloodstream. The effect of this is to switch on the heat conservation mechanism that will result in keeping more heat in the body. Alternatively, taking a hot drink will increase the temperature of the blood and switch on the heat-losing systems, such as sweating, that will in time cool you down! (See Figure 4.28.)

Make a flow chart to show how these effects come about. Next time you are feeling hot try these two effects.

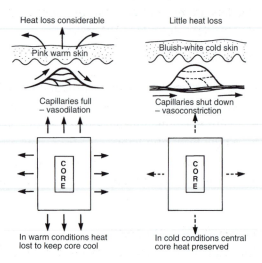

Figure 4.28 Temperature regulation

Human body systems

Structure and functions of blood

Blood

Blood consists of straw-coloured plasma in which several types of cells are carried (see Figure 4.29). Plasma is mainly water in which various substances are dissolved, such as gases like oxygen and carbon dioxide, nutrients like glucose and amino acids, salts, enzymes and hormones. There is also a combination of important proteins collectively known as plasma proteins; these have roles in blood clotting, transport, defence and osmosis.

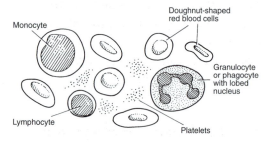

Figure 4.29 Different blood cells

The most numerous cells in the plasma are red blood cells (erythrocytes) which are bi-concave in shape, very small and packed with iron-containing haemoglobin that is responsible for combining with oxygen from the lungs. In the mature state, these cells have lost their nuclei (and consequently their power to divide) in order to have a larger surface area and carry more haemoglobin. They have a limited life of approximately 120 days.

White cells or leucocytes are larger cells, which are less numerous and have various roles in defending the body against invasion. There are several types, but the most numerous are the granulocytes, phagocytes or polymorphs that are capable of engulfing foreign material such as bacteria and carbon particles. Granulocytes carry lobed nuclei and granules scattered throughout the cell material. Large monocytes are also efficient at engulfing foreign material (phagocytosis) and both granulocytes and monocytes are able to leave the circulation and travel through tissue.

Lymphocytes are smaller cells containing round nuclei and clear cytoplasm. They assist in the production of antibodies which form part of the plasma proteins. Thrombocytes or platelets are not full cells but products of the fragmentation of much larger cells. They play a vital role in blood clotting.

The functions of blood can be listed as follows:

- main system of transport throughout the body – oxygen, carbon dioxide, nutrients such as amino acids and glucose, hormones, antibodies, urea, etc.
- defence against disease – clotting, action of leucocytes
- temperature regulation – distribution of heat from warmer places such as the liver and muscles to cooler places like limbs to maintain an even temperature
- aids in reproduction by stiffening the penis during insemination of the female.

Lymphatic system

The lymphatic system also forms part of the cardiovascular system. The lymphatic system begins as closed-ended *lymphatic capillaries* which lie in the spaces between cells (see Figure 4.30). They unite to form larger and larger vessels passing upwards eventually to join the great veins in the neck. At several points in this lymphatic circulation, the lymph fluid passes through small nodules known as *lymph nodes*, which are scattered about the body in groups.

Lymph nodes contain lymphocytes and macrophages which destroy any microbes which have entered the lymphatic vessels from the tissue spaces. They do this by initiating the antigen-antibody response (sometimes called the *immune response*) and by macrophages carrying out *phagocytosis*, which destroys the microbes.

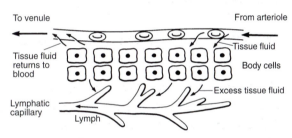

Figure 4.30 The relationship between blood capillaries, cells and lymphatic capillaries (lymph vessels)

The cardiovascular system

The heart is a muscular pump which forces blood around a system of blood vessels, namely arteries, veins and capillaries. Blood carries dissolved oxygen to the body cells and at the same time removes carbon dioxide and water. However, blood also distributes heat, hormones, nutrients and enzymes around the body as well as transporting urea between the liver and the kidneys for excretion with many other products.

The adult heart is the size of a clenched fist located in the thoracic cavity in between the lungs, protected by the rib cage (see Figure 4.31). It is surrounded by a tough pericardium that contains a thin film of fluid to reduce friction.

The heart is a double pump, each side consisting of an upper chamber (the atrium) and a lower chamber (the ventricle). The right-

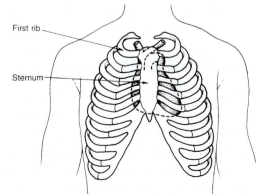

Figure 4.31 The position of the heart

sided pump contains deoxygenated blood and is totally separate from the left side that contains oxygenated blood. Each chamber has a major blood vessel either entering or leaving the heart. The veins pour blood into the atria and the ventricles bear arteries that carry blood away from the heart.

It is helpful to remember that atria have veins, ventricles have arteries: A and V in each case, never two As or two Vs.

The right pump receives blood from the body tissues, having off-loaded its oxygen, and pumps the blood to the lungs for re-oxygenation. The left pump receives blood from the lungs, fully loaded with oxygen, and distributes it to the body tissue. You will notice that the blood travels twice through the heart in one circuit around the body. This is known as a double circulation. Figure 4.32 illustrates this, but notice how the right and left halves have been artificially separated.

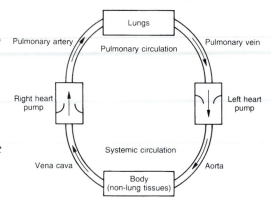

Figure 4.32 Double circulation: blood flows through the heart twice in one circuit

One circulation is to and from the lungs and is known as the pulmonary circulation. Whenever you see or hear the word pulmonary you will know that it is referring to the lungs; so the artery taking blood from the right ventricle is the pulmonary artery and the vein returning blood from the lungs to the left side of the heart is the pulmonary vein(s), in fact there are four of these. The other circulation is called the systemic circulation because it carries blood to and from the body systems, except the lungs of course!

The main artery of the body is the aorta which leaves the left ventricle, and the main vein returning blood to the right atrium is the vena cava. There are two divisions of this vein, the superior and inferior venae cavae returning blood from the head/neck and remainder of the trunk respectively.

The semi-lunar valves are located where the main arteries leave the ventricles. All these valves have the same purpose – to ensure that blood only flows one way through the heart.

You will also notice the septum dividing the right and left sides of the heart, valve tendons and papillary muscles in the ventricles. The papillary muscles contract and pull on the valve tendons a tiny fraction of a second before the main ventricular muscle contracts, so that the contraction does not force the tricuspid and bicuspid valves inside out. The valves make noises when they close, but not when they are open (rather like clapping your hands) and these noises are the heart sounds that doctors listen for with a stethoscope.

Theory into practice

Ask to borrow a stethoscope and listen to either your own or a partner's heart sounds. They make sounds rather like lubb, dup, lubb, dup.

By counting each pair of lubb, dups for the duration of one minute, you would have a very accurate measurement of heart rate.

The events that occur during one complete heartbeat are more correctly called the **cardiac cycle** (see page 147).

Think it over

Study the labelled diagram of the heart (Figure 4.33) and find all the major blood vessels you have studied.

You will need to examine the diagram of the heart again to see four valves labelled. Two of these, the tricuspid and bicuspid, are located at the junctions of the atrium and ventricle on each side.

You can remember these because the TRIcuspid valve is on the RIghT side (a rearrangement of the letters) so that the other side, the left, must be the bicuspid valve.

The *myocardium* is the name for the heart muscle.
The *endocardium* is the name of the smooth endothelial lining of the cavities.

Superior vena cava

Arch of aorta

Semi-lunar valve or pulmonary valve

Pulmonary artery

Endocardium

Myocardium

Left atrium

Right atrium

Bicuspid valve

Tricuspid valve

Semi-lunar valve or aortic valve

Right ventricle

Left ventricle

Inferior vena cava

Septum

Branch of coronary artery

The *chordae tendineae* and *papillary muscles* tie the edges of the valves to the ventricular wall and stops the blood from flowing backward.

Figure 4.33 A section through the heart

Heart murmurs are extra sounds heard between the normal heart sounds, some are significant and indicate heart problems, while others carry no significance. They are usually the result of disturbed blood flow.

The cardiac cycle

If the heart rate, at rest, is counted at around 70 beats each minute, then the time for each beat is $1 \div 70$ minutes or $60 \div 70$ seconds. This works out as approximately 0.8 seconds for each beat of the heart.

If this is represented by 8 small squares, each to the value of 0.1 second, then we can produce a diagram as shown in Figure 4.34. If we wish to show events happening in the atria and ventricles during this period, we can have two 'timelines'. The shaded squares represent when the cardiac muscle is contracting and the plain squares, relaxation.

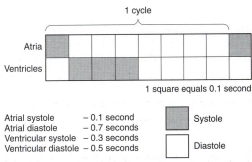

1 cycle

Atria

Ventricles

1 square equals 0.1 second

Atrial systole	– 0.1 second
Atrial diastole	– 0.7 seconds
Ventricular systole	– 0.3 seconds
Ventricular diastole	– 0.5 seconds

Systole

Diastole

Figure 4.34 Timed events in the cardiac cycle: allocations of systole and diastole

Contraction phases are called *systole* or *systolic periods* and relaxation periods *diastole* or *diastolic periods* (see Figure 4.35). These names are also used for the two figures in a blood pressure measurement.

The events in the cardiac cycle can be described as follows:

1 Atria contract, blood is pushed into ventricles under pressure.
2 Ventricles bulge with blood, pressure forces the tricuspid and bicuspid valves shut. This causes the first heart sound to be heard with a stethoscope; it sounds like 'lubb'. Atria relax and begin to fill with blood.
3 Ventricles begin contraction, pressure in blood rises and forces open the aortic and pulmonary valves.
4 Systole in the ventricles pushes blood into the aorta and pulmonary artery. These are elastic walled and begin to expand.
5 Ventricles begin to relax and blood falls back with the effect of gravity for a few moments and catches in the pockets of the semi-lunar valves of the aorta and pulmonary artery, pressing them together and closing off the opening. This causes the second heart sound which, through a stethoscope, sounds like 'dup'.
6 Tricuspid and bicuspid valves are forced open and blood rushes from the filled atria into the ventricles during their diastolic phase. On being filled to about 70 per cent capacity, atrial systole occurs and the heart has completed the cycle at the point where it started.

Note: in a healthy heart, both the two atria and the two ventricles contract simultaneously.

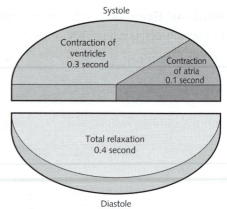

Figure 4.35 Cardiac cycle: at rest

Blood vessels

These tubes, together with the heart, make up the circulatory system. The main types of blood vessel are:

- arteries
- veins
- capillaries (see Figure 4.36).

Each type has functional and anatomical differences, which are summarised in the table below.

Each organ has an arterial and a venous supply bringing blood to the organ and taking blood away respectively (see Figure 4.37). The link vessels supplying the cells of the tissues of the organ are the *capillaries*. A protein-free plasma filtrate driven out of the leaky (selectively permeable) capillaries becomes the tissue or interstitial fluid which supplies the cells. It is through the

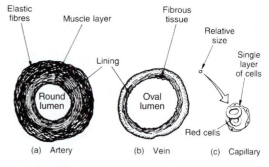

Figure 4.36 Blood vessels, transverse sections

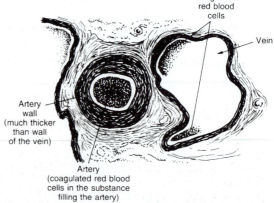

Figure 4.37 Transverse section through a vein and an artery

blood and tissue fluid that raw materials for respiration, hormones, enzymes, etc. get to the cell organelles. This is also the route for communication, as the circulatory system must go to all organs (see Figure 4.38).

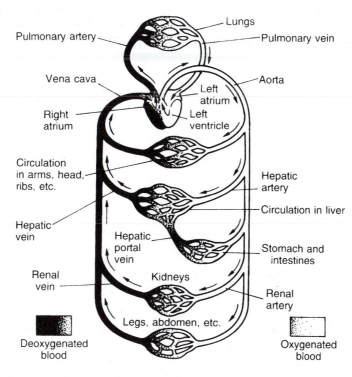

Figure 4.38 The human circulatory system

Arteries	Veins	Capillaries
Functional differences	**Functional differences**	**Functional differences**
Carry blood away from heart to organs	Carry blood to heart from the organs	Connect arteries to veins
Carry blood under high pressure	Carry blood under low pressure	Arterioles and capillaries cause greatest drop in pressure due to overcoming the friction of blood passing through small vessels
Usually contain blood high in oxygen, low in carbon dioxide and water	Usually contain blood low in oxygen, high in carbon dioxide and water	Delivers protein-free plasma filtrate high in oxygen to cells and collects up respiratory waste products of carbon dioxide and water.
What are the exceptions?		
Large arteries close to the heart help the intermittent flow from the ventricles become a continuous flow through the circulation		

Arteries	Veins	Capillaries
Anatomical differences	**Anatomical differences**	**Anatomical differences**
Large arteries close to the heart are almost entirely made of elastic tissue to expand and recoil with the outpouring of blood from the ventricles during systole	Veins have thinner walls than arteries	Capillaries have walls which are only one cell thick
	Veins have oval spaces in centre (lumina)	Capillaries have leaky walls (permeable) enabling small molecular nutrients and dissolved gases to exchange with cells
Arteries have thick walls with corrugated lining and round lumens	Veins over a certain diameter contain valves which prevent blood flowing backwards under the influence of gravity	No cell can lie more than a few cells from a capillary
Walls consist of three layers, endothelial lining, muscle and elastic tissue, and an outer tough fibrous layer	Veins usually lie between skeletal muscles which squeeze blood flow onwards during musclar activity	Capillaries often smaller than red blood cells which must distort to pass through
	Walls have three coats but far less muscle and elastic tissue and more fibrous tissue	

Cardiac output

Each ventricle has a capacity of approximately 70 ml of blood. This is called the stroke volume as it is the quantity expelled at each beat of the heart. With moderate exercise and stressful circumstances the stroke volume can increase to 110 ml or as high as 140 ml in strenuous activity! Heart rate at rest varies a great deal, but in untrained people it is usually between 60 and 80 beats per minute. Cardiac output is the volume of blood expelled in one minute so is the result of heart rate multiplied by stroke volume.

Think it over

George is a highly trained athlete whilst his friend Ali watches sport on television. Find each man's cardiac output at rest using the following data:

	George	Ali
Stroke volume	90 ml	70 ml
Heart rate at rest	58 bts/min	70 bts/min
Cardiac output	ml/min	ml/min

Comment on the differences in the data between the two men and suggest reasons for the differences. What do you think would happen to their relative cardiac outputs if the two men had to run vigorously to catch a bus?

Cardiac muscle

The muscle which makes up the heart walls is not found anywhere else in the body. The muscle fibres form a branching network along which nervous impulses pass with great speed. One remarkable feature of cardiac muscle is its ability to contract rhythmically without being supplied by nervous impulses; this is called myogenicity. When isolated from a nerve supply, the atrial muscle contracts at a faster rate than the ventricular muscle; however, in a healthy heart both rates of contraction are governed by the autonomic nervous system (see Figure 12.1, page 480).

Nervous conduction through the heart

A cluster of special cells lies in the upper part of the right atrium and every few moments they become excited, sending nerve impulses across the branching network of the atrial muscle fibres to cause contraction. This cluster is called the *sino-atrial node* (shortened to the S-A node) or more commonly termed the *pacemaker*, because this is indeed what these cells do. These impulses are caught by yet another group of cells forming the *atrio-ventricular node* (A-V node) and relayed to a special band of tissue made of large *Purkinje fibres*, adapted to conduct impulses efficiently. The A-V node delays the transmission to allow the atria to complete their beat. The Purkinje fibres form the *Bundle of His* (or A-V bundle) which crosses the fibrous ring separating atria and ventricles, and then divides into *left* and *right bundle branches* running either side of the septum before spreading over the ventricles (see Figure 4.39).

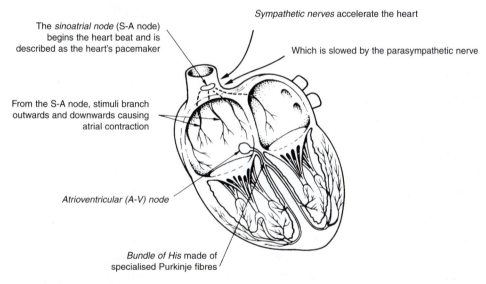

The *sinoatrial node* (S-A node) begins the heart beat and is described as the heart's pacemaker

Sympathetic nerves accelerate the heart

Which is slowed by the parasympathetic nerve

From the S-A node, stimuli branch outwards and downwards causing atrial contraction

Atrioventricular (A-V) node

Bundle of His made of specialised Purkinje fibres

Figure 4.39 The heart's conduction system

Impulse conduction is very fast so that the two ventricles beat together to force the blood around the body organs.

If the conduction system fails, artificial pacemakers can now be fitted which supply electrical stimuli from their batteries to stimulate the cardiac muscle direct.

Nervous control

Despite this elaborate conduction system, the heart also has a nervous control to allow for an almost instant response to the dangers and stresses of everyday life. There are two sets of nerves constantly making a play for control over the heart's rate by influencing the S-A node, which is only rarely allowed to beat at its own pace. Both nervous commands form part of the *autonomic nervous system* which co-ordinates and controls the internal organs (or viscera) of the body. One set continuously tries to calm the heart down, slowing its pace and reducing the strength of the beat. This is the *parasympathetic* branch of the autonomic nervous system, which unceasingly aims for peace and contentment. The other branch is the *sympathetic*, aiming for increased strength of heartbeats and a stirring of pace. It is called into action during muscular work and stress (see Figure 4.39). The sympathetic branch is closely associated with the release of the hormone *adrenaline*.

Pulse

A pulse can be felt whenever an artery crosses over a bone, thus there are many places in the body where pulses can be felt. The most common places for feeling a pulse are at the wrist and in the neck. The wrist pulse is felt below the thumb on the inner side of both arms and the neck pulses on either side of the trachea inside the strap muscle of the neck.

Theory into practice

Practise finding your own and your partner's wrist and neck pulses and record the number of beats in 15 seconds. Multiply by 4 to obtain the rate per minute.

Blood pressure

Blood pressure (BP) is the pressure exerted by the blood on the walls of the blood vessels and is generated by the contraction of the left ventricle during the heartbeat. The new units for measuring BP are kilopascals (kPa), but you will find that most establishments still record in the older traditional units of millimetres of mercury.

A blood pressure reading looks like a fraction, but it is not. It is two figures separated by a line; the upper figure represents systolic BP at the height of ventricular systole while the lower diastolic figure is the pressure when the ventricles are relaxed.

The highest BP is found in the aorta, large and medium arteries and after that there is a gradual drop in pressure throughout the circulation, falling to zero as the blood returns to the right atrium (see Figure 4.40).

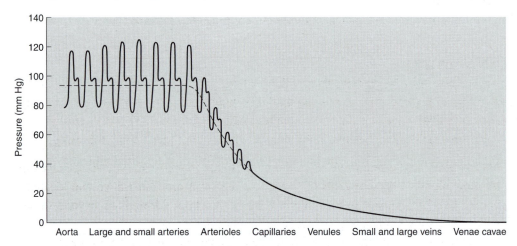

Figure 4.40 Blood pressure in the main vessels of the circulation

The arterioles account for the greatest drop in BP as the blood flows through them. They have muscular walls that can contract (producing vasoconstriction) or relax (vasodilation) and this is under the control of the vasomotor centre in the brain.

Vasoconstriction causes BP to rise, but the arterioles are not the only factor involved in controlling BP (see below).

Think it over

Imagine that your are lying in bed, your head, heart and legs are in the horizontal plane and your heart is delivering blood to every part of your body. Then the alarm clock rings and you leap out of bed to get ready for work. Your head is now much higher than your heart and your legs are far lower. If your BP did not change to drive blood up to your head, you would faint, becoming horizontal again. Changing BP depends on a combination of adjustments of blood volume, resistance from the arterioles (vascular resistance), stroke volume and heart rate.

Blood volume

It might appear surprising that blood volume can change and so influence blood pressure. The spleen acts as a reservoir of blood and can add more blood to the system when necessary. The veins, also, being thin-walled can allow blood to pool in the lower legs (see below on venous return).

Blood flow

This is the volume of blood which flows through a tissue in a period of time – usually mililitres per second. The speed or velocity of blood flow is inversely proportional to the cross-sectional area of the blood vessels it is flowing through. The aorta has a wide lumen but it is only one single vessel, whereas there are milions of capillaries with a huge cross-sectional area between them although they are microscopic. This means that blood flow through the aorta (40 ml per second), large arteries and veins is rapid whereas blood flow through the capillaries is very slow, in fact less than 1 ml per second.

Think it over

Why is it important that blood flows only slowly through capillaries?

Venous return

This is the return of blood from the capillaries back to the right atrium of the heart. As seen in Figure 4.40 the pressure in capillaries, venules and veins is quite low. Although this pressure difference is small it is usually enough to keep blood moving and so maintain cardiac output, but two additional boosts are provided by the following:

- The skeletal muscle pump. Veins in the lower limbs also contain valves opening only to allow blood to flow towards the heart. As the veins are thin-walled and located between skeletal muscle groups, blood is prevented from falling back beyond these valves when the contracting leg muscles squeeze the veins.
- The respiratory pump. We will see that to effect inhalation a negative pressure is produced in the thorax by the descending diaphragm muscle. At the same time this causes a positive pressure in the abdomen below. Consequently blood moves from the abdominal veins to the thoracic veins down the pressure gradient.

In these ways, blood is returned to the heart to complete the systemic circulation.

Functions of the cardiovascular system can be listed as follows:

- circulate blood around the body
- assist with absorption, transport and distribution of digested food materials
- assist with the elimination of waste products of metabolism
- create blood pressure that is vital to distribute body fluids
- transport dissolved gases to their appropriate destinations to maintain respiration
- transport blood cells and antibodies important in the defence of the body to appropriate locations
- regulate the temperature of the body
- transport hormones to their target organs
- regulate the flow of blood to appropriate organs when required, such as during exercise or in critical situations.

Breathing and respiration

There are two definitions crucial to your understanding of the respiratory system. These definitions are as follows:

- Respiration – this is the release of energy from the breakdown of food molecules.
- Energy – best described as a stored ability to do work.

Aerobic and anaerobic respiration

There are two types of respiration – aerobic and anaerobic. **Aerobic** respiration is the type usually carried out by our body cells and involves the use of oxygen from the air around us. It is very efficient and produces a lot of energy for work by the body, such as pumping blood around the body, digesting food and walking.

Anaerobic respiration takes place when the muscle cells are working so hard that the amount of oxygen required to release the energy cannot be taken in sufficient quantities by the lungs and air passages to carry out aerobic respiration. It can be thought of as a temporary emergency shortcut for the body. It is much less efficient than aerobic respiration and produces less energy; it also causes toxic waste products, such as lactic acid, that can only be allowed to accumulate for a short period. Running at maximum speed for a few minutes uses energy mainly produced anaerobically, whilst running longer races – such as the 1500 metres or even a marathon – means that energy must be produced by aerobic respiration. This is why athletes tend to specialise in races of particular distances.

It is aerobic respiration which takes place most of the time. The link between the respiratory system and respiration is described below.

The respiratory system comprises the anatomical structures and the physiological processes that take the vital oxygen into the body and transport it to the body cells where aerobic respiration can be carried out and, at the same time, eliminate its waste products. Respiration and energy release can only take place inside body cells.

The word equation for aerobic respiration is:

Food (glucose sugar) + oxygen = energy + carbon dioxide + water.

The chemical equation for respiration is:

$C_6H_{12}O_6 + 6O_2 = 6H_2O + 6CO_2$ + energy.

$C_6H_{12}O_6$ represents one molecule of glucose sugar, $6O_2$ and $6CO_2$ is six molecules of oxygen and carbon dioxide and, finally, $6H_2O$ is six molecules of water.

Carbon dioxide and water are waste products and need to be eliminated from the body.

The study of the process of respiration is facilitated by subdivision into four distinct parts:

- breathing
- gaseous exchange
- transport in the blood
- cell respiration.

Breathing

The chest or thorax is an airtight box containing the lungs and their tubes, the bronchi (see Figure 4.41). There are two lungs (right and left), each with its own bronchus, which unite to form the windpipe or trachea. The trachea joins the back of the throat or pharynx, which connects with both mouth and nose, which are of course open to external air. All these tubes are lined with mucus-secreting ciliated cells and have either C-shaped rings or small plates of cartilage in their walls to prevent collapse. Mucus is the sticky white jelly-like material used to lubricate and trap dust particles that can enter by external passages.

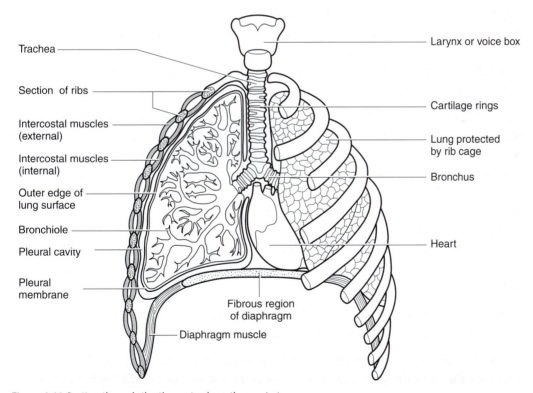

Figure 4.41 Section through the thorax to show the respiratory organs

The lungs themselves have a thin, outer covering of membrane called the pleura and are located behind the chest wall which is also internally lined with pleura. Between the two layers of pleura is a thin film of moisture, which exerts surface tension, so allowing the two layers to slide up and down but not allowing them to pull apart easily. This means that when the chest wall moves, the lungs are usually pulled with them.

Think it over

Read the preceding paragraph again and study Figure 4.43. You will have heard of the condition known as pleurisy and might know that there are two types – 'wet' and 'dry' pleurisy. It can be painful to breathe if you have pleurisy. What do you think has happened to the chest of a client who has pleurisy?

Forming the wall of the chest, outside the pleura, is the bony rib cage with two sets of oblique muscles joining them together – these are known as the intercostal muscles (*inter* means between; *costal* means ribs). A sheet of muscle called the diaphragm forms the floor of the chest. The diaphragm is dome-shaped, with the highest part in the centre and the edges firmly attached to the lowest ribs. The chest is an airtight cavity with the trachea being the only way for air to enter.

Rhythmic breathing is controlled by a part of the brain known as the respiratory centre and the process is shown in the flow chart in Figure 4.43 (see also Figure 4.42). It is necessary for you to know one of the gas laws to understand this. Volume and pressure of a gas are inversely related. In simple terms, when volume gets larger, pressure decreases and vice versa.

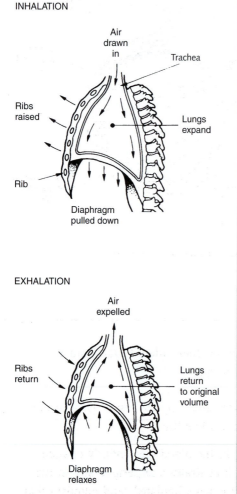

INHALATION

Air drawn in

Trachea

Ribs raised

Lungs expand

Rib

Diaphragm pulled down

EXHALATION

Air expelled

Ribs return

Lungs return to original volume

Diaphragm relaxes

Figure 4.42 Changes during inhalation

Nervous impulses from the brain cause the diaphragm and intercostal muscles to contract

| Diaphragm flattens and the intercostal muscles cause the ribs to move upwards and outwards | Volume of the chest increases, **so the** pressure inside the chest must **decrease** |

| Surface tension between the pleura drags the lungs with the chest wall. As they expand, they fill with air | Air, containing oxygen rushes down the trachea and bronchi to equalise the pressure with the external environment – **inhalation** |

| After a few seconds, the nervous impulses stop arriving and the elastic tissue in the lung causes recoil: the diaphragm rises and the ribs lower | The volume of the chest decreases, **so** pressure **increases**, causing air to rush out of the trachea – **exhalation** |

| The cycle repeats after a few minutes because the respiratory control centre becomes active again sending more nervous impulses |

Figure 4.43 The process of breathing

Key issue

A wound in the chest wall provides a 'shortcut' for air and destroys the surface tension between the pleura, causing the lung to collapse. It is essential to place a large sterile or clean pad over the wound as quickly as possible to prevent this from happening. Although a healthy person can manage with only one functioning lung, in this case oxygen-carrying blood will have been lost and the casualty may be in shock – making the situation life-threatening.

Gaseous exchange

Inside the lungs, smaller and smaller branches of the bronchi, called bronchioles, open into thousands of air sacs, each consisting of a cluster of alveoli. Each air sac with its alveoli and bronchiole looks rather like a bunch of grapes on a stem.

The wall of each alveolus is only one cell thick and surrounded on its outside by tiny blood vessels called capillaries – these, too, have walls only one cell thick. The air in each alveolus is separated from the blood in the capillary by very thin walls, only two flat cells thick. A film of moisture in which the respiratory gases dissolve lines each alveolus. The walls of the alveoli contain elastic fibres capable of expansion and recoil.

The process by which gases exchange across these walls is called **diffusion** (see Figure 4.44).

Dissolved oxygen will pass from the high concentration in the alveolar air across the two thin walls into the blood in the capillary that has previously unloaded most of its oxygen to the cells of the body. Dissolved carbon dioxide and water have been picked up from the body cells as waste products of respiration and are high in the blood, but low in the alveolar air, so they pass in the reverse direction. Exhalation removes them into the atmosphere.

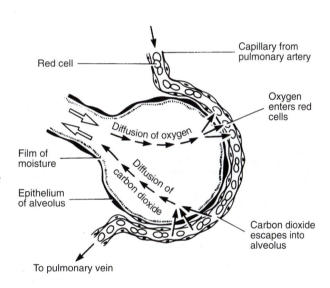

Figure 4.44 Gaseous exchange in the alveoli

Think it over

Figure 4.45 below shows a vertical section through the chest. Identify the features represented by the letters A to G and describe their purpose.

The respiratory centres in the brain alternately excite and suppress the activity of the neurones supplying the respiratory nerves that control breathing.

Nervous receptors sensitive to chemicals dissolved in the blood (particularly oxygen, carbon dioxide and hydrogen ions) are located both centrally and peripherally in the body. These chemoreceptors initiate reflexes which when stimulated send impulses that cause alterations in breathing activity.

The main factors that affect breathing and respiration are:

- exercise
- emotion
- altitude
- adrenaline release.

All of these increase ventilation to an appropriate level and when the stimulating factor is removed, ventilation returns to normal levels.

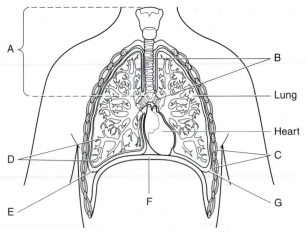

Figure 4.45 Vertical section through the chest

Excretion

As you take in the raw materials to sustain life and living processes, so waste products are produced as a result of the chemical reactions that make up the metabolism. Waste products can be gases, such as carbon dioxide, water, salts and nitrogenous materials. Carbon dioxide and some water can be removed by exhaling air from the lungs, but the main route out of the body for most of the water, salts and nitrogenous materials is in the urine produced by the kidneys and voided to the exterior from the bladder and urethra.

You may also think that faeces or stools eliminated from the rectum or back passage are also waste material. In fact, most of this material has mainly passed through the centre of the body (from the mouth to the anus) and therefore, has not become part of the 'flesh' of the body. The exception to this is the brown coloration of the faeces that is a pigment left from the breakdown of old red blood cells.

Excretion can be defined as *the elimination of waste products of metabolism from the body.* It is carried out by the:

- lungs
- kidneys
- liver
- skin.

Assessment activity 4.6

Compile a three-column table using the excretory organs listed above in the first column and write in the second column the substances actually excreted by those organs. In the last column write in the way those substances are excreted. For example, the lungs (first column) excrete carbon dioxide and water (second column) in exhaled air (third column). You may need to research some of the other information in a biology textbook.

The renal system

The renal system consists of two kidneys and the tubes leading from them to the bladder called the ureters, the bladder and the urethra (see Figure 4.46). The only difference between males and females is that the urethra in the male is longer and also serves as part of the reproductive system as it is used to convey semen (spermatozoa and gland secretions) during copulation. Short renal arteries leave the aorta to enter each kidney and renal veins carry the blood from the kidneys to the inferior vena cava. The kidneys are dark red in colour because they receive one quarter of the cardiac output.

The kidneys
Each kidney holds approximately one million microscopic units called nephrons that are responsible for producing urine (see Figure 4.47). Urine travels to the bladder down the ureters and is voided at regular intervals from the bladder via the urethra.

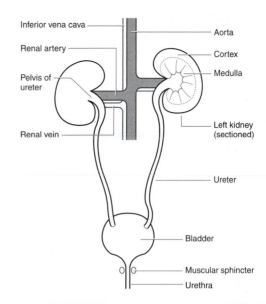

Figure 4.46 The renal system

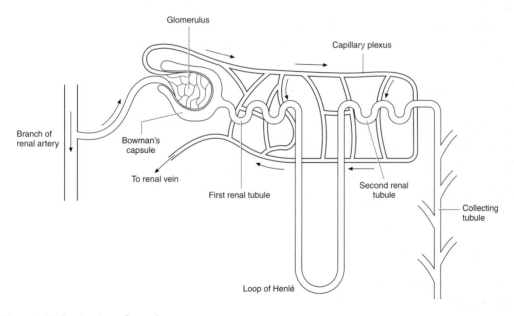

Figure 4.47 The structure of a nephron

The renal artery enters the kidney and breaks up into many tiny capillaries that form knots called *glomeruli*, held tightly inside the first cup-shaped part of the nephrons – the Bowman's capsule. The capillary, which exits from each glomerulus, is narrower than that which entered, resulting in a 'traffic jam' of blood and raised pressure. The pressure is responsible for forcing out about 10 per cent of the plasma through the one-cell thick wall of the Bowman's capsule and glomerulus to enter the cavity of the Bowman's capsule.

Note that blood cells and plasma proteins are too large to be filtered and remain in the blood. This process is called ultrafiltration and it is dependent on the fairly small glomerular pressure.

Think it over

If an individual suffers from a haemorrhage or severe shock, their BP falls due to a lack of circulating blood; this leads to a fall in glomerular pressure and a decrease in the amount of renal filtrate produced. Why is this an advantage in the short term?

The fluid is called glomerular or renal filtrate and it is not yet urine. It consists of water, urea, salts, glucose, amino acids and other dissolved materials. Many of these are useful to the body and cannot be wasted, so the rest of the nephron is concerned with re-absorption of useful materials and tailoring the composition of urine to suit the needs of the body at any given time.

Think it over

John has a cardiac output of 5.75 dm^3/min. How much renal filtrate will he produce in his kidney nephrons in one hour?

We have already looked at the need for food and the fact that glucose and amino acids are used for energy, growth and repair, so they must be saved and returned to the blood. The first coiled part of the nephron tubule is closely surrounded by a capillary network, and is concerned with reabsorption of all glucose, all amino acids, 88 per cent of water and salts, particularly sodium and chloride ions, as these are important chemicals of body fluids.

There is no control over the selective reabsorption in the first renal tubule and the volume that passes on through the rest of the nephron is markedly reduced.

Key issue

Many people believe incorrectly that diabetes mellitus is a problem associated with the kidneys, probably because diabetic people can excrete urine loaded with sugar. In fact, the first renal tubule is able to reabsorb all the glucose from the renal filtrate in a non-diabetic person. When a diabetic person has an abnormally high blood sugar, perhaps three or four times greater than normal, then the renal tubule is simply not long enough to reabsorb all the glucose and the rest passes on into the urine, a condition known as glycosuria.

The renal filtrate passes on to the loop of Henlé and is now much reduced in volume, containing water, salts and urea. The concentration of urea has now increased significantly because of the reduced volume. This part of the nephron carries out a special task of producing a high sodium concentration in the surrounding medulla and this is responsible for concentrating urine. The second part of the renal tubule after the loop of Henlé tailors the water and salt concentrations to suit the body's circumstances, and it requires the assistance of the endocrine system in managing this.

Diuresis means a copious flow of urine and there are many natural substances which act as *diuretics*, such as tea and alcohol. You may have heard of a client or a relative who takes 'water' tablets; these are diuretic medicines and are often prescribed for people with a high BP.

Think it over

Why should diuretics help to reduce blood pressure?

It is worth knowing that one of the most important hormones in the body is called anti-diuretic hormone (ADH) which is produced by the pituitary gland and the hypothalamus in the brain. The name of this hormone should tell you that it helps to reduce the flow of urine.

As the filtrate passes down the second renal tubule the water is reabsorbed into the blood if antidiuretic hormone is present in the bloodstream. If the water has been reabsorbed, then it has left the filtrate, so the amount of water in the urine has been reduced and the volume is smaller. ADH is produced when body water is getting short and therefore the blood is more concentrated than it should be.

A hormone from the adrenal cortex called *aldosterone* similarly controls the amount of sodium in the body.

The filtrate runs through the area known as the medulla and this is an area where sodium has built up to a high concentration. Surplus water leaves the filtrate by osmosis in this area.

Urination

Once the relevant hormones have controlled the filtrate content, the fluid is known as urine and it flows from the tip of each kidney pyramid through the pelvis of the ureter, down the ureter itself to collect in the bladder. As the bladder approaches 70 per cent capacity, nervous impulses are sent to the brain and an individual feels the need to urinate. At a convenient time, the bladder muscle contracts, sphincters relax and urine is forced out through the urethra to the exterior. If the warning signals are continually ignored, then the bladder will empty itself automatically. This is what happens in babies before their nervous systems and muscular co-ordination are sophisticated enough to provide control. It can also happen in older people who may have suffered strokes or nervous and muscular degeneration so that they have lost control. Losing control over urination is termed incontinence.

The kidneys of some people fail to work effectively (renal failure) and they must either have regular dialysis to remove the waste products by a kidney machine or have a kidney transplant.

Digestion, absorption and assimilation of food

The purpose of digestion is to change the large complex molecules that make up our food into small soluble molecules which are capable of being absorbed through the wall of the gut into the bloodstream, in order to be used for energy in respiration and other raw materials. You will probably already be familiar with the main chemical components of food as shown in the table below.

Note: Protein, carbohydrate and fat form the bulk of our diets and are called **macronutrients**; vitamins and minerals are only required in tiny amounts and are called **micronutrients**.

In order to break the macronutrients down into small molecules, various parts of the digestive system produce biological catalysts called **enzymes**. Enzymes are specific to the material they break down and most names of enzymes end in -ase, so they are easily recognisable.

Chemical component in food	Types of food containing this component	Purpose of this type of food	End-product of digestion as small soluble molecule
Protein	Meat, fish, milk, cheese, eggs, soya bean	To provide raw materials for making new cells and repairing damaged cells	Amino acids
Carbohydrate	Bread, rice, pasta, sugar, cereals, cakes, sweets	To provide energy for respiration	Simple sugars such as glucose
Fats (lipids)	Butter, margarine, oils such as sunflower and olive oil, milk, cream, eggs	To protect vital organs and insulate the body, to carry some vitamins To provide materials for hormones (steroids) and cell membranes	Fatty acids and glycerol
Vitamins	Green vegetables, fruits, milk, fish liver oils, cereals, nuts	Do not provide kilojoules for energy, but are essential to many chemical processes in the body	Not required
Mineral salts	Similar to vitamins	To take part in chemical reactions, form important body fluids and pigments like haemoglobin	Not required
Fibre	Cereals, bread, fruits and vegetables	To prevent constipation, assist in preventing bowel disorders, give feeling of fullness so curbs appetite	Not digested
Water	Various foods and drink	To allow body fluids to flow, provide solvent for other chemicals, help regulate body temperature and eliminate waste products of metabolism	Absorbed into the bloodstream without change

Relatively few molecules of enzyme are required to break down many food molecules as enzymes themselves are not used up in the reactions. Enzymes are sensitive to temperature, working best around body temperature, and they are also sensitive to the pH of their surroundings. Some, like gastric protease, prefer acid conditions, some like lipase prefer alkaline conditions while salivary amylase prefers a neutral pH of 7.

The digestive system is a tube that extends from the mouth to the anus; it is dilated, folded and puckered in the various parts of its length. You will need to learn the names of the regions, their main purpose and the outcome of their activities. The whole structure is also known as the alimentary canal (see Figure 4.48).

Ingestion is the act of food being taken into the mouth, here it is mixed with saliva, chewed and rolled into a small ball suitable for swallowing (a *bolus*). Saliva contains an enzyme called salivary amylase and this starts the process of breaking down carbohydrate starch. Many people do not chew their food for long these days as food is well cooked and refined so the amylase has only a short time to work before the bolus passes quickly down the oesophagus into the stomach.

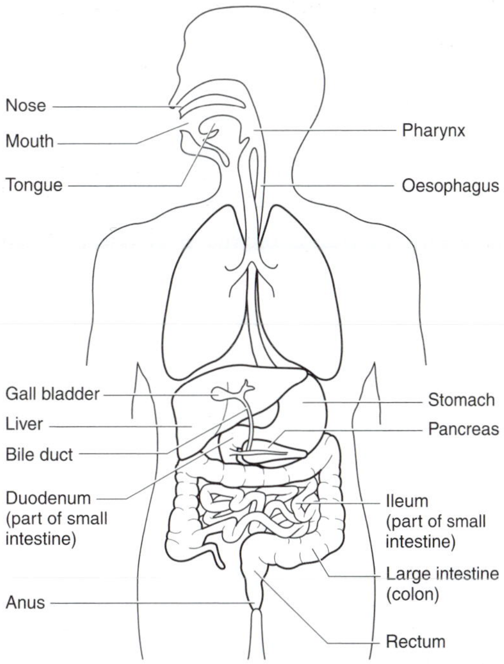

Figure 4.48 The alimentary canal

In the stomach

Food stays in the stomach for up to three hours and the strong muscles in the wall of the stomach churn the food into a loose paste called *chyme*. During this time, gastric glands in the stomach produce (gastric) protease often called pepsin which is poured onto food and this begins to break down proteins. Unlike the amylase, that prefers neutral conditions, pepsin favours acid conditions and hydrochloric acid also from the gastric juice is secreted onto the food simultaneously. The acid activates the pepsin to work and also helps to kill bacteria in raw foods. In babies, another enzyme, called renin, is produced to solidify and digest milk proteins. The pH of the stomach contents falls to 1–2.

The small intestine

Protein and carbohydrate have started to break down by the time food leaves the stomach to enter the small intestine. Two very important organs pour juices onto the chyme in the first part of the small intestine to help further breakdown.

- The liver pours bile on to the chyme. Although bile does not contain enzymes, it contains important bile salts which reduce dietary fat into tiny globules (emulsification). Bile also contains pigments that are the waste products from degraded haemoglobin released from worn-out red blood cells.
- The pancreas pours an enzyme-rich juice onto food that continues the breakdown of all three major food components:
  - protease or trypsin that acts on proteins
  - amylase that continues the breakdown of starch
  - lipase that digests fats, which have been emulsified by liver bile.
- An abundance of alkaline salts raises the pH of the gut contents in this region to 7–8 as the pancreatic enzymes work best in an alkaline medium.

The intestinal wall itself contains glands which produce enzyme-rich juices, such as:

- maltase (maltose sugar from malt to glucose)
- lactase (lactose sugar from milk to glucose and galactose)

- sucrase (sucrose cane sugar to glucose and fructose)
- dipeptidase (dipeptides to individual amino acids).

These work either on the surface or inside the epithelial cells.

The rest of the small intestine is concerned with the absorption of the end-product of digestion into the bloodstream. As well as being very long and folded, the inside wall contains thousands of tiny projections to increase the internal surface area for absorption. These are called *villi*, and each is thin-walled (one cell thick) and well supplied with both a capillary network and a branch of the lymphatic system called a lacteal. In addition, each lining epithelial cell contains hundreds of tiny microvilli which can only be seen through an electron microscope. An enormous increase in surface area is created by the villi and microvilli, ensuring fast and efficient absorption of nutrients (see Figure 4.49).

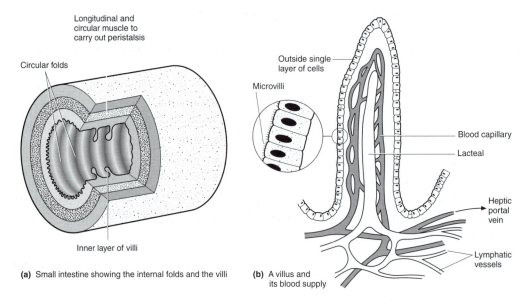

(a) Small intestine showing the internal folds and the villi

(b) A villus and its blood supply

Figure 4.49 The small intestine contains thousands of villi and microvilli

The end-products of protein and carbohydrate digestion, namely glucose and other monosaccharide sugars and amino acids, diffuse through the walls of the villi into the blood capillaries, whilst the fatty acids and glycerol pass into the lacteals. (This means 'like milk'.) Lacteals and lymphatics unite into larger vessels and discharge eventually into the large veins close to the heart. It is a circuitous way for fat products to enter the blood, but avoids the discharge of a lot of potentially harmful fat direct into the bloodstream.

Amino acids and simple sugars, such as glucose, pass directly into the capillaries of the villi and these join up to form the hepatic portal vein that carries these products to the liver and breaks up into liver capillaries. A portal vein is one that starts and ends in capillaries, unlike most other blood vessels which have capillaries at only one end.

The end-products of digestion have been absorbed into the blood and are transported either to cells, if the raw materials are required immediately, or to storage depots around the body or broken down.

The liver

One of the largest storage organs in the body is the liver. Glucose is turned into glycogen to be stored here and in the muscles. A hormone called insulin is responsible for this. When the glycogen stores are full, excess glucose is converted to fat and insulin is again responsible for this conversion. Amino acids, surplus to the needs of the body, cannot be stored and the liver breaks them down in a process called **deamination**.

Amino acids (and their parent proteins) are nitrogen-containing compounds, and the nitrogen part is detached and converted into a substance called **urea** that is excreted from the blood by the kidneys (see page 159). The rest of the molecule can be used for energy. The liver also stores fat-soluble vitamins until they are required.

Think it over

In the Western world, most people consume excess protein in their diet and it is degraded through deamination into urea, making extra work for livers and kidneys; in underdeveloped countries, however, protein foods are in short supply and many people suffer serious health problems because of protein deprivation.

Mineral salts dissolve into ions in the digestive juices and are absorbed into the blood along with amino acids and glucose. Water-soluble vitamins follow the same route, but fat-soluble vitamins are transported with the fatty acids and glycerol via the lymphatic system to the liver.

Fatty acids are converted to triglycerides and used to:

- make external and internal cell membranes along with protein molecules
- manufacture steroid hormones
- protect delicate body organs against knocks (fat becomes liquid at body temperature)
- form a long-term store of energy underneath the skin and around organs
- insulate the body against heat loss.

Fibre/cellulose is not absorbed at all and passes out as part of the body motions or faeces.

The large intestine

As food passes along the alimentary canal, the digestive glands have poured large volumes of enzyme-rich juices onto the food. The body cannot afford to lose this quantity of essential water, so the purpose of the large intestine is to return this water into the blood by reabsorption. By the time the food residue has reached the last part of the large intestine, known as the rectum, a semi-solid motion has been formed. Faeces contain cellulose, dead bacteria and scraped-off gut lining cells. It is coloured brown by the bile pigments.

Think it over

When the alimentary canal is irritated by toxins (poisons) from bacteria such as *Salmonella*, the food is rushed along the gut too fast for much watery juice to be reabsorbed and so the faeces are far more fluid, a condition we call diarrhoea. The irritation may also cause vomiting upwards. This loss of water can cause serious dehydration problems, particularly serious in babies and the elderly who have inefficient water balance systems.

Monitoring the nature, colour and consistency of faeces and vomit can be important with some clients. Loss of blood from either end of the gut indicates a medical problem such as gastric ulcer, haemorrhoids, colitis, polyps or cancer of the bowel. If the blood loss is high up in the intestine, the blood itself becomes partially digested and the faeces appear black; this is called melaena. Loss of blood from the gut should always be investigated.

Key issue

There are more than 25,000 cases of cancer of the large intestine each year in the UK, accounting for 20 per cent of all deaths from cancer. The disease is much more common in Western countries and current thinking is that diets which are high in red meat and fat and low in fibre content are probably to blame. There is also a genetic factor, with siblings and children of affected victims being more likely than the average person to contract the condition. Contrary to public opinion, this type of cancer can produce no pain until late in the disease. Changes in the production of faeces, bowel habits and blood mixed in with the faeces are more likely to alert attention to the condition than pain.

Assessment activity 4.7

Make a table to show the different regions of the alimentary tract, the digestive secretions, enzymes produced and their effects.

Structure and function of bones and muscles

As well as providing support for the soft tissues of the body, bones also provide a store of calcium, help in the manufacture of red blood cells, enable movement to take place with the action of muscles and offer protection to vital organs. Tiny bones in the ear assist with transmission of sound for hearing.

The *axial skeleton* (down the centre of the body) is composed of the skull, vertebral column or spine, the ribs and the sternum or breastbone. The shoulder and hip girdles, arms and legs make up the *appendicular skeleton*. Bones can be flat, irregular or tubular in shape. The bones that make up the long bones of the arms and legs are tubular, being hollow in the centre, rather like girders in construction. This composition makes them very strong yet light and quite difficult to break. The hollow centre contains marrow that is used to make red and some white blood cells. (In adults, many fewer bones are used in blood cell manufacture and much of the marrow becomes fatty (see Figure 4.11).)

There are two types of bone; the hardest being compact bone forming the shaft of the bone and lining the heads of bone. Spongy or cancellous bone contains spaces between plates of bone and predominates in the ends of the long bones. The spaces in spongy bone are often used to make blood cells too.

Bone itself is composed of a series of concentric rings in which calcium phosphate and carbonate are deposited (see Figure 4.11). On the edge of each ring or lamella there are spaces called lacunae in which bone cells or osteocytes are located. These cells produce the calcified material that gives the hardness to bone and then become imprisoned within it. In the centre of each set of rings (Haversian systems or osteones) lies a channel containing blood vessels and nerves.

Think it over

When you see bones in college they appear to be rather lifeless, but bone is a dynamic tissue which is constantly being replaced and just as alive as any other tissue. If you have ever broken a bone, you will know how much pain the injury produced.

Bones cannot move by themselves: they need muscles to pull them into a different position. Muscles always pull, never push. This means that there must be at least two muscles to effect a movement; one muscle pulls to displace the bone and the other pulls to return the bone to its former position.

Muscles would not be able to cause bones to move if they were just attached to one long bone that, as you have learned, is very strong. Muscles need to act across two or more bones where they meet to form a joint. To be able to pull a bone a muscle needs to shorten or contract and so they are made of contractile fibres with non-contractile ends attached to the bones; these are called tendons.

Muscles need to be supplied with energy-releasing materials and oxygen because they perform strenuous work, particularly during exercise or energy. A large amount of glucose from the digestive process eventually ends up in the muscles where it is stored as glycogen. The glycogen breaks down to supply the energy for the muscles to contract.

However, muscles do not contract on their own; they must have exciting nervous impulses sent along the nerves to the muscles. This multi-system performance is a very good example of body systems interacting together.

Skeletal muscle, also known as voluntary and striated muscle, is under the control of the will. The fibres are long and cylindrical, showing dark and light banding with many nuclei. Each one contains many myofibrils embedded in a soft cytoplasm; myofibrils contain the contracting proteins. The nerve endings terminate in special neuromuscular junctions that allow the nervous impulses to be converted into co-ordinated contractions of the myofibrils. When a muscle is not contracting it is said to be relaxed.

One of the best examples of bone and muscle working together can be seen in the flexing and extending of the forearm. Flexing means decreasing the angle between two bones and extending is the reverse action.

Assessment activity 4.8

Study Figure 4.50, which shows the bones of the arm and some of the major muscles attached to it.

Answer the following questions:

a Which muscle contracts to cause flexion?

b What will the other muscle shown be doing and why?

c Which joint is involved in this action?

d Thinking about the action of flexing the forearm, why is it important for the tendons to be non-contractile?

e Describe the action of the two muscles involved in straightening or extending the arm.

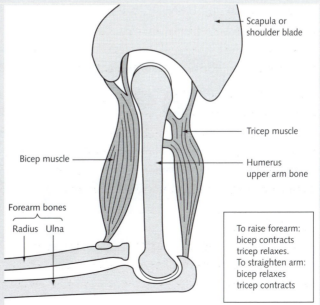

To raise forearm:
bicep contracts
tricep relaxes.
To straighten arm:
bicep relaxes
tricep contracts

Figure 4.50 Muscle action and the forearm

Sexual reproduction

The cells of the human body contain nuclei with 46 or 23 pairs of chromosomes that contain units of heredity or genes. The number of chromosomes is very important in a species because any deviation from this number produces abnormalities in human life. When humans reproduce they do so sexually; in other words a cell nucleus from a male cell unites with a nucleus from a female cell to form a new 'combined' cell (called fertilisation) from which the new being will form. The male and female cells are known as gametes because each cannot develop further unless it unites with a gamete from the opposite sex. Male gametes are spermatozoa produced in large numbers by the male testis and delivered in glandular fluids into the female body by tubes or ducts that emerge through an erect penis capable of insertion into the female vagina (see Figures 4.51 and 4.52).

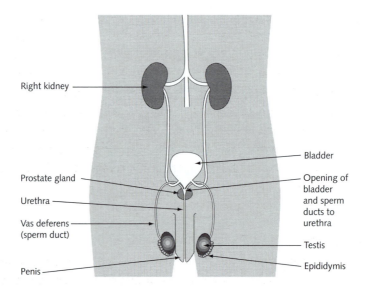

Figure 4.51 The male reproductive system

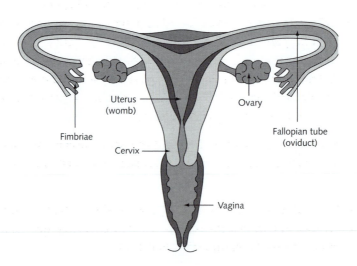

Figure 4.52 The female reproductive system

Female gametes or ova are usually produced singly every four weeks by the ovary. The ovum enters the oviducts and travels slowly towards the uterus or womb. It may or may not become fertilised during this journey, depending on whether insemination or sexual intercourse occurs at the right time.

The importance of the species chromosome number was mentioned above and so both gametes undergo a special chromosome reduction division during their development within the testis or ovary. This is called meiosis and the effect is to reduce the chromosome number of each sperm and ovum to 23 single chromosomes. Therefore, when fertilisation takes place, the 23 pairs are restored for the developing new life. You will realise that each new individual has half their chromosomes from the mother and half from the father. There can be a random shuffling of the genes on the chromosomes during meiosis and this means that children from the same mother and father can have quite different characteristics.

When fertilisation has taken place, the resulting cell – known as a zygote – undergoes many cell divisions to form the embryo, its coverings and the umbilical cord through which it receives nourishment during the pre-birth stages. After about 11 days, when the tiny embryo has reached the uterus, it begins to embed itself in the thick wall of the uterus where it undergoes further growth and development for about 40 weeks. This period is known as gestation and, at the end, uterine muscle contractions expel the foetus (the name given to an embryo after two months) from the mother's body through the vagina. The process of bringing live young into the world (as opposed to laying eggs) is known as *viviparity*. You will learn more about human growth and development in Unit 7.

The nervous system

To conserve energy, the body systems need to work together in harmony to produce maximum efficiency. This efficiency should not be impaired even when external and internal changes take place. The role of the nervous system is to control and co-ordinate the different body systems and to respond appropriately to changes in the environment.

The central nervous system (CNS) is composed of the brain and spinal cord and the cranial (from the brain) and spinal nerves form the peripheral nervous system that connects the CNS with all parts of the body (see Figure 4.15). Within the CNS are hundreds of thousands of nerve cells or neurones with long processes wrapped in connective tissue that form the nerves (see Figure 4.16). Neurones are excitable cells (similar to muscle cells) which respond to stimuli by creating tiny electrical impulses that can cause muscles to contract or glands to secrete.

Stimuli received by sense organs scattered around the body initiate impulses which travel along sensory nerves to the CNS, or impulses can be generated by the workings of mind and intelligence.

Control of internal organs and processes such as heart and breathing rates, peristalsis (gut movements), balance and sexual intercourse are carried out by the autonomic system of nerves connected to the brain and spinal cord.

'Action' neurones that run *from* the CNS to cause muscles to contract or glands to secrete are known as motor or efferent neurones. Neurones that run from sensory receptors *towards* the CNS are sensory or receptor neurones. Some neurones connecting these two types are relay or connector neurones and these exist in the CNS. Communication between neurones occurs at a specialised location called the synapse where the incoming nervous impulses cause chemicals to be released into the tiny space of the synapse, to enable the excitatory 'message' to move onwards. If the impulses are too few or too infrequent the 'message' may fade away at this point and go no further. This can be very helpful in reducing the number of excitatory stimuli reaching the CNS, for example you would not wish to be conscious of the feel of your clothes on your skin all day and every day!

Think it over

Try to think of more examples of situations when it is helpful not to be bombarded with sensory impulses.

Sometimes it is important that the nervous system reacts very quickly without conscious thought through the brain, such as in an emergency to prevent injury. This is a reflex action that is rapid, automatic and a response to a specific stimulus. If you stepped on a sharp point in bare feet, you would rapidly pull your foot away – this would help to prevent injury with the minimum amount of movement and energy expenditure. Only two or three neurones are involved and the route taken would be into the spinal cord via the receptor neurone involved, round the cord in an arc and out again via the efferent neurone to the appropriate muscles. There may be a connector neurone involved within the spinal cord or not. Synapses take more time to cross than an impulse travelling down the nerve fibre, so reducing the number of synapses makes the reflex much faster. The brain is involved at a slower pace although it is only a matter of fractions of a second. You know this because you would shout something, look at the foot and perhaps rub the area.

To summarise, the nervous system:

- controls and co-ordinates body systems
- responds to changes in the environment with maximum efficiency
- controls and co-ordinates the processes carried out by internal organs, including many examples of homeostasis
- reduces injuries through reflex actions
- receives sensations and causes appropriate actions
- promotes thinking and intelligence.

The endocrine system

Some glands in the body pass their secretions directly into the bloodstream and not down tubes or ducts. The older name for these glands was ductless glands but now they are called endocrine glands and the active materials in their secretions are hormones. Hormones cause a change in a target organ that may be close at hand or some distance away. Some hormonal secretions affect only one place in the body, but others have an effect on the entire body. The major hormones and their actions are shown in the following table.

Endocrine gland	Major hormones	Summary of the actions of the hormones
Hypothalamus – also part of the brain	Releasing and inhibitory factors that control other endocrine glands	Stimulation and inhibition of many glands, particularly the pituitary gland
Pituitary gland – anterior part	Growth hormone	Skeletal, muscular and soft tissue growth
	Adrenocorticotrophic hormone (ACTH), also known as corticotropin	Stimulation of the hormone cortisol from the also adrenal cortex
	Follicle stimulating hormone (FSH), also called follitropin	Stimulates the production of gametes from the gonads
	Luteinising hormone or lutropin	Causes ovulation and the formation of the corpus luteum in females. Causes testosterone to be secreted from the testis in males
	Prolactin	Stimulates breastmilk formation after childbirth
	Thyroid stimulating hormone or thyrotropin	Stimulates the thyroid gland to produce thyroxine
Pituitary gland – posterior part	Antidiuretic hormone also known as vasopressin	Causes water reabsorption in the second renal tubules and collecting ducts
	Oxytocin	Causes rhythmical contractions of uterine muscle in childbirth
Thyroid gland	Thyroxine	Regulates growth and development and controls the basic metabolic rate
Parathyroid glands	Parathyrin	Controls calcium in blood and body tissues
Adrenal glands – the medulla	Adrenaline and noradrenaline	Stimulates the fright, flight and fight response to stress. Involved in the regulation of blood sugar
Adrenal glands – the cortex	Cortisol	Involved in regulating blood sugar and repair of body organs damaged in degenerative diseases
Pancreas (islets of Langerhans)	Insulin Glucagon	Regulation of blood sugars
Ovaries	Oestrogen and progesterone	Growth and development of primary and secondary sexual organs and female secondary sexual characteristics
Testes	Testosterone	Growth and development of primary and secondary sexual organs and male secondary sexual characteristics

Most are stimulatory but a few are inhibitory. If endocrine glands over-secrete or under-secrete there can be adverse effects on the body; some irregularities can be life-threatening, while others have less harmful effects.

Endocrine glands and their hormones control and co-ordinate the behaviour of other cells and in this regard they have a similar role to the nervous system. Their action is much slower than the nervous system because hormones travel to their target organs via the bloodstream. They are chemicals that are usually protein or steroid in nature. Some endocrine glands are compact organs, such as the thyroid and pituitary glands. Others are scattered groups of cells embedded in other tissues, such as the pancreas and the testis. The major compact glands are the thyroid, parathyroids, adrenals and the pituitary. The major diffuse glands are the testis, ovary, pancreas and those associated with the digestive system.

Assessment activity 4.9

Make a list of all the hormones you have heard of and describe some of their effects. Make a study of one particular endocrine gland, giving the actions of its hormones and some effects of over- and under-secretion. The table above will provide a starting point for your references.

What is the difference in co-ordination and communication carried out by the nervous and endocrine systems?

Assessment guidance

This unit is assessed internally by your tutor, but will be also be considered by your external verifier to make sure that you have covered all the specifications.

1 **The role of the main components of the human body cell and tissues**
   You will need to demonstrate the following:
   a) Understanding of the structure and function of cell components visible under the light and the electron microscope. You can show this by annotated diagrams of the structure of both microscopic cell diagrams.
   b) The differences between simple and compound epithelial tissues and connective tissues and relate their structures to their functions. You can do this by producing illustrations of sections through the skin, bladder lining and lungs, with accompanying notes.
   c) That you know the features and functions of the types of connective tissue found in relation to the skin and a joint. Produce neat, labelled diagrams of adipose tissue, tendon, ligament, bone and cartilage with brief notes relating to their functions. Bio-viewers are ideal for this type of work. See also 3 c) and 4 f).
   d) Recognition of the three types of muscle tissue found in the stomach wall, uterus, heart and muscles attached to the knee joint, relating each structure to function. To do this, produce diagrams of the three different muscle types with accompanying notes. You will also need to have examined microscopic or bio-viewer slides provided by your tutor. See also 4 f).
   e) That you are familiar with the appearance of nervous tissue such as that found in the spinal cord and can relate function to structure. A bio-viewer slide will be adequate for this.

2   Describe the processes involved in the exchange of materials between the cell and its immediate environment.

You will need to do the following:

a) Carry out practical experimental work to demonstrate diffusion, osmosis and the rate of diffusion, drawing accurate conclusions that show a clear understanding. Assessment activity 4.3 on page 134 will provide a foundation for this work and stimulate further progress to enable a higher grade to be achieved.

b) Explain osmotic potential and active transport with illustrative examples.

3   Outline the processes of homeostasis that operate to maintain the internal environment surrounding cells

You will need to demonstrate the following:

a) That you understand why body cells must be isotonic with their surroundings and how this is achieved. You can do this by producing an illustrated report of 'the how and why of osmoregulation'.

b) The role of gaseous exchange in the maintenance of the internal environment. You can produce a detailed illustrated report explaining breathing, respiration and gaseous exchange, which will support this assessment criterion and also 4 c). You should include reference to the maintenance of the internal environment in your account.

c) How the body maintains its temperature within a normal range.

4   Outline the major structures and functions of human body systems

You will need to demonstrate the following:

a) An explanation of the structure and functions of blood. To do this, produce an illustrated table of the components of blood, listing the main features and functions of plasma and the different types of cells.

b) That you can describe the main functions of the cardiovascular system – a list of functions will be satisfactory for this.

c) That you can explain breathing and respiration; you should be able to cross-reference to 3 b).

d) A definition of excretion and an investigation into the production of urine. You can do this by producing a report into renal function. This assessment evidence can be combined with 3 a).

e) That you know how food is digested, absorbed and assimilated. You could produce an illustrated report explaining how a simple meal of your own choice becomes digested, absorbed and used in your body.

f) The structure and functions of bone and muscle; this work can be included in 1 c) and d) with appropriate cross-references.

g) That you can outline the processes involved in creating new individuals; you can produce annotated diagrams of the male and female reproductive systems and a simple flow chart showing a few pairs of chromosomes in the male spermatozoon and female ovum and how they unite to form a new individual. Do not attempt to show 23 pairs of chromosomes as the diagrams would be too confusing, but note that in the interests of clarity only six or the number of your choice is displayed. Identify where meiosis has taken place.

h) Compare the communication and co-ordination carried out by the nervous and endocrine systems. You can produce a three-column table to show your comparisons – an example is provided for you below.

Chart to show a comparison of the communication and co-ordination carried out by the nervous and endocrine systems		
Feature to compare	Nervous system	Endocrine system
Speed of communication and co-ordination	Acts extremely fast, a nervous impulse can travel down a myelinated nerve fibre at 100 m/s	Is restricted by the speed at which blood travels as hormones are delivered by the bloodstream

End of unit test

1 Describe the differences in structure and function of the two main types of endoplasmic reticula.

2 What are nucleic acids and where are they located in a cell?

3 Which of the following statements are true and which are false?
  a Lysosomes are concerned with the manufacture of proteins.
  b The plasma membrane is a single-layered structure that limits the cell.
  c Chromosomes can always be seen inside a nucleus.
  d Mitochondria carry out the last stages of glucose oxidation.
  e The nucleolus is an important source of RNA.

4 Define diffusion and osmosis and state three clear differences between the two processes.

5 Why is drinking hot tea more beneficial in cooling the body in hot weather than eating ice cream?

6 Put these areas of the alimentary canal in order from mouth to anus: large intestine, stomach, oesophagus, small intestine, rectum.

7 Explain why muscles responsible for movement never occur singly.

8 Where precisely would you find the following:

Haversian canal   Pancreas   Inspiratory centre   Thyroid gland   Effector neurone.

9 Describe the events that follow drinking 1dm^3 of orange juice rapidly in terms of osmoregulation.

10 Describe a major effect of the following hormones: adrenaline, insulin, antidiuretic hormone, thyroxine.

11 Explain how the nervous system, bones and muscles interact to lift the forearm.

12 Explain the differences between the following:

Ligament and tendon   Cartilage and bone   Receptor and effector neurones
Simple and compound epithelia.

13 Complete the following table, shading the inappropriate boxes, the first line is provided as an example.

Feature	Plasma	Red blood cell	White blood cell	Platelet
Bi-concave shape		Yes		
Has lobed nuclei				
Concerned with blood clotting				
Concerned with defending the body				
Contains large numbers of lysosomes				
Contains no DNA				

14 Explain the features of the alveoli in the lungs that make diffusion of oxygen more efficient.

15 Explain why red blood cells must be isotonic with plasma and the two possible consequences if tonicity is disturbed.

References and further reading

Fullick, A. (1994) *Heinemann Advanced Science: Biology*, Oxford: Heinemann
Moonie, N. (2000) *AVCE Health and Social Care*, Oxford: Heinemann
Soper, R. *et al.* (1992) *Biological Sciences 1 & 2*, Cambridge: Cambridge University Press
Toole, G. and Toole, S. (1994) *Understanding Biology for Advanced Level*, London: Hutchinson

This unit is designed to provide a background to aspects of chemistry and physics relating to human physiology and applications in the health and allied industries. It is not possible for the unit to cover all the chemistry and physics that you could encounter in your future career, but it will provide a stepping stone from which to explore particular subjects in further detail.

As everyone who reads this unit will have a different understanding of physics and chemistry, some of you will need to work your way through section by section whilst others will be able to skip some parts and be able to concentrate on those areas where your knowledge and understanding aren't so strong.

Finally, a word about the numerical understanding required to cope with the mathematics that underpins many concepts within physics and chemistry. It is possible, for the most part, to have an understanding of principles without necessarily comprehending the underpinning maths. As such, the mathematics in this chapter has been kept to a minimum and should be within the grasp of anyone who has studied to GCSE level.

What you need to learn
- Atomic and molecular structure
- Physics and chemistry of homeostasis
- Physical principles of specific human functions
- Medical applications

Atomic and molecular structure

The structure of matter
Whatever you breathe, eat, smell or touch is composed of what is called **matter.** All matter is made up of unimaginably tiny particles called **atoms** and **molecules.** Atoms are the smallest particle of matter that can take part in a chemical reaction and molecules can be regarded simply as the products of such reactions.

Matter can exist as a solid, liquid or gas, the difference between these being how tightly packed the atoms or molecules are. So when you touch something solid, such as your skin, the atoms and molecules of which it is made are packed together quite closely, whereas the air you breathe is made up of atoms and molecules that are much farther apart from one another (see Figure 5.1).

Atoms are composed of even smaller particles called **protons, neutrons** and **electrons.**

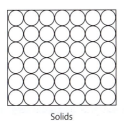
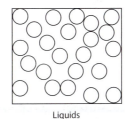
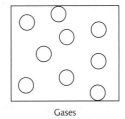

Solids   Liquids   Gases

Figure 5.1 The molecular make-up of solids, liquids and gases

Protons and neutrons make up the central portion of the atom known as the **nucleus** and the electrons move around the nucleus. Another important feature of these particles is that protons are positively charged and electrons are negatively charged, whilst neutrons have no charge.

Atoms can have different numbers of protons, neutrons and electrons and as such they have different properties. Substances that are made up of atoms containing the same number of protons are called **elements**.

Of the 114 (at the last count) known elements only four make up over 96 per cent of the human body – hydrogen, carbon, oxygen and nitrogen. Another 3.9 per cent is composed of what are called the trace elements, calcium, sulphur, phosphorus, potassium, chlorine, iodine, iron, sodium and magnesium. A number of other ultra trace elements are needed in even smaller quantities and include copper, molybdenum, cobalt, zinc, boron, fluorine, aluminium, silicon, vanadium, chromium, manganese, tin and selenium. These elements are identified in the periodic table shown in Figure 5.2.

For each element the number of protons it contains is called the **atomic number** or proton number. The number of protons usually equals the number of electrons. Another value, the **mass number**, is used to describe the total number of protons and neutrons in the atom.

Some elements can exist in different forms known as **isotopes**. Isotopes contain the same number of protons but different numbers of neutrons. So isotopes of an element have the same atomic number but different mass numbers. As most elements exist as a mixture of isotopes the **relative atomic mass** is used to show the average mass of the different isotopes in relation to their abundance. Many isotopes are radioactive and some of them are used in medical techniques to be considered later in this unit.

In 1869 Dmitri Mendeleev developed the periodic table (Figure 5.2). The elements are arranged in order of the number of protons they contain, i.e. atomic number. The table also shows the relative atomic mass of each element starting with hydrogen which has one proton. The table also reflects the arrangement of the electrons around the nucleus of each atom. This arrangement of electrons is called the electronic structure of an atom. The electronic structure contributes to the properties of elements and enables us to predict the type of chemical bonds they form with each other to make molecules.

Up to GCSE level the structure of atoms is based upon the model proposed by Neils Bohr in 1913. In this model the electrons move around the nucleus in orbits, rather

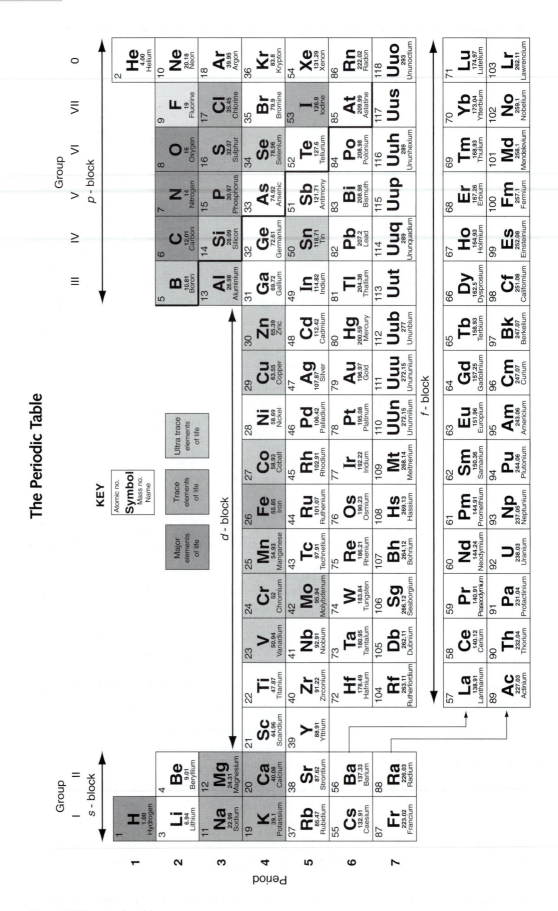

Figure 5.2 The periodic table

like the planets move around the sun. The element hydrogen can be shown as in Figure 5.3.

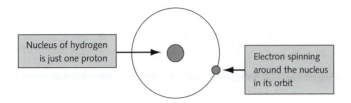

Figure 5.3 Nuclear model of the hydrogen atom

For this level it is more appropriate to think of the electrons occupying regions in space called **atomic orbitals** rather than specific orbits (see Figure 5.4). This is the basis for the Quantum Theory of electronic structure that helps to predict amongst other things the shape of molecules. Shape is crucial to the function of many molecules within the cells and tissues of the human body.

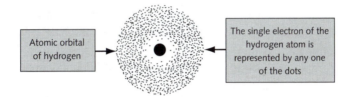

Figure 5.4 Orbital model of hydrogen atom

Quantum theory determines that orbitals have size and shape that ensures electrons are kept as far apart as possible from one another and that each orbital can only contain up to two electrons.

Different orbitals form part of **electron sub-shells** that are in turn grouped into **electron shells**.

Electron sub-shells are identified by the letters s, p, d and f, each of which contains one or more atomic orbitals. There is one s orbital, three p orbitals, five d and seven f orbitals.

Electron shells are identified by a **principal quantum number** (n). The first shell has a principal quantum number 1, the second shell 2, the third 3 and so on.

The arrangement of electrons can be depicted using the notation:

Principal quantum number *Electron sub-shell* Number of electrons in atomic orbitals

For example, potassium, atomic number 19, has the following arrangement of electrons:

$1s^2 2s^2 2p^6 3s^2 3p^6 4s^1$

where 1, 2, 3 and 4 are the principal quantum numbers, *s* and *p* are the electron sub-shells and [1], [2] and [6] are the number of electrons in the atomic orbitals.

The arrangement of electrons in the orbitals and shells for the first 10 elements is shown in the table below.

Elements are arranged into groups or periods in the periodic table.

Element	Atomic number	Electronic structure
Hydrogen	1	$1s^1$
Helium	2	$1s^2$
Lithium	3	$1s^2 2s^1$
Beryllium	4	$1s^2 2s^2$
Boron	5	$1s^2 2s^2 2p^1$
Carbon	6	$1s^2 2s^2 2p^2$
Nitrogen	7	$1s^2 2s^2 2p^3$
Oxygen	8	$1s^2 2s^2 2p^4$
Fluorine	9	$1s^2 2s^2 2p^5$
Neon	10	$1s^2 2s^2 2p^6$

The group indicates the number of electrons in the outer shell of an element whilst the period indicates the principal quantum number of the outermost shell. The table is sub-divided on the basis of the electron sub-shell that contains the outermost electrons. Elements whose outermost electrons are found in the *s* sub-shell are called *s*-block elements. Elements whose outermost electrons are found in the *p* sub-shell are called *p*-block elements. Elements whose outermost electrons are found in the *d* sub-shell are called *d*-block elements. Elements whose outermost electrons are found in the *f* sub-shell are called *f*-block elements. Elements in different blocks tend to have similar general properties:

- *s*-block elements are metals that are very reactive
- *p*-block elements are all non-metals
- *d*-block elements are all metals, but have different physical and chemical properties from the *s*-block elements.

The size and shape of *s*, *p* and *d* orbitals or electron sub-shells is governed by some rather complex mathematics that enable us to comprehend their three-dimensional shape which then determines the size and shape of molecules they form. In addition, the electrons within the outermost electron shell not only determine the position of an atom within the periodic table but also the type and number of bonds that one element will form with another. It is important to note in relation to this that the electron shells of helium and neon are full as are all other elements found in group 0 of the periodic table. These elements are known as the noble gases and are very stable and unreactive due to their electron shells being completely filled.

Assessment activity 5.1

In groups, share out the elements of life as identified in Figure 5.2. For each element:

a identify its atomic structure
b find out as much as you can about its properties and its role in the body.

Produce a sheet to show the structure of your element(s) and summarise other information researched. Finally, produce a few questions on your elements for others in the group to answer. This will mean everyone has read and understood each other's work enabling the assessment criteria to be met.

Bonding and molecules

Why do elements come together to form molecules?

Essentially, elements want to achieve the stability of the group 0 elements by having their outer electron shells filled. So in the case of hydrogen, with one electron in the 1s orbital, another electron is needed to fill this orbital and achieve a stable state like that of helium. Carbon, on the other hand, has four electrons in its outer shell (two in the 2s orbital and two in the 2p). To achieve stability, carbon would either have to lose or gain four electrons. It is easier for carbon to gain four electrons rather than lose four.

In order to lose or gain electrons, atoms of elements can either share electrons between each other to form covalent bonds or give electrons away to, or gain them from, other atoms to form **ionic bonds**.

Covalent bonds

Covalent bonds form between non-metal elements where atoms would have to lose or gain too many electrons to form ionic bonds. Covalent bonds result from atoms of non-metal elements sharing outer shell electrons so that they attain the electronic configuration of the group 0 elements.

When a covalent bond forms between atoms of the same element the electrons are shared equally (see Figure 5.5).

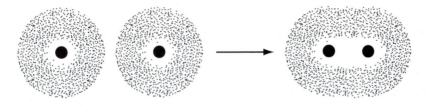

Figure 5.5 Two hydrogen atoms come close enough together for the attractive force between the protons and electrons of each atom to enable the electrons to be shared

When a covalent bond forms between atoms of different elements the shared electrons will tend to be attracted to the nucleus of the element with the greatest attraction for electrons. This is determined by the number of protons in the nucleus and the overall size of the electron shell. Thus, an atom with more protons in the nucleus will have a greater electron affinity whilst an element with a large overall electron shell size will have less affinity for electrons as the electrons are further away from the nucleus and the attractive force of the protons. This attraction for electrons is termed **electronegativity** and atoms lying towards the top right-hand corner of the periodic table are more electronegative, as shown in Figure 5.6.

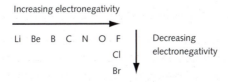

Figure 5.6 Change in electronegativity in relation to position of element in periodic table

Covalent bonding between atoms of different elements can result in molecules exhibiting **polarity**. The electrons involved in bonding spend more time around the more electronegative atom so conferring an overall negative charge on that part of the molecule. The other atom or atoms in the molecule will therefore appear positively charged.

In many covalently bonded molecules there may be little difference in electronegativity between the atoms or where there is more than one polar bond, the polar effects may cancel each other. Such molecules are termed **non-polar**.

Polarity in molecules can have important biological consequences and the one of most significance is that exhibited by water molecules.

Water molecules are composed of two hydrogen atoms covalently bonded to one oxygen atom (see Figure 5.7). The oxygen atom has eight, positively charged protons in its nucleus that attract the negatively charged electron of each hydrogen atom more strongly than does the proton of hydrogen. This makes the oxygen appear slightly negatively charged and each hydrogen slightly positively charged. Under normal circumstances you would expect the two polar bonds to cancel each other out. This indeed would be the case if the bonds between the hydrogen atoms and oxygen were all in a straight line, i.e. a linear molecule. However, the bonds are angled (for reasons we haven't the space for here), so the water molecule exhibits polarity.

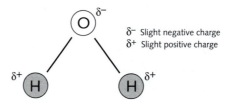

Figure 5.7 Diagrammatic representation of water molecule

As a result, when water molecules are close together the positively charged hydrogen of one molecule is attracted to the negatively charged oxygen of another molecule. This attractive force is known as a **hydrogen bond** (see Figure 5.8). Whilst it is much weaker than a covalent or ionic bond it is enough to cause water to exhibit a number of unique properties that are considered in more detail in the section on Water, solutions, pH and buffers (see page 200).

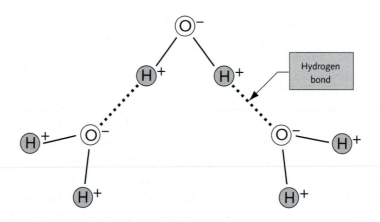

Figure 5.8 Hydrogen bonding between water molecules

Some covalently bound groups of atoms can exhibit the properties of ions (see below) forming **complex** or **polyatomic ions** (see table below). These are important constituents of body chemistry and contribute to a number of physiological functions, particularly the buffering of body fluids (see Water, solutions, pH and buffers, page 200).

Polyatomic ion name	Polyatomic ion
Hydroxide	OH^-
Carbonate	CO_3^{2-}
Phosphate	PO_4^{2-}
Sulphate	SO_4^{2-}
Hydrogen carbonate	HCO_3^-

Ionic bonds

Ionic bonds tend to form between certain elements, such that one or more elements give away electrons whilst others accept them in order to achieve electron configuration similar to that of the nearest group 0 element. Elements that give away electrons are found in groups I and II of the periodic table, i.e. the *s*-block (metal) elements, e.g. sodium, potassium, calcium, magnesium. Elements that gain electrons are found in groups VI and VII, i.e. the *p*-block (non-metal), e.g. chlorine, iodine, oxygen. Thus atoms of the metal elements give electrons to the non-metal elements to produce inorganic compounds.

As the number of protons is unaffected by the formation of a bond the gain or loss of electrons will result in the atom having an overall positive or negative charge and is consequently known as an ion. Since the metal elements lose electrons in forming ionic bonds the atoms become positively charged ions and are called **cations**. The non-metal elements in gaining electrons become negatively charged and are called **anions**.

A non-metal can only accept so many electrons due to the repulsive forces occurring between the electrons as they are added. With metals it becomes more difficult to remove second and third electrons due to the attractive forces of the atom's nucleus, such that anions with a charge of 4- are very rare.

When electrons have been transferred from a metal element to a non-metal element, the molecule produced is held together by the forces of electrostatic attraction between the different ions.

Atoms of elements that can lose or gain more than one electron can form different types of ions, depending upon the number of electrons they gain or lose (see table on page 184).

Inorganic elements and molecules

Whilst the term **inorganic** is somewhat out of date, it helps to distinguish those elements and molecules that are not based on carbon since these form the basis of organic chemistry. If you look at the periodic table (page 178) you will see that there are 25 elements other than carbon that are present in the human body. These include the bulk elements hydrogen, oxygen and nitrogen that contribute to the structures of both organic and inorganic compounds. The table below identifies a number of these elements, their general function, the form or forms in which they can be found within the body and the amount an adult male requires per day.

Mineral	Symbol	Atomic Number	Ionic form	Alternative names	Function	Daily requirements
Fluorine	F	9	F^-	Fluoride	Required for bone development, prevents tooth decay	
Sodium	Na	11	Na^+		Essential to maintain water balance, nerve conduction and muscle contraction	1200 mg
Magnesium	Mg	12	Mg^{2+}		Enzyme action	400 mg
Phosphorus	P	15			Component of proteins, nucleic acids and ATP, required for teeth and bones	
Sulphur	S	16			Component of two amino acids found in many proteins	
Chlorine	Cl	17	Cl^-	Chloride	Essential to maintain water balance in blood and interstitial fluid	1800 mg
Potassium	K	19	K^+		Nerve impulse conduction and muscle contraction	3000 mg
Calcium	Ca	20	Ca^{2+}		Calcification of bone and teeth, blood clotting, contraction of muscle, release of neurotransmitters in nerve cells, intracellular transport	1000 mg
Iron	Fe	26	Fe^2 Fe^{3+}	Iron II Iron III	Essential component of haemoglobin and needed by some enzymes involved in ATP production	18 mg
Copper	Cu	29	Cu^+ Cu^{2+}	Copper I Copper II	Enzyme activity	2 mg
Iodine	I	53	I^-	Iodide	Vital to hormone production in thyroid gland	130 mg

The majority of inorganic elements occur as ions in solution or are part of polyatomic ions as previously mentioned. As can be seen from the table, some can exist in more than one ionic form that relates to their ability to donate electrons in redox reactions.

Key issues: Free radicals

The following extract from 'Age-old story', in *New Scientist* (23 January 1999) gives an indication as to some of the effects of highly reactive atoms or molecules called free radicals. Free radicals are simply atoms or molecules with an unpaired electron that attack other atoms or molecules to gain an electron, turning them into free radicals in the process. Their existence may come about as a result of chemical reactions or the effect of ultraviolet light or other forms of radiation.

'It turns out that two of the most important substances for life do most of the damage: oxygen and sugar. **Aerobic respiration**, in which oxygen is used to break down complex organic molecules such as fat and carbohydrate to release energy, produces highly reactive by-products called **free radicals**. These have the potential to wreak havoc, particularly in the vicinity of mitochondria, where respiration occurs. As a result, the small but vital amount of DNA inside mitochondria is especially vulnerable. Less reactive radicals, such as hydrogen peroxide, diffuse through the cell and into the nucleus, where they may damage the DNA in chromosomes as well. Fats also come under attack wherever they occur in the body, for example in membranes or as part of hormones and eye pigments. The harmful form of blood-borne cholesterol, **low-density lipoprotein** (LDL) is also attacked, which might seem a good thing. But when LDL is oxidised by **free radicals**, it changes into a form that cannot be recognised as 'self' by the immune system, making it a target for autoimmune attack. This process may contribute to the development of fatty plaques in arteries. Fortunately, antioxidant vitamins such as E and C can soak up **free radicals**. Enzymes also play a part. Catalase, for example, converts hydrogen peroxide into water. It has been estimated that there are as many as 10,000 instances of free radical damage per cell per day. Most of these chemical dents are patched up by the body's repair mechanisms, but not all. Over the years, the damage accumulates.'

Assessment activity 5.2

Carry out your own research into free radicals that attack the body, their structure, how they arise, the damage they can cause and how they are dealt with. Write up your research as a report.

Organic molecules

Organic molecules are often referred to as the chemistry of carbon compounds, since organic chemistry is based upon the enormous range and variety of compounds that carbon forms. Carbon compounds are the foundation of life and the numbers and complexity of compounds that exist is due to the ability of carbon to form strong covalent bonds with itself or other atoms to produce stable chain or ring structures. As already mentioned, in living material there are only a few other elements involved in bonding with carbon to create the vast number of organic chemicals that make up our bodies.

Another reason why there are so many organic compounds is due to the existence of isomers, compounds with identical molecular composition but different structures and properties. The potential number of isomers increases as the number of carbons per molecule increases as shown in the following table.

Formula	Number of isomers
C_8H_{18}	18
$C_{10}H_{22}$	75
$C_{20}H_{42}$	366,319
$C_{40}H_{82}$	60 billion

Because of the structural complexity of organic compounds a system for naming them has been developed that is based upon the following:

1 The name given to the main part of the molecule. This will be a chain with the most carbon atoms or a ring.
2 A suffix (word ending) that identifies the main reactive part of the molecule called the principal functional group.

3 One or more prefixes (word beginnings) that identify any atoms or groups of atoms (substituents) replacing a hydrogen on the main chain or ring.

4 A number that identifies which carbon of the main chain or ring a substituent is located on.

This system has resulted in organic compounds with similar structures being allocated to different groups. These groups include the alkanes, alkenes, alcohols, aldehydes, ketones and carboxylic acids. As each group has the same basic structure they are termed the homologous series.

The alkanes are *saturated hydrocarbons* in that every carbon atom in the molecule is bonded to either another carbon or hydrogen.

Methane   Ethane   Propane

The alkenes are *unsaturated hydrocarbons* since they contain double bonds between adjacent carbon atoms. Here the suffix is changed from -ane to -ene as in ethene, propene, butene, etc. An alkene can have two different isomeric forms called *cis* and *trans* that describe the position of the atoms on the carbons adjacent to the double bond.

Ethane (*cis*)   Ethane (*trans*)

In alcohols a hydrogen is replaced by a hydroxyl (–OH) group and the suffix is changed to -ol, as in methanol and ethanol. When you get to propanol the –OH group could be on any one of three carbon atoms, so this time a number is introduced to identify its location, e.g. propan-2-ol or propan-1-ol. There can be more than one –OH group so the alcohol becomes a diol (2, –OH groups) or triol (3, –OH groups) as in propan-1,2,3-triol.

Methanol   Ethanol

Propan-1-ol   Propan-2-ol

Aldehydes and ketones contain a carbonyl group (>C=O). In aldehydes the carbon atom is bonded to at least one hydrogen, whereas in ketones the carbon is bonded to two other groups.

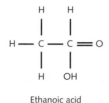

Glyceraldehyde   Dihydroxyacetone

Carboxylic acids contain a carboxyl (–C=O) group and the suffix -oic and acid are used as in ethanoic acid (commonly called acetic acid). As the name implies, carboxylic acids have acidic properties, since the OH group can dissociate to give H^+ ions.

Ethanoic acid

Amines contain an amino (–NH$_2$) group and the suffix -amine is used. Amines have alkaline properties.

These families of organic compounds are the basis of carbohydrates, lipids, proteins and nucleic acids, i.e. complex molecules that form the structural and functional components of cells, tissues, organs and systems of the human organism.

Carbohydrates

Carbohydrates are made up of the elements carbon, hydrogen and oxygen, generally in the ratio of 1C:2H:1O. The carbohydrates are split into three main groups:

1 Monosaccharides are the building blocks of carbohydrates and include glucose, fructose, galactose, ribose and deoxyribose – the major monosaccharide sugars to be found in the body. Glucose, fructose and galactose are all structural isomers with the molecular formula $C_6H_{12}O_6$. Glucose acts as the main source of energy for cells within the body and is the only source of energy for the central nervous system which has no store of glycogen or fat. Fructose acts as an energy source for spermatozoa.

The difference between the three monosaccharides is in the functional groups they carry and their positions within the molecule. Glucose and galactose both contain an aldehyde functional group, as a result of which they are called aldoses. The two sugars differ due to the position of hydroxyl groups they carry. Fructose has a ketone functional group and is consequently termed a ketose sugar. The functional groups give the sugars some of their characteristic properties and are a means by which they can be identified.

Ribose has the molecular formula $C_5H_{10}O_5$, is an aldose sugar and is an important component of ribonucleic acids. Deoxyribose has one less oxygen than ribose and is the sugar of deoxyribose nucleic acid.

2 Disaccharides are made up two monosaccharide monomers and include the sugars sucrose, lactose and maltose. The disaccharide sucrose is composed of one glucose and one fructose unit and is the sugar you put in your tea. Lactose, composed of one molecule each of galactose and glucose, is the sugar in breast milk, and maltose, made up of two glucose units, is the sugar found in malted cereal grains. The addition of many more glucose units to maltose leads to the formation of starch or glycogen, depending upon how the glucose units are joined together.

3 Polysaccharides include starch and cellulose, found in plants, and glycogen, an energy source for humans stored within the liver and muscles. All these polysaccharides are polymers of the monosaccharide glucose.

The formation of disaccharides and polysaccharides results from condensation reactions between monosaccharides and the resulting bond that links them together is known as a **glycosidic bond**.

Lipids

Lipids are a diverse group of compounds, the most widespread of which are the **triglycerides** that are based on esters of the alcohol **glycerol** and three **fatty acids**.

Fatty acids are so called because they contain the **carboxyl** functional group which has acidic properties. Fatty acids have the general formula RCOOH where R is a chain of carbon and hydrogen atoms. Most fatty acids have between 14 and 22 carbon atoms in the chain that give these compounds many of their physical and chemical properties.

Sometimes the long chain 'hydrocarbon tail' contains double bonds (C=C) and as such are said to be **unsaturated**. The form of the double bond, i.e. *cis* or *trans* can have a dramatic effect on the shape of the hydrocarbon tail and therefore the properties of the molecule. Fatty acids with no double bonds are said to be **saturated**.

Another important group of lipids are the **phospholipids**, so called because they contain a phosphorus (P) atom. The phosphorus occurs as part of a phosphate group that replaces one of the fatty acid groups in a triglyceride. This structure endows certain physical properties on the phospholipid molecule that has important biological consequences. The molecule is commonly represented as shown in Figure 5.9.

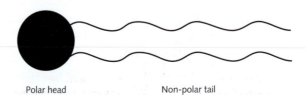

Polar head   Non-polar tail

Figure 5.9 The phospholipid molecule

The head of a phospholipid is polar due to the charge carried by the phosphate group and as such is soluble in water, whereas the non-polar hydrocarbon tail is not. The water soluble, polar head is termed **hydrophilic** (water loving) whilst the non-polar tail is **hydrophobic** (water hating). The consequence of this is that in an aqueous (water) solution phospholipid molecules will arrange themselves so that the hydrophilic heads are exposed to the water, but the tails are not. There are two possible ways by which this can occur (see Figure 5.10).

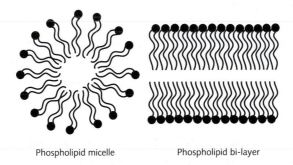

Phospholipid micelle   Phospholipid bi-layer

Figure 5.10 Phospholipid molecules in water

The phospholipid bi-layer is the foundation of all living cell membranes.

Proteins

Proteins have a wide range of functions within the human body, from supporting structural components to transport and protection, acting as enzymes and as hormones.

All proteins are made up of monomer units known as **amino acids**. There are over 10,000 proteins found in the human body, all composed of different arrangements of up to 20 amino acids.

Amino acids are so called because they possess an **amino** functional group ($-NH_2$) and a **carboxylic acid** functional group ($-COOH$), and they have the general structural formula shown in Figure 5.11, where R is hydrogen or some other group of atoms. This group is responsible for the unique properties each amino acid displays.

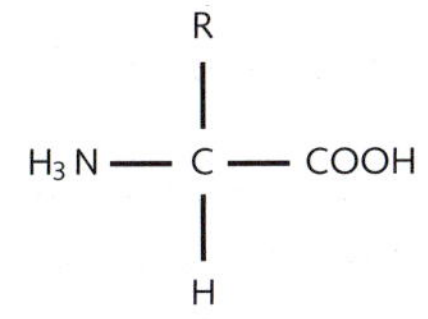

$$H_3N \longrightarrow \underset{\underset{H}{|}}{\overset{\overset{R}{|}}{C}} \longrightarrow COOH$$

Figure 5.11 Structural formula of a generalised amino acid

Because they possess both acidic (carboxylic) and basic (amino) groups amino acids can exhibit both acidic and basic properties (see Figure 5.12). Substances that do this are called **amphoteric**, a feature that gives both amino acids and proteins the capacity to act as buffers.

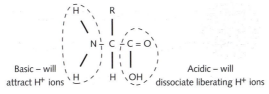

Basic – will attract H^+ ions   Acidic – will dissociate liberating H^+ ions

Figure 5.12 Structural formula of a generalised amino acid showing amino and carboxylic acid functional groups

Amino acids can form a variety of chemical bonds, the **peptide bond** resulting from a reaction (condensation) between the amino group of one amino acid and the carboxylic group of another. This creates a dipeptide which has an amino group at one end and a carboxylic group at the other, both of which can combine with other amino acids to produce a **polypeptide**.

The number and sequence of amino acids in a polypeptide is known as the **primary (1°) structure** that determines the biological function of a protein (se Figure 5.13).

Figure 5.13 Diagrammatic representation of primary structure of a protein in which each shape represents a different amino acid

The **secondary (2°) structure** of proteins takes into account the folding of the polypeptide chain into a β-pleated sheet and/or a α-helix (see Figure 5.14). These two structures are held together by hydrogen bonds between carbonyl and amino groups projecting from the sides of the chain. Many, but not all, of the proteins in the human body have some part of the polypeptide chain folded in this way.

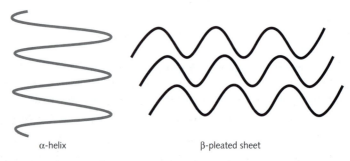

α-helix   β-pleated sheet

Figure 5.14 Diagrammatic representation of secondary structure of a protein

Collagen, a protein found in tendons and other connective tissue, is formed from three polypeptide chains, each of which has an α-helix structure that is then twisted around to produce a triple helix structure that prevents collagen, and therefore tendons, stretching.

The polypeptide chain of most proteins undergoes more extensive folding to produce a three-dimensional globular structure. This is termed the **tertiary (3°) structure** that is held together by ionic bonds, disulphide bridges (a covalent bond between two sulphur atoms projecting from different parts of the polypeptide chain) and hydrophobic interactions as seen in lipids (see Figure 5.15).

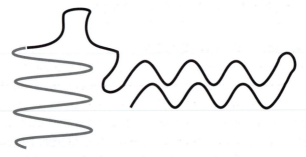

Figure 5.15 Diagrammatic representation of the tertiary structure of a protein incorporating α-helix and β-pleated sheet secondary structures

Finally, many large, complex proteins consist of more than one polypeptide chain held together by hydrophobic interaction, hydrogen and ionic bonds. This is the **quaternary (4°) structure** and refers to the specific arrangement of the folded polypeptide chains.

In addition to amino acids, proteins may interact with '**prosthetic groups**' – the groups of atoms also known as co-factors, that can be particularly important in the functioning of protein. Many vitamins act as co-factors.

As the shape of proteins is critical to their role any change to the structure will affect function. As such, proteins are sensitive to changes in temperature and pH, either of which will disrupt the bonds holding the protein molecules in its secondary or tertiary structure – resulting in the protein becoming **denatured**.

Haemoglobin is a protein that exhibits all levels of protein structure.

Nucleic acids

Nucleic acids provide the template for the production of all the proteins within our body. They are based upon polymers of a sugar, a phosphate group and nitrogen containing bases. There are two types of nucleic acid:

1 Ribonucleic acid or RNA is composed of phosphate, the sugar ribose and the bases guanine, adenine, cytosine and uracil.
2 Deoxyribonucleic acid or DNA also contains phosphate, but the sugar is deoxyribose and the bases are guanine, adenine, cytosine and thymine.

The basic monomeric unit of a sugar, phosphate group and base is called a nucleotide. RNA exists in different forms but consists of no more than a few hundred nucleotides forming a single-stranded molecule. DNA contains thousands of nucleotides forming two strands that are twisted around each other in a double helix and held together by hydrogen bonds between what are termed complementary bases. The sequence of bases in DNA provides the genetic code for the production of all the proteins a living organism needs, whilst RNA helps to translate this code, gene by gene, into protein production.

Assessment activity 5.3

Carry out practical investigations on the identification of carbohydrates, lipids and proteins, relating results obtained to the structure and function of these macromolecules.

Physics and chemistry of homeostasis

Transport between compartments

The concept of homeostasis was introduced in Unit 4. You will have learnt that homeostasis is the maintenance of the body's internal environment in the face of constant disruption from external or internal events. One aspect of the homeostatic process is the requirement to move substances between the various compartments that separate the internal from the external environment. The internal compartments are the intracellular and extracellular fluids, and the blood, which acts as the link between these and the external environment (see Figure 5.16).

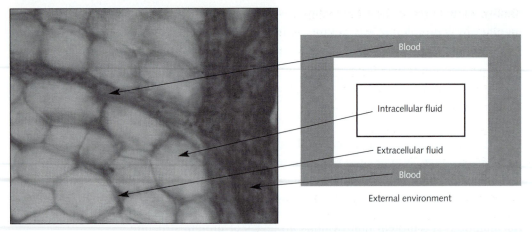

Figure 5.16 Photomicrograph of stained adipose tissue related to model of body compartments

Movement between these compartments is based upon the basic chemical and physical principles of diffusion and include simple diffusion, facilitated diffusion and osmosis.

Simple diffusion

Molecules and ions within a solution are continually moving about due to the **kinetic energy** (the energy of motion) they possess. The random mixing of molecules and ions is called **diffusion**.

If a particular ion or molecule is present in high concentration in one area and in low concentration in another area, the difference in concentration between the two areas creates a **concentration gradient**. As a result, particles from the region of high concentration diffuse to the region of low concentration. Such movement is called **net diffusion** and the substance is said to be moving along or down its concentration gradient. The point at which there is no further net diffusion results in all the particles in solution being in **equilibrium**.

In describing the diffusion of gases within say the respiratory and cardiovascular systems it is common to talk about the partial pressure of gases in air or solution and the movement of a gas from an area of high partial pressure to one of low partial pressure. The behaviour of gases and the concept of partial pressure are based upon a number of physical principles known as the gas laws (though not all need to be considered here).

Avogadro's law states that equal volumes of all gases, measured at the same temperature and pressure, contain the same number of particles (atoms or molecules).

Boyle's law looked at the relationship between pressure and volume of fixed masses of a gas and found that volume is proportional to the inverse of pressure, such that a decrease in volume caused an increase in pressure:

$$V \propto 1/P$$

In order for air to enter the lungs the pressure inside the alveoli of the lungs must be lower than the pressure outside the body, i.e. atmospheric pressure. The expansion of the thoracic cage by contraction of the diaphragm and muscles between the ribs (intercostal muscles) causes an increase in volume within the thoracic cavity. According to Boyle's law, this increase in volume will result in a decrease in pressure in the lungs so that air is drawn into the alveoli from outside.

Dalton's law looks at the relationship between gases in a mixture and states that the partial pressure of a gas in a mixture is the pressure created by that gas if no other gases are present. Atmospheric air is a mixture of oxygen (21 per cent), carbon dioxide (0.04 per cent), nitrogen (79 per cent), water vapour and other gases present in negligible amounts. On the basis of Dalton's law, atmospheric pressure is the sum of all the partial pressures of each gas:

Atmospheric pressure = $pO_2 + pCO_2 + pN_2 + pH_2O$

The partial pressure of each gas in a mixture can be determined by multiplying the percentage of the gas in the mixture by the total pressure of the mixture. Pressure is measured in pascals, although it isn't uncommon for the older style of unit – mm Hg – to be used (1 pascal = 1 newton m^{-2} = 0.0075 mm Hg). At sea level the atmospheric pressure is 101 kPa or 760mm Hg and the partial pressure of oxygen is:

$$pO_2 = \frac{21}{100} \times 101 = 21.2 \text{ kPa}$$

and for carbon dioxide:

$$pCO_2 = \frac{0.04}{100} \times 101 = 4 \text{ kPa.}$$

pO_2 and pCO_2 of alveolar air, oxygenated blood, deoxygenated blood and for extracellular fluid are as follows:

	Alveolar air kPa	Oxygenated blood kPa	Deoxygenated blood kPa	Extracellular fluid kPa
pO_2	14.00	14.00	5.33	5.33
pCO_2	5.33	5.33	6.00	6.00

Looking at the table, and remembering that diffusion is from an area of high partial pressure to one of low partial pressure, it can be seen that oxygen will diffuse from the alveoli into deoxygenated blood passing through the pulmonary capillaries and carbon dioxide will diffuse in the opposite direction (blood to alveoli).

Assessment activity 5.4

With reference to the above table, what happens to oxygen and carbon dioxide between oxygenated blood and tissue fluid?

At high altitude there are fewer molecules of air so air pressure is less though the proportions of each gas remain the same. For every 5000 m increase in height, air pressure is roughly halved. Above 3000 m we begin to suffer from altitude sickness.

Determine the partial pressures of oxygen and carbon dioxide in the air we breathe at 5000 m and 10,000 m. Compare these values with the values of pO_2 and pCO_2 for deoxygenated blood. What are the consequences?

Research altitude sickness in relation to the physics and chemistry of the blood and other homeostatic mechanisms that attempt to 'acclimatise' the body.

Henry's law explains the solubility of gases and states that the quantity of a gas that will dissolve in a liquid is proportional to the partial pressure of the gas and its solubility coefficient when the temperature remains constant. The solubility of carbon dioxide is high, whilst that of oxygen and nitrogen is low. This explains why CO_2 can be carried around the circulatory system dissolved in the plasma where it reacts with water to form carbonic acid whilst oxygen needs the assistance of the blood protein haemoglobin. Together with Dalton's law it also explains why deep-sea divers get 'nitrogen narcosis' and decompression sickness or the bends.

Because diffusion is dependent on the kinetic energy of the particles, anything that increases the kinetic energy, such as heat, will result in particles moving more rapidly such that diffusion occurs more quickly. Thus, the warming of air entering the lungs assists in the rapid diffusion of gases.

Within the body, substances may have to diffuse across several layers, e.g., plasma membranes, basement membranes, connective tissue. Here the rate at which the particles diffuse will be dependent not only upon the concentration of such particles but also the thickness of the membranes, etc., and the total surface area through which they are passing. These parameters are related through **Fick's law**:

$$\text{Rate of diffusion} \propto \frac{\text{Surface area} \times \text{Difference in concentration}}{\text{Thickness of membrane}}.$$

Facilitated diffusion

Urea, glucose, fructose, galactose and certain vitamins diffuse through the plasma membrane by **facilitated diffusion**. In this process, the substance moves along or down its concentration gradient with the help of specific membrane proteins that serve as water-filled **channels** or **transporters** for particular substances. The rate of diffusion is determined by the concentration gradient between the inside and outside of the cell for that particular substance and by the number of substance specific channels available.

Glucose is an important molecule that crosses the membrane by facilitated diffusion in the following manner:

1 The glucose molecule attaches to the protein channel on the outside of the membrane.
2 The protein molecule changes shape.
3 Glucose diffuses into the cell.
4 An enzyme called glucokinase catalyses the attachment of a phosphate group to glucose to make glucose-6-phophate.

Note: The change in shape of the protein allows the glucose molecule to enter the cell and glucokinase ensures that the concentration of glucose within the cell is always very low, so favouring the movement of glucose into, rather than out of, the cell.

Osmosis

This involves the net diffusion of a solvent (water in living systems) through a **partially** or **selectively permeable membrane** and is described in terms of **water potential, solute potential** and **pressure potential**.

Water potential describes the kinetic energy of water molecules and can be measured in units of energy, e.g. joules, but is more commonly expressed in units of pressure, i.e. mm Hg or pascals. The greater the concentration of water molecules in a system, the greater the total kinetic energy and the higher the water potential. Pure water has the greatest water potential as it has the highest concentration of water molecules. In terms of the activity of water molecules there will always be a movement from an area of higher water potential to one of lower water potential, which is just another way of describing diffusion from an area of high concentration to one of low concentration.

If a substance or solute is added to pure water, the concentration of water molecules is reduced and the water potential is lowered. This lowering of the water potential due to the addition of a solute is called the **solute potential** and is always a negative value. The greater the concentration of solute, the lower (more negative) the solute potential.

A tissue cell is composed of between 75 per cent and 90 per cent water, with solutes making up the remainder and is surrounded by extracellular fluid containing about 90 per cent water and 10 per cent solutes. Consequently, extracellular fluid has a higher water and solute potential than the cytoplasm. This means that the water molecules in the tissue fluid have a greater kinetic energy and will be moving around more rapidly than the water molecules in the cytoplasm. Water molecules will move from a region of higher energy, or higher water potential, to one of lower energy or lower water potential, such that there is a net movement of water molecules into the cell.

If there is an increase in **hydrostatic pressure** within a system the water potential increases. This increase is known as the **pressure potential** and tends to be a positive value. A tissue cell taking in water by osmosis has a lower solute potential compared to that of the surrounding tissue fluid and as a result the pressure potential increases, due to the resistance created by the cell membrane. When the pressure potential plus the solute potential equals the water potential there will be no further movement of water molecules:

Water potential = Solute potential + Pressure potential.

However, animal cell membranes exert little if any resistance so that an increase in water potential outside the cell, or a lowering of solute potential inside the cell, will result in movement of water molecules into the cell. The cell subsequently increases in size until the cell bursts. Alternatively, an increase of solute potential inside the cell or a decrease in water potential in the tissue fluid (or a lowering of the solute potential) will result in a net movement of water out of the cell which will cause the cell to shrink and the cell membrane. Thus it is extremely important for water, solute and pressure potential of tissue fluid to be in equilibrium with the cytoplasm.

The concentrations of substances within body fluids is crucial to maintaining homeostasis since any great departure from the 'norm' will result in changes in osmotic potential that could lead to cell disruption.

Assessment activity 5.5

Carry out practical investigations on diffusion and osmosis, applying findings to the homeostasis of body fluids between intracellular and extracellular compartments.

Theory into practice

Moles, molar and molar equivalents

When a patient in hospital is placed on an intravenous (IV) drip for the purpose of providing nutrients, preventing dehydration or for the delivery of drugs, it is essential that the fluids being introduced into the bloodstream don't cause disruption of blood cells.

As a result, the constituents of a drip must be isotonic with that of the blood cells, i.e. the concentration of water molecules and solutes are the same as the intracellular fluid of blood cells. It has been found that a 0.9 per cent solution of sodium chloride (a saline solution) is isotonic with blood cells – 0.9 per cent sodium chloride means that there is 0.9 grams of salt in every 100 cm^3 of water.

Whilst the majority of IV drips are expressed in terms of percentage concentration some may be shown in moles/litre, moles dm^{-3} or milliequivalents. A mole is the relative atomic mass in grams of any element or molecule. As drips are solutions the amount of solute expressed in moles/litre or moles which is the same as moles dm^{-3} is calculated using the formula:

$$\text{Moles dm}^{-3} \text{ (molarity)} = \frac{\text{Mass dm}^{-3}}{\text{Relative molecular mass}}.$$

If we consider a 0.9 per cent saline solution, the relative molecular mass is the relative atomic mass of sodium plus chlorine. If you look at the periodic table (see page 178) you will see that these are 23 and 35.5 respectively, so

Relative molecular mass NaCl = 23 + 35.5 = 58.5.

The mass of sodium chloride = 0.9 g in 100 cm^3 water = 9.0g dm^{-3}.

Therefore:

Molarity = 9.0 ÷ 58.5 = 0.15 moles dm^{-3}.

Some solutions are expressed in terms of molarity. This refers to the number of molar equivalents of solute per dm^3 of solution and is used to express concentrations in relation to particular types of reaction, i.e. redox and acid-base reactions.

Chemical reactions

A chemical reaction can simply be regarded as the change of one substance into another, or the combination of atoms or molecules. In order for a change to take place chemical bonds have to be broken and new ones made. The process of breaking bonds requires energy whilst the formation of bonds releases energy. The energy required to break bonds usually comes in the form of heat, but may also result from light or electrical energy. The amount of heat required or released in a reaction will vary depending upon conditions such as pressure, the amount or concentration of substances involved and the presence or absence of catalysts.

Chemical reactions are subject to the laws of thermodynamics. The first law states that energy can be neither created nor destroyed only converted from one form to another. Thus in a chemical reaction, energy usually in the form of heat is converted to the energy of chemical bonds or when chemical bonds are broken the energy stored in the bonds (**potential energy**) is released as heat. The second law states that any change in a system leads to an overall increase in disorder or **entropy**.

The heat energy of a chemical reaction is known as **enthalpy** and is a consequence of the first law of thermodynamics. In reactions where energy is required the enthalpy change is positive and the reaction is termed endothermic or endergonic. In reactions where heat energy is released, the enthalpy change is negative and the reaction is exothermic or exergonic. Enthalpy changes can be represented graphically as energy level diagrams where the energy changes of a reaction over time can be represented (see Figure 5.17).

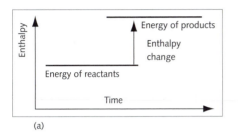
(a)

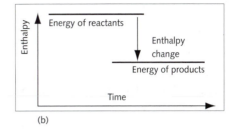
(b)

Figure 5.17 Enthalpy diagrams for (a) endothermic reaction and (b) exothermic reaction

The input of energy increases the **kinetic energy** of the molecules or atoms. The molecules move around more quickly and are consequently more likely to collide, at which point electrons in the outer shells rearrange themselves so bonds are broken and formed. The point at which the electrons are disrupted before becoming part of new bonds is called the transition state of a chemical reaction and the energy that is needed to enable reactants to change into the products is called the activation energy. This can be seen in the enthalpy diagram for an exothermic reaction (Figure 5.18).

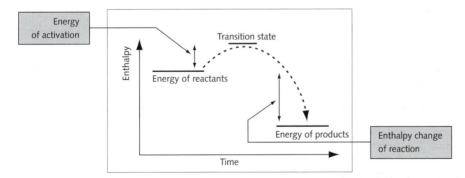

Figure 5.18 Enthalpy diagram for an exothermic reaction showing the transition state

Since part of the reason substances react is due to their colliding with each other, then any factor that allows this to occur more quickly will increase the speed or rate of reaction. Such factors include the following:

- The concentration of reactants – this increases the number of reactant molecules such that they will be closer together, thereby increasing the chance of collisions.
- Pressure – increasing the pressure of gaseous substances increases the number of reactants in a given volume, so increasing the chance of collisions.
- Surface area – the greater the surface area of solid reactants, the faster the rate of reaction.
- Light – light as a form of energy affects the rate of certain reactions, e.g. the formation of vitamin D in the skin is dependent upon light energy.

- Catalysts affect reaction rates – a catalyst is a substance that affects the rate of reaction without being chemically changed itself.

In humans, and the vast majority of other living organisms, the temperatures at which they operate are such that the chemical reactions that need to take place would take too long if they occurred at all, since they may not possess enough kinetic energy to collide or reach transition states. However, living organisms are able to overcome this problem by the use of enzymes that act as catalysts, reducing the activation energy needed to reach the transition state whereby a reaction takes place. As a consequence, reactions can take place at body temperature at very fast rates, i.e. 1000 molecules of substrate per second for each molecule of enzyme. The other advantage of enzymes as catalysts is that they enable a reaction to happen without being altered themselves, so they can be recycled over and over again.

The action of enzymes is known to involve an interaction between the enzyme and the substrate molecule or molecules that are involved in the chemical reaction. This interaction is called the lock and key hypothesis or, more accurately, the induced fit hypothesis. The enzyme as a protein has a shape resulting from its three-dimensional structure, as we have already seen. Part of the enzyme molecule, called the active site, is shaped so that the substrate molecule fits into it. When this happens the enzyme-substrate complex (as it is now termed) becomes activated so the chemical reaction can take place (see Figure 5.19). Once the reaction is complete the products will be a different shape to the substrate and will no longer fit the active site on the enzyme so will fall out. This leaves the enzyme free to react with another substrate molecule.

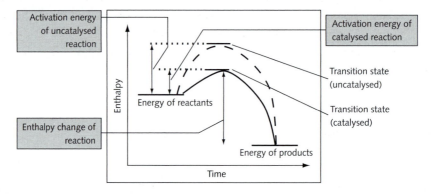

Figure 5.19 Enthalpy diagram to show effect of enzyme catalysed reaction on activation energy

Chemists identify two main groups of chemical reaction: redox and non-redox. Within each group there are three other types of reaction identified, as shown in the table below.

Non-redox		Redox	
1	Combination reactions where two or more reactants combine to form a product	1	Combination
2	Double replacement reactions where two reactants exchange atoms or groups of atoms	2	Single replacement where one element replaces another in a compound
3	Decomposition reactions where a single reactant gives two or more products	3	Decomposition

Chemists, biochemists and biologists talk about all sorts of different types of reaction but all fit into the above categories. Within the human body a wide range of enzyme catalysed reactions occurs and the term **metabolism** is used to describe all the different chemical reactions that are taking place. Metabolism includes both redox and non-redox reactions that involve combination and decomposition, although biologists often refer to combination reactions as anabolic reactions and decomposition reactions as catabolic reactions. Thus metabolism is the sum total of all the anabolic and catabolic reactions occurring within the body.

1   Anabolic reactions are combination reactions where atoms, ions or molecules combine to form new, larger molecules. Such reactions lead to the synthesis of new materials, such as carbohydrates and proteins, and require energy to make them take place. The formation of carbohydrates and proteins from the combination of more simple molecules involves the removal of hydrogen and hydroxyl groups from the participating reactants. The hydrogen and hydroxyl groups form water molecules such that these combination reactions are termed **condensation**.

$$
\begin{array}{ccc}
\underset{\substack{\text{H}\\\diagdown\\\diagup\\\text{H}}}{\overset{\text{R}}{\underset{\substack{|\\\text{H O}}}{\text{N–C–C–OH}}}} +
\underset{\substack{\text{H}\\\diagdown\\\diagup\\\text{H}\;\;\diagdown\\\;\;\;\;\text{H}}}{\overset{\text{R}}{\underset{\substack{|\\\text{H O}}}{\text{N–C–C–OH}}}} \rightarrow \text{H}_2\text{O} +
\underset{\substack{\text{H}\\\diagdown\\\diagup\\\text{H}}}{\overset{\text{R}\qquad\qquad\text{R}}{\underset{\substack{|\;||\quad\;|\;|\;||\\\text{H O}\;\;\;\text{H H O}}}{\text{N–C–C–O–N–C–C–OH}}}}
\end{array}
$$

    Amino acid 1   Amino acid 2   Dipeptide

Esterification is a specialised condensation reaction involving the combination of a alcohol and an organic acid to form an ester. The formation of a triglyceride (the ester) from glycerol (the alcohol) and three fatty acids is an example of esterification that occurs in fatty tissue. This type of reaction is a condensation reaction since water is removed in the process.

$$
\begin{array}{ccccccc}
\text{CH}_2\text{OH} & & \overset{\text{O}}{\overset{||}{\text{HO-C-R}}} & & \text{CH}_2\text{OC-R} \overset{\displaystyle\text{O}}{} & & \\
| & & \overset{\text{O}}{\overset{||}{}} & & |\;\;\overset{\text{O}}{\overset{||}{}} & & \\
\text{CHOH} & + & \text{HO-C-R}' & \rightarrow & \text{CHOC-R}' & + & 3\text{H}_2\text{O} \\
| & & \overset{\text{O}}{\overset{||}{}} & & |\;\;\overset{\text{O}}{\overset{||}{}} & & \\
\text{CH}_2\text{OH} & & \text{HO-C-R}'' & & \text{CH}_2\text{OC-R}'' & & \\
\end{array}
$$

glycerol   3 fatty acids   triglyceride   water

[R, R' and R" represent different alkyl groups in the above chemical equation, where an alkyl group is a long hydrocarbon chain.]

2   Catabolic reactions are decomposition reactions that include both non-redox and redox reactions.

An example of a non-redox reaction is the breakdown of glycogen to glucose in the liver in response to falling blood glucose. It involves the splitting of glucose molecules from the ends of the glycogen by the enzyme catalysed addition of water. This decomposition reaction is termed **hydrolysis**. The glucose produced enters the bloodstream to restore blood sugar levels.

Many catabolic reactions are redox reactions that involve the breakdown or decomposition of larger molecules into smaller ones with the release of energy. Traditionally, redox reactions referred to the addition of oxygen and as a result one substance would become oxidised whilst the other was reduced. It is now deemed to involve the transfer of electrons to and from different substances, though in biological systems this can involve the transfer of hydrogen atoms. The chemical that loses the electrons (or hydrogen atoms) is oxidised whilst the one that gains electrons becomes reduced.

In every cell of our body glucose is broken down to produce energy by a whole series of redox and non-redox reactions that can be summarised by the chemical equation:

$$C_6H_{12}O_6 \; + \; 6O_2 \; \rightarrow \; 6CO_2 \; + \; 6H_2O \; + \; \text{ENERGY}.$$

glucose	oxygen	carbon dioxide	water

One of the reactions involves the production of pyruvic acid. If there is no oxygen available to continue the breakdown process, i.e. cells are respiring anaerobically, then the pyruvic acid is oxidised to lactic acid, i.e. lactic acid gains two electrons. When oxygen becomes available the reaction is reversed so that lactic acid is reduced to pyruvic acid with the loss of two electrons.

```
COOH                                            COOH
|                add 2H (2H+ + 2e-)             |
C=O          ─────────────────────────►         CHOH
|            ◄─────────────────────────         |
CH3              remove 2H (2H+ + 2e-)           CH3

pyruvic acid                                    lactic acid
```

Assessment activity 5.6

Carry out experiments on the effects of substrate concentration, pH and temperature on the activity of enzymes and relate the findings to the importance of enzymes in human physiology.

Solutions

Water, solutions, pH and buffers

Water possesses a number of unique properties such that life would not exist without it. Estimates of water content show that over 90 per cent of blood plasma is water; muscle contains about 80 per cent water and more than 50 per cent of most other tissues is water, such that some 75 per cent of total body mass is water. As well as being the most abundant cell component, water is effectively responsible for transporting all the nutrients required by cells, the oxygen used by cells and the waste products they produce.

The importance of water, and its job as the 'solvent of life', are a consequence of the physical properties unique to this compound.

Water *boils at 100°C*, yet in comparison with other similar compounds the boiling point should be –100°C. On the same basis, the melting point of water at 0°C is very high and it also has a high heat of vaporisation (this is the heat required to turn liquid water into gaseous water or water vapour). This enables many terrestrial animals to maintain their body temperature through sweating and panting, body heat being used to evaporate the moisture on the skin.

Water has a very *high specific heat capacity* (the amount of energy required to raise 1 kg of a substance by 1°K). This again helps to stabilise body temperature as it takes a lot of heat to increase the temperature of water, so warm-blooded organisms will not get too hot, nor will they cool down very quickly.

As water cools, its *density increases to a maximum at 4°C*. Below this temperature the water molecules become arranged in a lattice structure, with large spaces between them. As a result ice is less dense than water and floats. Ice covering a body of water acts like the glass of a greenhouse, allowing the heat of the sun to penetrate to the water below whilst preventing heat escaping. This enables aquatic organisms to survive in the water under the ice for many months. The reason why ice and water appear blue is that only certain wavelengths penetrate into deeper waters, i.e. blue and green colours whilst red and orange are absorbed.

Another feature of water turning to ice is that as it freezes a large amount of heat is released which actually helps in slowing down the freezing process. This is called the *heat of fusion*.

Water has a *high surface tension*. A watery film called surfactant found between the pleural membranes of the lungs creates a surface tension that contributes to the process of breathing.

All the above properties are a consequence of the polarity of water molecules and their ability to form **hydrogen bonds** between themselves or other polar molecules as has already been shown.

Solvents and solutes
The polarity of the water molecule allows water to act as an excellent solvent. A **solvent** is a substance (solid, liquid or gas) in which another substance (solid, liquid or gas) called the **solute** will dissolve.

Most substances carrying a positive or negative charge will dissolve in water as the polar water molecules can surround the charged ions or groups, holding them in suspension. As a consequence any substance that carries a charge will dissolve in water, the water molecules literally surrounding the solute particles.

When a salt, such as sodium chloride, is added to water the ions become separated by water molecules and are said to be **dissociated** (see Figure 5.20). The extent to which dissociation occurs is dependent upon the solubility of the salt such that in a solution of a salt there will be an equilibrium between the number of salt molecules and its dissociated ions.

$$NaCl \rightleftharpoons Na^+ + Cl^-$$

The use of two arrows is to show that there is an equilibrium between the amount of sodium chloride and sodium and chloride ions. Changing conditions will increase or decrease the amount of salt and its dissociated ions, i.e. the chemical equation can shift in either direction.

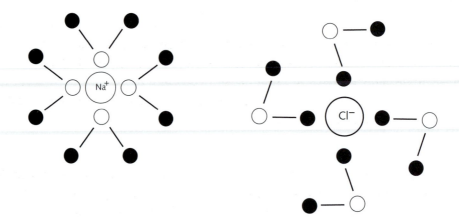

Figure 5.20 Dissociation of sodium chloride by solvating action of water molecules

pH

Water is also capable of dissociating into the ions H^+ and OH^-.

$$H_2O \rightleftharpoons H^+ + OH^-$$

The concentration of each ion in pure water has been determined as 1×10^{-7} mol dm^{-3}. The addition or removal of H^+ causes a solution to become **acidic** or **basic (alkaline)** and any substance that has the ability to donate hydrogen ions is called an **acid** whilst any substance that accepts or removes hydrogen ions from solution is called a **base**. Therefore any change to the concentration of hydrogen ions changes the acidity of the solution.

The number of hydrogen ions in solutions of different acidity or alkalinity varies enormously, e.g. gastric juice formed from hydrochloric acid produced by the stomach lining contains 10^{-2} moles (0.01 moles) of hydrogen ions, whilst human blood contains some 3.98×10^{-8} moles (0.000 000 0398 moles) of hydrogen ions, a change in concentration of around 100,000 times. Consequently, to help comprehend these very small numbers acidity is measured on the **pH** scale. pH is based upon logarithmic values of the hydrogen ion concentration:

$$pH = -\log[H^+]$$

where $[H^+]$ = hydrogen ion concentration.

This enables acidity to be measured on a scale from 0 to 14 where a change in pH of 1 represents a ten-fold change in hydrogen ion concentration. Thus, gastric juice has a pH of around 2 and blood a pH of about 7.4. Pure water has a pH of 7.

When we exercise there is an increase in the amount of carbon dioxide entering the bloodstream as a result of increased cellular respiration. The carbon dioxide dissolves in the water of the plasma and most of it reacts with water catalysed by the enzyme carbonic anhydrase to form carbonic acid. Carbonic acid then dissociates to form hydrogen carbonate and hydrogen ions that increase the acidity of the blood.

$$H_2O + CO_2 \underset{\text{anhydrase}}{\overset{\text{Carbonic}}{\rightleftharpoons}} H_2CO_3 \quad \text{Carbonic acid}$$

$$H_2CO_3 \rightleftharpoons HCO_3^- + H^+$$

> The hydrogen ions increase the acidity of the blood

Vigorous exercise means that actively respiring cells, particularly skeletal muscle cells do not have enough oxygen available to catabolise glucose for energy production. Such conditions are termed anaerobic and result in the oxidation of pyruvic acid to lactic acid (see redox reactions). Lactic acid dissociates in solution to release hydrogen ions that can exacerbate the effects of carbonic acid.

Buffers
Generally, large changes in pH cannot be tolerated by living organisms and as such they regulate their internal environment to resist or control pH. This is done by the use of **buffers**, mixtures of weak acids and their soluble salts. If the hydrogen ion concentration increases (pH goes down), buffers react with the extra H^+ ions so removing them from solution to keep the pH constant. Conversely, if the hydrogen ion concentration decreases (pH goes up) the buffer releases hydrogen ions into solution to keep the pH constant. There are three main buffer systems within the body:

1 Carbonic acid-hydrogen carbonate system – uses carbonic acid as the weak acid and sodium hydrogen carbonate as the soluble salt.
2 Phosphate system – uses sodium dihydrogen phosphate as the weak acid and sodium monohydrogen phosphate as its soluble salt.
3 Protein system – the most abundant buffer in the body cells and blood plasma, this system utilises the carboxylic acid and amino groups of these molecules. When the number of hydrogen ions in solution increases, leading to a fall in pH, the amino groups will mop up the excess hydrogen ions. If the pH rises, the decrease in hydrogen ions results in carboxylic acid groups dissociating to release hydrogen ions and so restore pH.

The pH of blood and extracellular fluid is maintained between 7.35 and 7.45 by all the above systems.

Colloids, suspensions and viscosity
True solutions are where the solute particles are generally less than 1 nm in diameter and distributed throughout the solvent. Sweat and urine are dilute solutions of salts and waste materials in water.

Solutions where the molecules are between 1 nm and 1000 nm in diameter are called **colloids**. The surfactant that lubricates the lungs is a colloid and cell membranes are colloids based on phospholipids and proteins.

Suspensions are solutions in which the solute particles are greater than 1000 nm and as such can only remain dispersed if continuously agitated.

Blood is regarded as a suspension of blood cells, although it also acts as a solution and a colloid. Plasma is composed of 92 per cent water and about 1 per cent dissolved gases, ions and waste materials, the remaining 7 per cent are proteins, the size of which gives plasma its colloidal properties.

Another feature of blood as a liquid is its viscosity or stickiness. This has important consequences for our health since blood travels through tubes (blood vessels) of different diameter and a resistive force occurs between the viscous blood and the walls of the blood vessels that reduces blood flow. The blood flowing nearest the walls of the blood vessels is affected more than that in the middle, but as the blood vessels get narrower the effect increases. The flow of a fluid is related to its viscosity and the radius of a tube through which it is flowing. By halving the radius of a blood vessel, blood flow decreases by a factor 16. In heart disease, where high levels of blood cholesterol lead to the development of atherosclerotic plaques in arteries (particularly the coronary arteries), blood vessel size is markedly decreased so the rate of flow of blood is affected dramatically – which consequently reduces nutrient and oxygen supply to tissues.

Assessment activity 5.7

Carry out investigations on the effects of exercise on respiratory function and relate results to homeostatic mechanisms controlling pH.

Physical principles of specific human functions

Sound and hearing

When you throw a stone into a pond, the surface of the water is thrown into a series of ripples that moves outwards from where the stone landed. When the stone lands on the water it pushes water molecules close to it out of the way. These water molecules then push against other water molecules, so that the disturbance spreads across the water surface as a wave. What has happened is that the kinetic energy of the stone has been transferred to the water. However, because the water molecules can interact with each other (remember hydrogen bonds) they have a push-me pull-you effect on each other. This pushing and pulling effect between the water molecules gives the water elasticity or 'springiness' and results not only in the effect being carried through the water (the movement of the wave) but also means that more than one wave is produced (the ripples).

Although we can't see it, the same happens when air is disturbed. When you slam a door the air molecules in the doorway are pushed together or compressed. Because some air molecules have been pushed together others are pulled apart, creating a region where there is less air. This is referred to as rarefied air and is often used in talking about the air at high altitudes because there is less of it. The compression and rarefaction of the air from slamming the door travels across the room disturbing the curtains on the other side. The difference in the wave in a pool of water and that created by the door slamming is in the way it travels. The wave in the pool is known as a **transverse wave** whilst that of the air is a **longitudinal wave**.

What has all this got to do with sound? Well, when you listen to your stereo the loudspeakers vibrate and in doing so 'push at and pull on' the air next to it. This creates waves (sound waves) of compression and rarefaction that reaches our eardrums (see Figure 5.21). The eardrum or tympanic membrane is springy like the water surface, so that a wave of compressed air pushes against it. The rarefied air that follows allows the eardrum to spring back. The number of waves of compression and rarefaction created by

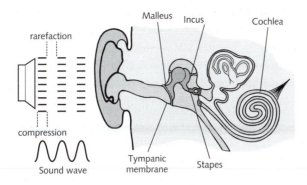

Figure 5.21 Diagrammatic representation of sound waves generated by a loudspeaker being perceived by the ear

the vibrating speaker will create the same number of vibrations in the eardrum. This is called the **frequency** of the sound, that is measured as the number of waves or cycles per second or hertz (Hz). The vibrations of the tympanic membrane are transmitted to the much smaller oval window via three tiny bones or ossicles called the malleus (hammer), incus (anvil) and stapes (stirrup). The lever system of these bones, together with the difference in size of the two eardrums, creates an amplification effect of around ×30. The vibration of the oval window creates waves within the fluid (perilymph) of the cochlea of the inner ear (just like the stone being thrown into water), that is transmitted across another membrane (the basilar membrane), to move the hair cells in the organ of Corti that triggers nerve impulses to the hearing centre of the brain so that we perceive the sound.

The loudspeaker can vibrate more or less rapidly, so producing sound waves of different frequencies that stimulate different groups of hair cells to enable us to differentiate between sounds on the basis of their frequency or pitch. The human ear can detect sound waves between 20 Hz and 20,000 Hz (20 kHz).

Above 20,000 Hz sound waves are called **ultrasonic** waves that can have frequencies as high as 600 million Hz (600 MHz). Such high frequency sound waves are used in **ultrasound** scanning. Sound waves of less than 20 Hz are termed **infrasound**. Dogs can detect ultrasound frequencies as high as 45,000 Hz and bats up 120,000 Hz. Elephants, on the other hand, are able to detect infrasound frequencies as low as 5 Hz.

Turning up the volume of your stereo causes the speaker to vibrate more. This does not mean it vibrates more rapidly but that the backwards and forwards movement of the speaker is larger. You can think of this as throwing a larger stone into the water. More energy is transmitted from the stone to the water so that the waves are bigger. In terms of the stereo speakers, the larger movement of the speaker causes the sound waves to be bigger. The size of the wave is termed its **amplitude** and is commonly referred to as the **intensity** of the sound (see Figure 5.22). The effect of this on the ear is to cause the eardrum to make a larger movement, which consequently makes the perilymph move more, increasing the stimulation of the hair cells so a louder sound is heard. However, loudness and intensity are not the same as two people may perceive a sound of the same intensity to be of a different loudness, i.e, loudness is subjective.

The most intense sound that the human ear can bear without being damaged is more than 1000 billion times more intense than the quietest sound, called the threshold of

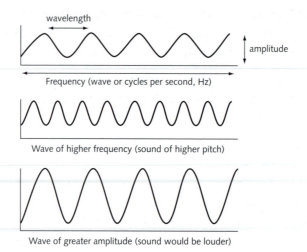

wavelength

amplitude

Frequency (wave or cycles per second, Hz)

Wave of higher frequency (sound of higher pitch)

Wave of greater amplitude (sound would be louder)

Figure 5.22 Sound waves

hearing. As the range of hearing is so large intensity of sound is measured in multiples of 10, i.e. a **logarithmic** scale. The intensity at the threshold of hearing is assigned a decibel rating of 0dB. The table below shows what happens to the decibel rating for every ×10 increase in intensity.

Intensity	Decibel	
0	0	Threshold of hearing
10	10	
100	20	
1000	30	
10,000	40	
100,000	50	
1,000,000	60	
10,000,000	70	
100,000,000	80	
1,000,000,000	90	
10,000,000,000	100	
100,000,000,000	110	Pop concert
1,000,000,000,000	120	
10,000,000,000,000	130	Threshold of pain
100,000,000,000,000	140	
1,000,000,000,000,000	150	
10,000,000,000,000,000	160	Instant perforation of eardrum

As you can see, for every ×10 increase in intensity the decibel rating increases by 10. Therefore, being at the front of a rock concert that records a decibel rating of 110 dB is 100,000,000,000 more intense than the quietest sound you can hear! Instant perforation of the eardrum occurs at 160 dB, with 130 dB being the threshold of pain which occurs when the ossicles of the middle ear are vibrating so strongly that they bang against the wall of the middle ear. Sustained noise of more than 85 dB can cause permanent damage to the inner ear.

One of the problems with using the decibel scale to measure intensity is that humans are able to hear some frequencies louder than others. As a consequence, different decibel scales have been devised to measure sound intensity at different frequencies.

The distance from the start of one wave or compression to the start of the beginning of the next is called the **wavelength**. Wavelength is a function of the speed of the sound wave and its frequency and are related by the equation:

$$\text{Wavelegth } (\lambda) = \frac{\text{Speed}}{\text{Frequency}}.$$

The speed of the sound wave is governed only by the type of medium through which it is travelling. As we perceive sound through the air, then the speed is more or less constant at around 340m sec^{-1}. As we hear sound between frequencies 20 and 20,000 Hz the wavelength varies between 17 m (at 20 Hz) and 1.7 cm (at 20,000 Hz).

The speed of sound is affected by the density of the medium it is travelling through, such that the greater the density, the greater the speed. This results from the molecules of which the medium is composed being more closely packed together, so a sound wave will be transmitted more rapidly from molecule to molecule. In water the speed of sound is around 1,230 msec^{-1} and in a solid such as steel is around 6000 msec^{-1}. Temperature also affects the speed of sound due to the increased kinetic energy of the molecules through which it is travelling. So, the speed of sound in air at 0°C is 331 msec^{-1} and at 20°C it is 343 msec^{-1}.

When sound waves hit an object that is larger than the wavelength then it can be either **reflected** and/or **refracted**. The reflection of sound is demonstrated when you hear an echo. The sound waves are bouncing off the object in front of us. In order that we hear the echo, the object must be fairly solid and be far enough away for the difference in the sound emitted being distinguished from the echo. If the object is compressible, such as water, part of a sound wave will be reflected and part will pass into the water – refraction (see Figure 5.23). This may seem a bit odd, but next time you are in the bath stick your head under the water and get someone to shout at you. You will hear the sound, though not as loudly as you would if your head was out of the water. **Refraction** occurs at the boundary between two mediums through which sound travels. It involves the sound waves changing in wavelength, speed and direction as they pass from one medium to the other.

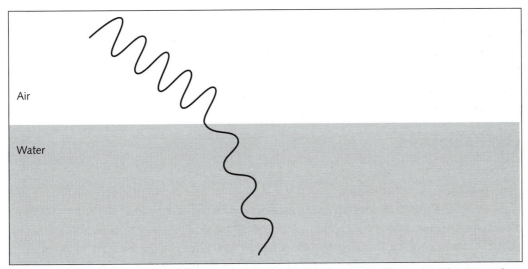

Air

Water

Figure 5.23 Change in wavelength, frequency and direction of sound wave moving from one medium to another (air to water)

Another feature of sound waves relates to us being able to hear conversations taking place in a different room. This is called **diffraction** and occurs when the wavelength of sound is greater than the distance around an object, such that some of the wave passes around the object. See what happens to the waves from throwing a stone into water when they meet an object in their path. The waves appear to bend around the object and the same thing happens with sound waves.

Two other properties demonstrated by sound waves are **interference** and the **Doppler effect**. Interference refers to the effect created by two waves meeting whilst travelling through the same medium. The effect can be to increase or decrease the amplitude of the wave so that the sound gets louder or quieter. In the latter case this phenomenon can be exploited to protect people working in noisy environments. The Doppler effect refers to the apparent change in frequency of the sound waves perceived by the ear when the object producing the sound is moving whilst the observer is stationary or *vice versa*. This happens when a plane passes overhead or a police car sounding its siren goes past. In effect it results from the sound waves being squashed together in front of the moving object and being farther apart behind it. This occurrence is exploited in ultrasound scanning equipment where, for example, the movements of the foetus or the ultrasound probe can be translated into an image of the foetus.

The perception of sound relies on the compression and rarefaction of particles in the medium through which the sound is travelling. If there are no 'particles', then no sound can be heard. This can be demonstrated by placing an alarm clock inside a bell jar from which the air is gradually evacuated, i.e. a vacuum is created. As the air is removed the alarm gets quieter until it cannot be heard at all. This has led to sound waves being described as a mechanical wave.

Assessment activity 5.8

Produce an annotated labelled diagram of the ear and how sound is transmitted to the inner ear from an external source.

If your college has access to audiometry equipment, investigate the hearing of different people within your group and explain what the resultant audiograms show. Alternatively, contact your local hearing impaired service and ask if they can make some audiometry equipment available or some copies of audiograms.

Ask the college's health and safety officer, or contact your local environmental health office, to see if they have a sound level meter available to investigate sound levels in different environments. This could be extended to obtaining information on complaints to environmental health about sound as a nuisance.

Light and sight

Light can also be considered to travel as waves, but no physical medium is required. If it were, then the light from the Sun would never reach us since space is a vacuum.

Light travels as waves termed **electromagnetic waves** that are produced by the vibration of electrons within atoms on the Sun's surface. These produce waves of oscillating electrical and magnetic fields that subsequently travel through the vacuum of outer space, eventually reaching Earth. Were it not for the ability of electromagnetic waves to travel to Earth, life would not exist.

Electromagnetic waves include radio waves, microwaves, ultraviolet and infra-red radiation, X-rays, gamma rays and countless other forms of electrical and magnetic energy. All such waves can be distinguished from one another in terms of their wavelength and/or frequency and like sound waves the amplitude can vary. Electromagnetic waves also exhibit the properties of reflection, refraction, diffraction, interference and the Doppler effect.

In terms of human vision light waves pass from the object through, and are refracted by, the cornea and then the lens to be focused upon the retina, that is composed of light sensitive cells called rods and cones. These cells trigger nerve impulses that are transmitted to the vision centre of the brain, which visualises the object. Defects of the cornea and/or lens can result in the light not being focused on the retina, such that corrective lenses have to be used in front of the eye to correct the sight. An optician carries out an eye test to check if there is any visual defect and to determine whether light from an object is being focused behind (long sight) or in front of (short sight) the retina. If the former, convex lenses are used to correct the problem and if the latter concave lenses (see Figure 5.24). Lenses of different curvatures will be tried. This will alter the amount of refraction until a lens is selected that refracts the light onto the retina. Alternatively, lasers can be used to literally remove slivers of cornea to alter its refractive properties in order to focus the light on the retina.

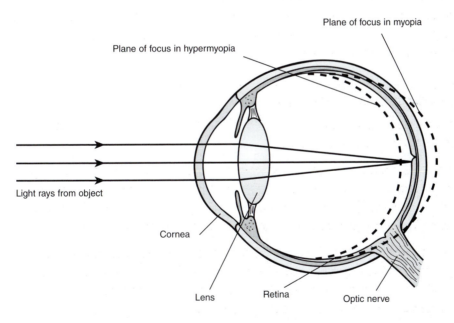

Figure 5.24 The focusing of light from an object by the cornea and lens onto the retina in a 'normal' eye and where light would be focused in a hypermetrophic and myotropic eye

Why do objects appear coloured? Materials absorb different parts of the electromagnetic spectrum and reflect others (see Figure 5.25). We see those parts or mixtures of wavelengths that are reflected. However, we only see those colours that are found within the visible part of the spectrum because the light sensitive cells (cones) in the retina responsible for colour vision are only sensitive to wavelengths in the red, green and blue sectors of the spectrum.

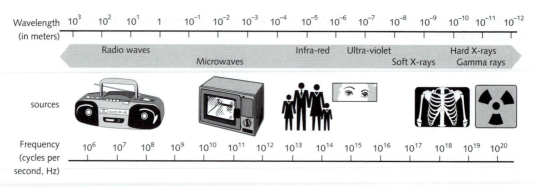

Figure 5.25 The electromagnetic spectrum

Assessment activity 5.9

How do we see colour? Explain the physics behind the perception of coloured objects.

Medical applications

An increasing range of diagnostic and therapeutic equipment is used within medicine and allied fields that is based upon the principles of electric currents, magnetism and electromagnetism.

Electricity

We have all experienced the effect of removing nylon clothing leading to the production of static electricity. Static electricity results from electrons being removed from atoms or molecules, in this case the molecules that make up the surface of the skin and the hairs on the body, to create areas of negative charge (on the clothing). The removal of electrons from atoms and molecules will leave them with an overall positive charge because of the protons they contain. As a consequence, the nylon material clings to the skin as it is removed due to the forces of attraction between the areas of negative and positive charge. The hairs on the skin will stand on end as they are all positively charged so repel each other and if you remove the clothing in the dark you can hear crackles and see sparks that are the negatively charged electrons literally jumping back from the material to the positively charged skin.

The uncontrolled flow of electrons in this example is the basis for the controlled flow of electrons that is current electricity. In current electricity electrons are made to pass along materials called conductors. The most effective conductors are metals as their molecular structure is based upon cations surrounded by a sea of electrons that can be made to move. The movement of electrons along a conductor requires a force called an electromotive force supplied by a battery or electrical generator. Another way of looking at the electromotive force is that it creates a difference in potential energy between two points that is termed the potential difference, measured in volts. The flow of electrons represents the conversion of potential energy to kinetic energy and is termed the current, which is measured in amperes or amps. The flow of electrons can be impeded which is the basis of electrical resistance and is the reason why some materials are regarded as insulators since they conduct electricity poorly, if at all. Resistance is measured in ohms. The relationship between potential difference, current and resistance is summarised by the equation:

$V = I \times R$

where V = voltage
      I = current
  and R = resistance.

Current electricity exists in two forms: a direct current, as supplied by a battery, or an alternating current, as supplied by a generator. In an alternating current the electrons move back and forth rather than along the conductor, however the effect is not unlike a car hitting the back of a line of stationary vehicles. Whilst the car is brought to a halt its potential energy is transmitted to the next car and so on, until it reaches the car at the front. Read electrons instead of cars and you should hopefully see how the current flows along the wire. Resistance to the flow of an alternating current is termed impedance.

Magnetism

Magnetism can be regarded as a side effect of the flow of electricity. It can be fairly easily shown that when a current is passed along a wire, the needle of a compass placed close to the wire will be deflected. The deflection of the needle results from the creation of a magnetic field that encircles the wire (see Figure 5.26).

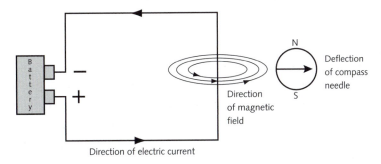

Figure 5.26 Magnetism and electric currents: representation of a magnetic field produced by a current flowing through a wire

Wrapping a coil of wire around a bar of iron and passing a current through the wire magnetises the iron, turning it into an electromagnet, but only whilst the current flows. A compass placed at either end of the electromagnet will be deflected in opposite directions, showing that the electromagnet has polarity due to the nature of the magnetic field.

Although an electromagnet made of iron loses its magnetism when the current is switched off, a more permanent magnet can be made if steel is used. A permanent magnet introduced into a coil of wire will induce an electrical current to flow in the wire, but only whilst the magnet moves. This is called electromagnetic induction and is the basis for the production of an alternating current by a generator.

The relationship between electricity and magnetism can be extended to the understanding of electromagnetic radiation that includes light and an almost limitless range of phenomena that make up the electromagnetic spectrum. Light has been discussed in terms of electromagnetic waves, but it can also be thought of as travelling as packets of high-energy particles called photons.

Radiation

Radioactivity is the spontaneous disintegration of the nucleus of many, but not all, isotopes of atoms that results in the emission of radiation in the form of alpha, beta and gamma radiation as well as positrons and electron capture. As atoms disintegrate, the radioactivity of a substance decreases. The time required for this activity to decrease by half is called the **half-life** and is characteristic of each radioactive isotope. It ranges from fractions of a second to several thousand million years.

Alpha (α) radiation results from the emission of the nuclei of helium (two protons and two neutrons) by the decay of elements such as radium, plutonium, uranium, and radon. Being positively charged they are deflected by magnetic fields. As the largest radiation particle, alpha particles are capable of doing the most damage. Because of their size they cannot penetrate the skin, but the element radon occurs as a gas and is released in the mining of uranium. Breathing in radon gas can lead to lung cancer. The radon decays to other radioactive particles that in turn decay with the emission of α-particles which pass into the cells lining the lungs to damage the DNA. Mutated DNA may then become cancerous.

Beta (β) radiation is fast moving negatively charged electrons that have arisen from the decay of a neutron into a proton. They are deflected by magnetic fields and are more penetrative than α-radiation, requiring a thin sheet of aluminium to stop them.

Gamma (γ) radiation is the emission of high-energy photons, i.e. electromagnetic radiation, with a wavelength of 10^{-12} m. They are unaffected by magnetic fields, are the most damaging form of electromagnetic radiation and are able to penetrate lead of 1 m thickness.

Positrons are electrons with a positive charge produced by the decay of protons and are the basis of Positron Emission Tomography (see page 215).

Electron capture involves the collapse of an orbiting electron from the outer shells of large atoms into the nucleus. The electron collides with a proton that changes it into a neutron with the emission of X-rays. X-rays can penetrate different materials but are stopped by dense objects.

There are at least 30 radioactive isotopes or radionucleides being used in modern medicine, from ovarian cancer therapy using californium 252 to the tracing of physiological processes using magnesium 28, with many more being used for general scientific and medical research. The number after the name refers to the atomic mass of the isotope.

X-rays are a form of electromagnetic radiation with a wavelength of between 10^{-8} m to 10^{-12} m, created by bombarding a tungsten target with high-speed electrons inside a device known as the X-ray tube. To generate the stream of electrons, an alternating current (AC) electricity is transformed up to 35–150 kilovolts and applied across a small wire (the cathode). Electrons emitted from the cathode are accelerated across the cathode ray tube to strike a metal disk (called the anode) causing the production of high-energy photons or X-rays.

Diagnostic and therapeutic techniques

The application of electromagnetic radiation and radioactivity to diagnostic and therapeutic techniques is increasingly wide ranging and cannot be covered comprehensively here. A brief introduction to a number of techniques will be discussed which will hopefully whet your appetite to research these or other topics in more detail.

Radiography

X-rays were discovered in 1895 and within six months X-ray machines were being used to locate bullets in wounded soldiers. X-rays penetrate the soft tissues of the body but are stopped by dense material such as bone. An X-ray image is called a radiograph and is produced by passing a beam of X-rays through the patient's body onto a sheet of photographic film sensitive to X-rays. The patient's bones absorb more rays than do the muscles or internal organs, and so the bones cast the sharpest shadows on the film or plastic. As a radiograph is a photographic negative, the shadows of the bones show up as light areas. Other parts of the body allow more X-rays through than the bones do and so cast shadows in varying shades of grey.

Radiographs of soft tissues can be obtained by introducing X-ray dense materials into the body through, for example, the ingestion of barium meals for investigating ulcers or cancer of the gut or the injection of contrast materials into the lungs, kidneys and other organs

Fluoroscopy is the use of X-rays to produce a moving image of an X-ray on a fluorescent screen, although today television screens and image intensifiers are used.

Digital imaging using computer technology to enhance radiographs from conventional X-rays or fluoroscopy will ultimately replace traditional radiographs. X-ray detectors beneath or around the patient produce a digital signal that can be visualised on a computer, enhanced and stored for future use or for the exchange of information for research and training purposes.

Computer tomography (Computer Axial Tomography – CAT)

Computer Tomography or CT scanners were developed in 1972 and are X-ray images of slices of the human body. The X-ray tube is rotated around the body together with a detector that transmits images to a computer. By repeating the process at slightly different positions a stack of images can be obtained to give a three-dimensional picture.

Dynamic spatial reconstruction (DSR) takes CT one step farther. Instead of using a single rotating X-ray machine to take single slices and add them together, DSR uses about 30 X-ray tubes. The images from all the tubes are compiled simultaneously, rapidly producing a three-dimensional image. Because of the speed of the process, multiple images can show changes over short periods of time and begins to give an idea of function as well as structure.

Digital subtraction angiography (DSA) uses a CT scan to obtain a three-dimensional X-ray image of an organ such as the heart, which is then stored in a computer. A radiopaque dye is then injected into the circulation, and a second X-ray computer image is made. The computer subtracts the first image from the second one so that the main image is of the flow of injected dye (see Figure 5.27). DSA can be used in real time so that, for example, a catheter can be observed as it is introduced into a coronary artery during angioplasty, the insertion of a tiny balloon into a coronary artery to compress material clogging the artery.

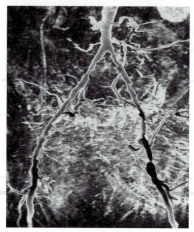
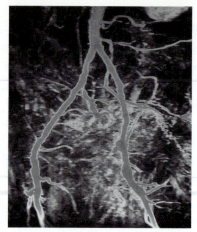

Standard DSA image of leg arteries

Computer enhanced image to highlight edges of arteries

Figure 5.27 Images of arteries

Magnetic Resonance Imaging (MRI)

MRI uses powerful magnetic fields that cause protons of hydrogen atoms in water molecules within the body to line up. Radio waves are then directed at the patient which displace the hydrogen atoms. When the radiowaves are turned off the hydrogen atoms realign under the influence of the magnetic field (see Figure 5.28). It takes different lengths of time for the hydrogen atoms to become realigned in different tissues. Computers analyse this information to produce very detailed, coloured images of slices of the body which like CT scans can be made three-dimensional (see Figure 5.29 and 5.30). It is a very sensitive technique for detecting tumours.

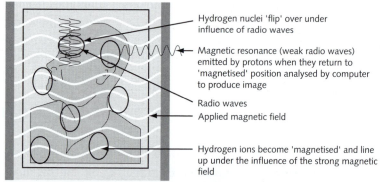

Hydrogen nuclei 'flip' over under influence of radio waves

Magnetic resonance (weak radio waves) emitted by protons when they return to 'magnetised' position analysed by computer to produce image

Radio waves
Applied magnetic field

Hydrogen ions become 'magnetised' and line up under the influence of the strong magnetic field

Figure 5.28 Diagrammatic representation of MRI

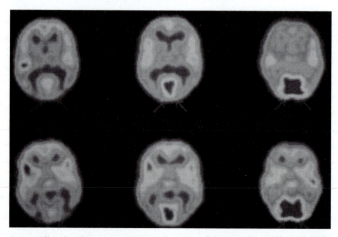

Figure 5.29 MRI scans of brain showing activity when patient is asked to:
1 close their eyes   2 open their eyes   3 view a complex scene

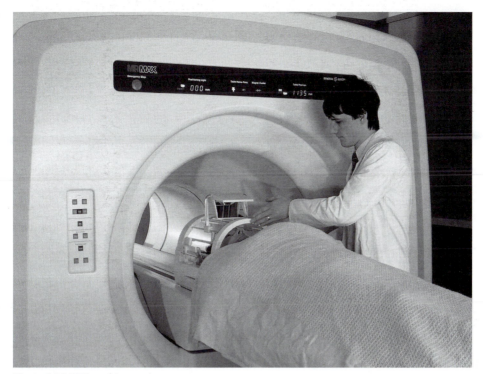

Figure 5.30 MRI machine

Positron Emission Tomography (PET)

PET scans are able to identify the metabolic states of various tissue. Chemical reactions are continually taking place in active cells and in doing so are using energy supplied by the breakdown of glucose. In PET, radioactively labelled glucose is given to the patient which is then taken up by cells. The decay of the radioactive elements in the glucose results in the emission of positrons. The positrons collide with electrons to produce gamma rays that are detected by scintillation detectors (see Figure 5.31).

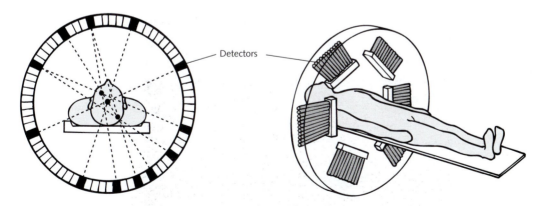

Figure 5.31 Diagrammatic sections through a PET scanner

Scintillation detectors and gamma cameras

When some materials absorb ionising radiation they emit photons of light. Such materials are called scintillators and the light they produce can be detected by photomultiplier tubes. The scintillator and photomultiplier tube works as shown in Figure 5.32.

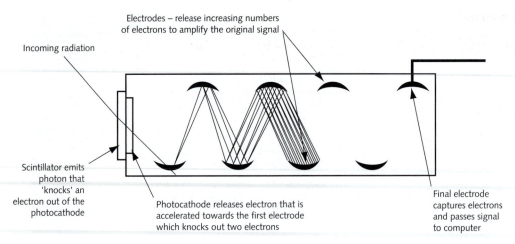

Figure 5.32 How a scintillator works

A gamma camera uses a scintillator attached to an array of photomulplier tubes. When a radioactive material is introduced into the body the radiation emitted strikes the scintillator which then emits photons that are detected by the photomultiplier tubes to create an image of radioactive material within the body. This technique is used for bone scans or to examine kidney function using different radioactive sources.

Lasers

Laser stands for Light Amplification by Stimulated Emission of Radiation. Lasers work by atoms of the 'laser material' being stimulated by the use of intense light flashes, so that electrons in the atoms are 'pushed' from their usual or ground state orbital into outer orbitals where they will possess more potential energy. The electrons return to the ground state, releasing energy in the form of a photon (light). This photon is capable of 'releasing' photons from other excited atoms. As long as the electrons in the excited atoms are moving from the same outer orbitals to the ground state then all the photons produced will be of the same wavelength. Mirrors at either end of the 'laser material' reflect the photons back and forth through the medium so more and more electrons become 'excited' and on returning to their ground state release more and more photons. As a mirror at one end is only half silvered some light in the form of laser light is allowed through. Laser light is extremely intense and is of one wavelength. The table below shows some different types of laser, the type and wavelength of light they generate and their use.

Laser type	Wavelength (nm)	Uses
Argon fluoride (UV)	193	
Krypton fluoride (UV)	248	
Nitrogen (UV)	337	
Argon (blue)	488	
Argon (green)	514	Glaucoma, diabetic retinopathy
Helium neon (green)	543	

(continued)

Laser type	Wavelength (nm)	Uses
Helium neon (red)	633	
Rhodamine 6G dye	570–650	
Ruby ($CrAlO_3$) (red)	694	
Nd:YAG (NIR)	1064	
Carbon dioxide (FIR)	10,600	Skin

Note
UV = ultraviolet
NIR = near infra-red
FIR = far infra-red

Carbon dioxide, YAG and argon lasers are the most commonly used in medicine. They have found a role in microsurgical techniques such as cataract surgery, repair of detached retinas, sealing of bleeding blood vessels, diagnosis, location and treatment of tumours, cosmetic surgery for the removal of skin blemishes or tattoos, stretch marks and even dental surgery.

Radiotherapy

Whilst radiology has grown to encompass diagnostic imaging techniques that use radioactivity as well as X-rays, radiotherapy is about the therapeutic use of radioactive materials in the treatment of cancer.

Radiotherapy may be used on its own or in conjunction with cancer chemotherapy and surgery to destroy tumours or it can be given as a palliative treatment to ease the pain of cancer.

There are two main forms of radiotherapy, each of which uses different methods of irradiating the tumour:

1 Internal radiotherapy
   a) Brachytherapy – the implantation of radioactive material close to or inside the tumour. Caesium 137 is commonly used for cancer of the cervix, uterus or vagina as the implant can be given as a suppository that irradiates the tumour rather than normal tissue.
   b) Radioisotope treatment – the drinking or intravenous injection of a radionucleide.

2 External radiotherapy
   a) Total body irradiation is often used for patients who are having a bone marrow transplant if they have leukaemia, for example. A large single dose, or six to eight smaller doses, of radiation is given to the whole body to destroy the cells of the bone marrow. The new bone marrow, usually from a donor, is then implanted.
   b) Irradiation of smaller areas of the body will utilise different machines depending upon whether the cancer is internal or on the skin. A patient may have traditional X-ray or CAT scans to help locate any tumour prior to treatment.

Chemotherapy

Chemotherapy is considered by many as the treatment of cancer by chemical means, but it is traditionally the use of chemical drugs to treat or prevent any disease. The development, testing and marketing of drugs is a multimillion pound business and incorporates a wide range of associated disciplines, particularly pharmacology which is the study of drugs and their action.

One aspect of pharmacology, called pharmacokinetics, looks at the administration of drugs into, their distribution around, their absorption into the different parts of the body and elimination from the body. Another side of pharmacology called pharmacodynamics considers where and how drugs act on cells, tissues and organs.

Think about any drug treatment you may have received from your doctor or the local hospital or that has been self-administered. Most of the time you will have taken drugs orally in the form of a pill or liquid. You may have had an injection, in which case this could have been into a vein (intravenous), muscle (intramuscular) or under the skin (subcutaneously). Other sites of injection are into the brain (intracranial), the spine (epidural) or the abdomen (intraperitoneal).

Other ways of administering drugs are by inhalation, for say asthma, through the skin, as in the use of nicotine or hormone replacement therapy patches or a skin cream, under the tongue, as in giving aspirin to a heart attack victim, or by suppository into the vagina or rectum for thrush or haemorrhoids.

Most drugs are either injected straight into the bloodstream or diffuse into the blood from the site of administration. Diffusion of the drug will depend on its solubility (whilst most drugs are water soluble, many are fat soluble), its molecular size and any interaction it may have with other substances in the body or in which it may be dissolved. Once in the bloodstream the drug has to get to the site of action. Some drugs may affect the whole body whereas others will have been produced to target specific cells, tissues or organs. Whilst the cardiovascular system will transport the drug around the body it may have obstacles to cross such as the blood-brain barrier, mucous membranes, cell membranes or placenta. Equally there may be parts of the body where it isn't desirable for the drug to end up, such as an embryo or foetus. Another factor that may effect a drug's efficacy is the length of time the drug acts for and the intensity of its effects. We all know that antibiotics, such as penicillin, need to be taken regularly and until the course of treatment has been completed as the antibiotic has to reach and maintain a concentration over a long enough period to destroy the bacteria in the body.

Many drugs have side effects and these are usually a result of the drug being distributed to most – if not all – parts of the body that causes such effects as the drug is acting on cells and tissues that it wasn't intended for. Elimination of the drug will be through all bodily secretions via the lungs, kidneys, liver and gall bladder, salivary glands or, in breast feeding mothers, the breast milk.

Drugs act for the most part at the molecular and cellular level of organisation, though the action of some drugs may be little understood except that they are known to produce the desired response in a particular organ or tissue. Some drugs may be aimed at having one effect but can have secondary effects that are also of benefit.

At the molecular level drugs will interact with specific molecules that may be cell membrane receptors, enzymes, components of metabolic reactions or nucleic acids. Whatever the molecule, the intermolecular action is related to the shape and size of both the drug and interacting molecule in the same way that enzymes work in catalysing reactions.

The consequence of activity at the molecular level will be to affect the activity of cellular organelles such as mitochondria, the nucleus and the plasma membrane which will affect the function of that particular cell type and therefore the action of a tissue composed of those cells.

Penicillin works by blocking the synthesis of bacterial cell walls. Morphine fits into receptors on nerve cells preventing the transmission of nerve impulses, hence its use in pain relief for childbirth and cancer. Amphetamines used as antidepressants also fit nerve cell receptors but have the effect of stimulating nerves.

Problems associated with drugs, apart from side effects, are their potential for abuse and the effects of tolerance with prolonged usage.

Assessment activity 5.10

Research diagnostic and therapeutic techniques in modern medicine and analyse their effectiveness in the management of named conditions.

Research the action of a drug.

End of unit test

1 A negatively charged ion is called a _____ .

2 Atoms of different elements have different numbers of _____ .

3 The polar covalent bond in water molecules enables them to form what other type of bond?

4 Why does ice float?

5 Why is water known as the solvent of life?

6 What is the name of the covalent bond between two glucose molecules called?

7 Enzyme are types of _____ that speed up chemical reactions without being altered themselves.

8 A patient was put on an intravenous drip of pure water by accident. What would you expect to happen? Your answer should include reference to water, solute and pressure potential.

9 The air pressure in the interpleural space (the space between the lungs and the chest wall) is 754 kPa and that in the alveoli is 758 kPa. If atmospheric pressure is 760 kPa is the person breathing in or out? Explain your answer.

10 The following table shows the partial pressures of oxygen and carbon dioxide gases in the blood entering the lungs and in the air within the alveoli. Explain what happens to the movement of these two gases as the blood flows through the lungs.

	Alveolar air kPa	Blood entering lungs kPa
pO_2	14.00	5.33
pCO_2	5.33	6.00

11 Glucose is generally supplied for intravenous injection as a 5 per cent solution. What would this be in terms of molarity?

12 Explain why vigorous exercise increases the acidity of the blood and how the blood buffers such changes.

13 The diagram shows the structure of the amino acid methionine. Circle and label the amino and carboxylic acid functional groups.

```
        C O O H
        |
H₂N — C — H
        |
        C H S H
```

14 Suggest why blood may best be described as a colloid rather than a solution.

15 Explain what is meant by the term frequency and how we hear sounds of different frequencies.

16 Explain how sound waves can effectively travel round corners.

17 Suggest why a light wave can travel through a vacuum but a sound wave cannot.

18 Use a diagram to show the correction of hypermyopia using an appropriately shaped lens.

19 Name a medical diagnostic technique that uses electromagnetism.

20 Explain why soft tissue appears dark and dense tissue light on an X-ray plate.

21 Suggest how radioactivity can be used for diagnostic as well as therapeutic purposes in medicine.

22 With reference to the action of drugs explain the importance of molecular shape.

References and further reading

Aldridge, S. (1994) *Biochemistry for Advanced Biology*, Cambridge: Cambridge University Press

Burton, G. *et al.* (1994) *Salters Advanced Chemistry – Chemical Storylines*, Oxford: Heinemann

Burton, G. *et al.* (1994) *Salters Advanced Chemistry – Chemical Ideas,* Oxford: Heinemann

Elliott, A. & McCormick, A. (2001) *Health Physics*, Cambridge: Cambridge University Press

ILEA Physics Project Team (1989) *Advanced Physics Project for Independent Learning*, London: John Murray

Raffan, J. and Ratcliff, B. (1995) *Foundation Chemistry*, Cambridge: Cambridge University Press

Tortora, G. J. and Grabowski, S. R. (2000) (9th edn) *Principles of Anatomy and Physiology*, Chichester: John Wiley

Kingsland J. (1999) 'Age-old story', *New Scientist*, Vol. 161, Issue 2170, 23 January 1999

6 Vocational practice

This unit is designed to assist you in gaining maximum benefit from the programme of structured work placement that is part of your Health Studies National Diploma or Certificate course. The unit is an essential part of your qualification and sits alongside your 400 hours of work experience in different care settings. The clients and staff in the care settings will appreciate and value the theoretical and practical experience you will achieve as you progress through the unit.

The unit brings together knowledge from many other units and will help you gain competence in real health care practice. You will learn how to acquire basic skills, how to evaluate your own performance and develop an action plan for personal career goals. You will investigate particular features of each care setting and make comparisons between them, review management structures and find out about the roles and responsibilities of care employees. Achieving this unit will give you confidence for your future in health care.

As you will compile the evidence for this unit throughout the two years of your programme, it carries the value of *two* units.

What you need to learn

- Common and particular features of each vocational placement undertaken
- Base knowledge and skills to be an effective practitioner
- Principles of team work, work relationships, roles and responsibilities
- Equal opportunities
- Care programmes
- Personal career goals

Common and particular features of each vocational placement undertaken

Work experience may take various forms: it may be one six-hour day every week in term-time or block placements of one or two weeks each term at a period of time designated by your tutor. It might even be a combination of both, producing a front-loaded experience programme. Block placements are usually to be preferred for continuity. Some educational establishments may be fortunate enough to allow each student to select their placement; others will have little or no choice because of the difficulty in obtaining a sufficient number of placements. You should remember from the outset that your tutors have worked extremely hard to get the vocational placements for you and be reliable, punctual, polite and enthusiastic in your approach.

Wherever possible, you should attempt to cover a wide variety of placement care settings and not be blinkered from the start. Occasionally, students will declare that they only wish to work with children, for example, and be resentful and uninterested if they have to work with elderly clients. This is a poor start to caring, as all carers must be able to value the equality and diversity of all service users and be able to respond to their needs. Such students would be well advised to consider a course of study related to children only, as they are unlikely to be useful carers in other fields. An open, enquiring mind and a willingness to learn in all areas is required from the beginning of your programme of studies.

Many students are anxious to gain vocational placements in hospitals, probably because this is where they see their future career, or it seems exciting and dramatic, apparently at the cutting edge of health care. Hospital trusts are now very aware of the expensive litigation they can face if clients are disadvantaged by the results of their programme of care; they are also short of staff and under pressure to cut waiting lists, meet government targets and balance budgets. As a result, many trusts are increasingly reluctant to offer vocational placements, so do not be disappointed if you cannot access your local hospital. It is worth remembering that more people are cared for in other settings than in a hospital, with clients' homes representing the largest percentage of all. There are so many other varieties of care settings in which you can develop your caring skills and knowledge that this should not concern you at all and will be to your advantage when you eventually begin your professional training.

Assessment activity 6.1

Allow two or three days to carry out the research for this activity and, if possible, work in groups of three or four – eventually comparing group results in a plenary session.

Research all the different types of care settings in your neighbourhood using local information, telephone directories, family and friends, libraries and any other appropriate sources of information. Think very broadly – it does not matter if the setting is large or small, public or private, residential or day care, or managed by a charity. When the group feels that their list is complete, write the names on strips of card and mix them up. Exchange cards with another group and distribute them among group members, with each individual telling the group the name on the card, and a few sentences about the type of care given in the care setting and the service users. Two groups join and clear up any gaps in knowledge, seeking assistance from the tutor if required. Finally, all groups join and discuss their results before making a large wall chart display of the cards with accompanying notes. The display should be titled, 'Types of care settings in our locality'. A display such as this will assist in the planning of your programme of vocational placements.

You may be fortunate in knowing the whole of the first-, and even, second-year programme of vocational placements or simply the first or next placement. It is clearly useful to know well in advance where you will be going, but the disadvantage is that changes may occur, such as withdrawal of funding or re-location and that can mean your tutors have to reassess the programme. Whatever the extent of your knowledge, *it is crucially important that you record accurately the knowledge and skills that you gain in each placement and do not wait until you have almost completed your course of study.* Your Vocational Practice Log of evidence that you will collect externally is the assessment for this unit. As you read the unit through ensure that you also read the assessment guidance on each section.

Placement structure

You have learned that there is a wide variety of care settings and each will have a set of policies, procedures and a statement of aims, sometimes called a mission statement or a statement of principles.

Statement of principles for a primary school

Children are happy when they are learning how to do things. We want our children to learn how to read and write, how to play together, how to discover, how to make things and last, but not least, how to behave towards each other, teachers, parents and society in general.

Aims are broad general statements of the purpose of the organisation and are usually fairly short.

A policy is a formal written statement explaining what to do within an organisation or work setting; workers must abide by the policies of the organisation. Policies usually arise from European or government requirements and can exist at international, national or local levels.

Policies will cover many areas such as health and safety, manual handling and lifting, confidentiality, equal opportunities, bullying and harassment and dealing with aggression and violence. You will find these policies operating in all care sectors, so it is a good place to start. If there are several students working at your vocational placement try to make sure that a copy of each policy is available at a particular place where it can be accessed by students; this may be in the workplace or in the educational establishment. It is costly and time-consuming for workplace staff to provide multiple copies at different times for different students.

Big teaching hospitals will have a very large number of policies and procedures – probably over two thousand – and you will not be able to manage more than a few of these; smaller units, such as residential homes, will have only a few so be aware of this type of incompatibility.

Procedures detail the steps an employee should take in a particular situation such as a fire, when faced with violence, etc. A procedure should be followed as laid down in the written document and if not followed will undoubtedly lead to a post-incident investigation. Procedures exist to help employees in difficult situations and have been agreed by management and employees as the best way forward. Policies and procedures exist to protect clients *and* staff from harm in the workplace.

Roles and responsibilities of the staff structure

The size of the establishment or organisation also affects the staff structure, proportion of management to other staff and the mix of skills found in the care setting. A nursing home might only have a few qualified nurses on the payroll and a majority of 'hands-on' care assistants with or without NVQs. A busy hospital will have a much larger number of state registered nurses and still have many care assistants. A specialised setting such as a hospital dealing with transplant operations and heart by-pass surgery, will have an even greater proportion of qualified staff. A privately run playgroup might have only three paid staff, so whether the care setting is run by the state (i.e. statutory), privately owned or run by voluntary agencies (such as charities) will also make a difference to the management structure and proportion of staff.

Nearly all care settings will produce an annual report or information leaflet and these will usually provide the staffing information. A website providing statistics such as the proportion of nurses and doctors in hospitals to 100 patients can be found at: www.goodhospitalguide.co.uk. You can also compare one hospital with another this website. You will have to ask someone for this information at a smaller care setting.

You may also be able to obtain one or two copies of job and person descriptions for vacancies in the establishment. A job description clearly sets out the roles and responsibilities for the person holding that position. A person description sets out the knowledge, skills and abilities required for the job, for example a person dealing with the general public might be required to have excellent communication skills, be patient and even-tempered and dress appropriately.

A role will carry certain rights and obligations including who to report to and who reports to you. There may be in-built authority with certain roles, for instance head-teachers and principals in schools and colleges. Most organisations have a hierarchy that is a 'higherarchy' – from a majority of lower grade employees at the bottom to one or a few higher grade personnel at the top; this is often known as a pyramidal hierarchy.

Assessment activity 6.2

Draw a pyramid diagram of the staff structure at one of your placements, stating the roles and responsibilities of each member of staff.

Service users: how their needs are met in each setting

You will need to find out about the people who use the services of your placements. This will involve:

- single or mixed genders
- age ranges
- general or particular environments, such as a local community or a broad regional basis
- social classification – mixed or specific, for example a private hospital is more likely to take service users from the middle and upper social classes whereas a local authority nursery for single working mothers is more likely to have service users from the lower social classes.

Service users can have their needs met in many different ways

You must be careful not to stereotype service users, and are required to give a broad picture only. You will also need to provide an outline of the reasons why service users need the services and how their needs are met by the service.

Assessment activity 6.3

1 Describe the range of service users in this care setting.
2 What are the main reason(s) for using this service?
3 How are the needs of the service users met in this setting?

Services and resources provided by associated organisations

Many care settings have links with other organisations that carry out different tasks associated with the service. In a residential home for the elderly, for example, there might be visiting hairdressers, physiotherapists and chiropodists and certainly visiting doctors. Social services might be involved with financial assistance for many service users, charities for elderly people might help with clothing and local communities with fund-raising and social events. You will only find out about such links by being alert and asking for information from the care workers.

The WRVS has links with many other organisations

Case study

Jade lives with her 2-year old daughter Sylee in a two-roomed flat in a West Indian community that is part of a large city in the United Kingdom.

Her partner, also West Indian, left when she became pregnant and does not support her financially at all. She was living solely on benefit income and found it very hard to cope; neighbours are helpful but also have very little money to spare. This year, the local authority set up a non-fee-paying nursery/playgroup for children aged 2 to 5 years in an abandoned school and Jade was lucky enough to get a place for Sylee. At first, the place was for mornings only, three days each week. Last month, Jade was offered a full-time place and now she has found a job working in a large department store and is earning extra money to help with daily living expenses. She only pays for Sylee's meals in the nursery; these are prepared and delivered by the local authority from a school nearby. When Jade got to know more people using the nursery she found that at least 70 per cent of the children had single parents and the rest had at least one unemployed or disabled parent. As well as the qualified care staff, the local college and a secondary school supply volunteers on placements from the Health and Social Care and Child Care programmes.

- Describe the links the nursery has with other organisations. What benefits does this bring?

Role and performance in each student placement

You may be given a written sheet of general guidance by your tutors before you attend your placement or may be provided with verbal instructions. You should use this information to assist you in writing a job description for yourself in the placement. This should include:

- your aims for the placement
- your objectives in the placement
- the tasks you will be expected to perform.

The aims are broad general statements of your expectations from the placement whilst objectives are measurable goals, which you can expect to achieve during your period in the setting. You will find the headings for this unit useful in defining your goals.

Theory into practice

Imagine that next week, you will be going to a local residential home for elderly people for your first two-week block vocational placement. Write a job description for this placement before you go, stating your aims, objectives and expected tasks. You may need to look through the headings of this unit first.

With any learning it is essential to evaluate performance after the experience. Your aims and objectives might have been totally unrealistic for the skills, knowledge and abilities that you possess initially and by evaluating your work and performance after each placement you will soon become an expert at job descriptions! You should also find that your skills, knowledge and abilities become increasingly sophisticated as you progress through your placements over the two years of your programme. Do not be afraid of self-criticism, many students feel that they must always say good things about themselves. Being able to criticise one's own performance is a higher level skill and consolidates learning. Some examples of evaluation of personal performance are provided below:

- I was pleased with the way I comforted Mrs K because I empathised rather than sympathised with her loss.
- I felt that my irritation with Mr B showed in my body language and I was ashamed of myself later on. I need to learn to be more tolerant of demanding clients.
- When chatting to a care assistant about something personal that a client told me I forgot about confidentiality. I need to be more alert about confidentiality, it is easy to forget.
- I avoid talking to a severely deaf client because I am embarrassed when I speak loudly and feel everyone around is listening. I am discriminating against this client because of his disability due to my personal feelings.

You can see how these statements are producing good self-evaluation and should lead to an improved performance. With no analysis, there will be no change in behaviour.

Base knowledge and skills to be an effective practitioner

Having a job means being paid for the time and effort that you give to the workplace, but having a vocation means a sense of being called to the occupation. When you feel called upon to be a carer you will wish to make a difference to your clients, in other words you will desire to be an effective practitioner having a specialist knowledge and appropriate caring skills. Below you will find lists of basic tasks that you will be expected to perform in most placements.

Links between theory gained and practice in the health and care field

It is important to realise that, however many lectures you attend, books that you read or accounts that you write, you will not be effective in your placement and subsequent career, if you don't use your knowledge practically. You will need to show that you can transfer the knowledge that you gain into your practice. There are numerous ways of doing this, for example:

- demonstrating how you put equal opportunities theory into your workplace by anti-discriminatory practice or challenging (politely) a view or opinion of someone else that is not acceptable to you
- respecting confidentiality in your placement
- using your knowledge of psychology to help someone through a difficulty
- using your communication skills in appropriate ways, such as checking understanding, asking open questions and not being judgemental
- helping a client with meal planning and using your knowledge of the components that constitute a healthy diet
- promoting a healthy lifestyle with different clients
- being aware of potentially harmful environmental problems
- using knowledge of growth and development or human physiology to appreciate and be alert to potential problems
- planning research to aid practice.

These are necessary general statements and you will be able to find many other links over your two-year programme. By actively considering such links, you will not only increase your personal development, but improve your practice and increase the service that you are able to give to clients.

Developing skills

It is essential that you take the opportunity to work with different client groups because you will develop different skills with each group; although there will be many common themes with each placement, you will manage each situation differently. Intellectual stimulation, for instance, will be quite different with elderly people, adults, people with learning disabilities and children. Your practical care skills will also be quite different with different groups.

Assessment activity 6.4

Using only the four client groups mentioned above, devise suitable activities that will provide for *both* social and intellectual needs and explain why you have chosen these activities.

Think it over

Using 'assisting with toiletting' as an example of a practical skill, brainstorm all the important points you should be aware of and then say how these might differ between helping a 3-year-old child in a nursery and an elderly lady with limited mobility and moderate arthritis. When you are doing this exercise remember that all clients should be encouraged to be as independent as possible.

A whole unit in this book – and an essential unit in this qualification – is devoted to communication in the caring professions (see Unit 2). You may think that you are a good talker already, but that is not enough. Talking is very personal and you may have to think again about the way you speak with clients. General chat mainly revolves around expressing one's own views, asking closed questions and using language that might be all right with one's peers, family and friends, but not with vulnerable clients. It takes a lot of practice to get it right and can be frustrating at first; you will not be used to trying to edit and review what you want to say in your head before you say it. Students often say that they cannot do it but you do have to keep trying. Not only do you have to re-think what you say but also the way you say things and who you are saying them to. There would be no point in using Cockney rhyming slang to a Scotsman, and similarly there is no point in using modern slang to an 85-year-old lady – neither party would understand you! You would need to use simple, short sentences without complex words when speaking with a client with learning disabilities or a young child. Negatives can also have a confusing effect on certain client groups which 'home' in on certain words ignoring the negative. 'We are not going swimming today' can send some clients dashing off to fetch their bathers and towel, much to the frustration of the carer!

You will find that your communication skills develop rapidly on contact with different client groups and you will be able to analyse your performance better after a course year (and some varied placements). You will also gradually improve your knowledge and skills enough to judge when you need to refer something you have seen, done or heard to a supervisor. At first, you will probably refer most events or none at all depending on your personality, but later you will develop a better sense of proportion. It is probably wise to refer more rather than less!

As you gain more experience of your clients and the settings, you will understand their physical, social, emotional, spiritual and intellectual needs and be able to help meet these needs. Some clients will yearn for peace and quiet and need to be left alone whereas others may need social intercourse and intellectual stimulation. If you are unsure, ask the client and then you will know. Do not try to guess their needs, you may guess completely wrongly and give the appearance of not caring for them as people. Remember that people have a right to choose the care they receive and the way in which they receive it.

Communication skills

The importance of non-verbal and verbal communication should not be under-estimated. In this section, you will be considering how to overcome communication barriers. When you fail to get through to someone, you have to think about possible barriers in the interaction. When you have identified the problem you will see how to overcome the barrier.

First, is it you? Here are some of the points you may be failing to address:

- Are you not listening actively?
- Have you checked the client has understood at frequent intervals?
- Are you distracted by something else?
- Are you interrogating the client by asking repeated closed questions?
- Did you introduce yourself and your purpose?
- Have you adopted a poor position and/or posture?
- Is your body language implying that you are disinterested in the client?
- Is your voice too quiet/loud/fast/shrill/low/anxious?
- Are you giving poor responses, such as dismissing the client's feelings?
- Did you make the conversation too complex?
- Did you summarise and close the dialogue appropriately?
- Did you let the client down the last time you spoke?
- Have you respected the client as a person with feelings and rights?

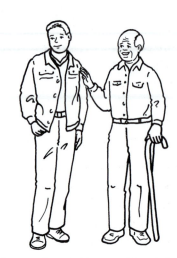

Are you distracted by something else?

This is a daunting list and you can probably think of other items to add to it but you will be able to check through this very quickly. Once you have identified the error you will know how to overcome it. Assuming that you feel that you have done your best with these points, you now have to consider other barriers – probably still your error as you should have checked on these points at the start of your conversation or better still, before beginning the conversation at all!

Figure 6.1 will provide you with food for thought! You will be able to overcome barriers to communication when you have identified the difficulty.

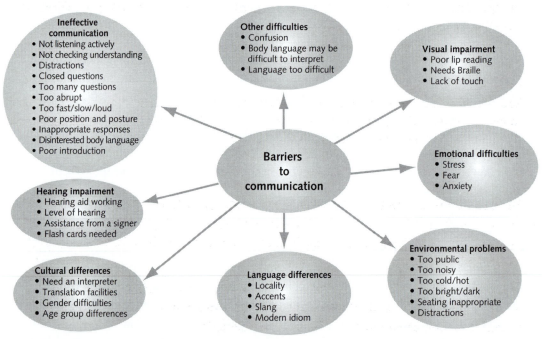

Ineffective communication
- Not listening actively
- Not checking understanding
- Distractions
- Closed questions
- Too many questions
- Too abrupt
- Too fast/slow/loud
- Poor position and posture
- Inappropriate responses
- Disinterested body language
- Poor introduction

Other difficulties
- Confusion
- Body language may be difficult to interpret
- Language too difficult

Visual impairment
- Poor lip reading
- Needs Braille
- Lack of touch

Barriers to communication

Emotional difficulties
- Stress
- Fear
- Anxiety

Hearing impairment
- Hearing aid working
- Level of hearing
- Assistance from a signer
- Flash cards needed

Cultural differences
- Need an interpreter
- Translation facilities
- Gender difficulties
- Age group differences

Language differences
- Locality
- Accents
- Slang
- Modern idiom

Environmental problems
- Too public
- Too noisy
- Too cold/hot
- Too bright/dark
- Seating inappropriate
- Distractions

Figure 6.1 Possible barriers to communication

Clients with communication problems

When someone speaks a language other than English and an interpreter is not available, try to learn a few appropriate words yourself and introduce picture flash cards with the English words on. Remember that non-verbal language is the major part of communication so, touch, smile, open posture and friendly demeanour are equally important as words.

People who have impaired hearing may need to be referred to an audiologist for a hearing aid or repair to an aid. Sometimes a new battery or cleaning is all that is required. Similarly, clients who are visually impaired may need suitable glasses to watch facial expressions and pick up on non-verbal communication. It is not unusual to hear an individual say, 'Wait until I get my glasses on so that I can hear you'. Do not shout at clients; rather repeat your message a few times clearly in a moderate voice. Some severely deaf clients may have a text messager attached to a mobile phone (using a type-talk service) on which they can communicate.

People who are confused or have learning difficulties respond to short, simple repeated messages at the right level. It is important to leave enough time to get the information across and not to become impatient with the client. Picture boards and flash cards can again prove useful, but should not entirely take the place of verbal and non-verbal communication.

Assessment activity 6.5

Suggest different ways of communicating with a client who is totally deaf when you need to ask if they would like:

- a drink
- a biscuit
- to see a visitor.

Analyse the different ways of communicating, and evaluate which is most suitable for this situation.

Confidentiality

You should respect confidentiality with all clients at all times unless you have fears for someone's safety; if you do feel the need to pass on information to your supervisor, then you must immediately tell the client. You will find more information on confidentiality in Unit 1.

Interactive styles in health and care professionals

You will develop different skills in different placements working with different people. You are unlikely to be involved in medical care, but highly likely to be asked to assist clients with daily living activities such as:

- menu planning
- assisting with food and drink
- accessing and using toilet facilities
- maintaining personal hygiene and appearance
- shopping
- cleaning and tidying

- supporting clients through communication
- helping clients to become comfortable
- reading to clients
- writing letters for clients
- assisting with simple mobility
- accompanying clients
- promoting leisure interests.

You should not be involved in lifting and handling of clients unless you have had recognised and appropriate training from a person qualified to give such training. You should not be involved in answering any questions dealing with the details of a client's care with family, friends or other care staff. As a general rule, you should not answer the telephone although sometimes you may be given permission to do so. You must be aware of the need to obtain a client's permission for any aspect of care work. A client has the right to refuse any part of their care and any refusal or rejection must be reported to the supervisor.

You are a person with values, beliefs and interests special to you. These personal factors will have influenced your development, personality and behaviour; you must understand that it is exactly the same for your clients. You will instantly be drawn to some people and enjoy caring for them but there will be others that you don't instinctively like. As an effective carer, you must be able to suppress these prejudices and look into yourself to analyse your feelings.

A good carer reflects on actions, thoughts and feelings. This is called being a reflective practitioner and the purpose of this is to identify the areas in your own personal development which need further work. At the end of a day in placement, look back at the support you have given your clients and try to identify any difficulties, anxieties or awkward moments that you might have avoided with a different approach. You might do this by mentally running through a checklist such as the one below.

Key issues

Reflective practice checklist
1. How did I approach the work I carried out?
2. Was my approach positive?
3. How did the way I worked affect the client?
4. How did the way I worked affect my colleagues?
5. How was my verbal and non-verbal communication?
6. Which part of today did I do well?
7. What were the reasons for my good performance?
8. Which part of today did I not do so well?
9. What were the reasons for the poorer performance?
10. How could I have performed better?
11. What have I learned today?
12. Performance rating out of 10?

Dealing with inappropriate behaviour and abuse

Inappropriate behaviour is behaviour not usually seen in the circumstances of the care setting; often distressing, sometimes violent, occasionally oppressive or simply ignoring the needs of others around are examples of such behaviour. Inappropriate behaviour can come from clients, visitors or care workers. In some cases you will be able to understand why the individual is acting in this manner, in other cases you will not. Understanding the reasons behind the behaviour does not change its acceptability. In most cases you will be able to refer the matter to a supervisor, as you should not be working on your own. There are certain generic guidelines for dealing with inappropriate behaviour, but you must realise that each situation will be unique and sizing up the problem quickly will help.

Key issues

Generic guidelines for dealing with inappropriate behaviour

1 Try to assess the size of the problem as quickly as possible and consider the approach you will use.
2 Get help if there is not enough care staff around.
3 Keep calm.
4 Think clearly.
5 Be clear in what you say.
6 Try to get the client into a private area.
7 Repeat the request and give your reason but don't enter into an argument.
8 Use frequent eye contact but don't stare.
9 Be assertive but not aggressive.
10 Give your client personal space.
11 Empathise with the client.
12 Let the client back down in a way that will not belittle or humiliate them.

Try to anticipate trouble and defuse it before it happens; knowing and understanding your clients will help you to do this.

Think it over

Mr J is a client in the residential home where you are working for two weeks vocational placement. He likes to sit in a particular chair to watch the television in the communal living room. A new client, Mrs M, came into the room straight after the evening meal, and occupied Mr J's chair. He is an ex-army man with a brusque manner and Mrs M is a timid client prone to bouts of weeping since her husband died. You anticipate the problem that might arise when Mr J enters; how will you approach Mrs M and what might you say to her? Is it necessary to refer the matter to a supervisor?

Although Mr J is brusque and may distress Mrs M a great deal he is not likely to be violent. Most of the generic guidelines above will be appropriate for dealing with violent people as well but in addition you will need to know:

- how to get out of the space as quickly as possible
- how to summon help – sound an alarm, shout for help, call security or police
- not to let the attacker get between you and the door
- remove any potential weapons if it is easy to do so.

Above all, keep yourself safe; you are a student and not trained to deal with attackers. Even if there are other people such as clients in the room, as an untrained person you will be more use bringing trained staff to their aid.

Think it over

On page 224 you learned about policies and procedures. Find out the appropriate steps to take in your placement when dealing with aggression and violence.

Sitting alongside inappropriate behaviour, there is the problem of abuse. This can occur in many forms (see Figure 6.2).

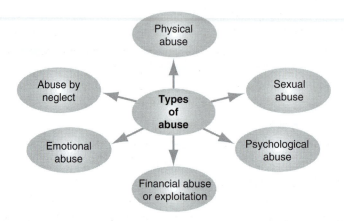

Figure 6.2 Abuse can occur in many forms

Assessment activity 6.6

Over a period of three months collect cuttings/photocopies from newspapers or magazines or refer to TV documentaries related to different forms of abuse. Obtain a copy of one placement's policy on dealing with abuse.

In a small group discuss a small selection of cases in the following ways:

- Which client group was being abused?
- How many clients were involved?
- Who were the abusers?
- What type of care setting was involved?
- How long did the abuse continue?
- What was likely to be the short- and long-term effects on the client?
- What signs might you have noticed if you had been working in that care setting?

Why do you think the abuse started?

What could you have done about it? (Your placement policy can be used here.)

You might find it helpful to repeat this exercise again using different cases before your study programme is finished to reinforce the importance of awareness of abuse.

Information

Lack of information or misinformation is probably the most likely cause of most daily difficulties arising in caring for people. Sometimes the mishap is easily overcome, many times it can mean a delay but, on other occasions, it can have disastrous or tragic consequences.

Think it over

Here are some examples of lack of information or being given the wrong information. What might be the implications of each?

1. Mrs F has two buses to catch and a long walk from her home to the first bus stop. She has her first appointment with the cardiovascular clinic on 12 September. On arrival, she finds that the receptionist had written the date incorrectly and she should have attended on 2 September. She recalls that the receptionist was distracted by a telephone call in the middle of her appointment-making.
2. The renal consultant had not received the documents relating to a case conference, he failed to attend and five other important, busy care workers could not progress and their time was wasted.
3. Jo asked her friend what time the external assessment was set for on the next day, she arrived two hours late at the time she was told and missed the session. She had to wait until the following year to complete her qualification.
4. The tired house doctor omitted to prescribe an essential medicine for a client. The client developed life-threatening symptoms and became a medical emergency.

Reasons for sharing information can be:

- to safeguard a client's care and life
- to prevent the waste of resources
- to prevent delays
- to value other people
- to communicate all the information to prevent errors and make decisions
- to ensure continuity of care.

Assessment activity 6.7

1. Brainstorm all the different ways of passing on information to other people.
2. For each way of transmitting information say how the information could be recorded.
3. For each way of transmitting information say how the information could be stored.
4. Discuss the advantages and disadvantages of each method of recording information.
5. Discuss the advantages and disadvantages of each method of storing information.

When you have completed the activity above, you will have an excellent base for comparing the different methods of recording and storage of information in your various placements.

You can form your own opinions about the effectiveness of storage of information during your placement by observation and experience. For example, how easy was it to find a particular placement policy?

Think it over

You probably communicate with some people by email or text messages. Think about the advantages and disadvantages of both these methods of communication particularly at speed.

Some confidential information must be kept in a secure location for access only by permitted personnel. You need to find out how the information is kept secure. Could it be simply behind lock and key or is it in computerised files protected by a password that is changed regularly and only known to a few key workers?

Taking a 'worst case scenario', imagine how care workers would feel if a client had been diagnosed with an untreatable cancer and written case notes had been read by another client who had disclosed the information to the person before the care workers had time to do so. The sick client then left a suicide note and killed herself because of the leaked information. Imagine if the 'nosy' client had mistaken two similar names! Fantasy, you might think, but these things do happen. It is also not infrequent for an individual to overhear a conversation about a service user who is a relative or friend, both inside and outside a care setting.

Make sure that you have read the organisation's policy on confidentiality and always abide by its contents.

Principles of team work, work relationships, roles and responsibilities

Every care setting consists of networks and teams of people working together and it is essential that each network or team member fulfils their duties to ensure maximum efficiency in delivering service to the client. If you have worked on a team project you will know how annoying, frustrating and angry people can get if one team member fails to carry out their responsibility. You will also know that the whole project can be abandoned or jeopardised under such circumstances, even though other people have worked really hard. In a care setting where you are dealing with vulnerable people, it is unforgivable to jeopardise the delivery of care. Co-operation means getting things done more efficiently.

Limits of their roles and competence in vocational practice

As a student on vocational practice, you will be expected to join one or more teams of carers. You will be one of the lowest levels of people in that team, but you can still be of great benefit. Your role will be limited by the guidelines that you have been given by your tutor or a placement supervisor. The guidelines will differ in different placements and you should be prepared for this. At all times, you must remember that the team has the primary function of delivering the best possible care to the client group. You will not be the most important person in the placement and there will be times when you feel in the way because the care workers have certain duties which must be carried out.

You can, however, always be observant, willing, responsible and enthusiastic about the tasks you are given to do. Make notes on questions you want to ask and find suitable times to seek answers from appropriately qualified people. Taking coffee breaks with some of your team members is often useful, rather than arranging a break time to fit with a friend in the same establishment.

Many students feel 'task-orientated', in other words they feel guilty if they are not actually doing something rather than talking to clients. There is no need to feel like this – talking to clients in an appropriate way is valuable to both parties. This does not mean telling clients all about your personal relationships or talking about yourself all the time, it means treating the client as a real person and finding out how they feel about things and generally being a reflective practitioner.

You should always introduce yourself to a client and explain the purpose of your presence. Never let a client believe that you are a qualified carer, even though this might seem quite flattering. If you do not know how to do something that you are asked to do, always say so politely and ask if you might observe so that you can carry out the task at a later date when you are competent.

Occasionally a carer may ask you to do something that is not permitted by your guidelines, so you must explain why you cannot do it at this time.

Take the time to discover the limits of other roles and responsibilities in the team such as care assistants, hospital porters, etc.

Assessment activity 6.8

Create a table that shows your responsibilities on placements and the responsibilities of two other people in different roles whom you work with. How do they differ?

Roles and relationships

Staff, clients, students, relatives and visitors

Relationships depend upon good communication between people and treating each person as an individual with unique needs, views, beliefs and choices. Where these can be seen to exist, relationships will form by right. Relatives and visitors are usually very important to service users and bring an interest in life outside the establishment. There are some exceptions to this and sometimes a client will not wish to see a relative or visitor. The client has that choice and the carer must communicate that information in a polite yet assertive way.

Relatives and friends may act as informal advocates for the client but should not dictate the care programme to care staff or make demands or suggestions that counter the client's wishes. In the past, hospital consultants and doctors were often viewed by everyone else as 'demi-gods' whose wishes must be carried out immediately, but this is slowly changing and more and more people will now challenge the medical staff as and when necessary. Nurses were traditionally seen as the 'handmaidens' of the doctors. They are now qualified professionals, often graduates, able to manage staff, plan care programmes, prescribe some medicines and act as advisers on health and illness; they are, quite rightly, now held in a higher regard by clients and the general public.

Students are expected to maintain relationships of a professional nature with staff and clients and to be polite and courteous to relatives and visitors. You will not be required to give or to receive information from people who visit the client in any aspect but refer to the supervisor in all matters.

Fontana (1990) writes that those who have good relationships with clients in a caring field also:

- convey a respect for them and show an ability to listen
- put them at ease but avoid emotional over-involvement
- clarify the help that can be given and cannot be given
- accept justifiable criticism
- avoid undue exercise of professional power.

Assessment activity 6.9

Practise making a pattern diagram of relationships between yourself and the people you know well. Try to give their roles in relation to you alongside their names.

Skills required to work effectively in a team

All care organisations work in teams and networks, largely because care is a 24-hour commitment and involves a multitude of skilled practitioners, 'hands-on' care assistants, administrative personnel, technicians, porters and security people, to name only a few groups. When individuals cannot work together, the atmosphere is unpleasant for the remainder of the team, everyone begins to question the roles they perform and the whole performance suffers. On the other hand, when people do work together within a team, there is pride in performance, everyone tries to do their very best and efficiency soars. In this situation there is a pleasant camaraderie and individuals enjoy job satisfaction even when times are difficult.

Communication and co-operation, both formal and informal, between team members is essential to make everyone aware of events and pull together. A large number of formal meetings that interfere with the actual caring role can be seen as irrelevant, whereas shared informal coffee breaks can forge team links in a very effective way.

Key issues

The team works together in an effective way when members:

- have the same professional objectives
- are able to contribute to discussion and action
- feel valued
- can be creative in their approach
- share responsibility
- suppress personal differences in the interests of team harmony
- have different skills and talents which are put to good use and complement each other.

Employees who are excluded deliberately or accidentally get extremely upset and resentful of the situation. Lack of communication is one of the most common causes of care service breakdown; sometimes it is an oversight due to forgetfulness or being called away at a crucial time, or there may be mislaid or lost information that is vital to the next course of action.

Think it over

Think of an incident when you could not perform to the best of your ability due to lack of information or misinformation. How did you feel about the end result and about the person(s) who let you down?

Have you ever failed to communicate properly to someone else? How did that turn out?

Punctuality is very important in employment and especially so when working with a team of people. A team may not be able to proceed if one member is missing and everyone's time is wasted. The late member can have no idea of the effort other people have made to arrive on time and the annoyance and frustration that can build up against them.

It is always prudent to arrive a little early for work or placement and to do this you must allow extra time for late transport, busy traffic, etc. This often simply means rising an hour earlier and preparing the items you need for work the night before. This is particularly important if you have a social occasion the evening before work as you are more likely to wake up later. Ensure that you have a good alarm clock or someone reliable to give you an alarm call. Continually being late is one of the most damaging factors to you personally and very few people believe your excuses for being late – however inventive you are!

You have already learned that in many situations, such as dealing with unacceptable behaviour, you should refer to others. Being able to do this is also part of working within a team. Team members will have different skills, strengths and abilities and to use these to good effect other team members must be prepared to refer problems to them. This must not be viewed as getting rid of a problem onto someone else, but as providing the best service. However, this must not stifle professional, social and personal development in others; there is everything to be gained by reflecting on the expert's actions and asking questions at suitable times, eventually gaining confidence and competence to perform similar tasks under the expert's supervision. As a student, you may be able to use this strategy in some simple tasks but are more likely to be able to observe the development of other workers in the care setting.

Assessment activity 6.10

Draw up a table that shows what skills you need to work effectively as a member of a team. Show which skills you are good at, and which you might need to improve on.

Causes of stress in the workplace and the effect on service users and staff

A large number of books have been written about the causes and management of stress in general and quite a number written solely about the stress involved in the various aspects of caring professions. Unit 8 also discusses the meaning of stress, various models of stress analysis and management of stress (see page 517). This unit asks you to look at the causes of stress in the workplace and how it affects clients and staff.

'Burnout' is a term used to explain how a person can feel after a long period of stress (chronic stress) when they feel stripped of motivation and enthusiasm. They are devoid of creative thinking and feel they cannot cope with anything more. Very often it can be a prelude to a complete breakdown and therefore should be taken seriously.

Care staff are continually being asked to perform more tasks and work longer hours because there is a chronic shortage of qualified care workers. It takes several years to fully train a qualified carer and, although the government has initiated various schemes to improve recruitment, there remains an imbalance between the number of clients needing treatment and the number of care staff. Hospitals are particularly hard-hit by staff shortages and care staff from overseas are being encouraged to come to Britain.

Think it over

It is always useful to make daily use of media reports, but do not believe *everything* that you read! For one week, take time to read daily and specialised media reports concerning care staff shortages, extended roles, longer working hours and stress levels.

Keep a log of everything you find and note the effects on clients and staff. Investigate stress levels, the causes and the effects in your different vocational placements. Compare your findings.

The most common *physical* symptoms of stress are:

- headache
- stomach disorders
- chest tightness
- lower back pain
- neck tensions
- chronic constipation.

Other symptoms of stress can be:

- insomnia
- loss of efficiency
- loss of concentration
- irritability
- breakdown of relationships
- lack of motivation
- depression.

You have learned that it is very important to have successful relationships in teams of people working together. Where there is conflict between care workers and/or service users, there is also stress. Many people can 'switch off' when they have finished the day's work, but some people will brood over any conflict for a very long time. People can find release for their feelings by talking to others, increasing physical activity, experiencing a period of solitude or even just going into an empty room and shouting their feelings out loud.

Equal opportunities

You will have come across several references to equal opportunities already in this book, particularly in Unit 1. You have also learned in this unit about valuing people as individuals and respecting the beliefs and views of others.

You will need to find out about the equal opportunities policies and procedures in *each* vocational placement that you carry out and analyse how these relate to the national and legal framework. To do this you will need access to the national and legal framework. Three most important documents/organisations for you on this topic will be:

- Commission for Racial Equality: www.cre.gov.uk
- Equal Opportunities Commission: www.eoc.org.uk
- Human Rights Act 1998: www.hmso.gov.uk/acts/acts 1998/19980042.htm/

Other useful information can be obtained from:

- Department for Work and Pensions: www.dwp.gov.uk/
- Opportunity for All: www.dwp.gov.uk/publications/dwp/2001/oppall-third/index.htm
- Age Concern: www.ageconcern.org.uk
- British Association of Social Workers: www.basw.co.uk
- Salvation Army: www.salvationarmy.org.uk

You should obtain leaflets (many are free) or download the appropriate information before you go on your first placement so that you are in a position to start checking the relationship of the policies and procedures to the national and legal framework.

Some policies may discriminate positively for a particular group of people in order to 'pump-prime' against deep-rooted prejudice. You can find more information on this in Unit 1, page 15.

Effectiveness

You will need to judge the effectiveness of the policies and procedures in each vocational placement. You will be able to think of several ways to do this if you observe and listen to the events around you. When the Queen opened a new parliamentary session in November 2001, she quoted a passage from Burke: 'To promote evil it is only necessary for good men to do nothing'. We could substitute injustice for 'evil' and people for 'men' and this quote would be highly relevant to equal opportunities practice. Bearing this in mind, you could focus on the presence *and absence* of action to promote equity.

Here are some suggestions:

- Do equal opportunities issues or rights appear regularly on the agenda of meetings?
- Are clients advised of their rights?
- Have you seen or heard anyone supporting clients to achieve their rights?
- Have you seen or heard any discriminatory behaviour?
- Was this behaviour challenged by anyone?
- Are complaints procedures explained to clients?
- How many complaints have been received in the last 12 months?
- Were complaints resolved satisfactorily as far as the clients were concerned?
- Have you seen any clients being assisted by an advocate?
- What is the gender mix of carers in the setting?

You can also consider practical care tasks in this way:

- Can individuals choose and wear their own clothes?
- Can they go to bed in their own time?
- Is there a choice of food at meal times?
- Are clients' religious beliefs catered for?
- Are people from ethnic minorities supported with their cultural differences, language, gender of carer, etc?

You will be able to use these ideas to form your own list of questions that are specific to the care setting in which you are working.

When you are compiling your questions, you will also be collecting examples of practice relating to theory and evaluating the effectiveness of equal opportunities practice. It should then be possible to suggest improvements from your evaluation of your answers.

Challenging discriminatory behaviour

Discriminatory behaviour can take many forms in different care settings and with different individuals; you will need to be able to identify the behaviour and know how to challenge it – which can be difficult to do, especially when the person is a good friend or someone in a superior position.

Many discriminatory remarks are hidden in humour or the individual responds with, 'I was only joking'. Other remarks are intended to put a person down, undermine them or even be absolutely cruel. On many occasions, the discrimination occurs through sheer ignorance of knowledge about different cultures practised by ethnic minority groups of people or failing to recognise the need to provide care programmes appropriate to different cultures. Ageism, sexism, racism and discrimination against disability, sexuality and unemployment is still prevalent in today's society despite legislation. Much of this is bound up with use of inappropriate language such as:

- dolies, yobs – unemployed people
- wrinklies, oldies, old folks, dearies – for elderly people (even 'the elderly' on its own is discriminatory)
- cripples, spastics – these are very unpleasant terms for people with disabilities
- Pakis, coons, wogs, Paddies – these are unacceptable terms for people from different ethnic groups.

In care it is unacceptable to call clients by their condition – the renal case, the stroke in bed 3, etc.

It is also discrimination to do nothing when you hear discriminatory remarks or to say: 'It's not my problem', 'I'm not going to cause trouble' or 'I will wait to see if anyone else takes it up first' or similar remarks.

You may find this rather worrying that, by doing nothing, you are also part of the discrimination. For many people, discrimination is only seen as a positive action against someone and they would be shocked to be implicated by the negative aspect. Take heart from the fact that very few people have *not* been guilty of this in the past either by not wishing to cause trouble and not get involved or simply not knowing how to manage the situation. However, the individual who is being discriminatory will continue to do so if never challenged and the effects on those being discriminated against will continue to be damaging to their physical and mental health.

Many members of the general public continue to be unaware of their discriminatory behaviour even when they have had equal opportunity training!

Case study

Mrs S and her partner Mr B were purchasing some cut flowers in a large supermarket to take to a friend in hospital. A middle-aged male employee was wrapping the flowers chosen and handed to him by Mrs S whilst the two men were chatting idly. Mrs S handed over the money for the flowers and the supermarket loyalty card in her name. When the purchase was completed, the employee handed the wrapped flowers, the change and the loyalty card to Mr B. When Mrs S complained about that, both men were astonished and Mr B explained quickly that he had no intention of keeping the change. Mrs S tried to make both men see that that was not the point; she felt no respect had been paid to her right to receive the items back herself. She said that if she had been a child buying flowers for her mother, she would have received change and purchase back herself. Both men thought that she was making a mountain out of a molehill, although Mr B did eventually see the point afterwards. Mrs S explained that most discrimination is so inbred that people just don't think about it.

Do you think that Mrs S was justified in her complaint?

Was this an example of sexism?

Would you have picked up on this type of discrimination or just accepted it?

What do you think might have happened if Mrs S had used a wheelchair and been accompanied by Mr B?

Do you think the incident would change the way the employee behaved next time?

Did Mrs S challenge the employee in the correct way?

You would challenge most types of discrimination by direct conversation with the individual concerned in a private room in a polite, but firm manner. If the matter is not resolved, then ask for support from your colleagues and supervisor. Where there is a lack of provision for people, then the most appropriate method of challenge is asking for the matter to be discussed at a unit meeting and if necessary request training. Where there is any risk to people, then the unit manager, health and safety officer or police should be informed.

Empowerment

In the past, professional carers such as nurses, doctors, social workers and carers generally made decisions about clients because they considered themselves to be experts on people. Nowadays, people are considered to be the experts on their own social, emotional and cognitive needs but not necessarily on their physiological care. Whereas historically the carer had the power, it is now generally perceived that clients should have the power to control their lives as much as possible and that carers should assist clients to make their own decisions whenever possible. This is known as **empowerment**.

Many clients are not able to work towards their own decisions because of their vulnerability due to illness, confusion, disability, dementia and old age. In these situations, the carer is required to reach out to the client or their advocate using empathy and understanding and work towards an agreement, which fits in with the client's lifestyle, culture and beliefs. A relative or family friend may be important in acting as advocate, by providing details of the client's identity that are unknown to the carer.

In addition to all the other policies and procedures that you have learned about, most care settings will have policies and procedures on empowerment to guide the caring staff on their approach. You will need to find out about the ways in which empowerment is managed in each vocational placement.

Most care settings have policies and procedures on empowerment to prevent situations like this

Care programmes

A care programme exists to identify the most appropriate ways of achieving the objectives identified after the assessment of the client's needs, to provide the best service possible with the available resources. Everyone who receives a service should have a care programme that fits resources to the client and not the client to resources. Some care programmes will be very simple whereas others will involve a number of agencies and a number of teams of different specialist carers – a so-called multi-discipline approach. Duplication, a waste of resources, and a failure to provide some aspects of care will result if the care programme is not fully understood by all personnel involved and constantly reviewed, as the client's needs change.

How information is gained about clients and their needs

Unit 2 emphasised the importance of effective communication skills. The carer who is assessing the client's needs must use these to develop a working relationship with the client to gain as much information as possible about their problems, identity, values and beliefs in order to plan an effective care programme. The carer must make sure that from the outset the client is aware of the carer's role and is given as much information as possible about the nature of the service provision. Frequently, clients and/or relatives have grandiose views about the services that can be provided and the carer must clarify any misconceptions at the start.

Carers should bear in mind the influences that they personally might have on the client during the assessment of needs. Some clients will maximise their needs whilst others make every effort to minimise the amount of help they require. It can be very useful to have present a relative or friend who knows the client well during the assessment; the client should be asked if there is such a person who can help them.

At regular intervals, the carer should summarise the information obtained so far and ask for confirmation. The needs assessor may, also, with the client's permission contact other people or agencies who have been working with the client in order to gain extra information. The client should be absolutely clear about who will be contacted and the nature of the enquiry and the carer must be absolutely clear that permission has been granted. All care professionals are bound by confidentiality policies and by appropriate legislation and

It is important to gain as much information as possible to plan an effective care programme

these must be adhered to. A representative from an outside agency, which has been involved with the client, can be asked to attend the needs assessment to provide a fuller picture. The client should be empowered by these 'helpers' and remain in control wherever possible.

The care setting will have appropriate documentation for completion and procedures in place for the needs assessment process. You will be required to find out how the assessment process operates in your vocational placement.

Own contribution to the planning for client needs

In this part of the unit, you are asked to take part in a care-planning meeting and make some contribution to the arrangements. You may be able to report on any observations that you have made or any events witnessed. However, you must not wait until a meeting is held to report anything; it might be important to report back to care staff immediately and this may feature in the planning meeting.

How agreement is made to provide appropriate services

Once the assessor has developed a working relationship with the client, a pre-arranged meeting is held in an appropriate setting, frequently the client's home. The assessor, client and carer should be present and appropriate representatives of agencies or advocates, as the client deems suitable to assist. At this meeting, the needs of the clients are explored; some clients will confuse 'wants' with 'needs' such as wanting a ground floor apartment to overcome difficulties with stairs whereas installation of a stair-lift will meet the need. As the needs become unravelled, the assessor will need to know those needs that concern the client most and those that concern the carer the most.

The assessor also needs to look at motivation; in other words which need is the client most eager to get sorted and for which need(s) are they willing to accept intervention? It might seem strange to you that a client can identify a need yet not require any help to address that need, but such a situation is quite common. Many people resist change or do not wish to feel they are becoming dependent on others.

The assessor will need to classify the needs into immediate needs, acute short-term needs and chronic long-term needs, and prioritise their plan. The next stage is to agree the objectives to be met in satisfying the prioritised needs; each objective must be capable of being measured and this can be quite difficult with qualitative goals such as improving social contact or emotional stability.

Any agency that is going to supply a service for the client should receive copies of the assessment documentation and care plan. The individual who has carried out the assessment usually becomes the care manager for the client and is responsible for the implementation of the plan and the coherence of the agencies involved, including the relatives and friends of the client as and when necessary. The broad aim of the care plan is to promote as much independence for the client as possible and enable the person to do as much as possible for themselves. The care plan will detail the activities involved, the day and time and who will provide the service – if indeed one is required.

How care programmes are reviewed

As each care plan is constructed, arrangements for monitoring and reviewing the care plan should be made and recorded. There can be several reasons for monitoring care plans:

- to ensure the objectives of the care plan are being achieved
- to ensure the contributions from different agencies are satisfactorily co-ordinated
- to ensure the care services are meeting quality standards
- budget control
- support for the participants
- to make minor adjustments to the care plan
- to prepare for review.

The care manager should carry out monitoring by telephone calls, observations, visits, surveys or letters. The same person is responsible for reviewing the care plan after a specified interval of time. After a period, the care plan 'ages' and major modifications need to be made. Reviews are necessary because:

- needs require re-assessment
- objectives require change
- objectives require checking and reasons for success and/or failure noted
- costs and quality of care need to be evaluated and revised
- services may need to be revised
- any needs not met require to be assessed
- further dates for monitoring and review need to be established.

Ideally the care manager should again carry out this review. The views of the client and carer are of paramount importance in checking progress and quality of care, but the opinion of service representatives is also valuable.

You will need to provide examples from your vocational placements of review situations and how evaluation is carried out in particular care settings.

Assessment activity 6.11

In each of your placement settings, record examples of how the care planning cycle identifies and meets clients' needs. What was your involvement, and that of other members of staff in the planning, delivering and reviewing of the care cycles in each setting?

Personal career goals

As well as learning about care and care services in your vocational placements, you will also be learning and developing your own knowledge, skills and abilities about *yourself*. During this time, you might confirm your initial ideas about your own career prospects or change them in the light of your increasing experience. Both of these options are perfectly all right and you should carry out planning and research to further your career goals. The final part of this unit helps you to do that by requiring you to make and monitor your personal and career plans and map your existing and proposed status against career requirements.

Personal career plan

In this plan you will need to consider all your possible career goals and the intended care area(s) in which you would like to work. For example, you might have chosen occupational therapy as your main career goal but decide that you would be far happier working in a community care setting rather than a large hospital. You need to consider all possible options in that setting; using the same example there may be opportunities for working with children, young disabled adults, elderly people or those with a particular disability like the loss of a limb. As your experience increases, the list of possible options will grow.

Qualifications, skills and attributes required and measure own status against them

As you identify your career goals, you will need to research the necessary requirements for those areas and can then match the qualifications you have already gained and those you are working towards against them. Qualifications open doors but you will also need to match your skills and abilities too. It is important to be both realistic and realise your own potential. If you do not enjoy studying for long periods at a time and have found examination success hard to come by, then it is probably not sensible to aim to be a doctor, surgeon, psychologist or pathologist for example. You could, however, consider nursing, pathology technician or community psychiatric nursing, depending on your personal views. If you do not like studying very much and prefer to learn in a more practical way, then National Vocational Qualifications alongside a job in the area are likely to form your best route after your National Diploma or Certificate. Which of these might be chosen might rest with whether you like to work face to face with people, like to work in a team or more in an office or laboratory environment. There are many different aspects to consider and research, and your tutors will not expect you to make decisions at the beginning of your programme – but they will expect you to investigate and research your favoured options.

Career action plan

In a career action plan, you will detail the actions and their time scales to achieve your career objectives. Once again you need to be realistic, particularly with time scales, which have a habit of slipping! You will measure progress against your goals and adjust when appropriate, providing the reasons why adjustment is necessary. This will be an ongoing action plan for your programme duration.

For further assistance on these action plans and maps, see Assessment guidelines below.

Assessment guidelines

It is crucially important that you record accurately the knowledge and skills that you gain in each placement and do not wait until you have almost completed your course of study. This is an essential unit, equal in depth and breadth to other essential units. However, it is a unit that cannot be completed by lecture notes, but from material and experience from your vocational placement. All your work from vocational practice will be placed in a file or portfolio called the Vocational Practice Log (VPL).

Sketchy, inadequate notes made during your period of time in the placement will cause great difficulty for you later on. If you can show that your progress, development, powers of analysis and evaluation have advanced from the first year of the course to the second, that will be exactly what your tutors are looking for. You will benefit from completing your first-year vocational placement reports in the VPL before the commencement of the second year and comparing your skills and knowledge gained from the first year with that gained towards the end of your course.

Record your findings from each placement in your VPL with dividing pages between each placement; alternatively, you might prefer to divide your file into evidence collection sections, such as policies, procedures, equal opportunities practice, care programmes, etc., and have a box or code at the top indicating the placement reference.

About a week before you begin your vocational placement, and with your tutor's agreement, pay an informal visit, trying to familiarise yourself with the route you have to take and the length of time you will be travelling. You will then have some idea of the length of time it will take you to reach your destination on the correct day of starting, but do remember that the starting time can make a difference. For example, if you visit one afternoon but actually need to travel between eight and nine o'clock in the morning, it could take you twice as long. You will not wish to arrive late on any morning, and certainly not the first one!

It is useful to telephone first to enquire whether you might introduce yourself when you carry out your journey practice. On this occasion, do not stay too long (carers are busy people), ask any questions that you are worried about which you know your tutor cannot answer and pick up any leaflets to read when you arrive home. Most residential and nursing homes will have publicity leaflets and many other care settings will also produce information. If you are fortunate, the supervisor will show you around and introduce you to other members of staff. If you have a placement in a large facility such as a hospital this will be more difficult, but you will be able to walk around the public areas without hindrance.

Ensure that you read all the necessary information before you arrive on the correct day. Your tutor will inform you about the need for uniform, name badges and the location for the first meeting, together with any particular information that you will require. If you are working with certain client groups, you will need to be 'police cleared'. This is nothing to be afraid of and involves completing a form, which your tutor will forward to the appropriate authorities. You can also find out if you need to sign a form of registration to indicate that you are on the premises and who to telephone if you are delayed or absent through illness. Most educational establishments will provide you with guidance notes on your student roles and responsibilities. These notes are generic and you may find that there are extra guidelines in specific placements.

Students are often anxious and fearful on their first few attendance days, worried that an emergency might happen and they cannot deal with it, worried that someone might shout at them or complain loudly or that they will be ignored. It would be the same on the first day at work and everyone feels like this – the feeling will soon wear off. In an emergency, call the nearest member of staff; you are not expected to handle emergencies or crises. Do not let yourself be ignored, offer to help other members of staff in a courteous way and stay calm and reassuring if a client becomes distressed – call a member of staff. You will not know whether this is a common occurrence and a feature of the clients' illness – most will be! Talk to someone at the placement about it in a quiet moment and you will feel much better about it.

Placement structure

Aims, policies and procedures

You will need to record the key features of the aims, policies and procedures in your workplaces and put these in your file. Photocopying the policies at your own expense is acceptable but if you then place it in your VPL without reading it through carefully, it will be of little use, whereas teasing out the key features will commit the policy to memory much more effectively. It will also be much easier to compare this list with your next placement's policies than using the whole document. Plan to do this in your first few days in the placement. Find out about other policies operating in the placement and perform the same exercise.

You will find that it is much easier to remind yourself about the key features of documents when you need to consider other evidence, such as linking theory to practice, confidentiality and equal opportunities, rather than work from whole policies. Do not attempt to summarise a large number of policies and procedures or you will find time passing so quickly that you will have little time left for anything else. Tackle the major topics that you will find useful for other sections of this unit, such as:

- equal opportunities, including empowerment
- bullying and harassment
- dealing with violence and aggression
- fire emergency
- lifting and handling
- confidentiality
- health and safety.

If you have difficulty in understanding the wording and terminology used in such documents, make some notes identifying the problems and in a quiet, suitable moment ask a professional carer to go over these with you.

Role and responsibilities of the staff structure

There are several ways to find out about the roles and responsibilities of different levels of staff in care settings:

- You can ask members of staff, choosing a suitable time.
- You can ask them about their person and job descriptions.
- Visit the personnel section or the employment manager of the organisation.
- Use a search engine for local organisation websites under the type of care setting.
- Write a few letters to care organisations who are advertising job vacancies.
- Use the latest edition of *Career* or other career guidance references in the library.
- Look at job specifications on notice boards in care settings or job centres.
- Look at job vacancies advertised in specialist medical, nursing and social service magazines.

You will see a job description in Figure 6.3 for a position advertised on a hospital website.

Title: **D/E GRADE NURSES**

Closing Date: 31/12/02

Area: Nursing: General

Grade: D/E

Salary:

Description: FULL OR PART TIME

We require staff nurses from varying backgrounds to complement the established teams on both sites. We require nurses who prefer to work at night (although posts will be rotational and day duty will be required to meet training and development needs). The wards accommodate medically stable patients, most of whom need nurses who are well educated in all aspects of medical nursing with expertise in social aspects of care. There is emphasis on the multi-disciplinary approach therefore applicants must have good communication skills.

D GRADE NURSING JOB DESCRIPTION JOB TITLE: Registered Nurse

GRADE: D

RESPONSIBLE TO: Ward/Unit Sister/Charge Sister

PROFESSIONAL RELATIONSHIPS: Ward/Unit multi-disciplinary team; Clinical/Directorate manager

JOB PURPOSE: The postholder will have responsibility for assessing, implementing and evaluating under supervision, the care needs of group patients.

PATIENT CARE RESPONSIBILITY: To provide safe, individualised, patient centred care. To participate in the maintenance and development of professional standards incorporating evidence based practice. This will be expected to include participation in the audit of clinical indicators for nursing care. Appropriate delegation, supervision and teaching to junior staff. To communicate effectively with patients, relatives and multi-disciplinary team utilising verbal and written communication methods.

DEVELOPMENT AND TRAINING: To participate in preceptorship, mentorship and clinical supervision to develop personal and professional competence. Accept responsibility for identification of personal development needs. Maintain active registration, including when appropriate attendance at formal education.

WIDER RESPONSIBILITIES: Work with UKCC Code of Conduct. Be aware of and follow Trust policies, procedures. D Grade nurses will not routinely be rostered to take charge. They may however at times be expected to take on this responsibility for personal development purposes or in the absence of a senior nurse. To act at all times as an Ambassador for the organisation. To respond positively and contribute to management of change projects, i.e. in link nurse roles or project groups. This will be expected to include initiatives such as Clinical Governance.

Reproduced with the permission of the Royal Liverpool and Broadgreen University Hospitals NHS Trust
Figure 6.3 A job description for a nursing position.

Service users

You will need to provide an outline description of the service users in each placement and a broad picture of the reasons behind their involvement in the setting. This will incorporate a similarly broad view of how the needs of the service users are met in the setting. You will have some idea of these areas from publicity literature of the setting but check that the overall picture is correct by discussion with staff members. This evidence can be confined to a few paragraphs; you must not ask service users systematically, using direct questions relating to the problems that led to their referral and their physical, emotional, intellectual or social well-being. This might cause too much stress and would probably offend some clients. During your placement experience, you may be able to amplify your evidence further because of the relationships you make. Remember that outline statements are all that is required and you must respect confidentiality at all times.

Services and resources provided by other organisations

This will largely depend on the type of placement you are working in – a small privately owned playgroup may have very few associated organisations whereas a community care establishment may have several associates such as diverse voluntary groups, physiotherapy and occupational therapy visits, psychology services, etc. You will need to ask staff and be vigilant in your observation of visitors to the establishment to obtain this evidence.

Role and performance in each student placement

You will have a basis for this work from your tutor's and/or placement guidelines and together with the placement diary that you should keep, be able to write a job description for yourself about halfway through the placement. Review your job description as your placement ends, to update if necessary. It is easier to do this by keeping your word-processed work on a floppy disk. Keep one or two disks for vocational placement only.

Convert your diary notes to floppy disk every few days and then complete and print out your work to put in the VPL.

You should use a tabular format that can be utilised for each placement and easily compared during each year of your programme. If you print a chart similar to the one below in landscape format you will have more space in the columns.

Name:		Placement dates:	
Title of vocational placement:			
Nature of client group:			
Aims of placement	*Objectives of placement*	*Expected tasks*	*Comments on performance*

*The final column will assist you with evaluating your own developing skills and communication skills.

You should try to become more sophisticated in your terminology as you gain experience and become more reflective in your practice. You should be able to evaluate your work as you progress. After you have completed each sheet at the end of a placement, write a reflective report and an evaluation of performance.

As you work through your placements, you will find some of the expected tasks are similar, but some will be very different. You can, however, make your aims and objectives very different by challenging yourself to complete more difficult objectives. An example is suggested below for your communication skills.

Placement 1	Practise different ways of introducing yourself and find the best way for you. Practise asking open questions and some closed questions and note the client's responses
Placement 2	Practise open questions and reflecting feeling
Placement 3	Practise opening and closing conversations with clients and summarising at the end
Placement 4	Practise total active listening
Placement 5 or as appropriate to the setting	Find and use ways to overcome barriers in communication
Placement 6	Practise prioritising any of the client's difficulties and ways to make the client progress towards making their own decisions. Do I offer the client individual choice? Do I treat clients as unique individuals? How do clients react to me?

You could make charts like this for other skills and abilities so that you have a plan for developing and improving your performance with each placement and in preparation for making the links from theory to practice. This will also help you with your personal action plan (see below). In every placement you should remind yourself of the need to respect confidentiality.

Demonstrate the base knowledge and skills to be an effective practitioner

When you complete the skills and abilities planning charts above, you will clearly be able to show the links between the theory gained in lectures and the practice in the vocational area. You will also show the range of skills needed to fulfil the placement role and how to overcome barriers in communication. The ideal way is to be pro-active in your search for evidence. The last thing you want to be doing is reaching the end of your placements and trying to remember events that took place several months ago, producing second-rate poor evidence or having no evidence at all for some sections – despite having been on five or six placements. Read through the unit specifications or this unit a few times before you go into each placement and plan ahead. Remember that some placement settings will give more scope in experiencing issues like dealing with barriers to communication, so be prepared to modify your plans as you learn about each care setting.

Organisations will not expect you to deal with inappropriate behaviour in care settings, although you are required to write a report on strategy for dealing with such behaviour. You can do this at an appropriate time for you, but place it on a list of 'things to do' in your VPL to remind you. However, you are likely to witness other staff having to deal with such behaviour from clients of all ages, so be observant and watch the staff closely so that you can provide witness examples. There is a tendency when viewing incidents of this type to pay more attention to the individual causing the disturbance – after all, in many situations, this is exactly why the individual acts this way. Try to pay more attention to the professional staff and the methods for dealing with the disturbance and make notes in your break time. Keep your report on disk for modification when you have a practical incident to add.

With the permission of your supervisor, try to put aside one (or two) mornings or afternoons, perhaps during visiting time, to find out about the recording and storage of information in each placement. This does not mean you have to look at confidential files – just determine the methods used. You will also need to find out how staff share information and what the reasons are for sharing information. After your first placement, when you have one set of information, try to set up a generic sheet on a computer to ask the same questions on the remaining placements with appropriate spaces for you to complete during your working time. This will not only save you time later on, but also provide you with a suitable format for comparisons at the end of the placement activity.

Demonstrate a working understanding of the principles of team work, work relationships, roles and responsibilities

You must be able to show that you are working within the limits of your role and competence in the placement. You will have the evidence for this from:

- your job description (see above)
- the expected tasks from your chart (also above)
- a work placement report.

The latter should be available from each vocational placement; your tutor may hold these reports and you can ask for a photocopy.

You should write a report based on these documents to demonstrate the limits of your role and your vocational competence. Put this report on your 'things to do' list. You should also find the evidence to demonstrate the skills required for working effectively in a team. To recap, you are looking for evidence of punctuality, communication skills, willingness to refer and to involve others.

Two additional items for this list are reports explaining a range of roles and relationships and the causes of stress in the workplace and the effect on service users and staff. Use several diagrams in your work on roles and relationships as these illustrate links between people and roles rather well (see Figure 6.4).

You might find that one care setting is suitable (with permission from the supervisor) for devising your own questionnaire to research the causes and effects of stress. You should get your questionnaire checked through by both your tutor and the placement supervisor if permission is granted. Use your survey as an example of primary research within your report.

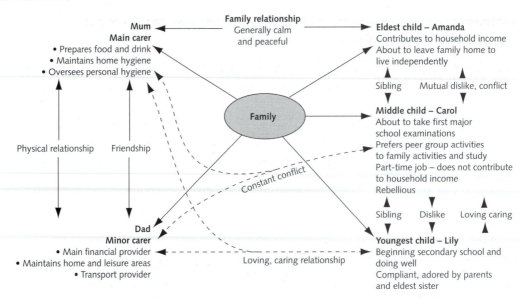

Figure 6.4 An example of family roles and relationships

Demonstrate an understanding of the practice of equal opportunities in the health and care field

You will need to write a report on the equal opportunities policy and procedure in each workplace and analyse how effective these are in the setting. You will have a sheet in your file outlining the key features of the relevant equal opportunities documents in each placement.

Examine the bullet points on pages 241–2; your answers to these questions should form a basis for your analysis of effectiveness. These responses will also help you to explain how staff and clients are empowered in each setting and this can be amplified by looking at the key features of the policies and procedures in use in the workplace.

How can staff be empowered? Here are some suggestions to explore:

- Are staff trained and developed in areas of concern to them?
- Can they contribute to the agenda of meetings?
- Are they freely able to contribute in meetings or do they feel intimidated?
- Can staff bank on support from managers?
- Will managers act as advocates for staff if required?
- Are members of staff confident about their roles and responsibilities?

You can probably add more bullet points to this list in specific settings that you work in.

Finally, in this section you will need to identify examples of challenging discriminatory behaviour that you have met or read about. This should go on the 'things to do' list. As well as practical examples, stay alert for articles in the media that you can use.

Demonstrate an understanding of the development, provision and review of care programmes

You may prefer to leave this section until your second year and make steady progress with the other sections in the first year. You must be able to observe some care planning meetings and have the opportunity to participate in at least one meeting. Participation will not be major and you will only be able to do this if you know the client and have developed a working relationship with them. Make sure that you record your contribution to use as evidence.

After the meeting has finished you will need to describe how information was gained about the client and their needs and how agreement was reached to provide services. Do not leave this until later or you will find that you have forgotten some valuable points. If you feel that your memory is not as good as it might be, you could ask all participants if they would mind if you took some notes on the *care planning process*. Ensure that the client knows that you are not making notes on their difficulties and allow them to see your finished notes if required. Preferably, practise active listening and avoid note-taking. If you can observe more than one care-planning meeting, then you will be very fortunate and only require to remember differences in the processes.

Identify and develop an action plan for personal career goals

This is a section that you can start even before you have been on a vocational placement! In fact, you can benefit from an early start and half-yearly monitoring, review and reasoned evaluation.

Begin by making a diagram of three or four potential career goals and possible options within those areas. You will produce something like the example shown in Figure 6.5 for a student who likes working with elderly people.

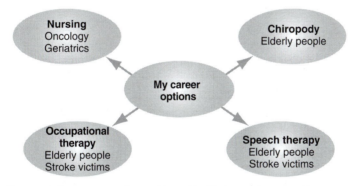

Figure 6.5 Career options for working with elderly people

This student has four career options at present – you may have more or less than this; remember that you can add or subtract career options as you progress through your course, ideas alone are a good start but you need to research the personal qualities and qualifications needed to realise these ambitions. The latest careers books in your libraries will provide you with the basic information, and then actually talking to carers practising those professions will provide insight. You can often do this informally at open days or evenings, so look out for these and take every opportunity to attend. Many career guides incorporate self-tests and exercises to find and develop the natural aptitudes of their readers in the search for the most suitable careers (see References and further reading at the end of this unit).

The best way of providing the evidence for your research findings and your personal action plan is to set up two tables (in landscape format) on your disk that you can keep reviewing and adding to. Try reviewing and updating your sheets every four months or at the end of each term (this can be a permanent feature of your 'things to do' list), printing out copies for your VPL after each update.

Your first table might look like the one below, but with more entries:

Career research plan: Maisie Dolojor

Career option	Entry qualifications required	Desired personal skills and attributes	Date of entry and current status	I need to work on...
Geriatric nursing	BTEC National Diploma Health Studies		21.12.02	
		Good health	Current health good	My fitness
		Intelligence	Reasonably intelligent	Reading more
		Ability to make relationships	Can form and sustain relationships	Client relationships
		Empathy and understanding	Learning more about this every day	Putting this into placement practice
		Ability to work in a team	Think I could	Putting this into placement practice
		Ability to work one-to-one	Think I could	Putting this into placement practice
		Excellent communication skills	Improving, less shy than I used to be	Putting this into placement practice
		Confidentiality	New to me	Putting this into placement practice
		Good management skills	Not very good, no opportunity	Putting this into placement practice
		Personal organisation	Could be better	Keeping to my time schedules and punctuality
		Time management	Not good	
		Equal opportunity practice	New to me	Putting this into placement practice
		Even-tempered	Placid	More enthusiasm
		Good personal hygiene	Yes	
		Common sense	People say so	
		Practical	Limited at present	Doing some voluntary work in vacations

A new Diploma student might produce this type of table and then incorporate the items to be worked on in the placement plans to improve skills and abilities so that they can show improvement in personal development at the next chosen review date. The student would need to produce a table for each career option. This is, if you like, a macro career plan and the following table would be a micro career plan to manage personal actions.

Personal Action Plan				
Date	*Personal actions required*	*Aims*	*Time scale*	*Progress*
21.12.02	Improve personal fitness by walking to college every day	To improve general health and stamina	Year one	
	Read one library book each week – seek guidance on choice from librarian	Improve literary skills and general knowledge	Term one	
	Visit Mr Kitch (elderly neighbour who lives alone) once a week	Practise improving one-to-one relationship building – voluntary work	Year one	
	Completing assignments on time with a plan of action	Improve personal organisation and time management	Course duration	

A student would usually have more items than this and include those that they wished to develop from vocational practice.

End of unit test

1 Explain the differences between aims and objectives.

2 Distinguish between policies and procedures.

3 Name three possible barriers to communication.

4 Explain the difference between an open and a closed question.

5 What is affirmative action?

6 Provide an example of affirmative action.

7 Provide two reasons for planning a client's care programme.

8 Why is it necessary to review care programmes regularly?

9 Name three possible causes of stress in a care setting.

10 Name two pieces of legislation that are important in protecting client files.

11 What skills are important in team work?

12 Explain the way that you would behave when confronted by an angry client or relative.

13 What is the role of a student on vocational placement when asked for information on a client by a relative?

14 What is an advocate? Explain when an advocate may be required.

References and further reading

Breakwell, G. (1990), *Facing Physical Violence*, Leicester: British Psychological Society

Fontana, D. (1990), *Managing Stress*, Leicester: British Psychological Society

Fontana, D. (1990), *Social Skills at Work*, Leicester: British Psychological Society

Hopson, B. and Scally, M. (2000), *Build Your Own Rainbow*, Cirencester: Management Books

Lee, E. (1997), *Mental Healthcare*, Basingstoke: Macmillan Caring Series

Lindon, J. and Lindon, L. (1997), *Working Together for Young Children*, Basingstoke: Macmillan Caring Series

Lore, N. (1998), *The Pathfinder: How to Choose or Change Your Career for a Lifetime of Satisfaction and Success*, New York: Simon and Schuster Books

Moonie, N. (2000), *AVCE Health and Social Care*, Oxford: Heinemann

Nolan, Y. (2001), *Care S/NVQ*, Oxford: Heinemann

Parry, G. (1990), *Coping with Crises*, Leicester: British Psychological Society

Smyth, T. (1992), *Caring for Older People*, Basingstoke: Macmillan

Spink, C. (1996), *Equal Opportunities Guide*, London: Kogan Page

Lifespan development

This unit looks at the different life stages during human growth and development. It deals with the different major life events, life chances, diversity and equality issues that affect people's development, including psychological theories of development.

What you need to learn

- Life stages
- Psychological theories of lifespan development
- The influence of life events

Life stages

It is traditional to see life as involving certain definite periods of development. Terms like infant, child, adolescent and adult have been used for centuries to classify the age-related status of individuals. During the last century it was common to assume that there was a universal pattern to both physical and social development. During infancy, childhood and adolescence, a person would grow physically and learn the knowledge and skills they needed for work. Adulthood was a time when people would work and/or bring up their own family. Old age was when people would retire. Children would be grown up by the time their parents reached old age.

An American theorist, Havighurst, described the developmental tasks of the different life stages (1972). Some examples of these stages are listed below:

Infancy and early childhood
- Learning to walk
- Learning to take solid foods
- Learning to talk
- Learning bowel and bladder control
- Learning sex differences and sexual modesty

Later childhood
- Learning physical skills necessary for ordinary games
- Learning to get along with peers
- Learning an appropriate masculine or feminine role
- Developing basic skills in reading, writing and calculating
- Developing concepts necessary for everyday living
- Developing conscience, morality and a scale of values

Adolescence
- Achieving new and more mature relations with peers of both sexes
- Achieving a masculine or feminine role
- Accepting one's physique and using the body effectively

- Achieving emotional independence of parents and other adults
- Preparing for marriage and family life
- Preparing for an economic career

Early adulthood
- Selecting a mate
- Learning to live with a marriage partner
- Starting a family
- Rearing children
- Managing a home
- Getting started in an occupation

Middle age
- Assisting teenage children to become responsible and happy adults
- Reaching and maintaining satisfactory performance in one's occupational career
- Relating to one's spouse as a person
- Accepting and adjusting to the physiological changes of middle age
- Adjusting to ageing parents

Later maturity
- Adjusting to decreasing physical strength
- Adjusting to retirement and reduced income
- Adjusting to the death of one's spouse
- Establishing satisfactory physical living arrangements

Manuel Castells (1996) argues that life has changed so much that the notion of adolescent, adult and later life tasks and transitions is no longer relevant for many people:

'Now, organisational, technological and cultural developments characteristic of the new, emerging society are decisively undermining this orderly life cycle without replacing it with an alternative sequence. **I propose the hypothesis that the network society** (the world today) **is characterised by the breaking down of rhythmicity, either biological or social, associated with the notion of a life cycle.**'

Biological, social and economic influences on development are changing because:

- Science is now prolonging life and health for many people – retirement need not be seen as necessary at a set age.
- Reproduction no longer has to start in early adulthood. It is now possible for women to give birth in their 50s!
- People's life plans no longer necessarily focus on taking on a set job role for 'adult' life.
- Retirement can be optional and even a temporary condition that can take place at almost any age.
- Gender, family and reproductive roles are no longer perceived as fixed. One in five women will not have children in their life. A substantial number of people may not marry. Two in every five marriages end in divorce.

We now live in a rapidly changing world where many people can choose their own style of living and plan families, careers and social roles with less and less reference to age. Even so, there are some generalisations about biological, social and emotional development which can be made at the beginning of the new century. These generalised patterns of development may help health workers to understand the needs of people who become clients in the next decade or so.

Definition of terms: physical growth and development

Infancy (0–2 years)

Every individual has a unique pattern of growth and development. This is because there are so many factors influencing our progress. It would be logical to say that each one of us begins from the moment a sperm nucleus from the father joins with the nucleus from the mother's ovum, but the exact time of this process, known as *fertilisation*, is usually unknown. To obtain a more recognisable starting date, doctors will ask a pregnant woman for the starting date of her last menstrual period and add on two weeks. The period when the ovum is available for fertilising by the sperm is halfway between menstruations.

There is, however, a great deal of controversy over when an embryo becomes a human being. This has largely arisen from discussions about abortion. In Britain, the Abortion Act (1967) allowed termination of pregnancy up to the 28th week of gestation; but, after lengthy debates in Parliament, the limit was reduced to the 24th week. The debate continues, however, as babies can now survive if born at 24 weeks, owing to the great advances made in modern techniques. Many groups think that the limit should be reduced even further. Some pressure groups (such as Life) and many individuals consider that all abortion is wrong and human life is sacred from the date of fertilisation.

The fertilised ovum, now known as a *zygote*, is one of the larger cells in humans and is just visible to the naked eye. Imagine the smallest dot you can make with a very sharp pencil and this is about the right size. After a short rest period it begins to divide, first into two cells, then four, eight and so on. Quickly the tiny structure becomes a ball of smaller cells – a *morula*. These cells begin to become organised into different areas. Some will be destined to form the new human being, but for a while the majority of the cells are preparing to become its coverings and developing placenta. It is important that these parts are ready to secure the food supply for the developing being as soon as the structure enters the womb, or uterus, of the mother. All the time so far has been spent in travelling down the fallopian tube leading from the ovary into the uterus. At about a week old, the tiny structure, a hollow ball of cells known as a *blastocyst*, arrives in the uterus. The next few days are vital to the embryo. It must bury itself in the *endometrium*, the thickened lining of the mother's uterus and secure a food supply before the mother's next menstruation is due. If this does not happen, the blastocyst will be swept out of the mother's body with the products of menstruation and will die. Once embedded in this way, a process called *implantation*, the tiny embryo releases a hormone into the mother's blood which prevents the next menstruation.

Never again will growth be so rapid. By the third week after fertilisation (week 5 of the pregnancy calculation), the embryo has grown to be 0.5 cm long and has started to develop a brain, eyes, ears and limbs. Some individuals might class the development of the brain as being significant in the date of becoming a human being. There is even a tiny heart pumping blood to the newly formed placenta to obtain nutrients and oxygen from the mother's blood.

The embryo continues to grow and develop at a fantastic rate until at week 8 all major organs have formed and there is a human-looking face with eyes, ears, nose and mouth. Limbs have formed fingers and toes, and the body length has increased to 3 cm (see Figure 7.1). The name changes again – from now until birth it is called a *foetus*.

Growth and development of internal organs continues and the next main stage is at 20 weeks. The mother will begin to feel movements of the foetus, weak at first but

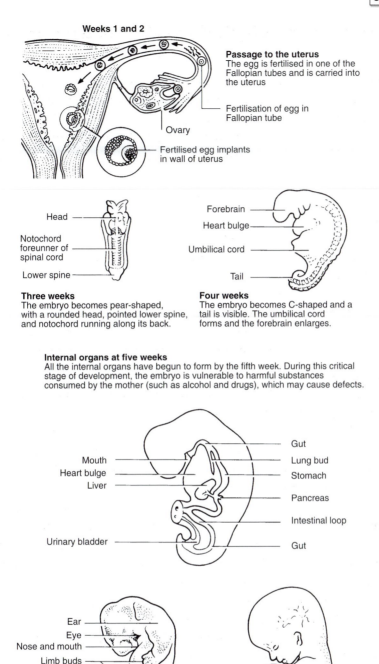

Weeks 1 and 2

Passage to the uterus
The egg is fertilised in one of the Fallopian tubes and is carried into the uterus

Fertilisation of egg in Fallopian tube

Ovary

Fertilised egg implants in wall of uterus

Head

Notochord foreunner of spinal cord

Lower spine

Forebrain

Heart bulge

Umbilical cord

Tail

Three weeks
The embryo becomes pear-shaped, with a rounded head, pointed lower spine, and notochord running along its back.

Four weeks
The embryo becomes C-shaped and a tail is visible. The umbilical cord forms and the forebrain enlarges.

Internal organs at five weeks
All the internal organs have begun to form by the fifth week. During this critical stage of development, the embryo is vulnerable to harmful substances consumed by the mother (such as alcohol and drugs), which may cause defects.

Mouth

Heart bulge

Liver

Urinary bladder

Gut

Lung bud

Stomach

Pancreas

Intestinal loop

Gut

Ear

Eye

Nose and mouth

Limb buds

Umbilical cord

Six weeks
Eyes are visible and the mouth, nose and ears are forming. The limbs grow rapidly from tiny buds.

Eight weeks
The face is more 'human', the head is more upright, and the tail has gone. Limbs become jointed. Fingers and toes appear.

Figure 7.1 Embryo development

getting stronger as the pregnancy progresses. The midwife can hear the heart beats through a trumpet-shaped instrument called a *foetal stethoscope*. The heart beats are very fast and difficult to count without experience.

The foetus is clearly male or female because the external sex organs have developed and the total length is now around 24 cm. The weight of the foetus is close to 0.5 kg already.

As you can see from the table below, at 9 months (40 weeks) the foetus is ready to be born. It is around 50 cm long and weighs around 3.5 kg.

Time in months of pregnancy	Length in centimetres	Weight in kilograms
1	0.35	Almost none
2	3.5	0.05
3	8.5	0.1
4	15	0.2
5	23	0.4
6	30	0.75
7	38	1.5
8	45	2.0
9	51	3.5

A newborn infant, often called a *neonate*, is a helpless individual and needs the care and protection of parents or others to survive. The nervous system which co-ordinates many bodily functions is immature and needs time to develop. The digestive system is unable to take food that is not in an easily digestible form such as milk. Other body systems, such as the circulatory and respiratory systems, have undergone major changes as a result of birth – the change to air breathing and physical separation from the mother. A few weeks later, the baby's temperature regulating system is able to function properly and fat is deposited beneath the skin as an insulating layer.

Key principles of development

The term 'growth' is used to describe a change in the quantity of some variable. For example, a child might become taller as they get older. We would say that they had grown taller. The word 'growth' does not explain what has happened – only that height has increased. If we assumed that the child's genetic programme is primarily responsible for an increase in height, then we might use the term 'maturation' to explain what we believed was happening.

The term 'development' describes changes which might be complex and qualitative as well as quantitative. The word 'development' is used to describe most intellectual, social and emotional change, where complex factors interact to create different patterns of change in different individuals.

Although development is a continuous process, it is not an even one affecting all parts of the body equally. However, development always follows the same sequence. The upper part of the body, particularly the head and brain, progresses extremely rapidly, while the lower part of the body, particularly the lower limbs, follows more slowly. This type of development is said to be **cephalo-caudal** and it means 'from head to tail'. Arms and legs, called 'the extremities', develop later than the heart, brain and other organs in the midline of the body. So as well as being cephalo-caudal, development is also from the midline to the extremities (see Figure 7.2). The reason for this is not hard to find: most vital organs are controlled by the

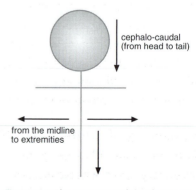

Figure 7.2 The sequence of development

brain and protected by the trunk. As the baby is dependent on the mother for nourishment, limbs are not essential to early survival.

Think it over

Look back at Figure 7.1 showing early development and you will notice the unusual overall shape of the infant's body and the strange proportions of the different parts compared to the whole. For example, measure the length of the whole 8-week-old foetus and then measure the length of the head only. You will find that the head is approximately 50 per cent of the total length, whereas the arms and legs are quite small and weak.

Early childhood (2–8 years)

During childhood, different parts of the body grow at different rates.

The nervous system, sense organs and head grow very rapidly from birth to 6 years. A 6-year-old's head is 90 per cent of the adult size, and they can wear a parent's hat! The reproductive organs remain small and underdeveloped until the onset of puberty (approximately between 10 and 15 years), and then they grow rapidly to reach adult size. General body growth is more steady, reaching adult size at around 18–20 years, but with three 'growth spurts' at 1, 5–7 years, and puberty.

Think it over

Look at Figure 7.3. Write notes on the changes you can see between birth and 8 years.

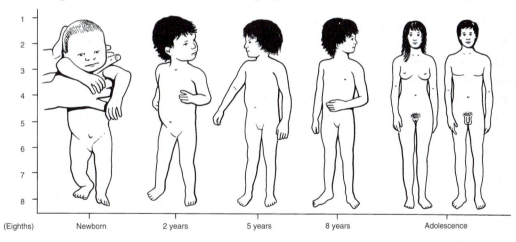

Figure 7.3 Growth profiles from birth to adolescence

When the skeleton first forms it is made of a flexible material called *cartilage.* This is slowly replaced by bone which is visible on X-rays. Each bone passes through the same sequence of changes of shape as it reaches maturity in a healthy adult. Bone age is, therefore, a useful measure of physical development. Height and weight standards are often associated with age, but are less useful because of the enormous differences which can occur in different individuals.

Puberty and adolescence (9–18 years)

Both boys and girls enter puberty between the ages of 10 and 15 years; this is when the secondary sexual characteristics develop and the sexual organs mature so that reproduction becomes possible. Puberty is the physical change which accompanies the emotional changes of adolescence and is caused by the hypothalamus part of the brain influencing the pituitary endocrine gland to secrete hormones known as gonadotrophins. In girls the gonadotrophin stimulates the ovaries to produce the hormone oestrogen and, in boys, the testes produce testosterone. Experts are still not sure why the hypothalamus seems to be important. Pubertal changes have occurred earlier in western countries with improved nutrition. It is also well recognised that, in the condition of anorexia nervosa, reproductive processes fail when an individual's body weight drops significantly.

Puberty is accompanied by a growth spurt in height, and weight increases are due to muscle building in boys and fat accumulation in girls.

Around the age of 10 to 11, but sometimes starting earlier, the breasts of girls start to swell, and pubic hair begins to grow. This is followed around one to two years later by the first menstruation, called the menarche. One hundred years ago the menarche occurred at an average age of 14.8 years; in 1988 it had reduced to 12.5 and a current research project indicates that it is now closer to 10 and 11, with breast budding and pubic hair appearance around 8 and 9. Early menstruation is often scanty, irregular and of brief duration; puberty is said to be complete when full, regular expected menstruation occurs. During this time, the pelvic bones widen, underarm (axillary) hair appears and fat is deposited around the body to produce a curvaceous figure with full breasts (see Figure 7.4).

The whole process takes three to four years to complete and very little growth in height occurs after puberty. Oestrogen is the hormone largely responsible for the physical changes but a second hormone produced during the second half of each menstrual cycle, i.e. progesterone, promotes glandular development of breasts and uterine linings.

Puberty in boys lags behind that of the girls by about two years, so at some time girls can be both taller and heavier than boys; boys eventually overtake girls in height and weight by the end of puberty (see Figure 7.5). The table below identifies male and female secondary sexual characteristics.

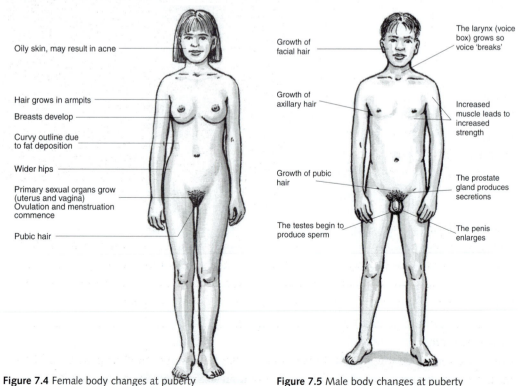

Figure 7.4 Female body changes at puberty

Oily skin, may result in acne

Hair grows in armpits

Breasts develop

Curvy outline due to fat deposition

Wider hips

Primary sexual organs grow (uterus and vagina) Ovulation and menstruation commence

Pubic hair

Figure 7.5 Male body changes at puberty

Growth of facial hair

The larynx (voice box) grows so voice 'breaks'

Growth of axillary hair

Increased muscle leads to increased strength

Growth of pubic hair

The prostate gland produces secretions

The testes begin to produce sperm

The penis enlarges

Male	Female
1 Enlargement of testes and penis	Enlargement of breasts and nipples
2 Pubic, facial, underarm hair growth	Pubic and underarm hair growth
3 Increased muscle and bone size leads to increased strength	Increased fat deposited under skin leads to increased curvy shape
4 Voice deepens (breaks)	Onset of menstruation

Influences on growth

Inherited characteristics

Height and build are thought to be controlled by a number of genes as well as environmental influences. An individual's height, for example, may depend on the proportions of 'tall' and 'short' genes that they have inherited from their parents. Tall parents may have more 'tall' genes than shorter parents and are thus likely, but by no means definitely, to pass on more 'tall' genes to their children. Average height parents are more likely to pass on fairly equal mixtures of 'tall' and 'short' genes. However, during certain types of cell division that precede the production of ova and sperm, there are random exchanges of genes. It is quite possible for a child of average parents to have a larger 'allocation' of 'tall' or 'short' genes than any brothers or sisters and so to be unusually tall or short.

Environmental factors

Children who live in deprived or disadvantaged circumstances may have their growth and development affected by poor home situations, such as inner city high-rise flats with no recreational areas and damp infested interiors. Parents who smoke cigarettes tend to have smaller than average children who do less well at school. Alcoholism in families affects the health and welfare of children, as do any other circumstances that cause anxiety in the home environment. Living close to nuclear establishments has recently been shown to affect children's health, particularly in the incidence of serious diseases such as cancer.

Many different factors produce people with different growth patterns

Nutrition and diet

Malnourishment will affect growth directly, and this could be the influence of too little food or food of the wrong type. A child whose main meals consist of chips or similar foods with inadequate protein, fruit and vegetable content, may appear well nourished, but lacks essential foods to promote healthy growth and development.

Think it over

How far do you think genetic influences affect the height and build of people and how far are issues such as diet and lifestyle involved in influencing shape and size?

Physical development

Adulthood and middle age (19–65)

After puberty, there is little further growth in height but muscle building often continues with increased work and leisure pursuits. Some weight gain is often experienced slowly from the mid-20s onwards, usually as a result of less strenuous activity and more sedentary work patterns. This is by no means universal and depends very much on the the influences dictated by lifestyle.

Between the ages of 45 to 55, females experience a decline in fertility, eventually resulting in complete cessation. This is called the 'menopause'. Menstrual periods become irregular, sometimes scanty and sometimes heavy, and may be accompanied by night sweats and feelings of bloatedness as well as mental and emotional changes such as anxiety, tiredness, confusion and periods of weepiness.

Males can experience physical changes in the same way, although of course not the menstrual changes. These form the basis of the so-called 'male menopause' ascribed to a decline in the levels of testosterone. At least 20 per cent of men are thought to experience changes due to low testosterone levels as they get older. The figure may even be as high as 50 per cent.

Men are still able to father children well into their 70s and 80s – assuming the absence of disease and that they were fertile in the first place.

As people get older, they begin to show some wrinkles, greying hair, 'middle age spread', less elastic skin, less muscle firmness and a reduced inclination to be strenuously active (see Figure 7.6). The eyesight begins to change. The focal point for accurate work such as reading gets farther and farther away and reading glasses usually become necessary. One in two people over the age of 60 will experience significant hearing loss.

Loss of hair may affect both sexes in the middle years of life, but it is much more common in men. Hair loss in men occurs first from the temples, then the crown of the head, with a gradual widening of the bald area to the sides of the head.

Older people are usually less active than younger people, but often still continue to take in the same amount of food. This usually results in a gradual thickening of the trunk, arms, and legs, often called 'middle age spread'. Many people regard this as an inevitable stage in getting older, but generally it is a result of not matching food (and therefore energy) intake with energy output.

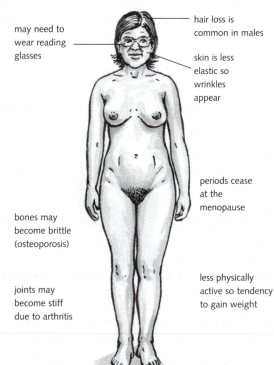

may need to wear reading glasses

hair loss is common in males

skin is less elastic so wrinkles appear

periods cease at the menopause

bones may become brittle (osteoporosis)

less physically active so tendency to gain weight

joints may become stiff due to arthritis

Figure 7.6 Some physical changes become obvious as people get older

Later adulthood (65+)

Physical and mental changes occur as time passes. Not many people live to be over a hundred years old – the average life span is around 85 years of age in the West.

Sexual activity may decline only a little or a lot, very often depending on the usual life pattern of the individual. Elastic tissue, present in many organs, degenerates with age and this is most readily seen in wrinkled skin. Blood capillaries are more fragile so bruising occurs from relatively small injuries.

The number of nerve cells in the central nervous system steadily decreases from quite a young age and they are irreplaceable. This loss, unnoticed at first, begins to show as we get older. It results in poorer memory, difficulty in learning new skills quickly and slower reaction times. Senses are less acute, particularly taste, smell and hearing.

The progressive loss of hearing which can come with age is known as *presbyacusis* – sounds are less clear and high tones less audible. It occurs with the degeneration of the sensory hair cells of the cochlea (in the inner ear) and of nerve cells.

The focusing power of the eye weakens with age, beginning at around 45. Often after the age of 65 there is little focusing power left – *presbyopia*.

As the body ages it gradually loses its sensitivity to cold, so when body temperature drops an old person may not feel the cold.

Heart, breathing and circulation all become less efficient, causing difficulty with climbing stairs and hills, and with strenuous exercise. A healthy young adult has a blood pressure around 110/75 mm of mercury, but around the age of 60 years this is 130/90 or higher.

Muscle thins and weakens, whilst joints become less mobile and total height shrinks. Wound healing and resistance to infection decline with age. Functions of organs like the kidneys and the liver slowly decline.

However, there are positive aspects to growing older. Despite the decline of physical systems, a combination of tolerance, wisdom and experience built up over the years enables older people to avoid the mistakes made by younger, inexperienced people.

Healthy older people may have greater emotional control and a more developed understanding of their self concept than younger people. Socially, older people may have more time to appreciate people and their environment.

Developmental abnormality and delay

Developmental abnormality is a general term that may simply be a variation from normal in the structure or physiology of a cell, tissue or organ. Alternatively, the term may refer to a physical malformation or deformity such as a curvature of the spine or a mental or behavioural problem such as aggressive attitudes towards other children.

Developmental delay happens when a baby or young child has not shown new abilities within a 'normal' time range and is displaying a type of behaviour not usually seen at a particular age. The term is generally restricted to children under the age of 5 years. Remember that when the words 'normal' time range are used, there may be an incredibly long time range considered as normal such as in walking ability or bladder control.

Causes of developmental delay may not be known, but some of the major known causes are:

- brain damage (before, during and after birth, or during infancy)
- poor interaction with carer(s) usually parents
- severe disease of organs or organ systems of the body
- serious visual disability
- serious hearing disability
- low intellectual ability
- poor nutrition or starvation.

Developmental progress is checked as a matter of routine if the child is taken regularly to baby and well-child clinics and problems may be highlighted by the health professionals who carry out the checks. More commonly, parent carers are the first to notice that their child is not acquiring new skills at the same rate as other children of the same age and contact their health visitor or family doctor. A full assessment is carried out consisting of:

1 full developmental assessment
2 thorough physical examination
3 visual testing
4 hearing tests.

The child may then be referred to an appropriate specialist for advice and/or therapy. Professionals will try to estimate the severity of the developmental delay and its probable cause. Appropriate treatment or therapy will be advised so that the child can be assisted to achieve its maximum potential.

You should remember that a premature baby (born before 37 weeks of the pregnancy) will develop the new skills and abilities somewhat later than a baby born at full term. For example, a baby born four weeks early will be approximately four weeks late in learning to smile. However, the premature child has usually caught up with other children of the same age group by its first birthday.

Biological and social consequences

Biological consequences of a developmental disturbance can depend on the specific nature of the delay, For instance, a child with cerebral palsy which affects all aspects of motor (muscular) control will have difficulty in controlling head movements and make slow movements. Some affected children have stiff, contracted muscles, others floppy (hypotonic) muscles and some writhing movements. There is enormous variation in the degree of disability and intelligence amongst those with cerebral palsy. This disorder may cause feeding difficulties, sitting up and walking disabilities, problems with speech or lack of bladder control and the possibility of serious renal infections. The variation is immense, but it is also important not to stereotype children with cerebral palsy; many affected children are able to lead independent, normal lives with a near-normal life expectancy.

Other developmental disorders resulting in physical disability include:

- toxoplasmosis
- rubella
- drugs known as teratogens, such as thalidomide
- irradiation
- spina bifida.

Social consequences usually arise from the perceptions of other people or society in general to the person with a disability (see Figure 7.7).

Figure 7.7 Some of the possible negative perceptions of society towards people with disabilities

---

Assessment activity 7.1

In small groups of three or four discuss the effects of other people's perceptions on the person with the disability. Write the effects you have suggested on a flip chart and discuss in a class plenary session. Afterwards, make your own notes on the key consequences.

Has this activity changed any of your attitudes or behaviour to someone with a disability? Discuss this.

Impact of disability

The impact of disability within the family unit can be enormous. Some families withdraw to protect themselves from pity and curiosity which results in social isolation. Other families become expert on the disability and seek as much help from services as they can, thus widening their social horizons, knowledge and skills. Caring for a disabled person can change relationships within a family. Often non-disabled siblings feel that they do not get enough attention from parent carers and disruptive behaviour patterns may emerge. This can also happen to the partner of the main parent carer and many marriages break up as a result of the increased tensions and frustration.

The carer's own quality of life diminishes as so much time and effort is given to the affected child; this can lead to resentment, bitterness, anger and, frequently, depression due to feeling more and more trapped. If the marriage or partnership fails the situation can deteriorate further. In many situations, if the main carer is the mother, there may be covert or overt feelings of guilt, particularly if the disability arose during pregnancy. In addition to all this, there is often a paucity of financial resources and a lack of suitable, willing helpers to act as surrogate carers. A large number of young carers, such as brothers and sisters, become involved at an early age and subsequently wish to enter one of the caring professions as a result of childhood experiences.

Models of disability

A model is a framework of theory around which people can work. There are two major models of disability that you need to be aware of:

- the medical model
- the social model.

Medical model

The medical model is based on the medical causes of disability, in other words if you have a hearing impairment it may be due to the dysfunction of the cochlea in the inner ear. The Disability Discrimination Act is based on the medical model because the causes of disability are attributed only to medical causes.

Key issue

Disability Discrimination Act (1995)

A person has a disability if they have a physical or mental impairment which has a substantial and long-term effect on their ability to carry out normal day-to-day activities if it affects one or more of the following:

- mobility
- manual dexterity
- physical co-ordination
- continence
- ability to lift, carry or move everyday objects
- speech

- hearing
- eyesight (unless corrected by spectacles)
- memory – ability to concentrate, learn or understand
- perception of the risk of danger.

The medical model has been criticised for its:

- narrowness
- implication that the individual is flawed, faulty and second class
- lead into 'discrimination' being used to describe the lack of opportunities for disabled people who cannot carry out 'normal' activities because of impairment(s)
- ignorance of the large number of social factors which may also influence 'day-to-day' activities
- use of value judgements, that other means of speech, mobility, communication, etc. are abnormal
- implication that the legitimate requests for adjustments to buildings, walkways, for example, are to accommodate the abnormal.

Social model

The social model of disability, developed in the early 1970s, stated that disablement was the result of any behaviour or barriers that prevented people with impairments choosing to take part in the life of society. It does not imply that impairments and physiological differences do not happen, but says that aspects of life can be changed so that disablement does not occur. In the example above, hearing impairment is only a barrier to day-to-day living because a British Sign Language interpreter is not provided. This model does not attach value judgements on 'normality' but describes disablement as a consequence of social organisation – which could be changed. It is the discrimination produced by the social organisation which produces disablement.

Lifespan: social, emotional and cultural change

The life story of an individual person will involve the interaction of their genetic structure with the social context and events that make up a person's environment. Human development can also be influenced by the interactive nature of human behaviour and thought. People are not simply moulded into shape by circumstances – people can make choices and interact with their environment in a way which will influence how they adapt to their environment.

This section provides an overview of life stages and describes some of the social, cultural, and emotional issues to which people have to adapt.

Infancy

On average, infants will follow a moving person with their eyes during the first month of life. They will also show an interest in face-like shapes. By 2 months of age an infant will start to smile at human faces and may indicate that they can recognise their mother. By 3 months an infant may make sounds and smile when an adult talks. At 5 months, infants can distinguish between familiar and unfamiliar people. By 6 months an infant may smile at a mirror image.

It is as if babies come into the world prepared to make relationships and learn about others. Infants try to attract attention, they will smile and make noises to attract adults. It may be the case that infants have an in-built need to make a relationship that will tie or bond them with their carer. The development of a social and emotional bond of love between a carer and infant is one of the key developmental issues during infancy.

Early childhood

A child's attachment to parents and carers is just as strong as in infancy, but children no longer need to cling to carers. As children grow older they start to make relationships with other children and learn to become more independent. Young children still depend very much on their carers to look after them, however, and they need safe, secure, emotional ties with their family.

Close emotional bonds provide the foundation for exploring relationships with others. Attachments within a family setting provide a child with opportunities to learn from others. As a child grows they will copy what other adults and children do. Children learn attitudes and beliefs by watching the behaviours of parents, brothers, sisters and other relatives toward them. Parents and families create a setting or context in which children learn expected social behaviour. This process of learning social rules is called **socialisation**.

Socialisation

Socialisation means to become social – children learn to fit in with and be part of a social group. When children grow up within a family group, they will usually learn a wide range of ideas about how to behave.

Families and similar social groups develop attitudes about what is 'normal' or right to do. Sociologists call these beliefs '**norms**'. Each family will have 'norms' that cover how people should behave.

By the age of 2 years, children usually understand that they are male or female. During the socialisation process, children learn how to act in masculine or feminine ways. Boys may copy the behaviour of other male members of the family, and girls may copy the behaviour of other female members. Sociologists call this learning a gender (male or female) role. Learning a role means learning to act as a male or female person.

During childhood, children learn ideas about what is right or wrong. They learn the customs of their culture and family, they learn to play gender and adult roles, and they learn what is expected of them and what they should expect from others. Socialisation teaches children ways of thinking, and these ways of thinking may stay with a person for life.

Primary socialisation

Not everything that a child learns during first (or primary) socialisation within the family group is learned by copying adults. Children also spend time watching TV, listening to radio and playing computer games. Children will be influenced by the things they see and hear over the media as well as their experiences within the home.

Assessment activity 7.3

Using yourself, a parent or similarly aged adult and an elderly person you have come to know through one of your vocational placements, write a report to:

a) describe the biological (physical) and social aspects of development
b) highlight the aspects that relate to the major theories on social and emotional development
c) discuss with reasons the relative importance of biological and social perspectives at each life stage.

Cultural influences

Children are influenced by the family and friendship groups that they grow up with. But every family and friendship group is different. Families and small social groups are influenced by the culture that surrounds them. The culture that surrounds a child will be influenced by assumptions and expectations associated with:

- ethnicity
- religion
- social class
- lifestyle
- geographical location.

The culture which surrounds a family or small group will create different assumptions within that group. These assumptions are referred to as norms or expectations as to what sort of behaviour is appropriate (as mentioned above). Different family habits about meal times, for example, will be strongly influenced by the lifestyle of that family. Ethnicity, religion and social class will strongly influence a family's lifestyle and therefore what the child comes to believe is 'normal'. Small groups of teenagers will also form expectations of what behaviours are 'normal'.

Culture will create a major influence on individuals throughout their lifespan. Different people have different beliefs about what is morally right and wrong, about norms of politeness and about what people should aim for in life. All these differences will be influenced by the ethnicity, religion, social class and lifestyles that an individual identifies with.

Friendships

Young children enjoy playing with others and will often see children that they play with as being their friends. However, 3- and 4-year-olds will often show a need or even a preference for being with parents rather than with friends. This is sometimes called 'safe base behaviour' where the child seeks affection and reassurance from parents. By 7 years most children will express a preference for playing with others rather than needing the security of being in close contact with carers.

Friendships become increasingly important as children develop independence. Older children will see friendships as based on trust. Friends are special people who are trusted – not just people who are available to play with.

As children grow older they become increasingly independent. Friendship groups become increasingly important and can exert a major influence on behaviour. For a few individuals the norms and beliefs of friends may conflict with the values and norms learned during primary socialisation.

Secondary socialisation

As children grow older they go to school and learn to read and use computers. The range of influences on them grows larger. Even though children make friends and learn new ideas at school, however, the main group experience for most children will still be with their family and kinship group. Children's needs for love and affection and the need to belong to a group will usually be met by the family. If a child is rejected or neglected by the family, they will be at risk of developing a low sense of self-worth and poor self-esteem.

During adolescence the importance of the family group begins to change. Between 11 and 15 years of age adolescents bcome very involved with their own group of friends. Most adolescents have a group of friends who influence what they think and believe, usually people of the same age. This is the second influential group to which people belong, and it creates a second type of socialisation, that sociologists call secondary socialisation.

After the age of 12 or 13, a person's sense of self-worth is likely to depend more on the reactions of others of the same age than on what parents say. During adolescence it is important to be accepted and to belong with friends. Adolescents may tend to copy the way other adolescents behave, although they usually retain the values and cultural norms they learned during primary socialisation.

Think it over

Try to remember when you were 14 or 15 years old. Can you recall what you and others in your class at school thought about the following topics? What sort of beliefs and values did your parents have at that time? Which beliefs are closest to your beliefs now?

1 It is important to get a good job.
2 It is bad and dangerous to use drugs.
3 It is important to go out and have a good time.
4 Wearing the right clothes to look good is a priority.
5 Saving money is a priority.

Socialisation does not finish with secondary socialisation. People continue to change and learn to fit in with new groups when they go out to work and when they start new families.

Primary socialisation   = First socialisation within a family or care group.

Secondary socialisation = Later socialisation with friends and peer groups.

Change and transition during adolescence

Adolescence can involve major pressures to change and adapt as people go through rapid social and physical development. Sources of pressure may include the following:

- The need to make new friendships when transferring schools.
- Coping with change within a family group. (Nearly one in four children may expect divorce or the loss of a parent within their family before the age of 16. One in eight children will live with one or more step parents.)
- Coping with academic pressures to succeed and achieve good school results.
- Developing friendship networks and making relationships with 'best friends'.
- Balancing the beliefs and demands of family and the beliefs and values of friendship groups.
- Understanding sexuality and making sexual relationships.
- Coping with the transition from school to work – some adolescents and young adults experience a loss of self-esteem during this transfer.

Toward late adolescence people will begin to think about, plan or take on job responsibilities. Adolescence is a time when many people actively seek new experiences in order to explore the world and develop skills and knowledge needed for later life. Fifty years ago, the change from adolescent exploration to taking on adult responsibility was often quite obvious. Starting work or marriage could mean the start of a settled adult lifestyle. Nowadays, many people continue to explore social relationships and are constantly learning new skills and knowledge for most of their adult life. For many people the transition from adolescent social lifestyles to 'adult social lifestyles' is no longer clearly marked in western culture.

Early adulthood

In the United Kingdom the right to vote begins at 18, and 18 years of age is usually taken as defining the social category of adulthood. Early adulthood is often a time when people continue to develop their network of personal friends. Most young adults establish sexual relationships and partnerships. Marriage and parenthood are important social life events which are often associated with early adulthood.

Think it over

Look at the table below which describes the number of sexual partnerships that people claim to have had in the previous year. The pattern seems to suggest that as people become older there is an increasing tendency to have just one partner. Is this to do with age, or is it to do with culture, or is it both?

Number of sexual partners in the previous year: by gender and age (1998)

England		Percentages				
	16–19	20–24	25–34	35–44	45–54	All aged 16–54
Males						
None	48	14	7	8	11	13
One	24	49	78	80	82	71
Two or more	28	38	16	13	8	16
All males	100	100	100	100	100	100
Females						
None	30	17	9	10	13	13
One	37	53	81	86	85	76
Two or more	33	30	10	4	2	11
All females	100	100	100	100	100	100

(N.B. Figures have been rounded up or down to the nearest whole number)

Source: Health Education Monitoring Survey, Office for National Statistics and Health Education Authority

As in all periods of life, early adulthood involves the need to adapt to social and emotional pressures. The demands of family and careers are a source of growing pressure for many young adults.

Balancing work and relationships is not the only change or transition to which young adults need to adapt. Adult life can contain a range of transitions and changes which create a need for social and emotional adaptation.

Holmes and Rahe (1967) produced a catalogue of life events to which people frequently have to adapt. Barrie Hopson (1986) states that this general index was found to be consistent across European countries and with the cultures of Japan, Hawaii, Central America and Peru. Naturally, the amount of work needed to readjust to a life event differs for each individual. Each person has particular vulnerabilities, strengths and weaknesses. The Holmes-Rahe scale is no more than a general overview originally researched in the USA in the 1960s (see table below).

The value scale suggests that on average the death of a partner involves ten times the change, and perhaps the threat, that being caught for speeding does. Changing to a new school is half as stressful (on average) as a new sibling being added to the family.

The Holmes-Rahe scale may be a useful list of changes and transitions which might happen to adults. But it is important to remember that few people are 'average'. In your own personal life you may rate some issues as far more or less stressful than the scale suggests.

Life event	Value
Death of partner	100
Divorce	73
Marital separation	65
Going to prison	63
Death of a close family member	63
Personal injury or illness	53
Marriage	50
Being dismissed at work	47
Marital reconciliation	45
Retirement	45
Change in health of family member	44
Pregnancy	40
Sexual difficulties	39
Gaining a new family member	39
Business or work adjustment	39
Change in financial state	38
Death of a close friend	37
Change to different line of work	36
Change in number of arguments with partner	35
Mortgage larger than one year's net salary	31
Foreclosure of mortgage or loan	30
Change in responsibilities at work	29
Son or daughter leaving home	29
Trouble with in-laws	29
Outstanding personal achievement	28
Partner begins or stops work	26
Begin or end school	26
Change in living conditions	25
Revision of personal habits	24
Trouble with boss	23
Change in work hours or conditions	20
Change in residence	20
Change in schools	20
Change in recreation	19
Change in religious activities	19
Change in social activities	18
Mortgage or loan less than one year's net salary	17
Change in sleeping habits	16
Change in number of family get-togethers	15
Change in eating habits	15
Holiday	13
Major festival, e.g. Christmas	12
Minor violations of the law	11

Reprinted from Journal of Psychomatic Research, Vol. II, Holmes, T. and Rahe, R., Social Readjustment Rating Scale, p214, © 1967 with permission from Elsevier Science.

Middle adulthood

Early adulthood is particularly associated with starting a career, making relationships and partnerships and, for many people, starting a family. 'Middle adulthood' from 46 to 64 years of age is likely to be more associated with maintaining work roles, relationships and meeting family commitments. Early adulthood may focus on developing a lifestyle which has to be developed and maintained as life progresses. The issues identified by Holmes and Rahe (1967) are relevant across the whole of the adult lifespan.

One of the distinctions between middle and early adulthood is the increasing significance of having to support parents as well as children. Some 'middle age' adults find that time pressures actually increase as they become older and that it can be very difficult to balance the demands of financing their chosen lifestyle, meeting commitments to own children, commitments to parents, commitments to a partner and/or friends, and commitments to the local community.

Stress

'The paradox of prosperity' (Salvation Army/Henley Centre, 1999) reports that:

- 82 per cent of the UK population (15 and over) claim to suffer from stress.
- almost a quarter of the UK population claims to have suffered a stress-related illness in the previous year (1999 figures)
- workplace absenteeism, largely attributed to stress, cost UK businesses £10.2 billion in 1998.

Later adulthood

The age at which men can access the state pension in the UK is 65. In the future this will also become the age at which women can access the state pension (it is still 60 years of age at present). Therefore 65 is seen as a possible age to use as a social definition of being 'elderly'.

Most 65-year-olds do not see themselves as old, however, and some writers distinguish between the 'young-old' (65 to 80) and the later years (80-plus). Many 80-year-olds will still reject the term 'old' however!

As with all periods of life there are immense variations in how life is experienced. A person's social class, wealth, health, gender and ethnicity may have far more significance on the type of life they lead than their age as such. Key age-related issues include the following:

- Retirement – the great majority of people over 65 do not undertake paid employment in order to maintain their lifestyle.
- Free time – the majority of people over 65 no longer have to care for children, although some may act as carers for relatives or friends. For those who are free of work and care

Retirement can give people time to indulge in their interests and hobbies

pressures, retirement can represent a time of self-development when they can indulge interests in hobbies, travel, socialising, and learning for its own sake. For some others, retirement and loss of a care role creates a feeling of uselessness and loneliness.

- The risk of disability – as life progresses, physical impairments may influence mobility, hearing, vision, memory and general performance of daily living activities.
- A person's enjoyment of later adulthood may be influenced by the level of financial resources they have; their perceived health including what people believe they can do; and their network of support from community, family and friends.

Successful ageing

What counts as successful ageing may vary from one culture to another. One hundred years ago, just reaching the age of 70 might have been seen as a wonderful achievement in its own right. The roles open to older people may vary depending on their family and community context. Elders have been traditionally respected in many Asian and Caribbean communities. For some people, cultural and family tradition will provide a secure sense of achievement and purpose in later life. An older person who is fortunate enough to belong to a culture or family which provides a secure role in later life may simply perceive growing older as a positive and natural development. The idea of successful or unsuccessful ageing may be difficult to understand.

For many people in Europe, adapting to later life presents a range of social, economic, mental and physical challenges. Successful ageing implies the ability to lead a happy and fulfilled life given a range of threats and uncertainties which may face many older people.

Expectations

Successful ageing involves the ability to avoid, minimise, or adapt to loss, change and threat. An individual's ability to avoid unwelcome changes, or to adapt to change will depend on the economic, social and emotional resources which they have developed during their life.

For many people, successful ageing will be influenced by the lifestyles, relationships and habits that they have established earlier in life. The type of work that a person undertook in adulthood will influence the savings and pension arrangements that the person will have. The friendship and family networks that the person established during their adult life may continue to support them during later life. A person's expectations and perceptions of ageing will be influenced by their experiences from childhood onwards. An individual's self concept in later life will be strongly influenced by adult life experiences.

Preparation

In terms of preparation for later life, the following principles may have general relevance for many people.

1 Physical exercise

   A lifestyle which involves moderate physical exercise may help to prevent cardiovascular disease and preserve flexibility and balance. Cardiovascular disease might contribute towards a loss of intellectual performance as well as a range of mobility and other health problems. Moderate physical exercise may help to prolong life as well as to maintain physical and mental abilities.

2   Maintaining social networks

Maintaining a healthy sense of self-esteem and self concept may be easier if an individual has a satisfying social life. Friends, family and community links can provide physical and emotional support during later life.

3   Avoidance of stress and poverty

Some people argue that money does not create happiness. Whether or not this is true there is evidence that low income is associated with poor health (Blaxter, 1990; the Acheson Report, 1998). A lack of financial resources is likely to provide a cause of stress for many people. People who are dependent on state benefits may also tend to have less choice with respect to their housing and the environment in which they live. Adequate financial resources help to enable people to feel in control of their lives. Financial planning represents an area of preparation which may contribute to successful ageing, even if only to avoid the stress of poverty.

4   Developing a positive view of self and ageing

Successful ageing and happiness have a lot to do with expectations and the way in which an individual makes sense of life. Where individuals have deeply held religious, philosophical, or cultural views which supply a sense of purpose, they may find it easy to maintain a sense of self-esteem. Where people see themselves as being socially useless or isolated, it may be harder to maintain self-esteem. An individual who thinks about facing a process of decay and decline may feel depressed. Someone who can perceive the whole of their life as important and meaningful may be able to adapt to physical changes in a positive way.

Think it over

At what stage of life would you plan to ensure that your relationships, health, wealth and self concept would help you to age successfully?

You might find this a difficult question – perhaps because so few people do plan for later life. Many people feel that they cannot control their life and that establishing resources for later life is a matter of luck rather than judgement! How far does socialisation influence a person's belief that they can be in control of their own life?

The final stage of life

For many people the final stage of life will involve a major process of emotional adjustment. The cultural norms and social support networks which surround an individual will have a major influence on how they adjust to dying.

Some people will fear death and refuse to think about it. Other people may have strong religious or personal beliefs which protect them from stress. Some older people may feel ready to let go of life as they experience physical decline. Some older people will prepare for their own death by thinking through and reflecting on the purpose of their lives and the things that they have achieved.

Some people who face death may want to see family, friends and relatives. Some people perceive the act of dying as being socially important. Some individuals may need social support to help them cope with the process; others may prefer to die alone. Each individual may have their own personal social and emotional needs at this stage of life.

Death as the final stage of growth

Being ready to die, not angry, afraid or depressed, might represent the final achievement a person makes during their life. Self concept develops across our lifespan and the sense of self that we invent is never really finished until we die. Our lives will have influenced others and have left a mark on the history of the world. The world might not be exactly the same if you had never existed.

Many of the world's great religions believe that the self that we have created (or soul) is in some way 'kept on record', and that God will re-create this self in heaven or in some other type of afterlife. Acceptance of death may involve making sense of finishing a life, but a sense of self-esteem will be important during the process of dying, just as in every other stage of adult life.

The following table outlines how we adapt to life events at each stage in our lives.

Period of life	Life event
Infancy	Emotional attachment and bonding
Childhood	Adapting to social roles and norms Learning social skills Making friends
Puberty	Adapting to own sexuality Developing new friendships Adapting to norms of peers Developing social skills
Early adulthood	Adapting to demands of work and finance, relationships/family
Middle adulthood	Adapting to change in roles Coping with unwanted change
Late adulthood	Adapting to reduced stamina and possibly to disability
The final stage of life	Making sense of one's own life and accepting death

Intellectual development

Cognitive development

Cognitive development covers the development of knowledge, perception and thinking. Over the past 40 years, the study of cognitive development has been dominated by the work of Jean Piaget (1896–1980) and his colleagues. The study of 'object permanence' and 'conservation' refer to aspects of Piaget's theory of development. Piaget originally developed his theories of cognitive development by observing and questioning young children. When his own children, Jacqueline, Laurent and Lucienne were born, Piaget was able to illustrate his theory by observing their actions.

Piaget's theory of cognitive development specifies that children progress through four stages:

1   the sensorimotor stage – learning to use senses and muscles (birth–$1\frac{1}{2}$ or 2 years)
2   the pre-operations stage, or pre-logical stage (2–7 years)
3   the concrete operations stage, or limited logic stage (7–11 years)
4   the formal operations stage – formal logic/adult reasoning (from 11 years).

Piaget believed that the four stages were caused by an in-built pattern of development that all humans went through. This idea and the linking of the stages to age groups are now disputed. There is some agreement that Piaget's theory may describe some of the processes by which thinking skills develop.

1   Sensorimotor stage
Throughout life we have to learn to adapt to the circumstances and puzzles that we come across. This process starts soon after birth.

To begin with, a baby will rely on in-built behaviours for sucking, crawling and watching. But babies are active learners. Being able to suck is biologically necessary so that the baby can get milk from its mother's breast. The baby will adapt this behaviour to explore the wider range of objects by sucking toys, fingers, clothes, and so on. If the baby is bottle-fed, they will be able to transfer this sucking response to the teat on the end of the feeding bottle. Learning to respond to a new situation, using previous knowledge is called *assimilation*. The baby can assimilate the bottle into their knowledge of feeding. Later, when the infant has to learn to drink from a cup, they will have to learn a whole new set of skills that will change the knowledge of feeding. This idea of changed internal knowledge is called *accommodation*. People learn to cope with life using a mixture, or balance, of assimilation and accommodation as their internal knowledge changes. (See Figure 7.8.)

Infant sees object

Infant watches carer hide object

Infant may act as though object has ceased to exist

Figure 7.8 The sensorimotor stage

Spatial awareness

Young infants do not have adult eyesight. Their brains and nervous systems are still developing and their eyes are smaller in proportion to their bodies. They are effectively short-sighted, able to see close detail better than more distant objects. Piaget's observations convinced him that infants were unable to make sense of what they saw. If a 6-month-old child was reaching for a rattle and the rattle was covered with a cloth, then the child would act as if the object had now ceased to exist. It was as if the object had been absorbed into the cloth!

Think it over

The world for the infant might be a very strange place. If we close our eyes we will be able to use our memory for spaces, 'our spatial awareness', to walk around a room with our eyes shut. According to Piaget, young infants have no memory of visual objects when they close their eyes. If they can't see an object, it no longer exists.

Piaget believed that young infants would have great difficulty making sense of objects and that they were unable to use mental images of objects in order to remember them.

Infants will also have great difficulty in making sense of objects. If a feeding bottle is presented the wrong way round, the young infant will be unlikely to make sense of it. The infant may not see a bottle as we would – they will see an unusual shape (see Figure 7.9).

As adults, we have a vast visual or spatial memory for objects – but something of the sensorimotor experience might be imagined by looking at illustrations.

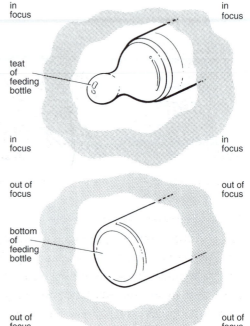

Figure 7.9 An infant will not recognise a feeding bottle if it is offered the wrong way round

---

Think it over

Look at the picture opposite. What do you see? Can you see a picture of both an old and a young woman? If not, it may be because you are not familiar with the visual patterns involved. Try to get a friend or colleague to help you see both images.

Piaget guessed that the young infant may be unfamiliar with almost everything that surrounds them. An infant would be unable to interpret what objects like feeding bottles were, or even to know that their own body ended and that there was an outside world.

Toward the end of the sensorimotor period, children would begin to internalise picture memories in their minds. Piaget noticed this in his daughter, Jacqueline, at 14 months of

age. Jacqueline had seen an 18-month-old child stamping his feet and having a temper tantrum. The next day, Jacqueline imitated this behaviour. Jacqueline must have been able to picture the behaviour in her mind in order to copy it later.

At the end of the sensorimotor period, children are regarded as being able to remember images and to make sense of objects that they see.

Object permanence

The sensorimotor period ends when the child can understand that objects have a permanent existence. The child knows that objects still exist even if they are not looking at them (see Figure 7.10).

Figure 7.10 Understanding the concept of object permanence (around 18 months)

2 Pre-operational stage

Pre-operational means pre-logical. During this stage Piaget believed that children could not operate in a logical or rational way. Between 2 and 4 years of age, children were pre-conceptual – they could use words and communicate with adults, but they might not really understand what they were saying. For example, a 2-year-old might use the word 'cat' to mean any animal that they see, and might not really have the same idea of a cat that an adult has. By 5 years of age a child might name objects correctly, but still not understand the logic behind things that they say. Pre-operational children don't always understand how *meaning* works in language.

Egocentricity

The pre-operational child is not only pre-logical but, according to Piaget, the child is also unable to imagine other people's perceptions. In a now famous experiment, Piaget showed 4–6-year-old children a model of three mountains. Piaget moved a little doll around the model and asked the children to guess what the little doll could see. Piaget gave the children photographs which showed different views of the mountain. The children had to pick out the photograph that would show what the doll saw. Children were also invited to try using boxes to show the outline of the mountains that the doll could see.

The young children couldn't cope with this problem. They chose pictures which showed what *they* could see of the model mountains. Piaget concluded that children could not understand other people's perspectives. Children were centred on their own way of seeing things – they were *egocentric*. Egocentric means believing that everyone will see or feel the same as you do. To understand that other people can see things from a different view, a child would need to de-centre their thoughts. Piaget believed that pre-operational children could not think flexibly enough to imagine the experiences of other people.

Observations of play might suggest that Piaget's view of egocentric thought is correct. Young children might speak with other children when they play, but they do not always seem to listen to others or watch others for their reactions. Piaget believed that emotional and social development were strongly influenced by cognition. The child's ability to reason and use concepts would lead the development of social skills and emotional development. Children might learn to de-centre and understand others' viewpoints when they could use concepts and make mental operations that would free them from being dominated by the way things look. This freedom from egocentricity and the ability to think logically come with the development of concrete operations.

3 Concrete operations stage

Children in the concrete operations stage can think logically provided the issues are 'down to earth' or concrete. Children can solve logical puzzles provided they can see examples of the problem that they are working with. The concrete stage implies an ability to think things through and 'reverse ideas'. Very young children have problems with verbal puzzles like, 'If Kelly is Mark's sister, who is Kelly's brother?' At the concrete stage, children can work out the logic of the relationship – Mark must be Kelly's brother if she is his sister. They can explore relationships in their minds. In terms of spatial ability, 7–11-year-old children are likely to be able to imagine objects as they would look from various directions. Drawing ability suggests that mental images are much more complex and complete.

Children of 8–11 years may tend to concentrate on collecting facts about topics that interest them. But their real understanding may still be limited compared to older children and adolescents.

4 Formal operations stage

When children and adolescents develop formal logical operations they have the ability to use their imagination to go beyond the limitations of everyday reality. Formal operations enable an adolescent or adult to see new possibilities in everything. Piaget stressed the ability of children to use formal deductive logic and scientific method in their thought. With formal logic, an adult can develop hypotheses about the puzzles that life sets. The adult with formal operations can reason as to why a car won't start. Adults can check their hypotheses out. Perhaps the car won't start because there is an electrical fault. Perhaps the fuel isn't getting into the engine. Is the air getting in as it's supposed to? Each hypothesis can be tested in turn until the problem is solved.

Hypothetical constructs and abstract thinking

The adolescent or adult with abstract concepts and formal logic is free of the 'here and now'. They can predict the future and live in a world of possibilities.

Although Piaget originally emphasised logic; the ability to 'invent the future' may be the real issue of interest for many adolescents. For example, an 8-year-old will understand how mirrors work and even understand that people can dress differently, change the way they look, and so on. The 8-year-old is likely to accept that the way they look is just 'how it is', and is very unlikely to start planning for

… but adolescents see themselves differently

a change of future image. With hypothetical constructs an adolescent can plan to change their appearance and future.

Was Piaget's view of cognitive development the whole story?

Over the past 30 years a range of research has built up which suggests that human development is not as straightforward as Piaget's theory of stages would suggest.

Object permanence

Berryman *et al.* (1991) quote research by Bower (1982), which suggests that 8-month-old infants have begun to understand that objects have a permanent existence. Bower monitored the heart beat of infants who were watching an object. A screen was then moved across so that the infant couldn't see the object for a short while. When the screen was removed, sometimes the object was still there and sometimes it had gone. Infants appeared to be more surprised when the object had disappeared. This should not happen if 8-month-old infants have no notion of object permanence.

Bower suggests that infants can begin to understand that their mothers are permanent from the age of 5 months. Infants begin to understand that their mothers move and exist separately from other events. Berryman *et al.* (1991) state: 'It seems that Piaget may well have underestimated the perceptual capabilities of the infant, and that some sensorimotor developments take place at an earlier age than he suggested'.

Conservation

The reason why children got 'logical' tasks wrong may not be that they are completely illogical or egocentric. Part of the reason why children got the tasks wrong may be that they did not fully understand the instructions they were given. Another reason may be that Piaget was right and that young children do centre on perception. They judge things by the way they look. Even so, this may not mean that they have no understanding of conservation.

Bruner (1974) quotes a study by Nair. There is a classical experiment where children are asked to fill two jars to the same level with water. When one jar is poured into a container of a different shape, the children will often say that the volume of water has changed because the shape of the jar has changed. The adult experimenter started with the two full, clear plastic jars and got the children to agree that there was the same water in each.

The adult then floated a small plastic duck on one jar of water, explaining that this was now the duck's water.

Children could now cope with the change. Many children would now say that the two amounts of water were the same when one jar was poured into a different container because the duck kept his water.

Children may be able to make logical judgements if the problems are made simple and put in language that they can understand. Bruner believed that in the original jars problem, young children may have centred their attention on the way the jars looked. Young children might have understood that water stayed the same, but they became confused because their picture (or iconic) memory suggested that height should make volume bigger.

Egocentricity

Piaget believed that young children were unable to de-centre their perception from the way things looked, to be able to understand logical relationships. Pre-operational children were supposed to be egocentric to the point where they could not imagine that anyone could see or experience things differently from themselves. Harris (1989) reports that children as young as 3 years of age do understand others' perspectives and do try to comfort others even though they are not themselves distressed. Hayes and Orrell (1993) quote research from Barke (1975) who found that 4-year-old children could choose a view that a *Sesame Street* character could see – and from different positions. Hayes also quotes research from Hughes (1975) who found that young children were able to hide a doll from another doll using partitions. The children could imagine who would see things at different angles.

Piaget's belief that pre-operational children are completely egocentric may not be safe. Modern research does not confirm his original findings.

The influence of inherited and environmental factors on cognitive development

Piaget believed that cognitive development was due to an *interaction* between environmental learning and genetic influences. He understood that genetic influences and environmental influences combined to create a new system, on which development depended.

The system which enables a person to learn and understand involves the regulation of knowledge through *assimilation* and *accommodation*. For example, consider the experience of learning to swim. Learning to float to begin with is not easy – you have to get the feeling of how it works. Once you've got the idea, then it's easy. This learning comes in a kind of automatic way. You may not be able to remember how you did it. Piaget thought that learning to float was 'regulated' by an automatic correcting and 'fine tuning' action. He called this *autonomous regulation* – you gradually get the 'feel' of how to do something.

If you are going to swim, you will have to experiment with arm and body movements. At first you may get it wrong and take in mouthfuls of water. Eventually you may get the action right. You learn by activity or by what Piaget called *active regulation* – trial and error type of learning.

A lot of skills, such as listening or non-verbal communication, are learned by active trial and error and fine-tuning of our behaviour. We do not learn them by thinking about them but through practice.

If you want to be a really good swimmer and enter swimming competitions, you will probably need *conscious regulation* of your learning. This is where you do work out and conceptualise what you are doing. You will need to work out a training routine, you will

The ability to use concepts can help in the improvement of skills

need the right diet, you may need to improve the way you turn your body and use arms and legs to swim. To get it right you may need to get your mind involved. The same applies to learning to listen, to communicate with people in care, or to reassure people who are upset. Basic skills might be developed naturally or unconsciously, but advanced skills require the ability to analyse or to evaluate what you are doing using concepts.

Piaget believed that people often started to learn from practical action. Skills could be dramatically improved by learning to use concepts to analyse action, and then autonomous, active and conscious regulation systems could be used together. With the ability to use concepts, mature learners can imagine a situation or skill that they want to improve. Imagination may even help competitive swimmers to improve their skills.

It may be that children do learn skills by learning practised actions and only later being able to conceptualise them. Some adults may be able to learn by using concepts before they try practical activities.

Think it over
Think of a skill that you have. Did you learn it through practical work? Could you improve it by analysing and evaluating it?

Intellectual development during adulthood and later life
Many adults will need to continue to develop their mental skills. Adults who work in professional jobs may develop special mental skills where they control and monitor their own thought processes. This ability is sometimes called *metacognition*. Many adults will specialise in particular styles or areas of mental reasoning.

Zimbardo (1992) suggests that adulthood may involve learning to cope with continual uncertainties, inconsistencies and contradictions. Logic alone may not be sufficient to cope with life. Skilled judgement and flexible thinking are needed. Some psychologists have gone on to call this adult stage of advanced thinking a *post-formal stage* – adding a fifth stage to Piaget's theory. As people grow older, happiness may depend on thinking skills that many cultures have referred to as wisdom.

Influences on development – an overview
Each person will develop unique physical and personality features. No one person is exactly the same as another owing to the immense complexity of interaction between factors which influence development. It is possible, however, to identify three different types of influence:

1   The development of each person will be influenced by their **genetic inheritance**.
2   Each person will be influenced by the **environment** in which they develop. Environmental influences include nutrition, housing, cultural context and economic circumstances.
3   The developing **self concept** of each person will cause that individual to interact with their environment in unique and unpredictable ways.

Human development involves the interaction of all three types of influence. People are not simply determined or fixed either by their genetics, or by social influences or even by their own ideas and wishes!

The interaction of genetics and environment

Genes control the sequence of human development, so many abilities like walking and talking seem to 'unfold' from within a growing child. This unfolding process is often called maturation. Maturation is not simply a matter of genetics, however. The environment a person grows up in will influence how development unfolds.

For example, a foetus may grow according to a genetic pattern, but growth will also be influenced by the diet and habits of the mother. Alcohol may damage the foetus's nervous system at certain stages of development. If a mother smokes it can harm her unborn baby. Diet during pregnancy may also influence the lifespan health of the child.

Environmental explanations

Environmental influences can be understood as working at different levels. Children are immediately affected by the behaviour of people in their family. But people in the family are influenced by wider issues, such as culture and economics. One way of looking at influences is set out in Figure 7.11.

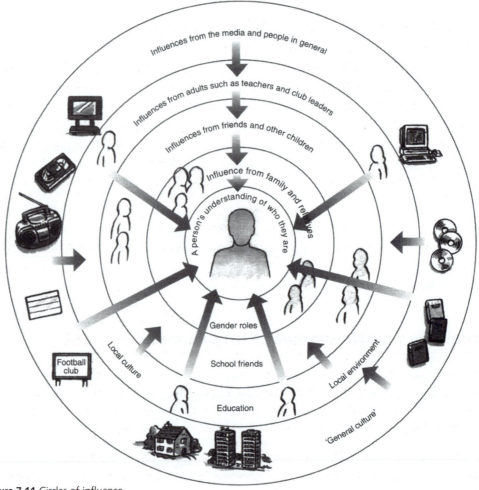

Figure 7.11 Circles of influence

Self concept

The way a person makes sense of the world they live in will have a central influence on their behaviour and on what happens to them during their life. A great deal of individual happiness and misery may be caused by an individual's interpretation of life. For example, if you believe that you are 'no one' unless you are wealthy you may become suicidal if you fail to 'strike it rich'. On the other hand if you believe that friendships are more important than money, you could be happy despite being poor.

Assessment activity 7.5

1 Make a list of lifespan development stages using Havighurst's stages. Analyse the degree to which your life and your friends' lives will fit the stages set out by these authors. Work out what social and biological factors influence lifespan development today and discuss your ideas with others to clarify theories of development. Try to evaluate the relative importance of biological and social influences in your discussion work.

2 Write a short report on the concepts of normal and delayed lifespan development using your own experience of other people's lives.

Promoting good health across the lifespan

Health campaigns have different time spans and cover diverse target areas. Many are focused on issues raised in the government publication 'Our Healthier Nation' (1998), for example accident prevention, cancer, coronary heart disease and strokes and mental health. A more recently publicised campaign is 'Five-a-day', referring to the need to consume more fruit and vegetables (at least five pieces each day) in our diets. To encourage children to eat more fruit, a National School Fruit Scheme will be introduced in 2004 when children in nursery education and 4- to 6-year-olds in infant schools will be given a free piece of fruit every day. To find out about current national health campaigns like this, either contact your local health promotion unit (HPU), or log onto:

www.open.gov.uk and use h for health in the index
www.doh.gov.uk – this website will provide you with the address, telephone number and email address of your local HPU as well.

Psychological theories of lifespan development

There is no single theory which explains the social, emotional and intellectual development of people. Psychology provides a range of different perspectives on human development. A perspective is a way of looking at something. There are many different ways of looking at lifespan development and trying to make sense of it.

Each perspective makes different assumptions about what influences human development. Each perspective can help us to understand influences on development because each perspective may be useful in drawing our attention to important issues. The perspectives listed below are more than just theories, they are more like eye glasses which can make the world look different – depending on which pair of glasses you put on. Probably the three best known are the behaviourist, psychodynamic and humanistic perspectives. The table below sets out some of the key features associated with these three viewpoints.

Perspective	Key theorists	Key features
Behaviourist	Pavlov, Watson, Thorndike, Skinner and Bandura	The environment controls how we develop. Our behaviour is controlled through **classical conditioning** and **reinforcement**. Bandura emphasised that people also learn through **imitating** the behaviour of others
Psychodynamic	Freud, Erikson and Bowlby	**Early experience** has a major impact on the development of our conscious and **unconscious mind**. Adult personality and behaviour are governed by the unconscious as well as the conscious mind. Bowlby stressed the importance of **attachment** as a key feature of early experience
Humanistic	Rogers and Maslow	Neither the environment, nor our early experience control our personality and behaviour. People have an in-built tendency to develop their potential – this is called **self-actualisation**. Problems with conditional regard (Rogers) or unmet deficit needs (Maslow) prevent people from fulfilling their potential. An individual's view of themselves (**self concept**) will control the development of their personality and behaviour

As well as the three well-known perspectives outlined above, key authors such as Piaget, Vygotsky and Kohlberg have developed theories of how we learn to think and reason. Sometimes these theories are described as 'developmental' because they explain how cognitive (or thinking) abilities develop; sometimes they are called 'constructivist' because they emphasise that people build or construct an understanding of the world that they live in. The important thing is to understand how the different perspectives and theories can help us to interpret the influences on human development.

Behaviourism

Behaviourists believe that learning is the main force that controls human development. People are understood as being immensely adaptable; they will adapt to the environment and life experiences that they encounter.

The Russian physiologist, Ivan Pavlov (1849–1936), and American psychologists, John Watson (1878–1958) and Burrhus F. Skinner (1904–90), all worked to develop theories of learning. These theorists believed that the environment controlled behaviour. The way people developed skills and abilities was entirely due to the learning experiences which they encountered.

Behaviourist theorists believe that theories of conditioning and reinforcement can explain human social and emotional development.

Conditioning

In 1906, Pavlov published his work on conditioned learning in dogs. Pavlov had intended to study digestion in dogs, but his work ran into difficulties because his animals anticipated that their food was due to arrive. Pavlov became interested in how the dogs learned to anticipate food.

Pavlov was able to demonstrate that dogs would salivate (or dribble) whenever they heard a noise, such as a bell being rung, if the noise always came just before the food arrived. The dogs had learned to 'connect' or associate the sound of the bell with the presentation of food. It was as if the bell replaced the food; the dogs' mouths began to water to the sound of the bell. The dogs associated sounds with food. This learning by association was called **conditioning**.

Examples of conditioning

Suppose you were riding as a passenger in a car, and the car was involved in an accident. Perhaps you receive minor injuries. You might understand how the accident happened and realise that it is unlikely that this kind of accident will happen next time. However, next time you go to get into a car, you might find that you have become anxious and afraid. Just a single bad experience is sometimes all it takes for you to develop a conditioned association between riding in a car and pain and shock. It will not matter how you think or reason. Conditioned learning will affect you at a deep emotional level. You will be unable to stop your anxiety by reasoning things through.

Conditioning is not always about unpleasant experiences. Very enjoyable experiences may cause conditioned associations of pleasure. A simple example might be having a really enjoyable meal at a restaurant. You might associate enjoyment with the restaurant and seek to repeat the experience as often as possible. Some problems that people develop, such as a constant need to go shopping, may involve conditioned associations of pleasure with the activity of shopping. The person gets pleasure but also some very large bills!

Watson undertook a range of research which showed how conditioning works in both animals and children. He demonstrated how both rats and birds developed fixed patterns of behaviour due to conditioning. He also demonstrated that he could create a conditioned fear in a young child. The child, known as Albert, was conditioned to become afraid of a pet white rat. When Albert was shown the rat, Watson would bang a steel bar with a hammer in order to create a loud unpleasant noise. The unpleasant noise became associated with the rat and Albert became afraid whenever the rat was presented. Albert also became afraid of things that looked like the white rat, such as a fur coat, a rabbit and a false beard. Watson was able to demonstrate the power of conditioned learning at a time in history when researchers did not work with the ethical principles that would be applied nowadays! (It is not known whether Albert remained afraid of animals during his later life or not!)

Skinner's theories of conditioning

Skinner argued that learning is caused by the consequences of our actions. This means that people learn to associate actions with the pleasure or discomfort that follows from action. For example, if a child puts some yoghurt in their mouth and it tastes nice, the child will associate the yoghurt with pleasure. In future the child will repeat the action of eating yoghurt. On the other hand if the yoghurt does not taste good the child may avoid it in future. This principle is similar to the law of effect – behaviour is controlled by past results associated with actions.

Skinner developed a new set of terminology to explain learning by association. Behaviour that operates on the environment to create pleasant outcomes is likely to strengthen or reinforce the occurrence of that behaviour. Behaviour operates on the world and so Skinner used the word 'operants' to describe behaviours which create learned outcomes. The term **operant conditioning** is used to describe learning through the consequences of action.

The terminology of conditioned learning
- **Classical conditioning** (Pavlovian conditioning) – learning to make association between different events.
- **Operant conditioning** (Skinnerian conditioning) – learning to repeat actions which have a reinforcing or strengthening outcome. In other words, people learn to repeat actions which have previously felt good or are associated with 'feeling better'.
- **Reinforcement** – Skinner believed that learning could be explained using the idea of reinforcement. Reinforcement means to make something stronger. For example, reinforced concrete is stronger than ordinary concrete; when a military base is reinforced, it becomes stronger. A reinforcer is anything that makes a behaviour stronger.

How conditioned learning influences behaviour and development
Some habits may be directly learned by classical conditioning, whilst many of our interests and achievements in life may have been influenced by operant conditioning or reinforcement. Pleasant and unpleasant experiences may affect our social, emotional and intellectual development.

Compare the two stories of Sarina and Jodie.

Sarina walks to school each morning with friends. Her friends enjoy talking to her and are always pleased to see her. At school Sarina is quite good at completing her work, teachers often praise her and write positive comments on her work. Sometimes people will say things like, 'Ask Sarina to help, she's very clever'. Sarina looks forward to school and likes to work hard in class.

Jodie travels to school alone. At school she is picked on by some older girls who try to steal her pocket money. Jodie is a little slower than the other girls in her class and is sometimes 'told off' for not putting things away in time or not completing work. Because Jodie gets bullied she is not 'popular' and does not get a lot of social attention from the other children.

How will conditioning theory predict the future for these two children?

Sarina gets a lot of positive reinforcement for mixing with others and for working with teachers and doing school work. Mixing with others feels enjoyable, doing work feels enjoyable; therefore these behaviours are reinforced and will get stronger. Sarina is likely to try harder and work longer than others because of reinforcement.

Jodie does not get much reinforcement from mixing with others or trying to do her work. Because Jodie is bullied she finds school 'punishing'. Punishment is the opposite of reinforcement and it will block Jodie's social behaviour and development. Teachers do not reinforce Jodie's attempts to study and so she is likely to withdraw from academic work. Punishment can stop behaviours in the same way that reinforcement can increase behaviour. Jodie may experience a process such as that described by learned helplessness in Unit 2.

Jodie's social, intellectual and emotional development may be blocked by her learning experiences whereas Sarina's development is reinforced. Sarina may go on to become very happy and successful in adult life because of the learning experiences she receives. Jodie may find it hard to get on with others and may be less successful. Theories of conditioned learning offer an explanation of Jodie's lack of success.

It is very important to remember that life experiences cause conditioning. Most conditioning happens without anyone planning or intending it. Reinforcement and punishment frequently take place in educational and social care settings. They happen whether or not anyone intended reinforcement or punishment to happen.

The concepts of conditioning and reinforcement offer some useful tools for understanding the ways in which life experience can influence human development. However, they may not explain the whole complexity of human experience.

'Imitation learning'

Albert Bandura (born 1925) argues that conditioning only partly explains what is happening when people learn. He argues that people also learn from what they see and hear and that people often imitate or copy others without external reinforcement or conditioned association taking place.

Bandura was able to demonstrate in a famous experiment done in 1963 that children will copy the behaviour that they see adults do. Children who saw adults behaving aggressively toward a 'bobo doll' were much more likely to get aggressive toward the doll when they had a chance to play with it than were children who saw more usual behaviour. This experiment confirmed that we are not just influenced by reinforcement, we are also influenced by what we see in the media and what happens to other people. Bandura argues that people will model themselves on other people who appear to be being rewarded or 'reinforced'. People copy or model themselves on people they associate as being like themselves, but who seem successful.

Think it over

If people imitate what they see others rewarded for, how might the following life experiences influence a person?

- Seeing an elder brother or sister praised for school achievement.
- Seeing a friend being praised and looked up to because of violent behaviour.
- Seeing a neighbour do well buying and selling shares on the Internet.
- Seeing a person gain respect and being 'looked up to' because they deal in drugs.
- Seeing a person being praised and thanked for caring for a relative.

Learning undoubtedly influences human development, and conditioning and imitation learning almost certainly go a long way to explain how neighbourhoods and local environments influence people at an individual level. Theorists like Skinner believed that learning theory could explain the whole of a person's development. Skinner even went so far as to suggest that language was learned entirely through reinforcement. Personality and ability were also explained in terms of environmental influences. Nowadays few people would accept such an extreme view. Individual biological differences and maturational processes almost certainly interact with learning to cause people to develop as they do. Learning theories are useful in helping to explain individual differences in development, but they may not be sufficient on their own to explain human development.

Psychodynamic theory

Sigmund Freud (1856–1939) developed a theory of human development which emphasised the interaction of biological drives with the social environment. Freud's theory emphasises the power of early experience to influence the adult personality.

Freud's theories are usually called psychodynamic theories; they are sometimes referred to as psychoanalytic theories because Freud founded a method of therapy called psychoanalysis. Psychoanalytic therapy involves exploring the impact of early experience on the mental functioning of a person.

Psychodynamic refers to the broad theoretical model for explaining mental functioning. 'Psycho' means mind or spirit and 'dynamic' means energy or the expression of energy. Freud believed that people were born with a dynamic 'life energy' or 'libido' which initially motivates a baby to feed and grow and later motivates sexual reproduction. Freud's theory explains that people are born with biological instincts in much the same way that animals such as dogs or cats are. Our instincts exist in the unconscious mind – we don't usually understand our unconscious. As we grow we have to learn to control our 'instincts' in order to be accepted and fit in with other people. Society is only possible if people can 'control themselves'. If everybody just did whatever they felt like, life would be short and violent, and civilisation would not be possible. Because people have to learn to control their unconscious drives (or instincts) children go through stages of psychosexual development. These stages result in the development of a mature mind which contains the mechanisms that control adult personality and behaviour.

Freud's stages of psychosexual development

Oral stage: Drive energy motivates the infant to feed; activities involving lips, sucking, biting, create pleasure for the baby. Weaning represents a difficult stage which may influence the future personality of the child.

Anal stage: Young children have to learn to control their muscles, and in particular, the control of the anal muscles. Toilet training represents the first time children have to control their own bodies in order to meet the demands of society. The child's experiences during toilet training may influence later development.

Phallic stage: Freud shocked Europeans a century ago by insisting that children had sexual feelings towards their parents. Freud believed that girls were sexually attracted to their father and boys were sexually attracted to their mother. These attractions are called the Electra and Oedipus complexes, named after characters in ancient Greek mythology who experienced these attractions. As children develop they have to give up the opposite-sex parent as a 'love object' and learn to identify with the same-sex parent. Children's experience of 'letting go' of their first love may have permanent effects on their later personality.

Latency: After the age of 5 or 6, most children have resolved the Electra and Oedipus complexes (Freud believed that this was usually stronger and more definite in boys, i.e. girls often continue with a sexual attachment to their father!). Children are not yet biologically ready to reproduce so their sexuality is latent or waiting to express itself.

Genital: With the onset of puberty adolescents become fully sexual and 'life drive' is focused on sexual activity.

Think it over

Freud's theories are often hard to accept in a society which is 'out of touch' with nature, but have you ever watched animals such as kittens develop? Young kittens focus all their energy on getting milk from the mother cat – life energy seems almost visible. As kittens grow to young cats they will sometimes attempt to mate with their parents! Freud's theories were based on the idea that people are animals – but animals that have to adapt their behaviour to the needs of society. Perhaps we adapt so far, that we forget or even deny our inner 'animal' drives?

Freud's mental mechanisms

Freud believed that we were born with an *id*. The 'id' is part of our unconscious mind that is hidden from conscious understanding. The 'id' is like a dynamo that generates mental energy. This energy motivates human action and behaviour.

When a young child learns to control their own body during toilet training the 'ego' develops. The 'ego' is a mental system which contains personal learning about physical and social reality. The 'ego' has the job of deciding how to channel drive energy from the unconscious into behaviour which will produce satisfactory outcomes in the real world. The 'ego' is both unconscious (unknown to self) and conscious (a person can understand some of their own actions and motivation).

The 'super ego' develops from the ego when the child gives up their opposite-sex parent as a 'love object'. The 'super ego' contains the social and moral values of the parent that has been 'lost' as a potential partner.

Throughout adult life a person has to find a way to release drive energy that is compatible with the demands of society and with the demands of the 'super ego' (see Figure 7.12). Sometimes people may feel sandwiched between the demands of their biology and social pressures. Typically today's world often creates pressure to 'have a good career' and please parental values by 'doing well'. For some people the desire to enjoy their sexuality and perhaps have children may conflict with the pressure to achieve. The way people cope with these pressures will be strongly influenced by childhood experiences in the oral, anal and phallic stages according to Freudian theory.

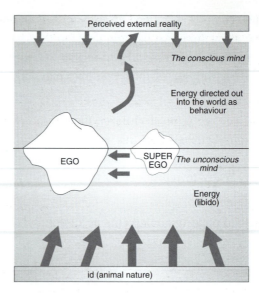

Figure 7.12 Freudian mental mechanisms

Erikson's stages of development

Erik Erikson (1902–94) based his theory on Freud's psychodynamic ideas. Erikson's first five stages of development are similar to Freud's and are developed from Freud's theory. The major difference between Freud's and Erikson's theory is that Erikson believed that people continue to develop and change throughout life. Freud only explained how early experience might influence adult life. Erikson believed that the events of adolescence and beyond were equally important to understanding people's personality and behaviour.

Erikson originally stated that there were eight periods of developmental crisis that an individual would have to pass through in life. These crises were linked to an unfolding maturational process and would be common to people of all cultures because they were 'psychosexual' in origin rather than linked to issues of lifestyle or culture. How an individual succeeded or failed in adapting to each crisis would influence how their sense of self and personality developed. The early stages of development provide a foundation for later development. Each stage is described in terms of the positive or the negative outcomes that may happen following the developmental stage. Many people achieve an in-between outcome.

Erikson's eight life stages are:
1   Basic trust versus mistrust
2   Self-control versus shame and doubt
3   Initiative versus guilt
4   Competence versus inferiority
5   Identity versus role confusion
6   Intimacy versus isolation
7   Generativity versus stagnation
8   Ego-integrity versus despair.

The explanation for these stages is as follows:

- **Basic trust versus mistrust (1)**
  Birth to $1\frac{1}{2}$ years. Infants have to learn a sense of basic trust or learn to mistrust the world. If children receive good quality care this may help them to develop

personalities which include a sense of hope and safety. If not, they may develop a personality dominated by a sense of insecurity and anxiety.

- **Self-control versus shame and doubt (2)**
  $1\frac{1}{2}$ to 3 years. Children have to develop a sense of self-control or a sense of shame and doubt may predominate. They may develop a sense of willpower and control over their own bodies. If this sense of self-control does not develop, then children may feel that they cannot control events.

- **Initiative versus guilt (3)**
  3 to 7 years. Children have to develop a sense of initiative which will provide a sense of purpose in life. A sense of guilt may otherwise dominate the individual's personality and lead to a feeling of lack of self-worth.

- **Competence versus inferiority (4)**
  Perhaps 6 to 15 years. The individual has to develop a sense of competence, or risk their personality being dominated by feelings of inferiority and failure.

- **Identity versus role confusion (5)**
  Perhaps 13 to 21 years. Adolescents or young adults need to develop a sense of personal identity or risk a sense of role confusion, with a fragmented or unclear sense of self.

- **Intimacy versus isolation (6)**
  Perhaps 18 to 30 years. Young adults have to develop a capability for intimacy, love and the ability to share and commit their feelings to others. The alternative personality outcome is isolation and an inability to make close, meaningful friendships.

- **Generativity versus stagnation (7)**
  Perhaps 30s to 60s or 70s. Mature adults have to develop a sense of being generative, leading to concern for others and concern for the future well-being of others. The alternative is to become inward-looking and self-indulgent.

- **Ego-integrity versus despair (8)**
  Later life. Older adults have to develop a sense of wholeness or integrity within their understanding of themselves. This might lead to a sense of meaning to life or even to what could be called 'wisdom'. The alternative is a lack of meaning in life and a sense of despair.

Both Freud's and Erikson's views of human development are based on the notion that human biology creates a 'life trajectory' where stages of crises are inevitable. Both Freud and Erikson accept that individual social experiences will interact with biology to create an individual personality. The psychodynamic view of development emphasises the importance of individual experience and the interaction of biological stages and the environment. The relationship between children and parents is seen as a key influence on the development of personality. Personal development is understood in terms of definable stages.

Think it over

Thinking back over your own life, did you experience times of crisis linked to issues like competence or inferiority in your own school life?

Do you think that your life will involve change through periods of crisis or more gradual and gentle change?

John Bowlby: attachment, bonding and maternal deprivation

Bowlby (1953) states, 'What occurs in the earliest months and years of life can have deep and long-lasting effects'. Bowlby studied mothers and babies in the mid-1940s, just after the end of World War II. Bowlby had noticed that some baby animals would make very fixed emotional bonds with their parents. For example, baby ducklings would attach themselves to, and follow, whomever they presumed to be their mother. Wild ducklings will naturally attach themselves to the mother duck. Bowlby had studied research which showed that ducklings would attach themselves to humans if humans were all that was around during a critical period when the duckling needed to bond.

Bowlby's studies of infants led him to the conclusion that human babies were similar to some types of animal, such as ducks. Bowlby believed that there was a biological need for mothers and babies to be together, and that there was a sensitive or critical period for mothers and babies to form this attachment, which is known as bonding. Bowlby (1953) stated, 'The absolute need of infants and toddlers for the continuous care of their mothers will be borne in on all who read this book'.

If the bond of love between a baby and its mother was broken through separation, Bowlby believed, lasting psychological damage would be done to the child. If a mother left her infant to go to work every day, or just once to go into hospital, there might be a risk of damage. Bowlby believed that children who suffered separation might grow up to be unable to love or show affection. Separated children might not care about other people. Separated children might also fail to learn properly at school, and might be more likely to turn to crime when they grew up. This theory that children who are separated from their mother would grow up to be emotionally damaged is known as a theory of maternal deprivation – being deprived of a mother's attention.

Humanistic theories

The psychodynamic and behaviourist perspectives represent two major 'schools of thought' in psychology. Another perspective which is important is the humanistic view of development. The humanistic perspective is sometimes described as a 'third force' or as an alternative to both the psychodynamic and behaviourist viewpoints.

The humanistic perspective can be harder to understand than the psychodynamic and behaviourist viewpoints. Behaviourism sees human behaviour as being caused by influences in the environment. The psychodynamic viewpoint emphasises the importance of early experience. Although ideas like conditioning and ego defences can be complicated, at least they fit with the common assumption that everything must have a cause. Humanistic theorists do not try to explain people's behaviour in terms of searching for causes in the environment. Development and behaviour are influenced by our own understanding of self. It is the way we have come to understand our own self concept that is important, not our early experiences or conditioning.

Carl Rogers

Carl Rogers (1902–87) created a theory of human emotional and social development. This theory argues that each person is born with an in-built need to grow and develop to their full potential. This need is called the 'self-actualising tendency'. Each person has their own individual, unique experience of life and will self-actualise in different ways. In a perfect world people would be free to grow and develop according to their own inner needs. In a perfect world everyone would be able to spend their time developing their physical, social or practical skills as they wished. People who were free to learn and grow would experience the world in a way that would enable them to live fully. They would follow their own instincts, they would be healthy, spontaneous, flexible and creative. Such people would also be able to truly experience events and sensations undistorted by the need to conform to social roles or be controlled by others.

Naturally, we do not live in a perfect world. Many people develop a self concept which does not fit with the needs of their own inner self-actualising tendency. People deny and distort their experience of life in order to maintain a working self-concept. Many people do not lead truly happy or fulfilling lives because they live their life trying to conform to the demands and wishes of other people.

Rogers identified 'conditional positive regard' as the main factor that caused people to develop an understanding of themselves that did not fit with their inner needs. Conditional positive regard means that you are only friendly towards people who meet your expectations of what is good. Conditional positive self-regard means that you only like yourself if you meet the standards that other people set for you. People like to be liked; many people adopt the values and beliefs of other people around them, not because these values and beliefs meet their real psychological needs – but because they want to be liked.

Case study

For example, a girl born in the 1970s might have been gifted with athletic abilities. Her inner tendency to self actualise might have included a deep enjoyment of athletic pursuits. Parents and friends may not have supported her tendency to develop these skills. In some communities in the past, the female gender role implied that girls should not be athletic. Parents might have criticised the girl for exercising. Friends may have threatened her by suggesting that she would become muscular and unattractive. Eventually, the girl would get more praise if she avoided exercise. Inwardly, she might feel that she should develop her abilities, but she might deny and suppress these feelings in order to 'look good' to others. By pleasing other people and doing what they wanted the girl would be responding to conditional positive regard. The consequences of this would be that the girl would develop a concept of herself as a non-athletic person. This concept would involve a denial and distortion of her true nature; it might prevent her from developing in a psychologically healthy way.

Nowadays, many people live within a culture where making money is seen as the purpose of life. Activities that bring in money are good. Jobs that involve making a lot of money are praised. People may be criticised for using their time to learn music or art if this does not make money. Taking a career in health work might be criticised if the earnings are less than in other jobs. Getting conditional positive regard might depend on maximising the amount of money you can earn. Some people might follow their own inner actualising tendency, others might put the need to earn money first in order to please others and look good. Rogers would have argued that it is difficult to lead a fulfilled and happy life, if you seek to look good and please others all the time.

Abraham Maslow

Rogers identified some very important issues relevant to the way people develop and live their lives. His theory is sometimes criticised as being too optimistic with respect to the potential for giving unconditional positive regard. We do live in an imperfect world, many people may continue to develop self concepts which are dependent upon the conditional regard of others. Abraham Maslow (1908–70) developed a theory of self-actualisation which was similar to Rogers. Maslow's theory accepts that many people will fail to self-actualise and live happy and fulfilled lives, because their basic needs will not be met.

Maslow believed that humans have an in-built framework of needs. We have a range of deficit needs which have to be met before we can truly develop to meet our full potential. This means we have:

- physiological needs – food, warmth, shelter, sex, etc.
- safety needs – to feel physical and emotionally free from threat
- a need to belong – a need for social inclusion and attachment to others
- self-esteem needs – a need for respect and to develop a secure sense of self/self concept (see Figure 2.5, page 39).

If any of these needs are not met, then an individual will invest their time and energy in meeting these needs rather than in progressing to the higher levels of development.

In an ideal world everyone would have their physical, safety and belonging needs met from birth. Everyone would grow up in a safe, secure, loving network of carers. The task of childhood and adolescence would be to develop a secure sense of self-esteem. Once self-esteem is established, adulthood could focus on the full development of a person's potential. Full development would include in-depth intellectual and artistic skills. In a perfect world each person would be 'free' to self-actualise (see Figure 2.5, page 39). Self-actualisation means 'becoming everything one is capable of becoming'.

People who achieve self-actualisation might have special qualities, including:

- a more accurate perception of reality
- greater acceptance of self and others
- greater self-knowledge
- greater involvement with major projects in life
- greater independence
- creativity
- spiritual and artistic abilities

People who self-actualise achieve a high degree of satisfaction from life.

Maslow believed that only a few people have the chance to achieve self-actualisation in North American or European culture. The majority of people spend most of their life struggling with deficit needs, feeling stressed and worrying about issues such as money or about self-esteem.

Think it over

'The paradox of prosperity' (1999), a paper prepared for the Salvation Army by the Henley Centre, argues that although material prosperity is increasing in western society, the chances of a fulfilling life are decreasing. By 2010 more people will experience life stress, fewer people will find satisfying relationships, fewer people will feel secure and 'safe' and fewer people will be able to meet the conditions for self-actualisation.

Maslow's theory offers a simple overview of balanced developmental needs and appropriate goals for living. His views may be useful in informing our understanding of quality of life.

Developmental theory

Piaget – stages of cognitive development

Whilst Freud and Erikson seek to explain emotional development, Piaget developed a stage theory of cognitive or intellectual development. Piaget's theory is described on pages 282–7.

The work of Lawrence Kohlberg

Piaget provided a theory of intellectual development. But Kohlberg developed these ideas further with specific reference to the way people develop their sense of ethical and moral reasoning.

Children's beliefs about what is right and wrong are strongly influenced by the beliefs of the people they live with and mix with. The way children talk about what is right and wrong is influenced by their level of intellectual development. Kohlberg (1976) published his ideas about how children and adults might progress through six different stages of moral thinking. These stages are outlined below:

1 **Punishment and obedience.** Things are wrong if you get told off or punished for doing them. You should do what you are told because adults have power.

2 **Individualism and fairness.** You should do things that make you feel good or get praised, and avoid things that get you punished. It is important to be fair to everyone. For example, 'If I help you, you have to help me!', 'If I get pushed in a queue, then I have the right to push other people!' There is a simple belief that everyone should be treated in exactly the same way. For example, if everyone gets the same food, this must be fair. Children at this stage will find it hard to work out that 'the same food' is not fair because it will discriminate against some people and not others. If everyone is given meat, this will be good for some people, but not for vegetarians!

3 **Relationships.** As children grow older, relationships with others become important and children begin to think about the way they are seen by others. At this stage, children start to think about 'good' behaviour as behaviour that pleases others. Being good is about meeting other people's expectations of you. Ideas of loyalty, trust and respect come into children's thoughts and feelings. For example, a child might think, 'I can trust my friend to keep a secret because she is a "good person"'.

4 **Law and order.** Adolescents and adults start to think in terms of a 'whole society'. Rules and laws are seen as important as they enable people to get on with each other. Being good is not only about relationships with friends and family, but also about relationships with people in general.

5 **Rights and principles.** Some adolescents and adults develop an understanding of what is right or wrong in terms of social principles and values. Laws are valid and must be obeyed because of social consequences or the principles of justice which should govern society. Laws can be changed depending on the needs of society.

6 **Ethical philosophy**. Adults who reach this stage will believe in a system of ethical reasoning. The individual will follow a system of values and principles which can be used to justify and guide action. Laws and regulations are judged in relation to the individual's own system of reasoning, and individuals take personal responsibility for their own actions.

These levels of moral judgement are strongly influenced by the level of cognitive development and education that an individual has received. The first two stages rely on pre-logical or pre-operational thinking. Stages three and four are associated with concrete logical thinking. Stages five and six require formal logical thought. Many adults do not develop clear systems of reasoning about moral and ethical issues. Research quoted by Cohen (1981) suggests that the majority of adults may not generally use formal (or operational) thinking in their daily lives. The majority of adults probably do not develop to stages five and six as outlined in Kohlberg's theory.

Think it over

When people you know discuss equal opportunities what sort of debate takes place? Do people concentrate on what can happen to you if you break the rules or on things being the same for everyone? Such a debate might suggest that moral thinking is at stages one or two. Do people discuss equal opportunities in terms of relationships or the need for a just society? This might put the debate at Kohlberg's stages three or four. If people discuss the relativity of value systems, or the ethical context of equal opportunities, then this would be a discussion at stages five or six.

In real life much adult debate might focus on stages two to four.

Other theories – a footnote

This section has described some of the major psychological perspectives and theories which are frequently used to explain emotional and personality development. It is important to note that sociobiological explanations often seek to explain human development in terms of the unfolding of a genetic pattern. Very often human development is interpreted in terms of possible evolutionary advantages that specific genetic patterns might confer. Genetic inheritance undoubtedly exerts a major influence on each individual's development. It may be important to consider the influence of genetic inheritance as an influence on personality as well as an influence on physical development.

A diagrammatic overview of the theories is set out in Figure 7.13.

Case study

Stephen is now 20 years old. He appeared to enjoy a healthy and happy childhood but he never did very well at junior school. When Stephen was 12 years old his mother and father got divorced and his mother remarried. Stephen did not get on well with his new stepfather. Stephen stayed at school until he was 18 but never did very well in his exams. He went to work for a DIY store as his first job but found that he couldn't get on with the other staff. Stephen left his job because of arguments with his employers.

The different theories of development would explain issues in Stephen's life in different ways.

Behaviourist theories – conditioning (Pavlov and Skinner)

Perhaps Stephen did not get sufficient reinforcement to motivate him to be successful in school work? Perhaps Stephen's environment conditioned him to avoid certain activities or learn to give up on some tasks?

Learning theories – imitation (Bandura)

Perhaps Stephen did not grow up in a culture where success in academic work was rewarded? Perhaps Stephen copied role models who were not successful in academic work?

Psychodynamic theory (Freud, Erikson and Bowlby)

Freud and Erikson's theory would explain Stephen's actions in terms of unconscious struggles in the mind. Perhaps his inability to get on with others is linked to his relationship with his mother and rivalry with his stepfather? Perhaps Stephen's emotional development and achievement at school has been disturbed because of tensions between his parents? Erikson's theory would emphasise the struggle Stephen might have to develop a working identity or sense of self. Parental conflict and poor relationships with others might prevent Stephen from developing an effective identity. Perhaps this will interfere with his ability to relate to others, love and work?

Bowlby might have questioned whether Stephen had developed a secure attachment to his mother during the first years of his life. It could be that the divorce triggered deep unconscious problems to do with an unsatisfactory level of security and attachment. Stephen's problems with work might be a symptom of deeper emotional problems which date back to early childhood.

Humanistic theory (Rogers and Maslow)

Rogers might have been concerned that Stephen has not grown up in an environment which has encouraged him to build a positive sense of himself that fits with his potential. Perhaps Stephen has experienced contradictory pressures to please different people in different ways. Perhaps he has been unable to develop a satisfactory, positive self concept that fits his needs.

Maslow might have emphasised the deficit needs which are probably unmet in this case study. Stephen's need for emotional safety and for love and belonging may not have been met – perhaps since the age of 12 when his mother and father got divorced. Maslow might have also questioned whether Stephen had had a chance to meet his self-esteem needs. Without a sense of self-esteem, emotional safety and belonging Stephen might find it hard to cope with life.

Cognitive theory (Piaget)

Perhaps Stephen did not have the right kind of experiences to help him develop effective 'internal' mental theories of intellectual and social development?

Genetic determinism

Theories which emphasise genetic explanations would probably explain poor academic performance and poor social skills in terms of a lack of aptitude or genetic potential for these activities.

Freud/Erikson: early experiences influence adult life

Mental mechanisms are influenced and created by developmental crises

Piaget: children progress through stages of cognitive development

Child matures in stages
Adults may facilitate or
help but children build
their own systems of
thinking

I can work it out

Skinner and Bandura: children are conditioned to learn from their experiences

Reinforcement or punishment

That's good!

Learning by imitation: Bandura

I like this. I'll keep doing it

I can copy that

Unconditional regard

The child is free to develop — Inner experience guides development

Conditional regard

We won't like you unless...

The child develops a sense of self based on what others would like him or her to be like

Figure 7.13 Overview of theorists

There may be some truth and value in all of these theories.

Think it over

Thinking about your own life, how would you analyse your own experience using the theories in this section? Can you find some value or relevance in each theory?

Assessment activity 7.6

Write a report in your own words that explains the major psychological theories of lifespan development, pointing out the similarities and differences that you discover. Giving reasons for your statements, say how the major theories have influenced the progress of modern caring skills and care practice.

The influence of life events

Life events and change

Buddhist religion teaches that apart from birth and death the only certainty in life is that there will be change. Each individual will experience change differently. Changes such as moving house, losing a job, or divorcing a partner, may be immensely stressful for some people. Yet other people may be able to cope with these changes with relative ease. Going to school, getting a job, leaving home, marriage, parenthood, retirement, grief and ageing are all common events that involve change. Many individuals will not experience all of these life events.

Some life events result in a permanent change to an individual's self concept. Life events that change self concept often involve:

- a sense of **loss** for the way things used to be
- a feeling of **uncertainty** about what the future will be like
- a need to **spend time** and/or money and/or emotional energy sorting things out
- a need to **learn** new things.

There are some common life events that can change an individual's understanding of themselves and we will consider a selection of these in turn.

Starting school

Some people are taught at home because of travelling problems or personal needs. But most people go to school and many people will remember their first day.

Starting school can involve a sense of loss. This might be the first morning your mother and family have left you to cope with lots of other people on your own. You might cry because you miss them.

Starting school usually gives children a sense of not knowing what to expect from all the strange new people they meet. Starting school involves spending time and energy learning lots of new things – how to find your way in the building, how to get on with other people, what you have to do and so on.

How positive or negative was your first day starting secondary school? Do you have any relatives who started infant school recently? How positive or negative was their first day? Rate experiences on the scale below:

1	2	3	4	5
Stressful, frightening	Not good	All right	Good	Great fun, exciting

Some children miss their families, some children are frightened by other children and teachers. Some children get confused about what to do (e.g. at lunchtime, in the playground or using the school toilets) and find school hard to cope with. Starting school could be a negative experience.

Some children feel safe even though their parents or carers are not with them. Some children feel that it is exciting to meet new people. They may feel excited rather than afraid. Some children might find school interesting and may be proud that they are 'grown up' enough to start school activities. Starting school can be a positive experience, involving increasing independence – it all depends on how each child is helped to cope with the change. It may also be easier for a child who has older brothers or sisters at the school as the place will be more familiar than it is to an eldest or only child.

The birth of a sibling

Gaining a new brother or sister may change a child's relationship with their parents. Children's reactions to the new member of the family can be very varied and reactions differ depending on how old a child is and how large the family is. Very often children have mixed emotions. Children may feel pleased that they have a new brother or sister, but they may also feel jealous that their new sibling gets the attention that they would like for themselves. Some positive and negative feelings associated with gaining a new brother or sister are listed below.

Positive	Negative
The child feels important because they can help to care for the new infant	The child may feel rejected because parents spend more time with the baby
The child is pleased because there are more people to play with	The child may think of themselves as having been replaced in their parents' affections
The child feels increased self-esteem because they are the older child	The child may feel that their attachment to their parents is threatened
The child makes a new attachment with the brother or sister	The child may feel that they are in competition with the new brother or sister

Leaving home

Moving out from the family home can be a major life event. Sometimes, leaving home happens gradually. A person might go away to study or work but return home at weekends or at the end of term. Sometimes people may leave home to marry and the major life event is getting married. Some people leave home after a dispute with parents

– some people 'run away' rather than leave. Some people do not leave their family home during their early adult life.

For some people, leaving home is a great change. Some people will miss their family and feel a loss of company. Some people will feel uncertain about their future and unsure about how to cope with a new house or flat. People who leave home will need to spend a lot of time and energy sorting their new home out. There is much to learn about paying bills, buying food and doing your own laundry and housework. Many people will find that the change is a positive experience. People who feel that they have been forced to leave, perhaps to find work, or because of arguments, might see the change as a negative life event. For many people, 'having your own place' is the final thing you need to be an independent adult.

Marriage

In Britain, marriage is the legal union of one man to one woman. Gay and lesbian couples are currently excluded from being legally registered as married, although gay and lesbian marriages can be formally acknowledged and certificated in London. Some other cultures permit a husband to have more than one wife or a wife to have more than one husband. But the legal definition of marriage in Britain restricts marriage to one man and one woman.

Many heterosexual couples now live together without marrying, some go on to marry after living together for some years, but about half of all couples who live together do not go on to marry the partner they have lived with. Current trends suggest that perhaps about one in five people will never be married during their lives.

Marriage involves a commitment to live with a partner permanently. It ties financial resources and networks of family relationships together. Marriage is a big change in life. It can involve moving house and leaving your family. This may cause a sense of loss. Many people feel some anxiety about getting married: are they marrying the right person, will they both get on together, what will living together forever be like? Getting married and coping with married life involves a lot of time, money and energy. Living with a partner involves a lot of learning about their needs and their ways.

Marriage is a big change in life

For some people, marriage is amongst the most positive changes that can happen in life. But other people may regard it as involving a loss of freedom or even as a relationship where one person dominates or exploits another.

Think it over

How positively or negatively do you and your friends see marriage? Discuss in a group your personal experiences in relation to marriage. Do you know people who are happily married? What do you think about divorce?

Case study

Davinder is 21 years old and is about to complete her studies for a university degree. Davinder is a Sikh. She has lived in a Sikh community in the UK all her life. Davinder has thought about marriage a lot during the past few years. Many times, she has discussed with her family the possibilities and whom she might marry. Davinder's family are very concerned that she should make a good marriage with someone of an equal educational status.

Davinder has met Sohan and thinks he is attractive and intelligent. Davinder's family know Sohan's family and have agreed that they would make a good couple. Sohan has visited Davinder's family and an 'engagement' ceremony has taken place at their local gurdwara (or temple). Davinder has been given a gold ring by Sohan's mother.

Davinder is now looking forward to her wedding day. She is extremely happy and excited. She will be very important; she will go through a ceremony that will mark a major change in her life. After the ceremony she will live with her husband and not with her original family. Everything about this change is welcome. Davinder will wear red and gold, lucky colours. There have been many gifts exchanged between the families. Davinder feels a mixture of joy and anticipation.

After the wedding she will be different; she will have her own house, and she will have a husband to care for, although she will not be with her own family. The change almost makes Davinder feel a bit 'giddy' when she thinks about it.

Davinder will find marriage positive because she wants to be married. She has had a great deal of support from her family and feels that she has some idea of how to cope with her new role. Marriage is a major change that Davinder has looked forward to for a long time. She is sure that Sohan will be a good husband.

Divorce

At present roughly one in three marriages is likely to end in divorce. Half a century ago many people stayed married – despite being unhappy with their partner. In the past it was often difficult to get a divorce and there were likely to be serious problems over money and finding somewhere to live following divorce – particularly for women.

Divorce is much more common nowadays, but many people who divorce go on to re-marry. Each year over a third of marriages are likely to be re-marriages. Nearly a quarter of children in Britain may expect their parents to divorce before they are 16 years old. Although many people experience divorce negatively, it may often be better than living in a stressful relationship. Sometimes people develop a new and more positive self concept following divorce. Agencies such as Relate provide counselling services to help people to understand the emotions involved in partnerships. Counselling may help some people to decide whether it is best to divorce or not.

Childbirth and parenthood

Becoming a parent involves a major change in life. Many parents experience their relationship with their child as an intense, new, emotional experience. There may be strong feelings of love and a desire to protect the child. Becoming a parent also involves losses. Parents can lose sleep because the baby wakes them up. Parents may find that they can't go out so much and they can easily lose touch with friends and social life. Parents can lose money because they either have to pay for child care or give up full-time work to care for their child. Parents can lose career opportunities if they stay out of full-time work to bring up a family. These losses can sometimes place a relationship or marriage under stress. Sometimes a parent can even become jealous of the time and attention that a child receives from the other parent.

Becoming a parent is likely to involve some anxiety about the new role of being a parent: 'Will the baby be all right?', 'Is the baby well?', 'Is the baby safe?', 'Am I being a good mother/father?' New parents usually seek advice from family, friends, doctors and health visitors. Parenthood involves a lot of pressure on time, money and energy. A new infant will need clothes and toys, nappies, cot, high chair, food, car seat and so on. An infant needs lots of attention. Carers will need time and emotional energy to care for the child. Parents often need advice on caring skills – there is often new learning to be a good parent and always lots to learn about the child as a new relationship develops.

Think it over

Parenthood involves a great mixture of problems and joy for many people: do the problems outweigh the joy amongst the people you know, or does the joy outweigh the problems?

Retirement

Many people born in the 1940s–70s grew up expecting to work for an employer until they were 60 or 65. Often, people expected to stay with the same employer for the last 15 or 20 years of their working life.

The nature of work and employment are now rapidly changing. Many people will work as self-employed or temporary workers in the future. Retirement may become very flexible, with some people effectively retiring in their 40s and others continuing to take on work in their late 60s and 70s. Retirement can represent a major change for people who have worked in a demanding full-time job and then suddenly stop working.

A sudden break from full-time work might cause a feeling of loss. Work roles influence self concept. A person's self concept and self-esteem can change following retirement. A person may lose their routine, and perhaps their work friends, when they retire. Some people may not be prepared for the leisure time they have, and may not be sure what to do each day. Some people say that retirement makes them feel useless – they are retired because they are of no use to anyone.

People who have to live on the state pension alone may experience a loss of income. Some older people live below the poverty line.

On the positive side, people with private pensions and savings often have the time and money to travel and thoroughly enjoy themselves. Some people see retirement as a time of self-fulfilment, a time when they harvest the rewards of a lifetime's work. Retirement can lead to greater freedom and the opportunity to spend more time with family, relatives and friends.

Death of a loved one (bereavement)

People can lose their partners at any stage of life. However, as couples grow older the chances that one person will die increase. Bereavement means losing someone you loved. Bereavement causes a major change in people's lives. There is a very strong sense of loss – you might lose the main person that you talked to, the main person who helped you; you lose your sexual partner, a person you shared life with and a person who made you feel good. Living without a partner can involve great uncertainty. Your partner may have helped with sorting out household bills or with shopping or housework – now you have to do it all yourself. Bereavement can mean you have to learn to live a new life as a single person again. Coping on your own can take a lot of time and energy.

People who try to cope with a major loss often experience a feeling of not being able to believe that their partner is really dead. Later, people may become very sad and depressed as they miss the person in their life. People may feel strong emotions of anger or guilt as they struggle to cope with loss. Finally, people have to learn to live what might feel like a new life as a single person again. Few people describe bereavement as a positive life event, but the final outcome need not be sadness or grief. Over time people can change and can take a positive outlook on life again.

The following case study tries to illustrate the emotions and changes that an individual might go through during bereavement.

Case study

Jack had been married for 22 years when his partner unexpectedly died of a heart attack. They had been very close. When Jack was first told about the death he showed little reaction. Friends had to persuade Jack not to go into work the next day. Jack had said that it would give him something to do, take his mind off things. Later, at the funeral, Jack said that he felt frozen inside and that he did not want to eat. It was some weeks later that Jack said he felt better because he could talk to his partner, sitting in a chair late at night. Jack admitted that he never saw his partner, he just felt her presence.

As time went on, Jack said that he felt he could have done more to prevent the heart attack; if only he had noticed some signs, if only they hadn't smoked. Jack felt angry with their local doctor. His partner had seen the doctor only two months before. Surely, if the doctor was any good, he should have noticed something! On occasions, Jack just became very angry and bitter about how badly everything had gone; perhaps he was to blame?

Months later, Jack explained that he had sorted his life out a bit. Whereas his partner had used to organise things, he had now learned to cope alone. He explained that he spent time with a close friend, 'a shoulder to cry on' as he put it.

After a year and a half, Jack still misses his partner but he now says that the experience has made him stronger: 'It's as if I understand more about life now. I feel that if I could cope with this loss – well, there isn't much I can't cope with'. Jack has now become involved with the local voluntary support group for people who are bereaved. He says that helping others has helped him: 'It has given me new meaning and purpose in life. I think everything in life has a purpose – things are meant to happen to you. I had a good life before and now I've got a new life to lead.' Jack says that 'Life feels OK now'.

In the case study Jack has come through the experience in a positive way, even though he will always wish that his partner had never died. Bereavement can lead people to start what might feel like 'a new life'. Bereavement need not be understood as totally negative.

Trauma and abuse

The word 'trauma' means a wounding experience. Abuse may often result in wounding experiences. Abuse can include criminal acts of violence or acts of neglect. Some forms of abuse are listed below:

- physical abuse – this includes hitting, wounding or any act which causes physical pain or distress
- sexual abuse – this includes the sexual exploitation or humiliation of others
- emotional abuse – this includes bullying, blaming, and damaging or threatening others' self-esteem
- financial abuse – this includes taking other people's property or money
- neglect – this includes failing to provide food, medical care, affection or attention.

Abuse and trauma can cause lasting damage to a person's sense of self-esteem. Experiences of abuse in childhood may result in the individual failing to develop a sense of self-confidence and self-worth. Some victims of abuse may be more at risk of becoming withdrawn and depressed as their life progresses.

Other victims of abuse may become perpetrators of abuse when they achieve a position of power. For example, a person who has been put down and bullied may repeat that behaviour with their own children. Some victims of abuse may become self-destructive, others may fail to make loving relationships or to keep a job.

In general, it is likely that experiences of abuse and trauma during childhood may have a negative impact on the individual's mental health and well-being in later life.

Impact of social marginalisation

The term 'social marginalisation' means to put people at the edge of the community – outside the opportunities which other people enjoy. The government uses the term 'social exclusion' to refer to the same problem. Whichever term is used, it refers to the fact that some people are born into an environment that offers less chance of leading a healthy and fulfilled life than for other people. Some people are disadvantaged in terms of their opportunity for social and economic development.

The government set up the Social Exclusion Unit in December 1997 to explore ways of improving opportunity and reducing social exclusion. This group produced a report in 1999 called 'Opportunity for All – tackling poverty and social exclusion'. In this report it states:

> 'Our aim is to end the injustice which holds people back and prevents them from making the most of themselves. That means making sure that all children, whatever their background and wherever they live, get a first class education, giving them the tools they will need to succeed in the adult world. And it means making sure that children can live and play in clean, safe environments, and that the community in which they live is thriving and supportive. Put simply, our goal is to end child poverty in 20 years' ('Opportunity for All', p.1).

The government says its goal is 'that everyone should have the opportunity to achieve their potential. But too many people are denied that opportunity. It is wrong and economically inefficient to waste the talents of even one single person'.

'Opportunity for All' also states that:

- the number of people living in households with low incomes has more than doubled since the late 1970s
- one in three children live in households that receive below half the national average income
- nearly one in five working-age households has no one in work
- the poorest communities have much more unemployment, poor housing, vandalism and crime than richer areas.

The report goes on to say that the problems which prevent people from making the most of their lives are as follows (see Figure 7.14):

- *Lack of opportunities to work.* Work is the most important route out of low income. However, the consequences of being unemployed are more far reaching than simple lack of money. Unemployment can contribute to ill health and can deny future employment opportunities.

- *Lack of opportunities to acquire education and skills.* Adults who are without basic skills are substantially more likely to spend long periods out of work.

- *Childhood deprivation.* This is linked with problems of low income, poor health, poor housing and unsafe environments.

- *Disrupted families.* The evidence shows that children in one-parent families are particularly likely to suffer the effects of persistently low household incomes. Stresses within families can lead to exclusion and, in extreme cases, to homelessness.

- *Barriers to older people living active, fulfilling and healthy lives.* Too many older people have low incomes, a lack of independence and poor health. Lack of access to good quality services is a key barrier to social inclusion.

- *Inequalities in health.* Health can be affected by low income and a range of socio-economic factors, such as access to good quality health services and shops selling good quality food at affordable prices.

- *Poor housing.* This directly diminishes people's quality of life and leads to a range of physical and mental problems. It can also cause difficulties for children trying to do their homework.

- *Poor neighbourhoods.* The most deprived areas suffer from a combination of poor housing, high rates of crime, unemployment, poor health and family disruption.

- *Fear of crime.* Crime and fear of crime can effectively exclude people within their own communities, especially older people.

- *Disadvantaged groups.* Some people experience disadvantage or discrimination, for example, on the grounds of age, ethnicity, gender or disability. This makes them particularly vulnerable to social exclusion.

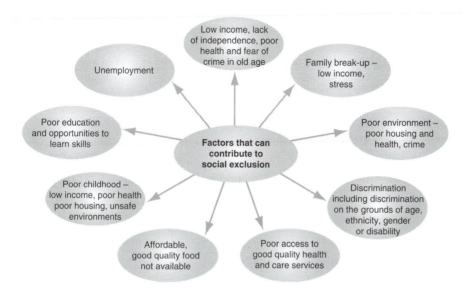

Figure 7.14 Factors which can contribute to social exclusion

Causes of social marginalisation

The Social Exclusion Unit paper, 'Opportunity for All' (1999) explains that some communities are 'trapped outside mainstream society'.

The problems deprived communities face include:

- unemployment
- lack of educational opportunities
- high crime rates
- poor health
- poor services.

Growing up and living in the most deprived neighbourhoods may greatly restrict an individual's chance of developing their full intellectual, social or emotional potential. The problems of poor facilities and crime may prevent employers from starting businesses. Poor facilities and crime may help to cause unemployment. Unemployment may contribute to poor facilities because people have little money to spend. Growing up in a neighbourhood with widespread unemployment, crime and poor facilities may do little to motivate children to work hard at education. If people do not achieve a good standard of education they may find it harder to get jobs. The problems 'feed off' each other, creating housing estates and areas which are stressful to live in. Neighbourhoods may have a major impact on a person's life chances of growing up to lead a fulfilled life.

Unemployment

The 'Opportunity for All' paper notes that 'Unemployment rates are twice as high in the 44 most deprived local authority districts compared with the rest of England'. Inner cities often have 'extreme concentrations of joblessness', perhaps because inner city residents do not have the education and skills needed for the jobs that are available. The report also notes that race discrimination is likely to be a factor in creating unemployment in many communities.

Crime

The 'Opportunity for All' paper notes that 40 per cent of all crime may happen in just 10 per cent of areas in England. 'The most deprived local authority districts in England experience poor housing, vandalism and dereliction two or three times higher than the rest of England.'

Poor services

The 'Opportunity for All' paper notes that 'Of 20 unpopular local authority estates in England surveyed in 1994, none had a supermarket or a range of shops, and no more than five had a post office, a GP/clinic, a launderette or a chemist'. Poor communities tend to have:

- a poor range of shops
- above average cost for food and essentials (one study found that food in small shops can cost 60 per cent more than in supermarkets)
- poor public transport
- poor access to information technology and even telephones
- poor access to financial services.

The disadvantages found in some housing estates and communities mean that life is both more stressful and shorter than for people in wealthier areas. The 'Opportunity for All' paper quotes a study which suggests that mortality (death) rates are 30 per cent higher in the most deprived local authority districts in England as compared with the rest of the country.

Education

Education levels in the poorest communities are lower than for the country generally. The government regards the improvement of primary and secondary school achievements as a major priority, in order to equip people with the skills needed to achieve jobs and careers.

The Acheson Report (1998) notes that schools in deprived neighbourhoods are likely to suffer more problems than schools in more affluent areas:

'Schools in disadvantaged areas are likely to be restricted in space and have the environment degraded by litter, graffiti, and acts of vandalism. This contributes to more stressful working conditions for staff and pupils. Children coming to school hungry or stressed as a result of their social and economic environment will be unable to take full advantage of learning opportunities. Stress, depression and social exclusion may reduce parents' capacity to participate in their children's education.' (Acheson, 1998, pp. 38–9.)

Social class is a major factor which influences access to higher education. In 1998–9, 31 per cent of people under the age of 21 were undertaking a higher education course at university or college. But 72 per cent of young people from the professional classes were taking a higher education course compared with only 13 per cent of children from an unskilled background (*Social Trends*, 2000). *Social Trends* notes:

> 'Young people (aged 21 and under) from the partly skilled and unskilled socio-economic groups are particularly under-represented in higher education in Great Britain. The participation rate for the unskilled group more than doubled, from 6 per cent in 1991/92 to 13 per cent in 1998/99. However, their participation rate is still only a fraction of that for the children of professional families. This, in part, reflects lower achievements at A-level and equivalent for these groups.'

It is likely that the combined effects of poor resources, low expectations and the need to earn money often influence young people from low income families to give education a low priority.

The government is now introducing new initiatives such as 'Connexions' and Educational Maintenance Allowances to encourage young people from low-income families to achieve A-levels and access to higher education. In the past there were strong environmental influences which tended to exclude people from a working-class background from the higher levels of educational achievement.

Cultural influences

The term 'culture' is used to identify different patterns of beliefs, customs, expectations and patterns of behaviour which exist in different social groups. Different ethnic groups may have different values or norms that define the expectations for members of that community. An individual's culture is also influenced by religion and by social class or lifestyle factors.

An individual's family and the local area or community where they grow up may also influence the norms and expectations that a person develops. Figure 7.15 summarises some influences on the norms of expectations that an individual will develop.

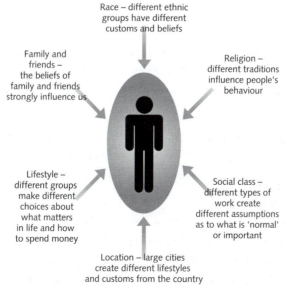

Figure 7.15 Some factors which influence cultural norms

People develop different beliefs, values, habits and assumptions because of the social experiences they have during their life. Culture can influence how people understand themselves, because different cultures create different ideas about what is normal or right to do. These ideas may be referred to as 'norms'. Some norms which influence what we think of as right or wrong to do are listed below.

Different norms about food

Different religions forbid different foods. Muslim and Jewish people do not eat pork. Most Hindus and Buddhists do not eat any meat.

Different ethnic traditions surround the way food is eaten. White Europeans will eat cold food, such as bread, with their fingers but not hot food. Asian customs allow certain 'hot foods to be eaten with the fingers'. Many British people will not eat snails, frog legs, snake, insects, dog or cat. But snails and frog are eaten by other Europeans and some other cultures do not restrict what can be eaten.

Different norms about education

Children born into middle-class families are likely to be taught that they must do well at school and have a good career. Children in other families may not be socialised in the same way. Asian and South East Asian cultures often stress the importance of educational achievement.

Different norms about behaviour

Some families and communities may emphasise norms about keeping appointments, never being late, and being organised for work. Other families may emphasise relationships and being honest with friends. Different communities have different views on issues like drug taking. Some families see using drugs as a very serious crime, others do not think this way.

Different norms about sex, marriage and gender roles

Different religions and different families and communities have different beliefs about marriage. Many religions teach that sexual behaviour is only acceptable within marriage. Some communities have beliefs that women who become pregnant outside marriage bring shame on their family. Other families and communities believe that sexual behaviour is entirely a matter for individual free choice.

A person's sense of self and what they think of as being important will be influenced by the norms of other people around them. What a person expects to eat, how much they value education, their attitude to drugs and sex, will all be influenced by culture. Culture will also influence how people understand themselves. For example, whether a person thinks they are good or not will be influenced by culture. Self-esteem (how much people value themselves) will be influenced by cultural expectations. The development of a sense of self or identity is a critical task that must be achieved if an individual is to lead a successful life – according to Erikson. Some more detailed theory on the development of self concept can be found earlier in this unit.

Alternative models for the provision of care

Cultural differences in health

There is evidence of major differences in the general health of different ethnic community groups. The Department of Health published a Health Survey for England in 1999. This survey recorded self-reported bad or very bad health by age and ethnic identity. Some results from the survey are shown in Figure 7.16. They suggest that older people in the identified ethnic communities suffer very much poorer health than the general population.

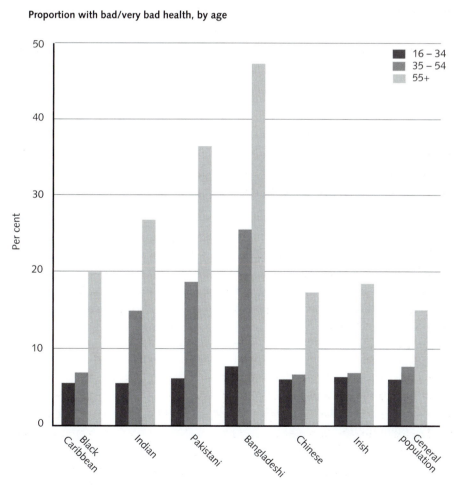

Proportion with bad/very bad health, by age

Source: Department of Health Survey, 1999
Reproduced with permission of Department of Health

Figure 7.16 People with bad health according to age and ethnic identity

The government's Social Exclusion Unit states that people from minority ethnic communities are at a disproportionate risk of social exclusion. The Social Exclusion Unit's publication, 'A National Strategy for Neighbourhood Renewal' (2000) states:

> 'There is a significant lack of information about minority ethnic groups in society, and about the impact of policies and programmes on them. But the available data demonstrates that, while there is much variation within and between different ethnic groups, overall, people from minority ethnic communities are more likely than others to live in deprived areas and in unpopular and overcrowded housing' (pp. 1–2 of summary to the report).

The Social Exclusion Unit's report emphasises the links between deprivation and membership of various ethnic minority communities. People from ethnic minorities make up 6.5 per cent of the population of Britain but 56 per cent of these people live in the 44 most deprived local authorities in Britain. Section 2.36 of the report states: 'Infant mortality is a hundred per cent higher for children of African-Caribbean and Pakistani mothers, compared to white mothers'. Section 2.37 of the report states: 'Some ethnic groups are also at much greater risk of suffering specific conditions or diseases than white people. For example, Pakistani and Bangladeshi people are more than five times more likely to be diagnosed with diabetes than white people, and African Asian, Indian and African-Caribbean people three times more likely. Pakistani and Bangladeshi people are also more likely to suffer coronary heart disease than other groups (50 per cent more than whites). African-Caribbean women have higher rates of diagnosed hypertension than others (80 per cent more than whites).'

Key issue

Go to http://www.cabinet-office.gov.uk or look for 'Social Exclusion Unit' on the Internet. See if you can get the most recent information on the health needs of ethnic minority communities.

Specialist services to meet the needs of minority communities

The government's 'National Strategy for Neighbourhood Renewal' concludes that much of the variation in the quality of health between ethnic minorities and the general population is due to differences in economic prosperity. Measures designed to improve employment opportunities may therefore improve the quality of health for ethnic minority groups.

In addition to policies aimed at improving the economic status of disadvantaged groups, the national strategy document includes the following strategies for meeting the needs of minority communities:

- The Department of Health's race equality agenda requires Health Authorities Primary Care Groups and Primary Care Trusts to 'give due regard to identifying and meeting local population health service needs, including those of minority ethnic groups' (section 7.4). Monitoring and target and target setting mechanisms must be used to ensure that inequalities in the health of ethnic minority communities are addressed.
- 'Mental health services are required to plan and implement their activities in partnership with local communities in order to ensure that they meet the needs of

minority ethnic communities and performance measures have been defined that include monitoring the experience of services by minority ethnic groups' (section 7.5).

- The government will develop action plans for improving services for older people from ethnic communities in partnership with local minority ethnic-led voluntary organisations.
- The government will 'produce training material for social care staff to work with minority ethnic older people and those with mental health problems' and fund projects to improve service delivery and share good practice (section 7.6).
- The government will gather additional information on teenage pregnancy and produce good practice guidance for local co-ordinators of services relevant to teenage pregnancy in order to meet the needs of local ethnic communities (section 7.7).
- The government will work closely with the black African voluntary sector to increase awareness of HIV and AIDS.
- 'Make explicit the need for coronary heart disease services... to be accessible to everyone taking account of race, culture and religion' (section 7.8).

Assessment activity 7.7

Write a report that contains some examples of how social and cultural influences can cause people's lives to develop in different ways. Explain how social exclusion might restrict the opportunities open to individuals. Explain the sources of discrimination and disadvantage that may exist for some members of ethnic minority groups.

Biological and environmental factors

What are genetics?

Jones (1993) explains that genetics is a language, 'A set of inherited instructions passed from generation to generation'. Jones argues that genes are like the words in a language. The way genes are arranged can be seen as the rules for language – a grammar. Genetics also has a literature, 'The thousands of instructions needed to make a human being'.

Genes contain the information or 'the instructions' needed to make living organisms. At a molecular level this information is held in DNA (deoxyribonucleic acid). Each cell nucleus in a living person contains this genetic material.

Every individual person is a unique creation made from the inseparable and intertwined influences of genetic instructions and experience. To be alive, you will have had to have a code (genetics) to guide the construction of your body. That body could not have been built if there were no materials and no environment to build it in. Some individuals may have a genetic design or potential to grow tall, but they will not achieve this potential if they do not have enough protein in their diet as a child. The environmental and genetic influences interact. An individual, a phenotype, is the result of an interactive process, not just an example of an underlying genotype or genetic pattern.

Some very powerful genetic influences

We have known for many years that particular conditions result from genetic influences. Genes are carried on chromosomes. Usually a person has 23 pairs of chromosomes in each cell nucleus. These pairs are made up of one set of chromosomes from the mother and one set from the father. It is possible for a person to be born with three 'number 21' chromosomes, instead of two. Where this happens, the three-chromosome pattern causes 'Down's syndrome'. A person with Down's syndrome may have a learning disability and may have a physical appearance which includes a rounded face and shorter height. The extra genetic material on the additional chromosome clearly has a strong influence on the individual's development.

Richards (1993) identifies Huntington's disease and hereditary ovarian and breast cancer as two areas of disease which are linked to a *dominant genetic pattern*. This means that it only requires one parent to have the genetic pattern for children to inherit the illness. Increasing knowledge has enabled tests to be designed to show whether a person is carrying one of these genetic patterns. These patterns could lead their children to develop an illness later in life. Counselling can be offered to people who are found to carry the genes for these illnesses, to enable carriers to plan their lives and avoid passing the genes on to children.

Genetic influences and environmental factors

Dominant genes and chromosome abnormalities may have dramatic influences on individuals. Most genetic influences are likely to be more complex.

A rare disease which is caused when two carriers produce a baby is phenylketonuria or PKU. People with PKU cannot process phenylalanine, a substance found in most diets. So in the past, babies with PKU became poisoned. They did not develop intellectually and were likely to die from their genetic defect. Nothing can be done to change the genetic make-up of people with PKU. But nowadays most babies have no problem with the illness. At birth, they are tested for PKU and a special diet can be given if the test is positive. The special diet means that the genetic inability to process phenylalanine has no effect. So people with PKU grow up to be healthy and intelligent. PKU is caused by genetics, but is made harmless by the right environment.

Think it over

Are genetic or environmental influences most important when thinking about PKU? The answer may be that it is a mistake to try to separate genetic and environmental influences. In some senses, PKU is 100 per cent genetic and 100 per cent environmental.

Findings at the Patterson Institute for Cancer Research in Manchester (1995) suggest that about one person in ten inherits a general susceptibility to cancer.

Some genetic diseases only happen if a person also catches a virus to trigger the disease response. Some cancers are genetic but come into operation because of diet. Some genes may cause cancer if triggered by chemicals or radioactive substances.

Are genetic or environmental influences at work here?

One of the reasons for studying the human genetic code is to find answers to the puzzles of genetically inherited disease. There may be ways in which environmental influences, drugs, vitamins and so on, can influence the effects of our genetic code. The environment may often be able to 'un-cause' the consequences of our original genetic plans.

How the environment can modify genetic influences

If genetics and environment are inseparable when understanding disease, then what of studies of personality and ability? Plomin (1989) reviews research on the heritability of personality and intellectual factors. Personality traits and intelligence test results provide measures which can be studied in relation to potential inheritance. This area is highly controversial, but Plomin claims evidence that traits like extroversion and ability are influenced by genetic inheritance. Plomin also finds evidence that genetic influences are inseparably linked to environmental influences. It is not simply that intelligence or personality is passed from parents to children.

Think it over

Imagine a man in his 40s. He goes to his doctor with complaints of being short of breath, sometimes feeling dizzy, and being generally unfit and unwell. The doctor discovers high blood pressure. If the doctor knew a little more about the person he could diagnose the situation as follows:

'Well as I see it, you are unemployed. Your social habits involve excessive drinking, smoking, lack of exercise, and a poor high-fat, high-sugar diet. Your life situation provides you with little chance of changing your ways. Your family won't really support you to change your lifestyle – you are poor. Frankly you have little chance of recovery – expect to die!'

Alternatively, the doctor could have said:

'Well, tests of your genetic pattern suggest that you are at risk of developing heart disease. Some people are lucky, but I'm afraid you've inherited a tendency to heart disease – nothing I can do about that, it was all fixed before you were born – expect to die!'

Hopefully there are no doctors who would behave as in these two examples. The advice actually given would be more like:

'You have a history of heart disease in your family and it seems that you are not doing the right things to help yourself. I can't help you with money, jobs or family, but there are some things that we could do – would you take up an exercise programme if you had someone to help you? Would you follow a diet? Would you give up smoking? Can you find a sense of purpose that would make these things possible? You aren't guaranteed to live a long life if you can do these things – but at least you can try!'

The first two reactions are deterministic. The make-believe doctor is interpreting the social or the genetic pressures on an individual as fixing (or determining) what will happen. Social influences do affect people – statistics provide evidence of this. Genetic influences do affect people. But what happens to a person depends on the interplay of these factors. They also depend on the reaction of the individual. There are different levels of explanation that can be used for any area of human behaviour.

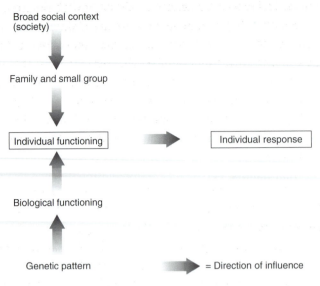

Figure 7.17 Different levels of explanation for behaviour

Society, belief systems, wealth, and social roles, all have a strong influence on the way families and friendship groups behave. Individuals are socialised to behave in terms of the norms and values that they learn in these groups. Genetics also influence our biological nature. Aspects of ability, temperament and susceptibility to disease will also influence how we react. The influences of biology and social groups have been interacting in us since our birth.

The interaction of nature and nurture

The debate about inherited and environmental influences is sometimes referred to as the *Nature* (inherited influences) *versus Nurture* (environmental influences) debate. This is a poetic way of putting the issues that may go back to Shakespeare. Shakespeare created the character Caliban in his play *The Tempest*. Caliban is described as a person 'upon whose nature nurture could never stick'. This means that he was fixed by inheritance. The nature–nurture debate was going on long before genes or chromosomes were discovered.

The nature–nurture debate will continue to run and run

Can criminal behaviour be influenced by genes? Professor Patrick Bateson, writing in *The Independent* (18 February 1995) commented on articles claiming that biological make-up might hold the key to criminal behaviour, or that unemployment might be the cause. He said, 'The sad thing was the determinism that accompanied the media coverage of the claims. It was obvious that, in certain quarters, the dreadful old nature–nurture debate was rampant once again.' Later, he states, 'By degrees, both sides in the nature–nurture dispute have come to appreciate that behavioural development cannot be treated as though it were wholly under the control of the genes or wholly influenced by the environment.'

It is possible to look at issues like temperament, language learning and the in-built reactions of babies and say that these are all genetic, and so, therefore, a certain proportion of language or personality is genetic. Bateson argues that this is wrong. To explain why, Bateson uses the example of baking a cake. A cake is more than the ingredients that go into it. A cake is the result of a process. When a cake is mixed and later baked, the butter, sugar, eggs, flour, milk, raisins and water all alter. The taste of the cake and the texture of the cake is different from the taste of the cake mixture. Bateson argues that human development is a process. The contribution of environment and the contribution of genetics is impossible to separate:

> 'You would not expect to recognise each ingredient and each action involved in cooking as a separate component in the finished cake… The development of individuals is an interplay between them and their environment. Individuals choose and change the conditions to which they are exposed; then they are themselves changed by those conditions to which they are exposed.'

The question as to how much human development is due to environment and how much is due to genetics could be answered by saying that it's a bit of both. But even this answer is wrong. The influence of both nature and nurture is an influence on a process. Development is a process. Jones (1993) states:

> 'An attribute such as intelligence is often seen as a cake which can be sliced into so much "gene" and so much "environment". In fact the two are so closely blended that trying to separate them is more like trying to unbake the cake. Failure to understand this simple biological fact leads to confusion and worse.'

Human beings are infinitely more complex than mixing and baking a cake. The cake stays baked – it becomes a finished product. Humans are never finished. Human learning and change continue until an individual dies. Although the cake metaphor is limited, it does provide a way of understanding why it is unwise to separate the influences of nature and nurture.

A conclusion would appear to be that nature and nurture cannot be usefully abstracted from the process of development, but that nature and nurture form a process of interaction which progresses across the lifespan of any organism. Environment may completely override genetic influences, as in PKU, or genetic influences may sometimes have powerful effects, depending on the environment with which they interact.

A European perspective

The UK has been a member state of the European Community (EC) since 1973. Together with 11 other countries – Belgium, Denmark, France, Germany, Greece, Ireland, Italy, Luxembourg, the Netherlands, Portugal, and Spain – in 1991 they signed the treaty of European Union. The EU or European Union has comprised 15 member states since 1994 when Austria, Finland and Sweden joined (see Figure 7.18). Further countries are negotiating to join the Union.

Figure 7.18 The 15 countries of the EU (as at 2002)

Munday (1996) provides an analysis of social support within Europe. Munday quotes Abrahamson's 1992 models of welfare within Europe. According to this analysis, there are four distinct approaches towards social care within the different states that make up the European Union. These four approaches or models are described as:

- the Latin welfare model
- the institutional or corporatist model
- the residual welfare state model
- the social democratic welfare model.

The Latin welfare model is exemplified by Greece, and associated with provision in Spain, Portugal and Italy. Here people rely heavily on their own family, communities, the Church and charities for social care and economic support.

The institutional or corporatist model is particularly associated with Germany and Austria. Here, workers access independent welfare organisations through insurance and other arrangements associated with their employment. People who are not permanently employed may be disadvantaged compared to people who work full-time for large corporations.

The residual welfare state model is particularly associated with the UK. Here, the state still continues to co-ordinate and provide some services, but the state is withdrawing from this role and encouraging people to rely increasingly on family, voluntary and commercial sector provision of social care services.

The social democratic welfare model is exemplified by countries such as Sweden and Denmark. Here, the state takes responsibility for providing social care and welfare support. Private sector and voluntary sector provision is limited.

There are considerable variations in the level and nature of provision within the European Union. There are also variations in the level of provision within member states. For example, services in Spain vary from one region to another. Different patterns of welfare provision are partly due to the historical and economic circumstances of the different member states. The wealthier member states have historically been able to fund a larger scale of state-provided welfare provision. Political tradition has also influenced models of provision. State intervention to support individuals and families has been a tradition in France and Denmark.

Key issue

The European Commission for Employment and Social Affairs provides extensive information on social policy within Europe. The Mutual Information System on Social Protection in the EU member states and the European Economic Area provides comparative tables on social protection in the member states. This information can be accessed from http://europa.eu.int/comm/employment

- Working in a group, you might each like to select one issue such as maternity benefits, family benefits or health care and analyse the different levels of provision provided across the different member states of the EU.

End of unit test

1 Read the case study below and answer the questions that follow.

Case study

Matthew has always lived on a crowded housing estate on the fringe of the capital with his mother and stepfather. He was very distressed when his parents divorced ten years ago, but has come to accept his new family. Matthew is now 17, working for important examinations that will influence his future. He has spent considerable time with a careers adviser but is still confused about his plans on leaving school.

School life has not been easy for Matthew; an only child, he found it difficult to make friends with other children and had trouble learning to read. He was well behind the reading ability of his peers by the age of 10.

Matthew enjoyed physical games at school but his chronic asthma restricted his ability. This also led to him being bullied for a while and he began to dislike school. At secondary school, Matthew worked hard and began to find schoolwork more interesting and easier to do, resulting in some good GCSE grades and a place in the sixth form.

a) Describe the major changes in personal relationships that might have occurred as Matthew passed through infancy, early childhood, childhood and adolescence.

b) The psychodynamic perspective stresses the importance of early experience in influencing personality. Explain some key stages that this perspective might have predicted for Matthew.

c) Matthew developed chronic asthma but others living in the same locality did not. Suggest some reasons for this.

d) Matthew lagged behind his peers in his reading ability. Suggest four explanations, which might account for differences in learning performance as children develop.

e) If the housing estate where Matthew lived also had high unemployment and crime levels, suggest how these environmental influences might have affected Matthew's education and career perspectives.

f) Matthew enjoys being at school now and finds learning much easier; explain how this change has occurred, linking your ideas with 'skills development'.

g) Place the following motor skills into gross and fine categories:
   i) stands without support
   ii) builds a tower of six or more cubes
   iii) catches a ball
   iv) runs up and down stairs one foot at a time
   v) uses a pincer grasp to pick up fine objects
   vi) holds a rattle without dropping it
   vii) rolls from front to back.

2 Describe the symptoms that could be alleviated in a middle-aged female by hormone replacement therapy.

3 List four secondary sexual characteristics that feature in a male passing through puberty.

4 The psychodynamist Eric Erikson believed that late adulthood involved a particular life crisis. Give the main points of the eighth crisis which older people may expect to experience within this theoretical perspective.

References and further reading

Acheson, D. (1998) *Independent Inquiry into Inequalities in Health*, London: HMSO

Bandura, A. (1989) 'Perceived self-efficacy in the exercise of personal agency', *The Psychologist* 2 (10), 411–24

Bee, H. (2001) *Lifespan Development*, Needham Heights, MA: Allyn and Bacon

Berkman, L. F. and Syme, S. L. (1979) 'Social networks, lost resistance and mortality', *American Journal of Epidemiology*, 109, Oxford: Oxford University Press

Berryman, J. *et al.* (1991) *Developmental Psychology and You*, London: BPS Books and Routledge

Black, D. *et al.* (1980) 'The Black Report' in Townsend, P. *et al.* (1988) *Inequalities in Health*, Harmondsworth: Penguin

Blaxter, M. (1990) *Health and Lifestyles*, London: Routledge

Bowlby, J. (1953) *Child Care and the Growth of Love*, Harmondsworth: Penguin

Bowlby, J. (1969) *Attachment and Loss*, Vol. 1, London: Hogarth Press

Bruner, J. (1974) *Beyond the Information Given*, London: George Allen & Unwin

Castells, M. (1996) *The Rise of the Network Society*, Oxford: Blackwell

Catell, R. B. (1963) 'Theory of fluid and crystallised intelligence: A critical experiment', *Journal of Educational Psychology* 54

Clarke, A. M. and Clarke, A. D. B. (eds) (1976) *Early Experience: Myth and Evidence*, Somerset: Open Books

Cohen, D. (1981) *Piaget: Critique and Reassessment*, London: Croom Helm

Denny, N. W. (1982) 'Ageing and cognitive changes', in B. Wolman (ed.) *Handbook of Developmental Psychology*, Harrow: Longman Higher Education

Erikson, E. (1963) *Childhood and Society*, New York: Norton

Fantz, R. (1961) 'The origin of form perception', *Scientific American* 204, 1097–104

Gardner, H. (1984) *Frames of Mind*, New York: Basic Books

Goleman, D. (1996) *Emotional Intelligence*, London: Bloomsbury

Gross, R. (1992) (2nd edn) *Psychology*, Sevenoaks: Hodder & Stoughton

Harris, P. (1989) *Children and Emotion*, Oxford: Basil Blackwell

Havighurst, R. J. (1972) (3rd edn) *Developmental Tasks and Education*, Oxford: David McKay

Hayes, N. and Orrell, S. (1993) (2nd edn) *Psychology: an Introduction*, Harlow: Longman

Hayes, N. (1995) *Psychology in Perspective*, Basingstoke: Macmillan

Henley Centre (1999) *The paradox of prosperity*, Salvation Army/Henley Centre

Holmes, T. H. and Rahe, R. H. (1967) 'The social readjustment rating scale', *Journal of Psychosomatic research* 11, 213–18

Hopson, B. (1986) 'Transition: Understanding and managing personal change' in Herbert, M. (ed.) (1986) *Psychology for Social Workers*, London: British Psychological Society and Macmillan

Jones, S. (1993) *The Language of the Genes*, London: Flamingo/HarperCollins

Klinnert, M. (1984) 'The regulation of infant behaviour by maternal facial expression', *Infant Behaviour and Development* 7, 447–65.

Kohlberg, L. (1976) 'Moral stages and moralization: The cognitive-developmental approach' in Lickona, T. (ed.) *Moral Development and Behaviour*, New York: Holt

McGarrigle, J. and Donaldson, M. (1975) 'Conservation accidents', *Cognition* 3, 341–50

Mead, G. H. (1934) *Mind, Self and Society* (ed. Morris, C.), Chicago: University of Chicago Press

Pinker, S. (1995) *Language instinct*, Harmondsworth: Penguin

Plomin (1989) 'Environment and genes', *American Psychologist* 44 (2) 105–11

Rose, S., Lewontin, R. C. and Kamin, L. J. (1984) *Not in our genes*, Harmondsworth: Penguin

Rutter, M. (1981) (2nd edn) *Maternal Deprivation Reassessed*, Harmondsworth: Penguin

Schaffer, H. R. and Emerson, P. E. (1964) 'The development of social attainments in infancy', *Monographs of Social Research in Child Development* 29 (94)

Schaie, K. W. (ed.) (1983) *Longitudinal Studies of Adult Psychological Development*, New York: Guilford Press

Segall, M. H. *et al.* (1990) *Human Behaviour in Global Perspective*, Needham Heights: Allyn and Bacon

Social Exclusion Unit (1999) *Opportunity for All*, London: HMSO

Social Trends, Vol. 30 (2000) London: HMSO

Sorce, J. F., Emde, R. N., Xampos, J. J. and Klinnert, M. D. (1985) 'Maternal emotional signalling', *Developmental psychology* 21, 195–200

Stopford, V. (1987) *Understanding Disability,* London: Edward Arnold

Walker-Andrews, A. (1986) 'Intermodel perception of expressive behaviours: Relation of eye and voice?', *Developmental psychology* 22, 373–7

Wason, P. (1974) *Psychology of Reasoning: Structure and Content*, Cambridge, Mass: Harvard University Press

Wolf, D., Rygh, J. and Altshuler, J. (1984) 'Agency and experience: Actions and states in play narratives' in Brehterton, I. (ed.) *Symbolic Play*, London: Academic Press

Zimbardo, P. G. *et al.* (1992) *Psychology and Life*, London: HarperCollins

Zimbardo, P. *et al.* (1995) *Psychology: A European Text*, London: HarperCollins

Our Healthier Nation: a Contract for Health 1998, London: The Stationery Office

8 Health promotion

This unit covers a broad range of issues which relate to the promotion of health. It opens by considering the various perspectives on health, including the biomedical model and the social model, comparing these with your own understanding of health and other lay viewpoints. It explores the factors which underpin good health before moving on to consider differing types of health promotion activity including primary, secondary and tertiary prevention.

You will learn about the differing and complementary approaches to health promotion and the people and organisations who play a part in promoting health, before considering the ethical issues which face them. You will also consider the constraints on health promoters, be they financial, political or simply lack of knowledge.

You will explore the opportunities for health promotion around specific topics and target audiences and how the current national policy is supporting those types of initiative. You will consider the role of major organisations like the NHS and the role of the private sector and mass media in promoting health.

Finally, you will consider more practical aspects of being a health campaigner or educator – such as what targets you might focus your work around, how to select the appropriate leaflets and posters and how to plan, implement and evaluate an effective health promotion campaign.

What you need to learn
- Concepts of health and health promotion
- Ethical issues
- Key themes
- Health promotion campaigns

Concepts of health and health promotion

Think it over

What do you think about when you hear the phrase 'health promotion'?

Write down words, phrases, pictures it makes you think about.

Now try to write a couple of sentences, which will be your starting definition for health promotion. Keep this to hand – you will come back to it throughout this first section

Models of health

Lay models of health

The term 'lay' refers to a non-professional viewpoint, i.e. the models of health held by the public at large (as summarised by Stainton Rogers (1997) in the table below) as opposed to professionally or scientifically phrased perspectives. For many people, the term healthy is usually associated with not being ill, i.e. a negative perspective which is best summarised as not knowing what you had till you lost it. More positive perspectives might talk about building up your strength, being on good form or having resistance to infections; these are aspects of physical health which emphasise the need for strength and robustness for everyday life.

Lay health model	Description
The body as a machine	Has strong links to the medical model of health in that it sees illness as a matter of biological fact and scientific medicine as the natural type of treatment for any illness
Inequality of access	As above, this perspective is rooted in a reliance on modern medicine to cure illness but is less accepting because of an awareness that there are great inequalities of access to treatment
The health promotion account	This model emphasises the importance of a healthy lifestyle and personal responsibility, for example if you are overweight it is simply a matter of your own choice of diet and a lack of exercise which has led to this
God's power	Health is viewed as part of spirituality, i.e. a feature of righteous living and spiritual wholeness. This might be seen in abstinence from alcohol consumption because it is an impure substance which is unholy but also can lead to immoral activity
Body under siege	The person exists in a sea of challenges to their health, be they communicable diseases, such as colds and flu, or stress at work, etc.
Cultural critique of medicine	Science and the medical model on which health care is based can oppress certain groups (i.e. they can take away their rights to self-determination); this could be the way health care manages pregnancy as an example of oppressive practice against women or the treatment of minority ethnic groups
Robust individualism	Best summarised as 'It's my life and I will do with it what I choose'
Will power	Suggests that we all have a moral responsibility to remain healthy. This relies on strong will power to manage our health, e.g. to eat the right things, take regular exercise and drink moderately

It can be seen that people's notions of what being healthy means can vary widely and are shaped by their own experiences, knowledge, values and expectations as well as what others expect them to do.

Think it over

What are your own views on health? To assess this, complete the Health quiz below to consider what the most important aspects of your own health are to you. When you have finished the exercise ask yourself:

- Was this what I expected to find?
- Which of the lay perspectives can I see in my own answers?
- How might the outcome vary if I was to complete this when I was 20 or 40 years older?
- How might someone with a physical disability have answered?
- How might someone living on benefits have answered?

Health quiz

What does being healthy mean to you?

In Column 1, tick any statements which seem to you to be important aspects of your health.

In Column 2, tick the six statements which are the most important aspects of being healthy to you.

In Column 3, rank these six in order of importance – put '1' by the most important, '2' by the next most important and so on down to '6'.

For me, being healthy involves:	Column 1	Column 2	Column 3
1 Enjoying being with my family and friends	....	....	....
2 Living to be a ripe old age	....	....	....
3 Feeling happy most of the time	....	....	....
4 Being able to run when I need to (e.g. for a bus) without getting out of breath	....	....	....
5 Having a job	....	....	....
6 Being able to get down to making decisions	....	....	....
7 Hardly ever taking tablets or medicines	....	....	....
8 Being the ideal weight for my height	....	....	....
9 Taking part in lots of sport	....	....	....
10 Feeling at peace with myself	....	....	....
11 Never smoking	....	....	....
12 Having clear skin, bright eyes and shiny hair	....	....	....
13 Never suffering from anything more serious than a mild cold, flu or stomach upset	....	....	....
14 Not getting things confused or out of proportion – assessing situations realistically	....	....	....
15 Being able to adapt easily to changes in my life, such as moving house, changing jobs or getting married	....	....	....

16	Feeling glad to be alive	....	....	....
17	Drinking moderate amounts of alcohol or none at all	....	....	....
18	Enjoying my work without much stress or strain	....	....	....
19	Having all the parts of my body in good working order	....	....	....
20	Getting on well with other people most of the time	....	....	....
21	Eating the 'right' foods	....	....	....
22	Enjoying some form or relaxation/ recreation	....	....	....
23	Hardly ever going to the doctor	....	....	....

Medical models

Probably the most widely known model of health is that which first developed in the early part of the nineteenth century and has come to dominate all others in the western world, i.e. the biomedical model. Its history lies in the developing understanding of how the various parts of the body might work together to ensure good health. This scientific view of health and body functioning is summarised by Jones as shown below.

The medical model of health (Jones, 1994).

- Health is predominantly viewed as the absence of disease.
- Health services are geared towards the treating of the sick.
- A high value is placed on specialist medical services.
- Doctors and other qualified experts diagnose and sanction treatment.
- Main purpose of health services is curative – to get people back to work.
- Disease and illness is explained by biological science.
- It is based in the understanding of how diseases arise, emphasising risk factors.
- A high value is placed on scientific research methodology.
- Quantitative scientific evidence is generally given higher value than lay or qualitative evidence.

Social model of health

Although the biomedical model has contributed greatly to increases in life expectancy, it is public health measures based on the social model of health which have contributed most to the decline in mortality during the twentieth century.

Think it over

Look at Figure 8.1 and then answer the questions:

- What period saw the greatest decline in mortality?
- Where does the introduction of the NHS fit in this time scale?
- What impact has the introduction of the NHS had on mortality rates?

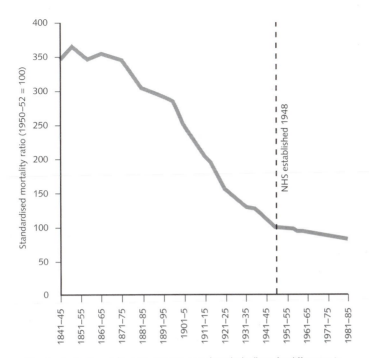

The standardised mortality ratio (SMR) is an index which allows for differences in age structure. Values above 100 indicate higher mortality than in 1950–52 and values below 100 indicate lower mortality.   (Source: OPCS)

Figure 8.1 Mortality trends, 1841–1985, England and Wales

A social model of health emphasises that to improve health it is necessary to address the origins of ill health; that is, the social conditions which make ill health more prevalent in some groups than others. Its underlying philosophy is that the health differences between individuals and social groups is the result of a complex mixture of behavioural, structural, material and cultural factors which together impact on health. The social model has strong links to the lay models of health because it recognises that people often have firmly held views about their own health, which are sometimes at odds with those of professionals. For example, the need to address damp conditions in housing and its link to childhood asthma might be prioritised by people living in those conditions as opposed to the need to tackle parental smoking, as prioritised by health services.

Think it over
- How has the environment in which we live changed in the last 100 years to improve health?
- What types of social and environmental issues would you include as key factors influencing health expectation today?
- What three things would you suggest as changes which would greatly improve the health of your local population?

Our environment has a great impact on our health

Holistic concepts of health

One of the most widely known descriptions of health is the 1948 World Health Organisation (WHO) definition: 'A state of complete physical, mental and social well-being'. However, this illustrates the difficulty in attempting to define health when you consider the alternative definitions shown below and the range of broad dimensions to health:

- **physical health** – concerned with body mechanics
- **mental health** – the ability to think clearly and coherently, strongly allied to –
- **emotional health** – the ability to recognise emotions and express them appropriately; the ability to cope with potentially damaging aspects of emotional health, e.g. stress, depression, anxiety and tension
- **social health** – the ability to make and maintain relationships with others
- **spiritual health** – can be about personal creeds, principled behaviour, achieving peace of mind or religious beliefs and practices
- **societal health** – the wider societal impact on our own individual health, e.g. the impact of racism on people from a minority ethnic culture, the impact on women of living in a patriarchal society and the impact of living under political oppression.

Definitions of health:

'A satisfactory adjustment of the individual to the environment.'
Royal College of General Practitioners (1972)

'By health I mean the power to live a full adult, living, breathing life in close contact with what I love. I want to be all I am capable of becoming.'
Katherine Mansfield (1888–1923)

'The extent to which an individual or group is able on the one hand, to realise aspirations and satisfy needs and on the other hand, to change or cope with the environment. Health is therefore seen as a resource for everyday life, not the objective of living: it is a positive concept emphasising social and personal resources as well as physical capabilities.'
World Health Organisation (1984)

8.1 Assessment activity

Consider the information given in Figure 8.1 and your own thoughts about the changing environmental impact over the last hundred years. Which model of health do you think this supports and why do you think this?

It is important to recognise that these are not alternative models of health but different dimensions of one health; together they build a holistic concept of health which embraces all the various aspects discussed previously.

Factors affecting health

Margaret Whitehead mapped the influences on health, reflecting the range of influences which a social model will recognise (see Figure 8.2).

If we base our investigation of health promotion on this model of health, then it is necessary to consider the environmental influences on health. These factors would include social class, gender, race, unemployment, age, disability, lifestyle and attitudes.

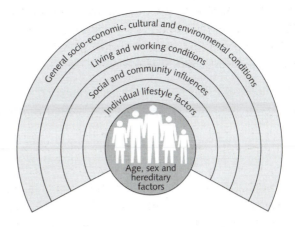

Figure 8.2 The Dahlgren/Whitehead model (1991) showing the underpinning influences of health inequalities

Disability

Disability is the consequence of an impairment or other individual difference. The disability a person experiences is determined by the way in which other people respond to that difference. It can have serious social consequences, which in turn can harm that person's health. In the past, being left-handed was considered a disability and left-handed people were banned from certain jobs. Today we are more accepting of that difference, but this does not apply for all such differences; for example, people with a disability are three times more likely to be unemployed, with all the attendant health impacts described below.

Social class

Social class has long been used as the method of measuring and monitoring health inequalities. Since the Black Report of 1988, it has been clearly identified and acknowledged that those from the lowest social groupings experience the poorest health in society.

Traditionally, social groups within society have been broken down into the six groups shown below; however, it has been accepted more recently that these groupings are no longer representative of the population.

	Social class grouping	For example
I	Professional	Doctors, engineers
II	Managerial/technical	Managers, teachers
IIIN	Non-manual skilled	Clerks, cashiers
IIIM	Non-manual unskilled	Carpenters, van drivers
IV	Partly skilled	Warehouse workers, security guards
V	Unskilled	Labourers

Therefore, for the 2001 census the National Statistics Office reclassified the population into eight layers as shown below.

The National Statistics socio-economic classification

1	**Higher managerial and professional occupations**
	1.1 Large employers and higher managerial occupations e.g. chief executives of major organisations
	1.2 Higher professional occupations e.g. doctors, lawyers
2	**Lower managerial and professional occupations** Middle management in bigger organisations, departmental managers, e.g. physiotherapy or customer services, teachers, etc.
3	**Intermediate occupations** e.g. clerks and bank workers
4	**Small employers and own account workers** e.g. painters and decorators or small manufacturing company owners
5	**Lower supervisory and technical occupations** e.g. builders, joiners, etc.
6	**Semi-routine occupations** e.g. unskilled labouring jobs
7	**Routine occupations** e.g. assembly line workers
8	**Never worked and long-term unemployed**

Source: Office for National Statistics

However we choose to classify the different social strata, most recent research suggests that it is the countries with the smallest income *differences,* rather than the richest countries, which have the best health status. Where income difference is large, such as in the UK, the following inequalities can be seen:

* Children in the lowest social class are five times more likely to die from an accident than those in the top social class.
* Someone in social class 5 is three times more likely to experience a stroke than someone in class 1.
* Infant mortality rates are highest amongst the lowest social groups.

Age

As one might expect, as people get older they are more likely to experience a wide range of illnesses. The health inequalities recorded above remain in the older generation, but are often compounded by the loss of income that comes with retirement. This significantly increases the proportion of the population who are living on benefits as compared to other age groups in the population. Another factor is the longer lifespan of women, which means that because women make up a higher proportion of the older population there are often higher rates of illnesses specifically associated with women.

Gender

Men and women have widely differing patterns of ill health. In the main this can be best summarised by saying that men suffer a higher rate of early mortality (deaths) whilst women experience higher rates of morbidity (illness). There are many specific examples which illustrate these points and they are linked to physiological, psychological and other aspects of gender characteristics influenced by the differing roles that the two genders are expected to adopt by society at large. Typically, men are less likely to access routine screening and other forms of health service, whilst women who are viewed as the carers in the family are more able to do so and therefore may be identifying potential health problems earlier. The result of these differences may be seen in the following examples:

- Men under the age of 65 are 3.5 times more likely than women to die of coronary heart disease.
- Suicide is twice as common in men as in women.
- Women experience more accidents in the home or garden whilst men experience more accidents in the workplace or doing sports activities.

Ethnicity

Black and minority ethnic groups have higher risks of mortality from a range of diseases such as diabetes, liver cancer, tuberculosis, stroke and heart disease. Infant mortality and mental illness have also been highlighted as problems amongst Afro-Caribbean men. However, establishing the cause of these variations has proved difficult. Medical interventions have tended to concentrate on cultural practices but this does not acknowledge the compounding factors of poverty and low employment levels in these groups. Racism also must play a part in the experiences of minority ethnic communities in contact with health services and should be seen as a causative factor in leading to a higher than average experience of poverty and unemployment in these groups.

Attitudes

If you look again at the lay definitions of health (page 332–3) it is possible to see how people's differing attitudes to health will influence their behaviour. A person who believes in the robust individualism model might well choose to smoke *and* take regular exercise, because these are both satisfying and that individual believes in their right to choose. This, however, would be a difficult position for someone who subscribes to the health promotion account or the will-power model – both of which emphasise personal responsibility to maintain health. In this situation that person's decision would appear to be contradictory. Therefore our own attitudes to health are essential to the behaviours we adopt.

Lifestyle

It is a common assumption that lifestyle choices are simply a product of our attitudes to health; as a consequence, people routinely make judgements about the behaviour of others. 'That woman shouldn't be smoking when she is pregnant' or 'That person who is overweight should go on a diet or take more exercise' might be typical examples of what is termed 'victim blaming', i.e. lifestyle as a choice we all make. But there is now considerable evidence that choice is quite limited in many cases, for example the vast majority of people who smoke are first recruited at a very young age before they are mature enough to make an 'adult choice'. The complex nature of the environment and its impact on health choices is also important. For example, choosing healthy nutritious food is as much a feature of availability in the shops and access to the shops which provide it, as it is of personal choice. Therefore it is unfair to make simple assumptions about people's health behaviours.

Unemployment

For a small minority of people unemployment actually leads to an improvement in health, but for the vast majority being unemployed leads to significantly poorer health. The unemployed have higher levels of depression, suicide and self harm and a significantly increased risk of morbidity and mortality across all classes. Men unemployed at both census dates in 1971 and 1981 had mortality rates twice that of other men in that age range and those men who were unemployed at one census date had an excess mortality of 27 per cent.

Assessment activity 8.2

Look at the Dahlgren/Whitehead grid for mapping health inequalities (Figure 8.2). Using these headings try to plot the issues which might impact on the health of the two case studies below:

- A teenage single parent, excluded from school, living alone in a council flat with little or no support from her parents, or
- A gay man, living with his partner, 'out' to close friends but not to work colleagues.

Components of health promotion

Health prevention is a term generally used to refer to action taken to prevent ill health before it starts. However, it is more accurately used to refer to a broader range of actions covering three levels: primary, secondary and tertiary prevention.

Primary prevention

This is an attempt to eliminate the possibility of getting a disease, such as the childhood immunisation programme. Other examples here would include smoking education as part of Personal and Social Health Education in schools or leaflets and posters for use in promoting healthy eating.

Secondary prevention

This addresses those people identified as being in the early stages of a disease, usually through early detection of symptoms. Action here focuses on addressing the underlying causes to alleviate any further symptoms. For example, action to address raised blood pressure taken by a doctor who identified those symptoms as part of a routine check-up for a patient. This might be drug therapy but equally could be a referral onto a physical activity scheme for promoting regular exercise, run as a collaboration with the local leisure services departments (usually referred to as an Exercise on Prescription Scheme). This sort of scheme might be used for people who are overweight and also for people with mild depression, so a range of secondary prevention issues could be addressed through one scheme. Alternatively, a 'stop smoking' group would be a secondary prevention initiative for someone who is already suffering from respiratory problems such as repeat infections, bronchitis, etc.

Tertiary prevention

This refers to the control and reduction (as far as possible) of an already established disease. This is not easily distinguishable from medical care but it is possible to consider issues such as increasing the capacity of the individual to manage their condition and their own health. This might refer to supporting and enabling people with a history of heart attacks to regain their confidence, in order to live a more fulfilling life in control of their own destiny as far as is possible. It could also apply to someone suffering from Parkinsons' disease being supported in learning about and managing their condition as independently as possible.

Approaches to health promotion

The term *health promotion* covers a wide range of different activities, all of which have a part to play in promoting health. None of these differing approaches is essentially the right way; they are simply different aspects which complement each other. The balance between them is very much a choice based on personal perspective, influenced by our own life experience, personal standpoints and values, as illustrated in the wide range of differing lay perspectives on health. Ewles and Simnett (1999) characterise these differing approaches under five broad headings which are summarised in the table below.

	Aim	Example: smoking
Medical	Freedom from medically defined disease and disability	**Aim** – freedom from lung disease, heart disease and other smoking-related disorders **Activity** – encourage people to seek early detection and treatment of smoking-related disorders
Behaviour change	Individual behaviour conducive to freedom from disease	**Aim** – behaviour changes from smoking to not smoking **Activity** – persuasive education to prevent people starting and persuade smokers to stop
Educational	Individuals with knowledge and understanding, enabling well-informed decisions to be made and acted upon	**Aim** – clients will have understanding of the effects of smoking on health, resulting in a decision whether or not to smoke, which they then act on **Activity** – giving information to clients about the effects of smoking. Helping them to learn how to stop smoking if they want to
Client-centred	Working with clients on the clients' own terms	Anti-smoking issue is only considered if clients identify it as a concern Clients identify what, if anything, they want to know and do about it
Societal change	Physical and social environment which enables choice of healthier lifestyle	**Aim** – make smoking socially unacceptable, so it is easier not to smoke than to smoke **Activity** – a no smoking policy in all public places. Cigarette sales less accessible, especially to children, promotion of non-smoking as social norm. Banning tobacco advertising and sports' sponsorship

Source: Ewles, L and Simnett, I (1999), *Promoting Health – A Practice Guide*, reproduced with permission of Ballière Tindall

Assessment activity 8.3

Evaluate the following examples of health education approaches to smoking. Try to identify what model of health promotion it is based on and the level of health promotion it illustrates:

- A practice nurse discussing an action plan for stopping smoking with a patient.
- A teacher showing a group of children a set of diseased lungs in a jar.
- A youth worker working with a group of young people to develop their decision-making skills.
- A community worker working with a group of single parents on an estate who have expressed a desire to stop smoking, to create their own support group.
- A doctor prescribing nicotine replacement therapy for a smoker who has been told by their consultant they have to give up.
- A national television campaign to encourage smokers to quit smoking with a quitline which offers support on how to quit.
- A person working with a quit smoking group for people who have suffered a heart attack.

Health promoters and their role

If you review the Dahlgren/Whitehead model of the determinants of health (page 337) it is possible to see how the promotion of health is multi-layered. It starts with the individual and their health and lifestyle choices, and moves on through local issues and organisations to broader influences at both national and international level.

International

Organisations operating at the international level include a range of charities such as Christian Aid, Oxfam, and Save the Children; as well as pressure groups such as Greenpeace and key statutory organisations like the United Nations, European Commission, World Health Organisation (WHO) and UNICEF. The WHO, in particular, has been instrumental in shaping and influencing health policy across many nations through its *Health For All by the Year 2000* programme. This has been crucial to a move away from medically dominated models of health promotion to a broader based approach encompassing social and environmental influences. The key feature of this programme was the introduction of the first targets for improving health.

National

The greatest potential for improving the health of the population lies at the national level with the government. Simply put, the single most effective action at any level to address the level of health inequality is to raise benefit levels. As the first health strategy, 'The Health of the Nation' (1992) identified, a cross-government commitment from all departments was required to raise health status. This recognition is again seen in the subsequent documents like the Acheson Report (1998) on tackling health inequalities and 'Our Healthier Nation' (1999), both of which identify key roles for a range of government departments including:

- Department of Health
- Department of Social Security
- Department for Education and Skills
- the Home Office
- Environment, Food and Rural Affairs
- Department of the Environment.

Think it over

Investigate the role these departments can play in promoting health. You can do this by visiting the website for the government health strategy, 'Our Healthier Nation' (see above): www.ohn.gov.uk/govwide/govwide

From here you will find links to the roles individual departments can play in the health strategy. What example can you find for:

* the Home Office
* Trade and Industry
* Education and Skills?

You can find examples of key targets and activities for the national government contribution to improving health on page 350 where it deals with the NHS plan, Health Improvement Programmes and the contribution of national policies across government.

However, the government alone is not the only national organisation which contributes to the promotion of health. There are many other national-level organisations which have a part to play in promoting better health. Some examples are shown in the table below.

Type of organisation	Examples
Voluntary organisations Produce educational materials such as those on sexual health issues from the Family Planning Association or safety from RoSPA. These organisations become acknowledged as being authoritative on their subject and may be the sole supplier of literature in that field. They also campaign on specific issues, e.g. MIND campaigning for improved mental health services	• Family Planning Association (FPA) • Royal Society for the Prevention of Accidents (RoSPA) • National Childbirth Trust (NCT) • National Association of Mental Health (MIND)
Professional organisations Set professional standards and codes of conduct, can strike off professionals who are proved to have breached them and therefore stop them practising. Nurses, for example, cannot be employed without a current registration with the UKCC; therefore it is an effective mechanism for managing the quality of their profession	• British Medical Association (BMA) • United Kingdom Central Council for Nursing, Midwifery and Health Visitors (UKCC) • Institution of Environmental Health Officers (IEHO)
Trade unions Advocate and negotiate for their members on issues such as pay and working conditions. They can also co-ordinate activity to campaign for changes to these, e.g. through strike action or working to rule, i.e. not undertaking agreed activities. For example, the teaching unions have had several periods when they have either withdrawn support for out-of-hours activities or resorted to strike action in response to government activity which affected their working conditions	• Public Sector workers (UNISON) • Teachers (NUT, AMMA, NASUWT) • Miners (NUM)
Commercial and industrial organisations There are roles for large private agencies here, for instance in delivering an efficient and effective rail network which which can reduce road traffic and hence pollution levels	• National Rivers Authority (NRA) • Railtrack

Local

Whilst national government policy will remain the most effective tool for enabling health to be promoted, it is at the local level that national policy is translated into practice. This relies on a range of local agencies working together effectively on health issues with a common purpose. Examples of local partner agencies and their potential roles are set out in the table below.

Agency	Role
Primary care trust	Has three key responsibilities: • improve the health of the local population • develop local primary health care services • commission other local health services in line with local health needs
Local authority	The provision of good quality affordable housing Tackling crime and issues of community safety e.g. through careful planning and design of estates The provision of leisure activities for all age groups The provision of safe areas for children to play Providing affordable nursery and crèche facilities to support working parents Tackling poverty through welfare rights advice and benefits take-up campaigns Tackling environmental issues of refuse, noise and dog fouling Attracting inward investment into an area Provision of sound, high quality education
Police	Increasingly the police are active partners in many local initiatives either through direct interventions such as those around drugs issues, or working through partnerships such as Community Safety, where the issues of crime and disorder can be addressed across organisational boundaries, e.g. working with the Youth and Community service to address youth-related problems. This might mean co-ordinating activity of these two services to address adult perceptions of neighbourhood nuisance involving young people
Council for Voluntary Services	An umbrella organisation for a wide variety of local voluntary sector organisations. The organisations they represent will vary from one area to another but usually have a high proportion of support groups for people with specific illnesses or disabilities. They offer a gateway for statutory organisations to communicate with many voluntary sector groups and carers

Informal networks

Finally, it is important to acknowledge the part that informal networks of families, friends and neighbours play in influencing our health decisions, beliefs and environment. It is now widely acknowledged that the vast majority of medical consultations are from lay members of the community. This is the consultation we have with other family members about how best to deal with our cold or flu, or the old lady on the landing above who knows a great deal about homeopathic remedies for backache. Lay knowledge is increasingly seen as an essential tool for screening out minor illness and ailment from the health care system.

Ethical issues

If you consider the wide variety of lay perspectives on health, and the various models of health promotion, it is easy to see how confusing it can be to try to define what is ethical and what is not in terms of health-promoting activity.

Decision making in health promotion

The danger with health promotion activity is that health promoters can become fixed on the goal of improved medical or physical health to the detriment of other aspects of holistic health. It is all too easy for professionals to adopt a judgmental approach, deciding what is best for the individual to the exclusion of that person's right to self-autonomy. It is important to remember that empowering people is an integral part of effective and ethical health promotion work. To enable health promoters to make ethical judgements about the work they undertake, the following questions can be considered:

- Will the people involved be able to choose freely for themselves?
- Will I be respecting their decision, whether or not I approve of it?
- Will I be non-discriminatory – respecting all people equally?
- Will I be serving the more basic needs before addressing other wants?
- Will I be doing good and preventing harm?
- Will I be telling the truth?
- Will I be minimising harm in the long term?
- Will I be able to honour promises and agreements I make?

These points are equally applicable for a one-to-one client/professional scenario, or a planner considering alterations to local roads in a housing estate. Here, for example, they might be asking themselves whether they have adequately involved the local people in the decision-making process and if they have respected their input, not valuing it differently to that of other professionals. The most challenging question is *who* to consult. It is impossible to consult a 'community' because no one person or group can accurately reflect the views of the entire community. So in this case the planner would have to consider a range of approaches, including postal surveys, consulting key people who work in the area, key people from the local community and any local community groups. Taken together these views might give a more accurate assessment of the situation.

Think it over

Review with a family member or friend an aspect of their health-related behaviour which they know is damaging to their health, for example continuing to smoke or not take sufficient exercise. Try to find out:

- the extent of their knowledge about that health issue – i.e. do they know and understand the relevant health messages?
- why they continue with that behaviour if they know it harms them
- how they feel when people ask them about it, as you are doing
- what their expectations of health professionals are – do they expect to be asked about it each time they visit their GP?

Constraints on health promotion

Financial constraints

Much local health promotion activity may be viewed as being relatively cheap in relation to the illness it seeks to prevent, but it is hard to measure the precise outcome of the work. The investment of two or three hours' time by a practice nurse to help someone quit smoking is considerably less expensive than the cost of extensive treatment for lung cancer. However, it is impossible to state categorically that the nurse's time led to that individual quitting, many other factors might have influenced the outcome, i.e. it isn't an *attributable* outcome.

Health promotion has historically had to compete against clinical treatments for funding where it is easier to attribute the outcome to the investment (the person receives their treatment and gets better), and in many cases the issues are significantly more emotive to deal with. It is possible that from the cost of one year's Factor VIII therapy for a child with haemophilia a local specialist health promotion service could be funded, so how does one make that choice and how do you justify that choice to the parents of the child?

Think it over

Promoting physical activity is probably one of the most cost-effective health promotion investments there is. If a person becomes more active it has great potential benefit on their physical, mental and social health.

Now imagine that you are trying to convince your local primary care trust to invest in an Exercise on Prescription Scheme for people who might benefit from being more active. Your scheme costs about the same as drug therapy for ten people with angina but the people who will make the decision are likely to understand that treatment better.

- Start by finding out what effects being active has on your health – this is the information you would need to enable you to market this approach.
- What model of health is it likely that the decision makers will be working to?
- How will this present problems for you in selling your proposal against a drug therapy?
- What problems might you have in identifying the future success of your scheme compared to the success of the drug treatment?

Political constraints

As one government leaves office and another arrives, wholesale changes may result in the landscape of health-promoting activity. For example, the concentration on individual responsibility in the Conservative government's 'Health of the Nation' White Paper (1992) is in stark contrast to the Labour government's 'Our Healthier Nation' health strategy of 1999. This

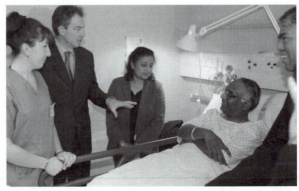

Political changes can mean changes in attitudes to health and health promotion

emphasises that health improvement relies on a contract between individual and government for each to play their part in the process, the individual taking responsibility for maintaining their own health and government providing a supportive environment, e.g. through job creation and environmental action.

Think it over

- Name three things that might influence health which might be changed as a result of a change in government.
- When politicians talk about health they are usually focusing on one aspect – what aspect is this and what model of health does it reflect?
- Why do you think politicians continue to talk about health in this simplistic way instead of in a broader holistic fashion?

The Black Report (1988) which illustrated the widening health gap between rich and poor in the country was suppressed by the Conservative government of the day, and the word 'inequalities' was largely replaced by the less emotive term 'variations' because of the government's sensitivity to that word. Government action in other areas led to compounding inequalities, e.g. the introduction of Clause 28 forbade schools from 'promoting homosexuality', creating a climate where schools felt unable to address issues of sexuality. The Conservative government of the time ensured that the initial HIV awareness campaign of the 1980s avoided any reference to risk-taking behaviours, which were deemed too sensitive for the public, and ran with a theme of 'AIDS – don't die of ignorance' (leaving many people to ask, 'What is this ignorance, and how do you catch it?).

Knowledge-based constraints

As the knowledge base for health promotion develops, health messages change – leading to confusion within the general population. A good example here is the change in physical activity recommendations for promoting a healthy heart. This has changed from 30 minutes of vigorous activity three times a week, to building up to 30 minutes of moderate activity on five days a week. It is not unusual, when asking people what they understand the current message to be, to receive either of these recommendations or a mixture of the two. This can place considerable demands on health promoters to remain up to date and can leave them in the same state of confusion as the rest of the population.

Developing new evidence on which to develop health promotion activities can be difficult. Health promotion is often excluded from scientific research networks because its approach runs counter to the prevailing scientifically based research culture. Here health promotion outcomes are less easy to measure, need to work in natural settings, and there is a need to evaluate the process as well as the end point.

Client groups

Every client group brings with it their own ethical considerations be it an individual or a whole population approach.

Smoking cessation advice for a client

Working with lifestyle change is fraught with ethical considerations. Two of the most important issues here would be the client's right to self-determination and the need to remain non-judgemental; for example, the role of the midwife in discussing smoking with a pregnant woman, where the midwife has considerable knowledge about the potential damage to the unborn child and the possibility of further health damage if the mother continues to smoke after the birth. However, to be an ethical health promoter she must respect the client's right to choose whether to continue smoking and not allow the client's decision to continue smoking (should that be the case) to change the relationship.

A community midwife can be a great source of support and information to pregnant women

Think it over

- What three pieces of information might the midwife most want to convey to the mother?
- What things will she have to be mindful of when having this discussion?
- Are there any specific issues which might present problems for her in doing this in the mother's own home?
- Why is it appropriate for her to have this discussion with the mother?

Children learning about healthy eating

With the government's initiative to ensure every child of primary school age is offered a piece of fruit each day, the issue of healthy eating is at the forefront of school health promotion work. However, there are many other attendant issues for consideration when addressing healthy eating in a Personal Social and Health Education lesson:

- Does the school have a nutrition policy to manage all aspects of nutrition on its premises?
- Does the school have a tuck shop or vending machines and, if so, are healthy choices available?
- If it generates essential income, what would be the likely impact of closing it to restrict sales of sweets and sugary drinks?
- Does the school canteen offer a range of foods with interesting healthy options as part of that menu?
- When discussing healthy eating with children are parents involved at all?
- Does the school have a policy on snacks which children can bring to school? (Some schools rule out crisps, chocolate and sugary drinks.)

An important aspect of introducing any policy is ownership. It is relatively easy to write or copy a policy from someone else, but the people who it affects do not 'own' it, that is they have no sense of it applying to them. Therefore, policy development of the type identified above often takes time in order to allow these people to be consulted and involved as much as possible along the way. This would allow a school time to identify to parents not only why they had decided to adopt a nutrition policy but also time to identify what the likely implications are for them as a parent of a child in that school. This reduces the likelihood of someone breaking the policy when it is introduced because everyone understands why and how it will operate. In some cases an amnesty period might be used. For example, for a smoking policy this would be three months when the penalties for breaching the policy would not operate; any breaches would not result in sanction or punishment but a polite but firm acknowledgement to what the penalty would be from the end of the amnesty period.

Screening

Screening was defined by the American Commission on Chronic illness in 1957 as *'the presumptive identification of unrecognised disease or defect by the application of tests, examinations and other procedures which can be applied rapidly. Screening tests sort out apparently well persons who may have a disease from those who do not'.*

Screening a well population is a contentious issue, with many attendant problems; for example, are we right to be medicalising a well population in this way? For health promoters there is considerable responsibility to consider what is an ethical position for discussion of screening programmes such as those for:

- breast screening
- cervical screening
- HIV screening of pregnant women.

These screening programmes raise many questions, not least of all the client's right to choose. In some cases, such as HIV screening of pregnant women, this is done without the women's consent as a part of a wider population screening programme to monitor HIV patterns, whilst in breast screening women below the age of 50 are not deemed to be at risk and are excluded from the programme.

Screening for some conditions remains an imprecise science. Media coverage of cervical cancer screening problems emphasises the difficulty of ensuring that all the people who take cervical smears are adequately trained and that the laboratory screening process itself has limitations and will inevitably miss some positive smears. The international debate for breast cancer is just as contentious, with a debate raging as to the effectiveness of the screening programme; some Scandinavian countries consider it to have little or no impact on survival rates for breast cancer.

Think it over

One of the most contentious screening programmes is that for breast cancer. There is conflicting evidence as to the effectiveness of the programme. If you were a nurse and someone asked you whether they should attend for breast screening, what would you tell them if you had the following background information available to you?

Background information

- Every year your chances of dying from breast cancer are 1 in 2400, after screening they may be about 1 in 2900 (Rodgers, 1990).
- Breast cancer screening offers the possibility of less radical treatment for breast cancer (Austoker, 1990).
- Treatment of breast cancer may include lumpectomy, mastectomy, radiotherapy, chemotherapy, hormone treatment.
- The woman's breast will need to be compressed to 4.5 cm (Forrest, 1990).
- 14,000 women will need to be screened to save one life (Rodgers, 1990).
- 142,000 women will be recalled with some false positives and some overdiagnosis (Rodgers, 1990).
- For every seven women found to have breast cancer, six will not live any longer as a result of early diagnosis (Rodgers, 1990).
- Some breast cancers will be missed at mammography (Skrabanek, 1989; Rodgers, 1990; Woods, 1991).
- Some cancers will develop in the three-year interval (Forrest, 1990).
- The cost of saving one life from screening is £80,000 (Rees, 1986).
- *Individual* benefit cannot be guaranteed (Skrabanek, 1989).

Assessment activity 8.4

Herneshire Local Authority has decided to impose a ban on smoking in public places, arguing that it is to protect the health of the local population and save medical costs in the county.

What are the ethical issues involved?

What steps would the local authority have to undertake before implementing this ban?

What constraints would there be?

You could debate this issue, using the headings: non-discrimination, freedom of choice, benefits, financial constraints, the advantages to different client groups.

Key themes

The recent emphasis on improving health in national policy has meant a need for local health promoters to ensure that their work addresses these targets and themes. As we have already seen, health promotion activity can struggle to identify funding unless it shapes its work along these major policy themes.

Health policy linked to key targets

'The Health of the Nation' was this country's first-ever health (as opposed to health services) strategy. It was published in 1992 with a stated aim of ensuring that 'action is taken whether through the NHS or otherwise, to improve and protect health'. It initiated action at three levels:

- The Department of Health was given the lead role.
- It commented on the contribution the state and individuals could make to improving the nation's health.
- It set a range of national health targets.

'Saving Lives – Our Healthier Nation'

This was the follow-up health strategy released by the Labour government as it came to power in 1999. 'Our Healthier Nation' proposed to tackle the root causes of ill health – including air pollution, unemployment, low wages, crime and disorder and poor housing. It focused on prevention of the main killers: cancer, coronary heart disease and stroke, accidents and mental illness and included a wide range of service providers including local councils, the NHS, and local voluntary bodies and businesses.

Main targets from 'Our Healthier Nation'	
Cancer	– To reduce the death rate in under-75s by at least 20%
Coronary heart disease and stroke	– To reduce the death rate in under-75s by at least 40%
Accidents	– To reduce the death rate by at least 20% and serious injury by at least 10%
Mental illness	– To reduce the death rate from suicide and undetermined injury by at least 20%

The NHS plan (2000)

The NHS plan was the Labour government's policy paper which outlined its intentions in modernising the NHS. It aims to tackle the health inequalities that divide Britain and set national targets for tackling health inequalities with the relevant supporting investment, such as:

- a £500 million expansion of the 'Sure Start' projects
- a new Children's Fund worth £450 million over three years for supporting services for children in the 5–13 age bracket which will improve educational achievement, reduce crime and improve attendance at schools, etc.
- a more effective welfare foods programme with increased support for breast feeding
- a 15 per cent cut in teenage conception rates
- to cut the number of smokers by at least 15 million by 2010
- every child in nursery, and aged 4–6 years in infant school, to be entitled to a free piece of fruit each school day.

Sure Start: case study of government action

The aim of Sure Start *To work with parents-to-be, parents and children to promote the physical, intellectual and social development of babies and young children – particularly those who are disadvantaged – so that they can flourish at home and when they get to school, and thereby break the cycle of disadvantage for the current generation of young children.*

Sure Start is a cornerstone of the government's drive to tackle child poverty and social exclusion. By 2004, there will be at least 500 Sure Start local programmes. They will be concentrated in neighbourhoods where a high proportion of children are living in poverty and where Sure Start can help them to succeed by pioneering new ways of working to improve services. At the time of writing, 128 have started work and another 66 programmes are working on their plans. Local programmes will work with parents and parents-to-be to improve children's life chances through better access to:

- family support
- advice on nurturing
- health services
- early learning.

The design and content of local Sure Start programmes will vary according to local needs. But it is expected that all programmes will include a number of core services:

- outreach and home visiting
- support for families and parents
- support for good quality play, learning and childcare experiences for children
- primary and community health care, including advice about family health and child health and development
- support for children and parents with special needs, including help getting access to specialised services.

Health Improvement Programmes

Introduced as part of the changes set out in the 1997 White Paper, 'The New NHS – Modern Dependable', the HImP was described as being 'an effective vehicle for making major and sustained impact on health problems... focusing action on people who are socially excluded'. All HImPs should include information about how national targets are being addressed, local health targets, action plans for delivering these targets, identify local health partnerships and this information should be made accessible to all. The key feature of the HImP, or its successor the Health Improvement and Modernisation Plan, is that they describe the local actions. Therefore, they identify what the targets are and what needs to be done to address them locally, including how the necessary finance will be made available to do that.

Health promotion topics

With such a broad agenda to cover it is hard to decide what areas of activity should be prioritised within health-promoting activity. The five topics selected here represent key national health concerns which relate to the targets set out in 'Our Healthier Nation'.

Diet

The proportion of both men and women who are overweight or obese has steadily increased since 1980. This is a major risk factor for a variety of illnesses but in particular, coronary heart disease (CHD). Poor diet, that is one containing too much fat and salt and not enough fruit and vegetables, is directly related to:

- diabetes
- raised blood pressure
- raised cholesterol levels
- weight gain.

All of the above are major factors in circulatory disorders such as CHD and stroke. Diet is also thought to account for about a quarter of all deaths due to cancer in this country and particularly colorectal and stomach cancer. The current trends show that the proportion of fat in our diets which contributes to many of these problems has remained the same since the early 1980s and shows little indication of reducing. In 1996, 61 per cent of men and 52 per cent of women were clinically obese with an increase in obesity amongst quite young children. This may relate to evidence found by the Department of Health (reported in 1989) that the main sources of dietary energy for children were bread, chips, milk, biscuits, meat products, cakes and puddings, whilst some vitamin intake levels were below the daily recommendation.

Exercise

Surveying the activity levels of the general population is a relatively recent phenomenon. Until the Allied Dunbar Fitness survey in 1995, the UK had no accurate picture of the current levels of physical fitness within the adult population. The results of that and other subsequent surveys have not been encouraging, with the message clearly being that we are an increasingly sedentary population. This may be caused by increased reliance on the car, children being transported by car due to safety worries of parents, less tolerance of children playing in the street, an increase in less active occupations and a wider range of other recreational activities such as play stations, PC games and multi-channel television.

Current recommendations are to build up to 30 minutes of moderate physical activity five days a week

Whatever the causes, the results are indisputable – we are less active as a nation, and this will contribute to a range of health problems, not just CHD but also a range of other illnesses, such as depression, osteoporosis, high blood pressure, diabetes and so on.

The current recommendation for physical activity levels which promote heart health is to build up to 30 minutes of moderate activity on five days a week.

Sexually transmitted disease

The government first set targets for improving the sexual health of the population in 'The Health of the Nation', where it focused on a reduction in rates of gonorrhoea and a reduction in the rate of conceptions amongst the under-16s by 50 per cent by 2000.

By the time of 'Our Healthier Nation' some of these priorities had changed, although tackling teenage pregnancy remained an issue with the UK having the highest rate of live births to teenage girls of anywhere in Europe. Therefore a target of reducing by half the rate of teenage conceptions by 2010 was retained, but with a fresh focus on teenage pregnancy as a social exclusion issue.

The government also recognised a worrying reversal in HIV trends with increasing levels of new infections and particularly amongst the heterosexual population. In 1996 nearly 3,000 new cases were recorded, emphasising concerns about complacency in the population and amongst young people in particular, where evidence showed a reduction in safe sexual practice and an increase in risky sexual behaviour, e.g. when holidaying abroad.

Clearly, lack of safe sexual practice also brings with it a risk of contracting other forms of sexually transmitted disease, and at this time there has been a steady rise in rates of both gonorrhoea and chlamydia. Between 1995 and 1997 there was a 53 per cent rise in rates of gonorrhoea and a 47 per cent rise in rates of chlamydia amongst the 16–19-year age group. These are both areas of considerable concern, with chlamydia particularly being the single most preventable cause of infertility in women.

Smoking

Smoking facts
- Tobacco smoking causes most lung cancers.
- It is implicated in a wide range of other cancers, including those of the nose and throat but also cervical cancer.
- Overall about one-third of cancer deaths can be attributed to smoking.
- Smoking also contributes to CHS and stroke rates.

The link between smoking and ill health is now well documented. 'Smoking is the single most important modifiable risk factor for CHD in young and old' ('Our Healthier Nation', section 6.5). A lifetime non-smoker is 60 per cent less likely to have CHD and 30 per cent less likely to have a stroke than a smoker. Smoking mirrors other patterns of ill health in that the highest levels are in the lowest social groups. Although the proportion of young people who smoke is similar across all social groups, by their mid-30s, 50 per cent of young people from higher social classes have stopped as opposed to only 25 per cent from the lowest income groups. The result is that about one-third of the smokers in the population are concentrated in only the lowest 10 per cent of earners in the country.

This reflects evidence that campaigning measures to reduce smoking levels have compounded this problem by encouraging those in higher social groups to quit, whilst having minimal effect on those in the lowest income brackets. Therefore some health promotion campaigning can compound health inequality. In its response to the problem the government released the tobacco White Paper 'Smoking Kills' in 1998, which included additional funding for a nationwide network of smoking cessation services to support smokers who wish to quit.

Skin care

The major cause of ill health associated with skin care is malignant melanoma or skin cancer. Skin cancer is distributed in the reverse pattern to other forms of cancer both regionally and by social class. That is, it is most common in the South West and East and in social classes 1 and 2. The incidence of malignant melanoma amongst men in class 1 is nearly five times that for men in class 5 and this is repeated for women where the difference is approximately twice that of class 5 for class 1. The table below shows the incidence of skin cancer by social class (1984).

Social class	Men	Women
I	150	(97)
II	108	111
IIINM	115	95
IIIM	57	67
IV	67	58
V	(34)	(51)

(National average rate shown as 100 – figures in brackets are those based on very small numbers)

The major cause of malignant melanoma (skin cancer) is exposure to the sun, which explains both the regional and social variations. In the northern areas of the country the number of days where lengthy exposure to the sun is likely is far fewer than in the south. The variations by social class are most usually explained by the use of tanning facilities and holidaying abroad, which those with greater disposable income can afford. Since the advent of the cheap package holiday this gap has narrowed as more and more people have greater access to holidays in hotter countries with stronger sunlight levels. Countries such as Australia have led the way in addressing this problem, with campaigns such as Slip (on a shift), Slap (on some sunscreen), Slop (on a hat), which have been adopted in many other areas worldwide.

Think it over

The current sun safety messages are:

* Seek the shade – especially at midday.
* Hats on – use a wide-brimmed hat.
* Apply sunscreen of at least SPF 15.
* Don't burn – it won't improve your tan.
* Exercise care – always protect the very young.

* How often do you see people following this advice?
* Why might people choose not to follow this advice?
* What wider principle does this illustrate?

Agencies involved

Delivering the health improvement agenda is clearly a multi-layered approach, as suggested above, with many partners at every level. Here we consider some key partners in the process.

Government

Government action to effect improvements in health take place across all departments, as we have already seen in the first health strategy 'The Health of The Nation'. This is illustrated through the work of the Department for Education and Employment, which has been instrumental in leading the development of the National Healthy School Standard and reducing the levels of unemployment through initiatives such as the Modern Apprenticeship and New Deal. The Social Security Department has been responsible for raising the levels of benefits and targeting them at those most in need, particularly families with young children as the Acheson Report recommended. This theme has been further supported by the introduction of the Sure Start and Sure Start plus programmes for supporting families in most need (see page 351).

On a wider front, the Department of Health has targeted additional resources for those areas identified as being at most need through the creation of Health Action Zones for large-scale health projects across a wide range of sectors, e.g. education, housing, etc. The Home Office has also played its part in addressing the issue of fear of crime through the introduction of Community Safety Strategies, which are local community plans to address crime issues through partnerships led by the local authorities.

Health services

The primary function of the NHS is to treat sick people. Although health promotion activity could and should be a feature of many health service roles (see examples described earlier), in practice this aspect of health activity is the poor relation to the primary goal of treating the sick. Recent government reorganisation of the NHS has emphasised its health improvement role, specifying that health authorities have the lead role in developing health improvements and giving primary care trusts, a primary function of 'to improve the health of their local population'.

There are several key roles within the health service for promoting health. Examples of these include:

- **public health doctors** – have a key role in assessing the patterns of ill health locally and identifying what types of health care provision and health promoting activities are required to improve health locally
- **health visitors** – have a public health role in local communities, working at a neighbourhood level to identify local health need and support community activity to address those needs
- **specialist health promotion services** – a small specialised service which supports the development of the health-promoting role of others, the development of new services and policies which can promote health locally.

Private sector

In the private sector, the commercial pressures mean that if an organisation doesn't generate an income it will quickly go out of business. However, as the public become more health conscious the private sector responds to serve that need; therefore it is not unexpected to see changes in the leisure industry, for example, where there is:

- an increasing number of leisure facilities
- a re-focusing on promoting active lifestyle rather than body building or elitist exercise
- a whole new market for sportswear and advice such as personal trainers.

This move within the market place has been coupled by developments in other areas, such as private practitioners in health fields such as alternative therapies, chiropractors, nutritionists, counsellors, etc. Increasingly, organisations buy in specific consultants for stress audits and advice on managing stress within organisations. In the home this response to a health-conscious population is probably best illustrated by the extent to which local supermarkets have responded to public concerns about genetically modified foods in the case of at least one retailer proclaiming that none of its products contain GM foodstuffs. A similar situation has developed for organically grown foods, where this niche market has gradually grown to occupy a significant proportion of the local produce on offer, the public clearly being prepared to pay the additional costs associated with those products.

Mass media

The mass media clearly has a major part to play in the health education of the public at large. It serves this purpose in two main ways.

The first is through paid-for publicity in the form of specific adverts carried on television, radio or in the printed media. This is usually national campaigning (due to the high cost), such as adverts to raise awareness of benefit entitlements, publicity for the national smoking quitline, HIV and safe sex awareness campaigns and the television 'stop smoking' adverts featuring John Cleese run at major quit periods such as New Year or in the run-up to National No Smoking Day.

Health promotion also often benefits from free media coverage of major campaign launches such as those for teenage pregnancy and National No Smoking Day. However, this type of media coverage brings with it many attendant problems, the most difficult being the lack of control over the final content of any article a health promoter may contribute to. Health is a very political issue and therefore news items about health issues present reporters with many opportunities to present the information in a particular light as a means of creating a more 'interesting' story. For example, the issue of tackling teenage pregnancy provides many opportunities for the media to reinforce the stereotypical view of feckless young mothers who get pregnant to obtain council housing accommodation, when the evidence simply doesn't support that view – but may be deemed as being less newsworthy.

Similar problems exist in gaining free coverage through the release of new health information. This can add to the confusion around a topic as the emphasis on the information can be influenced by the views of the reporter or paper, or the limitations of the new information can be missed, e.g. was this research sponsored by a company with a vested interest in the subject?

With the rapid rise in use of online services, people will increasingly be able to access information directly through the use of the Internet. Whilst greatly improving access, this will remove much of the control and screening which other forms of media provide, it is increasingly easy for people to set up their own websites and enable others to access information which is not regulated in any way.

Assessment activity 8.5

What examples of health information/campaigning can you find in the printed media? Collect any examples in your own newspaper and magazines over a seven-day period. This exercise will be more effective if you work with others to maximise the number of different papers and magazines you can cover.

- What examples did you find which were:
  - paid for advertising?
  - unpaid coverage of new information?
  - news coverage of new services/health-related projects?
- What are the messages being conveyed in these pieces?
- Did you find any examples of the same information presented differently in various papers and magazines?
- What problems do you think this might present for the health promoter seeking media coverage?

Health promotion campaigns

Health policy linked to campaigns

The link between national health policy and campaigning is probably best illustrated through the Ten Tips for Better Health set out in the introduction to 'Our Healthier Nation' (1997) by the Chief Medical Officer. These tips for health identified the balance the government wished to strike between national policy to address health inequalities and the individual's potential to manage their own health. Examples of the ways in which government has addressed these include the following:

- Smoking – the establishment of new smoking cessation support services in every district in the country. This is allied to major campaigns programmed at strategic times in the year, e.g. New Year and National No Smoking Day to encourage people to give up smoking and use the available services.

> **Ten Tips for Better Health**
>
> 1 Don't smoke. If you can, stop. If you can't, cut down.
>
> 2 Follow a balanced diet with plenty of fruit and vegetables.
>
> 3 Keep physically active.
>
> 4 Manage stress by, for example, talking things through and taking time to relax.
>
> 5 If you drink alcohol, do so in moderation.
>
> 6 Cover up in the sun and protect children from sunburn.
>
> 7 Practise safe sex.
>
> 8 Take up cancer screening opportunities.
>
> 9 Be safe on the roads: follow the Highway Code.
>
> 10 Learn the first aid ABC – Airways, Breathing, Circulation.

Source: 'Our Healthier Nation' (1997)

- Healthy eating – every child in the country is to be offered a piece of fruit in a similar scheme to the free school milk approach. The aim is to encourage children to adopt healthier diets.
- Stress – using the new NHS workforce plan to ensure that every NHS organisation has an anti-bullying policy in place to address one of the underlying causes of workplace stress.
- Skin cancer – promoting the sun awareness message by production of leaflets, posters, worksheets and games packs for primary school children.

Whilst these illustrate some of the types of government campaigning against key target areas within the health strategy, there are other illustrations, e.g. immunisation. The government sets national targets for achieving levels of coverage in key childhood immunisation. These targets are passed on to GPs who are given incentive payments for achieving these targets. Immunisation mainly occurs in younger children between the ages of 2 months and 5 years for diseases such as polio, measles, mumps and rubella.

Occasionally, other additional campaigns can arise from concerns about possible epidemics. Examples here would include government campaigns encouraging older people and key workers to be immunised against influenza. A similar situation arose with concerns about meningitis in teenagers, leading to a major national campaign to vaccinate older student groups.

Health promotion methods and materials

It is hard to quantify the extent to which individual face-to-face interaction can contribute to health campaigning. However, it is clear that the general public holds certain groups within society in high regard, e.g. doctors, nurses and teachers, and therefore respects the information they obtain from them. This creates considerable potential for promoting key health messages simply through the day-to-day routine of work. This might mean a doctor suggesting to someone that they consider giving up smoking when they attend for a health check, or a district nurse suggesting that moderate activity is still possible and potentially beneficial for an older client whilst visiting them at home.

Leaflets

Leaflets are the backbone of health education activity. They can serve a wide variety of purposes such as informing people about local services, providing information about specific health conditions, giving advice about specific health promotion issues or engaging people in thought about broader health considerations (see Figure 8.3). In many cases leaflets are designed to support specific health campaigns such as those for immunisation and National No Smoking Day. A leaflet may appear to be relatively simple, but it is important to consider a range of questions when designing or using a leaflet. For example:

- Who is the leaflet for? A drugs leaflet produced for secondary school children will not be appropriate for primary schools, for example.
- Who produced the leaflet? Will they have an interest in the information? If it is a commercial company, such as a pharmaceuticals company, will this mean it has been selective in its reporting of the information?
- How long ago was it first produced? Is the information still relevant or accurate? For example, information on drug-related harm changes very rapidly.

immunisation
THE SAFEST WAY TO PROTECT YOUR CHILD

inclu...
on recogr...

What is immunisation?

Immunisation gives protection against a disease by using a vaccine. It is the safest, most effective way of protecting your child against childhood diseases. It's free and easily available at your local GP surgery or health centre.

Childhood immunisation began in the UK in the late 50s and since then diseases such as polio and diphtheria have effectively disappeared. The Hib vaccine introduced in 1992 has led to a massive reduction in cases of Hib meningitis.

Immunisation begins at two months, so by the time your child starts school he or she is fully protected against a number of dangerous diseases. For medical reasons, a very small number of children cannot be immunised, so having your child immunised also helps to protect them.

As overseas travel becomes easier there is a risk that certain diseases will be brought back into the UK. We're lucky – immunisation is available to all children in the UK but in some countries this is not possible, and diseases such as polio and diphtheria still kill thousands of children each year.

...detailed information on
...s available from your local GP
...our doctor, practice nurse or
...advice if you have any
...munisation.

Meningitis and septicæmia – What to look for

Meningitis is an inflammation of the lining of the brain. Septicæmia is blood poisoning, which may be caused by the same germs that cause meningitis. Both are **very** serious and must be treated urgently.

The early symptoms of meningitis, such as fever, fretfulness, vomiting and refusing to feed, are also common with colds and flu. A baby with meningitis or septicæmia can become seriously ill within hours. The important signs to look out for are shown below.

In babies look for

- high pitched, moaning cry
- difficult to wake
- temperature of 39°C or above
- pale or blotchy skin
- red or purple spots that do not fade under pressure – do the **Glass Test**

In older children also look for

- stiffness in the neck – can the child kiss their knee or touch their forehead to the knee?
- drowsiness or confusion
- severe headache
- dislike of bright light

The Glass Test: Press the side of a glass firmly against the rash – you will be able to see if the rash fades and loses colour under pressure. If it doesn't change colour, contact your doctor immediately.

If your child becomes ill with one or more of these signs or symptoms, contact your doctor urgently. If you are still worried after getting advice, trust your instincts – take your child to the nearest accident and emergency department.

IF YOUR CHILD HAS A RASH OF RED OR PURPLE SPOTS OR BRUISES GET IMMEDIATE MEDICAL HELP.

Figure 8.3 A Department of Health leaflet on childhood immunisation

Immunisation timetable – a checklist for parents

When due	Which immunisations	Type	Common side effects	Date given
At two months	Polio	By mouth	None	
	Hib Diphtheria Tetanus Whooping cough	One injection	Possible small lump at site of injection Slight fever within 48hrs Small risk of high fever causing a fit	
At three months	Polio	By mouth	None	
	Hib Diphtheria Tetanus Whooping cough	One injection	As for Hib, Diphtheria, Tetanus, Whooping cough at two months	
At four months	. Polio	By mouth	None	
	Hib Diphtheria Tetanus Whooping cough	One injection	As for Hib, Diphtheria, Tetanus, Whooping cough at two months	
At 12 to 15 months	Measles Mumps Rubella	One injection	Fever and measles-like rash, 7–10 days after injection Small risk of high fever causing a fit	
3 to 5 years (usually before the child starts school)	Measles Mumps Rubella	One injection	As for Measles, Mumps and Rubella at 12–15 months but **less common**	
	Diphtheria Tetanus	One injection	As for Hib, Diphtheria, Tetanus, Whooping cough at two months	
	Polio	By mouth	None	
10 to 13 years (sometimes shortly after birth)	Tuberculosis (BCG)	Test plus injection	Irritation and soreness at injection site Blister or sore leaving a small scar	
School leavers 14 to 19 years	Diphtheria Tetanus	One injection	As for Hib, Diphtheria, Tetanus, Whooping cough at two months	
	Polio	By mouth	None	

Listed above are the immunisations currently recommended for children. **Common** side effects of the immunisations are shown. If your child has other symptoms, you should talk to your doctor, health visitor or nurse. For more information, you could consult the **Guide to Childhood Immunisations** booklet produced by the Health Education Authority in partnership with the Department of Health.

If your child has a slight temperature you should remove any excess layers of clothing or blankets, give extra drinks and paracetamol liquid, following the instructions on the bottle. If your child's temperature is 39°C or above, or they have a fit, you should contact the doctor immediately.

Immunisation protects your child against a number of childhood diseases. But it's not just for babies – to give maximum protection, your child must complete the **whole** programme.

Figure 8.3 A Department of Health leaflet on childhood immunisation (continued)

- Is the language level used appropriate to the target audience? Is it too adult? Does it include abbreviations or technical terms?
- Is it well designed? Will it grab the attention of the reader from amongst the other leaflets and posters? Will it connect specifically with the target audience?
- Are the key messages clearly identified or are there too many other distractions?
- For that particular leaflet and target audience, where is the best place to display it?

Think it over

Look at the Department of Health leaflet on childhood immunisation (Figure 8.3).

- What is the target group?
- How is the message being conveyed?
- Do you think it is effective?
- Why? Give your reasons.

Posters

Posters provide an excellent tool for first catching the attention of the target audience and supporting the key broad messages you might then develop in more detail within a leaflet. The table below shows the factors which draw attention to a poster divided into two groups.

Physical characteristics	Motivational characteristics
Size – the whole of the poster as well as parts within it like key lettering	Novelty – unusual features or surprising objects
Intensity – bold headings	Interest – items of interest to the target audience
Colour – use of primary colours such as red, green and orange	Deeper motivations – e.g. fashion and sex
Pictures – using photographs and drawings	Entertainment or humour

The key point of a poster is that it has to be eye catching and big enough to attract attention. It will need to be in colour or, if in black and white, to use this for impact or dramatic effect. Wording should be minimal and very bold. Posters need to be positioned carefully at places where the target audience will see them and routinely changed after a short period.

Assessment activity 8.6

Find an example of a poster campaign for a health promotion topic in your locality. Note down where the posters are placed and how many there are. Why do you think these places have been chosen?

Write a short report on the purpose of the campaign and evaluate its effectiveness. You could interview local people to find out how aware they are of the posters.

The role of the mass media in campaigning

Many people would view the use of the media as the most effective means of reaching the population to promote health, probably assuming that because it reaches a large number of people its effect will be correspondingly great. However, there are other considerations to take into account here.

The lay definitions of health show how people's differing attitudes to health will influence their behaviour, and, as we have already seen, it is important to avoid falling into the trap of assuming that our attitudes to health are solely responsible for determining our behaviour. Therefore it is important to acknowledge these underpinning factors, our own models of health, the attitudes to health they create and the impact of our environment when considering the role of the mass media in influencing health behaviour.

Having taken these factors into consideration it is not surprising to find that many research studies have now shown that the direct persuasive power of mass media is very limited. Expectations that the mass media alone will produce dramatic long-term changes in health behaviour are doomed to disappointment.

It is important to know what success can realistically be expected when using the mass media in health promotion work. Appropriate aims here might include using it to:

- raise awareness of health and health issues (for example, to raise awareness that the budget for running the NHS is limited and difficult choices about what to spend it on have to be made; or to raise awareness about the link between over-exposure to the sun and the risk of skin cancer)
- deliver a simple message (for example, that babies should sleep on their backs not their tummies; that there is a national advice line for young people wanting information about sexual health)
- change behaviour if it is a simple one-off activity (for example, phone for a leaflet) which people are already motivated to do and which it is easy to do. (Phoning for a leaflet is more likely if you are at home with a phone than if you're at a friend's house or if the nearest phone is a broken public one two streets away.)

The use of mass media is part of an overall strategy which includes face-to-face discussion, and personal help, and attention to social and environmental factors which help or hinder change. For example, mass media publicity is just one strand in a long-term programme to combat smoking.

What mass media cannot be expected to do
- Convey complex information (for example, about transmission routes of HIV).
- Teach skills (for example, how to deal assertively with pressure to have sex without a condom or take drugs).
- Change people's attitudes or beliefs. If a message challenges a person's basic beliefs, he is more likely to dismiss the message than change his belief (for example, 'My grandad smoked sixty a day till he died at 80, so saying I should stop smoking is rubbish').
- Change behaviour unless it is a simple action, easy to do, and people are already motivated to do it (for example, it will only encourage those people who are already motivated to be more active to start walking because this is an easy and accessible form of exercise, it will not do this for those who are not motivated to be more active).

How to plan, prepare and conduct a campaign

Dignan and Carr (1992) describe effective planning as 'requiring anticipation of what will be needed along the way towards reaching a goal. This statement implies that the goal is defined...' This means that to plan effectively requires a clear understanding of what you are trying to achieve and therefore that a health promoter should define clear aims and objectives before commencing any form of action (see Figure 8.4). Planning should provide you with the answer to three questions:

- What am I trying to achieve?
- What am I going to do?
- How will I know whether I have succeeded?

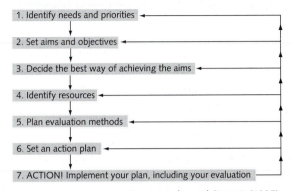

1. Identify needs and priorities
2. Set aims and objectives
3. Decide the best way of achieving the aims
4. Identify resources
5. Plan evaluation methods
6. Set an action plan
7. ACTION! Implement your plan, including your evaluation

Source: Ewles and Simnett (1995)

Figure 8.4 A flow chart for planning and evaluating health promotion

Setting objectives

It is important to start by differentiating between an aim and an objective:

- **Aim** – a broad goal.
- **Objective** – a specific goal to be achieved.

Any one aim may have several supplementary objectives within it, whilst objectives are usually defined as being SMART (see below).

Specific	Defined in clear terms
Measurable	When the work is finished we can see whether the objective has been achieved (or not)
Achievable	The target is realistic, i.e. within our power to change
Relevant	Is focused on addressing the issue within our broad aim
Timed	We have agreed a time scale by which we expect to have delivered this objective

Objectives which are not SMART are not aids to effective planning and may be aims which require breaking down further into specific objectives. Without this level of detail an objective becomes unmeasurable and therefore evaluation of the work is undermined.

Identification of target audience

Identifying your target audience for a campaign starts with the question – what is the health need which I should be addressing? The need for a campaign will usually come from one of four sources:

- **Normative need** – defined by an expert or professional according to their own standards. Where something falls short of this standard then a need is identified, e.g. percentage of people who are overweight or obese.
- **Felt need** – needs which people feel, i.e. things we want. For example, people might want their food to be free of genetically modified (GM) products.

- **Expressed need** – a felt need which is voiced. For example, the felt need to have GM-free food becomes an issue of public debate with pressure groups focusing on it.
- **Comparative need** – arises from comparisons between similar groups of people, where one group is in receipt of health promotion activity and the other is not. Examples here might be one school having a well thought out and planned Personal, Social and Health Education (PSHE) curriculum and another not.

Therefore as a health promoter the first action in undertaking any campaign is to identify the source of the need you are considering and this will identify who you are targeting.

Liaison with other agencies

Health promotion is rarely effective when the activity is focused within one organisation. As we saw at the beginning of this unit the causes of ill health are so broad that it requires a wide ranging response across agencies to influence health for the good. This is reflected in current government thinking through statutory duties to work in partnership on planning mechanisms such as the local community plan, Health Improvement Programme, community safety strategy, etc. When working with other agencies there are some key lessons to be learned, as shown below.

Effective partnership working is based on having:

- clear objectives
- a shared vision
- an understanding of where the partnership fits with other pressures/priorities
- an open approach to learning from the partnership
- partners with a strong ownership of the partnership
- the capacity to change mainstream service provision
- the right people with the appropriate level of authority to make this happen
- clear reporting and monitoring systems
- clear communication channels, within and across organisations
- the ability to pool budgets and release existing resources
- a commitment to evaluating their progress and the outcome of their work.

Source: Summarised from King's Fund findings (Autumn 2000)

Construct research tool

It is likely that as part of the work a health promoter will need to conduct some form of research. This might be to identify the need (as suggested earlier) or to assess whether they have achieved the objectives as part of the evaluation process. When carrying out any research it is important to consider the following steps:

1 Define the purpose of your research.
2 Review the existing literature – has your research already been carried out somewhere else?
3 Plan the study methodology for the investigation.
4 Test the methodology by carrying out a small-scale pilot.
5 Review the findings of your pilot and review your methodology in the light of these findings.
6 Carry out the research.

7 Analyse the information.

8 Draw your conclusions based on your findings.

9 Compile a report of your findings for the target audience identified in step one.

As part of the research you might choose to use various types of research tools, as shown in the table below.

Research tool	Comments
Questionnaire	• Useful for collecting information from large numbers of people • Needs to be as simple as possible – design and wording is key • Can be answered anonymously and therefore respondents may be more truthful • Cost-effective in that it can be distributed to large numbers of people at once • Needs careful piloting • Response rate is traditionally low
Personal interview	• Allows the development of a rapport which can encourage the subject to expand on their answers • Subject may be more expressive verbally than in writing • May provide information the interviewer hadn't thought to ask • Bias in the questioning and reporting is almost inevitable
Sampling	• Useful where collecting from the whole population or group is too costly or time consuming • Random (e.g. every tenth person on the electoral role) or quota (targets particular segments within a group, e.g. by age or sex) • Usually provides an accurate reflection of the population studied
Observation	• Might include an assessment of a person's behaviour, e.g. the make up of the weekly shop or physiological monitoring such as blood pressure or peak flow measurements

For more details on how to conduct research, see Unit 3.

Link to national campaigns

Inevitably, a high proportion of campaigning activity is linked to national campaigns. This is for two main reasons.

The first is that national campaigns are better resourced, for example through the provision of leaflets, posters, supportive media coverage, possibly small-scale funding and national advice on operationalising your work locally. In the past this role was taken on by the Health Education Authority which both produced the materials but also supported the role of local practitioners in activities for major campaigns such as National No Smoking Day and Drink-wise Day. However, the HEA has now been replaced by the Health Development Agency (HDA) which has a very different role, and the production of key campaigning materials has passed to the Department of Health. However, it is important to recognise that most government departments produce what might be considered campaigning material for health promotion. Examples might include:

- road safety pamphlets and cycling information from the Department of Transport
- energy conservation and recycling information from the Department of the Environment
- information for parents on helping children to read from the Department for Education and Employment
- advice on benefits from the Department for Social Security.

Most national campaigns support key national strategy and therefore offer opportunities for local agencies to identify how they are supporting government programmes locally. For example, all local health services will be expected to address the issues of smoking and therefore National No Smoking Day presents a high-profile opportunity to link in with a national campaign and report that action as part of the performance monitoring activity for the services involved.

End of unit test

1 Describe the key features of each of the following lay accounts of health:
  a The body as a machine
  b The health promotion account
  c God's power
  d Body under siege
  e Robust individualism
  f Will power.

2 Give five key features of the medical model of health.

3 Complete the following table to identify the relevant aspects of health or their key features:

Aspect	Description
	concerned with body mechanics
Mental health	
Emotional health	
	the ability to make and maintain relationships with others
Spiritual health	

4 Identify whether the following statements are true or false:
  a The disability a person experiences is determined by the way in which other people respond to that difference.
  b Since the Black Report of 1988, it has been clearly identified and acknowledged that those from the lowest social groupings experience the best health in society.
  c Because women make up a higher proportion of the older population there are often lower rates of illnesses specifically associated with women.
  d Suicide is twice as common in women as in men.
  e Black people and minority ethnic groups have higher risks of mortality from a range of diseases such as diabetes, liver cancer, tuberculosis, stroke and heart disease.

f Men unemployed at both census dates in 1971 and 1981 had mortality rates twice that of the rest of other men in that age range and those men who were unemployed at one census date had an excess mortality of 27 per cent.

5 Explain what each of the following means and give a suitable example for each:
  a primary prevention
  b secondary prevention
  c tertiary prevention.

6 Complete the following table to illustrate the five approaches to health promotion for promoting physical activity:

	Aim	Example: physical activity
Medical	Freedom from medically defined disease and disability	*Aim* – freedom from heart disease and other inactivity related disorders *Activity* –
	Individual behaviour conducive to freedom from disease	*Aim* – *Activity* – persuasive education to encourage the inactive to become active
Educational		*Aim* – clients will have understanding of the effects of being inactive on health, resulting in a decision whether or not to become active, which they then act on *Activity* – giving information to clients about the effects of inactivity. Helping them to learn how to manage a more active lifestyle if they want to
	Working with clients on the clients' own terms	
Societal change	Physical and social environment which enables choice of healthier lifestyle	*Aim* – *Activity* – encourage alternative transport options, showers at work, etc. Provide on-site exercise facilities encourage flexible working to enable people to access facilities as the norm. Banning tobacco advertising and sports' sponsorship

7 Give three examples of international agencies with a role in promoting health and a suitable example of the work they might undertake.

8 Place the following organisations into the relevant category in the table below:

IEHO   MIND   UNISON   BMA   NCT   NRA   UKCC
NUM   Railtrack   NUT   FPA   RoSPA

National agencies which can contribute to health promotion	Examples
Voluntary organisations	
Professional organisations	
Trade unions	
Commercial and industrial organisations	

9 List five issues which a health promoter would need to consider for ethical decision-making in a piece of health promotion work.

10 Complete the following passage by filling in the missing words:

Wholesale changes may result in the landscape of health-promoting activity when governments change. For example, the concentration on _____ in the Conservative government's _____ White Paper is in stark contrast to the contract between individual and government for each to play their part in the Labour government's 'Our Healthier Nation' health strategy of _____.

The _____ which illustrated the widening health gap between rich and poor in the country was suppressed by the government of the day, and the word _____ was largely replaced by the term 'variations' because of its sensitivity to that word. Government action also compounded inequalities, e.g. through the introduction of _____ which forbade schools from 'promoting homosexuality' creating a climate where schools felt unable to address issues of _____ . The government of the time ensured that the _____ _____ of the 1980s avoided any reference to risk-taking behaviours, which were deemed too sensitive for the public and ran with a theme of _____ , leaving many people asking – what is this ignorance, and how do you catch it?

11 Describe three features of screening programmes which contribute to them remaining a contentious issue.

12 What were the four headline targets for improving health in 'Our Healthier Nation'?

13 Describe the role and main features of the Health Improvement Programme.

14 Identify which of the following statements are true or false:
  a The proportion of both men and women who are overweight or obese has steadily declined since 1980.

  b The current trends show that the proportion of fat in our diets has remained the same since the early 1980s.

  c In 1996 61 per cent of men and 52 per cent of women were clinically obese.

  d The current recommendation for physical activity levels which promote heart health is to be vigorously active for at least 30 minutes 3 times per week.

  e Between 1995 and 1997 there was a 53 per cent rise in rates of gonorrhoea and a 47 per cent rise in rates of chlamydia amongst the 55–60-year age group.

  f A lifetime non-smoker is 60 per cent less likely to have CHD and 30 per cent less likely to have a stroke than a smoker.

  g The incidence of malignant melanoma amongst men in class 5 is nearly 5 times that for men in class 1 and this is repeated for women where the difference is approximately twice that of class 1 for class 5.

15 Identify the two main routes for gaining media coverage of health promotion events and give examples of each.

16 You have been asked to select a leaflet promoting healthy eating to schoolchildren, for use by school nurses in schools. What issues will you take into consideration in your selection?

17 If you were asked to design a poster, list three physical and three motivational issues you would take into consideration during your design process.

References and further reading

Acheson, D. (1998) *The Independent Inquiry into Inequalities in Health,* London: HMSO

Benzeval, M., Judge, K., Whitehead, M. (1995) *Tackling Inequalities in Health, an Agenda for Action,* London: King's Fund Publishing

Ewles, L. and Simnett, I. (1999) *Promoting Health – A Practical Guide,* London: Ballière Tindall

HM Government (1992) *The Health of the Nation,* HMSO

HM Government (1997) *The New NHS: Modern Dependable,* HMSO

HM Government (1997) *Saving Lives: Our Healthier Nation,* HMSO

Jones, L. (1994) *Social Control of Health and Health Work,* Basingstoke: Macmillan

Jones, L. and Sidell, M. (1997) *The Challenge of Promoting Health – Exploration and Action,* Buckingham: Open University

Jones, L. and Sidell, M. (1997) *Promoting Health – Knowledge and Practice,* Oxford: Macmillan Education

Moonie, N. (2000) *Advanced Health and Social Care,* Oxford: Heinemann

9 Health and society

This unit examines the relationship between social structures within society and the influences they can have on the health and well-being of populations and individuals. The unit provides essential information, which will be called upon again and again in other units of study as you work towards completion of this award. Therefore, it is important to develop a sound understanding of the sociological theories and applications that are drawn upon throughout your studies.

What you need to learn

- The relationship between the structure of society and social and cultural aspects of health
- Discrimination and inequalities in health care
- Health status in a social context

The relationship between the structure of society and social and cultural aspects of health

The way society is organised can and does have a profound impact on social and cultural aspects of health. For example, society can be divided into separate groups or communities and the way in which these groups find themselves living can seriously affect their health in a positive or negative way. However, before we can explore the effects of societal structure on health we need to be aware of some basic sociological terminology and exactly what is meant when we discuss certain aspects of human life.

Social structure

Social classifications are systems or ways of measuring similarities and differences between and within population groups. We know that some people, for example, die at a much younger age than others; we also know that women tend to live longer than men. It is through the study of difference and sameness in society that we can find out why these phenomena take place. In theory, once a cause has been identified for negative (or positive) difference, i.e. dying at a younger age or living longer, action can be taken by governments and society to provide equality for all people.

When sociologists are studying social structures and health and illness they tend to concentrate on several specific areas of human life. These are:

- social class
- culture
- the family
- education
- employment and unemployment.

Having insight into these areas of human life in any country allows sociologists and other researchers to make population comparisons with other countries. For example, we know that the USA tends to have a population that is more overweight than the population in the UK (although we are quickly catching up!).

Definitions

- **Social class** – the way society is organised into different layers (stratifications/strata), often using wealth and power as the measure of difference. Some sociologists would argue that social class no longer exists and that individuals do not define themselves through the class in which they live. Others would argue that social class is 'alive and well' and people are aware, and in many cases proud, of their class. We know that the social class a person belongs to will affect their health status in a variety of ways; one example being the length of time a person is likely to live and the amount of good health or poor health they are likely to experience during their lifetime.

- **Culture** – we all belong to a particular culture of our own. It can be classed as the way we live our lives following the rules, traditions and norms of the groups or society to which we belong. In other words, culture is something we learn from the people we live with. The learning of our culture helps us to function effectively within the social systems and organisations of our world; for example, knowing how to behave in school, work, leisure, families, etc. Culture also has a major impact on health status; for example, people who do not eat meat either through choice or tradition are unlikely to contract CJD; on the other hand, groups of people who traditionally do not undertake any form of exercise are at an increased risk of cardiovascular disease (heart disease).

- **The family** – at one time 'the traditional nuclear' family was seen as the ideal. This kind of family has certain characteristics, for example it is small and consists of a married mother and father with two or three children. However, we know that this form of family structure is not necessarily the norm. For example, we have reconstituted families (step families), where one or both parents have been married before, there are many single parent families, as well as more same-sex family groups, and of course many families have couples who co-habit and never marry. No matter what type of family a person comes from, the effects upon their health status will be felt for the rest of their lives. One example could be that a child learns to cook and eat the same foods as the parents, therefore if a poor (perhaps high-fat, low-fibre) diet is the norm throughout childhood this will continue through the next generations – along with the ill health that it is likely to result in.

- **Education** – some would argue that this is possibly the most important institution in society. All social groups experience some form of education, whether from family or from external organisations. In the western world this usually consists of attending an educational establishment such as a school from the age of 3 or 4 until adulthood. The purpose underpinning education would depend on the theoretical approach that you adopt. For example, functionalists would see education as having three broad functions. These are:
  - to help maintain society by integrating young people into the cultural values of their society
  - to ensure that young people discover their true abilities, thus enabling them to choose the best job for their abilities

– to make sure that society will have sufficient skills and knowledge to enable the modern society to take its place in a global economy.

From our point of view, education is another system that has the potential to affect our health status. Examples could include: sex education and the way it contributes towards a reduction in unwanted pregnancies and sexually transmitted disease; biology and food technology education can inform the student of ways of maintaining a balanced, healthy lifestyle; and, of course, drug and tobacco education can contribute towards combating drug abuse throughout society. However, we need to remember that education should continue throughout life (lifelong learning) and, therefore, adults are also subject to health education and the potential changes to health it offers.

- **Employment and unemployment** – in some ways employment and unemployment can be explored together. They are the opposite side of the same coin. However, we do have some difficulties when exploring employment. In the first place we need to decide whether we are discussing formal employment, i.e. going to work, earning a wage, paying income tax, etc., or whether we are talking about employment that could be classed as informal or unregulated; examples here might include housework, informal caring for others or perhaps something like unpaid child minding.

For the purpose of this unit we are talking about employment that is often classed as 'earning a living', i.e. formal employment that involves going to work, having an employer (or being an employer) and earning a salary or wage. The effects of employment upon health are enormous. We know that people in low-paid, dangerous work are more likely to die young from accidents and heart disease (possibly brought on by a poor standard of living) than are those people in highly paid, comfortable work.

Comparing Britain to the USA and parts of Europe

This is not an easy task because in order to compare accurately we should be comparing 'like with like'. However, no two countries are ever the same (think about culture, for example). In this case we can compare to a degree because all the countries are classed as 'western'. This means that in the main they are wealthy countries sharing in global wealth to the benefit of their residents. They have wealthy sections in their populations and people who live below the poverty line. In both cases their experience of health and illness is very similar to our own populations.

We can argue that the USA and Europe's major cause of death and ill health is heart disease and cancers, as it is in Britain. Screening programmes and health education programmes in Northern America involve similar activities and information to the UK programmes. It is also notable that the child health and maternal health of the population is also very similar.

Key issues

Find out about the heart disease and breast cancer statistics for Britain and the USA. Identify the preventive action taken by both countries and compare your findings with those of another person.

Carry out the same process for a European country of your own choice, but this time use heart disease statistics for comparison.

Now that we have explored some of the basic terminology and links to health status used in this unit we can explore further how each of these concepts has the potential to affect health and well-being.

Social class structure

Features of social class

As we have already said, social class is a way of measuring people. Researchers and politicians use the information gathered to make decisions about the policies and laws required to achieve the best possible conditions for society. When social class was first identified in the eighteenth century, people were measured through the job they held (mostly agricultural workers). This became known as the Registrar General's Social Classification.

Throughout the twentieth century, people (especially men) have continued to be classed by the job they hold. However, the classifications have become more and more difficult to handle as the number and type of jobs have changed and developed.

Key issues

Look at the table on page 337 and then answer the following questions.

- How many classes are there?
- What are these classes based on?
- What is the main difference between the middle classes and the working classes?
- Which class do you think accounts for most of the population in Britain?

It is likely that you have noted that there are five social class groups (known as divisions or stratifications). Each social class is based on the occupation of the person being classified. Answering the question about 'the main difference' is more problematic.

If you look behind the information presented you are likely to see that education and income are the two main differences between the middle classes and the working classes. In other words, one section of the population is more likely to have access to the 'good things in life' than are the other section of the population. Inequalities!

It is notable in contemporary society that the middle classes IIIN and IIIM are the most numerous in terms of job occupations in Britain.

A new system of classifying people into social groups was used in the 2001 census (see table on page 338). (This is a method used by researchers to collect data relating to human populations. Every ten years demographers carry out a national survey to find out about the lifestyles, income, and education, etc. of the general population. Completing the information is compulsory.)

What is a demographer?

A researcher who counts people according to their social characteristics; for example, age, housing, gender, occupation, marital status.

Aspects of culture

We have already discovered that all people belong to a cultural group of one sort or another. Simply put, this is a group of the population who share the same beliefs and traditions as each other. These shared ideas and values help the individual to recognise themselves (self-identity) and ways in which they might be different from other groups of the population. Factors which have a strong role to play in the development of culture, are shown in Figure 9.1.

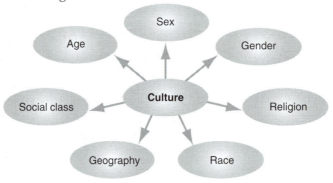

Figure 9.1 Factors in the development of culture

Each of these factors has the potential to affect our health status in one way or another.

Age

The age group we belong to has a strong role to play in our culture and clearly has an impact on our health. It may be that people over retirement age feel that they should no longer frequent public houses and social clubs (because they are for/used by younger people); this could lead them to becoming isolated and lonely which will clearly affect their intellectual and social well-being. Another example of age affecting health status could include a reluctance to exercise in a public place for fear of ridicule or fear of leaving the home.

Ethnic group

This is perhaps best explained as those people who 'share the same gene pool' or biological features. They are individuals who have the same origins and ancestors in the long term. The ethnic group you belong to can clearly affect your health status. We know that some ethnic groups, for example people from the Asian subcontinent, are more likely to develop heart disease and diabetes than are others. Other effects of ethnicity could include inherited diseases such as sickle cell anaemia.

Gender

In exactly the same way as age affects the cultural norms of a group of people so does gender. In the first instance we need to be clear about what we mean when we use the word *gender*. Sociologists usually see a difference between sex and gender. Sex is the biological difference between males and females whilst 'gender' is the role taken on by individuals to enable them to fit into society's expectations of them as either a male or a female.

The way you are brought up will affect the beliefs and values you hold about yourself. Clearly this also has the potential to affect health and well-being; for example, women may feel the need to strive for an unnaturally thin body shape, whilst men may feel that they should be 'strong and muscular'. In both cases food choices and exercise habits will be affected. If, however, we are talking about the difference between male and female we return once more to the issue of longevity, i.e. women tend to live longer than men (who are more at risk of heart disease). It also used to be that more men than women died of lung disease (through their smoking habits) but now we are seeing a rapid increase in the number of women also dying from lung cancer as the number of female smokers rises.

Social class

This element of our culture is another very powerful factor in terms of our health status. It is our social class which often denotes how much money we will have to spend on life's necessities (such as housing, food and heating) and luxuries (such as a car and membership of a gym). Each of these clearly has the potential to affect our lifestyle and therefore our health experience. However, it is also social class that gives people a 'strong sense of belonging', which in turn defines our friendship networks. For example, do we mix with drug users or pushers or people who spend their time in other dangerous activities or do we spend our time with people whose priorities are education, exercise and work? How we spend our time and who we spend it with, will ultimately affect the health choices we make and our experience of illness or health and well-being.

Some sociologists would argue that as traditional working classes are no longer relevant because of 'status' being measured by wealth and possessions, new social groups come into being. For example, if class is based on income and living standards where do homeless/jobless people fit into the class structure? They are often dependent on state benefits, which Saunders (1990) would argue leads to these people being classed as an 'underclass'. Therefore, we can see that these people are already disadvantaged in terms of housing and Maslow's most basic needs, so it is likely that they are also disadvantaged in the health stakes. For example, they are more likely to suffer from diseases of the chest such as bronchitis; living on cold damp streets will also result in bone and joint disorders; furthermore, lack of food and basic hygiene is also going to affect their overall health status in a negative manner.

Key issue

Look back at the social class chart on page 338 and discuss with another person the implications of being called an 'underclass'. Examine the situation from the point of view of a homeless/jobless person, the middle classes and a politician.

Geographical location

Another very powerful factor that influences our cultural norms and health status is our environment. The country, city or even the electoral ward that we live in can be closely linked to health. Equally, the regional area of our towns and cities can also have an influence of its own. For example, people from the south of England are notably healthier than are people from the North. This could be due in some part to higher levels of income and the traditional work patterns that have evolved over time. Whatever the difference is, people living in the south-east of England are more likely to live longer than those people living in (say) Glasgow, for example. Still using Glasgow as an example, we know that this city has a high incidence of drug misuse and a high rate of people living on or below the poverty line. What might be the connection here do you think?

Again, people who live in mainly rural communities are likely to develop a different culture and health experience to those people who live in cities. People living in rural communities are often poorer than those in the cities, resulting in poor levels of health.

Theory into practice

Find statistical evidence of some of the differences between people who live in a rural area and those who live in an urban area. Make notes of the effects this may have on their health and well-being, and how this in turn could affect the health and care services.

Profile of Britain

The populations in Britain are constantly changing. Human life is never constant. People migrate from one country to another, people grow older and babies are born. All of these events change a population profile.

Within Britain there is a diverse range of peoples and cultural groups. From our earliest records different cultures have lived, settled and helped to develop the country we have today. For example, the Romans lived here over two thousand years ago and in 1066 the French settled in England and brought with them their customs and ways of living. From the 1950s onwards people from the (New) Commonwealth also settled in Britain to work and develop (in particular) the cotton industry following World War II. The people who worked in these industries often found themselves in low-paid, physically demanding work. Their housing tended to be poorer than that of the white, indigenous populations and their status within society generally lower than average.

As a result of this their health status was also likely to be poorer than the indigenous population.

As the need to track and record population difference and similarity has become greater (especially through inequalities in health), the 1991 census asked respondents to identify their ethnic status for the first time. The following classifications were offered to those filling in the forms:

- White
- Black – Caribbean
- Black – African
- Black – other (please specify)
- Bangladeshi
- Pakistani
- Indian
- Chinese
- Any other ethnic group (please describe).

As a result of the data collection we are now able to gain a fuller picture of the living and working conditions of a range of different population groups. Health status can be explored and the data collected used to plan services and policies to meet the needs of all populations and communities, no matter what their background.

In contemporary Britain there are several major changes, which have been or are affecting our populations. For example, people now live to a much older age than ever before. The average life expectancy for women is about 78 years of age and for men about 75 (see Figure 9.2). If you then remember that many more older people will live well into their 80s we can see that this will have a huge impact on the country's services and systems. The longer people live, the more likely it is that they will suffer some form of ill health.

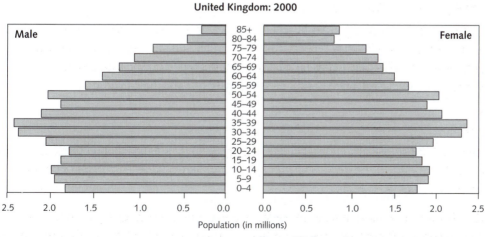

United Kingdom: 2000

Population (in millions)

Source: US Census Bureau, International Data Base

Figure 9.2 The population pyramid

Think it over

Use the population pyramid (in Figure 9.2) to identify the numbers of older people in the UK. What might be the implications of a rising, older population for health care, pension provision and housing?

In addition to more people living longer there are also differences in the number of births. In the main, the birth rate is dropping but in some areas more births are taking place. The most important point to note about this part of the British profile is that the babies born now are more likely to live than they were 50 or 100 years ago. Again, this has implications for our services and systems.

Theory into practice

Find out what the birth rate is for your area. What might be the long-term effects (20 years) of this on health care services and education provision in your area?

Assessment activity 9.1

Using the country you live in, describe the current social and class structures of the population. Include graphs and charts to demonstrate your findings before identifying possible future changes in the population profile.

Effects of personal beliefs and preferences on health

It is now well documented that the way a person is socialised (brought up) will affect the way they think about health and the way they live their lives. For example, in a 1973 study of middle-class people Herzlich found that people saw 'health' as being a lack of disease or illness. Other people describe 'health' as being physically fit and strong, which could mean that they believe in the value of exercise and healthy eating. On the other hand, the World Health Organisation (1946) described health as: 'A physical, social and mental well-being and not simply the absence of disease or infirmity'. This would indicate that there is much more to health than just being physically fit.

Think it over

What do you think health is? What parts of health does the WHO definition include? How important do you think each part is in contributing to overall well-being?

Whatever *you* think health is, your thoughts and attitudes towards your own (and others') health will have been influenced by the people around you and your experiences of life. In some social class groups it is noticeable that the attitude towards health is 'fatalistic'. In other words, it does not really matter what you do – if you are going to be ill, then you will be! These people see their health as being out of their control. Others have a different attitude towards health. They may feel that eating healthily and taking regular exercise will keep them fit and free of disease. They clearly believe that they do have (some) control over their health status.

It is important to remember that the environment will also affect the way you think and behave. For example, people who are unemployed and perhaps living in poor quality housing, experience much more ill health than people in high-paid employment. If this is how their parents (and their parents before them) lived, then we could reasonably expect them to feel that perhaps there is nothing they can do to give themselves a long and healthy life (i.e. fatalistic view).

Think it over

Lynda is a keen fell runner (just like her mother before her); she runs 30 miles a week regularly and eats a low-fat, high-carbohydrate diet. She is fairly relaxed and stress free. On the other hand, her friend Fiona does not take any exercise and 'comfort eats' to relieve the stress of her demanding job. She does not see any point in making herself miserable – after all, what will be will be. Her parents died at an early age and so did her grandfather from a heart attack.

The way we choose to live our lives is known as our 'lifestyle' and many health professionals would argue that our lifestyle has a direct effect on our health and well-being. It is now generally accepted by all populations 'that health is to a considerable extent, dependent on behaviour and in one's own hands' (Blaxter, 1990).

Research has demonstrated many connections between individual behaviour (lifestyle) and disease and ill health. For example, the link between smoking and lung cancer is well established and the link between lack of exercise and heart disease is also becoming clearer. However, people still make choices which place them in an 'at risk' situation from their lifestyle choices.

Theory into practice

Discuss the links between other lifestyle issues, for example diet, alcohol and stress to identify disease or illness attached to them. Why do you think people make 'unhealthy choices' in relation to their lifestyle? Find evidence from national or local research to demonstrate the links between lifestyle and ill health. How might this affect the funding and running of hospital services?

Health professionals often concentrate their health education activities on persuading 'at risk' individuals to change their unhealthy behaviours. For example, we are all used to seeing the 'Quit smoking' adverts on the television or the 'Don't drink and drive' adverts at Christmas.

Think it over

What do you think might be the difficulties for a health educator in changing an individual's lifestyle behaviours? Remember to include the influence of culture and social class in your deliberations.

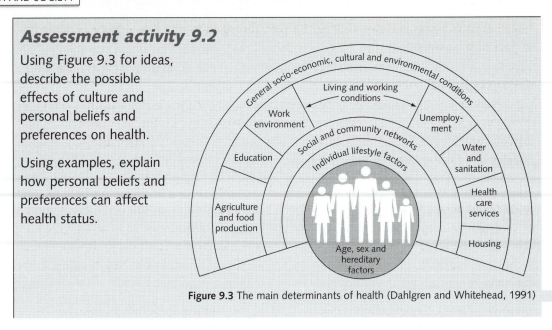

Assessment activity 9.2

Using Figure 9.3 for ideas, describe the possible effects of culture and personal beliefs and preferences on health.

Using examples, explain how personal beliefs and preferences can affect health status.

Figure 9.3 The main determinants of health (Dahlgren and Whitehead, 1991)

Factors affecting families' health and well-being

Social class

We have already explored some of the issues relating to social class and health earlier in this chapter. However, there are many other issues which we have not yet touched upon. Sociologists and health professionals use social class as a way of comparing the health status of different groups in the population. Their research is identifying many major issues which need to be addressed in Britain. For example, we know that families who live in the south of England (usually higher class groups) have better health than families who live in the North (including Scotland). Arguably, this could be due to some of the following reasons:

- more employment in the South
- higher wages paid in the South
- the South has warmer weather
- better access to health services in the South
- less deprivation and poor housing in the South.

But this is not the end of the story! Researchers have shown that inequalities relating to the social class of the family do not only exist in the North/South divide, they exist in the same region and even in the same town. This means that in a town, for example Blackburn, in the north of England, some wards (electoral districts) with lower social class families (made up of low skilled or unemployed people) have high levels of poverty and deprivation, with poor, damp housing and therefore ill health related to these damp conditions. It is also the case that their children often do not achieve as high a level of education as other social class groups, which can mean they will never 'escape' the conditions their families live in.

On the other hand, other wards in Blackburn (with higher social class families) have a better standard of living with good quality housing, gardens, parks and access to facilities such as leisure centres and supermarkets, leading them towards a better health status than their nearby neighbours. We can see then, that an individual's or family's social class (i.e. high or low) will affect health through the way it affects every other aspect of their lives.

Geography of the community

However, social class is not the only factor to affect a family's health and well-being. We have already explored the effects of the North/South divide, the ward differences in towns and cities and touched upon rural differences, but there are other geographical factors to consider as well.

These include the way that health and social care services are funded. For example, it is possible to access treatment and services in some areas of the country but not in others. This is a result of prioritising funding towards certain services and not others. This is known as treatment (or care) by postcode. Clearly if a family cannot access the health care services they need, then they will be disadvantaged and their health will suffer as a result.

Further geographical differences are the location of health and social services; for example, most of the teaching hospitals are in the south of England in the more affluent areas. This can mean that access to the most 'up-to-date' medical provision is limited to those areas. There has also been the suggestion that all the 'best' doctors set up practice in the more affluent areas (where their patients are in better health anyway!), leaving the poor, the sick and the infirm (in less affluent areas) with less well qualified doctors and health care workers.

Think it over

What do you think might be the result of some of the best services in health care being located in the South? What are the implications for people living in both the south and north of Britain?

Attitudes and beliefs

We have already seen that a family's attitudes and beliefs towards health and well-being will affect their health status. If the parents of a child smoke it is likely that the child will also take up the habit. If the family diet consists of high-fat foods and convenience foods, that is the diet the children are likely to follow for the rest of their lives. Remember the people who have a 'fatalistic attitude' towards their health? We can argue here that they are unlikely to seek help or use preventative services in time to make a real difference to their life expectancy. On the other hand, those people who feel they can make a difference to their longevity will follow all the 'expert' advice available and even come up with preventative actions themselves.

Think it over

Why do you make the food choices that you do?

Factors affecting groups' and communities' health and well-being

This section of the unit continues to link very closely with the issue of social class and the environment. It is clear that if a community feels that it is disadvantaged and that there is nothing it can do to change its health or social status (think of the unemployed and the way they often feel hopeless and helpless), it will have no motivation to 'fight' to change their circumstances.

> **Motivation?**
>
> That surge of enthusiasm that makes you *want* to do things. People who are well motivated can often take control of their lives and plan for continued improvement to their life chances.

Sometimes whole groups of the community feel disempowered and disenchanted with what they have, or more often 'have not', in comparison with other community groups. Some minority groups do not have equal access to the health and social care services. They may also find that their children are attending schools with poorer league tables than other schools and so the disadvantage moves from one generation to the next.

It is in the hope of changing this situation that community action groups are often formed. These may be led by members of the community or by health and social care professionals. In each case, the action is designed to improve the life chances of the individuals within that community.

Case study

The Mill Hill Community Action Group was formed by a small group of parents who wanted to start a playgroup for their pre-school children. They got together to find out how they could obtain premises and funding for the playgroup. They started by following the suggestion of one of their members to invite their local councillor to a meeting so that they could state what they wanted and find out how she could help them to achieve their aims.

What might be the advantages to the Mill Hill Community Action Group of working together to achieve their aims?

Case study

Parents against Speed

This is a community action group who formed to work together to get traffic calming measures in place after two children were killed when trying to cross the road to the playing fields. They formed a lobbying committee who attend all the council meetings to make sure the group's 'voice' is heard.

Key issue

Find out about community action groups in your area. Make notes about their priorities and methods of working before exploring the health related links in their work. A useful source of information is the library or Citizen's Advice Bureau.

Community action is not just about dealing with services, it can also be about enabling a community to learn new skills in order to bring about a better standard of living. There are many funding agencies involved in supporting community groups in this way.

For example, the European Structural Fund was established to target money into those areas of social deprivation where extra finance is needed to bring about improvements in health and well-being. One example is the use of European money to train members of the community to work as advocates for those people without a 'voice'. In a similar way the Single Regeneration Budget is also targeted to improve areas and communities and to bring about lasting change to both living conditions and health status for the families involved.

Community action aims to bring about a better standard of living

Community groups and other organisations access the money through a system of 'bidding'. This means that they have to suggest a project or activity that meets the needs of the funders (in bringing about improvements). This is then compared to the list of criteria and if all is well the activity can be funded. This could be for a short period of time, i.e. months, or for as long as five–six years.

A key role for some health/social care professionals is in writing bids to obtain the money for the communities or in training the communities to write the bids themselves, so that they can use the money to the advantage of their community.

Key issue

Research your own area (or another if necessary) to find out if there are any funded community action/development programmes. Identify the funding being used and the purpose of the action. What are the expected health/development benefits to the local population?

Other community action may take the form of 'lobbying'. This is where community groups (and sometimes individuals) try to change laws and processes often because they feel there is a better way of managing a particular issue. For example, Greenpeace is a lobby group and so is Friends of the Earth. Age Concern would also argue that it has a lobbying role on behalf of its service users, as would many disability campaigners and groups.

Think it over

Find out about a lobby group with a health and social care role that you are interested in. What are its main aims? Who does it represent? What action does it take when trying to bring about change?

Discrimination and inequalities in health care

Inequalities in health

We have already introduced the fact that there are major health and status differences between population groups; for example, the employment differences between the people in the north and south of the country and the way they contribute to inequalities in living conditions. However, as we have already noted there are also the differences in the health experiences of our populations. It has been argued for many years that these differences or inequalities could be as a result of gender and/or social class.

Gender

Whether you are born male or female has the potential to affect your health status. We already know that women live longer than men. We also know that men are more likely to have a heart attack than are women (at least up until the age of menopause, when women develop the same risk as men). So what might be the reasons for this?

The natural selection theory would argue that women are stronger than men and therefore, live longer.

Behavioural theory would put forward the argument that men are more likely to be risk takers, for example smoking, consuming alcohol and taking more dangerous jobs than women (although this is beginning to change).

Structural theory would say that women have been protected from dangerous jobs and situations through the laws of the land.

Key issue

Working with another person, choose one of the theories identified above to research further. Prepare a short presentation of your findings to give a report to your colleagues.

Social class

Health can almost certainly be argued to relate directly to the social status of a person. In other words, the social group to which you belong has the potential to affect your health and your life chances. Perhaps some social classes should carry a 'health warning'!

Life chances was first described by Max Weber who pointed out that a person's social class extended way beyond the amount of money they could earn, to include other important factors; for example, the quality of their life and the positive or negative chances that might be offered to them as they progress through life.

Case study

A company manager is usually well paid and lives in good housing with a garden; owns a family car as well as a car paid for through work. He often receives company 'perks', such as a season ticket to the football and has opportunities open to him for career advancement.

• Compare this situation to that of a worker in a fast-food restaurant.

In this case study it is unlikely that the worker in the fast-food restaurant will have the same opportunities and life chances as the company manager. They have very few options open to them for career advancement, are unlikely to earn high wages and will stay that way; and the only company perk might be free food that, if typical of fast foods, is high in fat, sugar and salt and low in fibre and useful nutrients. Not much of a perk!

There is evidence that strongly points to poor health status for the lower working-class populations. This should hardly be surprising that people from the lower social groupings often experience unemployment, low income, poor life chances and to live in poor housing in poor surroundings isolated from other population groups.

Think it over

Which health risks are commonly associated with these living conditions? Find empirical evidence to support your findings.

It is likely that you will find data relating to, for example, chronic bronchitis, coughs and colds, perhaps you have linked the conditions to asthma and other chest disease. You might even have made a link between low income, poor diet and heart disease and cancers. We can also add a range of other issues to the social class/health status debate, as outlined below.

Health expectations
People living in poor conditions often do not expect to have good health. As already discussed, if this is what you are used to, then this is what you learn to expect. But even this can be taken further. It is likely that these people will be unaware of their rights as a patient or client within the health and social care services. It may be that they are aware of their rights but then do not know how to action them. This can result in missed treatment opportunities or failure to access support services to their best advantage.

Language and culture
People who use a different language from the service provider are also at a disadvantage in the 'health stakes'. This point is not just about having English as a first language, it is also about the use of language and, in particular, jargon.

People who have a different language from their health care professional are at a clear disadvantage. Not only must they communicate through a third person (perhaps an interpreter) and suffer the possible indignities that this may bring with it if they ever do 'make the appointment', but they must also rely on others to tell them about their rights and make appointments for them in the first place.

It is now well accepted that there are different regional dialects (accents) which in themselves can cause communication difficulties. But there are also differences in how the social groupings speak and use language. For example, people from the higher social classes are more likely to be well educated and therefore use 'long, complicated words' which people from other social classes may not understand.

Think it over

What might be the possible results of a service user from the working classes having a consultation with a higher social class health professional?

There is research to show that doctors tend to spend more time with their patients who are from a higher class (something similar to their own) than they do with their patients who are from a working-class background. Why do you think this is? Perhaps the expectations of the health professional differ from their patients?

Another difference between population groups that can contribute towards health inequalities is culture. We have already explored some of the implications of culture for health but, again, we can explore this subject to a greater level when we begin to examine the inequalities that exist.

The culture we have often dictates the way we should behave in certain circumstances. This can lead to difficulties with the health care service. For example, if you are from a culture that says a person should only be examined by a health professional of the same sex, and there is no one available, then you are disadvantaged and may even forgo the examination rather than break with tradition or taboo. This can (and often does) result in life-threatening conditions, such as cervical cancers, going undetected until it is too late for remedial action to be taken.

Stereotyping

This is where people have particular, set ideas about how a person or group of the population will respond or behave, in other words suggesting that some people are 'all the same'. For example, a practice receptionist may think that all teenage mothers are incapable of caring for their baby in an appropriate way or a school nurse might think that all children from a particular background do not eat fruit and vegetables. It is immediately clear that there are inherent dangers with stereotypical thinking. It is possible that client rights will be infringed – leading to discrimination and unequal services.

This appears to argue in the face of all we have explored up until now about population groups and families. However, there are always exceptions within any community and these must be allowed their individuality.

The Black Report

This report came about because the Secretary of State for Health in the late 1970s was concerned about the difference in death rates between the higher and lower social classes. The research was designed to identify the reasons for the difference in mortality rates. It was the first major study undertaken of social class difference and was led by Sir Douglas Black, a physician and researcher. The main aspect of the research used occupational class as the measure for exploring difference.

It highlighted the fact that people from low income groups died at a much earlier age than did those people from a higher income background. The Black Report also highlighted the health differences experienced by people from black and minority ethnic groups. Evidence was also provided in the report to demonstrate the regional differences in health and life expectancy and that sex differences were widespread across the country.

Key issue

Obtain a copy of the Black Report (1980) and read about the major differences in health status. Make a list of the recommendations made by the report and then decide if these are still relevant today, more than 20 years since publication.

Whitehead's Inquiry ('The health divide', 1987)

This followed on in 1987 from the work carried out by the Black Committee and explored more deeply the issues of poverty and deprivation. This research confirmed the findings of the Black Report and indicated that nothing had changed since its publication. However, 'The health divide' also noted that there were differences in the way that people were able to gain access to the services that they needed. Overall the report concluded that:

> 'In general, death rates in adults of lower working ages have declined more rapidly in the higher than the lower occupational classes... Indeed in some respects the health of the lower occupational groups has actually deteriorated' (Whitehead, 1987).

In other words, health status had become even more of a problem for the lower working classes.

Effects of culture and geographical situation

We already have an outline idea of how culture and geographical location might affect the health of different groups of the population. This section enables you to take this information further to give you some practice in reading and interpreting the data and statistics involved.

Key issue

Working with another person, use the information in Figure 9.4 to prepare a short presentation on the changes in the causes of mortality for males and females between 1911 and 1999. Briefly explain why you think the changes have occurred.

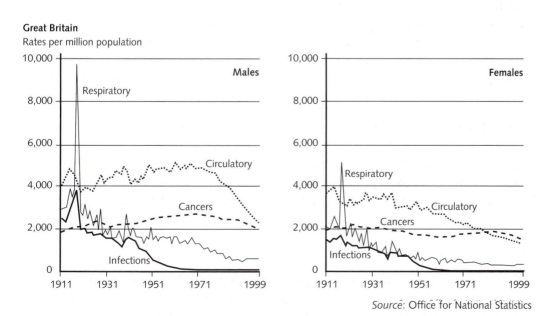

Great Britain
Rates per million population

Source: Office for National Statistics

Figure 9.4 Mortality, people aged 15–74: by gender and major cause

Assumptions and oppressions

This section continues with some of the issues of stereotyping and discrimination that we have already begun to explore. It is possible to affect the health and well-being of another individual or group of the population simply through the care practices that we provide. The way we use language to refer to people from different social groups or those with specific needs can also be oppressive and discriminatory.

People who have been marginalised within health and social care have challenged the policies and practices of service planners and providers; for example, action groups representing the interests of HIV-positive people and those people with disabilities.

As a result of being marginalised throughout the years, women and black and ethnic minority voices in particular demanded to be heard during the 1970s and 1980s. It is as a result of continuous campaigning by groups such as these that we now have policies and practices designed to support positive, anti-discriminatory practice.

Case study

Myra is a receptionist in a busy GPs' surgery. Yesterday she was very busy when Doris, a gypsy traveller, came in and asked her for an appointment. Doris explained that she was not a patient but had just arrived in the area.

Myra refused to give her an appointment. As she said to the practice nurse, 'Our doctors have better things to do than be pestered by the likes of them.'

- What beliefs and attitudes do you think Myra holds towards travellers?
- How might her beliefs and attitudes affect the health and well-being of Doris?

Looking at the case study above, it is possible that your thoughts have centred around the fact that Doris did not get her immediate health needs seen to. In this case you are right, but it is possible to take this discussion to a deeper level. For example, not only did Doris not get to see the doctor but she is likely to have felt embarrassed, angry and disillusioned about the whole situation. This in turn could have the following results: Doris will probably:

- continue to have the health problem (unless it resolves itself)
- avoid that particular surgery in the future
- not seek further health advice
- develop low self-esteem and self-value
- not ask for help when she or other family members really need it
- have a low opinion of the value of health care and so will not use available preventative services
- become another statistic of early death rates.

We can see that the receptionist's assumptions, and indeed oppression, of Doris because of her preferred mode of living has clearly affected her health as an individual. However, the damage does not stop here.

Case study

When Doris gets home, she invites the rest of her group in to discuss the situation further. She tells them not to bother visiting that GP as the receptionist is hostile to travellers. She advises that if any of them have health problems whilst they are in this area they should call on the accident and emergency services instead.

- What might be the implications of the GP receptionist's actions for travellers?
- What expectations do you think travellers are likely to have of the health service if this is the kind of response they regularly experience?

Over a period of time a whole community's expectations can be influenced by the treatment they receive at the hands of health care professionals. If we start by accepting the fact that a community is a group of the population who share common experiences, such as their environment, the way they live or the way they are treated, then we can see that Doris's experience will have reinforced their expectations of the health care system, as most of them will already have some experience of this kind of discrimination.

In addition to the discrimination Doris experienced there is also the issue of the Care Value Base (see Unit 1, page 3). Myra clearly demonstrated a lack of respect and value for Doris which breaks the principles of the Care Value Base, and Doris certainly did not get her rights from a public service that should treat everyone as an equal.

Key issue

Find out what the principles of the Care Value Base are and how they have the potential to affect the health and well-being of a client and social carer.

Travellers are not the only groups of the population to suffer from assumptions and oppression. The National Health Service as an institution has been accused of institutional paternalism and indeed racism; in other words, that paternalism and discrimination is inherent within the entire service. We need to remember that when health care services started in the 1940s they were developed for a white, middle class society. This can mean that the approaches and services required for today's client have to be different, and in some cases made appropriate, if they are to meet the needs of whole communities.

Key issues

Find out how, in the past, male consultants could be guilty of paternalistic practices with women.

Working with another person, discuss ways in which people from minority ethnic communities could be disadvantaged through their experience of the health and care services. What action is your own local health and care service taking to ensure equal opportunity for all?

Health status in a social context

Individuals

So, how easy is it for an individual to make changes to their own health status? To explore this issue we could start by examining our own health behaviours. For example, make a note of all the things that you have ever started to do to improve your own health and well-being, such as take up swimming once a week, eat less fatty foods, etc.

Now tick all those that you have successfully integrated into your lifestyle (in other words, those things that have become normal, everyday routines or behaviours). If you are anything like me and millions of other people there will be very few to tick – if any at all!

Making changes on an individual level is not easy. Think about how hard it is for someone to give up smoking or lose weight. However, it is clearly not impossible, as many have actually achieved changes. It would appear that if all support mechanisms are in place they may well encourage an 'individual to stick with it'.

The stages of change model (Prochaska and DiClemente, 1984) demonstrates how individuals go through several stages of the change process before they succeed in changing their behaviour (see Figure 9.5).

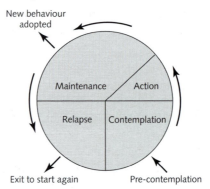

Figure 9.5 The stages of change model (adapted from Prochaska and DiClemente, 1984)

- **Contemplation** (thinking about change)
  At this point the client is aware that there is something that needs changing. It might be that they have developed a cough and feel that the time has come to stop smoking. This stage could last a few hours or several years!
- **Action** (preparing and making changes)
  Now the client has decided to take action. They stop smoking! And hopefully progress to the next stage of the change process.
- **Maintenance** (maintaining change)
  If they can stay off the cigarettes they begin to feel in control and empowered to maintain the change. At this point the client can exit the cycle because they no longer even think about the need for a cigarette. They are in control.

There are another two stages in this model. One is 'relapse', which is the stage a person might fall back into before they have 'another go' at quitting the cigarettes and the other is pre-contemplation (not interested in changing). This is the stage before a client is even aware that there could be a problem with their health behaviours. However, once they have become aware they rarely go back to pre-contemplation.

Think it over

What might be the support requirements from the health and social care services for an individual at each stage of the change process? You will need to think about information, support, guidance, counselling, etc.

Access to information

In order to pass successfully through each stage of the change process clients need help from a range of health professionals. For example, once an individual has decided to 'quit smoking' they need access to information such as:

- where and when support classes are held
- how they can obtain nicotine replacement therapy.

Without access to the information they need the individual may well fall at the first hurdle. Counselling services can also be useful to enable individuals to recognise problems and sometimes the 'root' cause associated with lifestyle behaviour. However, counselling is also used to enable individuals to explore the best approaches for them to bring about change in their lives.

Key issue

Find out about problem-solving approaches used in counselling for change and person-centred, non-directive approaches. Compare the two approaches. Which do you prefer and why?

Overcoming barriers

Often clients need help to overcome barriers to lifestyle change. Tones (1995) developed the health action model, which explored the reasons why people behave in certain ways. You will see by looking at Figure 9.6 that for change to occur self concept and self-esteem are important factors. Alongside these are the important factors of motivation, beliefs and attitudes and the normative system (social pressures and expected behaviours).

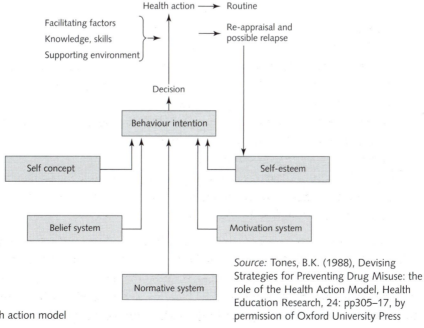

Source: Tones, B.K. (1988), Devising Strategies for Preventing Drug Misuse: the role of the Health Action Model, Health Education Research, 24: pp305–17, by permission of Oxford University Press

Figure 9.6 The health action model

As an example, if an individual decides to make changes to their eating habits the following must be involved:

- a belief in themselves (self-esteem)
- feelings that this is the 'right' thing to do (belief system)
- information on healthy eating (knowledge)
- costs of new food choices need to be within the individual's budget (supporting environment)
- readily available food choices (facilitating factors)
- transport to go and purchase the items (facilitating factor)
- finance to purchase the foods (facilitating factor)
- a liking for the new tastes (motivation factor)
- family approval and support (normative system).

We can see that if any of these aspects do not fit with the required new health behaviour the individual is not likely to succeed in making changes.

Key issue

Find out more about the health action model (a good health education text will be useful for this activity).

Overcoming barriers

It might help you to think about barriers to lifestyle change as falling into three categories:

- personal barriers, such as preferences, habits, motivation, enthusiasm
- environmental barriers, such as transport, availability of resources, finance
- social barriers, such as family support, cultural norms, acceptability to others.

Health and social care professionals can help individuals with each of these barriers in a variety of ways. We have already seen that the need for accurate and relevant information is paramount to facilitate change. However, this information needs to be given at an appropriate time in the change process; for example, it will not be effective to tell clients about nicotine replacement therapy if they have not yet accepted the need to give up smoking.

Sometimes an individual just needs to talk to others about their feelings and, in some cases, symptoms. In this way support from health professionals either on a 'one to one' basis or small-group counselling can be invaluable.

Think it over

What methods are often used to support clients who are trying to change their behaviours with alcohol and food habits?

The rise in consumerism

As if there is not enough to contend with when people want to change their behaviours, they also have to deal with consumerism. Every product you can think of usually has some element of advertising attached to it. Think of people who are trying to reduce their weight visiting the supermarket. How do they manage to 'get out' without filling their trolleys full of high-fat, high-sugar products? Look at smoking advertisements on bill boards, often depicting an 'anti hero' to attract the attention of young adults. Television programmes continually target children and adults with all the good things in life: the simply 'must haves', bigger and better televisions, everything with a remote control – not exactly an incentive to participate in regular physical activity!

How does the individual beat the rise of consumerism? Perhaps with the help of group support?

Groups

We have already explored the contribution that community action groups can potentially make to an improved health status for their local populations. However, there are other issues that can be included in the discussions about a 'group's' role within the arena of change. For example, identifying need is a key issue for bringing about health improvements. This is often referred to as listening to 'local voices'.

Identifying need

There are various ways in which this could be carried out. These include:

- focus group research
- telephone interviews
- postal questionnaires
- community profiles
- working with 'significant others' or 'gatekeepers'
- rapid appraisal.

Whichever method is chosen it will not be an easy task. No two members of the community ever agree on everything! Although local people may have certain issues or problems in common, they may well differ on methods of dealing with them. Some people within the community may have their own agenda to drive forward and are willing to use any method within their means.

Groups from the community will often work alongside agencies, which have a specific role of enabling change. Agencies can be from a wide variety of sectors. For example:

- education
- health
- social care
- environmental health.

In some cases, training may be the key factor in enabling members of the community to develop the skills of advocacy or there could be a role for some people as interpreters. The list is endless.

Health forums are often used as a way of bringing local people, voluntary sectors and health professionals together to meet regularly in order to find ways of dealing with health issues that relate to them and their communities.

Another way of working in groups is known as 'rapid appraisal'. This is a method of collecting data which is then used to create a list of priorities which the statutory agencies can use in their planning.

Data on health issues is collected from a variety of sources, for example secondary sources could include information from public health reports; national census data could be used as well as any other research that had been carried out for the area. Primary sources could include meetings with local groups and agencies as well as key individuals to inform the data collection.

Case study

A rapid appraisal approach was used by Dale and colleagues (1996) to find out the views of service users and service providers about 'out of hours medical care' in London.

The researchers made a list of all the service providers in the area and held meetings with key representatives. The information collected was then reviewed by representatives from the community before final reports were created.

The main advantage with this method of collecting information is the speed with which data can be collected. However, as you can see the method relies very heavily on key informants who may not always fully represent the community they are connected with.

Assessment activity 9.3

Select a group of the population who share similarities such as social class, age, ethnicity or disabilities and identify the factors which could affect their health and well-being. You should include issues of gender and race in your answer. What obstacles might they face when attempting to bring about improvements in their health status?

Evaluate the possibilities of success or failure in their attempts to bring about change on an individual and group basis.

Government

Within this section we explore some of the national initiatives that are being driven by the government to improve health status, in particular, Health Action Zones and 'The New NHS'. However, there are many more initiatives that you might be interested in finding out more about, for example:

- Saving Lives: Our Healthier Nation
- Healthy Living Centres.

Health Action Zones (HAZ) were created to encourage many agencies (private, statutory and voluntary) to come together in areas of greatest need and deprivation to tackle the causes of ill health and high mortality rates. They have a remit to develop new ways of working in partnership to address inequalities in health and well-being. There are approximately 30 areas with Health Action Zone status across England. However, the funding for health improvement initiatives such as this has to be applied for in the form of a 'bid'. This means that areas of equal need are competing with each other for funding. There is an argument that this just adds to inequalities in health. Some politicians and health professionals argue that the funding should be part of mainstream provision.

Where an area has successfully applied for Health Action Zone status they have extra finance to tackle the causes of ill health. This could mean the money is spent on housing, education or services (see Unit 10, page 404 for more information on HAZ).

Key issue

Locate a Health Action Zone on the Internet. Make notes of its priorities and actions taken to reduce ill health and high mortality rates.

The New NHS

The White Paper, 'The New NHS, Modern and Dependable' (1998) brought structural changes to the way health and social care provision is arranged.

Three developments were identified for the New NHS. These are:

- NHS Direct – a 24-hour telephone advice line for the public staffed by nurses
- GPs and hospitals directly connected to the NHSnet information superhighway (to speed up out-patient appointments)
- anyone with suspected cancer to see a specialist within two weeks of their GP deciding they need to be seen urgently.

In addition, the New NHS sought to:

- drive quality in the new NHS
- drive efficiency in the new NHS
- bring quality and efficiency together.

All this means that there are new responsibilities and roles for health authorities, hospital trusts and the Department of Health. For example, primary health care groups (trusts) have been formed to purchase (commission) care services for their own localities. There are representatives from the medical and social care professions on the group as well as representatives from nursing, health education and the voluntary and community sectors. This has created stronger links between health and social care services.

Health authorities have a primary role in drawing up three-year Health Improvement Plans for their own localities and populations. All agencies should work within this framework to bring about improvements in health and well-being.

Key issues

Find out about your primary health care trust. Find out who is represented and what their roles and responsibilities are.

Obtain a copy of your local area Health Improvement Plan (the health authority will be a useful contact here).

It is clear that the implications of these changes relate to both service user and the staff employed within the health and social care arena.

For service users:

- better, quicker services
- seamless provision
- 24-hour access to health information
- less 'red tape' for access to services
- national standards of care guaranteed.

For staff:

- new working arrangements
- more career opportunities
- development of new skills
- working within a coherent framework to improve health
- less red tape.

Health Improvement Programmes

Each health authority is charged with developing a Health Improvement Programme for their local population (see Unit 8, page 351). However, the health authority is expected to work with others to develop joint strategies for improving the health of their entire population, especially concentrating on those identified as suffering from inequalities. Organisations identified for joint working to bring about improvements in health are:

- primary care trusts (charged with making this a 'kingpin' of all their policies)
- local authorities
- Health Action Zones
- education.

Assessment activity 9.4

Select a policy initiative of your own choice to review and evaluate.

Give a brief description of the policy including when it was implemented and who it is aimed at. Explore the policy content to explain the methods and approaches that are being used to improve health status in the target population.

Evaluate whether or not you think the policy initiative will be successful in terms of improving health status, giving your reasons for the judgement made.

Obstacles

In a way, the barriers and obstacles to change have been dealt with throughout this unit. You may find it helpful to re-read some of the issues relating to the individual experiencing barriers to change before exploring the dynamics of group and community change.

Individuals involved in change often lack confidence in themselves and in the success rates of the new health behaviour. Think about how many people still say such things as, 'Uncle Fred smoked until he was 93 and it didn't do him any harm!' Bringing about change, as we have already seen, requires positive self-esteem, locus of control, confidence, motivation and support from others; without this, change is unlikely to occur.

We already know that it is hard enough for the individual to change their own lifestyle behaviours without help and support from a range of health professionals. Consider then how much more difficult change on a group and community level must be.

Health professionals who work in the community development area place great value on developing the community and working in partnership with community groups. Focusing their efforts on small sections of the community can be highly rewarding. But in reality the impact on community change in terms of overall public health improvements is likely to be minimal. Furthermore, we often find that the 'community' may have other priorities and fail to agree within themselves priority action/developments. Remember no two people think alike about everything!

Theories of group and community change (Rogers, 1983) demonstrate the process involved in that change. For example, we know that community leaders are often the innovators of change. In many instances these people are of a higher social class than the rest of the community. In some examples, the innovators have been the health workers involved with the community. The next line of change is with those people with influence in the community who are called 'early adopters'. In other words, the individuals have followed the lead of the innovator and then adopted the changes. The final group to change and accept the new ways are the 'late adopters'. These are the very last people to come on board. When you now remember that this process can take many years (think culture, norms and peer pressure), community change is an extremely slow process. However, this is not the end of the story because as you might expect there will always be a minority of the community who never change and adapt to the new health behaviours.

Think it over

What are the implications for the health and social care services of people who never adapt to change?

End of unit test

1   Identify three different social class groups that can be found in the Registrar General's Social Classification. For each group that you have identified, give two examples of an occupation that someone within that group might work in.

2   Briefly describe the changes that have occurred to the social classification system since the first system designed by the Registrar General.

3   What might be the major differences in health between people from a higher social class grouping and those from lower social classes?

4   What are the major demographic changes that have occurred in the country in which you live? Give two reasons why they might have occurred.

5   Evaluate the likely impact of the demographic changes that you have identified on the health and social care services.

6   Briefly describe the possible effects of culture and upbringing on an individual's health status.

7 Briefly outline the health issues that affect women in particular.

8 How might ethnicity affect the health and well-being of families living in the UK today?

9 For your local region, briefly describe the aims and content of a national policy that has been implemented to improve the health status of individuals.

10 Explain how the policy you have chosen aims to improve the health status of those who would be considered most in need of support.

11 Discuss the possible difficulties facing an individual who wants to give up smoking. Suggest some realistic ways of overcoming these barriers.

References and further reading

Ahmad, W. (1993) *Race and Health in Contemporary Britain*, Buckingham: Open University Press

Black, D. (1980) *Inequalities in Health* (The Black Report)

Blaxter, M. (1990) *Health and Lifestyles*, London: Routledge

Dahlgren, G. and Whitehead, M. (1991) *Policies and Strategies to Promote Social Equity in Health*, Stockholm: Institute for Future Studies

Dale, J. and Shipman C. (1996) *Creating a shared vision of out-of-hours care: using rapid appraisal methods to create an interagency-community-orientated approach to service development*, British Medical Journal, 312, 1206–10

Hart, N. (1998), *The Sociology of Health and Medicine*, Lancashire: Causeway Press

Hawtin, M., Hughes, G., Percy-Smith, J. and Foreman A. (1996) *Community Profiling*, Buckingham: Open University Press

Merry, P. (2001), *Wellard's NHS Handbook*, East Sussex: JMH Publishing

Prochaska, J. and DiClemente C. (1984) *The Transtheoretical Approach: Crossing Traditional Boundaries of Therapy*, USA: Krieger Publishing Company

Rogers, A., Pilgrim D. and Lacey R. (1993) *Experiencing Psychiatry*, Basingstoke: Palgrave Macmillan

Tones, B.K. (1995) *Making a change for the better*, Healthlines, November, 17–19

Townsend, P., Phillimore, P. and Beattie, A. (1988) *Health and Deprivation: Inequality and the North*, London: Routledge

Trowler, P. (1995) *Investigating Health, Welfare and Poverty*, London: Collins Educational

This unit opens with an introduction to the concept of public health – what we mean by the term, how it has evolved and the types of models of health on which public health activity is founded. You will learn about a range of organisations and individuals and their roles in the public health process.

A key aspect of public health is the mapping and control of diseases. This introduces the concept of epidemiology where you will learn about how disease is studied, what causes disease, how we can prevent or detect disease and what measures are taken where diseases are either endemic or epidemic.

The section on occupational health provides information about the provision and role of those people employed in occupational health and safety, and the relevant legislation that has been applied for keeping individuals free from harm.

The final section of the unit takes public health into the arena of environmental health and explores the potential for ill health that can be created by the global and local environments in which we find ourselves.

What you need to learn

- Public health
- Epidemiology
- Approaches to occupational health
- Environmental health issues

Public health

Concepts of public health

The public's health v public health

When using the term *public health* it is important to understand its meaning. The definition used in the Report on Health Inequalities of 1998 defined it as:

> 'the science and art of preventing disease, prolonging life, and promoting health through the organised efforts of society'.

This definition is still widely used because it reflects:

> 'the essential elements of modern public health – a population perspective, an emphasis on collective responsibility for health and on prevention. In this definition the role of the state is identified as tackling the underlying causes of ill health, i.e. not just focusing on disease but on poor housing, environment and employment status, often referred to as socio-economic factors. It relies on a multi-disciplinary approach which emphasises partnership with the populations served'.

The report identified three key aspects to the public health role:

- minimising and where possible removing damaging environmental, social and behavioural influences on health
- the provision of services to restore the sick to health
- where this isn't possible, to reduce to a minimum suffering, disability and dependence.

Therefore to distinguish the two, public health is an activity to promote better health within the community whilst the public's health is a measure of the state of that community's health. So the public's health can be used as a measure of the success of public health!

Think it over

If you were a modern-day public health doctor, what examples of local or national issues would you be working on to improve health locally that might fall into the three categories of action identified by Acheson:

- minimising the harm caused by socio-economic conditions
- health service provision
- supporting people with incurable conditions?

History of public health development

Public health, as we know it today, originated from the nineteenth-century Poor Law system, and the Victorian Sanitary Reform Movement. Industrialisation and the rapid growth of cities during this period led to concerns about environmental problems such as poor housing, unclean water supplies, 'bad air', and the impact that these had on the health of the working population.

The first national Public Health Act (1848)
At this time, Edwin Chadwick was an active campaigner on a number of public health issues, including poor housing and working conditions and sanitary reform. Chadwick's *Report on an inquiry into the sanitary conditions of the labouring population of Great Britain* (1842) contained a mass of evidence supporting the relationship between environmental factors, poverty and ill health. It recommended the establishment of a single local authority, supported by expert medical and civil engineering advice, to administer all sanitary matters. Six years later, the national Public Health Act was passed, and the first Board of Health was established.

John Snow and the Broad Street pump
Infectious diseases were still a major cause of death, and at this time the cause of epidemics such as cholera, yellow fever, typhus and typhoid was attributed to miasmas (bad smells and gases). In 1854, John Snow was interested in the role of drinking water in the spread of cholera, and had observed that people who had drunk water provided by one water company were more likely to contract the disease than those who had not. Having identified the source of the infection as polluted water, he went on to remove the handle of the Broad Street water pump and halt the outbreak of cholera in Soho, London.

By plotting the cases of cholera on a map, Snow was able to establish that all those falling ill were getting their water from a single pump, which drew its supplies from the sewage-contaminated River Thames. People using nearby wells to obtain their water had escaped infection. The connection between cholera and contaminated water was therefore established, before bacteriology was able to identify the causative organism.

John Simon and the 1866 Sanitary Act

The third 'founding father' of public health succeeded Edwin Chadwick in his role in public health administration. John Simon was a physician by profession and became Medical Officer to the Board of Health in 1855. Advised by a team of scientists and engineers, Simon was instrumental in helping a number of towns to install their first sewage systems throughout the 1850s and 1860s. In 1866 the Sanitary Act placed a duty of inspection on local authorities and extended their range of sanitary powers.

Medical officers of health

Another well-known historical figure is William Henry Duncan, who was the first local medical officer of health (for the City of Liverpool) appointed in 1847. Duncan's role was set out in the Liverpool Sanitary Act of 1846, which made provision for the appointment of 'a legally qualified medical practitioner' with powers to:

> '... inspect and report periodically on the sanitary state of the said Borough, to ascertain the existence of diseases, more especially epidemics increasing the rate of mortality, and to point out the existence of any nuisances or other local causes which are likely to originate and maintain such diseases...'

Other local authorities soon followed suit, and appointments of medical officers of health eventually became compulsory for every local district in the 1872 Public Health Act.

Throughout the first half of the twentieth century infectious diseases were still a major cause of death, but developments in bacteriology led public health practice to focus on isolation, disinfection and personal hygiene, alongside immunisation and vaccination, as the major means of controlling disease. Alongside these developments, there was also a growing concern over continuing high rates of maternal and infant mortality, as well as the poor physical condition of army recruits. As a result, medical officers of health began to take on responsibility for promoting the health of specific groups within the community, such as expectant and nursing mothers, and young children.

This led to the development of community health services such as mother and baby clinics and the Schools Health Service, all located within the local authority. Medical officers of health worked alongside other professional groups concerned with promoting health and well-being of individuals and communities, including environmental health officers, community midwives, health visitors and social workers. This arrangement continued up until the NHS reorganisation of 1974.

The new public health and the rise of health promotion

During the 1970s and 1980s, however, a new, more integrated approach to public health began to emerge. The Lalonde Report (1974), in Canada, was a major influence, followed shortly afterwards by a number of other health strategies such as the WHO's *Health for All 2000* (1977). This approach not only broadened the definition of health, but also took a wider view of the major determinants of health, particularly behavioural influences.

This very much influenced the development of a more pro-active model of health promotion, aimed at promoting health through the encouragement of healthy lifestyles. Risk factor reduction through individual behaviour change was seen as the key to improving health.

However, publication of the Black Report (1980) and 'The Health Divide' (1987), both of which clearly identified the relationship between poverty and ill health, led to a growing recognition of the importance of social and economic influences on health and disease, and was incorporated into the *Ottawa Charter for Health Promotion* (WHO, 1986), which defined the role of health promotion as:

- building healthy public policy
- creating supportive environments
- strengthening community action
- developing personal skills
- re-orientating health services.

A brief history of health promotion

1974	Lalonde Report, *A New Perspective on the Health of Canadians*
1976	*Prevention and Health: Everybody's Business* (DHSS)
1977	*Health For All by the Year 2000*, launched at 30th World Health Assembly
1978	Declaration of Alma Ata
1980	The Black Report: *Inequalities in Health* (DHSS)
1984	Healthy Toronto 2000, launched in Canada
1985	World Health Organisation: 38 Targets for Health in the European region
1986	*Ottawa Charter for Health Promotion* (WHO)
1987	Healthy Cities project launched
1987	*Promoting Better Health*: The Government's Programme for Improving Primary Care (DHSS)
1988	Adelaide Conference on Healthy Public Policy
1991	Sundsvall Conference on Supportive Environments
1990–93	Publication of: *Health For All in Wales*; *Health of the Nation* (England); *Scotland's Health: A Challenge to Us All*; *A Health Promotion Strategy for Northern Ireland*
1991	WHO revised *Health For All* targets
1998	The Acheson Report: *Independent Inquiry into Inequalities in Health*
1998	*Saving Lives: Our Healthier Nation*

Source: Jones L. 1997, The Challenge of Promoting Health, Palgrave Macmillan

Reproduced with permission of Palgrave Macmillan

Concepts of social and medical models of health

Biomedical model

Since the beginning of the nineteenth century the model of health which has come to dominate all others in the western world is the biomedical model. Its history lies in the developing understanding of human anatomy at that time, when dissection of body parts gradually developed the understanding of how the various parts of the body might work together to ensure good health. This scientific view of health and body functioning is summarised by Jones below.

The medical model of health – Jones (1994)

- Health is predominantly viewed as the absence of disease.
- Health services are geared towards the treating of the sick.
- A high value is placed on specialist medical services.
- Doctors and other qualified experts diagnose and sanction treatment.
- Main purpose of health services is curative – to get people back to work.
- Disease and illness is explained by biological science.
- It is based on the understanding of how diseases arise, emphasising risk factors.
- A high value is placed on scientific research methodology.
- Quantitative scientific evidence is generally given higher value than lay or qualitative evidence.

Source: Jones L. 1997, The Challenge of Promoting Health, Palgrave Macmillan
Reproduced with permission of Palgrave Macmillan

This is the model most frequently used by members of health care professions. In particular it is the foundation of most medical science and therefore is central to the practice of medicine. As a result, it is the cure which doctors focus upon – their approach being founded in an impression of what is normal and what is abnormal in terms of bodily function. It is most effective with short-term or acute illness, where a cause is identified and the relevant treatment administered.

The biomedical model is at its least effective with chronic illnesses, i.e. those which persist over longer periods of time and are managed rather than cured, such as Parkinson's disease, terminal care of the dying and other aspects of health care such as maternity care where the patient isn't actually ill.

Assessment activity 10.1

1 Identify three things which demonstrate how childbirth is medicalised as a result of the medical model dominating health care provision.
2 What tensions does this present for the mother in her relationship with her doctor?
3 What things can currently be offered to women to reduce this medicalisation?

Social model of health

Although the biomedical model has contributed greatly to increases in life expectancy, it is public health measures based on the social model of health which contributed most to the decline in mortality during the twentieth century.

A social model of health emphasises that to improve health it is necessary to address the *origins* of ill health, in terms of the social conditions which make ill health more prevalent in some groups than others. Its underlying philosophy is that the health of individuals and social groups is the result of a complex mixture of behavioural, structural, material and cultural factors which together impact on health. The social model has strong links to lay models of health (see Unit 8, page 332) because it recognises that people often have firmly held views about their own health, which are sometimes at odds with those of professionals. A good example of this clash of priorities might be the need to address damp conditions in housing and its link to childhood asthma, as prioritised by people living in those conditions, as opposed to the need to tackle parental smoking as prioritised by health services.

So the question remains, 'How do I define health?'. The answer might be to use the often-quoted 1948 World Health Organisation (WHO) definition 'A state of complete physical, mental and social well being; not merely the absence of disease and infirmity'. However, this definition is one of many (see below) and it has its limitations. It has an idealistic standpoint and static view of life (e.g. it makes no reference to the need to be able to change and adapt with life's changes), however it acknowledges the interrelating factors which impact upon health.

'A state of complete physical, psychological and social well-being and not merely the absence of disease and infirmity.'
World Health Organisation (1948)

'A satisfactory adjustment of the individual to the environment.'
Royal College of General Practitioners (1972)

'By health I mean the power to live a full adult, living, breathing life in close contact with what I love. I want to be all I am capable of becoming.'
Katherine Mansfield (1888–1923)

'The extent to which an individual or group is able on the one hand, to realise aspirations and satisfy needs and on the other hand, to change or cope with the environment. Health is therefore seen as a resource for everyday life, not the objective of living: it is a positive concept emphasising social and personal resources as well as physical capabilities.'
World Health Organisation (1984)

Health Action Zones

Health Action Zones (HAZs) are a modern-day public health initiative to target funding at areas of high health need and address the existing patterns of inequality. Their goal is to reshape services better to meet local needs, develop new approaches to partnerships between key public players and address health inequalities. These partnerships include the NHS, local authorities, community groups and the voluntary and business sectors. The aim will be to develop and implement an integrated health strategy in each of the areas granted HAZ status. Eleven first-wave HAZs commenced work in April 1998 including Lambeth, Southwark and Lewisham, Plymouth, Manchester, Salford and Trafford, Bradford, etc., with a further 15 second-wave HAZs in 1999.

Whilst HAZs are about bringing all the players together to find imaginative ways to make best use of existing resources through working in partnership, considerable additional resources have also been made available. HAZs are expected to develop co-ordinated approaches to the delivery of services that have an impact on health, ensuring engagement and synergy with other initiatives. For example, on employment issues, HAZs are expected to:

- ensure strategic co-ordination of health and employment initiatives locally, identifying impediments and potential flexibilities, e.g. exploring new ways of addressing the needs of disabled people in accessing work experience
- develop the HAZ partners' service provider role, e.g. explore new relationships with local employers which will help develop services to remove barriers for people with disabilities and focus upon employers' skills requirements and workplace support needs

- use the full potential of the NHS and other HAZ partners as employers, e.g. exploring how health service organisations can recruit locally through initiatives such as training programmes for target groups in areas of skill shortage.

Community involvement

The Ottawa charter emphasised the need to involve the public actively in the cause of strengthening community action.

Think it over

In 600 BC, Lao Tze summarised success in community involvement in these terms:

> 'Go to the people. Live amongst them. Start with what they have. Build with them. And when the deed is done, the mission accomplished, of the best leadership. The people will say, We have done it ourselves.'

Discuss in a group how Lao Tze expected people to improve their surroundings. How can this be applied to today's world? Who would Lao Tze expect to be living amongst the people in a modern setting?

Why should health services involve the public?

More locally, the 1998 discussion document 'In the public interest – developing a strategy for participation in the NHS' set out the agenda for promoting community involvement. Some of the reasons given in the document are summarised below.

- The public no longer accepts the view of experts unquestioningly because they are better informed about health.
- Science and technology cannot answer all our questions; some of these raise ethical, moral and political issues which require public debate, e.g. genetic screening of unborn children.
- The NHS must be responsive to the changing needs of a rapidly diverging population.
- Despite the innovation and progress in health care, health inequalities are continuing to widen.
- It is the right of citizens to have a say in the services which affect their health.
- Outcomes are improved by involving patients in their own care and treatment.
- Patients' experiences can be a valuable contributor to the education of health professionals.
- The NHS must address the inverse care law and the involvement of the public is one means of doing this.
- Communities can help solve problems as well as identifying them.

Theory into practice

The inverse care law can be summarised as 'The people who experience the poorest health make the least effective use of their health services'.

What reasons can you think of to explain this? You need to consider which groups in society experience the poorest health and then what types of barriers might exist for them in accessing their local health services.

How could involving local communities overcome this issue?

People routinely refer to 'involving the public' or 'community participation' and appear to be using these words interchangeably. However, the dictionary definitions show that these words have quite different meanings:

Informing – give information to, knowing the facts
Consulting – seek information or advice, take counsel, take into consideration
Involving/participation – include in its operation, share experience – to have a share or take a part.

Assessment activity 10.2

Imagine you are the chief executive of the local health authority faced with the possible need to close a hospital accident and emergency department in order to address concerns about the ability of the hospital to support that department. You feel it is important to involve the local population. What activities could you use to:

- inform
- involve
- consult

local people about the issues this raises?

Write a report that will inform the local population and reduce the fears that they may have about the possible closure of the hospital A & E department. Why is it your responsibility to allay the population's fears?

Roles of professionals and lay members in public health

Community Health Councils

The National Health Service and health issues in general are of interest and concern to many people. Community Health Councils (CHCs) exist to represent the interests of the public in the operation of the NHS. The Community Health Council represents the interests of the public to their local primary care group/trust (PCT), health authority and NHS Trust, ensuring their voice is heard in planning health services in both hospital and the community, as well as services provided by family doctors, dentists, opticians and pharmacists.

The role of CHC members includes contributing to informed comments on local health services and plans for changes, monitoring the quality of services provided, and making recommendations for improvement. CHC staff help individual members of the public who want information about NHS services, advice about dealing with a problem or help in making a complaint about their treatment.

A CHC has between 18 and 30 voluntary members who can join through one of three possible routes:

- Local authorities in the area nominate half of the members of each CHC. They do not have to be councillors.
- Voluntary organisations with an interest in health matters elect one-third of the members of each CHC.
- The remaining places are for people who make application as individuals and are appointed by the Secretary of State for Health.

As a CHC representative a member would be expected to:

- be a member of specialist working groups, for example looking at particular issues such as child health services or services for elderly people
- visit hospitals, clinics and health centres
- represent the CHC at meetings with health authorities, and other statutory and voluntary bodies
- contribute to comments on plans and proposals from health authorities, NHS Trusts and other bodies.

Watchdogs

The recent NHS reforms set out in the NHS plan to introduce mechanisms for improving public participation in the management of health care provision. They include a range of new initiatives which will act as watchdogs for local services:

- **Advocacy services** – for people who want to complain about the NHS. Patients or carers will be able to access this service directly to assist them in making a complaint about NHS services – if they wish to do so.

- **Patient surveys** – making the NHS publicly accountable. Since 2001, every acute hospital trust must undertake a new patient survey programme to use local patient views to improve the quality of patients' experiences. From April 2002, every NHS organisation is required to publish, in a new Patient Prospectus, an annual account of the views received from patients and the action taken as a result, to demonstrate that the NHS is acting on information gained from patients and responding to patients' priorities.

- **Patients' Forums.** The government intends to introduce Patients' Forums for every NHS Trust and PCT in England. They will be statutory independent bodies, made up of patients and others from the local community, with extensive powers to inspect all aspects of the work of trusts. They will elect one of their members on to the trust board, so allowing patients to elect a representative of the key decision-making body of every local NHS organisation for the first time. The forums should be able to:
  - elect one of their members to be a non-executive director of the local trust board
  - inspect every service that NHS patients use, including primary care services, and go behind the scenes, too
  - make their reports available to key decision makers in the community including the local Overview and Scrutiny Committees (OSC), and Local Strategic Partnerships about the views and concerns of patients
  - monitor Patient Advocacy and Liaison Services (PALS) and bring to the attention of the trust cases where this service is under-performing – where the service does not improve they should be able to recommend that it is replaced
  - report adverse incidents to the National Patients' Safety Agency
  - make reports and recommendations for improvement of services to the trust board based on the experiences, ideas and needs of patients and the wider public
  - contribute evidence to inform the Commission for Health Improvement (CHI) inspection and Health Select Committee inquiries.

Patient's Charters

The first Patient's Charter was one of the major policy initiatives of John Major's Conservative government of the early 1990s. It was introduced in April 1992 with the stated aim of: 'Improving the quality of care delivered to the patients' by recognising 'The importance of identifying and being responsive to patients' needs'.

However, after six years in operation a King's Fund study in 2000 found that it had fallen short of delivering these aims and the majority of NHS staff had become quite hostile to it. But this was balanced by some potential benefits which NHS staff could identify from the implementation of the charter:

1 It gave greater clarity about standards for both staff and patients.
2 Monitoring and performance of the NHS was more open.
3 It empowered patients, inviting them to voice their views about the service and help in its development.

Although the review concluded that 'the overwhelming view of the charter amongst those who had experience of it was that it was of limited usefulness' they did identify several areas of common interest to both patients and staff, which had become apparent through the introduction of the first charter:

- making available to the individual patient, comprehensive information regarding their condition, treatment and choices open to them
- making available to the wider public, comprehensive information about the full range of services available
- promoting a positive relationship between patients and NHS staff and, in particular, ensuring that each patient is treated as an individual and not a condition
- focusing on privacy and confidentiality for patients and on respect and dignity for both patients and staff
- improving access to the NHS as a whole including more flexible, patient friendly hours and targeting those groups who have traditionally found it difficult to get treatment.

Therefore, although staff were sceptical there was a clear rationale for introducing a revised charter which took account of the concerns raised about the first. The original Patient's Charter has now been replaced by 'Your Guide to the NHS' which was operational from April 2001 and for the first time emphasises both rights and responsibilities for patients.

Our commitment to you

We want the NHS to be a high quality health service. These are our aims as set out in the NHS Plan:

- The NHS will provide a universal service for all based on clinical need, not ability to pay.

- The NHS will provide a comprehensive range of services.

- The NHS will shape its services around the needs and preferences of individual patients, their families and their carers.

- The NHS will respond to different needs of different populations.

- The NHS will work continuously to improve quality services and to minimise errors. The NHS will support and value its staff. Public funds for health care will be devoted solely to NHS patients.

- The NHS will work together with others to ensure a seamless service for patients.

- The NHS will help keep people healthy and work to reduce health inequalities.

- The NHS will respect the confidentiality of individual patients and provide open access to information about services, treatment and performance.

The NHS will work better if you use the service responsibly

- Do what you can to look after your own health, and follow advice on a healthy lifestyle. Care for yourself when appropriate. (For example, you can treat yourself at home for common ailments such as coughs, colds and sore throats.)

- Give blood if you are able, and carry an organ donor card or special needs card or bracelet.

- Listen carefully to advice on your treatment and medication. Tell the doctor about any treatments you are already taking.

Think it over

As a nurse on a ward, what problems might you be presented with by identifying patients' rights to them through such a charter?

How might people view the list of responsibilities included to balance the rights?

Primary care groups

First described in the government's White Paper 'The New NHS, Modern and Dependable', the concept of the primary care group (PCG) was a means of restoring the balances of control within the NHS to local primary health care practitioners. This was to reflect their position as the patient's advocates, the people most in touch with local health care needs, unlike health authorities which were perceived as being too bureaucratic, bogged down with the commissioning of health services, often struggling to balance their competing roles of balancing the local health budget and acting as local champion for people's health needs.

Ultimately the PCG is governed by the health authority, although most PCGs have since moved on to become primary care trusts (PCTs) and have adopted a greater proportion of the health authority commissioning role and the increased autonomy which goes with it. The move to a more practitioner-focused organisation is reflected in the board of the PCG:

- 4 to 7 GPs
- 1 or 2 community or practice nurses
- 1 social services nominee
- 1 lay member
- 1 health authority non-executive member
- 1 PCG chief executive.

Key points here are that GPs clearly hold a majority on the board; they can reduce their numbers to increase the number of representatives from other professions but in so doing would lose this majority. The nurses on the board provide professional advice and a strategic view for the development of the nurse role, as well as being one of few professional non-doctors on the board. PCGs were initially offered four options for level of responsibility:

Level 1 Essentially to act as an advisory body for the health authority with no commissioning powers.
Level 2 To take responsibility for a portion of the health care budget, and to operate formally as part of the health authority.

Level 3   To become established as a free-standing body accountable to the health authority for commissioning care.

Level 4   To become established as a free-standing body, accountable to the health authority for commissioning care and with the added responsibility of providing community health services for the population (primary care trust or PCT).

Whilst some PCGs chose to go 'live' in April 1999 at level 1, many others, having previously experienced commissioning through GP fundholding and local commissioning pilots, chose level 2. Since then considerable progress has been made and by the time this book is published virtually all PCGs will have moved to level 4 status as primary care trusts. At this level they are largely independent of the health authority, holding almost all the local health budget. Primary care trusts both deliver local community health services (health visiting, district nursing, community physiotherapy, etc.), support and monitor local family doctor services (GPs are in an unusual position being 'Independent Practitioners' contracted to but not employed by the PCT) and commission secondary care services (hospital services). By 2004 it is likely that PCTs will have further evolved with the creation of 'care trusts' when PCTs take in local social service departments as well.

Health professionals

Improving health and preventing disease is the responsibility of those working to provide health care – especially in a primary and community care setting. The health promotion role of primary care dates back to 'Prevention and Health: Everybody's Business' (DHSS, 1976). This was followed some time later, by the 1990 GP Contract, which emphasised the importance of dealing with risk factor reduction, screening and lifestyle advice in a primary care setting.

One professional group with a long history of working in a primary and community care setting is, of course, nursing. Community nurses, community midwives, health visitors, school nurses, occupational health nurses, and nurses working in the control of communicable diseases all have a long tradition of public health practice, working with communities as well as providing care to individuals. More recently, nurses with public health skills and expertise have been employed in health authorities, contributing directly to the work of public health departments as well as supporting the development of primary care, and the role of the public health nurse has become established.

The public health contribution of nurses, health visitors and midwives was outlined in a recent report, 'Making it Happen' (Department of Health, 1995). This emphasised that nurses, midwives and health visitors were not only 'hands on' professionals, delivering care to individuals, but also had an important strategic role to play in the development and implementation of local health improvement initiatives. For example, there is the school nursing role in supporting the implementation of the National Healthy School Standard, working with teachers, governors, parents and pupils to develop healthy

School nurses develop healthy practice within school

policy and practice in the school environment, across a range of issues. The role the health visitor plays is also important, profiling and then responding to local health needs, possibly by supporting groups of young parents, or volunteers trying to set up a food co-op, etc.

Environmental health personnel

Although split apart from the public health medicine department by the 1974 reforms, the environmental health service has managed to retain a broad public health role covering housing, food safety, water supply, refuse disposal and pollution control. Increasingly, the emphasis on the key statutory duties of surveillance and enforcement has left little scope for developing a broader, comprehensive approach to the improvement of the public's health. Environmental health departments have therefore tended to focus their activities around the core statutory functions.

Food safety

The food safety team is responsible for ensuring that all food produced or sold locally is safe. Complaints are investigated and food samples taken for examination. Diseases which could be food or water borne are also investigated.

Health and safety

The commercial safety team is also responsible for enforcing health and safety legislation in the majority of workplaces locally, including offices, shops, places of entertainment, consumer and leisure services. All premises allocated to the local authority for enforcement are regularly inspected by the team who provide advice and education as well as formal enforcement action including prosecution, where appropriate. Many workplace accidents are required by law to be reported to the local authority and these are investigated to determine the cause and to prevent a repetition. Additional inspections are carried out at premises which require special licences, including places of entertainment and skin piercers.

Environmental protection

Environmental health also has a role in investigating complaints from the public about a range of environmental nuisances which can affect people's health, including noise, smoke, fumes, odour and dust. These are investigated and minimised wherever possible. Authorisations are given to certain industrial processes, strictly limiting their emissions of air pollution, together with the necessary carrying out of monitoring and enforcement. The team also identifies and investigates contaminated land sites.

Pest control

The pest control team treats rodent infestations in domestic and commercial premises throughout the district, as well as other public health pests, such as fleas, cockroaches and wasps. The team also undertakes an annual programme to control rats in the sewage system.

What is the role of the pest control team in improving public health?

Dog control

The dog control team enforces the dog fouling laws, provides advice and education on responsible dog ownership and removes stray dogs from the street.

Epidemiology

Epidemiologists are concerned with the health status of a population. They compare the health of groups within a given population, analyse the findings and attempt to provide explanations for any differences. Epidemiologists may be interested in: morbidity (levels of disease), mortality (rates of death), recovery from illness, use of services, etc.

The term epidemiology derives from the study of epidemics, although it actually covers a much broader approach including how and why epidemics occur, how and why they spread, what causes them and how they can be contained.

Basic terminology

Epidemiology has many terms which specifically apply to certain types of data routinely collected. Some of these are shown in the box below.

Some common terms used in epidemiology	
Standardised rates	Estimate of the rate for particular groups or in particular circumstances, such as by age group, for example heart disease rates for 60–65-year-olds
Perinatal mortality	Deaths occurring between week 24 of pregnancy and one week after birth
Infant mortality	Number of deaths per 1000 infants under 1 year old
Standardised mortality ratio	A comparison of death rates against the national average, e.g. for a particular area or age group. This usually sets the national average as 100 with figures above being higher than and those below, lower than 100.

Epidemiology involves estimating the frequency and distribution of diseases in populations and comparing how suspected risk factors may contribute to the frequency of the disease. Two key terms to understand here are incidence and prevalence.

Incidence

This is the number of new cases of a disease or disorder which arises over a set period of time; for example, the number of new cases of CJD in any one year, or the number of people infected with HIV by unprotected heterosexual sex in the last six months.

Prevalence

This is a measure of how many people are suffering from a particular condition or behaving in a particular way at any one time. This might be used to measure the prevalence of smoking, illegal substance use in the population or the current prevalence of measles.

Epidemiological studies to assess causes of disease usually fall into three categories: cross-sectional, case control and cohort study – as shown in the table below.

Type of study	Description
Cross-sectional	Usually uses a sample from the population to produce a descriptive study, often based on information drawn from questionnaires, tests such as blood pressure or cholesterol, or examination of records; for example, investigating exercise levels in the population, as the Allied Dunbar Fitness Survey did in 1995
Case control	Usually used to test a particular theory or hypothesis. A group of people with a particular condition compared with a similar group who do not have the condition and investigations carried out to assess what previous factors might have led to the current condition; for example, establishing that treatment with a particular drug during pregnancy leads to damage to the unborn child
Cohort study	Focuses on a group of people who exhibit a particular characteristic, for example people who smoke cigarettes, following them for an extended period of time to record what happens to them. It was this type of study which led to Sir Richard Doll identifying the health risks associated with smoking by tracking a group of smokers for 40 years by which time over two-thirds of the sample had died

Patterns and causes of diseases

Cause

We often hold quite simple views as to what causes disease, using a straightforward cause and effect model to explain our illness, such as the commonly held concept of 'catching a cold'. However, it is evident that in many cases the cause is far more complicated than we imagine and cannot be explained in these simple terms. These viewpoints tend to relate to simple disease patterns caused by micro-organisms for which the nineteenth-century microbiologist Koch defined rules for determining whether an organism causes a specific disease.

Koch's postulates for identifying whether a disease is caused by a particular organism

- The organism must be present in every case of the disease.
- The organism must be isolated and grown in pure culture.
- The organism when inoculated into a susceptible animal must cause the specific disease.
- The organism must then be recovered from the animal and identified.

Clearly these rules represent thinking from a much earlier time in medicine and today the cause of disease is viewed as a far more complex problem. A good example is that of lung cancer, where there is an overwhelming body of evidence linking cigarette smoking with lung cancer; however, some people can smoke for many years without developing lung cancer. Therefore smoking is one causal factor which, acting together with others, will trigger the development of the cancer. However, this picture is further complicated by the fact that quitting smoking reduces the number of cases of lung cancer without knowingly being able to affect other causal factors. For this reason the cause of a disease may be described as:

'An event, condition, characteristic or a combination of these factors, which plays an important role in producing the disease'.

Two key terms here are:

- **sufficient** – a cause is termed sufficient when it inevitably produces or initiates the disease
- **necessary** – a cause is termed necessary if the disease cannot develop in its absence.

Think it over

Four types of factor may play a part in the causation of a disease. These include:

- **predisposing factors** – e.g. age or sex which may make you more susceptible to a disease, such as breast cancer
- **enabling factors** – such as low income, poor housing, poor nutrition, etc. which may help the disease develop
- **precipitating factors** – such as exposure to the disease agent, be it an organism or a chemical
- **reinforcing factors** – e.g. repeated exposure or work patterns which aggravate an established condition.

Discuss in a group which types of factor play a part in the causation of lung cancer.

Establishing causes of disease

Establishing cause in modern-day diseases is clearly not as straightforward a process as Koch might have anticipated. With conditions such as coronary heart disease and cancer it is not usually a disease organism which is the causative agent but may be any one of several hundred potential factors.

However, it is possible to apply a systematic approach to establishing the cause of a disease and establish a causal link. This requires the answers to a series of questions which were first used by the US Surgeon General in 1964 to establish the link between smoking and lung cancer.

Guidelines for establishing causation

- Does the cause precede the effect?
- Does this association fit well with other knowledge about the disease?
- Have similar results been shown in other studies?
- How strong is the association between the cause and the disease?
- Is increased exposure to the cause mirrored by increased levels of disease?
- Does reduction of the disease result from removal of the cause?
- Is the study design which demonstrates this relationship sound?
- How many differing investigations have led to this same conclusion?

Range of pathogens

The term pathogen refers to any organism which causes a disease, and is derived from the Greek word *pathos* meaning 'disease'. The most common pathogens include those shown in the table below.

Pathogen	Description	Example
Viruses	A very simple life form, viruses are a piece of genetic information in the form of DNA or RNA, surrounded by a protein coat. They must enter a host cell and take over the host cell machinery for reproducing its own DNA/RNA to enable it to reproduce. The virus destroys the host cell to release it, when it has reproduced in sufficient numbers	**DNA viruses** Hepatitis B Herpes simplex **RNA viruses** Influenza HIV Rhinovirus (common cold)
Bacteria	Although more sophisticated than viruses, bacteria are still relatively simple single cell organisms. They can reproduce without the host's machinery and usually secrete toxic chemicals. Usually they either act as parasites living within our cells or form colonies which disrupt normal functioning	Anthrax Tetanus Staphylococcal food poisoning Meningitis Cholera Diarrhoea
Fungi	A group of simple organisms similar to plants but lacking the green pigment chlorophyll. Because they lack this they are unable to produce their own food and therefore act as parasites on other creatures. In humans usually they invade areas which provide appropriate conditions, e.g. warm and moist, therefore they are often found invading the mouth, genitals and folds in the skin	Candida (thrush and vaginal yeast infection) Athlete's foot
Protozoa	Single-celled organisms, more sophisticated than bacteria, usually found in water courses. Protozoa can invade body fluids and destroy cells either by parasitising them or directly destroying them	Amoebic dysentery Giardiasis Malaria Toxoplasmosis
Pathogenic animals	Larger multicellular organisms which cause disease by parasitising humans or causing injury in some other way	**Nematodes** Roundworm infection Trichinosis **Platyhelminth** Schistosomiasis Tapeworm Liver fluke **Arthropods** Mites and ticks

Host characteristics

The host is a crucial link in the chain of infection and is defined as the person or animal which provides a suitable place for an infectious agent to grow and multiply under natural conditions.

Infection by the disease organism may be unapparent or might lead to symptoms which may vary between mild and severe. If symptoms do develop, the time taken between infection and development of symptoms (termed the incubation period) may vary from a few hours or days, such as with food poisoning, to many years, e.g. HIV. Some organisms such as HIV may enter a latent stage where the disease organism lies dormant within the host and is virtually undetectable.

A suitable host will provide a point of entry, e.g. mucous membranes, respiratory or gastrointestinal tract, and the necessary conditions for the organism to grow and multiply such as appropriate temperature, nutrients, etc. The organism must also remain free from attack by the host's immune system; any previous contact between the host and the organism may have raised antibodies to the disease organism and as a result trigger a rapid immune response to the infection.

Health screening

Screening was defined by the American Commission on Chronic Illness in 1957 as 'the presumptive identification of unrecognised disease or defect by the application of tests, examinations and other procedures which can be applied rapidly. Screening tests sort out apparently well persons who may have a disease from those who do not'.

However, screening a well population can be a contentious issue, with many attendant problems; for example, are we right to be medicalising a well population in this way? Screening for some conditions remains an imprecise science. Naidoo and Wills set out a list of criteria for determining whether a screening programme will be effective (see box below).

Naidoo and Wills's criteria for screening programmes

1 The disease should have a long preclinical phase so that a screening test will not miss the symptoms.
2 Early treatment should improve the outcomes.
3 The test should be sensitive, i.e. it should detect all those with the disease.
4 The test should be specific, i.e. it should detect only those with the disease.
5 The screening programme should be cost effective, i.e. the number of tests performed should yield a number of positive cases.

Source: Naidoo, J. and Wills, J. (1996), Health Promotion – Foundations for Practice, reproduced with permisssion of Ballière Tindall

---

Think it over

Health workers sometimes use the two terms **screening** and **surveillance** interchangeably to talk about the same thing. Divide a page in two with a line, place one word on each side of the page and then quickly write down all the things that word makes you think about – don't leave out things which don't appear to be about health, try to capture all the feelings and thoughts that this word conjures up for you.

Can you see any differences between the way in which you think about these two words?

What messages might we be sending out to people through use of terms like screening and surveillance?

Cervical cancer screening

In England and Wales alone, between 4000 and 5000 women contract cervical cancer and 2000 women die from it every year. However, in general there has actually been a decrease in this disease: in developed countries, mortality declined approximately 30 per cent between 1960 and 1980 as a result of screening and prompt treatment. The disease occurs at about the same rate in all women of ages above 30, but there has been an increase in the 35 and under age group of 6 per cent in the last ten years. One in 20 deaths occurs in women under the age of 35.

Of all the four female cancers, cervical cancer has the strongest relationship with social class: it tends to hit the lower classes, who make less effective use of health services and are less easily influenced through the media. Cervical cancer is thought to be caused by a virus; there are several DNA viruses which have been implicated including the papilloma (wart) virus, the herpes simplex virus, the Epstein-Barr virus (thought to be the virus causing glandular fever) and the hepatitis virus. At the moment, the finger points most strongly at the wart virus.

There may be two kinds of cervical cancer: a slow-growing type with a detectable pre-invasive stage which is susceptible to treatment; and a more rapidly growing type which is harder to treat and which does not have the long pre-invasive stage. Some of the faster-growing cancers have been known to grow to the size of a football within four weeks, but fortunately these are relatively rare.

Infant screening

Some defects in young children are unlikely to be recognised by even the most astute of parents; in these situations only a trained health professional may identify potential problems if specific screening tests are carried out. Good examples here would include high-frequency hearing loss before an age when a child would normally be expected to start to talk or congenital dislocation of the hip before the age at which a child would normally walk.

From the moment of birth young children are routinely screened for specific conditions. A newborn baby will be screened for:

- height, weight and head circumference
- birthmarks
- heart defects
- congenital dislocation of the hips
- eye defects
- hearing
- a range of metabolic disorders.

Some or all of these tests are repeated at 2 weeks, 6–8 weeks, 3–4 months, 6–9 months, 18–24 months, 39 months and at 5 years. These will involve a range of health personnel including the midwife, health visitor, family doctor and school nurse who must all liaise effectively to track the health record of the child. This is usually through a 'patient held record' which is left with the parents or guardian.

Immunisation

As seen earlier in the section dealing with the history of the public health movement, infectious diseases are one of the greatest challenges to maintaining the health of the population. This is where immunisation programmes come in. It is possible to make people immune to certain diseases by challenging their immune system with a weak or inactivated version of the disease organism in order to stimulate the person to create antibodies to the disease. This will enable their immune system to respond quickly should they contract the disease later on, resulting in no more than mild symptoms instead of experiencing the worst aspects of the disease.

The immunisation programme creates what is known as 'herd immunity', that is, if enough people within the population are immunised the likelihood of any epidemic is greatly reduced. For this reason the government sets targets for immunisation rates for local health services to meet. Any regular fall below these levels signals a potential epidemic and becomes a serious cause of concern.

Routinely, children are immunised for diphtheria, typhoid, polio, measles, mumps, rubella, etc. These last three are seen as particularly contentious because some parents believe there may be a link between the MMR vaccine and autism. Whilst there is as yet no strong supporting evidence it has undermined public confidence in the vaccine and reduced the uptake by parents, which in turn risks the herd immunity and, consequently, an epidemic of measles or rubella for example.

HIV testing

The NHS is currently seeking to increase the availability and uptake of testing for HIV with the objectives of reducing undiagnosed HIV, ensuring early access to treatment and limiting further transmission. This will involve work with voluntary and community organisations to make people more aware of the benefits of testing and of where testing, treatment and care are available. In particular this will include promoting access to, and explaining the role of the local genito-urinary medicine (GUM) services and increasing the uptake of testing through primary care.

Theory into practice

Not sure what your GUM service is? Then find out all about it:

- When is it open?
- What services does it offer?
- What confidentiality is on offer?
- Do you have to register?
- Do you need a referral?
- Why might people not wish to be seen visiting it?

Screening through primary care

GPs also offer HIV testing and are especially useful for people who are reluctant to use GUM services (possibly because of the stigma associated with the use of these services). HIV testing has always been possible in primary care, but in the past people have been put off by concerns about GPs providing medical reports to insurance companies. New General Medical Council guidance advises GPs to discuss the information required with patients before completing medical reports, and reminds them that patients are entitled to see the reports before they are disclosed to anyone else. Updated advice from the Association of British Insurers and the BMA makes it clear that only positive HIV tests will affect insurance.

Antenatal screening

The introduction of antenatal HIV screening meant that in 1999, 73 per cent of pregnant women in Inner London had their infection diagnosed before delivery compared to only 50 per cent in 1998. Increased antenatal HIV testing is the key factor contributing to a decrease in mother-to-infant HIV infections. The Department of Health has set a national target of an 80 per cent reduction by the end of 2002 in the number of children with HIV acquired from their mothers during pregnancy, birth or through breastfeeding.

Negative attitudes and expectations get in the way of people accessing services such as these. Embarrassment, previous bad experiences and worries about confidentiality all create barriers between people and the services they need, whilst social exclusion, language, cultural difficulties and homophobia make those barriers harder to cross.

Genetic screening

Genetic science is progressing rapidly. Over coming years our expanding knowledge of genetics will have a major impact on our ability to predict an individual's level of risk of developing certain conditions. Ultimately the genetic revolution may lead to ways of preventing these diseases but in the meantime they allow people to be screened and their risks assessed more accurately.

Genetic screening is available for a wide variety of conditions and across all age ranges. Increasingly, parents are able to assess the health of their foetus before birth and have counselling as to the likely consequences for the child if any ill effects are found. These tests are available during pregnancy using amniocentesis to extract foetal cells from the amniotic fluid surrounding the unborn child. However, this carries a significant risk of spontaneous abortion and may present the parents with difficult choices if the tests prove positive for the condition. Most commonly the diseases screened for here are Down's syndrome, which occurs in about one in every 600 live births, rising to one in 80 for women over 40, Turner's syndrome and Klinefelter's syndrome.

However, screening the unborn presents considerable ethical issues to parents and raises the spectre of eugenics, i.e. the selection of children deemed 'pure or fit' and the abortion of any seen as less than. Disability protesters actively challenge any moves in this direction, pointing out that many people with disabilities are able to live rich and fulfilling lives which might have been terminated under these circumstances.

For adults, if we consider cancer screening as a specific example there are three distinct situations where genetic testing may be used:

- Relatively rare cancer syndromes which have clear patterns of inheritance. In these cases genetic testing is used to confirm diagnosis or to predict disease development in people who do not yet exhibit disease symptoms.
- Some common cancers which are due to single gene defects but where environmental or other factors can affect the development of disease. In these cases, presence of the gene defect (for example for some forms of breast, ovarian, or colorectal cancer) significantly increases the risk of getting the cancer. Therefore the person concerned may be offered routine testing to detect cancers early, or preventative treatment.
- For the majority of common cancers disease development is dependent on complex interactions between several genetic and environmental factors. Genetic testing in this area will determine the probability of an individual developing cancer and will facilitate the introduction of lifestyle modification programmes aimed at lowering the risk to reduce the incidence or prevent the disease.

Assessment activity 10.3

Write a report using epidemiological terminology to describe the major patterns and causes of two groups of diseases (e.g. lung cancer, HIV, heart disease) and evaluate the approaches that would be used to screen for or prevent them at both a national and a local level.

The spread and control of communicable diseases

Investigation and control

The purpose of investigating an outbreak or epidemic is to identify its main cause and the best means of controlling it. It is important to adopt a systematic approach in the investigation, which usually involves the following main steps:

- **Preliminary investigation** – to verify the diagnoses of the suspected cases and confirm that the epidemic exists. Initial thoughts about the source and spread of the disease may also start here.

- **Identification of cases** – certain diseases are termed notifiable, that is any cases identified in this country have to be reported to the public health department for follow-up. The communicable disease team will then try to establish who else may have been in contact with the disease and consequently may have contracted it. This is called routine surveillance and forms part of the process of establishing who has been infected; examples here would include cholera, hepatitis, HIV and other sexually transmitted diseases.

- **Collection and analysis of the data** – analysis of the data being gathered by the communicable disease team allows an assessment of whether there has been a significant rise in the levels of a specific disease and therefore whether the disease merits being placed in the outbreak or epidemic category.

- **Implementation of control measures** – once an outbreak or epidemic has been identified it is necessary to establish clear control measures based on evidence of previous effectiveness, which can initially halt the spread of the disease and subsequently reduce the numbers affected.

- **Dissemination and follow-up** – after any outbreak a report is compiled, drawing together the key features of the outbreak, its source of origin, pattern of spread, method of control and the outcome of the interventions used. Learning points for future practice would also be considered to improve the evidence base for future practice in that area.

Assessment activity 10.4

Imagine you are a nurse working in the GUM clinic and you have identified someone with gonorrhoea. You must now identify how that person contracted the disease which is usually spread by unprotected sexual intercourse. You must also identify who else might have been put at risk through contact with your patient:

- How will you go about finding out this information?
- What problems might this present for you?
- How do you think the patient might react?
- How will you approach the people they identify as being contacts who might have contracted the disease?
- How might the person you are contacting react?
- What types of issues might you come across when contact tracing sexual partners?

Managing outbreaks

The management of an epidemic involves treating the cases, preventing further spread of the disease and monitoring the effects of further control measures. Treatment is usually a simple matter unless the situation is complicated by social and/or environmental disruption; for example, the difficulties in controlling the inevitable outbreaks of typhoid and cholera which follow major natural disasters such as earthquakes. The problems presented by the damage to roads, sewerage, water supply and hospitals make the control of any outbreaks a major public health challenge.

Control measures will address two key problems: controlling the source of the infection and protecting people exposed to it. Occasionally, simply removing the source of an infection is sufficient; for example, in an outbreak of food poisoning once the source of the outbreak has been identified, the premises closed and any food from that source withdrawn from sale, the public is no longer at risk.

The true challenge and limitation of the epidemiological approach to the control of disease outbreaks is probably best seen in the history of HIV. By the end of 1982, one year after the first scientific paper on the new disease, epidemiologists had a clear picture of the fundamental nature of the disease's epidemiology. They understood the nature of the epidemic and the measures required to control its spread.

However, although the potential for a major epidemic has been controlled, through a variety of health education programmes and innovative service developments, the reality is that despite this knowledge HIV has continued to spread amongst specific sections within the population. These were initially gay and bisexual men and intravenous drug users, but more recently transmission rates are peaking in heterosexual women, young people, and most recently older people, and HIV is epidemic in sub-Saharan Africa. Therefore the answer is never so simple.

Epidemics

An epidemic is the occurrence of a disease in a community or region of a number of cases of a disease that is unusually large or unexpected for the given place or time (Bres, 1986). By contrast an endemic disease is usually present in a particular region at relatively high prevalence or incidence rates.

The characteristics of an epidemic may vary, based on a number of features including:
- the number of cases
- the size and type of population exposed
- previous experience of or exposure to the disease
- the time and place of the occurrence.

In some cases an epidemic may be identified from a rise in a particular disease in only a small number of cases. A classic example of this is the rise in the number of cases of *Pneumocystis carinii*, a very rare form of pneumonia, between 1977 and 1982 in New York. This form of pneumonia is normally only seen in patients with damaged immune systems but between 1977 and 1982 the number of cases rose from 2 to 88. It was this fact which lead to further exploration of the outbreak and the eventual identification of what became known as AIDS.

Therefore this was an epidemic which occurred over a period of several years, to a specific group within the population (gay men) and was identified because it differed markedly from the previous experience of the disease.

Epidemics are usually either point source or contagious. In a point source people are exposed almost simultaneously, i.e. together resulting in a rapid rise in numbers, possibly over a few hours, e.g. a food poisoning outbreak. In a contagious epidemic the disease is passed from person to person and the result is a slower rate of spread.

Key issues

Each year the government has a campaign in the autumn to encourage health workers and people over 65 to have flu vaccination.

Why do you think these two groups are singled out?

For each group consider the following:

- What messages would you use to market the vaccination?
- What venues you would use to market the vaccine.
- What approaches you could use to maximise the uptake of vaccine.
- What agencies or groups you could involve to help you achieve your targets for vaccination.

Chains of infection

Communicable diseases arise as a result of the interaction of the agent, the transmission process and the host. To control the disease one or more of these components may be changed. Whilst epidemiology strives to gain as much knowledge and understanding of a disease as possible to enable effective control, it is possible to implement effective control measures with only limited knowledge; as John Snow demonstrated with his action to remove the handle of the Broad Street pump, despite not having clear knowledge of the causative agent for the cholera outbreak (see page 400).

The infectious agent

A large number of organisms cause disease in humans, as we have seen in previous sections. The characteristics of an agent are important in determining the nature of the infection and its likely epidemic characteristics. Some of the key features which might be considered would include those shown in the table below.

Infectious agent	Characteristics
Pathogenicity	The ability of the agent to produce the disease, measured as a proportion of the number of people exposed to the agent who go on to develop the disease
Virulence	A measure of the severity of the disease
Infective dose	A measure of the number of disease organisms required to cause infection
Source of infection	The person or object from which someone acquires the infection

Transmission

This is the second link in the chain; it refers to the spread of the infectious agent through the environment or to another person. Transmission may be direct or indirect, as shown in the table below.

Direct transmission	Indirect transmission
Touching Kissing Sexual intercourse Airborne for short distance Transfusion Crossing the placenta Childbirth	Vehicle borne (contamination of food, water, farm implements, etc.) Vector borne (insects, e.g. malaria; animals e.g. BSE, toxicara, toxoplasmosis) Parenteral (injection with contaminated syringe)

Host

The host is the person or animal which provides a suitable environment for the infectious agent to grow and reproduce. Points of entry may vary from one agent to another and include skin, mucous membranes and the respiratory and gastrointestinal tract. Reaction of the host to the infection may vary and be dependent upon previous exposure to the condition.

Impact of travel

Travel patterns have changed significantly over the last 100 years. People from every social class can now often afford to travel abroad for their holidays. The speed of travel from one place to another has resulted in far-flung destinations being accessed by more people than ever before. It is often these more exotic destinations such as Africa, Asia and the Mediterranean that still have high levels of disease-inducing agents, for example the tsetse fly which can transmit malaria to the unprotected traveller.

As you might expect this has a real implication for health and the health care services. Travellers often fail to access appropriate health information prior to travel. This can lead to illness such as gastroenteritis, food poisoning, etc. or the more deadly diseases such as TB, malaria and typhoid – the list is almost endless! Other problems have been identified when cases of malaria were found to have originated in airports due to the transport and survival of the infected mosquito.

Far-flung destinations are being accessed more than ever before

Theory into practice

Recent research illustrates the possibilities of thrombosis occurring to passengers travelling on long-haul flights. Research this issue and discuss your findings in a group.

It is often the case that people are back from holiday before any symptoms show. This of course places a heavy burden on the health care systems in terms of treatment, screening and rehabilitation.

Think it over

Find out how your local public health/environmental health departments carry out 'contacts tracing'.

Global disease patterns

Researchers now argue that the world is so small (because of the ease of access) that we need to consider all disease in terms of the global environment.

This unit concentrates on three such diseases, i.e. typhoid, HIV and malaria. Although there are higher levels of the disease in some countries rather than others, prevention concerns us all. Global action needs to be taken to reduce incidence and prevalence.

Typhoid
Typhoid became less important in western countries such as the UK and America after about 1920. This was largely due to public health measures. However, this is not the same story for countries where poverty, famine and lack of public health facilities are the norm.

Globally there are as many as 33 million cases of typhoid every year. All countries carry some element of risk as the disease is transmitted in food and drinks. In the main, high-risk countries include Central Africa, the Indian subcontinent and western South America. Medium-risk countries would be those situated around the Mediterranean and low-risk countries are seen as Australia, North America and Europe.

HIV
According to the World Health Organisation there are approximately 38 million adults and children worldwide living with HIV/AIDS. Over 95 per cent of these people live in the developing world where there are limited resources for their support and treatment.

The figures for Western Europe are much less due to the preventative activities that take place. It is also interesting to note that the survival rate is significantly different for people living in the western world and those living in poorer regions of the world.

Look at these statistics:

- 1.4 million adults and children with HIV/AIDS in Latin America
- 640,000 adults and children with infection in Asia
- 420,000 adults and children in Eastern Europe
- 25.3 million in sub-Saharan Africa.

Think it over

Why do you think there is such a difference in figures between people living in Africa and those living in another country?

Malaria

Malaria actually causes the death of over 1 million people every year. The parasite responsible is found in as many as 90 different countries. Sub-Saharan Africa accounts for 90 per cent of all cases, whilst the remaining cases are found in countries such as India, Brazil and Colombia.

The most serious case of malaria affects the brain and kidneys, leading to unconsciousness and finally death.

Although malaria is mainly found in hot tropical countries there have also been cases in Russia, Turkey and Europe.

Approaches to occupational health

Provision of occupational health services

Good occupational health practice aims to support employers and employees in achieving the main aims of the business or service being provided. In more health-related terms, occupational health should lead, in the longer term, to positive outcomes for workers and businesses alike, in terms of a good quality of life inside and outside the workplace, access to the social and material advantages of work, reduced sickness absence, higher productivity, a good, responsible image for individual businesses and greater national wealth creation.

Legal requirements

All companies in the UK with five or more employees have a legal duty to maintain and implement safe systems of work under the 1974 Health and Safety at Work Act (HSWA). Occupational health services in the UK are an integral part of this process. They work within the spirit of the Act with the task of meeting the specific subordinate regulations relating to occupational health.

The HSWA places a wide ranging duty on employers to protect the safety, health and welfare, of their employees. Regulations made under the HSWA and other legislation place specific duties on employers relating to risk assessment, health surveillance, managing health, fitness for work, protecting the vulnerable and employing disabled people.

However, in contrast with legislation in certain other EU member states, none of these provisions places a duty on employers to provide or buy in occupational health services. Instead, the Management of Health and Safety at Work Regulations 1999 require employers (with certain exceptions) to appoint competent persons to fulfil their statutory responsibilities. The 1999 Regulations and associated Approved Code of Practice make it clear that the preferred way of complying is to appoint people from within the workforce.

The Safety Representatives and Safety Committees Regulations 1977 and the Health and Safety (Consultation with Employees) Regulations 1996 require employers to consult with employees on health and safety matters. In many cases, it is the workers themselves who know most about their immediate working environment and the types of risk to which they are exposed.

HSWA also places duties on employees to take reasonable care for the health and safety of themselves and others, to co-operate with employers in compliance with the latter's obligations, and not to interfere with or misuse anything provided in the interests of health, safety or welfare.

The Disability Discrimination Act 1995 (DDA) requires employers with 15 or more employees to treat disabled persons equally with non-disabled persons in all employment matters and make any reasonable changes to the premises, job design, etc. that may be necessary to accommodate the needs of employees with a disability. The DDA extends the definition beyond deafness, blindness, mental illness and physical impairment, to include severe disfigurement as well as progressive conditions such as HIV/AIDS, where disability develops some time after first diagnosis. Excessive selection procedures to exclude disabled people may be an offence under DDA. Occupational health support can help employers to avoid acting in a discriminatory manner.

The World Health Organisation says that occupational health work is:

> 'the promotion and maintenance of the highest degree of physical, mental and social well being of workers in all occupations by preventing departures from health, controlling risks and the adaptation of work to people and people in their jobs' (WHO, 1950).

Roles and responsibilities

Therefore, we can argue that occupational health services in the UK are concerned primarily with legislative compliance, preventative health and rehabilitation. The main roles and responsibilities of occupational health staff are:

- pre-employment screening
- during employment health screening and surveillance, for example noise and hearing or lung function tests and skin inspections
- to provide an impartial health advisory service to employers and employees
- the promotion of health and safety
- monitoring the working environment
- managing health promotion activities
- ensuring legal compliance
- confidential counselling
- rehabilitation for work returners after illness or injury
- minor treatment service
- staff training.

Different levels of service and the personnel involved

As we have already seen there is no law that requires any company of any size to have occupational health departments. However, the statutory requirements linked to screening and surveillance make it a sensible option for those companies employing large numbers of people (rather than always paying for an 'external service'). Where a company does decide to have its own occupational health department specific guidance must be followed. For example:

- the Chief Medical Officer is responsible for the issue and maintenance of all policies and standards relating to occupational health (HS/A.09)
- doctors, nurses and advisers are employed in occupational health subject to approval from the Chief Medical Officer or a regional medical officer

- the regional medical officer advises companies on the level of service required based on the numbers employed and the type of business provided
- the company must comply with current UK legislation relating to professional codes of confidentiality and data protection.

In the main, occupational health departments are staffed by qualified doctors and nurses (sometimes known as 'health advisers'). Nurses need to have an RGN background and have completed the Diploma or Degree in Occupational Health Nursing.

Qualified first aiders also have a role to play within the overall system of occupational health.

Think it over
What role do you think a qualified first aider might have in a company that manufactures car and aeroplane parts?

Key issue

Defence Medical Services The armed services are unique in offering fully co-ordinated primary care, occupational medicine, environmental health care, secondary care and public health medicine.

Find out why and how this is delivered and managed.

Issues of hazards, risk and methods of control in the workplace and environment

Identifying the range of hazards in different work environments

Nearly all workplaces have potential hazards and risks. In some cases this can be through the use of machinery and equipment, or it could be the substance involved in the production process. Another hazard is the working style of the employee; for example, do they always follow the guidance provided and do they attend regular training (perhaps in first aid or safe moving and handling practices)?

Hazards would usually include all of the following although there are many others that could be added to this list:

- fire
- machinery
- electrics
- hazardous substances
- manual handling
- noise, light, environment
- unsafe working practices.

Think it over
What might be the risks and hazards in a residential care home and a hospital?

Write a report that compares the differences between the residential care home and the hospital.

How risk is assessed and the stages of risk control

Identifying hazards in the workplace is now a statutory duty for every employer. The Management of Health and Safety at Work Regulations 1999 require employers to carry out risk assessments on all their activities. If carried out thoroughly this should give a clear picture of areas where there is the potential for accidents to occur.

In the main, the stages can be seen as:

- carry out the risk assessment
- remove or control the hazard
- train employees to use the control measures implemented
- monitor compliance
- plan for future risk assessments.

Once risks have been identified, control measures can be put into place (operationalised). Some of the measures include:

- relevant signs
- training
- personal protective equipment
- space
- supervision
- safe working procedures.

Case study

James is a theatre nurse and Ahmed a ward nurse; they both work busy shifts that involve changing the times of work, i.e. days and nights. Their employer is Westerly Hospital, a large general hospital that caters for all kinds of care. Surgical procedures are regularly carried out in this hospital, there are many frail older people that need to be moved from one place to another and both nurses use dangerous substances in the course of their daily routines.

- Prepare a risk assessment for the work that these nurses regularly become involved in.
- Plan a series of control measures for the risks you identify that will prevent or minimise any harm to both the staff and their patients.

Responsibilities

Everyone has a responsibility to identify and control risks to health and safety. The Health and Safety at Work Act requires the following actions:

- Employers have a duty to ensure the health, safety and welfare of their employees and members of the public (as far as can be reasonably expected).
- Trade union representatives have the power to appoint safety representatives from the workforce.
- People who control premises must make sure that there are no harmful emissions into the atmosphere.
- Manufacturers must produce user information for any equipment and other articles that have the potential to harm.
- Employees have a duty to co-operate with their employer to keep themselves and their colleagues free from harm.
- Inspectors from the Health & Safety Executive enforce the regulations.

Theory into practice

Using the Internet find the Health & Safety Executive website to find out more about risk assessment and control methods.

Find out what powers an inspector from the HSE holds within a workplace.

Legislation relating to health and safety in the workplace

Control of substances

The Control of Substances Hazardous to Health Regulations 1999 (COSHH) lays down the essential requirements for protecting people from dangerous substances. Any substance labelled as dangerous or hazardous is included (except lead and asbestos). For example, the words very toxic, harmful, irritant and corrosive would indicate they are covered by the COSHH regulations.

Other substances covered would include large amounts of dust, micro-organisms (including those found on clinical waste) and any substances that have a limited exposure time.

Case study

Miriam is opening a nursing and residential home for frail and sick older people. She is still learning about an employer's responsibility under the 1974 Health and Safety at Work Act and now she has just discovered that the COSHH regulations must also be followed.

- What duties and responsibilities does an employer have under the COSHH regulations for themselves, their staff and their clients?

Health and safety

The Management of Health and Safety at Work Regulations 1999 is a useful source of information in terms of an employer's duties. They outline the requirements in terms of risk assessment and the fact that every employer must appoint one or more competent people to help them meet the requirements of the legislation. You might also find it helpful at this point to obtain a copy of the health and safety guidelines for your place of work or study and then try to relate them to the information contained in this unit.

Moving and handling

The Manual Handling Operations Regulations 1992 are designed to ensure that safe action is taken when moving or handling equipment (and people). Over 25 per cent of reported accidents each year involve the manual handling of loads.

Under these regulations employers must take all the steps necessary to ensure that, as far as possible, injuries do not occur. Before any moving occurs, a full risk assessment must be carried out and appropriate control measures implemented. This often means that in the care sector, lifting equipment such as hoists and slings are used.

Emission control

In the UK the main pollution control act is the Environmental Protection Act 1990. However, the European Union produced a directive in 1996 (which had to be implemented in the UK by 1999) on Pollution Prevention and Control. Therefore, the Pollution Prevention and Control (England and Wales) Regulations 2000 came into force in August 2000.

Key issues

Obtain a copy of the summary for the Environmental Protection Act 1990 and make notes of the section relating to emission control.

Find out what impact the Pollution Prevention and Control Regulations 2000 are likely to have on local industry in your region or locality.

Responsibility of the individual

Again we have looked at this already in the unit but it is useful to be reminded that under the Health and Safety Act 1974, for example:

- all employees are charged with keeping themselves and their work colleagues safe from harm as well as preventing accidents
- protective clothing and equipment must be used at all times
- employees should know what action and procedures to follow in the case of an emergency
- employees must not misuse or mishandle any equipment or substance
- employees should be alert to risks and hazards and report them as soon as possible
- personal cleanliness must be a priority for any person exposed to harmful conditions.

Environmental health issues

Effects of the environment on health

This section aims to provide some understanding of the wide range of environmental factors that have the potential to influence health in either a positive or negative way. Perhaps a useful starting point is to explore exactly what we mean when we talk about 'environmental health'.

Think it over

What do you think the word 'environment' means? Look up a definition in a dictionary.

What about the word 'health'? What definitions can you find to explain the meaning of this word? (Looking back into the early sections of this unit might be helpful.)

Your definitions should have included the fact that 'environment' includes all external conditions in which we live; for example, the soil, climate, food production, housing and transport. We would also need to see these and other aspects of our environment in the terms of our culture, political views and social processes (for example the law and education). So we can see that 'environment' is much more than perhaps the town or city surrounding us.

Health is another difficult word to define. A useful starting point for this probably lies with the World Health Organisation's definition which we came across earlier: 'Health is a complete physical, mental and social well-being and not simply the absence of disease or infirmity'.

Here we can see that there are many aspects to our health. The main thing to note is the way our environment has the potential to affect positively or negatively any or all of the aspects of our health and well-being.

Local effects of the environment on health

In this case 'local' means our immediate environment, in other words the things that surround us; for example, the housing you occupy, the road or street that you live in, the workplace and the type of work you do are all classed as local factors. However, there are many more.

Think it over

Make a list of other local environmental factors that could have an impact on health and well-being.

If you have been thorough in creating your list it should include many more aspects of the local environment. For example, have you included waste disposal, railway lines and stations, litter, major road systems or parks and other recreational facilities? If not, you will need to rethink your list!

It is clear that each of the items listed above has the potential to affect our health adversely. However, there can also be positive health factors to be gained. For example, parks and recreational spaces can encourage us to participate in regular exercise or even just allow us the opportunity to experience time away from the stresses and strains of everyday life. On the other hand, it is now well documented that poor housing often leads to chest illnesses such as asthma and bronchitis. There is also some argument as to whether landfill sites have the potential to harm those people who live close to them and, of course, the argument still rages as to whether mobile phones and their masts have the potential, through the microwaves emitted, to cause cancer and possible brain damage in the people who use or live near them. Friends of the Earth would argue that phone masts are often situated in built-up areas, close to schools and on top of blocks of flats, thus having the potential to harm many people.

Home

The home environment links very closely with the local environment to the extent that in some cases they cannot be easily separated. For example, when we talk about the home we are including all the internal and external factors, such as gardens, driveways and garages. The interior of the home usually consists of a number of rooms designed for specific purposes. Each room has the potential to create negative or positive effects on health. In fact, there are aspects of the entire house that could affect well-being: think about the electricity supply, the wiring systems, electrical appliances, gas appliances, roof space and wall cavities. We also need to remember that in the home we often store cleaning materials that have the potential to harm our health. Then what about food preparation, cooking and storage? Again, food safety forms an important part of our environment.

We can also include indoor air pollution in an exploration of the home environment; for example, inhaling other people's tobacco smoke (passive smoking) is clearly a risk to health. There is also a risk to health in some homes from radon gas, which is naturally occurring in many areas.

Theory into practice

Carry out an environmental audit of your own home or immediate locality. Make a note of the factors that have the potential to affect health and well-being and then explain in what ways each could affect the health of a range of client groups, e.g. older people, children and adults.

Office

This is another environment that most people will come across in their normal daily routines. Not everybody works in an office, so you may need to think much wider to include other workplaces such as shops, classrooms, restaurants and leisure services. However, in general there are aspects of the typical office environment that would need to be taken into consideration when exploring the links with health. For example, ergonomics is the study of the relationship between people and their working environment. This is particularly important in relation to posture, work activities, space for movement and comfort and even light and dark.

These days more and more work is produced electronically, and again, this has the potential to create hazards such as repetitive strain injury, vision problems and others.

Key issue

Find out more about ergonomics and its relationship to health.

Macro-pollution

Once again we need to explore this by defining the key words involved in the term. *Macro* means large scale, in other words the opposite of micro, which is 'very small'. A useful definition of pollution is contained in the UK Environment Protection Act 1990:

> 'Pollution of the environment due to the release (into any environmental medium) of products from any process or substances which are capable of causing harm to man or any other living organisms supported by the environment.'

Therefore we can see that when we are talking about macro-pollution we need to include issues such as radiation, chemical pollution and carbon monoxide emissions. Other forms of pollution could also include noise and poor environments. Just think how derelict areas turn into 'eye sores' or 'blots on the landscape'. This is known as 'visual pollution'.

Radiation

There has been much research into the possible effects of nuclear radiation in areas of the country that are close to nuclear power stations, for example Sellafield on the Cumbrian coast. There have been several studies attempting to link radiation to childhood leukaemia and fertility issues in the workforce. We have already mentioned the possible dangers from mobile phone masts and the phones themselves. Although it was once thought that the main danger was caused through thermal heat there is now a growing opinion that, in fact, the main risk to health is through radiation transmitted by the equipment.

Chemical pollution

This type of pollution is arguably the greatest cause of damage to the environment. Chemicals contained in liquids, gases and solids are used in many aspects of industry. These range from the relatively harmless types (depending on your point of view) often contained in food and household products through to extremely harmful chemicals. However, not all links between chemicals and ill health are clear cut. For example, some individuals feel that organophosphates (used in pesticides) have affected their nervous system but there is no 'hard' evidence that this is so. On the other hand there are industrial chemicals, for example caustic soda, which are clearly known to 'burn'.

Where chemicals are known to be dangerous, health and safety precautions must be followed to eliminate any dangers. However, accidents do happen. If you check your newspapers you may well find information relating to chemical spillages into rivers and onto land. In most cases these accidents will cause the death of the organisms living in that environment, such as fish. However, in some cases the damage can also be transmitted to the human organism in drinking water or through bathing in affected waters. However, chemicals are not just restricted to spillages in water. There is also the possibility of chemical spillages during road traffic accidents. Dangerous chemicals have to be identified by their symbol on any vehicle transporting them from one place to another. This is to ensure that the authorities have the necessary information to protect themselves, the public and the environment from major damage.

Theory into practice

Find out about three dangerous chemicals of your choice. Make notes on the risk factors and the potential for harm to the human organism and the environment.

Carbon monoxide emissions

This is possibly one of the greatest environmental air pollutants in the world. It directly affects 'air quality', which in turn affects the air that we need to obtain our oxygen supplies. There is also research which demonstrates that pollution of the air is contributing towards the 'greenhouse effect'. Carbon monoxide is produced from a variety of sources, one of which is the motor vehicle. It is caused by the burning of carbon-based fuel. Other sources of carbon monoxide pollutants are power stations and heating boilers.

The need for environmental legislation

Environmental legislation is required to protect the environment from a range of dangerous substances and pollutants. For example, it was environmental legislation (the Clean Air Act of 1956) that brought about an improvement in air quality, particularly in those towns and cities with many factory chimneys. During the early part of the last century it was 'usual' to have thick yellow fogs (known as 'pea soupers') created by vast numbers of chimneys burning coal and belching out thick smoke. As you can imagine there were many deaths attributed to the smoke.

However, we now face other problems. As the industrial smog has reduced carbon monoxide, carbon dioxide and nitrous oxide emissions have increased on both a global and local scale. It is only through environmental legislation implemented at both of these levels that we will be able to protect the Earth.

Rio Summit 1992

The Earth Summit was held in Rio de Janeiro in June 1992. This world conference was called for by most of the world's leading countries. For the first time, a range of targets and agreements was set by the participating governments to develop international co-operation on environmental issues such as global warming. Returning carbon dioxide emissions to the 1990 levels by the year 2000 was one of the conventions specifically agreed at the summit. Other conventions agreed were a commitment to safeguarding biodiversity and reducing poverty on a worldwide basis.

As a result of the UK's participation in the Earth Summit action has been taken by the government and industry to contribute to these challenging targets.

Assessment activity 10.5

Research the effects of the Rio Summit from a global perspective. Identify any relevant action taken by the UK government to contribute to the conventions agreed.

Find out what the benefits to health and well-being might be through the reduction of carbon monoxide emissions.

The effects of global and environmental change

Deforestation

This is a particularly worrying issue in many countries. The 'cutting down' of trees and forests is having a huge impact on many populations. For example, despite the fact that tropical rainforests have a rich diversity of plants and animal species, the soil upon which they are based is usually of a very poor quality. Therefore, once the ground cover and trees have been removed nothing will grow. This ultimately means that people will starve because they can no longer grow or select their own food. Again, once the trees are removed the local people have no further commodities to sell, thus creating even more poverty and deprivation.

Deforestation is leading to increased poverty and deprivation

Ozone depletion

The ozone layer is a thin blanket of gas that covers the Earth at a height of about 20 to 25 kilometres. Its main role is to protect the Earth (and its population and environment) from dangerous ultraviolet rays (solar radiation) emitted from the sun. However, research has demonstrated that this layer of ozone is becoming thinner and in some places has even developed holes. There is an argument that one of the causes of this 'thinning' is CFCs (chlorofluorocarbons). If the ozone layer becomes too thin, more harmful ultraviolet rays from the sun will reach the Earth. This could result in:

- increases in skin cancers
- damage to crops and plants
- increased risk of sun damage to those people who usually work outdoors.

Grazing

This is the main method by which animals such as cows and sheep feed, and at first glance would seem to be harmless enough. Indeed, until the 1930s that is exactly what everyone thought. However, we now know better!

The animals eat the grass right down to its root. This means that the grass dies and is not replaced. Instead weeds are more likely to take root and the animals have to be moved to another area because they cannot eat the plant life. Over time, grazing areas are ruined and in many cases the top soil is blown away leading to other disastrous environmental effects such as the silting up of rivers and lakes.

Different farming methods

Over the years farming has changed significantly through the use of scientific developments. Pesticides and genetic modifications are just two of the major issues which have brought about change. However, there are other changes which also have an impact on the environment, as we have already seen, such as increased grazing and deforestation to increase grazing land.

Intensive farming methods have not been covered elsewhere and therefore, need to be covered here. Intensive farming often involves the use of enclosed areas where animals and birds spend their entire lives. Examples of these could include:

- battery hens
- pig lots.

The farmer can ensure maximum production from the animals involved using intensive farming methods. However, from an environmental point of view the waste products generated by this method of farming can be immense. Disposal then becomes a problem and in many cases land and water courses become polluted because of the intensive amounts of waste products.

From a humane point of view the creatures may be kept in appalling, stress-inducing conditions before they are slaughtered and enter the food chain.

Think it over

How might the food produced in this way be affected? Discuss in a group, the positive and negative effects of different farming methods.

Genetic modification

This is also known as genetically manipulating foods, in other words the plant has been changed by adding the genes from another plant. This could be the addition of a single gene or many genes.

The reason this is carried out is arguably to enhance some particular trait of the food in order to increase production; for example, to increase the size of say a tomato. Alternatively, plants are modified in order to give them immunity from certain predators or, as in the case of the tomato, to protect it from cold temperatures. Genetic modification can also produce crops which are drought and disease resistant which is of particular benefit to farmers in less-developed countries.

Modifying plant foods is not the only action taken by the food industry. Many animals are injected with hormones to produce more meat, cows can be treated with hormones to increase their milk production and even salmon have been treated to increase their size.

However, it has been argued that the presence of these 'extra' genes or hormones has the potential to harm human health. For example, where antibiotics are used in food production this could lead to an immunity in those people who eat the food and many people have developed allergies. In some cases interfering with 'mother nature' has arguably damaged the environment.

Use of pesticides

Pesticides are used in food production and storage, forestry and even in domestic gardening on a large scale. They are chemical substances or in some cases micro-organisms, such as bacteria and fungi, that are mainly used to prevent the spread of pests and insect-borne disease amongst crops and plants. However, research has demonstrated that one of the major chemicals involved (DDT) does not easily or quickly break down once it is in the environment.

Researchers have linked problems with pollution in rivers and lakes and deformities in birds and animals to those areas where there is a high and sustained use of pesticides. The problem that lies ahead is the potential dangers to the human population. There are many uncertainties regarding the long-term effects of the use of pesticides.

Key issue

Find out about DDT and the possible dangers it poses to the environment and living organisms including human beings. Draw a table that compares the benefits of using pesticides to the potential damage caused by DDT to humans and the environment.

Sustainable development

The idea of sustainable development was first introduced as early as 1980 and can perhaps be best described as:

> 'Development which meets the needs of the present (population) without compromising the ability of future generations to meet their own needs' (Brundtland, 1987).

The concept of sustainable development encourages the use of the environment in the best possible way so that human needs can be met over a long period of time, rather than finding quick, short-term answers that are likely to be damaging to the environment in the long run.

The problem with the concept of 'sustainable development' is how to implement it. If people are left to participate voluntarily there is the chance that immediate, pressing needs will drive action that is not sustainable in the long term. However, if laws are introduced to force governments

Visual pollution

and organisations to act in certain ways there is the risk of high costs for the sake of the environment. Perhaps the answer lies with some kind of in between action. What do you think?

Pollution

Pollution can be said to have occurred when the environment is negatively affected in some way. As we have seen pollution comes in many forms from air pollution to land, water and aesthetic pollution (visual). Many of these forms of pollution have the potential to effect long-term damage on both the environment and human health and well-being on a global and national scale. It is argued that pollution should be monitored and measured to allow action to be taken to reduce the amount of all kinds of pollution.

Assessment activity 10.6

Write a report on the changing effect of the environment on health, including an evaluation of the effects of global and environmental change. Discuss what role global and local environmental legislation should take.

Protection of the individual

The individual needs, and indeed has a right, to be protected in the home, the workplace and in public places. Legislation has been developed and implemented to make sure that each individual has access to that protection.

Home

Home covers a range of different residential environments from your own home to a place where you have 'chosen' to live. For example, people living in a residential care environment can expect to find all the necessary fire regulations for their health and safety in place along with other relevant environmental protection.

People living in their own homes are protected from harm by a range of legislation, for example laws making it illegal for a gas fitter to fit an appliance unless they are an approved CORGI registered gas fitter. Other legislation relating to waste collection and disposal by the local authority, clean water and sewage disposal would apply to individuals in their own homes. Schemes such as Neighbourhood Watch and 'Be a Good Neighbour' would also apply in terms of individual 'social' protection.

Workplaces

The 1974 Health and Safety at Work Act is the main piece of legislation affording protection to both the employer and the employee. This Act covers all people who are working with just a few minor exceptions. The main points are:

- employers have a duty to ensure the health, safety and welfare of their employees
- employers have a duty to make sure that members of the public are not put at risk
- employees have a duty to take reasonable care of themselves and their co-workers
- employees (and employers) must not misuse anything required in the interests of health and safety.

Theory into practice

Obtain a summary of the Health and Safety at Work Act 1974 and make a list of the main points affecting both the employer and the employee.

Public places

Individuals are protected in public places through a variety of different mechanisms including the role of the police, fire service and armed services. Other examples include: road traffic regulations in place for the safety of drivers, passengers and members of the public; many towns and cities have local legislation banning the consumption of alcohol in public places.

Think it over

Why would the banning of alcohol in public places protect individuals?

It is likely that you have thought about harassment and safety issues within this aspect of protection. It can often be the case that people who are under the influence of alcohol and other drugs may injure themselves and members of the public.

Other forms of protection in public places would also include the banning of tobacco smoking in those areas used by members of the public. For example, hospitals, shopping centres, colleges, cinemas and many public houses no longer allow smoking on their premises.

Role of environment agency

The Environment Agency is a public body charged with protecting and improving the environment in England and Wales. Its roles include:

- maintenance of flood defences (not coastal protection)
- maintenance of water supplies
- regulating industry
- improving the habitat for wildlife
- pollution prevention and control
- waste management.

It also has responsibilities in the areas of fishing and navigation. Some areas of its responsibilities are carried out by other agencies. For example, its role in regulating industry does not cover noise and smoke, which is dealt with by the local authority.

More information about the Environment Agency's work and responsibilities can be found on its website.

Role of public health officials

Public health officials cover a range of different job roles. The main ones are as follows:

- Director of public health – employed in health authorities and primary care trusts. They are charged with improving the health of local populations.
- Consultants in communicable disease – employed in the same way as the director of public health but charged with the control of infectious diseases. Responsible for managing outbreaks of disease such as meningitis, TB and others.
- Environmental health officers – employed mainly in local authorities. Responsible for all aspects of environmental health, including pest control, food hygiene, housing, hazards, industrial emissions, etc.
- Health and safety officials – employed by the Health & Safety Executive. Responsible for health and safety at work, emissions and pollutants, accident prevention.

In a broader sense the uniformed services, i.e. police, fire and armed forces, also have a role to play in public health.

Hygiene Regulations 1995

The main act that covers the entire food chain is the Food Safety Act 1990. This Act aims to make certain that all food for sale is safe to eat. However, in 1995 additional regulations came into being because of European Directives.

The general Food Hygiene Regulations 1995 state that food handlers must:

- avoid food contamination
- keep cuts and skin abrasions covered with waterproof dressings
- not smoke or spit in food areas
- wear protective clothing, which must be kept clean (see Figure 10.1).

Figure 10.1 The legal requirements on food premises

Air Quality – National Air Quality Strategy

The Air Quality Regulations and Strategy 1997 has been welcomed by all the different agencies involved who have said that air pollution 'kills many thousands and hospitalises just as many every year'. As an example, the Department of Health suggested that in Scotland as many as 800 people die due to particulate air pollution in any one year.

The Air Quality Regulations 1997 have now made it a statutory duty for local authorities to assess and manage the air quality in their area. They are advised to follow a step-by-step approach for assessing and managing the following pollutants which are most closely linked with public health:

- particulate matter
- nitrogen dioxide
- ozone.

The pollution which this strategy aims to deal with is mostly from carbon monoxide, lead, sulphur dioxide and benzene.

Key issue

Find out what your own local authority is doing about assessing and managing air quality in your area.

Waste: Section 33 Environmental Protection Act

The Environmental Protection Act 1990 covers a wide range of issues, one of which is Section 33 'Prohibition on unauthorised or harmful deposit, treatment or disposal etc. of waste'. This section contains too much detail for a text of this nature but basically states that a person shall not:

- deposit controlled waste on any land unless they have a licence
- treat, keep or dispose of controlled waste unless they have a waste management licence and then only in a manner that will not harm the environment or human health.

Also, waste carried in a motor vehicle must have all reasonable precautions applied. Any person found guilty of contravening this Act is liable to a prison sentence and a fine.

Think it over

Obtain a copy of Section 33 of the Environmental Protection Act 1990 to identify the fine detail. Why is it important that waste is properly disposed of by the relevant authority?

End of unit test

1 Briefly describe the role played by John Snow in the London cholera outbreak of 1854.

2 What are the key differences between the following two definition of health as suggested by the World Health Organisation?

> A state of complete physical, psychological and social well-being and not merely the absence of disease and infirmity.   *World Health Organisation 1948*

> The extent to which an individual or group is able on the one hand, to realise aspirations and satisfy needs and on the other hand, to change or cope with the environment. Health is therefore seen as a resource for everyday life, not the

objective of living: it is a positive concept emphasising social and personal resources as well as physical capabilities.　　*World Health Organisation 1984*

3　Give five reasons why it is appropriate to involve the public in discussions about developing and delivering local health services.

4　Identify whether the following statements about Community Health Councils (CHCs) are true or false:

  a　local authorities in the area nominate all of the members of each CHC from the local councillors

  b　voluntary organisations with an interest in health matters elect one representative to the CHC

  c　people can make applications (to become members) as individuals and are appointed by the Secretary of State for Health.

5　Describe three ways in which a school nurse addressing the issue of substance use contributes to the public health role.

6　Give a brief description of five key functions of an environmental health department.

7　Complete these definitions of key epidemiological terms:

  a　*Standardised rate:* Estimate of the rate for_____

  b　*Perinatal mortality:* Deaths occurring between week_____

  c　*Infant mortality:* Number of deaths per thousand infants_____

  d　*Standardised:* A comparison of death rates against_____

  e　*Incidence:* The number of new cases_____

  f　*Prevalence:* A measure of how many people are suffering from_____

8　Fill in the blanks to complete these descriptions of various epidemiological studies:

Cross-sectional　Usually uses a _____ from the population to produce a _____ study often based on information drawn from _____, examination of records and tests (e.g. for _____. and _____). An example of this kind of study was the Allied Dunbar _____ _____ in 1995 which investigated exercise levels in the population.

Case control　Usually used to test a particular _____ or _____. A group of people with a _____ _____ are compared with a similar group who do not have the condition and investigations are carried out to assess what _____ _____ might have led to the current condition. A study of this kind might try to establish whether treatment with a particular drug during pregnancy leads to _____ to the _____ _____.

Cohort study　Focuses on a group of people who exhibit a _____ _____. This type of study might involve following people who smoke cigarettes for an _____ period of time to record what happens to them. It was this type of study which led to _____ _____ _____ identifying the health risks associated with smoking by tracking a group of smokers for _____ _____ by which time over two-thirds of the sample had died.

9 Complete the following table by filling in the missing information.

Pathogen	Description	Example
Viruses		DNA viruses RNA viruses
Bacteria		anthrax tetanus staphylococcal food poisoning meningitis cholera diarrhoea
	A group of simple organisms similar to plants but lacking chlorophyll. As they lack chlorophyll they are unable to produce their own food and therefore act as parasites on other creatures. In humans they usually invade areas that provide appropriate conditions e.g. the warm and moist conditions provided by the mouth, genitals and folds in the skin.	
Protozoa	Single-celled organisms. They are more sophisticated than bacteria and are usually found in water courses. Protozoa can invade body fluids and destroy cells either by parasitising them or destroying them.	
Pathogenic animals		Nematodes – roundworm infection, trichinosis Platyhelminth – schistosomiasis, tapeworm, liver fluke Arthropods – mites and ticks

10 How did the American Commission on Chronic Illness define screening in 1957? What measures does the child health screening programme cover?

11 Give three examples of both direct and indirect modes of transmission for disease organisms.

References and further reading

Acheson, D. (1998) *The Independent Inquiry into Inequalities in Health*, London HMSO

Brown, A. (1992) *The UK Environment*, London: The Stationery Office Books

Ewles, L. and Simnett, I. (1999) *Promoting Health: A Practical Guide*, London: Ballière Tindall

Jones L. (1997) *The Challenge of Promoting Health*, Basingstoke: Palgrave Macmillan

Naidoo, J. and Wills, J. (1996) *Health Promotion: Foundations for Practice*, London: Ballière Tindall

Rogers, J. and Feiss, P. G. (1998) *People and the Earth*, Cambridge: Cambridge University Press

Diet and nutrition

Government food policies and guidelines have existed since the early twentieth century when many young men, recruited to fight in the Boer war, were found to be physically unfit for combat. This unit will introduce you to the influences that food and diet have on the health of individuals and a range of population groups.

The first section examines the influences that produce different nutritional profiles for a range of different population groups and this is followed by a comprehensive investigation of the chemicals that comprise our food. The next section is concerned with looking at some of the common diseases and disorders related to our food intake and then you will be required to assess and evaluate dietary information from a client using the knowledge and information you have gained through the unit.

What you need to learn

- Influences which produce different nutritional profiles for a range of population groups
- The function of major macro and micro nutrients in the context of a healthy diet
- Diet-related diseases and disorders
- Assessing and evaluating dietary intake

Influences which produce different nutritional profiles for a range of population groups

Today most people in the western world are able to choose what and how much they eat. Food is used to help us socialise, celebrate special festivals and to help us cope with tension and stress. One hundred years ago, however, under-nutrition was the major concern in the western world. Nowadays, the major concern is over-nutrition caused by poor dietary choices and the inclusion of excessive amounts of saturated and total fat, salt and energy foods in our food choices. Today we are urged to consider not only what, but how much, and the different proportions of the different foods that we eat, i.e. to balance our diet.

The concept of a balanced diet arose in an effort to eradicate the deficiency diseases, which are caused by a lack of essential nutrients in the diet. In the developed countries today these are no longer such a problem; instead, the so-called diseases of affluence give cause for concern, e.g. coronary heart disease and cancer.

This does not mean to say that under-nutrition does not exist in the western world. It does, and wherever people suffer from malnutrition the common link appears to be poverty. Under-nutrition results from inadequate supplies of nutrients. If the body does not receive the nutrients it requires, many of the deficiency diseases develop and, because the immune system does not function properly, infectious diseases are common.

The greatest risk from under-nutrition occurs during growth and development. Low birth weight is a leading cause of infant death all over the world, and reduced mental and physical capabilities are evident in those that receive a diet deficient in the essential nutrients.

The World Health Organisation (WHO) has developed dietary guidelines, based on the scientific knowledge that we have of the nutritional requirements for different individuals. To help people follow these dietary guidelines, different countries have developed food selection guides. The UK has published 'The Balance of Good Health', in which the recommended foods and proportions of food are shown on a dinner plate (see Figure 11.1 and pages 460–61). Food manufacturers are now required by law to include dietary information on the labels of tins, jars, bottles and packets of food.

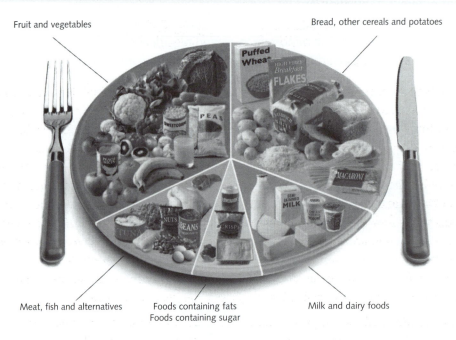

Figure 11.1 The recommended foods and proportions of foods needed for a healthy diet

The main dietary sources of energy for most people are carbohydrates, fats and proteins. Scientists have established recommended daily allowances (RDAs) for the essential nutrients. In the western world most of the protein and about three-fifths of the fat is derived from animal sources and the carbohydrates from simple sugars and starches. In other parts of the world the proteins are derived from plants not animals, e.g. beans, rice and corn.

Tropical diets are often deficient in protein, vitamins A, B1 and B3 and contain insufficient calories. They generally contain too many yams, cassava and maize (cheap foods deficient in protein), and not enough green vegetables, tomatoes and other sources of carotene. In countries where the diet is principally rice or maize vitamins B1 and B3 are likely to be deficient.

Assessment activity 11.1

Compare and contrast the nutritional profiles of the Third World with those of North America and Western Europe.

Influences on the food choices made by populations in the developed world

Factors that influence food choice in the developed world include age, gender, lifestyle, family and cultural background, education and geographical location (see Figure 11.2). Government policies and recent advances in biotechnology also have an effect on the choices available when the diet is being selected.

Figure 11.2 Factors influencing our choice of food

Food preferences begin during early life and only change when the individual is exposed to new people, places and situations. Geographical location, coupled with greatly improved transport links, mean that food choices have been extended over the last decade. Many different foods can now be grown in warmer climates and imported into the cooler western countries. This has not only extended the food choice of the western world but also extended the season and availability of the many traditional fruits and vegetables. Parental choice and cultural influences may limit food choice, and the individual who is unwilling to try new and unfamiliar foods often demonstrates this. Generally, pre-school and nursery children are willing to experiment and eat new varieties of food but when children start school they are more likely to be influenced by their peers. Adults caring for children should try to provide as many different food types as possible so that the diet becomes as wide, varied and as healthy as possible, as soon as possible.

Carefully designed education programmes can be used to establish, maintain, and reinforce good dietary practice. If used, these should be targeted at *all* social groups, recognising that those who already make sensible, health-promoting food choices, are more likely to be those people who belong to social classes 1, 2 and 3, i.e. the better-educated, middle-class, professional people.

However, old habits are very difficult to change and dietary habits established in our early family life are often very difficult to break. Even when we recognise that a particular food is bad for our health we may like it too much to give it up, e.g. eating too many biscuits or too much chocolate.

The major food production companies and larger supermarkets are now attempting to respond to health needs by providing, promoting and advertising more foods which are low in fat, sugar, and salt, i.e. foods that promote and maintain good health.

Unfortunately these foods are often expensive and only available at a limited number of outlets. They are not always available to the poorest members of society. The government White Paper 'Saving Lives: Our Healthier Nation' (1997) expresses concerns about the availability of healthy affordable food to the poorer members of the community. Government policies can help to improve the health of the nation by tackling issues such as low pay, unemployment and bad housing. All these factors contribute both to poor health and to poor dietary choices.

Influences responsible for the differences between the diet of the developed and the developing world

There are many factors responsible for under-nutrition in the developing world. These include:

- inadequate food resources
- inadequate means of distributing the food
- poor farming methods
- limited water supplies
- natural devastation, e.g. drought, fire, crop infestation
- war and civil unrest
- debt.

Large numbers of people in the developing world do not have enough food to eat and consequently suffer from malnutrition. One of the four main objectives of the WHO's Department of Nutrition for Health and Development is to develop and maintain global nutrition databases for keeping track of the world's major forms of malnutrition. The latest data from the WHO shows that nearly 30 per cent of infants, children, adolescents, adults and the elderly in the developing world are currently suffering from some form of malnutrition. The table shows trends and projections of the prevalence and number of malnourished children in developing countries, by region, to 2020.

Region	1970	1995	2020 status quo
Percentage underweight:			
South Asia	72.3	49.3	37.4
Sub-Saharan Africa	35.0	31.1	28.8
East Asia	39.5	22.9	12.8
Near East and North Africa	20.7	14.6	5.0
Latin America and the Caribbean	21.0	9.5	1.9
All developing countries	46.5	31.0	18.4
Numbers underweight (in milliions):			
South Asia	92.2	86.0	66.0
Sub-Saharan Africa	18.5	31.4	48.7
East Asia	77.6	38.2	21.4
Near East and North Africa	5.9	6.3	3.2
Latin America and the Caribbean	9.5	5.2	1.1
All developing countries	203.8	167.1	140.3

Source: International Food Policy Research Institute 2020, Brief 64, February 2000, World Health Organisation

The populations of many of the developing countries have been rising faster than their production of food. Lack of education means that not only is effective birth control not practised to limit the size of the population, and therefore the demand on the food supply, but also best use is not always made of the land available for the production of food. If those who farm the land do not know which plants provide the most nutritious foods, if they are not aware of the methods that they can use to farm their land more efficiently, and of modern methods of pest and disease control, they cannot choose to use them. Malaria and sleeping sickness are endemic in undeveloped countries. These diseases are debilitating and leave people so tired and exhausted that they are unable to work the land.

There is therefore an urgent need for the development and implementation of a comprehensive education programme covering *all* aspects of nutrition and including all stages in the production and distribution of food.

Education is not the only factor limiting good farming practice. The level of poverty in these countries is very high. Poor farmers do not have the money to buy modern agricultural machinery and expensive fertilisers, weed killers and disease-resistant seeds. In addition to this there are a number of external factors, often beyond the farmer's control, that influence the cultivation and production of food crops, e.g. natural disasters (floods, drought, plagues of pests, and disease), wars and civil disturbance.

Key issues

Name two recent examples where natural disasters have affected the food supply of large populations in the undeveloped world. Discuss measures that could be adopted by the western world to help resolve food shortages created by the disaster.

Poor people in under-developed countries usually eat the cheapest available food, such as rice, yams, cassava and maize. These are foods that are often low in protein and lack the essential minerals and vitamins; consequently those who consume only these foods often suffer from the deficiency diseases. The latest figures from the World Health Organisation show that the diseases resulting from a deficiency of vitamin A, and the minerals iron and selenium, zinc, calcium are still major causes of concern (see Figure 11.3).

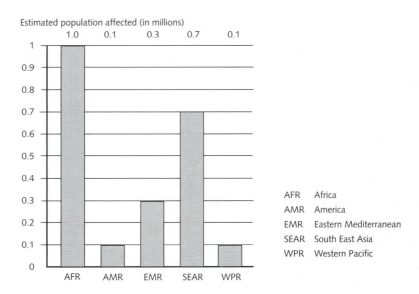

Source: Bulletin of World Health Organisation, 71 (6) 703–712, 1993

Figure 11.3 Estimated per cent of population of children under 5 years of age affected by vitamin A deficiency, by WHO region

In the western world the provision of an adequate supply of clean fresh water is taken for granted. In the developing countries, clean safe water is not always available. On a global scale it is estimated that about 250,000 people die each day from water-borne diseases, such as cholera, diarrhoea, malaria, sleeping sickness and typhoid. Drinking contaminated water causes approximately 80 per cent of diseases and over one-third of deaths in the developing world. More than one-third of the world's population is without a safe supply of drinking water and by the early part of the twenty-first century an estimated one-quarter of the world will be suffering from chronic water shortages. To ensure that basic human and environmental needs are met it is therefore important that a sound global water policy is developed.

Systems of government, education, transport and communications are all elements of the infrastructure that affect the sowing, growing, harvesting, and distribution of food. Food policies must be developed to ensure that there will be enough food available to feed the population of the world (see Figure 11.4). The developed countries have formulated food policies to maximise health; the developing countries must now formulate food policies to minimise hunger. Direct food aid should only be used as a short-term solution to the problem.

Region	% of stunted children	Number of stunted children (millions)
Africa	38.6	44.6
Asia	47.1	172.8
Latin America	22.2	12.1
Oceania	41.9	0.4
All developing countries	42.7	229.9

Source: The Worldwide magnitude of protein-energy malnutrition: an overview from the WHO Global Database on Child Growth in *Bulletin of the World Health Organization*, 71(6), 1993.

Figure 11.4 Prevalence of stunted children in developing countries

Assessment activity 11.2

Evaluate the influences that are responsible for the differences between the nutritional profile of the developing world and that of the North America and Western Europe.

Consider the diseases that can be caused by poor diet and explain how a good diet can alleviate specific conditions.

Biotechnological advances

Recent advances in food and biotechnology have led to the development of new and improved food products. Different methods of food preservation, e.g. fast freezing and freeze-drying, have resulted in food having a longer shelf life. Food no longer needs to be consumed as soon as it is harvested. Whole ranges of food have thus become available to a wider population over an extended period of the year.

Genetic engineering, a method of changing the inherited characteristics of organisms by altering their genetic composition, their DNA, has contributed to the development of new drug-resistant and pest-resistant varieties of food.

Think it over

One of the most controversial ways currently being developed to help pest control is the production of manufactured viruses to target specific pests. These are sprayed on the vulnerable crops. The viruses do not appear to harm other species and they appear to destroy themselves when they have killed the pest damaging the food crop. In a group, find out what you can about these viruses and discuss the possible advantages and disadvantages of this method of pest control.

The function of major macro and micro nutrients in the context of a healthy diet

Our diet provides the raw materials for all cellular activity. In order to maintain good health the diet should include proteins, carbohydrates, fats, vitamins, mineral salts, water and dietary fibre. We also require water. Although this has no energy value, it is required to enable the chemical reactions of the body to take place.

The role of proteins

Proteins contain carbon, hydrogen, oxygen, nitrogen and sometimes sulphur and other elements. They are built up from sub-units called amino acids. These have an amino group, $-NH_2$, and a carboxyl group, $-COOH$. The common naturally occurring acids all have the same general formula. That is:

$$\begin{array}{c} H \\ | \\ H_2N-C-COOH \\ | \\ R \end{array}$$

The amino acids differ in the nature of the R group. For example, when R = H, the acid is glycine (NH_2CH_2COOH), when it is CH_3, it is alanine ($NH_2CHCOOH$).

$$\begin{array}{c} | \\ CH_3 \end{array}$$

Proteins are formed by amino acids linking together. The amino group of one acid can react with the carboxyl group of another. Water is removed during this reaction and the two amino acids become joined by a peptide bond to form a dipeptide. The condensation reaction can continue and further amino acids are added to the chain to form a polypeptide. Proteins are made from long polypeptide chains containing from around 50 to many hundred amino acid residues. The chains are usually twisted and folded and are sometimes linked to other non-protein entities. Although there are only about 20 naturally occurring amino acids in food protein, they can be linked together in so many different sequences that there are an almost limitless variety of different proteins.

Proteins are not used in the form in which they are eaten. They are essentially a source of amino acids. During the digestive process the protein-digesting enzymes break them down into their constituent amino acids. These are then reassembled, by condensation reactions, to make the different types of protein required by the body (in the same way that a set number of Lego bricks of different colours can be used to make a wall and then knocked down and a new wall built with the coloured bricks in a different order) (see Figure 11.5).

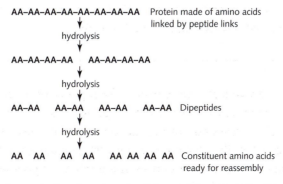

Figure 11.5 Protein broken down into constituent amino acids during digestion

449

Although we cannot make amino acids, we can in some cases convert one amino acid into another. However, there are eight amino acids that the body cannot make and these are called the essential amino acids. These essential amino acids must be contained in our food, and therefore provided in the diet, if the body is to remain healthy. Proteins obtained from animal sources generally include all the essential amino acids. These are said to be proteins of high biological value, first class proteins, or complete proteins. Vegetable proteins often lack one or more of the essential amino acids or they contain them in the wrong proportions. They are said to be proteins of low biological value, second class proteins or incomplete proteins. The essential amino acids occur in large quantities in milk, cheese or eggs and if these are included in the daily diet then the requirements of the body will be satisfied.

Think it over

Consider why it is important to include a number of different types of protein in our diet.

Functions of protein

The primary function of protein is to build body tissue. Proteins exist in the body in a variety of forms, for example: as enzymes, e.g. pepsin, lipase and trypsinogen; hormones, e.g. insulin, corticotrophin; respiratory pigments, e.g. haemoglobin and myoglobin; storage products, e.g. albumin in egg white; and the contractile proteins found in muscle, e.g. actin and myosin. They are essential components in a variety of activities, including transport, protection and support. Oxygen is transported round the body by combining with haemoglobin to form oxyhaemoglobin. Antibodies, involved in the immune response, and fibrinogen and prothrombin, proteins involved in the clotting mechanism in mammalian blood, provide protection, and the proteins collagen and elastin present in connective tissue, provide support for the body. In addition to these functions, proteins are an essential component of all cell membranes. Proteins are particularly important to the body during the time when new cells and tissues are being made, for example during pregnancy and growth. It is therefore important that growing children, adolescents and pregnant women receive adequate supplies of protein and foods containing all the essential amino acids in the correct proportions in their diet.

Key issue

When insulin is used to treat diabetes it must be injected into the patient. Why can't it be given to the client as a tablet?

Dietary sources of protein

Most dietary advice is to eat a combination of animal and vegetable protein to meet the recommended adult requirement of 0.8 grams per kilogram of body weight, for example a 60 kg adult will require 48 g of protein each day. Growing infants and young children require 0.9 grams per kilogram of body weight and pregnant women enough protein to supply both the mother's body and her developing embryo.

Role of carbohydrates

Carbohydrates are made from carbon, hydrogen and oxygen and occur as sugars, starch, cellulose and glycogen. Their primary function in animals is the production and storage of energy.

Monosaccharides

Monosaccharides are the simplest form of carbohydrate, with the general formula $(CH_2O)_n$. All monosaccharides are white crystalline solids that readily dissolve in water. They all taste sweet and are classified according to how many carbon atoms there are in each molecule. If n = 6 the resultant monosaccharide has the formula $C_6H_{12}O_6$ and is said to be a hexose sugar; if n = 5 the resultant sugar is said to be a pentose, and if n = 3 the sugar is called a triose. The hexose sugars include glucose, the most common sugar found in the human body.

CHO	CH_2OH
|	|
CHOH	CO
|	|
CHOH	CHOH
|	|
CHOH	CHOH
|	|
CHOH	CHOH
|	|
CH_2OH	CH_2OH
glucose	fructose

There are other monosaccharides with the same $C_6H_{12}O_6$ formula but with a different arrangement of the atoms within their molecules. These include fructose (fruit sugar) and galactose (present in milk sugar). The different arrangement of the atoms within the molecule causes the molecule to react in different ways.

Disaccharides

Monosaccharides are the building blocks of the more complex carbohydrates. In the same way that the amino acids are the building blocks of the proteins, monosaccharides can combine to form larger molecules. When two monosaccharide sugars combine they form a disaccharide. The reaction is reversible and under suitable conditions the disaccharide may be converted back to its original monosaccharide sugars. Disaccharide sugars include maltose, sucrose and lactose. Maltose, or malt sugar, found in germinating seeds, is formed by the combination of two glucose molecules.

Polysaccharides

Polysaccharides are giant molecules in which many monosaccharide units are linked together. The most common polysaccharides are starch and cellulose. Both starch and cellulose are made from glucose, but the manner in which the glucose units are linked together leads to differences in their properties. Glycogen, the storage form of carbohydrates in humans, is a highly branched polymer of glucose. Starch and glycogen are both insoluble in water and consequently provide a suitable form in which carbohydrates can be stored. Glycogen is stored in the liver and muscles of human beings and starch is stored in plants. The enzymes that break down the glycogen in the cells act only at the ends of the glucose chains and, because glycogen is so branched, it has many sites available for enzyme action and so the enzymes of the cells in which it is stored quickly break it down. Disaccharide sugars and the polysaccharides can be converted back to their constituent monosaccharide sugars and when this happens their solubility is restored. This change in solubility enables them to be transported through the body and to be used during respiration to release energy. The exception to this is the glycogen stored in muscle. This is not converted to blood glucose but is used to supply glucose for use by the muscle, especially during high-intensity and endurance physical activity.

The different nature of the chemical linkages between the monosaccharides in starch and cellulose, and the specificity of the digestive enzymes, make it possible for the human body to digest starch but not cellulose. Cellulose forms an important part of the human diet but it is not digested. It is dietary fibre and simply helps to maintain the normal healthy functioning of the human intestine by stimulating the peristaltic movements of the gut.

Pentose and hexose sugars are able to link with other molecules to form more elaborate compounds. An essential first stage of respiration involves a hexose sugar combining with phosphoric acid, and the nucleotides, the building blocks of the nucleic acids, are made as a result of a pentose sugar and an organic base combining together. Some sugars contain nitrogen. These carbohydrates are called mucopolysaccharides. The mucopolysaccharides are found in the synovial fluid of joints and are an essential component of the matrix of connective tissue.

Think it over

Would you classify fructose and galactose as pentose or hexose sugars?

Name two major polysaccharides. How does each play a part in the human body?

Dietary sources of carbohydrates

Carbohydrate in the diet is obtained as sugar, starch and cellulose. Foods that provide sugar include biscuits, cakes, confectionery, and fruits. Sucrose is often added to cereals, canned soups, fruit and drinks. Starch is found in bread, cereals, rice, peas, and beans, and cellulose is found in abundance in vegetables, particularly the green leafy vegetables such as spinach and cabbage.

Biological functions of carbohydrates

The combustion of the carbohydrates' starch and sugar during cellular respiration yields energy. The energy used by the cells comes from the carbon-hydrogen chemical bonds found in carbohydrates. The energy is incorporated into these bonds during photosynthesis when plants use the energy obtained from the sunlight to manufacture glucose and other carbon-containing compounds. The body is then able to use the energy that has been trapped and stored to enable it to build other compounds, carry out muscular movements, allow nervous transmission and maintain the ion balance within the cells at a constant value.

The amount of energy released from these food materials is usually measured in calories (cals) or, because a calorie is such a small measure, kilocalories (kcal):

- A calorie is the amount of heat required to raise the temperature of 1 gram of water 1 degree Celsius.
- A kilocalorie is the amount of heat required to raise the temperature of 1000 grams (1 litre) of water 1 degree Celsius.

The term calorie is often used inaccurately, in fact the value quoted on diet sheets and on the labels attached to food is really a value in kilocalories – and not calories as stated. Always use the terms accurately so that the instructions given to clients are clear and there is no doubt about any recommendations that you are offering to a client.

Key issue

Collect labels from a variety of food products. Use the labels to establish how much energy is provided by each food.

Dental health

There is a common misconception that all sugars are bad foods. It is true that foods high in simple sugars may provide few proteins, vitamins or minerals compared with the number of kilocalories that they supply. If, however, the sugar is the only source of kilocalories, or if the client is undernourished, then the consumption of simple sugars is not harmful – indeed it is probably beneficial. The problems arise when simple sugars are eaten *in place* of foods containing the vitamins and minerals essential for the normal healthy bodily functions.

Sugars consumed in large quantities have been shown to contribute to dental caries and dentists have become most concerned about the effects of eating sugar on teeth. Sugars, and indeed other carbohydrates, are metabolised by the bacteria present in the mouth to form acids and it is this acid that attacks the enamel of the teeth causing dental caries. If the acid attacks are frequent then the underlying tissue of the tooth is eventually damaged and ultimately the tooth is destroyed. Every time sugar is consumed the teeth are subjected to an acid attack. Constant 'snacking' on sugary foods therefore increases the risk of tooth decay.

Bacteria in the mouth may also affect the teeth by reacting with the sugars consumed to form a sticky substance called plaque. The plaque collects around the teeth and reduces the neutralising effect of the alkaline saliva present in the mouth.

Figure 11.6 shows the principal factors in the development of tooth decay. Eating cheese at the end of a meal helps to neutralise some of the acid bathing the teeth and thus helps to reduce tooth decay. Chewing sugar-free chewing gum also has the same effect.

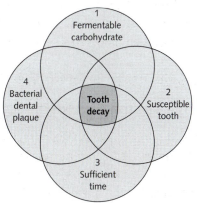

Figure 11.6 Principal factors in the development of tooth decay

Think it over

When a granny visits her grandchildren she always brings sweets and chocolate. The parents are worried about the number of sweets eaten by the children and concerned about the relationship of sweets and chocolate to tooth decay. The parents do not wish to hurt the grandmother's feelings. What advice would you give?

Sugars are frequently added to food to make them more palatable. These sugars are referred to as 'hidden sugars'. The ingredients of food are listed on the packaging but many busy shoppers do not always have the time, or indeed the desire, to read them. Thus large quantities of sugar are consumed inadvertently. Many medicines, particularly those prescribed for children, also often contain large quantities of sugar.

It has been part of our culture to use sweets and chocolate as a currency of affection and to give sweets and chocolate to children. Sweets and chocolate are also often used by tired harassed parents as rewards for good behaviour from their children. However, to improve the dental health of children it is important that sugary snacks should not be given to children throughout the day, and, by shopping carefully, the amount of hidden sugar in their diet should be reduced. Some examples of foods containing 'hidden sugar' are given in the table below.

Product	Portion (weight in grams)	Amount	Sugar per portion
Chocolate biscuits	15	2 biscuits	7
Ginger nut biscuits	20	2 biscuits	7
Ice cream	50	1 scoop	8
Tinned rice pudding	220	Half a tin	16
Fruit yoghurt	150	1 small carton	18
Baked beans	225	Half a medium tin	10
Jam	15	2 teaspoonfuls	10.5
Tinned tomato soup	200	Half a tin	5
Cornflakes	30	3 tablespoons	2
Sugar Puffs	30	3 tablespoons	17
Coca-Cola	300 ml	1 can	32
Polo mints	30	1 tube	30
Mars bar	52	1 bar	36

Note: All measurements in spoonfuls mean a 'rounded' spoonful; one rounded spoonful of sugar weighs approximately 4 grams

Role of fibre in the diet

As explained earlier, the chemical links between the molecules in some complex carbohydrates cannot be broken down during digestion. These complex carbohydrates help to provide bulk to the faeces and maintain the normal healthy functioning of the human intestine by stimulating the peristaltic movements of the gut. It is recommended that a healthy diet should include about 20–35 g of fibre per day. Including this amount of fibre in the diet will help to prevent the development of cancer of the colon as well as the more common diverticulosis. Foods providing dietary fibre include cereals, green vegetables, and many types of fruit, both dried and fresh.

Lipids

Lipids include fats and oils; fats are the solids and oil the liquids. Fats and oils do not dissolve in water. Like carbohydrates, fats contain carbon, hydrogen and oxygen; however, the proportion of oxygen present in a molecule of lipid is less than that in a molecule of carbohydrate. Fats and oils in food are mostly in the form of triglycerides, formed by a molecule of glycerol combining with three molecules of fatty acid. The fatty acids may all be the same, all different, or a mixture. The triglycerides are randomly mixed in fat (see Figure 11.7).

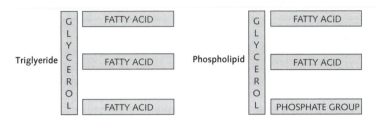

Figure 11.7 Triglycerides and phospholipids

Just as in the case of carbohydrates, the reactions can be reversed and when this occurs the lipid is split into its constituents, i.e. glycerol and fatty acids. If one of the fatty acids is removed a diglyceride is formed, if two fatty acids are removed a monoglyceride is formed. Most dietary fats are converted to monoglycerides and fatty acids by the digestive process. It is in this form that lipids are absorbed into the cells of the intestine.

Saturated and unsaturated fatty acids

If the molecule of lipid contains its full complement of hydrogen atoms the molecule is said to be saturated, if it does not it is said to be unsaturated. The body requires certain polyunsaturated fatty acids but is unable to make them itself. These are the so-called **essential fatty acids**. These fatty acids are particularly abundant in vegetable and seed oils and fish. They take part in the immune processes and vision, assist in the formation of cell membranes and help in the production of hormone-like substances. The body requires only very small quantities of these substances and sufficient amounts are usually present in the normal diet.

Think it over

Why is it important to include fish in the diet at least twice a week?

Phospholipids are lipids built on a backbone of glycerol. At least one fatty acid, is however, replaced with a phosphorous-containing compound (see Figure 11.7). Phospholipids are an important constituent of the plasma membrane and they aid the absorption of fats in the intestine.

Cholesterol

Steroids are an important group of compounds with properties similar to lipids. A typical steroid is cholesterol. Cholesterol is used to form part of the cell membrane, some hormones, e.g. oestrogen, testosterone, and bile acids. Cholesterol is found in animal products. It is made in the liver. If we do not eat enough cholesterol the body makes what it needs. If there is too much cholesterol in the blood then it may be precipitated and deposited in the bile duct or in the gall bladder forming gallstones. Alternatively some of the cholesterol may be deposited on the walls of certain arteries obstructing the free passage of the blood. This often results in an intravascular blood clot. If this occurs in one of the coronary arteries it causes coronary thrombosis or 'heart attack'. If the intravascular clot is formed in the brain the result is cerebral thrombosis or 'stroke'.

Biological functions of lipids in the diet

Many of the key functions of the body require triglycerides. These are used for the storage of energy, insulation and the transportation of the fat-soluble vitamins. They are also important in metabolism and as a constituent of plasma membranes.

Providing energy for the body

Although carbohydrates provide the most direct source of energy in the body, fats also supply energy. In fact the triglycerides that are eaten as part of the normal diet, together with those triglycerides stored in adipose tissue, provide the main source of energy for the body. In endurance exercise, e.g. long-distance running, carbohydrates supplement the energy supply. Overall about half the energy used by the body at rest or after light exercise is supplied from the fatty acids.

Think it over

What dietary advice would you give to an athlete preparing to run in the London Marathon?

Storage of energy

Like starch and glycogen, fat is energy-dense, insoluble and chemically stable. These properties make it a convenient form for storing energy. Fats are more energy dense than carbohydrates, yielding 9 kcal per gram. Carbohydrates and proteins yield only 4 kcal per gram. Any carbohydrate eaten in excess of immediate requirements is readily converted to fat for storage – as well we know when we try to lose weight.

Insulation

The fat deposits just beneath the skin, the subcutaneous fat, are mostly triglycerides. The function of this layer is principally for storage but it also acts as an insulating layer (see Figure 11.8). The thicker the layer of fat, the greater the degree of insulation it provides. People who live in very cold conditions often build a very thick layer of fat under the skin to insulate themselves against the weather.

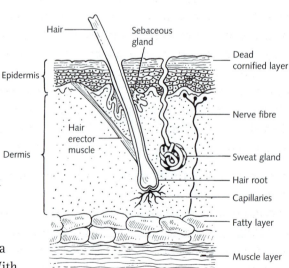

Figure 11.8 Vertical section of the skin to show the subcutaneous layer of fat

Those who suffer from anorexia nervosa end up losing most of their body fat. With the loss of this they also lose the insulating properties of the subcutaneous layer. In place of the subcutaneous layer anorexics often develop a layer of downy hair all over the body. The hair, called lanugo, tries to insulate the body by becoming erect and trapping a layer of air next to the skin, which then stops the warmth escaping from the body.

Protection
Fat is liquid at body temperature and is compressible. It may be deposited round the organs of the body, e.g. the kidneys and heart. As well as insulating the organs the fat deposits provide protection from injury.

Transportation of the fat-soluble vitamins
The triglycerides carry the fat-soluble vitamins, A, D, E and K, to the small intestine and assist in their absorption. People who, because of illness or disease, such as those with cystic fibrosis, do not absorb fat properly are likely to suffer from the deficiency diseases associated with the fat-soluble vitamins, especially those associated with vitamin K (haemorrhage) and vitamin D (rickets and osteomalacia).

Constituent of the plasma membrane
Phospholipids are an important constituent of the plasma membrane. (See also Unit 4 page 123 for more information on phospholipids.)

Dietary sources of lipids

Lipid fats or oils in the diet are obtained from a wide range of foods of both plant and animal origin. Plant sources include nuts, cereal germs, fruits, olives, and soya beans. Animal sources include oily fish, and red meat. Lipid oils and fats, from plant or animal sources, also increase the lipid content of the food when they are used in cooking or when they are added to food as spreads, dressings or creams. Oils and fats used in this way include: peanut, olive, palm, sunflower, soya bean, coconut, maize and rape seed oils from plants; lard, dripping, suet, ghee, butter, fish liver oils (cod and halibut), and fish oils (herring and pilchard) from animals.

Vitamins

These are carbon compounds required daily in very small amounts to help promote and regulate the chemical reactions taking place within the body. The absence of vitamins from the diet gives rise to deficiency diseases. Administering the missing vitamin can cure these diseases very quickly. The body cannot, generally, synthesise vitamins so they must be included as part of a normal healthy diet. Exceptions to this are vitamin D, which may be synthesised by the skin in the presence of sunlight and vitamin K, which may be synthesised by the bacteria normally present in the gut. Vitamins A, D, E and K are soluble in fat. The B vitamins and vitamin C are soluble in water. Except for vitamin K, the fat-soluble vitamins are not readily excreted from the body. The water-soluble vitamins, however, readily dissolve in the water of the cells and the excretory process then eliminates them. The fat-soluble vitamins are not readily excreted and these may accumulate in the body, if they are taken in large quantities, with toxic effects.

A number of studies have shown that a diet including fruit and vegetables is associated with a decreased risk of getting a number of diseases, including cancer. Fruit and vegetables are rich in carotenoids and these are known to block the effects of the many oxidising agents present in the food that we eat. Oxidising agents seek electrons and in doing so destroy biologically important molecules. A particularly active type of oxidising agent is the free radical. Free radicals are short-lived forms of compounds with an unpaired electron in their outer electron shell. This causes them to actively seek electrons and it is this that causes them to be destructive to areas of the cell such as the cell membrane and DNA. Since the carotenoids, as well as vitamins C and E, provide an alternative source of electrons for these free radicals and since they block the effects of the oxidising agents they are known as antioxidants.

The table below lists the essential vitamins and the effects of their deficiency.

Vitamin	Solubility	Major food source	Function	Deficiency
A (retinol)	Fat soluble	Fish liver oil, animal liver, dairy products Vitamin A is added to margarine All green vegetables contain carotene which is converted into retinol in the body	For vision For growth and functioning of epithelial tissue (surface tissues) especially those producing mucus	Night blindness Complete blindness eventually in children Dry skin
B_1 (thiamine)		Meat, wholemeal bread, vegetables	Enables energy to be released from carbohydrate	Beri-beri, a nervous disorder
B_2 (riboflavine)		Milk	Enables energy to be released from food	Rarely deficient
B_3 (nicotinic acid)	Water soluble	Meat, potatoes, wholemeal bread	Enables energy to be released from food	Pellagra (a skin disease)
B_5 (pantothenic acid)		Most food	Essential part of co-enzyme A	
B_6 (pyridoxine)		Meat, fish, eggs, some vegetables	Takes part in the metabolism of amino acids	
B_{12}		Liver, yeast extract	Essential for the synthesis of nucleic acids in dividing cells	Pernicious anaemia
Folic acid		Liver, white fish, raw leafy green vegetables	Essential for the synthesis of nucleic acids	Anaemia during pregnancy
Biotin		Liver, yeast extract, vegetables	Required for the metabolism of fat	
C (ascorbic acid)	Water soluble	Vegetables, fruit, particularly citrus fruits	Maintains connective tissue	Scurvy, bleeding from small blood vessels, and from teeth and gums
D (calciferol)	Fat soluble	Fish liver, butter, margarine, egg yolks Made by the action of sunlight on the skin Sometimes called the 'sunshine' vitamin	Maintains levels of calcium and phosphorus in the blood Regulates the exchange of calcium and phosphorus between the blood and the bones	Rickets (failure of growing bones to calcify) In adults, painful bones which may easily fracture
E (tocopherol)	Fat soluble	Plant oils		
K (phylloquinone)	Fat soluble	Dark green leafy vegetables	Essential for the clotting of blood	

Key issues

When vitamin supplements are used why is the risk of toxicity greater for vitamin A than for vitamin C?

Pregnant women are advised not to eat liver pâté during their pregnancy. Why is this advice given to this group of women?

Minerals

Mineral elements are those elements other than carbon, hydrogen, oxygen and nitrogen required by the body. They constitute about 4 per cent of the body mass. Some are present in large amounts; others occur in very small amounts and are referred to as trace elements. The major minerals are those required in excess of 100 milligrams a day. These include sodium, calcium, phosphorus, potassium and chloride. The trace elements include iron, zinc, iodine, copper and fluoride. Minerals contribute to body structure as well as to the regulation of the processes taking place within the body.

The functions of the minerals are many and varied. For example, calcium and phosphorus are required for the healthy formation of bone; calcium is a key component of muscle contraction; sodium, potassium and calcium take part in nervous transmission; iron is a component of haemoglobin; and iodine is necessary for the formation of thyroxine. Cooking does not readily destroy minerals but they may be leached out into the water during cooking and, if the water is not subsequently used, e.g. to make gravy, they may be lost to the body.

A lack of essential minerals can lead to the deficiency diseases mentioned at the beginning of this unit (and see below, page 470). However, an excess of, for example, sodium – because too much salt is present in the diet – can lead to problems of hypertension (i.e. high blood pressure).

The table lists the essential minerals, their dietary sources and diseases resulting from deficiency.

Element	Importance in mammals	Common food source	Deficiency diseases
Nitrogen	For the synthesis of proteins	Lean meat, fish	None likely
Sulphur	For synthesis of proteins, particularly hair, nails and the horny layers of the skin	Lean meat, fish	None likely
Phosphorus	For synthesis of proteins, DNA, RNA, bones and teeth and muscle contraction, essential for cell division and reproduction	Protein foods, especially milk, bread and cereals	Increased bone loss in elderly women
Potassium	For metabolism in the cells For the transmission of nervous impulses	Vegetables, meat, milk, fruit, and fruit juices	Increased blood pressure Slowing of heart beat Present in kidney failure
Sodium	For tissue fluids including blood For the functioning of the kidneys For the transmission of nervous impulses	Household salt, bread, cereals	Increased blood pressure particularly in those who are susceptible to it Increased calcium loss in urine

Element	Importance in mammals	Common food source	Deficiency diseases
Calcium	For bone and tooth structure For clotting of blood For muscle contraction	Milk, cheese, bread	Osteoporosis Increased blood pressure Kidney stones
Iron	Constituent of haemoglobin	Liver and certain vegetables, e.g. watercress, bread flour and potatoes	Iron deficient anaemia
Iodine	For the manufacture of thyroxine	Seafood, household salt	Goitre
Chloride	For tissue fluids including blood For functioning of gastric juice	Household salt	Deficiency unlikely
Fluoride	For tooth structure It confers hardness on bone	Milk, drinking water, tea	Deficiency unlikely
Magnesium	As a growth factor and for the development of bone For internal respiration needed for the activity of some enzymes	Milk, bread and other cereal products	Increased blood pressure particularly in those who are susceptible to it Weakness in those with kidney failure

Think it over

What dietary advice would you give to a 13-year-old girl if she says she never drinks milk because she can't stand it?

Recommendations for a healthy diet

In order to maintain our own health and promote that of our clients, we should choose, and eat, a well balanced diet. A poor diet, deficient in essential nutrients, has been linked to poor heath status. Such a diet has also been shown to be a leading factor in the development of diseases such as coronary heart disease, stroke, hypertension, some forms of cancer, osteoporosis and anaemia.

Guidelines for a healthy diet

The 'Balance of Good Heath' is a food selection guide produced jointly by the Health Education Authority, now the Health Development Agency, the Department of Health and the Ministry of Agriculture, Fisheries and Food, now the Department of Environment, Food and Rural Affairs. This document aims to help people understand and enjoy healthy eating. It is hoped that the leaflet will reduce the confusion about what healthy eating really means. The leaflet is based on the government's eight guidelines for a healthy diet:

- Enjoy your food.
- Eat a variety of different foods.
- Eat the right amount to be a healthy weight.
- Eat plenty of foods rich in starch and fibre.
- Don't eat too much fat.
- Don't have sugary foods and drinks too often.
- Look after the vitamins and minerals in your food.
- If you drink alcohol keep within sensible limits.

The guide applies to all people including those who are above the desired weight for height, vegetarians, and people of all ethnic origins. It does not apply to children under two years of age, those with special dietary requirements and those under medical supervision.

Food provides the nutrients that are required to help the body function effectively. No one single food provides all the nutrients in the required quantities, so a mixture of foods must be eaten. The 'Balance of Good Health' leaflet tries to make healthy eating easier to understand by showing the types and proportion of foods required to make a healthy and balanced diet in a pictorial form (see Figure 11.1 on page 444). The foods are divided into the five commonly accepted food groups:

* bread, potatoes and other cereals (group 1)
* fruit and vegetables (group 2)
* milk and dairy foods (group 3)
* meat, fish and other alternatives (group 4)
* foods that contain fat and foods that contain sugar (group 5).

Dietary advice should always be to include a variety of foods chosen from the first four food groups every day: more from groups 1 and 2, moderate amounts from groups 3 and 4 and sparingly of foods in group 5. If a different food is chosen from each group this will ensure the availability of a wide range of nutrients required to keep the body healthy and functioning efficiently. Foods in the fifth group are not essential for a healthy diet but they do add choice and palatability.

Ideal body weight

The 'Balance of Good Health' encourages us to eat at least five portions of fruit and vegetables each day. It also suggests that we eat increased amounts of bread, potatoes and cereals, in bigger rather than more portions. The 'Balance of Good Health' does not specify portion size, as we all have different needs and these needs are difficult to determine. All food should be eaten in moderation. Therefore, controlling portion size is important if we wish to maintain our ideal body weight and avoid obesity and its associated risks. If over a period, of say a week, a variety of foods is chosen from the same group the meals will be more interesting, eating more enjoyable and all the required nutrients will have been included.

Reduction of fat intake

Most fruit and vegetables are low in fat, unless butter, margarine or cream has been added, so eating these instead of foods higher in fat content will reduce the total fat that we eat. Eating fruit and vegetables also increases the amount of fibre, vitamins and minerals in our diet. Fruit and raw vegetables are therefore more appropriate snack foods than potato crisps, biscuits and cake. Providing fruit is not covered with syrup, sugar or cream, and vegetables do not have added fat or oil, they can be a useful addition to diets for those wishing to lose weight.

We can eat less fat by choosing leaner cuts of meat and lower fat versions of commonly eaten foods, and also by eating more starchy foods such as bread, potatoes, pasta and rice. Adding fat to these foods should be avoided or kept to a minimum. Changing the way in which we present these foods can help to reduce the amount of fat eaten.

Key issue

Record all the food that you eat over a period of 24 hours. Does it meet the recommendations of the 'Balance of Good Health' leaflet? If not, how can you improve your dietary intake to improve your health and well-being?

Reduction in alcohol intake

Alcoholic beverages provide energy but few or no nutrients and some of those who drink alcohol drink too much at one time. Excessive consumption of alcohol contributes to some of the leading causes of death in the UK. Cirrhosis of the liver, certain forms of cancer, accidents – both in the home and on the road – heart disease, nerve disease, obesity and suicide can all be the result of persistent alcohol abuse. The social consequences of alcohol abuse include divorce, family violence and poverty.

Those who abuse alcohol may also demonstrate nutritional problems. Changes in the metabolism of the body result in many vitamins being deficient, leading to the associated deficiency diseases; for example, a deficiency of niacin causes pellagra.

Current guidelines for safe drinking are different for men and women. Men, of all ages, who regularly drink between 3 and 4 units of alcohol per day, and women, of all ages, who regularly drink between 2 and 3 units of alcohol per day, are thought *not* to incur significant health risks (see Figure 11.9). Men who consistently drink more than 4 units of alcohol per day, and women who consistently drink 3 or more units of alcohol a day, are said to carry a progressive health risk.

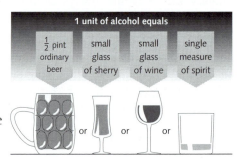

Figure 11.9 What makes a unit of alcohol?

Think it over

John drinks a glass of wine with his evening meal every night. After the evening meal he meets his friends in the local pub. Here they chat and drink at least two pints of beer. Using publicised leaflets work out how many units of alcohol he drinks daily. Is this within safe limits?

Reduction of salt intake

As well as limiting the amount of alcohol that we drink, we should also try to reduce intake of salt. To do this we should limit the amount of salt used in cooking and at the table and restrict the number of salty, highly processed, salt preserved, and salt pickled foods that we eat. Sodium intake tends to increase blood pressure particularly in those who are susceptible to developing a high blood pressure (hypertension). Many processed foods contain a large amount of salt (as well as sugar), which is another good reason to increase the amount of fruit and vegetables in the diet and reduce the numbers of processed food that we eat.

Reduction in sugar intake

It is as important to maintain a healthy weight as it is to maintain a nutritious diet, so it is vital to eat sugars in moderation and to remember the role of sugar and starch in tooth decay. The more frequently we eat sugar and starch, the more we expose our teeth to an acid attack. Adults should monitor their weight regularly and should aim to keep their Body Mass Index in the low twenties. Body Mass Index (BMI) is calculated by dividing the weight of the individual in kilograms by their height in metres squared. So:

$$\text{BMI (kg/m}^2) = \frac{\text{Weight (kg)}}{\text{Height (m)}^2}.$$

The BMI is then considered against the following values:

- Less than 20 underweight
- 20–25 normal weight (desirable range)
- 25–30 overweight
- more than 30 obese
- more than 40 very obese.

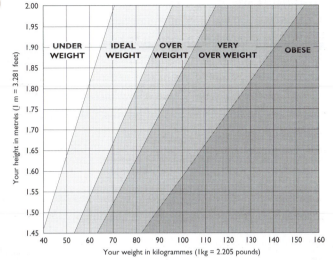

Figure 11.10 Are you the right weight for your height?

Once weight has stabilised it should be kept as steady as possible. The weight of an individual should not fluctuate either way by more than about 3 kg (or 7 lb).

Think it over

Work out your own BMI. Is it within the recommended limits? What changes can you make to your diet if it is not?

Benefits of a healthy diet

The benefits of eating a sensible healthy diet have been shown in each section covered so far. To summarise, these are:

- reduction of obesity and high blood plasma cholesterol levels and associated diseases
- reduced risk of constipation and bowel disorders
- reduced risk of some cancers
- improved energy balance and levels
- improvements in dental health.

Dietary requirements of particular groups

The government's 1999 White Paper, 'Saving Lives: Our Healthier Nation' set out two key aims. These are:

- to improve the health of everyone
- to reduce the health gap (any inequality in health).

There are four key areas to be targeted for action: cancer, coronary heart disease and strokes, accidents and mental illness. In addition there are plans to tackle other important health issues, namely sexual health, drugs, alcohol, food safety, water fluoridation and communicable diseases. The White Paper recognises that diet is central to health throughout life and that if the health of the nation is to be improved, then serious changes to the diet of a large part of the population will have to be made.

Nutrition for pregnant women

A varied diet containing adequate amounts of energy and nutrients is essential both before and during pregnancy. It is known that the diet of the mother influences the health of her baby. Before pregnancy it is important for the mother to be a healthy body weight. If she is underweight it is more difficult for her to conceive and it makes it more likely that her baby will have a low birth weight. Being very overweight before pregnancy increases her risk of having diabetes and high blood pressure during pregnancy.

During pregnancy the diet of the mother must provide sufficient nutrients to meet not only her needs but also the needs of her baby. Gaining too much weight during this time can raise the blood pressure of the mother-to-be, putting both lives at risk, and increases the chance of obesity in the future. However, it is equally important for the pregnant woman not to starve herself or go on a slimming diet.

Proteins are particularly important to the body during the time when new cells and tissues are being made and it is therefore important that the pregnant woman receives adequate supplies of protein and foods containing all the essential amino acids in the correct proportions in her diet.

It is important that all women who are in the early stages of pregnancy, or indeed those who are planning to become pregnant, take in a good supply of folic acid (one of the B vitamins). Folic acid is needed for the development of the baby's organs and tissues and has been shown to reduce the risk of spinal defects, such as spina bifida. The Department of Health recommends that women who are planning to become pregnant, in addition to their normal daily folic acid intake, should take 400 micrograms of folic acid supplement a day. They recommend that the tablets be continued until the twelfth week of pregnancy.

Vitamin A is essential for good health. However, it has been shown that eating large amounts of foods rich in vitamin A (retinol) during early pregnancy can lead to birth defects; therefore pâté, liver, liver sausage and cod liver oil should not be eaten during early pregnancy as they may contain large amounts of retinol. Another form of vitamin A (carotene) is not harmful. It is therefore acceptable for pregnant women to eat foods containing carotene, such as green and yellow fruits, mangoes, carrots and spinach.

Some women develop iron deficiency anaemia during their pregnancy. These women are usually given dietary advice to make sure that they are receiving adequate amounts of all nutrients, and in addition they are prescribed iron supplements. Iron deficiency anaemia during pregnancy can increase the risk of the baby having a low birth weight and the risk of the baby developing iron deficiency anaemia during the first years of life. If, during late pregnancy, the mother eats very little and if her fat stores are low, then the developing baby grows very slowly and this may increase the risk of heart disease and raised blood pressure later in its life.

Research into the effects of the consumption of caffeine by pregnant women has shown that caffeine reduces the absorption of iron by the mother-to-be, reduces the flow of blood through the placenta, and may contribute to the risk of spontaneous abortion.

Pregnant women are therefore advised to drink no more than two cups of coffee, and no more than four cups of caffeinated soft drinks, each day during pregnancy. Pregnant women should also limit the intake of caffeine from tea, over-the-counter medicines and chocolate. Some research workers suggest that caffeine and alcohol should be avoided altogether during pregnancy. The table below outlines dietary advice for pregnant women.

Foods to avoid	Safety tips
• Do not eat soft boiled eggs or foods containing raw eggs (Shop-bought products such as mayonnaise are safe because they're made with pasteurised egg) • Soft-whipped ice cream • Coleslaw and pre-prepared salads • Ripened soft cheeses, eg. Brie, Camembert and blue-veined cheeses • Undercooked meat and raw cured meats, e.g. Parma ham • Liver and products made from liver such as pâté • Unpasteurised soft cheese made from sheep or goats' milk	• Wash all salads, fruit and vegetables thoroughly • Buy only pre-packaged and date-stamped foods from delicatessen counters • Reheat cook-chill foods really thoroughly • Always wash your hands with warm soapy water before preparing food, and in between stages, especially if you've been handling uncooked meat • Use a fridge thermometer to ensure your fridge is below 5°C, and your freezer is below −18°C • Don't reheat food more than once • Cover and store raw foods at the bottom of the fridge; cooked foods at the top

Source: Boots spring/summer 2002, The Guide to Pregnancy and Early Parenthood Catalogue

Breast feeding

During pregnancy the developing baby obtains all its nutrients from its mother via the placenta. After birth, energy and nutrients are obtained from breast milk or formula milk. During pregnancy, hormones from the placenta stimulate the cells in the breast to grow and become ready to secrete the milk. After birth the mother produces more of the hormone prolactin and this maintains the changes in the breast tissue and enables the breasts to synthesise milk for the newly born child. A mother who is breast feeding needs extra energy and nutrients. The diet and the energy stores laid down during pregnancy supply this.

In the first three days after birth, colostrum – a special form of breast milk – is secreted. This contains less fat, more protein and more 'protective' factors than the milk that is later produced by the breast tissue. Following on from the colostrum, breast milk contains, on average, 1.3 per cent protein, 4.1 per cent fat and 7.2 per cent carbohydrates. Most of the protein found in this milk is synthesised by the breast tissue but some proteins enter the milk from the mother's bloodstream. The proteins transferred from the mother's bloodstream include enzymes, antibodies, white blood cells, growth factors and hormones. Some of the fats in the milk are synthesised by the breast tissue and some come from the diet of the mother. The breast tissue also synthesises the sugar galactose and glucose enters the milk from the bloodstream of the mother. These two sugars in the milk condense together to form lactose (milk sugar). Lactose is the main carbohydrate in human milk. Breast milk provides all the nutrients the baby needs for growth and development.

Diet for the lactating mother

The nutrient needs for the mother who is breast feeding are not significantly different from that of the pregnant woman. The lactating mother does have an increased need for energy, vitamins A and C and the mineral zinc but she no longer requires the increased iron and folic acid of pregnancy. Women who are breast feeding are advised to eat a balanced diet providing at least 1,800 kcal a day. The diet should include a moderate amount of fat and a variety of dairy products, fruits and grains. It is important that the nursing mother does not restrict her energy intake too much, as this will cause her milk production to decrease. The nursing mother should drink fluids every time she nurses the infant, as this increases the amount of milk that she produces.

Most substances that the mother eats are secreted in her milk so she should limit or avoid the amount of alcohol and caffeine that she drinks. The passage of flavours from mother's milk to her baby does however enable the baby to learn about the foods of its family long before weaning is started, a sensory experience denied to those infants who are fed on infant formula from a feeding bottle.

Think it over

What four pieces of advice would you give to a mother-to-be who wished to maximise her chances of having a healthy baby?

Suggest three advantages to a mother and her baby of breast feeding as opposed to bottle feeding.

Bottle feeding

If a mother finds feeding her baby herself difficult, or if she does not wish to breast feed her baby, she can use baby milk (infant formula) delivered from a bottle with a teat. Because cow's milk contains a high mineral and a high protein content (suitable for the development of calves) the human baby cannot tolerate cow's milk. Most baby milk is made from cow's milk that has been modified to make it closer in composition to human milk and thus suitable for feeding human babies. Infant formula generally contains lactose or sucrose for carbohydrate, heat-treated casein and whey from cow's milk, and vegetable oils for fat. Some infant formulas are based on soya protein and these are especially suitable for those infants who cannot tolerate lactose or the proteins found in cow's milk.

Infant formulas are usually in the form of a powder and they have to be reconstituted with the correct proportion of water. The water must be sterilised and cooled. The feeding bottles must also be carefully washed and sterilised in an effort to kill any bacteria that may be present. Infant formulas do not contain any antibodies so infections, particularly bowel and chest infections, tend to be more common in bottle-fed babies than in those babies who are given breast milk.

Weaning

Once the infant has reached the age of 4 to 6 months, milk no longer provides all its nutritional needs and additional foods must be provided. This is called weaning. Many different foods are used to wean the baby. The first food most commonly introduced is a cereal based on rice. Because the baby does not have any teeth and cannot chew its food the cereal is mixed with the milk, milk substitute or sterilised water, to make it semi-fluid and soft.

Vegetables, fruit, meat, fish and dairy products are then gradually introduced into the diet and as the child gets older the food is made more solid and less runny, eventually encouraging the baby to chew the food. Food prepared for infants should not have salt added to it and sugar should only be added if it is required to make the food more palatable, e.g. fruit that is naturally sour. Most food should be softened by cooking and then converted into a purée by mashing or chopping. Pre-prepared baby foods are available commercially and many parents find it more convenient to purchase their baby food from the local chemist or supermarket than to make it at home. However, most family meals (with the exception of spicy curries, etc.) can be adapted for a baby simply by adding liquid and mashing or liquidising the food. It is important to ensure that whatever type of food the baby is fed, the baby diet contains enough iron and that the iron is in a form that can be easily absorbed. Meat and meat products are valuable sources of iron and many commercially prepared baby foods have added iron.

Vitamins A, C and E in the form of liquid drops should also be given to infants fed on breast milk but not to those babies fed on infant formula as this already has added vitamins.

Nutrition for pre-school children

Because they are growing quickly, as well as becoming more active, children have a high energy requirement. A pre-school child does not have a large stomach and so is unable to eat large quantities of food at one time. These children require small frequent meals of food, which is high in energy and rich in nutrients. Meals given to children of this age should contain adequate supplies of protein, calcium, iron and the vitamins A and D. Protein is required for the growth and the replacement of cells, calcium for healthy teeth and bones, and vitamins A and D for the development of strong straight bones and the prevention of rickets. (Vitamin D is required for the absorption of calcium.) Whole milk is a rich source of nutrients and it is recommended as the main drink for children over 1 year of age. Skimmed or semi-skimmed milk does not provide enough energy and vitamin D for a growing child and it is not therefore recommended for children under 5 years of age. Children who attend playgroup or nursery sessions which last longer than two hours are eligible to receive a third of a pint of milk free on each day that they attend nursery. This is known as the Nursery Milk Scheme.

Children under 5 whose parents receive Income Support or the income-based Job-seeker's Allowance are also eligible to a free pint of milk each day under the Welfare Food Scheme.

It is, important to encourage the development of good dietary habits as early as possible and every effort should be made to manage the weight of the child so that the child does not become fat or obese.

Think it over

What dietary advice would you give to the organisers of a pre-school playgroup about the provision of a mid-morning or mid-afternoon snack for the children in their care?

Dietary requirement for school children

Children over the age of 5 start to express their own food preferences so it is very important that good dietary habits have become established within the family before the child starts school. Once at school peer pressure becomes important. Primary socialisation ensures that habits, both good and bad, established over the first five years of life, are very difficult to change. School meals can make an important contribution to the nutritional requirements of a child but, since the Education Act of 1980, there is no longer an obligation for schools to provide meals of a set nutritional standard. However, schools are actively encouraged to adopt voluntary nutritional guidelines. Children whose parents receive Income Support or the income-based Job-seeker's Allowance are eligible to free school meals.

All children should be encouraged to limit their intake of sweet sugary snacks as well as snacks with a high fat content.

Think it over

If you were making a packed lunch for an 8-year-old to take to school, what would you put in? You should specify what type of bread or roll (e.g. white or wholemeal), what sort of drink, and remember that the child must want to eat it! (i.e. it must be appealing as well as healthy.)

Adolescent diets

Growth and development are rapid during adolescence. Most girls begin a growth spurt between the ages of 10 and 13 and most boys between 12 and 15. Almost every organ in the body grows during this period, height and weight both increase and the secondary sex characteristics develop. During this growth spurt girls grow about 25 cm in height and boys about 30 cm. Before adolescence both girls and boys have an average of 18 per cent body fat. During adolescence this increases to about 28 per cent in girls and decreases to about 15 per cent in boys. Girls accumulate both fat and lean tissue; boys tend to accumulate lean tissue. During this period the demand for both energy and nutrients is increased. The greater growth spurt in boys means that boys require more energy and more protein than girls of a corresponding age.

One of the ways in which adolescents obtain extra energy is by snacking between meals. Often these snacks are foods that have a high fat content, e.g. potato crisps, cakes, particularly cream cakes, biscuits, sweets and chocolate. However, an over-indulgence in these foods can lead to tooth decay, obesity and an increased risk of chronic disease later in life, such as heart disease and some forms of cancer. Adolescents should be encouraged to moderate snacking and to make sensible food choices when they do snack. The poor dietary habits of adolescence often remain for life.

To enable the bones to grow and mineralise during adolescence there is an increased need for calcium in the diet. Boys should aim for 1000 mg of calcium a day and girls 800 mg of calcium a day. If teenage girls do not receive adequate supplies of calcium at this stage of their life they risk developing osteoporosis in later life.

During the teenage years adequate supplies of the mineral iron are also required. The onset of menstruation in girls means that extra iron is required to replace the blood lost during their periods. It is thought that about 17 per cent of adolescent girls suffer from iron deficient anaemia. It is therefore important that the adolescent diet also includes foods that are rich in iron. Vitamin C is thought to aid the absorption of iron so a food or drink containing vitamin C should accompany this food and if it is not eaten at breakfast time it could be eaten as a snack during the day.

Nutrition for adults

With the exception of pregnancy and lactation in women the basic nutritional requirements of adults between the ages of 18 and 50 do not change. When growth stops the energy requirements are reduced, but the actual amount of energy required by any individual depends on how active they are.

Older adults

Older adults are considered those people over 65 years of age. As people get older their energy requirements tend to fall but it is still important for them to eat a healthy balanced diet and to keep active. Gentle exercise ensures that a healthy appetite is maintained, mobility is increased, obesity is avoided and sleep patterns are maintained. Although the energy requirement, and therefore food intake, is reduced in older people it is still important that the food which they eat contains the right quantities of vitamins and minerals. Many older people do not eat very much and consequently have diets that are deficient in vitamin D and/or iron. This group of people should be encouraged to eat foods containing these nutrients.

Guidelines for healthy eating in older adults:

- Eat small regular meals.
- Ensure that the meal contains the essential nutrients.
- Eat in a well-lit sunny area.
- Ensure that the food looks appetising.
- Make food preparation easier.
- Make clearing up after the meal easier.
- Eat with family and friends.
- Have some gentle exercise before eating to help develop an appetite.

Groups with particular dietary preferences

Over time there has been a continual movement of people from one part of the world to another. This movement has influenced dietary practice, with new practices being accepted and others being abandoned. Over time the culinary practices of different cultures have become integrated.

Vegetarian diets are those that do not include meat or meat products. Those who eat this type of diet do so for ethical, cultural, religious or economic reasons (or a combination of these). There are many different types of vegetarianism. Vegans eat only plant foods. Lacto-vegetarians eat dairy produce as well as foods with a vegetable origin. Lacto-ovo-vegetarians include eggs as well as dairy products in their diet. By including these animal foods it makes it easier to ensure that the diet contains all the nutrients essential for health. Generally, the almost vegetarian diet is the healthiest – this is probably because it contains an abundance of vegetables and fruit (see Figure 11.11).

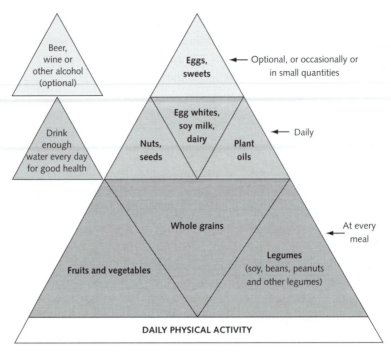

©2000 Oldways Preservation & Exchange Trust

Figure 11.11 Vegetarian diet pyramid – based on traditional eating patterns of healthy vegetarian people of many cultures

Diet-related diseases and disorders

Disorders of malnourishment

The health of the body is determined by its nutritional status. Failing health that is the result of dietary habits practised over a long time is termed malnutrition. The term malnutrition can refer to either under-nutrition or over-nutrition. Under-nutrition is failing health that results from dietary practices that do not meet nutritional needs; over-nutrition is when the nutritional intake exceeds the needs of the body. Continued nutrient deficiencies deplete the body stores. When the concentration of essential nutrients falls to a very low value the metabolic processes of the body slow or stop, giving rise to clinical signs or symptoms. Eating more essential body nutrients than the body needs leads to over-nutrition. To start with this causes no clinical symptoms. However, if the nutrients continue to increase the body may find them toxic and the result may be serious disease.

Kwashiorkor

Kwashiorkor is the Ghananian term meaning 'the disease that the first child gets when the new child comes'. It develops when babies are weaned from breast milk to the native yam and cassava. Breast milk is rich in protein whereas cassava and yam are deficient in protein so the child suffers from a deficiency of protein and does not get enough food to satisfy its energy needs. The child becomes listless, apathetic and does not thrive. Other signs and symptoms of the disease include flaky, scaly skin, reduced muscle mass, a swollen abdomen and changes in hair colour. In addition, these children hardly move and they do not cry. Many of these children die before they are 5 years of age. Many of these symptoms are linked to insufficient protein and energy-providing foods in the diet and providing a diet containing more food and a better balance may reverse them.

Marasmus

Marasmus means to 'waste away'. It occurs as an infant slowly starves to death. It is caused by a diet of foods lacking energy, protein and minerals. The condition is also known as protein-energy malnutrition or PEM. Marasmus commonly occurs in infants who are not breast fed or who have stopped breast feeding in the early months of life. Marasmus in infants is common in large towns and cities of poor countries and in areas of famine. An infant with marasmus needs large amounts of energy and protein and if these are not provided there is little chance of recovery.

Variations of these two diseases also appear in the western world, e.g. in hospitalised patients, particularly the very old and the very young, not receiving enough energy and other nutrients. This can be the result of a number of diseases, notably anorexia nervosa, cancer, AIDS, and some diseases of the intestine.

Diseases that link nutrition and the endocrine system

Diabetes

The hormone insulin brings about the regulation of the amount of glucose in the blood. The pancreas produces insulin and this keeps the blood sugar at a constant value by the process known as homeostasis. If for some reason the pancreas is unable to produce as much insulin as it should the level of blood sugar rises and diabetes mellitus develops. In this condition the blood glucose level rises (hyperglycaemia) and glucose appears in the urine (glycosuria). If left untreated the condition is fatal.

In the UK, diabetes is a common medical condition affecting around 1.4 million people. Insulin injections and diet treat this type of diabetes. A second type of diabetes is non-insulin dependent. It develops when the body produces some, but not enough, insulin to meet its needs or the insulin that is produced is not used properly by the body. This type of diabetes usually develops in people over 40 years of age. It is usually treated by diet or by diet and tablets, or very occasionally by diet and insulin injections.

The diet for people with diabetes is the same healthy diet recommended for everyone. There is not a special diet. Those guidelines laid out in the 'Balance of Good Health' should be followed. Regular meals based on starchy carbohydrate foods like bread, potatoes, pasta, cereals and rice will help to control blood sugar levels. Including foods with less sugar should reduce the amount of sugar in the diet and sweeteners can be used to sweeten drinks, desserts and cereals if desired. Jam and marmalade can be eaten in small amounts, but reduced sugar jams and pure fruit spreads have a lower sugar content than the regular variety. Snacks are important for diabetics and these should be chosen carefully. They should always be low in fat and high in fibre. Special diabetic foods offer no benefit to diabetics – they are unnecessary and can be expensive.

Diabetics should aim to be a healthy weight and take regular exercise as being overweight makes it difficult to control the diabetes and exercise helps to control weight.

Theory into practice

Devise a daily diet composed of three meals for a diabetic client.

Osteoporosis

Osteoporosis is a disorder in which there is a decrease in bone mass. The bone breaks down faster than it is formed and this results in an increased likelihood of fractures, a loss in height and a characteristic stoop. The cause of osteoporosis appears to be associated with a reduction in the amount of oestrogen in the body coupled with the amounts of calcium and vitamin D in the diet.

There are two types of osteoporosis, i.e. postmenopausal osteoporosis, which appears directly after the menopause, and senile osteoporosis, found in both men and women of advanced age. Hormone Replacement Therapy (HRT) with oestrogen slows bone loss in women at the menopause and it is recommended that those women at risk be given HRT at this stage in their life. The oestrogen present in the medication acts by increasing the absorption of calcium into the body, thus assisting in the maintenance of the bone. Smoking and excessive consumption of alcohol both affect bone strength.

Smoking lowers the oestrogen in the blood and alcohol is toxic to the bone cells. Those at risk from osteoporosis should be encouraged to have regular exposure to the sun, weight-bearing exercise and to increase their intake of both calcium and vitamin D, such as by including dairy foods in the daily diet.

Disorders with a dietary link

Coronary heart disease (CHD)

You will recall the link between heart disease, atherosclerosis, atheroma and a diet high in fat. Coronary heart disease is associated with atherosclerosis – the deposition of fatty material (plaques) on the lining of the arteries. Their deposition reduces the internal diameter of the blood vessel and consequently a reduced flow of blood through the tube (see Figure 11.12). If a blood clot is formed the artery becomes completely blocked, causing a sudden decrease in the supply of oxygen to the organ that it supplies. Sometimes fragments of the deposited plaque break off and travel through the bloodstream and this causes the smaller vessels to become blocked. The plaques increase in both size and number with age, especially in those people who have high levels of cholesterol in their diet. A diet high in fat, particularly from animal sources, raises the level of cholesterol in the blood plasma and this causes the deposition of fat on the walls of the arteries. Choosing a diet low in fat, especially saturated fat, and cholesterol will help to avoid CHD. Fat intake should be limited to 20 per cent to 30 per cent of the total energy intake and saturated fat to no more than one-third of that fat.

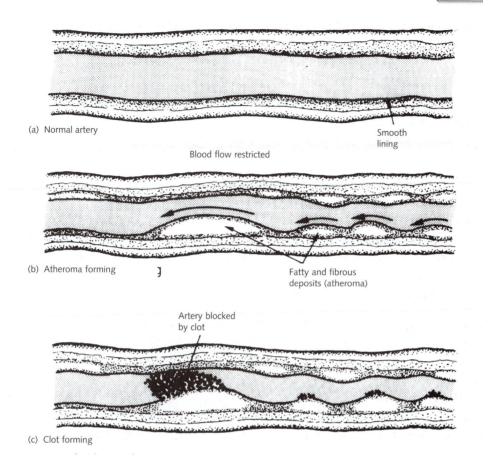

(a) Normal artery

Smooth lining

Blood flow restricted

(b) Atheroma forming

Fatty and fibrous deposits (atheroma)

Artery blocked by clot

(c) Clot forming

Figure 11.12 Atheroma and clot formation

Cholesterol should be limited to 200–300 mg per day. This can be achieved by choosing lean meat, fish, poultry and peas and beans as sources of protein, skimmed or semi-skimmed milk, and low fat milk products as well as limiting eggs to three or four a week. You will recall that fat should be removed from meat, skin from chicken, sandwiches made with thicker bread, using a reduced fat spread on one side only and food should be boiled, baked or grilled and not fried.

Liver disease

Cirrhosis of the liver is a chronic and progressive disease of the liver. The liver cells die and are replaced by scar tissue. This results in failure of the liver cells and high blood pressure in the portal vein. In the western world most (but not all) cases of cirrhosis are caused by long-term alcohol abuse. The liver is the main organ of detoxification and alcohol is a toxin. Heavy drinking causes the liver to become fatty and enlarged, leading to liver dysfunction. The liver cells become destroyed, scarring eventually appears and liver failure and death follow. Complete recovery is impossible but it is sometimes possible for some normal liver function to be returned.

A nutritious diet does sometimes help to prevent some of the complications associated with alcohol abuse. People who drink large amounts of alcohol often suffer from deficiencies of vitamin A, thiamin, niacin, folic acid, vitamin D, vitamin C and vitamin K – and consequently the vitamin deficiency diseases.

Gallstones

As we get older the gall bladder may function less effectively, so that gallstones may be formed and may collect in the bile duct and gall bladder. If bile is prevented from being produced, fat digestion is incomplete. A low-fat diet will help to control this condition. However, if this fails ultrasound treatment or surgery may be required to remove the gallstones.

Pancreatic conditions

The pancreas produces insulin, a hormone, you will recall, responsible for the control of blood sugar. If the concentration of sugar in the blood deviates from normal then the disease diabetes develops. You should refer to the previous section on page 471 describing the condition and the control of the different forms of diabetes, and how this relates to the diet and nutrition of those clients with the condition.

Diseases of the alimentary system

Carcinoma of the bowel

Cancer of the bowel is a growth of malignant cells in the colon or rectum of the large intestine. In the United Kingdom it is the third commonest form of cancer and the second commonest cause of cancer death. The consumption of dietary fibre may play a key role in the prevention of this form of cancer. Many other factors also contribute to the development of the disease, such as obesity, smoking, drinking more than two alcoholic drinks every day and lack of exercise, as well as deficiencies of vitamins C, D, folic acid and the mineral calcium. It is not yet known how dietary fibre affects the development of the cancer but it does appear that the fluid in the fibre dilutes the carcinogens in the intestine; these then become bound to the fibre and are evacuated from the body more quickly. The fibre provided by fresh fruits and vegetables tends to give the most protection from this kind of cancer.

Diverticular disease

Diverticular disease is a group of conditions affecting the large intestine. Small pouches of the inner lining of the bowel are forced out of the intestinal wall. The pouches are called diverticula. A person can have many diverticula. Diverticula do not present symptoms in most people. However, the little pouches can become filled with food and they may then become inflamed – giving rise to diverticulitis. When this happens, dietary fibre should be reduced and not restarted until there is no further pain.

Crohn's disease

This is chronic inflammation of the alimentary tract. It can occur in any part of the digestive tract but it is commonly found in the ileum and colon. The lining of the intestinal tract becomes inflamed and ulcerated and some areas of the gut may become obstructed. During a painful episode those who suffer from this condition may benefit from a diet limited in lactose fat and fibre.

Irritable bowel syndrome (IBS)

Many adults, particularly women, suffer from IBS and have attacks consisting of a combination of cramps, gassiness, bloating and an irregular bowel function. Although irritable bowel syndrome is uncomfortable it is a harmless condition. Many of those who have IBS appear to benefit from elimination diets that focus on the elimination of dairy products and gas-forming foods, e.g. beans. More frequent low-fat meals are also usually beneficial because large meals can trigger violent movements of the intestinal tract.

Food poisoning

Food may become contaminated with disease-causing organisms in a number of different ways. *Salmonella* and *E. coli* are two of the better known types of food poisoning. Other food poisoning bacteria include *Staphylococcus aureus*, *Clostridium perfringens* and *Listeria*. Food poisoning generally presents no serious risk but for some people it can be serious, e.g. infants, pregnant women and the elderly. For a number of reasons the risk of contracting a food-borne illness is high. Not only do consumers mishandle food (for example, not chilling foods) but also many of our meals are convenience foods, take-away, or ready-to-eat foods prepared and cooked by commercial organisations in large central kitchens. This centralisation of food production increases the risk of us catching a food-borne illness.

To avoid food poisoning we should ensure that:

- the food does not become contaminated during preparation (e.g. cooked and uncooked meats should not come into contact)
- any micro-organisms present are killed by cooking or reheating the food thoroughly in our own homes
- any micro-organisms that get into food do not multiply (i.e. ensure that the food is stored in the correct conditions).

Diseases with a psychological or an emotional component

Anorexia nervosa

Anorexia simply means loss of appetite. Anorexia nervosa is a psychological disorder, partly expressed by well-defined procedures associated with food. The signs and symptoms of the condition include extreme loss of weight, a morbid fear of obesity and weight gain accompanied by a distorted body image. Those suffering from anorexia nervosa see themselves as fat when in reality they are very thin. Young girls are the group most commonly found to be suffering from anorexia nervosa.

Bulimia

Bulimia is another psychological eating disorder. Concern about body weight and a distorted self-image lead to episodes of binge eating followed by vomiting, the use of laxatives and/or diuretics and other extreme measures to control weight.

Both disorders are potentially life threatening and both require long-term counselling with an experienced and sympathetic counsellor.

Food allergies and food intolerance

Food allergies and food intolerance are reactions that arise in certain people when they eat a particular food or a particular type of food. Acute reactions to food are the most serious but less serious forms of the allergic reaction are quite common. If the allergic response appears immediately after eating the food the problem can be solved by the avoidance of that food. The situation, however, is not always that simple: often the allergic response appears some time after eating the food, making it difficult to link the food and the allergic response. An allergic reaction to nuts is particularly problematic because small amounts of nuts or nut products often turn up in the most unexpected places. The difficulty in identifying presence of nuts and nut products in food has led to food manufacturers being required to label all foods that might contain even minute traces of nut.

The solution to any form of allergic response is for the affected person to have sensitivity tests or to exclude the apparently offending food from the diet for a number of weeks, i.e. the so-called exclusion diet. This makes the diagnosis of the condition a long and painstaking process.

Assessment activity 11.3

Using the websites of at least three different supermarkets, produce a leaflet to be used by a parent who has a family member with either an allergy to nuts, an allergy to cow's milk or the need for a diet free from gluten.

Plan a series of meals for a week and indicate suitable alternative foods for the family member with the allergy.

Food intolerance is when the adverse reaction to the food is difficult to link to the immune system. All the allergy tests are negative but the condition persists when certain foods are eaten. These conditions often respond to an exclusion diet. Diseases linked to food intolerance include migraine, irritable bowel syndrome, Crohn's disease and arthritis. Some widely used colouring agents, e.g. tartrazine and preservatives, cause food intolerance.

Coeliac disease

Coeliac disease is sensitivity to wheat gluten. The gluten in wheat products causes damage to the lining of the bowel and this causes those with the food intolerance to have constant diarrhoea. The treatment for this is a life-long avoidance of wheat and wheat products.

Lactose intolerance

There are some people who are deficient in the enzyme lactase and are therefore not able to digest lactose, the sugar found in milk. These people are said to be lactose deficient and they must adopt a life-long avoidance of milk and milk products.

In recent years Crohn's disease has been found to respond to an elimination diet. In this case the patient is given a liquid diet, containing all the nutrients necessary, for two weeks to rest the gut. Normal foods are reintroduced one at a time and the reactions of the patient closely monitored. Any offending foods are thus eliminated from the diet one by one.

The diagnosis of food intolerance must be made very carefully and the adoption of exclusion diets made with caution and under medical supervision. Patients who embark on an exclusion diet, feel better and then exclude even more foods can end up on a diet deficient in the essential nutrients.

Assessing and evaluating dietary intake

This unit has covered healthy eating guidelines, trends in eating habits and the use of food tables to assess basal metabolic rate and Body Mass Index. Now you must use the information that you have acquired with your clients.

Assessment activity 11.4

Select a client, preferably one from your placement. Using published dietary information, estimate the dietary requirements for this individual. Encourage the client to compile a daily record of all the food eaten over the next week. Evaluate the diet and determine whether it is providing the nutrients required for maintaining health.

Calculate the BMI of the client, then use published tables to determine if their weight is appropriate for their height. Offer dietary advice to the client, making sure that any advice that you give is appropriate to the client's needs.

End of unit test

1 Explain the difference between macro and micro nutrients.

2 Explain the relationship between proteins and amino acids.

3 State three functions of lipids in human physiology.

4 Why should a diabetic person consume carbohydrates in a complex form rather than as simple sugars?

5 Describe the chemical nature of a peptide link and say where it can be found.

6 What do condensation and hydrolysis mean?

7 What is ascorbic acid, its functions and chief source, and deficiency disorder?

8 What are the main sources of calcium and why is it important in the human body?

9 Jenny is 1.8 m in height and weighs 74 kg. Calculate her BMI and say whether this is within the normal range.

10 Jason has a BMI of 33, what advice would you give him?

11 Jason takes little exercise likes to go drinking pints with his friends and have a fish and chip supper at least three times each week. He is 20 years old, what risk is he taking?

12 What three precautions should a pregnant woman take in her food habits?

13 What nutrients are older people generally encouraged to consume?

14 Name two foods that will contain rich sources of the nutrients you have named in question 13.

References and further reading

Dickerson, J. W. T. (1985) *Clinical Nutrition for Nurses, Dieticians and other Health Care Professionals*, London: Faber and Faber

Fieldhouse, P. (1986) *Food and Nutrition for Nurses, Dieticians and Other Health Care Professionals*, London: Croom Helm

Fox, B. A. and Cameron, A. G. (1995) *Food Science, Nutrition and Health*, Sevenoaks: Hodder and Stoughton

Government White Paper (1999) *Saving Lives: Our Healthier Nation*, London: HMSO

McCance, and Widdosons (2001) *The Composition of Foods,* London: The Royal Society of Chemistry and Ministry of Agriculture, Fisheries and Food

Wardlaw, G. M. (1997) *Contemporary Nutrition Issues and Insights*, New York: McGraw-Hill

12 Applied physiology A

This unit will extend the knowledge that you have gained from studying Unit 4, Human anatomy and physiology. You will learn about the cardiovascular, renal and respiratory systems of the body and the relationship of these systems to each other. You will learn how the systems work together to maintain the normal physiological function of the body. You will recall from Unit 4 that the maintenance of a constant internal environment is called homeostasis and that homeostasis is important if the cells of the body are to function effectively. You will learn about the structure and function of the blood and how it is involved in the homeostatic mechanism of the body.

The final part of the unit explores the implications of disorder and disease to the systems, to the individual and to society

What you need to learn

- The structure and function of the cardiovascular, respiratory and renal systems
- The composition and function of blood
- Relationship between the cardiovascular, renal and respiratory systems and homeostatic mechanisms
- Implications of disorder and disease

The structure and function of the cardiovascular, respiratory and renal systems

The cardiovascular system

The system responsible for transport in the human body is the circulatory system. In human beings the circulatory system consists of blood vessels (the arteries, veins and capillaries) in which the liquid called blood is circulated. The blood vessels are usually tubular and the blood is circulated by muscular contractions of these vessels, or by an expanded and specialised blood vessel with a thick muscular wall called the heart.

Blood vessels

Each organ of the body has a major artery, supplying it with oxygenated blood from the lungs and a major vein collecting the deoxygenated blood from the organ and returning it to the heart and finally the lungs. All arteries divide to form smaller vessels called arterioles. Arterioles eventually end in very thin-walled vessels called capillaries. Capillaries further divide, branch, and ultimately join with the capillaries formed from the venules to form the capillary beds spreading through the tissues (see Figure 12.1). The capillaries leaving the capillary bed link up with the venules and veins so a continuous network is formed for the circulation of the blood through the body).

Structure of arteries, veins and capillaries

The basic structure of both arteries and veins is the same. Any differences are modifications made to the structure to accommodate the different functions of the two sets of blood vessel. The walls of both arteries and veins consist of three layers (see Figure 4.36, page 148). There is a layer of squamous epithelium lining the vessel, in contact with the blood contained in the vessel; a middle layer of smooth muscle and elastic fibres, called the tunica media; and an outer layer of fibrous connective tissue called the tunica externa. Arteries are the blood vessels leaving the heart and, with the exception of the pulmonary artery, they contain oxygenated blood. Veins return blood to the heart and, with the exception of the pulmonary veins, they contain deoxygenated blood. The blood contained in the arteries is at a much higher pressure than that in the veins and this results in the walls of arteries being thicker than those of the veins (Figure 4.36, page 148). The diameter of the arteries decreases as they move further away from the heart, the diameter of the veins increases as they get nearer to the heart. The walls of the veins have fewer elastic fibres and less smooth muscle than the walls of the arteries. As blood is under low pressure in the veins, backflow of the blood is possible. This is prevented by the presence of semi-lunar valves along the length of the veins. Movement of the blood through the veins is helped by the contraction of the surrounding muscles.

Refer back to the table on pages 149–50 which outlines the functional and anatomical differences between arteries, veins and capillaries.

The heart

The heart is situated in the thoracic cavity. About the size of a clenched fist, it is found between the two lungs, behind the sternum, in front of the oesophagus, protected by the rib cage. The heart is surrounded by the pericardium. The pericardium is a double-layered sac containing a thin layer of liquid to reduce the friction caused when the heart beats. The general inelastic nature of the pericardium prevents the heart from being either overfilled with blood or being overstretched. The pericardium is attached to the diaphragm and this anchors the heart firmly in position.

The walls of the heart are made of cardiac muscle, a special type of muscle found only in the walls of the heart (see Figure 12.1). Coronary arteries arise from the base of the aorta and pass over the surface of the heart. The coronary arteries supply the capillaries of the walls of the heart with oxygenated blood; the deoxygenated blood from the heart itself is collected up by the coronary veins and eventually returned to the right side of the heart.

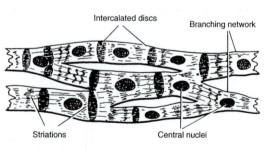

Figure 12.1 The structure of cardiac muscle

The heart is divided into four chambers. Two of these chambers are on the right-hand side of the heart, two on the left-hand side. The chambers on the right-hand side of the heart are separated from the chambers on the left-hand side by a thick wall. The blood contained in the chambers on the two sides never mixes. The two chambers at the top of the heart are called the atria (singular atrium) and the two lower chambers are called the ventricles. Both atria have thin walls and both the ventricles have thick walls. The septum separating the right and left ventricles is called the interventricular septum. The right atrium receives deoxygenated blood from the body, via the venae cavae, passes it to the right ventricle and from here it is pumped to the lungs to be oxygenated via the pulmonary artery. Oxygenated blood is returned to the left atrium from the lungs, via the pulmonary veins and passes to the left ventricle. The blood is then circulated to the rest of the body via the aorta. The blood goes through the heart twice and this is said to be a double circulatory system.

The distance that has to be travelled by the blood from the two ventricles results in the thickness of the walls of the right and left ventricles being different. The right ventricle pumps the blood to the lungs, a relatively short distance, the left ventricle pumps the blood to the whole of the body, a much longer distance and this results in the wall of the left ventricle being about three times as thick as its right counterpart. Although the walls of the two ventricles differ in thickness, the capacity of the chambers on both sides of the heart appears to be the same (see Figure 4.33, page 147).

Heart valves

Valves maintain the blood flow through the heart. Atrioventricular valves separate the atria from the ventricles. The atrioventricular valves are prevented from turning inside out by strands of connective tissue, which run from their underside to the walls of the ventricle. These are the so-called heartstrings or chordae tendinae. The atrioventricular valve between the right atrium and right ventricle is called the tricuspid valve; the valve between the left atrium and left ventricle is called the bicuspid valve.

Think it over

The wall of the right ventricle is not as thick as that of the left ventricle, there is therefore more space inside this cavity and there is room for a valve divided into three, i.e. it is tricuspid. The wall of the left ventricle is thicker than the right ventricle and there is less space, therefore the valve is divided into two not three, i.e. it is a bicuspid valve.

The bicuspid valve is sometimes called the mitral valve because it resembles a bishop's mitre. Pocket-shaped semi-lunar valves prevent reflux of the blood into the heart from the aorta and pulmonary artery leaving the ventricles (see Figure 12.2).

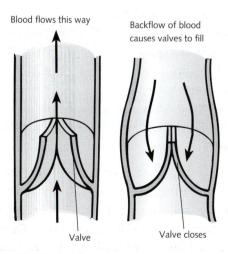

Blood flows this way

Backflow of blood causes valves to fill

Valve

Valve closes

Figure 12.2 Semi-lunar valves

The cardiac cycle

The cardiac cycle refers to the sequence of events when the heart beats to pump the blood around the body (see Figure 12.3). The heart pumps by means of alternate contraction (systole) and relaxation (diastole). During the cardiac cycle the following sequence of events takes place:

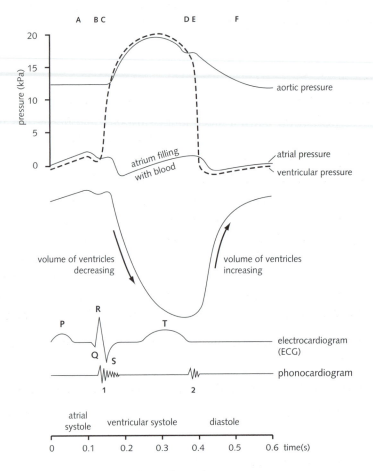

Figure 12.3 Pressures within the cardiac cycle

1   Deoxygenated blood, under low pressure, enters the right atrium. At the same time oxygenated blood from the lungs enters the left atrium. Both right and left atria are relaxed and gradually become distended. The tricuspid and bicuspid valves are both closed at this stage. As both chambers fill with blood they become distended and the pressure set up by the blood entering the atria forces the valves to open, releasing some of the blood into the ventricles. This period of relaxation is called diastole.

2   When atrial diastole ends, both atria contract – forcing the blood into the ventricles. This is called atrial systole. The ventricles then contract. The tricuspid and bicuspid valves are forced closed. As the ventricles both contract (ventricular systole), the pressure inside them increases, the semi-lunar valves in the aorta and pulmonary arteries are forced open and the blood is ejected from the ventricles past the valves and into the blood vessels leaving the heart. The first heart sound ('lub') is heard as the blood is forced against the closed atrioventricular valves on both sides of the heart.

3   Ventricular systole is followed by ventricular diastole. The high pressure developed when this happens forces some blood back towards the ventricles, causing the semi-

lunar valves to fill and close off the blood vessels leading from the heart. The movement of the blood against these valves causes the second heart sound ('dub'), i.e.
- ventricular systole gives rise to the 'lub' sound
- ventricular diastole gives rise to the 'dub' sound.

The whole cycle starts again with the blood entering the atria.

When the heart is beating at 75 beats per minute the time taken for one cardiac cycle is 0.8 seconds (see Figures 4.34 and 4.35, pages 147–48).

Pulse

Ventricular systole forces blood, in spurts, through the arteries. The arteries expand to accommodate the blood. The expansion can be felt as a pulse, especially where the artery passes over a bone and comes near to the surface of the body. In adults the pulse rate is usually between 60 to 80 beats per minute. It is faster in children and may be slower in very fit adults.

The pulse rate may increase with exertion, fear, fever and the loss of blood. During fainting, certain heart disorders and compression of the brain, the pulse is slowed down. The traditional place to take a pulse is just above the wrist. This is called the radial pulse. In an emergency, when the circulatory system is shutting down, the carotid pulse is felt because this comes straight from the aorta. The aorta carries blood directly from the heart. This pulse is found in the neck on either side of the larynx and it is usually felt by placing two fingers into the gap between the larynx and the muscle that runs behind the ear across the neck to the breastbone. Pulses can also be felt in the groin and temple.

It is often difficult to feel the carotid pulse in a baby so the brachial pulse on the inside of the upper arm is felt.

Pulse readings can also be read and recorded using digital monitors. Excitement, fear, embarrassment and movement can all cause significant changes to the pulse rate.

Theory into practice

Choose a partner. Take their resting pulse rate by placing the pads of three fingers in the hollow immediately above the wrist creases at the base of the thumb. Press lightly. This is the radial pulse. Do not use your thumb because this has a pulse of its own and you could end up recording your own pulse. Count and record the number of beats per minute after:

- at least 10 minutes' rest
- 5 minutes' light exercise
- 5 minutes' vigorous exercise.

Record the length of time taken for the pulse to return to the normal resting rate after exercise. Change with your partner and repeat. Record your findings in your assessment folder. If there are any differences between you and your partner try to explain them.

The beating of the heart

The heart will continue to beat rhythmically long after it has been removed from the body. The stimulation for the contraction of the heart comes from the cardiac muscle itself.

Heartbeat is initiated in the walls of the right atrium at a point close to where the great veins enter. This is called the sino-atrial node (SAN) or pacemaker of the heart. The impulses then pass across the two atria, accompanied by contraction. When the impulse reaches the junction of the atria and the ventricles it excites another area of specialised tissue called the atrioventricular node (AVN). The impulse then passes down an area of tissue, consisting of specialised cardiac muscle fibres, passing down the interventricular septum and spreading out over the ventricle walls. This specialised tissue is called Purkinje tissue. The walls of the ventricles are then stimulated and contract.

The muscle that makes up the heart is unique to the heart. It is able to contract rhythmically without being supplied with nervous impulses. It is said to be myogenic. The muscle of the atria and the muscle of the ventricles do not contract at the same rate. When isolated from a nerve supply the muscle from the atria contracts at a faster rate than the muscle from the ventricles. In a healthy heart, however, the nerves of the autonomic system govern the contraction of both atria and ventricles.

Although the pacemaker initiates heartbeat, the actual activity of the pacemaker is controlled by two nerves: the sympathetic nerve, part of the sympathetic nervous system, and a branch of the vagus nerve, part of the parasympathetic nervous system (see Figure 12.4). Both originate in the medulla oblongata of the hindbrain. These do not initiate beating of the heart but control the rate at which the heart beats. Stimulation of the sympathetic nerve fibres causes an increase in heart beat; stimulation of the parasympathetic nerve fibres a reduction in the rate at which the heart is beating. Blood is forced from the heart only during contraction. Blood flow is therefore intermittent. The blood flows rapidly during systole and more slowly during diastole. By the time the blood reaches the capillaries it is flowing at a constant rate. This change is made possible by the elasticity of the walls of the arteries. The amount of blood flowing out of the heart over a given period is called the cardiac output. The cardiac output depends on the volume of blood forced out at each beat, the stroke volume, and the heart rate.

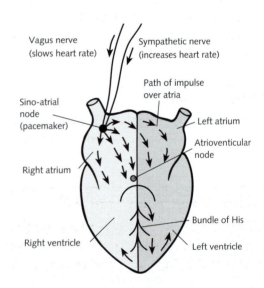

Figure 12.4 The initiation of heartbeat – ventral view of heart showing the spread of the electrical impulses that accompany contraction of the heart

Cardiac output

The cardiac output is the amount of blood leaving each ventricle of the heart and thus entering the arterial system in one minute. The cardiac output refers to the blood being pumped from each individual ventricle. The amount of blood being pumped by each ventricle is usually the same. It is known as the stroke volume. The heart rate is the number of heartbeats in one minute. So:

Stroke volume × Heart rate = Cardiac output.

Anything that affects heart rate or stroke volume obviously affects the cardiac output. Heart rate increases during exercise or as a result of disease and slows down during sleep.

Regulation of blood pressure

Blood pressure depends on a number of factors: heart rate, the strength of the heartbeat, the stroke volume and the resistance to the blood flow by the blood vessels. The contraction or relaxation of the smooth muscle in the walls of the blood vessels controls resistance to the flow of blood. Increased resistance causes a rise in blood pressure; decreased resistance, a reduction in blood pressure. A vasomotor centre in the medulla oblongata of the hind part of the brain controls this activity. Nerve fibres run from this centre to all the arterioles in the body. The activity of the vasomotor centre is controlled by impulses from stretch receptors in the walls of the aorta and carotid sinuses. If the parasympathetic fibres are stimulated there is a reduction in the blood pressure; accompanied by a reduced heartbeat. Conversely, if the blood pressure becomes low the impulse transmission along the sympathetic fibres increases and there is a rise in blood pressure and an increased heartbeat.

An increase in the supply of carbon dioxide affects blood pressure. A large amount of carbon dioxide produced as a result of the increased activity in a tissue causes the vasodilator centre in the brain to be stimulated. Impulses are then sent to the blood vessels and these constrict, causing the blood pressure to be raised and the flow of blood to be increased through the parts of the body where carbon dioxide is tending to build up.

Emotional stress and the resultant production of adrenaline also affects blood pressure. The effects of adrenaline are similar to the effects produced by the sympathetic nervous system and their function is to prepare the body for action by diverting the blood supply to where it is most needed.

Think it over

Stress increases the rate and strength of heartbeat. Why do you think our heart thumps and pounds when we are very frightened?

Assessment activity 12.1

On unlined A3 paper draw a large diagram of the heart. Label the different parts and to each label add short notes to describe any important anatomical features. Add short notes to the diagram to explain how the heart functions.

Produce a further series of drawings to help you to explain the electrical activity in the heart as it beats to circulate the blood. Underneath these drawings explain how blood pressure is maintained. What type of response is this? What advantages do you think this response gives to the body?

The structure and function of the respiratory system

The organs in which the exchange of oxygen from the air and carbon dioxide produced by the cells takes place are the lungs, and these are well adapted to allow gaseous exchange to take place. The lungs are found in the thorax. The thorax is bounded by the ribs and intercostal muscles and separated from the abdomen by a sheet of muscle called the diaphragm. Inside the thorax the lungs are surrounded by the pleural cavities lined with the moist pleural membranes (Figure 4.41, page 155).

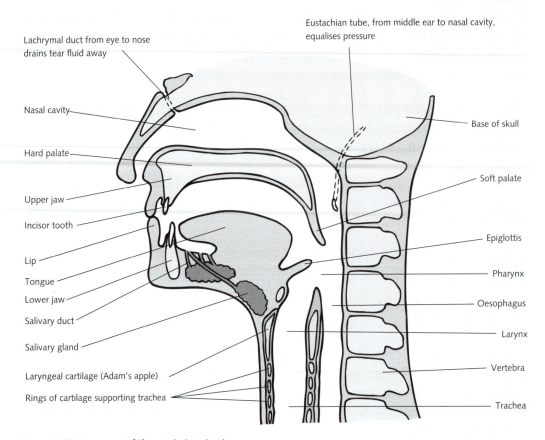

Figure 12.5 Upper part of the respiratory tract

The respiratory system consists of the nose, the trachea, the bronchi and the lungs. The openings of the nasal cavities are the nostrils. The right and left nasal cavities are separated by a septum. At the back of the nose the roof is formed from the base of the skull and the floor by the hard and soft palates (see Figure 12.5). The nasal cavities are lined with mucous membrane and these produce mucus that drains into the nasal cavity. Ciliated epithelium lines the nasal cavity. The bacteria, dirt, and dust particles breathed in become trapped in the mucus produced by the goblet cells of the epithelium and the mucus, together with the trapped dirt, is then moved by the beating of the cilia to the back of the throat where it is swallowed. The turbinated bones in the nasal cavity are convoluted and this makes it more likely that the air passing in through the nose will come into contact with the ciliated epithelium and be filtered. This also means that the air takes longer to travel through the nasal cavity and it is warmed and moistened as it passes up the nose. As well as warming, moistening and filtering the air there are also olfactory cells present in this region and they help with the sensation of smell.

The respiratory passage continues through the glottis, at the back of the mouth, into the windpipe or trachea. At the upper end of the trachea is the larynx or voice box. The entrance to the glottis is normally open to allow the free passage of air down the trachea. A cartilaginous flap, the epiglottis, closes the glottis when food or liquid is swallowed, to prevent the food or liquid from entering the air passageway, and just before coughing, when air is forced out of the lungs.

The larynx continues as the trachea. The trachea usually lies in the midline of the neck. It extends about 10 cm and then divides into two bronchi that then enter the lungs. The trachea is lined with pseudostratified ciliated epithelium. Goblet cells are interspersed in the epithelium. The cilia move the mucus, together with its trapped dirt particles, back to the back of the mouth where it can be swallowed and removed from the respiratory system via the alimentary canal. If it is not removed in this way, then it becomes deposited in the lungs and causes disease.

'C' shaped bands of cartilage and smooth muscle support the trachea. The muscle layer rests against the oesophagus and stretches a little as food passes down. This prevents the oesophagus from becoming blocked by the food as it passes down the alimentary canal. The 'C' shaped bands of cartilage stop the trachea from collapsing and allow the air to pass freely to the lungs.

The trachea branch into two bronchi. These enter the lungs and divide into many smaller bronchi before terminating in many finely divided bronchioles. Like the trachea these tubes are lined with ciliated epithelium and the cilia help to clear the respiratory system of accumulated unwanted mucus. The bronchioles have a smaller internal diameter than the bronchial tubes. The cartilaginous rings disappear, the mucus-producing glands disappear and the fine bronchioles are lined with flat cuboidal epithelial cells. Ultimately the bronchioles give way to the alveoli, the region where exchange of gases takes place.

The breathing cycle

The flow chart on page 156 (Figure 4.43) shows the breathing cycle and Figure 4.42, page 156 shows the changes which take place in the lungs during inhalation and exhalation. During normal respiration about 500 cm^3 of air is taken in and expelled. This is known as the *tidal volume*. During activity both the rate and depth of breathing increase; the more vigorous the activity, the greater the volume of air taken in and the greater the depth of breathing. The volume of air taken in in one minute is known as the *ventilation rate*.

Ventilation rate = Tidal volume × Frequency of inspirations.

For example, if a person has a ventilation rate of 15 breaths per minute and a tidal volume of 500 cm^3 their ventilation rate will be

15 × 500 cm^3 = 7.5 dm^3/min.

The lungs can readily adapt to changing needs. They have a capacity of about 3 dm^3 more than their tidal volume and this extra capacity can be brought into use when required. This is known as the *inspiratory reserve volume*. If after normal breathing you breathe out as much air as you can the extra air expelled is roughly 1 dm³. This volume is known as the *expiratory reserve volume*. The maximum volume of air that can be expelled from the lungs after a maximum inhalation is called the *vital capacity* (see Figure 12.6). The vital capacity varies according to the health and size of chest of the individual. The vital capacity of an average adult is between 4 and 5 dm³ and a very fit athlete has a vital capacity of 6 dm³. Even after the most forceful exhalation the lungs still contain some air. This is why the lungs do not totally collapse after expiration. The air remaining is called residual air. It is usually about 1.5 dm³.

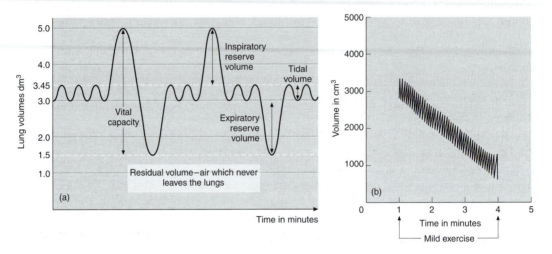

Figure 12.6 Spirometer chart to display lung volumes

Theory into practice

Using Figure 12.7 work out the following volumes to the nearest 00.5 dm³:

- tidal volume at rest
- tidal volume during exercise
- vital capacity
- residual volume
- total lung capacity.

Assessment activity 12.2

Revise the topics of breathing and respiration in Unit 4.

Prepare a talk for a small group of people describing the physiology of the nose, trachea, the bronchi and the lungs. Explain the functions of the lungs and bronchi to the group.

Ask them to trace the path of a molecule of oxygen from the time it enters the nose to the time it arrives in the alveoli of the lungs and explain how the oxygen is transported to the cells of the body to enable tissue respiration to take place. Keep a copy of any materials that you use to help you in the delivery of your talk and keep a record of the text that you use to deliver your message. Include it in your assessment folder.

Gaseous exchange

The process by which gaseous exchange takes place across the walls of the alveoli is called **diffusion**. Blood reaching the alveoli has a lower partial pressure of oxygen and a higher partial pressure of carbon dioxide than the alveolar air. The concentration gradient thus set up allows oxygen to diffuse into the blood and carbon dioxide to diffuse into the alveoli (see Figure 4.44, page 157). When the blood leaves the alveoli it will have the same partial pressure of oxygen and carbon dioxide as the alveolar air. As a result of the changes in the partial pressures the saturation of the blood with oxygen rises to about 95 per cent. The composition of the alveolar air, however, does not change much because the process of ventilation is continuous and air is constantly being passed in and out of the lungs.

Diffusion between the alveoli and the capillaries (see Figure 12.7) is helped by the following factors:

- The barrier between the capillaries and the alveoli is very thin.
- Body temperature helps the molecules to move faster.
- The partial pressure of the gases is high.
- The surface area of the alveoli and capillaries is large.
- A concentration gradient of the gases is maintained.

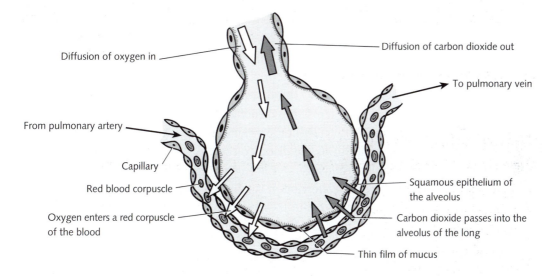

Figure 12.7 The exchange of gases at the alveoli

Think it over

Imagine how it would be if 90 per cent of your group stood at one end of the room and 10 per cent at the other, with everyone moving randomly around the room to music. Someone stops the music after ten minutes. Would you still have the same proportion of people in different parts of the room? Of course you would not, people would be much more evenly distributed. That is what diffusion is about: an 'equalling up' of moving molecules which were unevenly distributed in the first place. Place a line of chairs in the middle of the room and it would not make any difference to the result, it would just take longer to cross the barrier. Build a wall across the room (don't try this at home!) and it would make a difference – the barrier is now too thick to cross.

The structure and function of the renal system

The renal system consists of:

- right and left kidneys
- right and left ureters
- bladder
- urethra.

The urine, made in the kidneys, is transported down the ureters to the bladder, a temporary store, until it is released from the body by way of the urethra (see Figure 4.46, page 159).

Structure of the kidney

The kidneys are situated on either side of the abdomen. Each kidney is made up of a number of functional units called nephrons (Figure 4.47, page 159). Each nephron has the dual role of excretion and osmoregulation. You should now refer back to Unit 4 to remind yourself about these processes and their importance in the physiology of human systems.

The first section of a nephron, the Bowman's capsule, is found in the cortex of the kidney. The Bowman's capsule encloses a dense network of capillaries called the glomerulus. Between the outer and inner space of the Bowman's capsule there is a space, called the capsular space, lined with epithelial cells. The epithelial cells of the capsular space and the endothelia of the capillaries of the glomerulus are in very close contact and this, together with the thinness of the lining, allows exchange of materials to take place readily between the blood capillaries and the kidneys.

The Bowman's capsule leads into a long tubule. The first part of this is coiled. It is called the proximal convoluted tubule because it is the part of the tube that is nearest to the Bowman's capsule and it is convoluted. The proximal convoluted tubule leads to a U-shaped tube called the loop of Henlé. The first part of this loop (the descending limb of the loop of Henlé) passes right across the medulla of the kidney before returning to the cortex as the ascending limb of the loop of Henlé. When it reaches the cortex it once again becomes coiled and forms the distal convoluted tubule. The distal convoluted tubule, along with the tubules from several other nephrons, opens into a wider tube, the collecting duct. There are several collecting ducts and these open into the pelvis of the kidney. The pelvis expels its contents into the ureter and thence to the bladder where it is stored until it is ready to be eliminated from the body.

The blood passing into the glomerulus comes from the afferent vessel, a branch of the renal artery, and as such it is at a high pressure. Ultrafiltration causes liquid from the afferent vessel to pass into the capsular space of the Bowman's capsule. As the fluid passes from the capsular space down the kidney tubule useful substances are reabsorbed. Any glucose present in the filtrate is reabsorbed in the proximal convoluted tubule together with sodium, potassium, phosphate and hydrogen carbonate ions. Some substances, including some antibiotics and some drugs and toxins, are also passed into the tubule from the blood so that they can be eliminated from the body in the urine. About 85 to 90 per cent of water is reabsorbed in the proximal tubule and a great deal of the remaining water from the loop of Henlé, distal convoluted tubule and collecting duct. The permeability of these tubules, you will recall, is under hormonal control. The unwanted substances, including urea, are passed from the kidney, via the ureter, as urine, to the bladder for temporary storage prior to excretion.

In Unit 4, page 137, you learnt about osmoregulation and the composition of body fluids, so you should now go back and revise this section of the work.

Think it over

We tend to drink a lot of liquid on a hot day and a smaller quantity of liquid on a cold day. Despite this we tend to produce smaller quantities of more concentrated urine on a hot day and larger quantities of less concentrated urine on a cold day. Why is this so?

Assessment activity 12.3

Write an account describing the physiology of the kidneys including the renal corpuscles and renal tubules. Describe the relationship of the ureters, urethra, and bladder to the kidneys. Explain how urine is formed. Include diagrams in your work. Add all of this work to your assessment folder.

The composition and function of blood

Blood consists of several different types of cell suspended in watery straw-coloured liquid called **plasma**. The cellular components of blood, you will recall, are the erythrocytes (the red blood corpuscles), the leucocytes (the white blood corpuscles) and the thrombocytes (the blood platelets) (see Figure 4.29, page 144).

You should now read again and revise the information given about blood in Unit 4.

Erythrocytes

You will recall the following facts about the erythrocytes. They:

- do not have a nucleus
- are disk-shaped, to provide a larger surface area over which to absorb oxygen
- have a very thin flexible plasma membrane to enable them to squeeze through very small spaces and thus to transport oxygen more efficiently to the tissues
- have cytoplasm containing haemoglobin – the absence of a nucleus means that there is space for more haemoglobin in the cell
- have a diameter of about 8 μm and are about 3 μm in thickness
- carry oxygen from the respiratory organs to the tissues of the body
- live for about 120 days
- cannot divide
- cannot make new enzymes and structural proteins
- are made in the bone marrow
- are destroyed by the cells of the liver.

There are approximately 5 million erythrocytes in every ml of blood.

Normal destruction of erythrocytes

Because the erthrocytes progressively degenerate they have to be destroyed and this is carried out by the macrophages. The macrophages are large phagocytic cells found mainly in the liver, spleen and bone marrow. They break down the haemoglobin of the erythrocytes into its constituent amino acids, release the iron atoms and convert the residue of the haemoglobin molecule into brown pigment called bilirubin. The individual amino acids can be reused, the iron is stored in the liver until it is required for the manufacture of new red cells and the bilirubin is eliminated from the body as the bile pigments.

Leucocytes

These are the white blood corpuscles, which:

- are bigger and fewer in number than the erythrocytes
- have a nucleus, the nature of which varies
- have colourless cytoplasm that may be granular or agranular
- have the function of defence against disease
- number approximately 7000 white corpuscles per mm^3 of blood.

The leucocytes are divided into two main groups, i.e. granulocytes and agranulocytes. Granulocytes have a granular cytoplasm and a lobed nucleus. Because they have a lobed nucleus they are said to be polymorphic. There are three different types of granulocytes, known as basophils, eosinophils and neutrophils. The different granulocytes stain differently, depending whether an acidic or basic dye is used to stain them. When the granulocytes are stained with Leishman's stain (a mixture of an acid and a basic stain) the granules in the cytoplasm may stain red – in which case the granulocyte is said to be an eosinophil, blue – in which case the granulocyte is said to be a basophil, or remain unstained – the so-called neutrophil. There are about 1.5 per cent eosinophils, 70 per cent neutrophils, and 0.5 per cent basophils in blood. The granulocytes all originate in the bone marrow.

The leucocytes with a non-granular cytoplasm are called agranulocytes. These usually have a bean-shaped or spherical nucleus. Those with a spherical nucleus are called lymphocytes, and those with the bean-shaped nucleus, monocytes. There are about 24 per cent lymphocytes and 4 per cent monocytes in the blood. The lymphocytes produce antitoxins and the monocytes are phagocytic. Both lymphocytes and monocytes originate in the bone marrow and migrate to the lymph nodes and thence into the blood stream. The different types of leucocyte are identified in the table below.

Type	Occurrence in blood	Function
Neutrophils nucleus — granular cytoplasm Granules do **not** stain with Leishmann's stain	70%	Phagocytic
Eosinophils nucleus Granules stain red with Leishmann's stain	3%	Detoxification
Basophils Granules stain blue with Leishmann's stain	1%	Doubtful, but appear to be involved in the prevention of the coagulation of blood or lymph in obstructed tissues
Lymphocytes agranular cytoplasm	25%	Production of antitoxins
Monocytes agranular cytoplasm	1%	Phagocytic

Thrombocytes

These are:

- the smallest of all blood cells
- oval in shape
- enucleate, i.e. they do not have a nucleus
- really cell fragments formed from the megakaryocytes
- formed in the bone marrow
- involved in the clotting mechanism of the blood
- involved in the coagulation of the blood and vasoconstriction using the enzymes and chemicals which they contain.

There are approximately 0.25 million thrombocytes per mm^3 of blood.

Clotting of blood

When a blood vessel is damaged there is an immediate restriction to reduce the loss of blood. The surface endothelial cells of the blood vessel are forced close together so that they seal the blood vessel and the thrombocytes stick tightly together to form a platelet plug. Blood clotting then prevents excessive bleeding.

Clotting takes place in a number of stages (see Figure 12.8).

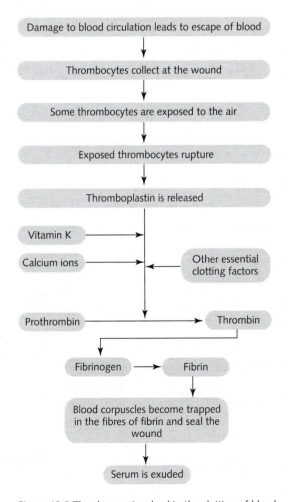

Figure 12.8 The changes involved in the clotting of blood

The thrombocytes contain an enzyme called thrombokinase. When the blood vessels are damaged thrombokinase is released and, as a result, prothrombin present in the blood plasma is converted into thrombin by a series of linked reactions. Some of these reactions require the presence of calcium ions as co-factors and others require phospholipids. Vitamin K is essential for the formation of the prothrombin and other clotting factors. The thrombin causes the blood plasma protein, fibrinogen, to be converted into a mesh of fine fibres called fibrin. The mesh so formed traps the red blood corpuscles and converts the free flowing blood into a gel. Once formed the blood clot becomes reduced in size due to the contraction of the fibrin fibres – a process called retraction. A pale yellow watery fluid called serum is exuded as retraction takes place.

Assessment activity 12.4

You have been asked by a colleague to produce a short revision booklet to help a group of trainee nurses in their revision of the blood. You are asked to describe the formation and function of the erythrocytes, leucocytes, and thrombocytes and to include an explanation of the normal destruction of these cells. You are also asked to add a section describing the normal clotting mechanism of the blood. Keep a copy of your work in your assessment folder.

Blood groups

Sometimes the blood from two individuals can be mixed with no observable effects but, on mixing, the red corpuscles sometimes clump together or agglutinate. Agglutination is caused because the erythrocytes have substances called antigens attached to their membranes and the plasma of different blood contains antibodies. It is when different antigens and antibodies meet that clumping or agglutination takes place.

Types of blood group

The most important antigens are the ABO antigens.

- A person who carries only A antigens is said to have blood group A.
- A person who carries only B antigens is said to have blood group B.
- A person who carries no antigens is said to have blood group O.
- A person who carries antigens A and B is said to have blood group AB.

In each case the plasma has antibodies against the blood antigens that are NOT present:
- A person who carries only A antigens has anti-B antibodies.
- A person who carries only B antigens has anti-A antibodies.
- A person who carries no antigens has both anti-A and anti-B antibodies.
- A person who carries antigens A and B has no antibodies.

Consequently it is important, when giving a blood transfusion, to give the patient blood of the right group. If the wrong blood group is given to the patient the blood agglutinates and death follows. Compatible blood groups are shown in the table.

Blood group of patient	Antibodies in plasma	Blood groups that can be used for transfusion
A	Anti-B	A, O
B	Anti-A	B, O
O	Anti-A and Anti-B	O
AB	Neither antibody A nor antibody B	A, B, AB, O

A person with blood group O used to be called a universal donor because their blood could safely be transfused into a patient with any blood group. A person with blood group AB used to be called a universal recipient because they can receive blood from any group. These terms are now not used because all blood must be cross-matched before a blood transfusion can take place.

Think it over

In mis-matched transfusions the red blood corpuscles release their haemoglobin. This then becomes 'stuck' in the glomerular pores of the kidney causing anuria, which results in the toxins accumulating. The toxins then have to be removed by dialysis until the haemoglobin becomes broken down and normal kidney function is restored.

Think it over

A road traffic accident results in a number of casualties. Three of these casualties require blood transfusions. One casualty is blood group A, one blood group AB and one blood group O. Identify the blood group of the blood that should be given to each patient. If there is a shortage of blood of an appropriate group, identify a suitable alternative.

Inheritance of blood groups

Blood groups are inherited from our parents. Their determination can be used in paternity suits when they can be used to determine whether a particular man could or could not have been the father of a particular child, not whether he is definitely the father. The human blood groups O, A, B, and AB are inherited by multiple alleles. Multiple alleles are defined as three or more alternative conditions of a single gene locus that result in different phenotypes. In any population an individual can have two, and only two, of the genes and any gamete only one of the pair. In the whole population there will be three or more different alleles. In the inheritance of the A, B and O blood groups there are three different alleles:

- gene a^A that causes the formation of agglutinogen A
- gene a^B that causes the formation of agglutinogen B
- gene a that produces no agglutinogen.

Gene a is recessive to gene a^A and gene a^B but neither gene a^A nor gene a^B is dominant to the other.

- Genotypes a^Aa^A and a^Aa result in the individual having blood group A.
- Genotypes a^Ba^B and a^Ba result in the individual having blood group B.
- Genotype a^Aa^B results in the individual having blood group AB.
- Genotype aa results in the individual having blood group O.

For example: A mother with blood group O will have the genotype aa. She will only produce eggs with the allele a. A father with blood group AB will have the genotype a^Aa^B. He will produce two types of sperm, those containing the allele a^A, and those containing the allele a^B. If an egg bearing the allele a is fertilised by a sperm containing the allele a^B the infant produced will be of blood group B. If an egg bearing the allele a is fertilised by a sperm bearing the allele a^A the offspring will be of blood group A. Only individuals with blood group A or blood group B are produced (see Figure 12.9).

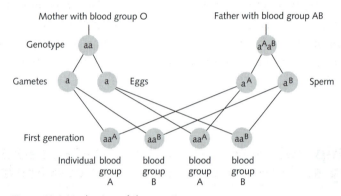

Figure 12.9 Mechanism of the genetic process

Nearly 12 other sets of blood types are inherited independently of the ABO blood types. These include the M-N factors and the series of Rh alleles. The frequency of different blood groups differs in different ethnic groups.

Think it over

Two women, Mrs Brown and Mrs Hilton, both gave birth to babies at the same hospital at the same time. Mrs Brown took home a daughter and named her Jennifer. Mrs Hilton took home a daughter and called her Alison. However, she was sure that the baby that she had taken home was not hers. She filed charges against the hospital. When blood tests were conducted the following results were obtained:

Client	Blood group
Mr Brown	O
Mrs Brown	AB
Mrs Hilton	B
Mr Hilton	B
Jennifer	O
Alison	B

Has there been a mix up of the two children? Explain your reasoning.

Rhesus factor

There is also another antigen that may be present in the membranes of the erythrocytes. This is the Rhesus factor, a factor first discovered in the blood of the Rhesus monkey. Any individual having this antigen is said to be Rhesus positive (Rh^+). If the antigen is absent, the person is said to be Rhesus negative (Rh^-). If Rh^- blood is exposed to Rh^+ blood, then anti-Rh antibodies are produced. This can happen if a Rh^- mother has an Rh^+ foetus. If the anti-Rh antibodies cross the placenta the red cells of the foetus can be destroyed. Generally the antibodies are not formed quickly or strongly enough to affect the first child but subsequent children can be affected. This is known as haemolytic disease of the newborn.

In the past, giving the child a complete transfusion of Rh^- blood treated the disease. These transfusions could be given whilst the child was still in the uterus. Now all men and women are tested for the Rhesus factor before they have children. When a Rh^- woman conceives a child by a Rh^+ man she is given an injection of a gamma globulin, containing antibodies against the Rh factor. This kills any Rh^+ cells that have migrated into the circulatory system of the mother from the foetus and prevents the mother from building up an immunity to the Rhesus factor. Any further children are not therefore exposed to the Rh antibodies. This technique has virtually eliminated the disease.

Relationship between the cardiovascular, renal and respiratory systems and homeostatic mechanisms

Interdependency of body systems

The systems of the body do not work in isolation (see Figure 12.10). To enable the body to function effectively the body systems must interact and work together so that the internal environment is kept constant – a process known as homeostasis. The cardiovascular and respiratory systems work together to ensure that oxygenated blood is circulated to the cells so that tissue respiration can take place and the renal system, working in harmony, then ensures that the excretory products produced during this tissue respiration are removed from the body. If the systems did not work together the materials essential for life processes would not be available at the correct time and the by-products of cellular activity would accumulate and be toxic to the cells of the body.

You should now revise the mechanism of homeostasis as described in Unit 4.

Assessment activity 12.5

1 Draw a large diagram on unlined paper to show the links between the heart, major vessels and the lungs. Underneath the diagram explain how the normal functioning of these systems maintain homeostasis in the body.

2 You are late for an important appointment. Identify the changes that will take place in the cardiovascular and the respiratory system as you hurry to your destination.

Keep a record of all your work and add it to your assessment folder.

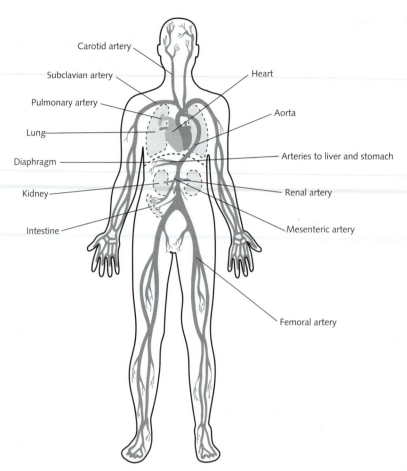

Figure 12.10 Location within body of cardiovascular, renal and respiratory systems

Implications of disorder and disease

The table shows the common disorders/diseases of the cardiovascular, respiratory, renal systems and the blood.

Disorder/disease	Body system affected	Signs and symptoms
Hypertension (high blood pressure)	Cardiovascular system	Dizziness, shortness of breath
Bronchitis	Respiratory system	Fever, chest pain, severe coughing, mucus coughed up from the respiratory tract
Nephritic syndrome	Renal system	Albumin and, sometimes, red and white blood cells appear in the urine
Asthma	Respiratory system	Attack often begins with coughing, wheezing and shortness of breath
Iron deficiency anaemia	Blood system	Pallor, shortness of breath, low vitality, dizziness, digestive disorders

Presentation of abnormal function

Heart attacks

Heart disease kills more people than any other disease in the developed world. There are many causes of heart attack. These include hypertension, atherosclerosis (narrowing of the coronary arteries), infection and congenital effects.

Hypertension

Those with hypertension or high blood pressure have an increased chance of having either a heart attack or a stroke. If the hypertension is treated, however, the risk is reduced. Although there appears to be genetic link, there are a number of other factors that can contribute to the development of hypertension. Blood pressure tends to increase with age but it is more likely to occur if an individual is overweight, does not exercise, has a diet that includes a high level of salt and fat, drinks large quantities of alcohol, smokes and is under a lot of stress. Weight reduction, a diet low in salt and fats and with more fibre, accompanied by an increase in exercise, can reduce hypertension and thus the risk of heart attack and stroke. A healthy young adult has a blood pressure reading of around 110/75 mm mercury. An older person usually has a higher blood pressure, usually of around 130–140/90–100 mm mercury. Someone suffering from hypertension will have a systolic blood pressure (the top value) exceeding 140 mm mercury or a diastolic blood pressure (bottom value) exceeding 90 mm mercury.

Asthma

Asthma (from the Greek word meaning 'panting') is a respiratory disease in which the smooth muscle of the respiratory tract contracts, causing the air passages to become constricted. The mucous lining of the tract swells and breathing becomes very difficult. The muscular spasm is sometimes triggered by an allergic reaction and sometimes caused by a respiratory infection. Asthma attacks are treated using a variety of drugs.

These drugs cause the muscle of the respiratory tract to relax and breathing then becomes much easier. An anti-inflammatory drug is usually taken regularly by asthmatics to prevent inflammation of the lining of the respiratory tract.

Assessment activity 12.6

The incidence of asthma among some groups of the population is increasing. Describe what asthma is. Choose an individual, for example a child, an athlete or a teenager, and describe the effects of asthma on their life. Include this work in your assessment folder.

Nephritis

One of the commonest diseases of the kidney is nephritis or inflammation of the kidney. The disease is more common in children than adults. Sometimes nephritis develops after a streptococcal infection. If the kidney tissue becomes destroyed as a result of repeated infection, then patients may develop a high blood pressure. If the kidneys are not working properly they allow the toxins to accumulate in the body – sometimes with disastrous results. In recent years dialysis has been used to remove these poisons from the blood. Transplantation is the preferred method of treatment for those suffering from chronic kidney failure because it is less expensive, it allows the patient to lead a normal life and it carries less risk. Dialysis tends to be used mostly whilst a person with a nephritic kidney is waiting for a suitable organ for transplantation.

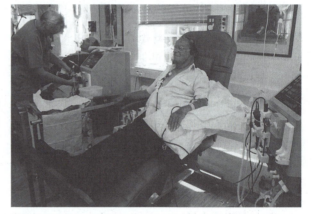
Kidney dialysis saves lives

Transplantation

Successful transplantation of body organs is quite difficult to carry out because donor organs contain antigens and they are therefore often rejected. To help overcome this, tissue typing is carried out before the donor organ is selected. Tissue typing ensures that donor and recipient antigens are matched as closely as possible. Immunosuppressive drugs are given to the patient to ensure that the immune system does not reject the donor organ.

Assessment activity 12.7

Research and describe the processes and outcomes of renal failure. The research may involve inviting a specialist speaker from a local hospital to speak to your group. In small groups, prepare your arguments for a group debate on the implications of dialysis treatment and renal transplantation to both the individual and society. Put together a summary of the group debate and include it in your assessment folder.

Iron deficiency anaemia

Anaemia is the abnormal reduction in the number of erythrocytes or in their haemoglobin content. This results in an inadequate delivery of oxygen to the tissues. Iron deficiency anaemia occurs when the body's need for iron increases, e.g. during pregnancy.

Assessment activity 12.8

At different life stages the body needs different amounts of iron. In a small group, research the causes and effects of iron deficiency anaemia. Discuss the differing needs of a child, a pregnant woman, and an elderly man. Summarise your findings and record them in your assessment folder.

End of unit test

1 Describe how arteries and veins differ in structure.

2 Explain how this difference is related to function.

3 List the stages of the cardiac cycle.

4 Explain why the brachial pulse is felt when taking the pulse of a baby.

5 Identify three factors that could affect pulse rate.

6 Which of the following statements are true and which are false?
   a Cardiac muscle is said to be myogenic.
   b The atrioventricular node of the heart is also known as the pacemaker.
   c When measuring the activity of the heart:
      Stroke volume × Cardiac output = Heart rate.
   d When we are stressed adrenaline is produced and blood pressure is increased.

7 Describe the passage of a molecule of oxygen from the air to the alveoli of the lungs.

8 What features of the alveoli of the lungs enable the oxygen to pass efficiently into the circulatory system?

9 Define the process by which oxygen is transferred from the alveoli to the blood and carbon dioxide is removed from the blood to the alveoli of the lungs.

10 Describe the sequence of events in the kidney following the consumption of five pints of beer on a cold day.

11 Describe how the structure of erythrocytes enables them to carry out their function more efficiently.

12 Explain why a person with blood group O used to be called a 'universal donor'.

13 Where precisely would you find:
   a the intercostal muscles
   b the liver

    c glomerulus

    d the diaphragm?

14 Give two reasons why transplantation is the preferred option when treating a patient with chronic nephritis.

15 Explain the purpose of tissue typing before transplantation is carried out.

References and further reading

Clegg, C. J. and Mackean, D. K. (1994) *Advanced Biology: Principles and Applications*, London: John Murray

Philips, W. D. and Chitton, T. (1989) *A-Level Biology*, Oxford: Oxford University Press

Soper, R. et al. (1992) *Biological Science*, Vols 1 and 2, Cambridge: Cambridge University Press

Toole, G. and Toole, S. (1995) *Understanding Biology for Advanced Level*, Cheltenham: Nelson Thornes

13 Health psychology

This unit offers an introduction to health psychology, looking at different theories of health/illness behaviour, including the concept of stress and coping strategies. Contemporary issues are considered, as well as the psychological factors involved in chronic/terminal illness.

What you need to learn

- Theories of health and illness behaviour
- Contemporary issues
- Stress management strategies
- Chronic and terminal illness

Theories of health and illness behaviour

Health psychologists who want to understand health behaviours use many of the same general psychological models and theories which explain any behaviour. One way in which we can understand factors which might determine health behaviours is to describe the thought processes which might be going on in someone's mind as they think about health behaviours.

Illness cognitions

Illness cognitions are common sense beliefs about being ill. These beliefs are key to understanding how people decide they are ill and cope with the implications of being ill. One of the most influential models of illness cognitions is that of Howard Leventhal and colleagues which was developed in the early 1980s. Leventhal's model has three main stages which will be examined in detail below (see Figure 13.1).

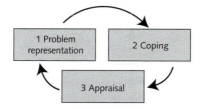

Figure 13.1 Leventhal's self-regulatory model of illness (1980)

Recognising that we are ill

The first stage in Leventhal's model is termed **problem representation**. It is at this stage that people make the decision that they are ill. Information for problem representations comes from three main sources:

- our own perception of internal sensations
- information from other people
- our previous experiences of illness.

Although we can detect many sensations of physical functioning we are generally unaware of them. For example, you probably don't normally think about the rumbling noises your intestines make after a meal, but if you had experienced pain in that area a few hours earlier, you might take more notice of the sensations in order to decide if something was wrong. The amount a person attends to internal sensations is referred to as **vigilance**. Hypervigilance, or an over-attendance to these internal sensations can lead to hypochondria where a person interprets normal internal symptoms as illness.

A second source of information for problem representations comes from our **lay referral system**. This is the informal social network of people who may provide health advice, such as family and friends. These people may offer advice when it is not asked for, e.g. after noticing that you are acting strangely. Alternatively, we may ask their advice on a symptom or sensation.

To get rid of a wart, first you need to get a piece of meat and bury it in the garden...

Our own **experience** and thoughts regarding illness provide a third channel of information to help us decide if we are ill. However, decisions that we are ill depend

Often we get more advice than we need from others or advice may not be sound! For example, would you follow this advice to get rid of warts?

very much on a person's understanding of physical conditions. Leventhal's research suggests that people describe illnesses in terms of four features:

- **Identity** – the signs and symptoms which identify the condition. People use the symptoms of an illness to give it a label. Once an illness has been given a label, people may expect or look for other symptoms.

- **Consequences** – the perceived consequences of the disease. The illness may have implications for physical self-image, social interaction, financial implications and emotional upset.

- **Causes** – theories as to the cause of illness. Research has found that most people try to make sense of their illness by determining its cause, e.g. genetic factors, stress, environmental hazards, own behaviour, bad luck, etc.

- **Time line** – beliefs surrounding the duration of the illness. We tend to classify illness as acute, recurrent or chronic in nature. This provides a clue as to how long we should expect to feel ill.

The combination of our internal perceptions, information provided from our lay referral system and our own understanding of illness allows us to come to the decision as to whether we are ill or not and what further action we need to take. It is important for health psychologists to understand how people make sense of their own illness, as this often provides the key to understanding why they follow the courses of action they do.

Coping with illness

Once we have decided that we are ill, we are motivated to cope with this problem. Although it might seem like the obvious choice to seek medical help, research suggests that this is not always the case. There are a number of ways of coping with illness and other problems. These can roughly be split into strategies to confront the problem, termed problem-focused coping, whilst emotion-focused coping aims to reduce the emotional consequences of the event.

Problem-focused coping can be characterised by constructive actions to resolve the problem. Examples of problem-focused coping with illness might include actions such as seeking medical help, taking rest, self-medication or planning to change behaviour patterns, e.g. give up smoking.

Emotional responses to feeling that one is ill may include fear, anxiety and worry. Thus people may engage in emotion-focused coping in order to reduce the negative impact of these emotions. One method might be to try to make oneself feel better through eating, drinking, smoking or using drugs. Denial is another form of emotion-focused coping where people try to forget that they might be ill. Giving vent to emotions in outbursts of anger and despair can also help people deal with the emotions caused by illness.

People engaging in emotion-focused coping will not necessarily seek medical attention, as this may provide confirmation that the illness is real and produce an increase in distress. Denial may be more common when people think that there is nothing they can do about the illness. In some situations, such as terminal illnesses, denial may be an effective coping strategy which allows people to stop worrying about their illness. Most illnesses are, however, treatable to a certain extent and under these circumstances, a delay in seeking medical help can lead to the problem becoming much worse.

Assessment activity 13.1

Write brief notes on the difference between problem-focused and emotion-focused coping. Make a list of the strategies you used to cope the last time you were ill. Separate these into problem-focused and emotion-focused strategies.

Appraisal

Following their coping strategy, Leventhal's model suggests that people go through a process of appraisal where they evaluate the success of their coping in conjunction with the health problem. For example, someone might redefine the signs they previously thought indicated a twisted ankle if, after a day's rest, the swelling disappears. Alternatively if the symptoms continue or worsen, they might decide that their current coping strategy of trying not to think about the pain and resting is not effective and they need to seek medical attention.

The entire process of problem representation, coping and appraisal continues until a state of normality is perceived. This process is illustrated by the following case study of Frank who had a heart attack. See if you can identify features of the self-regulatory model in Frank's account.

Case study

Illness cognitions during the experience of a heart attack

Frank breathed a sigh of relief as he got home from work. It had been a terrible day – his boss Chris had been complaining about his ability to meet his sales targets and he had performed badly in his review meeting. Later that evening, Frank began to feel pains in his chest. At first he thought he might have food poisoning, but remembered that someone had told him that food poisoning always takes 12 hours to develop. His next thought was that his lunch was too rich and had given him indigestion. After all, he had just had another slap-up meal in an effort to please a disgruntled client. It was probably the same as when he had gone out for the work's meal curry a week ago. As he had done on that occasion, he took a dose of indigestion remedy and decided to take the rest of the night off. As he fell asleep, Frank concluded that his initial diagnosis of indigestion had been correct as his symptoms had gone.

However, the following morning, as he was getting ready for work, Frank again felt the pains in his chest. His thoughts concerning food poisoning returned. However, his family who had all eaten the same foods the previous night reported themselves to be well and so he rejected this possibility. Frank's wife, seeing him to be in some pain, recommended that he go to casualty. This worried Frank further and he began to imagine all sorts of problems. Could it be a heart attack? Or was it something else, possibly even more serious, like cancer or liver failure? As his wife drove him to hospital, he began to worry about her and how she would cope were he to die or become unable to work.

Tests carried out in the emergency room confirmed that Frank was having a heart attack. Frank spent a lot of time thinking in the three weeks he spent in hospital following his heart attack. He decided that his heart attack had been brought on by over-work, and he now also remembered that an uncle had died young from a heart attack so Frank concluded that a weak heart must run in the family.

- Discuss the stages in Frank's illness representation. How do these fit Leventhal's model?
- Think back to the last time you thought you were ill. Does Leventhal's model fit your experiences?

The health belief model

The health belief model, devised by Rosenstock, predicts whether health behaviours will occur by considering two main thought processes, perceived personal threat and a cost-benefit analysis.

Threat is determined by:

- **susceptibility** – how vulnerable one feels to the negative outcomes of the behaviour
- **seriousness** – beliefs concerning how serious the negative outcomes would be
- **cues to action** – external or internal factors which start you thinking about the health issue.

The second part of the model, the cost-benefit analysis takes into account the balance between:

- **benefits** – the expected advantages of the behaviour
- **costs** – the perceived barriers and disadvantages of the behaviour.

The health belief model suggests that the likelihood of a person engaging in a behaviour is a combination of these two thought processes. These interrelationships are represented in Figure 13.2.

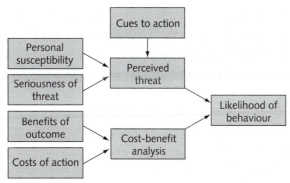

Figure 13.2 The health belief model

We can use an example of getting a flu jab to show how the health belief model might explain behaviour.

Case study

Health cognitions and getting a flu jab

John, a self-employed 52 year old, rates himself as fairly fit. We might expect that his rating of his susceptibility to catch flu is low. He thinks that having flu is a phrase that people use when they really mean they have a bad cold, and does not think it is a very serious condition. He never really even considers the possibility of getting a flu immunisation. He does not know the cost of getting a flu jab, but believes that it would be about £20, money he cannot afford to spend. He also has a bit of a fear of needles. He does not see any benefits to getting the flu jab and given the barriers he can see, it is probably unlikely, on balance, that he will ask his doctor for the preventative injection.

The following winter, one of John's friends has three weeks off work due to flu, and John's thinking about the matter changes. Knowing people who are catching flu, he thinks he might be more susceptible to catching it himself. He perceives flu as being more serious and a greater threat. Although his fear of needles has not disappeared, he weighs up the balance of the cost of the injection with the cost of being unable to work for a few weeks. On balance, this year he thinks he will get the injection.

- List the various thought processes John engages in under the headings of the health belief model.

Think it over

Consider the cues to action component of the health belief model. What might cue action for the following health behaviours:

- giving up smoking
- going for a dental check-up
- drinking 2 litres of water a day.

List as many types of cues to action as you can. How do these fit into commonsense models of illness?

The theory of planned behaviour

The theory of planned behaviour was developed by Izcek Ajzen (1991). It proposes that performance of health actions is initially determined by intention. Intentions are in turn determined by: our personal attitudes and beliefs regarding the behaviour and outcome; our ideas of what other people important to us think about these actions; and how easy it would be to take action (see Figure 13.3).

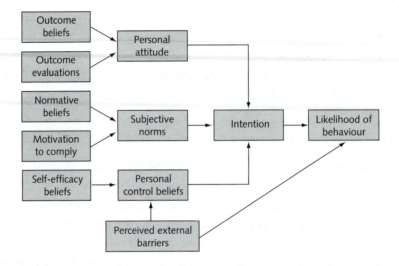

Figure 13.3 The theory of planned behaviour

Personal attitudes towards taking a behaviour are determined by:

- outcome beliefs – what we believe to be the outcome of taking the protective behaviour
- outcome evaluations – how worthwhile we consider the outcome.

Subjective norms are generated from:

- normative beliefs – what we think other people think about the behaviour and outcome, e.g. medical staff, family members, colleagues and friends
- motivation to comply – how motivated we are to act in line with others' views.

Personal control beliefs are determined by:

- external factors which might prevent us achieving our goals
- self-efficacy beliefs – how confident we are that we can achieve the change even in the face of barriers.

Let's return to the case of John's flu jab and see how this model would allow us to interpret his behaviour. The health belief model and theory of planned behaviour share some components in common. We already know that John believes that there are rewards to getting the flu jab. He believes that it will prevent him from catching the flu and that it will give him peace of mind over the winter. Both John's mother and his partner are constantly nagging him to get a flu inoculation. John finds it easy to brush off his mother's advice, but he takes more account of what his partner says, thus his motivation to comply with her views is high. However, even if his intention is there, many external and internal factors might get in the way of John getting his flu jab. If he was offered extra work, or if transport to the surgery was difficult, these perceived barriers, along with his fear of needles, would suggest that he would not get the flu jab.

Summary: predicting health behaviour

Health psychologists apply theories of health behaviour in order to promote behaviours which might prevent us getting ill (see Unit 8 on Health promotion), and to understand how people behave once they are ill (as in Leventhal's model, page 503). One of the health behaviours that health psychologists are particularly interested in understanding is how and why people respond to advice from health care professionals – or more importantly, why they don't!

Compliance

The term **compliance** is used to describe the extent to which people follow medical advice. Some researchers prefer the terms 'adherence' or 'concordance', as compliance implies giving in to demands whereas the terms of adherence and concordance recognise the patient as an active decision maker.

Non-compliance with medical advice is a common problem. For example:

- approximately one-third of people do not take short-course antibiotics as recommended.
- only about 50 per cent of patients with chronic diseases take medicines correctly
- approximately 25 per cent of transplanted kidneys are rejected due to recipients failing to correctly take anti-rejection drugs
- only 20–50 per cent of people comply with advice to change aspects of their lifestyle, i.e. give up smoking or improve their diet, even after major illness.

We might ask whether failing to follow medical advice to the letter actually matters. The answer is, probably not when we are talking about some acute conditions such as throat infections, although in terms of cost of drugs to the health service this still amounts to considerable waste. However, with chronic conditions, failing to take therapeutic levels of medicines can lead to further serious complications which are both expensive to treat and disastrous for the patient.

What factors influence whether people comply with health advice? Research has identified the following factors as important:

- **Understanding** – during consultations, medical personnel may use technical words or jargon which patients do not understand. The problem of patients' failure to understand information may be compounded by their reluctance to ask additional questions. It would appear to be a necessary condition for correctly following a medical treatment programme that the patient understands that treatment programme.
- **Memory** – if people are not able to remember the advice given, then they will be unable to follow it.
- **Complexity and duration** – a more complex or longer lasting treatment programme is less likely to be correctly followed than one that is shorter or simpler to complete.
- **Satisfaction** – people are more likely to comply with medical advice or attend appointments when they are satisfied with the advice given. In part this may link to the patients' expectations of the manner of the health professional or the treatment regimen.
- **Illness cognitions** – patients interpret the advice given to them in the context of their understanding of their illness and its treatment. This may lead to a conscious decision to vary the nature of their treatment in a manner which appears rational to

them but may not be ideal in medical terms: this is called creative non-compliance. This may occur if patients wish to test the effectiveness of the medication or its effects on their condition. Patients may also creatively non-comply if there are perceived high costs associated with the treatment, i.e. financial consequences, side effects or other impacts on their lifestyle.

- **Attitudes and beliefs** – cognitive models such as the health belief model and theory of planned behaviour (see above) can help us understand compliance. For example, medical advice to cut down on alcohol intake may be seen as a cue to action; however, a person may still go through a rational decision-making process regarding the value of following that advice.

- **Social environment** – the social environment may be seen to encourage compliance through monitoring from family and friends, or alternatively people may be unsupportive of the patient's treatment regime acting as temptations or providing contrary medical advice. The social environment may also produce barriers to compliance, such as a stressful family life deterring someone from giving up smoking.

Demographic and personality factors do not consistently predict adherence to medical regimens.

So what can be done to improve compliance?

- **Improving communication.** Practitioners can be helped to structure their consultations so that they spend adequate time listening to patients and in discussing treatment options. Research has found that stressing the importance of specific pieces of information, categorising information, and repeating key information during a consultation can improve the ability of patients to understand their treatment regimen. Use of effective questioning to elicit patient fears, or probing aspects of patient beliefs and negotiating treatment regimens can lead to increased satisfaction, and may avoid situations which produce creative non-compliance.

  Philip Ley's work has produced many techniques that health care professionals can use to enhance the ways in which health-related information is communicated to patients, clients and carers. One of the techniques he has devised is **explicit categorisation**. This involves highlighting the types of information being given. For example, a clinician using this technique might use a phrase such as: 'Right you'll want to know what's wrong, well I think you've got bronchitis'. This emphasises the type of information being given, i.e. diagnosis, and then presents the information. Studies suggest that presenting information in this manner leads to better memory, satisfaction and compliance with recommendations.

- **Providing written information.** This can provide a back-up to the verbal information given during the consultation and has been shown to increase compliance. When designing written information, care needs to be taken that it is easy to read and understand, i.e. simple words and short sentences.

- **Reminders.** These may act as cues to action for certain infrequent but important health behaviours, i.e. postcards or telephone reminders to attend appointments. Automated buzzers, pagers and drug calendars can prompt medication taking.

- **Reducing the complexity of regimens.** In some situations, it is possible to simplify the treatment regimen or to tailor it to the patient's lifestyle. Drug companies have also responded by providing easier methods of drug delivery such as patches and sustained release drugs.

- **External rewards.** Introducing fees for missed appointments, financial or gift incentives to maintain appointments, and reducing waiting times have been shown to improve appointment attendance rates.

Health psychologists can have an important input in exploring factors which lead to non-compliance in different illness scenarios, by designing interventions to improve adherence rates and evaluating the effectiveness of any such interventions. Given the huge cost of non-compliance to the health service this is a potentially useful and necessary role.

Assessment activity 13.2

Describe a time you received some specific medical advice. Did you follow this exactly? To what extent do the models of illness cognitions, the health belief model and the theory of planned behaviour explain your behaviour? Which aspects of your behaviour do the models not explain? Which do you feel is the best model?

Contemporary issues

Health psychologists apply models of health behaviour to help them understand specific behaviours. In the following examples, we consider three issues which can have a significant impact on health: smoking, alcohol use and obesity.

Smoking

Who smokes?
- There are about 1.1 billion smokers in the world.
- In the UK, just over a quarter of the adult population smokes.
- Roughly equal numbers of males and females smoke.
- The age group with the highest percentage of smokers is 20–24 years of age.
- Smoking is more common in people from lower social classes.

Smokers may damage their own health and that of other people

Health implications of smoking
Tobacco smoke contains more than 4000 chemicals. The most important components in terms of health are nicotine, tar and carbon monoxide.

- Nicotine causes a 'stress' like response, where the heart beats faster, blood pressure increases, blood becomes more prone to clotting and fats are released into the blood. These changes all put strain on the heart and blood vessels.
- Tar is the term given to the particles in tobacco smoke. Tar is a mixture of many chemicals, many of which are known carcinogens (cancer-causing substances).

- Carbon monoxide binds to red blood cells which normally carry oxygen in the blood. This reduces the amount of oxygen available and can cause tissue damage.

The main health problems which arise from smoking are due to the extra strain it puts on the circulatory system and the exposure to carcinogens. Smokers have a much higher risk of heart disease and angina than non-smokers. Although lung cancer is a well-known side effect of smoking, the risk of cancers of the mouth, lung airways and bladder are also increased. Smokers are also more likely to suffer from colds and other lung conditions, such as emphysema. Male smokers are more likely to be impotent with lower sperm count and it is estimated that fertility is lowered by 30 per cent in female smokers. Smokers also damage their appearance. Smoking causes staining to teeth, bad breath and discoloured, misshapen finger nails. Smoking causes damage to the structure of the skin, meaning that smokers have more wrinkles than non-smokers.

Smokers do not only damage their own health. The smoke breathed out by smokers and that which comes directly off their cigarettes can affect the health of other people. Passive smoking increases the risk of lung cancer, heart attacks and developing asthma, as well as being unpleasant to breathe in.

Children are at special risk from passive smoking. Those who are exposed to smoky environments are more frequently ill with coughs, colds, and other more serious lung and ear infections. They are more likely to develop asthma and once they have asthma, exposure to smoke can make the problem worse, triggering asthma attacks. Babies living in smoky environments are at higher risk of cot death, pneumonia, bronchitis and other chest problems. Babies can be damaged by tobacco smoke even before they are born. Smoke inhaled by pregnant women has been linked to lower birth weight of the baby, higher risk of miscarriage, premature birth and slowed child development.

Why do people smoke?

Given the well-known health risks of smoking, it is surprising that anyone still smokes. Reasons why people smoke have been found to vary from when they are just starting to experiment with cigarettes to when they are a totally addicted dependent smoker. The change in importance of various reasons at different stages is shown in this model devised by Stephney (Figure 13.4).

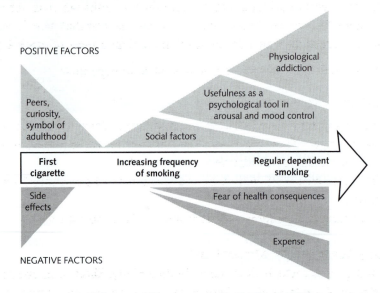

Figure 13.4 A psychology of the cigarette habit (Stephney, 1980)

Assessment activity 13.3

Write a short description of the importance of the different factors in Stephney's model (see Figure 13.4). Highlight which factors are most important in determining starting to smoke, becoming an established smoker and being an established smoker. How do these factors relate to the psychological theories discussed in the previous section of how health behaviour is determined? How might these factors affect people in different age groups?

The most important factors which tend to encourage people to experiment with smoking are psychosocial. Thus people may try their first cigarette out of curiosity, due to pressure from their friends, or to try to look older and rebellious. At this stage, the physical side effects of smoking can be very unpleasant, with many people feeling sick after their first few cigarettes.

Nicotine is an addictive drug. A drag on a cigarette delivers nicotine to the brain in 10 seconds. Nicotine increases levels of **dopamine** in the reward areas of the brain which leads to feelings of pleasure. Nicotine withdrawal effects can include headaches, irritability, inability to concentrate and inability to sleep. However, nicotine dependency takes a few years to become established. As people become dependent on nicotine, they may use it as a relaxant, or to calm them. Addiction plays an important role in continuing cigarette smoking.

Continuing smokers may find that increased worry about their health and the realisation of how much they spend on smoking become factors which encourage them to try to give up. However, by this stage their need to smoke is probably based more on addiction than social factors.

Alcohol

Defining problem drinking

Alcohol consumption is measured in units. One unit is equivalent to half a pint of beer/lager or cider, one small glass of wine or one measure of spirit. Recommended UK government safe levels of drinking are no more than 28 units per week for men and 21 units per week for women. In addition, it is recommended that men do not drink more than 4 units per day and women do not drink more than 3 units of alcohol per day.

People who are addicted to alcohol are termed **alcohol dependent**.

Who drinks?

- About 120 million people worldwide are classified as dependent on alcohol.
- In the UK, younger people are more likely than older people to exceed recommended guidelines for alcohol consumption.
- In the UK, more men than women exceed recommended guidelines for alcohol consumption.
- Alcohol consumption patterns do not differ greatly by social class.

Health implications of alcohol use

Alcohol is a depressant which slows down brain activity. Short-term effects of small amounts of alcohol are to produce feelings of relaxation and drowsiness, decrease in anxiety and lessening of self-consciousness. At higher levels, alcohol causes slurring of speech, visual impairments, loss of co-ordination, and loss of reasoning abilities.

Many of the negative effects of alcohol occur due to the lack of control people have when they are intoxicated. For example, people are far more likely to be involved in car accidents, engage in risky sexual behaviour, commit suicide, drown and be victims of fires when they have consumed alcohol. Alcohol also causes a number of social problems, with drink driving, increased levels of domestic violence, etc.

Long-term negative effects of alcohol are associated with abusive drinking patterns. These can include increased risk of liver disease (cirrhosis), stomach ulcers, heart and circulation disorders, cancers and brain damage. People can become addicted to alcohol although this takes some time. Withdrawal effects of alcohol addiction can be very serious – even fatal. Excessive use of alcohol by pregnant women can lead to a specific form of damage to their baby with characteristic mental impairments and physical abnormalities.

Why do people abuse alcohol?

Positive reinforcement of drinking behaviour can occur if people experience a reduction in anxiety or tension when drinking. Social factors are also important influences on drinking behaviour: both the example set within the home, and later peer groups influence young adults' drinking patterns.

Assessment activity 13.4

Which factors might explain why teenagers might see drinking alcohol or smoking as a symbol of success and adulthood status? How might the factors which encourage teenagers to drink or smoke differ from those of middle-aged people?

Obesity

Defining obesity

Your **Body Mass Index** (BMI) is calculated by the following formula:

$$\frac{\text{Weight (kg)}}{\text{Height (m)}^2}.$$

For example, someone who is 1.65 m tall and weighs 62 kg has a BMI of 22.8. (See also Unit 11 page 463.)

Classifications of BMI are as follows:

- less than 20   underweight
- 20–25   healthy weight
- 25–30   overweight
- more than 30   obese
- more than 40.0   morbidly obese

The BMI provides a rough rule of thumb for standard body compositions, although it doesn't work accurately for individuals with a particularly high muscle level, e.g. weight-lifters or a particularly low muscle level, e.g. older adults.

However it is important to consider that there are also cultural definitions of what is considered being overweight. These definitions change over time and also differ across cultures.

Who is overweight?

- The USA has the highest obesity levels worldwide.
- In the UK, over half the adult population is considered to be above the healthy weight category.
- Approximately 16 per cent of male and 18 per cent of female UK adults are obese.
- Prevalence of obesity increases by age, 5 per cent of 20-year-olds are obese compared to 20 per cent of those over age 60.
- In the UK and most other developed countries, obesity is more prevalent in lower social classes.

Marilyn Monroe was considered one of the world's most beautiful women in the 1950s, although by current contemporary standards of beauty, she might be encouraged to lose a few kilos

Health implications of being overweight

Being severely overweight or underweight leads to higher mortality risk. Obesity is a risk factor for many of the leading causes of death. Obesity increases the risk of developing coronary heart disease, cancer and diabetes. Obese people are at greater risk of complications in the operating theatre. Excess weight carried by obese people causes joint problems and can impair ability to exercise. Obesity has also been linked to higher levels of depression.

There is a great deal of evidence that society discriminates against obese individuals. For example:

- overweight children are rated as less likeable than children with disabilities
- obese adults are paid less than their thinner colleagues
- obese people are less likely to get married than thin people
- fat people are the butt of many jokes and are often portrayed in the media as weak willed, greedy, lazy and unattractive.

Given such discrimination, it is not surprising that some overweight people are depressed. It is obvious that some of the negative health implications of obesity are due to society's reaction to fatness rather than the physiological experience of being fat.

Why do people become overweight?

At a fundamental level, becoming overweight is all due to the balance between energy intake and energy use (see Figure 13.5). We gain energy from **food**. We lose energy from:

- **resting metabolic rate** – energy required when the body is 'ticking over'
- **physical exercise** – energy required to move
- **thermogenesis** – energy required to keep us warm
- **stress** – energy required by our mental processes.

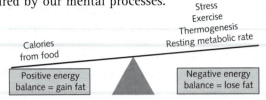

Figure 13.5 The energy balance

People only gain weight if they have a positive energy balance, i.e. the calories supplied by their daily intake of food exceeds their energy requirements. The excess is stored as fat.

Most people who are overweight are not increasing in weight, they are in energy balance. The amount of food that they eat is balanced by their higher energy requirements in terms of having a large body.

Explanations of obesity

- Studies of twins reared apart and families with adopted children suggest that we are more similar in weight to those we share our genes with than those we live with. This suggests that genes have a strong influence on body weight, however exactly how is not fully understood.
- People may be predisposed to gain weight due to having a low metabolic rate. This means that they are more efficient at using energy. Having a low metabolic rate may be important as a risk factor for becoming overweight. However studies generally show most overweight people to have similar metabolic rates to thinner people.
- Another factor which may influence weight is the number of fat cells. The number of fat cells may be under genetic control and fatter people tend to have more fat cells than thinner people. Being overweight in childhood also seems to be a particular risk factor.
- Set point theory suggests that each individual has their own individual ideal weight. The body strives to maintain this weight, increasing mental preoccupation with food and reducing metabolic rate when below set point and opposite effects when people are above the set point. This theory is supported by research which shows that it is difficult to make humans, or even rats increase or decrease their weight.
- Eating too much: the typical stereotype of someone who is fat is that they eat cream cakes and chocolate all day. It is notoriously difficult to accurately monitor food intake, either by using self-report diaries or using observation. Results of research are contradictory but generally it has been found that obese people do not appear to eat more than thin people. This may be because obese people need to eat about the same amount as thin people if currently maintaining their weight; however, it may be that overeating in the past has contributed to their being overweight in the first place.
- Over-responding to cues. It used to be thought that fat people eat for different reasons from thin people, often using food as an emotional comfort or eating when

they were not hungry. We are often cued by our environment to eat. Again, laboratory studies on this provide mixed evidence, and it is arguable whether people behave the same in a laboratory setting as they will in their daily life.

- Not exercising enough. Another stereotype of fat people is that they are lazy. Looking back at the energy balance model, we can see that less exercise tips the balance towards storing fat. Obese people tend to have lower levels of physical activity than thin people, but it is difficult to know whether this is a cause or result of being overweight. People who are overweight may find it uncomfortable to exercise and embarrassment may also cause them to avoid public exercise.

The explanation for obesity is important. People tend to be blamed for behaviour which is seen as within their control. Obese people often tend to cite physiological explanations for their obesity, whereas the lay perception is that it is all down to a lack of will power.

Should we try to make people lose weight?

Obesity is an expensive problem for the NHS; current estimates suggest that the costs of obesity in the UK exceed £195 million. Therefore it is in the public interest to get people who are overweight to slim down. However, dieting is a difficult enterprise. Looking at cognitive models, we might suggest that making someone feel bad about themselves for being overweight may encourage them to lose weight. However, if you make someone feel bad about themselves and they are unable to lose weight, then are you simply causing more harm?

Think it over

Working in small groups, debate the following issues:

- Do you think seriously overweight people should be encouraged to slim down?
- How overweight would someone have to be for you to want to make them lose weight?
- How would you go about motivating someone to lose weight?
- What would the psychological support be for your suggestions?
- What is the likely impact on cultural views of obesity of your campaign?

Stress

What is stress?

Stress is one of those terms which is frequently bandied around but which is very difficult to define.

Theories of stress have changed focus over time, from models which concentrated on the **physiological responses** of the body to **life events theory**, which focuses on the events encountered, and more recently to **transactional models** which emphasise the interaction of the person with their environment (see Figure 13.6).

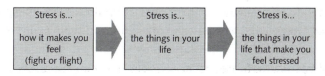

Figure 13.6 Development of stress model

Development of stress models

Stress as a physical response

The physical response to stress is all about a rapid mobilisation of energy.

Walter Canon (1939) outlined some of the most obvious immediate physiological changes which occur when a person or animal is stressed. The main changes which Canon observed are due to the activity of the sympathetic nervous system and the release of adrenaline and noradrenaline. He called these changes the **fight–flight response**, as they enable an organism to have energy either to fight or escape a situation.

You can feel some of the short-term effects of the stress response when you are briefly frightened: your breathing will become faster, you might feel your heart beating more, you feel shaky as your muscles are on a 'hair trigger' to enable faster reactions, your skin feels clammy as blood is diverted away from it, and your mouth goes dry as your digestive activity shuts down to conserve energy. Within your body other changes occur in your lungs to enable you to take in more oxygen, and various stored fats and sugars are released into the bloodstream to provide energy.

Hans Selye is credited with popularising the word stress as it is used today. Selye noticed that animals which were put in sustained stressful conditions all developed the same physical problems such as stomach ulcers, weight loss, abnormal changes in the size of glands (some shrunken, some enlarged), and impaired immune system functioning.

Selye (1976) proposed that when exposed to sustained stress there would be a standard response. He called this response the **general adaptation syndrome** and divided it into three phases.

- Phase 1 – **Alarm reaction**. Immediate reactions of the organism to the stressful conditions. This stage is similar to Canon's fight or flight response.

- Phase 2 – **Resistance stage**. The animal adapts to the demands of the stressor. However, this adaptation requires adaptation energy and this is gradually used up until the animal can no longer resist the stressor.

- Phase 3 – **Exhaustion**. At this stage, the animal's resistance to the stressor is so weakened that diseases become apparent.

Most of the long-term adverse changes that Selye observed were due to the effects of another hormone involved in the stress response, called cortisol. Cortisol has useful short-term effects, including mobilising energy stores and making us feel more alert. However, for various complex reasons, the long-term effects of cortisol are to down-regulate the immune system, disrupt the reproductive system, suppress the inflammatory response and even to damage areas of the brain which affect memory and mood.

Stress as a stimulus – life events theory

Life events theory focuses on stress as a stimulus. These can be classified by their seriousness and duration. Examples of major stressors are divorce, death of a loved one, or job loss. Luckily, these major events are rare sources of stress for most people, although their after-effects may persist for some time. In contrast, minor stressors such as being kept waiting, arguments with others or transport difficulties may pose a short-term source of stress on a daily basis. Sometimes, the regularity of an annoyance suggests that it is not simply a one-off event but a chronic stressor. Examples of chronic stressors include living in poor housing, being involuntarily childless, or stress at work or school.

Life events researchers measure the amount of stress for an individual by determining how many 'stressors' they have experienced in a certain time period. Often they use questionnaires which list agreed major or minor stressors.

Think it over

Create your own personal list of stressful life events: include at least five minor and five major stressors. Compare your list with that of a friend. How similar are the lists? How might your list differ from that of your parents/grandparents/children? What other types of items would you need to include to make the list relevant to them?

One of the main problems with this type of research is that it is difficult to generate a list which contains items which are relevant to all types of people but which is not so long that it becomes too cumbersome for people to complete.

Life events questionnaires are useful in research terms, as they enable a measurement of the amount of stress in a person's life. However, they rely on memory – which raises other problems. Some people forget things which have happened to them and some people are just grumpy and tend only to remember the bad things in life. These factors can make measuring stress using life events questionnaires difficult.

Transactional models of stress

Another model of stress suggests that an event is only stressful if a person thinks about it in that way. For example, it may be very stressful for one person to wait in a queue but for other people it poses no stress at all. Recognition that the meaning you attach to an event determines its stressfulness was one of the key ideas which swung models of stress towards their modern formulation, where stress is seen as an interaction between people and their environment.

Thinking about whether an event is stressful requires a two-stage appraisal:

- primary appraisal – assessment of the situation
- secondary appraisal – assessment of our ability to cope.

We only experience stress if the *perceived* demands of the situation exceed our *perceived* ability to cope. The word perceived is very important here as perceived demands and abilities to cope may not be realistic.

Within the transactional model of stress, factors which affect the appraisal process become very important. Some personality types are more likely than average to view events as stressful. People with these types of personality may be more susceptible to the health implications of stress. Conversely, some people seem to breeze through life brushing off difficulties that others would consider stressful.

Other factors which determine how stressful an event is are issues of control and social support. Something that is particularly stressful is the lack of control that the people involved have over the situation. Laboratory studies show that if a person is given a sense of control over a stressful event they have a reduced physiological reaction. This appears to hold in real life; people who work in demanding jobs, but have a high level of control, seem less affected by illness than people who do the same work but do not control any aspect of it.

Assessment activity 13.5

In your own words, describe the three models of stress. What are the similarities and differences between them?

Stress-illness link

There is lots of research evidence to suggest that people who have higher levels of stressful events in their lives have higher levels of illness. For example, one classic study found that sailors in the top third band for recent stress scores (based on a life events questionnaire) had 90 per cent more illnesses in the first two months of the cruise than those in the lowest scoring band.

Other evidence that stress causes illness comes from studying people who encounter naturally stressful events. At the extreme end of the scale, populations which are exposed to earthquakes, nuclear accidents and war, show higher rates of sudden cardiac death at the time of the disasters, and over a longer period of time levels of depression, cancer and heart disease may be increased.

At a more minor end of the scale, students coming up to their exams and people reporting more stressful life events generally have been shown to have higher rates of colds and other infections. Even getting a person to perform mental arithmetic out loud in a laboratory provokes potentially damaging physiological changes.

Other studies have focused on people in long-term stressful situations. For example, people caring for someone with Alzheimer's disease have been found to have slower healing rates than similar people of the same age; they also show other evidence of suppressed immune systems.

Key issue

Dutch researchers examined national health records for the weeks surrounding Holland's exit from the 1996 European Football Championships. They found that rates of sudden cardiac death and stroke were significantly higher on the day of the match compared to surrounding weeks – for men; the rates for women did not change significantly!

Physiologists term the strain put on the body by repeated experiences of stress the **allostatic load**. This has direct impact on the body leading to the characteristic findings of increased heart problems, depression, infections and slowed healing as shown above. However, stressful circumstances can also lead to ill health by affecting how people behave. Time pressures may prevent usual health enhancing behaviours, seeking escape may increase use of drugs, and worry may prevent people from getting enough sleep and paying enough attention to avoid accidents. Perversely, the people we seek out during times of stress may adversely affect our health by providing a source of infection which our weakened immune systems are unable to fight off. Generally, however, people who have higher levels of social support provided by family and friends to help them cope with stressful events tend to suffer fewer ill effects.

Stress management strategies

Typically it is not easy to remove the sources of stress in someone's environment. Therefore it is more effective to help people cope with stress.

Cognitive therapies focus on changing the way people think about the events in their lives. In one method, called cognitive restructuring, a client is asked to talk a therapist through the thoughts they have when they feel stressed. Often in these cases, people exaggerate the negative possibilities and have irrational thoughts leading to the appraisal of many events as threatening. For example, a reaction on realising that you failed an exam might be, 'I failed my exam, I'm really stupid, I'll never get any qualifications and will be stuck in a job I hate for the rest of my life'. Cognitive restructuring would encourage you to realise that even if you have failed this exam, you may have opportunities to retake the exam, that you are successful in other spheres of your life, and that even if you never pass that exam, there may be other ways for you to achieve your goals.

I can't believe I have failed my exam, but at least I will have a chance to retake it in a few months.

Cognitive restructuring can lead to success

Emotional expression, either through talking or writing about negative events, can be used as a cognitive strategy to help people manage their stress.

Stress inoculation is another form of cognitive therapy. In stress inoculation, the client imagines themselves in a stressful situation. They are then led by a therapist through a process of deciding how to cope with the stressful event. The client may practise or rehearse various strategies or skills, e.g. through role play. Finally the client is helped to apply their new coping strategies within their daily life and to learn how to be their own therapist in any new stressful situations.

Relaxation training teaches people how to reduce the physical consequences of stress. There are a wide range of relaxation techniques including progressive muscle relaxation, yoga, biofeedback training or meditation. First, the person uses one of these techniques regularly to enable them to relax in non-stressful situations. Once this skill has been gained, the person can use their relaxation training to reduce the physical sensations they feel when in a situation which causes them stress. This has benefits in making people 'feel' better but also reduces the allostatic load placed on the body and thus the eventual physical effects.

Behavioural strategies teach people skills to help avoid or minimise the stressors in their life. Thus a person might make a list of the positive and negative outcomes of a particular course of behaviour. This would then help them to feel more secure in their decision-making process and stop them worrying about issues. Time management may help people avoid stresses caused by lack of time to prepare, or assertiveness skills may help someone whose main source of stress is another person.

Prescription drugs can be useful in combating short-term severe stressors. However, many people turn to what are termed 'drugs of solace' such as alcohol, tobacco or to abuse anti-depressants when stressed. Although these may provide short-term stress relief, they are not a useful long-term strategy.

Exercise has also been shown to have beneficial stress management effects.

Assessment activity 13.6

Jenny is a working mother with two children. She finds her life gets on top of her sometimes. She doesn't have enough time to spend with her children and they are often in bed by the time she gets home from work. She finds she often gives in to requests from her boss to work late to finish assignments. She would like to get away from all her problems and often has to have a drink or two to help her calm down so she can get to sleep at night.

What stress management strategies would you recommend for Jenny? What would be the advantages and disadvantages of the strategies you recommend?

Assessment activity 13.7

'Experiencing an event such as divorce inevitably leads to illness.' Write brief notes to discuss this statement. Relate your answer to different models of stress and the role that coping and stress management strategies may have.

Chronic and terminal illness

An acute illness is one with a short duration which is resolved within a fairly short period of time. This may be due to recovery or death of the patient. Chronic illnesses have a longer time course, maybe lasting several years. Often the patient may not recover and be free of the illness but will rather have to manage the condition (e.g. diabetes, or lower back pain) and its health impact. Terminal illnesses are those which lead directly lead to death, however the gap between diagnosis and death may vary so that the condition may be either acute or chronic in nature. In this section we look at two chronic conditions, coronary heart disease (CHD) and HIV/AIDS.

Coronary heart disease

Statistics

- In 2000, coronary heart disease killed approximately 6.9 million people worldwide.
- CHD is the commonest cause of death in the UK, accounting for approximately 1 in 4 of all male deaths and 1 in 5 of all female deaths.
- UK death rates from CHD have been falling since the late 1970s although the improvement is slower than in Australia, Canada and other European countries.
- Scotland has one of the highest death rates from CHD in the world, the worst of all countries in the European Union.

What is coronary heart disease?

The arteries within the body supply oxygen-carrying blood to our tissues. **Atherosclerosis** is the name of a medical condition where your arteries become progressively furred up, in much the same way as do water pipes in areas with hard water. Coronary heart disease is the term given to this process of furred-up arteries in the heart. The build-up is known as **plaque**.

Atherosclerosis is a dangerous process. First, it gradually decreases the diameter of the blood vessels. Secondly, parts of the plaque may break off and risk blocking blood vessels elsewhere. Either of these events reduces blood supply, thus reducing the amount of oxygen reaching the tissue supplied by affected vessels.

Within the heart, temporary oxygen starvation of the heart muscle leads to pain called angina. More serious oxygen starvation can cause death of a part of the heart muscle (a heart attack) which can weaken the heart so much that it can no longer pump blood effectively or disrupt the heart beat so the pumping is uncoordinated and ineffective. Either of these two situations can be fatal.

Risk factors for coronary heart disease

Risk factors for coronary heart disease can be divided into causal and predisposing factors.

- **Causal factors**. We have very strong evidence to show that factors such as age, high cholesterol levels, high blood pressure and cigarette smoking directly affect the development of atherosclerosis.
- **Predisposing factors** are those which put you at a higher risk of CHD although they do not directly cause it. These include some factors which cannot be altered such as being male, or having a family history of CHD. However this category also includes many of the factors that health psychologists are interested in, such as obesity, sedentary lifestyle, depression, personality characteristics (hostility and Type A behaviour pattern – TABP), low levels of social support and high stress levels.

Type A Behaviour Pattern

In the early 1960s, doctors who treated people for coronary heart disease began to notice that their patients seemed to share certain personality characteristics such as being very hostile, impatient and distrusting of other people. These characteristics appear to be associated with a greater risk of heart disease.

Think it over

How many of the following 'Type A' personality characteristics do you have:

- hate being late
- like to eat very quickly
- have a strong need to be the best at everything
- like to be busy all the time
- do not suffer fools easily
- get annoyed at having to wait for anything?

Do you think you could or should try to change them?

Primary health promotion looks at reducing risk factors prior to the development of disease. Reducing levels of smoking, obesity, and the numbers of people with a sedentary lifestyle are important targets for health promotion campaigns. These health campaigns often rely on understanding and manipulating people's attitudes towards a healthier lifestyle. You can read more about health promotion campaigns in Unit 8 Health promotion.

Role of psychology in rehabilitation

Once a person has developed symptoms of coronary heart disease, health psychology has a role to play in aiding their rehabilitation. Part of this may be a continued emphasis on changing risk factors; however, it is also important to help people feel supported in coping with their chronic condition.

Cardiac rehabilitation programmes may focus on many aspects of changing risk factors, e.g. giving up smoking, adopting a healthier diet and reducing weight. Many of the stress management strategies discussed in the previous section can be useful in lowering the amount of stress in a person's life and thus their risk of coronary heart disease. Gentle exercise programmes have been developed for people recovering from CHD. Support groups composed of people with CHD or other chronic conditions may provide encouragement for behaviour change and in general coping. Support groups may be especially important for people who live alone or feel lonely.

Changing personality characteristics sounds impossible. However, programmes have been designed to help people reduce their Type A behaviour levels, often by getting them to cognitively restructure their thinking about stressful events, e.g. the slow checkout assistant in the supermarket is not doing it deliberately to wind them up. These programmes have been shown to reduce the re-occurrence of CHD requiring treatment compared to patients not receiving this intervention.

You might think that encouraging people to make lifestyle changes, after a serious event like a heart attack, would be easy. Look back at the cognitive models discussed on page 506 and you might think that experiencing a heart attack would provide quite a serious cue to action, as well as increasing perceptions of susceptibility and helping to tip the cost-benefit analysis towards benefits of reducing risk factors. Family and friends of a person who has had a heart attack would also be expected to provide a strong push to help them change risk behaviours. However, this is not always the case. Approximately, half of people on cardiac rehabilitation programmes drop out within one year, and many fail to sustain changes in lifestyle.

Assessment activity 13.8

Look back at the case study of Frank on page 506. What coronary risk factors does Frank have? What type of intervention programmes do you think might be likely to help reduce Frank's future coronary heart disease risk? With reference to the models of health behaviour and factors which increase adherence, how would you try to encourage Frank to make these lifestyle changes?

HIV/AIDS

Statistics

- More than 30 million people worldwide are infected with HIV. In some countries, 1 in 4 adults can be infected.
- In the UK in 2000, over 3400 people were newly diagnosed with HIV, adding to the approximate figure of 30,000 British people infected with HIV.
- Approximately half the new infections in the UK are the result of heterosexual contact.
- Rates of HIV infection are rising within the UK.

What are HIV and AIDS?

AIDS (acquired immunodeficiency syndrome) is the end stage of infection with HIV (human immunodeficiency virus). HIV damages CD4+ T cells. These cells are a component of the immune system and as their levels decline, the body becomes more vulnerable to infections such as herpes, bacterial and fungal infections, unusual forms of pneumonia and skin cancer which eventually lead to death. The time scale from initial infection with the virus to final stage AIDS can last from 10 to 15 years. There may also be a long gap between initial infection and diagnosis as HIV infection may produce no obvious symptoms for many years. HIV infection does not occur during everyday contact such as sharing facilities, holding hands or even kissing. The main routes of infection are through contact with an infected person during sexual intercourse, via intravenous drug use with shared needles, or from mother to child during birth.

Psychology and HIV

Changing risky behaviours

As a predominantly sexually transmitted disease, AIDS prevention efforts have focused on safer sex campaigns which highlight use of condoms and reducing riskier sexual practices. Initially, sexually active homosexual men were targeted in health promotion campaigns. However, the increasing levels of heterosexual transmission have led to a wider promotion of safer sex for all.

Intravenous drug users have also been targeted to reduce sharing of needles through greater awareness of this mode of infection and by increased provision of sterile needles.

The risk of transmission from mother to child can be cut by use of antiviral drugs and encouraging pregnant women to get appropriate antenatal care.

Health psychologists have played an important role informing the design of such health promotion campaigns. However, the success or otherwise of these efforts to change behaviour has also had an important impact on models of behaviour change. As with CHD, people do not always react as models would predict and often models need change or improvement.

Counselling

Counsellors can provide support to the person seeking an AIDS test. This is important not just to help people who may have to cope with potential diagnosis of a terminal illness but also to encourage people to examine the risk factors in their lives which have led them to consider themselves at risk of HIV infection.

For those who receive a positive diagnosis, counsellors can help people on a one-to-one basis to talk through the implications of being HIV positive and how to manage their illness.

Support groups

Despite increased public awareness of HIV and AIDS, there remains a strong prejudice towards people who are HIV positive. On disclosure of their HIV positive status, many people find themselves shunned by some of their former friends, colleagues and family members. Support groups for people who are HIV positive can provide others with whom to share the experience of having a terminal illness. Within the support groups, people may learn problem solving skills, stress management techniques and provide a source of support for each other. Support groups can also help family and friends of those with an HIV diagnosis.

The inclusion of HIV positive characters into popular soap operas and the public support of HIV-related campaigns by public figures has done much to educate the public on how you can and can't catch AIDS and reduce the stigma of HIV infection. For example, newspaper photos of the late Princess of Wales holding the hand of a person who was HIV positive caused people to think again about HIV and AIDS.

End of unit test

1 What are the three stages in Leventhal's illness cognitions model?

2 Complete the boxes of the health belief model with appropriate labels.

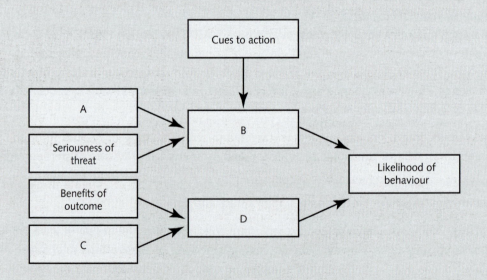

3 In 2002, there was a national debate about the value of vaccinating children with the MMR combined immunisation against measles, mumps and rubella as opposed to not vaccinating children or giving them vaccines to a single disease at a time. The table below lists various thoughts that a new mother might have. Which components of the theory of planned behaviour do they link to?

a	My GP is strongly in favour of the MMR vaccine
b	If I wanted to, it would be easy for me to take my child to the GP surgery to be vaccinated
c	It is very important to me to protect my child from catching measles
d	My best friend has decided not to get her child vaccinated against measles at all
e	I value the opinion of my GP and want her to think I'm a good mother
f	I do not think that the MMR vaccine will protect my child against getting measles

4 To work effectively, a complete course of antibiotics must be taken, even if symptoms disappear before the end of the treatment. What reasons do you think might be important in determining whether a person will follow the treatment as prescribed, or engage in creative non-compliance?

5 Betty smokes on average four cigarettes per day. Her brand of cigarettes costs £4.00 per pack of 20. Calculate how much money she spends on cigarettes per week and per year. How would you use this information to help Betty to change her smoking behaviour?

6 Which of the following physiological changes would you normally expect in response to a stressor:
  a decreased heart rate
  b sweating
  c increased blood pressure
  d increased saliva production
  e dilated pupils
  f slower reactions?

7 Some people say that beauty is in the eye of the beholder. Which model of stress would suggest that stress is also in the eye of the beholder? Why?

8 Look at the following strategies which you might use to cope before an exam. Which would you classify as problem focused and which as emotion focused?
  a Going to the library to find useful books.
  b Making a mind map of the topic area.
  c Eating lots of chocolate to cheer yourself up.
  d Asking teachers for some advice regarding exam topics.
  e Drawing up a revision schedule.
  f Going to the cinema to take your mind off the coming exam.

9 How would you categorise the following in terms of being an acute illness, a chronic illness or a terminal illness? Why?
  a Flu
  b Cancer
  c Arthritis
  d AIDS

10 Why might people with Type A Behaviour Patterns (TABP) be more susceptible to illness?

11 Which of the following are considered a risk factor for transmission of HIV:
a breast-feeding
b sharing bathroom facilities
c sharing intravenous needles
d holding hands
e kissing
f unprotected sexual intercourse?

12 How would you design a health promotion campaign to try to encourage people to practise safer sex by using condoms? Link your answer to aspects of the theory of planned behaviour.

References and further reading

Ajzen, I. (1991) 'The theory of planned behaviour', *Organizational Behavior and Human Decision Processes* 50, 179–211

Becker, H. M. (1974) *The Health Belief Model and Personal Health Behaviour*, Thorofare, NJ: Slack

Canon, W. B. (1939) *The Wisdom of the Body*, New York: Norton

Leventhal, H., Meyer, D. and Nerenz, D. (1980) 'The common sense representation of illness danger'. Rachman, S. (ed.) *Medical Psychology*, Vol. 2, New York: Pergamon

Ley, P. (1988) *Communicating with Patients: Improving Communication, Satisfaction and Compliance*, London: Chapman & Hall

Sapolsky, R. M. (1998) *Why Zebras Don't Get Ulcers: An Updated Guide to Stress, Stress-related Diseases and Coping*, New York: W H Freeman & Co

Selye, H. (1976) *The Stress of Life* (rev. edn), New York: McGraw-Hill

Smith, T. W. and Leon, A. S. (1992) *Coronary Heart Disease: a Behavioral Perspective*, USA: McNaughton & Gunn

Stephney, R. (1980) 'Smoking Behaviour. A psychology of the cigarette habit', *British Journal of Diseases of the Chest* 74(4)

Stroebe, W. (2002) *Social Psychology and Health* (2nd edn), Buckingham: Open University Press

Index